Wes Chow

Buick Re
and Century
Automotive
Repair
Manual

MW00823808

by Peter D du Pré
and John H Haynes

Member of the Guild of Motoring Writers

Models covered:

Regal: Regal, Regal Limited, Regal Sport Coupe

Century: Century, Century Custom, Century Limited, Century Sport Coupe, Century Special, Century Wagon

196, 231 (including Turbo), 252, 256, 301, 305, 307, 350, 403 and 455 cu in engines

ISBN 1 85010 386 0

Haynes Publishing Group
Sparkford Nr Yeovil
Somerset BA22 7JJ England

Haynes Publications, Inc
861 Lawrence Drive
Newbury Park
California 91320 USA

Library of Congress
Catalog card number
87–80839

Acknowledgements

Thanks are due to the Buick Motor Division of the General Motors Corporation for their assistance with technical information and the supply of certain illustrations.

The Champion Spark Plug Company supplied the illustrations showing the various spark plug conditions. The bodywork repair photographs used in this manual were supplied by Holt Lloyd Limited, distributors of "Turtle Wax", "Dupli-Color Holts", and other Holts products.

About this manual

Its aim

The aim of this manual is to help you get the best from your car. It can do so in several ways. It can help you decide what work must be done (even should you choose to get it done by a garage), provide information on routine maintenance and servicing, and give a logical course of action and diagnosis when random faults occur. However, it is hoped that you will use the manual by tackling the work yourself. On simpler jobs it may even be quicker than booking the car into a garage and going there twice to leave and collect it. Perhaps most important, a lot of money can be saved by avoiding the costs the garage must charge to cover its labour and overheads.

The manual has drawings and descriptions to show the function of the various components so that their layout can be understood. Then the tasks are described and photographed in a step-by-step sequence so that even a novice can do the work.

Its arrangement

The manual is divided into thirteen Chapters, each covering a logical sub-division of the vehicle. The Chapters are each divided into Sections, numbered with single figures, eg 5; and the Sections into paragraphs (or sub-sections), with decimal numbers following on from the Section they are in, eg 5.1. 5.2 etc.

It is freely illustrated, especially in those parts where there is a detailed sequence of operations to be carried out. There are two forms of illustration: figures and photographs. The figures are numbered in sequence with decimal numbers, according to their position in the Chapter — Fig. 6.4 is the fourth drawing/illustration in Chapter 6. Photographs carry the same number (either individually or in related groups) as the Section or sub-section to which they relate.

There is an alphabetical index at the back of the manual as well as a contents list at the front. Each Chapter is also preceded by its own individual contents list.

References to the 'left' or 'right' of the vehicle are in the sense of a person in the driver's seat facing forwards.

Unless otherwise stated, nuts and bolts are removed by turning anti-clockwise, and tightened by turning clockwise.

Vehicle manufacturers continually make changes to specifications and recommendations, and these, when notified, are incorporated into our manuals at the earliest opportunity.

While every care is taken to ensure that the information in this manual is correct, no liability can be accepted by the authors or publishers for loss, damage or injury caused by any errors in, or omissions, from the information given.

Introduction to the Buick Regal and Century

The seven year period that this manual covers marks a unique period of development in the history of the American automobile, particularly for Buick. 1974 marked the last year that truly large displacement engines were offered in Buick's "A" body automobiles (The Regal and Century lines). The great fuel shortage of early 1974 brought home the need for smaller and more efficient cars. Because of this, Federal regulations, and consumer leanings towards smaller autos, Buick has had to totally rethink just what a mid-size car is all about.

Beginning in 1976, Buick began down-sizing its entire line of automobiles and today the Century wagon is 23.6 inches shorter, overall, than it was in 1974. The Regal has shrunk, also, and is 12.4 inches shorter than it was in the mid-seventies. Wheelbase is also less than it used to be, having shrunk an average of 6.3 inches since 1974.

In spite of producing smaller cars, ride and comfort have not suffered as was first supposed, in fact they have been improved. Today's Buicks actually have more interior room than many earlier models. More room, less overall length and width, better comfort, greater economy, and improved styling are all hallmarks of the new Buick.

From a mechanical point of view, the cars remain basically unchanged in design since 1974. Suspension, brakes and drivetrains are virtually the same, except for very minor improvements. Engines are still available in V6 and V8 configurations, though the large 455 CID V8 is no longer available. The big change for Buick are the High Energy Ignition (electronic) introduced in 1975 and a turbocharger for the 231 V6, introduced in 1978. Another change for Buick is the introduction of other General Motors engines into its line up. Since 1977, engines installed in Buicks have been manufactured by Buick, Oldsmobile, Pontiac and Chevrolet. Detailed descriptions of these innovations, and others, are covered in detail in the appropriate sections of this manual. Stripdown procedures are basically the same for all years and the Haynes step-by-step photo coverage is applicable to all engine models. Differences between engine models are discussed in detail.

Contents

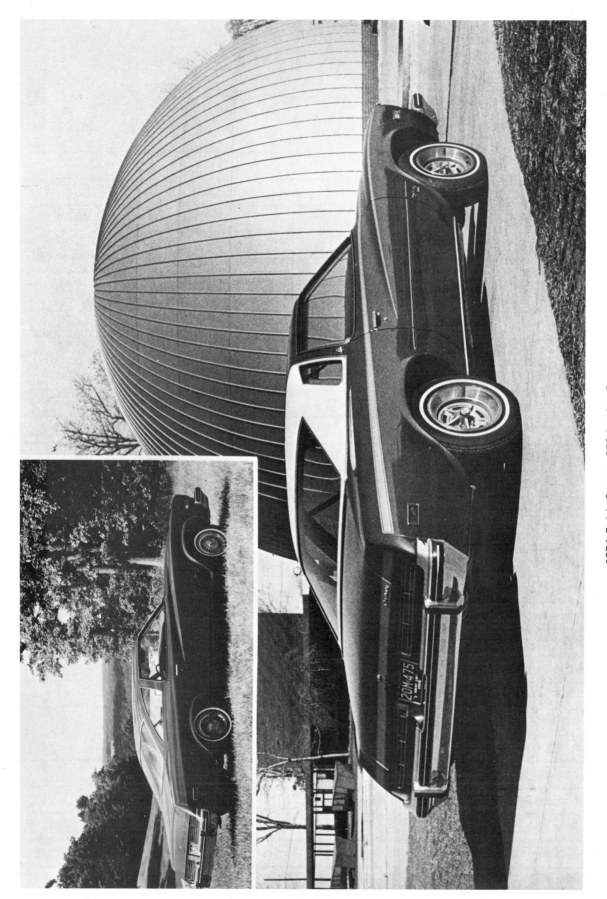

1974 Buick Century 350 Landau Coupe

1975 Buick Century Special

1976 Buick Century Custom Coupe

1977 Buick Century Sedan

1978 Buick Century Special Coupe

1980 Buick Century Limited Sedan

1974 Buick Regal 4-door Sedan

1977 Buick Regal Coupe

1979 Buick Regal Limited Coupe

1980 Buick Regal Sport Coupe

General dimensions and capacities

Dimensions (in inches)	Wheelbase	Length	Height	Width
1974				
Century 2-door coupes	112.0	209.5	55.0	79.0
Regal 2-door formal sedan	112.0	212.0	55.0	79.0
Century 4-door sedans	116.0	213.5	55.0	79.0
Regal 2-door sedan	116.0	216.0	55.0	79.0
Century 4-door wagons	116.0	218.2	55.9	79.0
1975				
Century 2-door coupes	112.0	209.5	53.5	79.0
Regal 2-door coupe/sedan	112.0	212.0	53.3	79.0
Century 4-door sedan	116.0	213.5	54.1	79.0
Regal 4-door sedan	116.0	216.0	54.1	79.0
Century 4-door wagons	116.0	218.2	55.3	79.0
1976				
Century 2-door coupe	112.0	209.7	52.8	79.0
Century Custom/Special	112.0	209.7	52.6	79.0
Regal 2-door coupe	112.0	213.5	53.6	79.0
All 4-door sedans	116.0	213.5	53.6	79.0
All 4-door wagons	116.0	218.2	55.3	79.0
1977				
All 2-door coupes	112.0	209.8	52.7	76.5
All 4-door sedans	116.0	213.6	53.6	79.0
All 4-door wagons	116.0	218.3	55.3	79.0
1978 through 80				
Century Special coupe	108.1	195.6	53.3	72.2
Regal coupe	108.1	199.6	53.4	72.2
Century Special sedan	108.1	195.6	54.2	72.2
Century Special wagon	108.1	194.6	54.5	72.2

Capacities

Cooling system

	US qts
1974	
350 CID V8	
W/heater	17.3
W/air conditioning or HDC (Heavy Duty Cooling) 20″	
fan shroud	17.6
W/air conditioning or HDC 22″ fan shroud	17.2
455 CID V8	
W/heater	19.4
W/air conditioning and/or HDC	19.9
1975	
231 CID V6	
Heater only	15.35
HDC	15.32
350 CID V8	
Heater only	16.88
HDC	17.16
1976	
231 CID V6	
Heater only	15.35
HDC	15.32
350 CID V8	
Heater only	16.88
HDC	17.16
1977	
231 CID V6	
Manual transmission	
W/heater and/or HDC	12.9
W/air conditioning and/or HDC	12.8

Automatic transmission
    W/heater or HDC 12.8
    W/air conditioning and/or HDC 12.7
305 and 350 CID V8 (VIN codes U and L)
    W/heater 14.8
    W/air conditioning 15.4
    W/HDC 16.9
350 CID V8 (VIN code H and J)
    W/heater 14.3
    W/air conditioning 14.9
    W/HDC 16.4
350 CID V8 (VIN code R)
    W/heater 15.3
    W/air conditioning 15.9
    W/HDC 17.4
403 CID V8 (VIN code K)
    W/heater 16.4
    W/air conditioning 17.0
    W/HDC 18.5

1978
196 and 231 CID V6
Manual transmission
    W/heater 13.1
    W/air conditioning 13.2
Automatic transmission
    W/heater amd HDC 13.0
    W/air conditioning and HDC 13.1
305 CID V8
    W/heater 19.2
    W/air conditioning 18.9
    W/HDC 19.6
350 CID V8
    W/heater 19.2
    W/air conditioner 18.9
    W/HDC 19.6

1979 and 1980
196 and 231 CID V6
    Manual transmission 13.4
    Automatic transmission 13.3
301 CID V8 (VIN code Y)
    W/heater 20.3
    W/HDC 20.8
301 CID V8 (VIN code W)
    W/heater 20.3
    W/air conditioning 21.0
    W/HDC 20.8
305 CID V8 (VIN code H)
    W/heater 17.6
    W/HDC 18.1
350 CID V8
    W/heater 17.6
    W/air conditioning 18.1
    W/HDC 18.1

Fuel tank capacity (approx)   US gallons
1974 through 1977 22
1978 through 1980 .... 18.1

Rear axle
1974 through 1980 (all) .... $4\frac{1}{4}$ pints

Engine oil
Refill (all) .... 4 qts
With new filter
    1979 amd 1980 Pontiac 265/301 engines .... 4 qts
    All others .... 5 qts

Spare parts and vehicle identification numbers

Spare parts

Spare parts are available from many sources and generally fall into one of two categories — authorized factory replacement parts and aftermarket replacement parts.

Authorized factory replacement parts: Your General Motors Corporation Buick dealer is the best source of parts which are peculiar to your Century or Regal car (major engine components, body panels, trim pieces, and so on). If your auto is still covered under terms of the factory warranty, the dealer is also the only place that you should buy all spares, as use of non-approved replacement parts will often invalidate your warranty.

Aftermarket replacement parts: Auto parts and discount stores are good places to purchase frequently needed components for your car (brake linings, filters, hoses, spark plugs, exhaust systems, etc.). Generally, routine maintenance items will cost considerably less at an aftermarket store than they will at a factory dealer. These stores often supply new or reconditioned parts on an exchange basis. You bring in the old part and "trade it in" on a new one, often at quite a saving. These stores are also a good place to purchase general maintenance items such as oil, grease, car wax, cleaners and head lamps. Other items such as tools and accessories are also available.

Wherever you purchase spare parts, it is essential to provide the parts counterman with correct information concerning the manufacturer, model, year, engine serial number and VIN code. It also helps to take along the old parts whenever possible.

Vehicle identification number (VIN)

This important code number is stamped onto a plate that is located on the upper left side of the dashboard and can be easily seen while looking through the car's windshield (from the outside). The VIN also appears on the title and the registration. This number is required by Federal law and gives such valuable information as where and when the atomobile was manufactured, the body style and model year of manufacture, and the type of engine installed in the car.

Buick vehicles use a variety of engines supplied by various GM divisions (Oldsmobile, Chevrolet, Pontiac); knowing the manufacturer of the engine is imperative to purchasing the correct spare parts. You can identify which type of engine your Buick has by using the VIN information supplied at the beginning of Chapter 2.

Body identification plate

Located on the upper surface of the shroud, the body identification plate contains information about the manufacture of the automobile and how it is equipped. This plate is particularly useful when matching body paint, interiors, and when having body repair work done.

Engine identification number

Due to the fact that various manufacturers have supplied the engines that are installed in Buick automobiles, the engine identification numbers may appear in different locations. The easiest way to determine who made the engine is to consult the VIN number. (Chapter 2 gives the details). Once you have identified the manufacturer, consult the figures in this section that show various locations of ID numbers. Some Buick engines have the ID number stamped on a pad located on the right front corner of the block. Other engines may have the number located on the front of the rocker arm cover on the left cylinder head. Finally, some engines have the number attached to the oil filler tube.

A   Typical VIN plate as seen from outside the car looking through the windshield

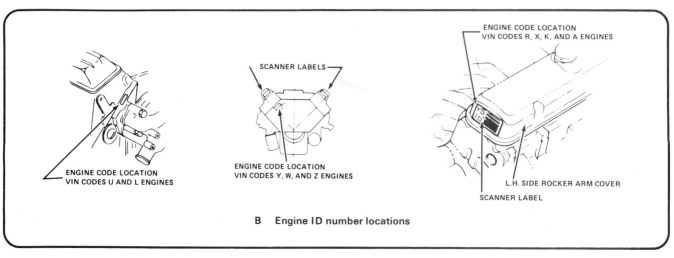

B   Engine ID number locations

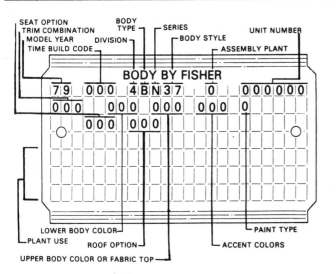

C   Typical body identification plate attached to the engine
     compartment firewall

Manual transmission number:

     3-speed Saginaw – Lower right-hand side of the case, adjacent to the cover.

     4-speed Borg Warner – Rear vertical surface of the extension housing.

     4-speed Muncie – Rear right-hand side of the case flange

     4-speed Saginaw – Lower right-hand side of case adjacent to the cover.

Automatic transmission number:

     The ID number for automatic transmissions is either on the right-hand vertical surface of the case or on the tag at the right-hand side of the transmission.

Rear axle number: Located on the right or left axle tube, adjacent to the center.

Generator: On top drive end frame

Starter: Stamped on outer case, toward rear.

Tune-up decal: Located in various positions inside the engine compartment (See Chapter 1 for details).

Maintenance techniques, tools and working facilities

There are a number of techniques involved in maintenance and repair that will be referred to throughout this manual. Application of these techniques will enable the home mechanic to be more efficient, better organized and capable of performing the various tasks properly, which will ensure that the repair job is thorough and complete.

Fastening systems

Fasteners, basically, are nuts, bolts, studs and screws used to hold two or more parts together. There are a few things to keep in mind when working with fasteners. Almost all of them use a locking device of some type; either a lock washer, locknut, locking tab or thread adhesive. All threaded fasteners should be clean and straight, with undamaged threads and undamaged corners on the hex head where the wrench fits. Develop the habit of replacing damaged nuts and bolts with new ones. Special locknuts with nylon or fiber inserts can only be used once. If they are removed, they lose their locking ability and must be replaced with new ones.

Rusted nuts and bolts should be treated with a penetrating fluid to ease removal and prevent breakage. Some mechanics use turpentine in a spout type oil can, which works quite well. After applying the rust penetrant, let it "work" for a few minutes before trying to loosen the nut or bolt. Badly rusted fasteners may have to be chiseled or sawed off or removed with a special nut breaker, available at tool stores.

If a bolt or stud breaks off in an assembly, it can be drilled out and removed with a special tool called an E-Z out. Most automotive machine shops can perform this task, as well as others (such as the repair of threaded holes that have been stripped out).

Flat washers and lock washers, when removed from an assembly, should always be replaced exactly as removed. Replace damaged washers with new ones. Always use a flat washer between a lock washer and any soft metal surface (such as aluminum), thin sheet metal or plastic.

Fastener sizes

For a number of reasons, automobile manufacturers are making wider and wider use of metal fasteners. Therefore, it is important to be able to tell the difference between standard (sometimes called U.S., English or SAE) and metric hardware, since they cannot be interchanged.

All bolts, whether standard or metric, are sized according to diameter, thread pitch and length. For example, a standard $\frac{1}{2}$ – 13 x 1 bolt is $\frac{1}{2}$ inch in diameter, has 13 threads per inch and is 1 inch long. An M12 – 1.75 x 25 metric bolt is 12 mm in diameter, has a thread pitch of 1.75 mm (the distance between threads) and is 25 mm long. The 2 bolts are nearly identical, and easily confused, but they are not interchangeable.

In addition to the differences in diameter, thread pitch and length, metric and standard bolts can also be distinguished by examining the bolt heads. To begin with, the distance across the flats on a standard bolt head is measured in inches, while the same dimension on a metric bolt is measured in millimetres (the same is true for nuts). As a result, a standard wrench should not be used on a metric bolt and a metric wrench should not be used on a standard bolt. Also, standard bolts have slashes radiating out from the center of the head to denote the grade or strength of the bolt (which is an indication of the amount of torque that can be applied to it). The greater the number of slashes, the greater the strength of the bolt (grades 0 through 5 are commonly used on automobiles). Metric bolts have a property class (grade) number, rather than a slash, molded into their heads to indicate bolt strength. In this case, the higher the number the stronger the bolt (property class numbers 8.8, 9.8 and 10.9 are commonly used on automobiles).

Strength markings can also be used to distinguish standard hex nuts from metric hex nuts. Standard nuts have dots stamped into one side, while metric nuts are marked with a number. The greater the number of dots, or the higher the number, the greater the strength of the nut.

Metric studs are also marked on their ends according to property class (grade). Larger studs are numbered (the same as metric bolts), while smaller studs carry a geometric code to denote grade.

It should be noted that many fasteners, especially grades 0 through 2, have no distinguishing marks on them. When such is the case, the only way to determine whether a particular fastener is standard or metric is to measure the thread pitch or compare it to a known fastener of the same size.

Since fasteners of the same size (both standard and metric) may have different strength ratings, be sure to reinstall any bolts, studs or nuts removed from your vehicle in their original locations. Also, when replacing a fastener with a new one, make sure that the new one has a strength rating equal to or greater than the original.

Tightening sequences and procedures

Most threaded fasteners should be tightened to a specific torque value (torque is simply a twisting force). Over tightening a fastener can weaken it and lead to eventual breakage, while under tightening can cause it to eventually come loose. Bolts, screws and studs, depending on the materials they are made of and their thread diameters, have a specific torque value (many of which are noted in the Specifications Section at the beginning of each Chapter). Be sure to follow the torque recommendations closely. For fasteners not assigned a specific torque, a general torque value chart is presented here as a guide. As was previously mentioned, the size and grade of a fastener determine the amount of torque that can safely be applied to it. The figures listed here are approximate for Grade 2 and Grade 3 fasteners (higher grades can tolerate higher torque values).

Fasteners laid out in a pattern (i.e. cylinder head bolts, oil pan bolts, water pump bolts, differential cover bolts, etc.) must be loosened and tightened in a definite sequence to avoid warping the component. Initially, the bolts or nuts should be assembled finger tight only. Next, they should be tightened one full turn each, in a criss-cross or diagonal pattern. After each one has been tightened one full turn, return to the first one and tighten them all one-half turn, return to the first one and tighten them all one-half turn, following the same pattern. Finally, tighten each of them one-quarter turn at a time until they have all been tightened to the proper torque value. To loosen and remove them, the procedure would be reversed.

Component disassembly

Component disassembly should be done with care and purpose to help ensure that the parts go back together properly during reassembly. Always keep track of the sequence in which parts are removed. Make note of special characteristics or markings on parts that can be installed more than one way (such as a grooved thrust washer on a shaft). Its a good idea to lay the disassembled parts out on a clean surface in the order that they were removed. It may also be helpful to make simple sketches or take instant photos of components before removal.

When removing fasteners from an assembly, keep track of their locations. Sometimes threading a bolt back in a part, or putting the washers and nut back on a stud, can prevent mixups later. If nuts and bolts cannot be returned to their original locations, they should be kept

	ft-lb	Nm
Metric thread sizes		
M-6	6 to 9	9 to 12
M-8	14 to 21	19 to 28
M-10	28 to 40	38 to 54
M-12	50 to 71	68 to 96
M-14	80 to 140	109 to 154
Pipe thread sizes		
$\frac{1}{8}$	5 to 8	7 to 10
$\frac{1}{4}$	12 to 18	17 to 24
$\frac{3}{8}$	22 to 33	30 to 44
$\frac{1}{2}$	25 to 35	34 to 47
U.S. thread sizes		
$\frac{1}{4}$ – 20	6 to 9	9 to 12
$\frac{5}{16}$ – 18	12 to 18	17 to 24
$\frac{5}{16}$ – 24	14 to 20	19 to 27
$\frac{3}{8}$ – 16	22 to 32	30 to 43
$\frac{3}{8}$ – 24	27 to 38	37 to 51
$\frac{7}{16}$ – 14	40 to 55	55 to 74
$\frac{7}{16}$ – 20	40 to 60	55 to 81
$\frac{1}{2}$ – 13	55 to 80	75 to 108

in a compartmented box or a series of small boxed. A cupcake or muffin tin is ideal for this purpose, since each cavity can hold the bolts and nuts from a particular area (i.e. oil pan bolts, valve cover bolts, engine mount bolts, etc.). A pan of this type is especially helpful when working on assemblies with very small parts (such as the carburetor, alternator, valve train or interior dash and trim pieces). The cavities can be marked with paint or tape to identify the contents.

Whenever wiring looms, harnesses or connectors are separated, it's a good idea to identify them with numbered pieces of masking tape so that they can be easily reconnected.

Gasket sealing surfaces

Throughout any vehicle, gaskets are used to seal the mating surfaces between two parts and keep lubricants, fluids, vacuum or pressure contained in an assembly.

Many times these gaskets are coated with a liquid or paste type gasket sealing compound before assembly. Age, heat and pressure can sometimes cause the two parts to stick together so tightly that they are very difficult to separate. Often the assembly can be loosened by striking it with a soft-faced hammer near the mating surfaces. A regular hammer can be used if a block of wood is placed between the hammer and the part. Do not hammer on cast parts or parts that could be easily damaged. With any particularly stubborn part, always recheck to see that every fastener has been removed.

Avoid using a screwdriver or bar to pry apart an assembly, as they

can easily mar the gasket sealing surfaces of the parts (which must remain smooth). If prying is absolutely necessary, use an old broom handle, but keep in mind that extra clean-up will be necessary if the wood splinters.

After the parts are separated, the old gasket must be carefully scraped off and the gasket surfaces cleaned. Stubborn gasket material can be soaked with rust penetrant or treated with a special chemical to soften it so that it can be easily scraped off. A scraper can be fashioned from a piece of copper tubing by flattening and sharpening one end. Copper is recommended because it is usually softer than the surfaces to be scraped, which reduces the chance of gouging the part. Some gaskets can be removed with a wire brush, but regardless of the method used, the mating surfaces must be left clean and smooth. If for some reason the gasket surface is gouged, then a gasket sealer thick enough to fill scratches will have to be used upon reassembly of the components. For most applications, a non-drying (or semi-drying) gasket sealer is best.

Hose removal tips

Hose removal precautions closely parallel gasket removal precautions. Avoid scratching or gouging the surface that the hose mates against or the connection may leak. Because of various chemical reactions, the rubber in hoses can bond itself to the metal spigot that the hose fits over. To remove a hose, first loosen the hose clamps that secure it to the spigot. Then, with a slip joint pliers, grab the hose at

Grade 1 or 2   Grade 5   Grade 8

D   SAE system bolt identification (slash marks indicate strength rating; increasing number of marks means higher strength)

E   Metric system bolt identification (numbers correspond to bolt strength; the higher the number the greater the strength)

F   SAE system hex nut identification (increasing dots represent an increasing strength rating)

G   Metric system hex nut identification (the higher the number, the greater the strength rating)

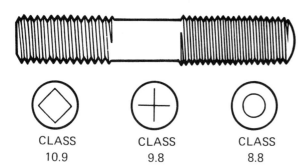

CLASS
10.9

CLASS
9.8

CLASS
8.8

H   Metric stud identification (large studs are marked with strength rating numbers which increase as strength increases; smaller studs are marked with a geometric code)

the clamp and rotate it around the spigot. Work it back and forth until it is completely free, then pull it off (silicone or other lubricants will ease removal if they can be applied between the hose and the spigot). Apply the same lubricant to the inside of the hose and the outside of the spigot to simplify installation.

If a hose clamp is broken or damaged, do not reuse it. Also, do not reuse hoses that are cracked, split or torn.

Tools

A selection of good tools is a basic requirement for anyone who plans to maintain and repair his or her own vehicle. For the owner who has few tools, if any, the initial investment might seem high, but when compared to the spiraling costs of professional auto maintenance and repair, it is a wise one.

To help the owner decide which tools are needed to perform the tasks detailed in this manual, the following tool lists are offered: *Maintenance and minor repair, Repair and overhaul* and *Special*. The newcomer to practical mechanics should start off with the *Maintenance and minor repair* tool set, which is adequate for the simpler jobs performed on a vehicle. Then, as his confidence and experience grows, he can tackle more difficult tasks, buying additional tools as they are

needed. Eventually the basic kit will be expanded into the *Repair and overhaul* tool set. Over a period of time, the experienced do-it-yourselfer will assemble a tool set complete enough for most repair and overhaul procedures and will add tools from the *Special* category when he feels the expense is justified by the frequency of use.

Maintenance and minor repair tool kit

The tools in this list should be considered the minimum required for performance of routine maintenance, servicing and minor repair work. We recommend the purchase of combination wrenches (box end and open end combined in one wrench); while more expensive than open-ended ones, they offer the advantages of both types or wrench.

Combination wrench set ($\frac{1}{4}$ in to 1 in or 6 mm to 19 mm)
Adjustable wrench – 8 in
Spark plug wrench (with rubber insert)
Spark plug gap adjusting tool
Feeler gauge set
Brake bleeder wrench
Standard screwdriver ($\frac{5}{16}$ in x 6 in)
Phillips screwdriver (No 2 x 6 in)
Combination pliers – 6 in
Hacksaw and assortment of blades
Tire pressure gauge
Grease gun
Oil can
Fine emery cloth
Wire brush
Battery post and cable cleaning tool
Oil filter wrench
Funnel (medium size)
Safety goggles
Jack stands (2)
Drain pan

Note: *if basic tune-ups are going to be a part of routine maintenance, it will be necessary to purchase a good quality stroboscopic timing light and a combination tachometer/dwell meter. Although they are included in the list of Special tools, they are mentioned here because they are absolutlly necessary for tuning most vehicles properly.*

I   Valve spring compressor

J   Piston ring compressor

K   Universal hub puller

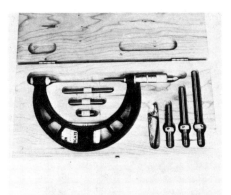

L   Micrometer set

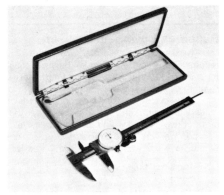

M   Dial caliper

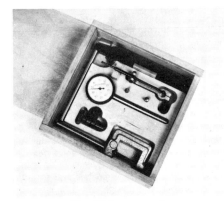

N   Dial gauge set

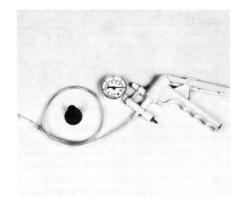

O   Vacuum pump

P   Brake shoe spring tool

Q   Piston ring expander

R   Hydraulic lifter extractor

S   Piston ring groove cleaner

T   Cylinder surfacing hone

U   Cylinder ridge reamer

V   Cylinder bore gauge

Repair and overhaul tool set

These tools are essential for anyone who plans to perform major repairs and are in addition to those in the Maintenance and minor repair tool kit. Included is a comprehensive set of sockets which, though expensive, will be found to be invaluable because of their versatility (especially when various extensions and drives are available). We recommend the $\frac{1}{2}$ in drive over the $\frac{3}{8}$ in drive. Although the larger drive is bulky and more expensive, it has the capability of accepting a very wide range of large sockets (ideally, the mechanic would have a $\frac{3}{8}$ in drive set and a $\frac{1}{2}$ in drive set).

Socket set(s)
Reversible ratchet
Extension – 10 in
Universal joint
Torque wrench (same size as sockets)
Ball pein hammer – 8 oz
Soft-faced hammer (plastic/rubber)
Standard screwdriver ($\frac{1}{4}$ in x 6 in)
Standard screwdriver (stubby – $\frac{5}{16}$ in)
Phillips screwdriver (No 3 x 8 in)
Phillips screwdriver (stubby – No 2)
Pliers – Vise grip
Pliers – lineman's
Pliers – needle nose
Pliers – circlip (internal and external)
Cold chisel – $\frac{1}{2}$ in
Scriber
Scraper (made from flattened copper tubing)
Center punch
Pin punches ($\frac{1}{16}$, $\frac{1}{8}$, $\frac{3}{16}$ in)
Steel rule/straight edge – 12 in
Allen wrench set ($\frac{1}{8}$ to $\frac{3}{8}$ in or 4 mm to 10 mm)
A selection of files
Wire brush (large)
Jack stands (second set)
Jack (scissor or hydraulic type)

Note: *Another tool which is often useful is an electric drill motor with a chuck capacity of $\frac{3}{8}$ in (and a set of good quality drill bits).*

Special tools

The tools in this list include those which are not used regularly, are expensive to buy, or which need to be used in accordance with their manufacturer's instructions. Unless these tools will be used frequently, it is not very economical to purchase many of them. A consideration would be to split the cost and use between yourself and a friend or friends. In addition, most of these tools can be obtained from a tool rental shop on a temporary basis.

This list contains only those tools and instruments widely available to the public, and not those special tools produced by vehicle manufacturers for distribution to dealer service departments. Occasionally, references to the manufacturer's special tools are included in the text of this manual. Generally, an alternative method of doing the job without the special tool is offered. However, sometimes there is no alternative to their use. Where this is the case, and the tool cannot be purchased or borrowed, the work should be turned over to the dealer, a repair shop or an automotive machine shop.

Valve spring compressor
Piston ring groove cleaning tool
Piston ring compressor
Piston ring installation tool
Cylinder compression gauge
Cylinder ridge reamer
Cylinder surfacing hone
Cylinder bore gauge
Micrometers and/or dial calipers
Hydraulic lifter removal tool
Balljoint separator
Universal-type puller
Impact screwdriver
Dial indicator set
Stroboscopic timing light (inductive pickup)
Hand operated vacuum/pressure pump
Tachometer/dwell meter
Universal electrical multi-meter
Cable hoist
Brake spring removal and installation tools
Floor jack

Buying tools

For the do-it-yourselfer who is just starting to get involved in vehicle maintenance and repair, there are a couple of options available when purchasing tools. If maintenance and minor repair is the extent of the work to be done, the purchase of individual tools is satisfactory. If, on the other hand, extensive work is planned, it would be a good idea to purchase a modest tool set from one of the large retail chain stores. A set can usually be bought at a substantial savings over the individual tool prices (and they often come with a tool box). As additional tools are needed, add-on sets, individual tools and a larger tool box can be purchased to expand the tool selection. Building a tool set gradually allows the cost of the tools to be spread over a longer period of time and gives the mechanic the freedom to choose only those tools that will actually be used.

Tool stores will often be the only source of some of the special tools that are needed, but regardless of where tools are bought, try to avoid cheap ones (especially when buying screwdrivers and sockets) because they won't last very long. The expense involved in replacing cheap tools will eventually be greater than the initial cost of quality tools.

Care and maintenance of tools

Good tools are expensive, so it makes sense to treat them with respect. Keep thim in a clean and usable condition and store them properly when not in use. Always wipe off any dirt, grease or metal chips before putting them away. Never leave tools lying around in the work area. Upon completion of a job, always check closely under the hood for tools that may have been left there (so they don't get lost during a test drive).

Some tools, such as a screwdriver, pliers, wrenches and sockets, can be hung on a panel mounted on the garage or workshop wall, while others should be kept in a tool box or tray. Measuring instruments, gauges, meters, etc. must be carefully stored where they cannot be damaged by weather or impact from other tools.

When tools are used with care and stored properly, they will last a very long time. Even with the best of care, tools will wear out if used frequently. When a tool is damaged or worn out, replace it; subsequent jobs will be safer and more enjoyable if you do.

For those who desire to learn more about tools and their uses, a book entitled *How to Choose and Use Car Tools* is available from the publishers of this manual.

Working facilities

Not to be overlooked when discussing tools is the workshop. If anything more than routine maintenance is to be carried out, some sort of suitable work area is essential.

It is understood, and appreciated, that many home mechanics do not have a good workshop or garage available, and end up removing an engine or doing major repairs outside (it is recommended that the overhaul or repair be completed under the cover of a roof).

A clean, flat workbench or table of suitable working height is an absolute necessity. The workbench should be equipped with a vise that has a jaw opening of at least 4 inches.

As mentioned previously, some clean, dry storage space is also required for tools, as well as the lubricants, fluids, cleaning solvents, etc. which soon becomes necessary.

Sometimes waste oil and fluids, drained from the engine or transmission during normal maintenance or repairs, present a disposal problem. To avoid pouring oil on the ground or into the sewage system, simply pour the used fluids into large containers, seal them with caps and deliver them to a local recycling center or disposal area. Plastic jugs (such as old anti-freeze containers) are ideal for this purpose.

Always keep a supply of old newspapers and clean rags available. Old towels are excellent for mopping up spills. Many mechanics use rolls of paper towels for most work because they are readily available and disposable. To help keep the area under the vehicle clean, a large cupboard box can be cut open and flattened to protect the garage or shop floor.

Whenever working over a painted surface (such as when leaning over a fender to service something under the hood), always cover it with an old blanket or bedspread to protect the finish. Vinyl covered pads, made especially for this purpose, are available at auto parts stores.

Jacking and towing

Jacking

The jack supplied with the vehicle should only be used to raise the car for changing a tire or placing jackstands under the frame. Under no circumstances should work be performed beneath the vehicle nor should the engine be started while the jack is being used as the only means of support. Before attempting to jack up your automobile, make sure it is parked on level ground. Block the wheels and put the transmission in 'Park' (automatic) or 'Reverse' (manual). Detailed instructions on jack positioning and use of the bumper jack are supplied in the car owner's manual.

Towing

If the driveline and steering are operable, the car may be towed with all wheels on the ground for distances up to 50 miles and at speeds of 35 mph or less. For each towing, the steering must be free, the transmission placed in 'Neutral' and the parking brake released. Hook towing cables or chains to the chassis, not to the bumpers or bumper brackets.

It is possible to tow your car for distances greater than 50 miles if the driveshaft is disconnected and removed from the vehicle. This is important. Transmission damage can result from towing a car with the driveshaft connected (particularly with automatic transmission).

Safety is always an important consideration. Use a tow bar whenever possible. Install a safety chain and obey all traffic laws. Remember that power brakes and power steering will not operate when the engine is not running. Also, the tow vehicle will require more maneuvering room and a longer braking/stopping distance when towing another vehicle.

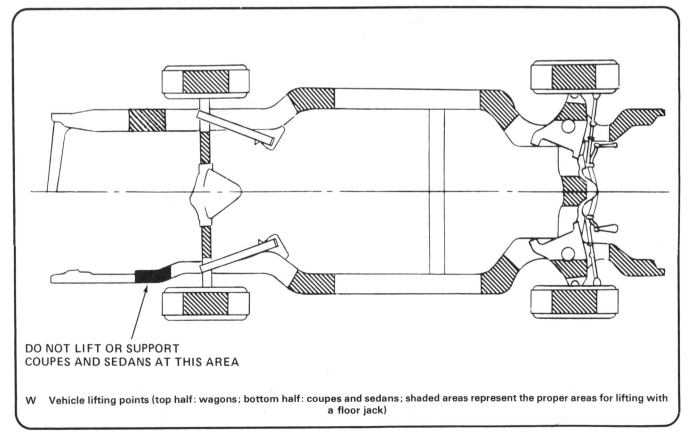

DO NOT LIFT OR SUPPORT
COUPES AND SEDANS AT THIS AREA

W   Vehicle lifting points (top half: wagons; bottom half: coupes and sedans; shaded areas represent the proper areas for lifting with a floor jack)

Automotive chemicals and lubricants

A number of automotive chemicals and lubricants are available for use in vehicle maintenance and repair. They represent a wide variety of products ranging from cleaning solvents and degreasers to lubricants and protective sprays for rubber, plastic and vinyl.

Contact point/spark plug cleaner is a solvent used to clean oily film and dirt from points, grime from electrical connectors and oil deposits from spark plugs. It is oil free and leaves no residue. It can also be used to remove gum and varnish from carburetor jets and other orifices.

Carburetor cleaner is similar to contact point/spark plug cleaner but it is usually has a stronger solvent and may leave a slight oily residue. It is not recommended for cleaning electrical components or connections.

Brake system cleaner is used to remove grease or brake fluid from brake system components (where clean surfaces are absolutely necessary and petroleum-based solvents cannot be used); it also leaves no residue.

Silicone based lubricants are used to protect rubber parts such as hoses, weatherstripping and grommets, and are used as lubricants for hinges and locks.

Multi-purpose grease is an all purpose lubricant used wherever grease is more practical than a liquid lubricant such as oil. Some multipurpose grease is colored white and specially formulated to be more resistant to water than ordinary grease.

Bearing grease/wheel bearing grease is a heavy grease used where increased loads and friction are encountered (i.e. wheel bearings, universal joints, etc.).

High temperature wheel bearing grease is designed to withstand the extreme temperatures encountered by wheel bearings in disc brake equipped vehicles. It usally contains molybdenum disulfide, which is a 'dry' type lubricant.

Gear oil (sometimes called gear lube) is a specially designed oil used in differentials, manual transmissions and manual gearboxes, as well as other areas where high friction, high temperature lubrication is required. It is available in a number of viscosities (weights) for various applications.

Motor oil, of course, is the lubricant specially formulated for use in the engine. It normally contains a wide variety of additives to prevent corrosion and reduce foaming and wear. Motor oil comes in various weights (viscosity ratings) of from 5 to 80. The recommended weight of the oil depends on the seasonal temperature and the demands on the engine. Light oil is used in cold climates and under light load conditions; heavy oil is used in hot climates and where high loads are encountered. Multi-viscosity oils are designed to have characteristics of both light and heavy oils and are available in a number of weights from 5W-20 to 20W-50.

Oil additives range from viscosity index improvers to slick chemical treatments that are supposed to reduce friction. It should be noted that most oil manufacturers caution against using additives with their oils.

Gas additives perform several functions, depending on their chemical makeup. They usually contain solvents that help dissolve gum and varnish that build up on carburetor and intake parts. They also serve to break down carbon deposits that form on the inside surfaces of the combustion chambers. Some additives contain upper cylinder lubricants for valves and piston rings.

Brake fluid is a specially formulated hydraulic fluid that can withstand the heat and pressure encountered in brake systems. Care must be taken that this fluid does not come in contact with painted surfaces or plastics. An opened container should always be resealed to prevent contamination by water or dirt.

Undercoating is a petroleum-based tar-like substance that is designed to protect metal surfaces on the under-side of a vehicle from corrosion. It also acts as a sound deadening agent by insulating the bottom of the vehicle.

Weatherstrip cement is used to bond weatherstripping around doors, windows and trunk lids. It is sometimes used to attach trim pieces as well.

Degreasers are heavy duty solvents used to remove grease and grime that accumulates on engine and chassis components. They can be sprayed or brushed on and, depending on the tire, are rinsed with either water or solvent.

Solvents are used alone or in combination with degreasers to clean parts and assemblies during repair and overhaul. The home mechanic should use only solvents that are non-flammable and that do not produce irritating fumes.

Gasket sealing compounds may be used in conjunction with gaskets, to improve their sealing capabilities, or alone, to seal metal-to-metal joints. Many gaskets can withstand extreme heat, some are impervious to gasoline and lubricants, while others are capable of filling and sealing large cavities. Depending on the intended use, gasket sealers either dry hard or stay relatively soft and pliable. They are usually applied by hand, with a brush, or are sprayed on the gasket sealing surfaces.

Thread cement is an adhesive locking compound that prevents threaded fasteners from loosening because of vibration. It is available in a variety of types for different applications.

Moisture dispersants are usually sprays that can be used to dry out electrical components such as the distributor, fuse block and wiring connectors. Some types can also be used as treatment for rubber and as a lubricant for hinges, cables and locks.

Waxes and polishes are used to help protect painted and plated surfaces from the weather. Different types of paint may require the use of different types of wax or polish. Some polishes utilize a chemical or abrasive cleaner to help remove the top layer of oxidized (dull) paint in older vehicles. In recent years, many non-wax polishes (that contain a wide variety of chemicals such as polymers and silicones) have been introduced. These non-wax polishes are usally easier to apply and last longer than conventional waxes and polishes.

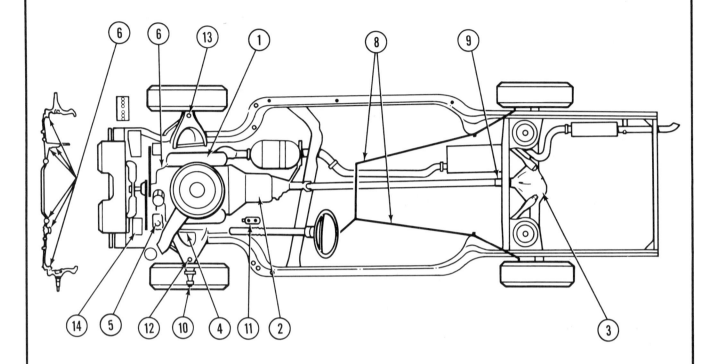

Recommended lubricants

Component	Lubricant type	Component	Lubricant type
Engine (1) *		**Steering box (4)**	GM 105 1052 grease
–30° to 20° F	SAE 5W – 20		
	SAE 5W – 30	**Power steering reservoir (5)** ..	GM Power steering fluid
0° to 60°F	SAE 10W		
	SAE 5W – 30	**Steering linkage (6)**	GM 6031 – M grease
	SAE 10W – 30		
	SAE 10W – 40	**Front suspension (7)**	GM 6031 – M grease
20° to 100°F	SAE 20W – 20		
	SAE 10W – 30	**Parking brake cables (8)**	GM 6031 – M grease
	SAE 10W – 40		
	SAE 20W – 50	**Drive shaft rear joint (9)**	GM 1050679 grease
	SAE 20W – 50		
		Front wheel bearings (10)	GM 1051344
* Engine lubricants should be labelled SE			Exxon Ronex MP grease
		Brake master cylinder (11)	Delco Supreme 11 or DOT-3 fluid
Transmission (2)			
Manual	SAE 80 GL5 gear oil	**Upper balljoints (12)**	GM 6031 – M grease
	SAE 90 GL5 gear oil	**Lower balljoints (13)**	GM 6031 – M grease
Automatic	Dexron II fluid		
Rear axle (3)		**Overflow reservoir (14)**	Coolant mixture (see Chapter 3)
Standard	SAE 80 GL5 gear oil		
	SAE 90 GL5 gear oil		
Limited slip differential	GM 105 1022 gear oil		

Troubleshooting

Contents

1 Engine will not rotate when attempting to start

1   Battery terminal connections loose or corroded. Check the cable
terminals at the battery; tighten or clean corrosion as necessary.
2   Battery discharged or faulty. If the cable connectors are clean and
tight on the battery posts, turn the key to the 'On' position and switch
on the headlights and/or windshield wipers. If these fail to function, the
battery is discharged.
3   Automatic transmission not fully engaged in 'Park' or manual
transmission clutch not fully depressed.
4   Broken, loose or disconnected wiring in the starting circuit. Inspect
all wiring and connectors at the battery, starter solenoid (at lower right
side of engine) and ignition switch (on steering column).
5   Starter motor pinion jammed on flywheel ring gear. If manual
transmission, place gearshift in gear and rock the car to manually turn

the engine. Remove starter (Chapter 5) and inspect pinion and
flywheel (Chapter 2) at earliest convenience.
6   Starter solenoid faulty (Chapter 5).
7   Starter motor faulty (Chapter 5).
8   Ignition switch faulty (Chapter 10).

2 Engine rotates but will not start

1   Fuel tank empty.
2   Battery discharged (engine rotates slowly). Check the operation of
electrical components as described in previous Section (see Chap.1).
3   Battery terminal connections loose or corroded. See previous
Section.
4   Carburetor flooded and/or fuel level in carburetor incorrect. This

will usually be accompanied by a strong fuel odor from under the hood. Wait a few minutes, depress the accelerator pedal all the way to the floor and attempt to start the engine.

5   Choke control inoperative (Chapters 1 and 4).
6   Fuel not reaching carburetor. With ignition switch in 'Off' position, open hood, remove the top plate of air cleaner assembly and observe the top of the carburetor (manually move choke plate back if necessary). Have an assistant depress accelerator pedal fully and check that fuel spurts into carburetor. If not, check fuel filter (Chapters 1 and 4), fuel lines and fuel pump (Chapter 4).
7   Excessive moisture on, or damage to, ignition components (Chapter 1).
8   Worn, faulty or incorrectly adjusted spark plugs (Chapter 1).
9   Broken, loose or disconnected wiring in the starting circuit (see previous Section).
10   Distributor loose, thus changing ignition timing. Turn the distributor body as necessary to start the engine, then set ignition timing as soon as possible (Chapter 1).
11   Ignition condenser faulty (Chapter 5).
12   Broken, loose or disconnected wires at the ignition coil, or faulty coil (Chapter 5).

3   Starter motor operates without rotating engine

1   Starter pinion sticking. Remove the starter (Chapter 5) and inspect.
2   Starter pinion or engine flywheel teeth worn or broken. Remove the inspection cover at the rear of the engine and inspect.

4   Engine hard to start when cold

1   Battery discharged or low. Check as described in Section 1.
2   Choke control inoperative or out of adjustment (Chapters 1 and 4).
3   Carburetor flooded (see Section 2).
4   Fuel supply not reaching the carburetor (see Section 2).
5   Carburetor worn and in need of overhauling (Chapter 4).

5   Engine hard to start when hot

1   Choke sticking in the closed position (Chapter 1).
2   Carburetor flooded (see Section 2).
3   Air filter in need of replacement (Chapter 1).
4   Fuel not reaching the carburetor (see Section 2).
5   Thermac air cleaner faulty (Chapter 1).
6   EFE (heat riser) sticking in the closed position (Chapter 1).

6   Starter motor noisy or excessively rough in engagement

1   Pinion or flywheel gear teeth worn or broken. Remove the inspection cover at the rear of the engine and inspect.
2   Starter motor retaining bolts loose or missing.

7   Engine starts but stops immediately

1   Loose or faulty electrical connections at distributor, coil or alternator.
2   Insufficient fuel reaching the carburetor. Disconnect the fuel line at the carburetor and remove the filter (Chapter 1). Place a container under the disconnected fuel line. If equipped with HEI system (1975 – 1980), disconnect wiring connector marked 'BAT' from distributor cap. If conventional system (1974), disconnect the coil wire from the center of the distributor cap. These steps will prevent the engine from starting. Have an assistant crank the engine several revolutions by turning the ignition key. Observe the flow of fuel from the line. If little or none at all, check for blockage in the lines and/or replace the fuel pump (Chapter 4).
3   Vacuum leak at the gasket surfaces or the intake manifold and/or carburetor. Check that all mounting bolts (nuts) are tightened to specifications and all vacuum hoses connected to the carburetor and manifold are positioned properly and are in good condition.

8   Engine 'lopes' while idling or idles erratically

1   Vacuum leakage. Check mounting bolts (nuts) at the carburetor and intake manifold for tightness. Check that all vacuum hoses are connected and are in good condition. Use a doctor's stethoscope or a length of fuel line hose held against your ear to listen for vacuum leaks while the engine is runnng. A hissing sound will be heard. A soapy water solution will also detect leaks. Check the carburetor and intake manifold gasket surfaces.
2   Leaking EGR valve or plugged PCV valve (see Chapter 6).
3   Air cleaner clogged and in need of replacement (Chapter 1).
4   Fuel pump not delivering sufficient fuel to the carburetor (see Section 7).
5   Carburetor out of adjustment (Chapter 4).
6   Leaking head gasket. If this is suspected, take the car to a repair shop or GM dealer where this can be pressure checked without the need to remove the heads.
7   Timing chain or gears worn and in need of replacement (Chap.2).
8   Camshaft lobes worn, necessitating the removal of the camshaft for inspection (Chapter 2).

9   Engine misses at idle speed

1   Spark plugs faulty or not gapped properly (Chapter 1).
2   Faulty spark plug wires (Chapter 1).
3   Faulty or incorrectly set contact breaker points (1974 models only). Also check for excessive moisture on distributor components and/or damage (Chapter 1).
4   Carburetor choke not operating properly (Chapter 1).
5   Sticking or faulty emissions systems (see Troubleshooting in Chapter 6).
6   Clogged fuel filter and/or foreign matter in fuel. Remove the fuel filter (Chapter 1) and inspect.
7   Vacuum leaks at carburetor, intake manifold or at hose connections. Check as described in Section 8.
8   Incorrect idle speed (Chapter 1) or idle mixture (Chapter 4).
9   Incorrect ignition timing (Chapter 1).
10   Uneven or low cylinder compression. Remove plugs and use compression tester as per manufacturer's instructions.

10   Engine misses throughout driving speed range

1   Carburetor fuel filter clogged and/or impurities in the fuel system (Chapter 1). Also check fuel output at the carburetor (see Section 7).
2   Faulty or incorrectly gapped spark plugs (Chapter 1).
3   Incorrectly set ignition timing (Chapter 1).
4   Contact points faulty or incorrectly set (1974 models only). At the same time check for a cracked distributor cap, disconnected distributor wires, or damage to the distributor components (Chapter 1).
5   Leaking spark plug wires (Chapter 1).
6   Emissions system components faulty (see Troubleshooting section, Chapter 6).
7   Low or uneven cylinder compression pressures. Remove spark plugs and test compression with gauge.
8   Weak or faulty ignition coil or condenser (1974 models, see Chapter 5).
9   Weak or faulty HEI ignition system (1975 – 1980 models, see Chapter 5).
10   Vacuum leaks at carburetor, intake manifold or vacuum hoses (see Section 8).

11   Engine stalls

1   Carburetor idle speed incorrectly set (Chapter 1).
2   Carburetor fuel filter clogged and/or water and impurities in the fuel system (Chapter 1).
3   Choke improperly adjusted or sticking (Chapter 1).
4   Distributor components damp, points out of adjustment or damage to distributor cap, rotor, etc. (Chapter 1).
5   Emission system components faulty (Troubleshooting section, Chapter 6).

6   Faulty or incorrectly gapped spark plugs. (Chapter 1). Also check spark plug wires (Chapter 1).
7   Vacuum leak at the carburetor, intake manifold or vacuum hoses. Check as described in Section 8.
8   Valve lash incorrectly set (Chapter 2).

12 Engine lacks power

1   Incorrect ignition timing (Chapter 1).
2   Excessive play in distributor shaft. At the same time check for worn or maladjusted contact points, faulty distributor cap, wires, etc. (Chapter 1).
3   Faulty or incorrectly gapped spark plugs (Chapter 1).
4   Carburetor not adjusted properly or excessively worn (Chapter 4).
5   Weak coil or condensor (Chapter 5).
6   Faulty HEI system coil (Chapter 5).
7   Brakes binding (Chapters 1 and 9).
8   Automatic transmission fluid level incorrect, causing slippage (Chapter 1).
9   Manual transmission clutch slipping (Chapter 1).
10   Fuel filter clogged and/or impurities in the fuel system (Chapter 1).
11   Emission control systems not functioning properly (see Troubleshooting, Chapter 6).
12   Use of sub-standard fuel. Fill tank with proper octane fuel.
13   Low or uneven cylinder compression pressures. Test with compression tester, which will also detect leaking valves and/or blown head gasket.

13 Engine backfires

1   Emissions systems not functioning properly (see Troubleshooting, Chapter 6).
2   Ignition timing incorrect (Section 1).
3   Carburetor in need of adjustment or worn excessively (Chapter 4).
4   Vacuum leak at carburetor, intake manifold or vacuum hoses. Check as described in Section 8.
5   Valve lash incorrectly set, and/or valves sticking (Chapter 2).

14 Pinging or knocking engine sounds on hard acceleration or uphill

1   Incorrect grade of fuel. Fill tank with fuel of the proper octane rating.
2   Ignition timing incorrect (Chapter 1).
3   Carburetor in need of adjustment (Chapter 4).
4   Improper spark plugs. Check plug type with that specified on tune-up decal located inside engine compartment. Also check plugs and wires for damage (Chapter 1).
5   Worn or damaged distributor components (Chapter 1).
6   Faulty emission systems (see Troubleshooting, Chapter 6).
7   Vacuum leak. (Check as described in Section 8).

15 Engine 'diesels' (continues to run) after switching off

1   Idle speed too fast (Chapter 1).
2   Electrical solenoid at side of carburetor not functioning properly (not all models, see Chapter 4).
3   Ignition timing incorrectly adjusted (Chapter 1).
4   Thermac air cleaner valve not operating properly (see Troubleshooting, Chapter 6).
5   Excessive engine operating temperatures. Probable causes of this are: malfunctioning thermostat, clogged radiator, faulty water pump. (See Chapter 3).

Engine electric

16 Battery will not hold a charge

1   Alternator drivebelt defective or not adjusted properly (Chapter 1).
2   Electrolyte level too low or too weak (Chapter 1).

3   Battery terminals loose or corroded (Chapter 1).
4   Alternator not charging properly (Chapter 5).
5   Loose, broken or faulty wiring in the charging circuit (Chapter 5).
6   Short in vehicle circuitry causing a continual drain on battery.
7   Battery defective internally.

17 Ignition light fails to go out

1   Fault in alternator or charging circuit (Chapter 5).
2   Alternator drivebelt defective or not properly adjusted (Chapter 1).

18 Ignition light fails to come on when key is turned

1   Ignition light bulb faulty (Chapter 10).
2   Alternator faulty (Chapter 5).
3   Fault in the printed circuit, dash wiring or bulb holder (Chapter 10).

Engine fuel system

19 Excessive fuel consumption

1   Dirty or choked air filter element (Chapter 1).
2   Incorrectly set ignition timing (Chapter 1).
3   Choke sticking or improperly adjusted (Chapter 1).
4   TCS emission system not functioning properly (not all cars, see Chapter 6).
5   Carburetor idle speed and/or mixture not adjusted properly (Chapters 1 and 4).
6   Carburetor internal parts excessively worn or damaged (Chap.4).
7   Low tire pressure or incorrect tire size (Chapter 1).

20 Fuel leakage and/or fuel odor

1   Leak in a fuel feed or vent line (Chapter 6).
2   Tank overfilled. Fill only to automatic shut-off.
3   ECS emission system filter in need of replacement (Chapter 6).
4   Vapor leaks from ECS system lines (Chapter 6).
5   Carburetor internal parts excessively worn or out of adjustment (Chapter 4).

Engine cooling system

21 Overheating

1   Insufficient coolant in system (Chapter 1).
2   Fan belt defective or not adjusted properly (Chapter 1).
3   Radiator core blocked or radiator grille dirty and restricted (Chapter 3).
4   Thermostat faulty (Chapter 3).
5   Freewheeling clutch fan not functioning properly. Check for oil leakage at the rear of the cooling fan, indicating the need for replacement (Chapter 3).
6   Radiator cap not maintaining proper pressure. Have cap pressure tested by gas station or repair shop.
7   Ignition timing incorrect (Chapter 1).

22 Overcooling

1   Thermostat faulty (Chapter 3).
2   Inaccurate temperature gauge (Chapter 10).

23 External water leakage

1   Deteriorated or damaged hoses. Loose clamps at hose connections (Chapter 1).
2   Water pump seals defective. If this is the case, water will drip from the 'weep' hole in the water pump body (Chapter 3).

3 Leakage from radiator core or header tank. This will require the radiator to be professionally repaired (see Chapter 3 for removal procedures).
4 Engine drain plugs or water jacket freeze plugs leaking (see Chapters 2 and 3).

24 Internal water leakage

Note: *Internal coolant leaks can usually be detected by examining the oil. Check the dipstick and inside of valve cover for water deposits and an oil consistency like that of a milkshake.*
1 Faulty cylinder head gasket. Have the system pressure-tested professionally or remove the cylinder heads (Chapter 2) and inspect.
2 Cracked cylinder bore or cylinder head. Dismantle engine and inspect (Chapter 2).

25 Water loss

1 Overfilling system (Chapter 1).
2 Coolant boiling away due to overheating (see causes in Section 15).
3 Internal or external leakage (see Sections 22 and 23).
4 Faulty radiator cap. Have the cap pressure tested.

26 Poor coolant circulation

1 Inoperative water pump. A quick test is to pinch the top radiator hose closed with your hand while the engine is idling, then let loose. You should feel a surge of water if the pump is working properly (Chapter 3).
2 Restriction in cooling system. Drain, flush and refill the system (Chapter 1). If it appears necessary, remove the radiator (Chapter 3) and have it reverse-flushed or professionally cleaned.
3 Fan drivebelt defective or not adjusted properly (Chapter 1).
4 Thermostat sticking (Chapter 3).

Clutch

27 Fails to release (pedal pressed to the floor – shift lever does not move freely in and out of reverse)

1 Improper linkage adjustment (Chapter 8).
2 Clutch fork off ball stud. Look under the car, on the left side of transmission.
3 Clutch disc warped, bent or excessively damaged (Chapter 8).

28 Clutch slips (engine speed increases with no increase in road speed)

1 Linkage in need of adjustment (Chapter 8).
2 Clutch disc oil soaked or facing worn. Remove disc (Chapter 8) and inspect.
3 Clutch disc not seated in. It may take 30 or 40 normal starts for a new disc to seat.

29 Grabbing (juddering) on take-up

1 Oil on clutch disc facings. Remove disc (Chapter 8) and inspect. Correct any leakage source.
2 Worn or loose engine or transmission mounts. These units may move slightly when clutch is released. Inspect mounts and bolts.
3 Worn splines on clutch gear. Remove clutch components (Chapter 8) and inspect.
4 Warped pressure plate or flywheel. Remove clutch components and inspect.

30 Squeal or rumble with clutch fully engaged (pedal released)

1 Improper adjustment; no lash (Chapter 8).
2 Release bearing binding on transmission bearing retainer. Remove clutch components (Chapter 8) and check bearing. Remove any burrs or nicks, clean and relubricate before reinstallation.
3 Weak linkage return spring. Replace the spring.

31 Squeal or rumble with clutch fully disengaged (pedal depressed)

1 Worn, faulty or broken release bearing (Chapter 8).
2 Worn or broken pressure plate springs (or diaphragm fingers) (Chapter 8).

32 Clutch pedal stays on floor when disengaged

1 Bind in linkage or release bearing. Inspect linkage or remove clutch components as necessary.
2 Linkage springs being over-traveled. Adjust linkage for proper lash. Make sure proper pedal stop (bumper) is installed.

Manual transmission

Note: *All the following Section references contained within Chapter 7.*

33 Noisy in neutral with engine running

1 Input shaft bearing worn (Sections 10 and 11).
2 Damaged main drive gear bearing (Sections 10 and 11).
3 Worn countergear bearings (Sections 10 and 11).
4 Worn or damaged countergear anti-lash plate (Sections 10 and 11).

34 Noisy in all gears

1 Any of the above causes, and/or:
2 Insufficient lubricant (see checking procedures in Chapter 1).

35 Noisy in one particular gear

1 Worn, damaged or chipped gear teeth for that particular gear (Sections 10 and 11).
2 Worn or damaged synchronizer for that particular gear (Sections 10 and 11).

36 Slips out of high gear

1 Transmission loose on clutch housing (Section 3).
2 Shift rods interfering with engine mounts or clutch lever (Section 2).
3 Shift rods not working freely (Section 2).
4 Damaged mainshaft pilot bearing (Section 9).
5 Dirt between transmission case and clutch housing, or misalignment of transmission (Section 9).
6 Worn or improperly adjusted linkage (Section 2).

37 Difficulty in engaging gears

1 Clutch not releasing fully (see clutch adjustment, Chapter 8).
2 Loose, damaged or maladjusted shift linkage. Make a thorough inspection, replacing parts as necessary. Adjust as described in Section 2.

38 Fluid leakage

1 Excessive amount of lubricant in transmission (see Chapter 1 for correct checking procedures. Drain lubricant as required).
2 Side cover loose or gasket damaged (Sections 7 and 8).
3 Rear oil seal or speedometer oil seal in need of replacement (Section 6).

Automatic transmission

Note: *Due to the complexity of the automatic transmission, it is difficult for the home mechanic to properly diagnose and service this component. For problems other than the following, the vehicle should be taken to a reputable mechanic.*

39 Fluid leakage

1 Automatic transmission fluid is a deep red color, and fluid leaks should not be confused with engine oil which can easily be blown by air flow to the transmission.
2 To pinpoint a leak, first remove all built-up dirt and grime from around the transmission. Degreasing agents and/or steam cleaning will achieve this. With the underside clean, drive the car at low speeds so the air flow will not blow the leak far from its source. Raise the car and determine where the leak is coming from. Common areas of leakage are:
    a) Fluid pan: tighten mounting bolts and/or replace pan gasket as necessary (see Chapter 1).
    b) Rear extension: tighten bolts and/or replace oil seal as necessary (Chapter 8).
    c) Filler pipe: replace the rubber oil seal where pipe enters transmission case.
    d) Transmission oil lines: tighten connectors where lines enter transmission case and/or replace lines.
    e) Vent pipe: transmission over-filled and/or water in fluid (see checking procedures, Chapter 1).
    f) Speedometer connector: replace the O-ring where speedometer cable enters transmission case.

40 General shift mechanism problems

1 Sections 4 and 5 in Chapter 7B deal with checking and adjusting the shift linkage on automatic transmissions. Common problems which may be attributed to maladjusted linkage are:
    a) Engine starting in gears other than 'P' (Park) or 'N' (Neutral).
    b) Indicator on quadrant pointing to a gear other than the one actually being used.
    c) Vehicle will not hold firm when in 'P' (Park) position.
    Refer to Sections 4 or 5 in Chapter 7B to adjust the manual linkage.

41 Transmission will not downshift with accelerator pedal pressed to the floor

1 Sections 6 and 7 in Chapter 7B deal with adjusting the downshift cable or downshift switch to enable the transmission to downshift properly.

42 Engine will start in gears other than 'P' (Park) or 'N' (Neutral)

1 Sections 9 in Chapter 7B deals with adjusting the neutral start switch used with automatic transmissions.

43 Transmission slips, shifts rough, is noisy or has no drive in forward or reverse gears

1 There are many probable causes for the above problems, but the home mechanic should concern himself only with one possibility; fluid level.

2 Before taking the vehicle to a specialist, check the level of the fluid and condition of the fluid as described in Chapter 1. Correct fluid level as necessary or change the fluid and filter if needed. If problem persists, have a professional diagnose the probable cause.

Driveshaft

44 Leakage of fluid at front of driveshaft

1 Defective transmission rear oil seal. See Chapter 7 for replacing procedures. While this is done, check the splined yoke for burrs or a rough condition which may be damaging the seal. If found, these can be dressed with crocus cloth or a fine dressing stone.

45 Knock or clunk when transmission is under initial load (just after transmission is put into gear)

1 Loose or disconnected rear suspension components. Check all mounting bolts and bushings (Chapter 1).
2 Loose driveshaft bolts. Inspect all bolts and nuts and tighten to torque specifications (Chapter 8).
3 Worn or damaged universal joint bearings. Test for wear (Chapter 8).

46 Metallic grating sound consistent with road speed

1 Pronounced wear in the universal joint bearings. Test for wear (Chapter 8).

47 Vibration

Note: *Before it can be assumed that the driveshaft is at fault, make sure the tires are perfectly balanced and perform the following test.*
1 Install a tachometer inside the car to monitor engine speed as the car is driven. Drive the car and note the engine speed at which the vibration (roughness) is most pronounced. Now shift the transmission to a different gear and bring the engine speed to the same point.
2 If the vibration occurs at the same engine speed (rpm) regardless of which gear the transmission is in, the driveshaft is NOT at fault since the driveshaft speed varies.
3 If the vibration decreases or is eliminated when the transmission is in a different gear at the same engine speed, refer to the following probable causes.
4 Bent or dented driveshaft. Inspect and replace as necessary (Chapter 8).
5 Undercoating or built-up dirt, etc. on the driveshaft. Clean the shaft thoroughly and test.
6 Worn universal joint bearings. Remove and inspect (Chapter 8).
7 Driveshaft and/or companion flange out of balance. Check for missing weights on the shaft. Remove driveshaft (Chapter 8) and reinstall 180° from original position. Retest. Have driveshaft professionally balanced if problem persists.

Rear axle

48 Noise – same when in Drive as when vehicle is coasting

1 Road noise. No corrective procedures available.
2 Tire noise. Inspect tires and tire pressures (Chapter 1).
3 Front wheel bearings loose, worn or damaged (Chapter 1).

49 Vibration

1 See probable causes under 'Driveshaft'. Proceed under the guidelines listed for the driveshaft. If the problem persists, check the rear wheel bearings by raising the rear of the car and spinning the wheels

by hand. Listen for evidence of rough (noisy) bearings. Remove and inspect (Chapter 8).

50 Oil leakage

1 Pinion oil seal damaged (Chapter 8).
2 Axle shaft oil seals damaged (Chapter 8).
3 Differential inspection cover leaking. Tighten mounting bolts or replace the gasket as required (Chapter 1).

Brakes

Note: *Before assuming a brake problem exists, check: that the tires are in good condition and are inflated properly (see Chapter 1); the front end alignment is correct; and that the vehicle is not loaded with weight in an unequal manner.*

51 Vehicle pulls to one side under braking

1 Defective, damaged or oil contaminated disc pad on one side. Inspect as described in Chapter 1. Refer to Chapter 9 if replacement is required.
2 Excessive wear of brake pad material or disc on one side. Inspect and correct as necessary.
3 Loose or disconnected front suspension components. Inspect and tighten all bolts to specifications (Chapter 1).
4 Defective caliper assembly. Remove caliper and inspect for stuck piston or damage (Chapter 9).

52 Noise (high-pitched squeak without brake applied)

1 Front brake pads worn out. This noise comes from the wear sensor rubbing against the disc. Replace pads with new ones immediately (Chapter 9).

53 Excessive brake pad travel

1 Partial brake system failure. Inspect entire system (Chapter 1) and correct as required.
2 Insufficient fluid in master cylinder. Check (Chapter 1) and add fluid and bleed system if necessary.
3 Rear brakes not adjusting properly. Make a series of starts and stops while the vehicle is in 'R' (Reverse). If this does not correct the situation remove drums and inspect self-adjusters (Chapter 1).

54 Brake pedal appears spongy when depressed

1 Air in hydraulic lines. Bleed the brake system (Chapter 9).
2 Faulty flexible hoses. Inspect all system hoses and lines. Replace parts as necessary.
3 Master cylinder mountings insecure. Inspect master cylinder bolts (nuts) and torque-tighten to specifications.
4 Master cylinder faulty (Chapter 9).

55 Excessive effort required to stop vehicle

1 Power brake servo not operating properly (Chapter 9).
2 Excessively worn linings or pads. Inspect and replace if necessary (Chapter 1).
3 One or more caliper pistons (front wheels) or wheel cylinders (rear wheels) seized or sticking. Inspect and rebuild as required (Chapter 9).
4 Brake linings or pads contaminated with oil or grease. Inspect and replace as required (Chapter 1).
5 New pads or linings fitted and not yet 'bedded in'. It will take a while for the new material to seat against the drum (or rotor).

56 Pedal travels to floor with little resistance

1 Little or no fluid in the master cylinder reservoir caused by: leaking wheel cylinder(s); leaking caliper piston(s); loose, damaged or disconnected brake lines. Inspect entire system and correct as necessary.

57 Brake pedal pulsates during brake application

1 Wheel bearings not adjusted properly or in need of replacement (Chapter 1).
2 Caliper not sliding properly due to improper installation or obstructions. Remove and inspect (Chapter 9).
3 Rotor not within specifications. Remove the rotor (Chapter 9) and check for excessive lateral run-out and parellelism. Have the rotor professionally machined or replace it with a new one.

Suspension and steering

58 Car pulls to one side

1 Tire pressures uneven (Chapter 1).
2 Defective tire (Chapter 1).
3 Excessive wear in suspension or steering components (Chapter 1).
4 Front end in need of alignment. Take car to a qualified specialist.
5 Front brakes dragging. Inspect braking system as described in Chapter 1.

59 Shimmy, shake or vibration

1 Tire or wheel out of balance or out of round. Have professionally balanced.
2 Loose, worn or out-of-adjustment wheel bearings (Chapter 1).
3 Shock absorbers and/or suspension components worn or damaged (Chapter 11).

60 Excessive pitching and/or rolling around corners or during braking

1 Defective shock absorbers. Replace as a set (Chapter 11).
2 Broken or weak coil springs and/or suspension components. Inspect as described in Chapter 11.

61 Excessively stiff steering

1 Lack of lubricant in steering box (manual) or power steering fluid reservoir (Chapter 1).
2 Incorrect tire pressures (Chapter 1).
3 Lack of lubrication at steering joints (Chapter 1).
4 Front end out of alignment.
5 See also Section 63 'Lack of power assistance'.

62 Excessive play in steering

1 Loose wheel bearings (Chapter 1).
2 Excessive wear in suspension or steering components (Chapter 1).
3 Steering gear out of adjustment (Chapter 11).

63 Lack of power assistance

1 Steering pump drivebelt faulty or not adjusted properly (Chapter 1).
2 Fluid level low (Chapter 1).
3 Hoses or pipes restricting the flow. Inspect and replace parts as necessary.
4 Air in power steering system. Bleed system (Chapter 11).

64 Excessive tire wear (not specific to one area)

1   Incorrect tire pressures (Chapter 1).
2   Tires out of balance. Have professionally balanced.
3   Wheels damaged. Inspect and replace as necessary.
4   Suspension or steering components excessively worn (Chapter 1).

65 Excessive tire wear on outside edge

1   Inflation pressures not correct (Chapter 1).
2   Excessive speed on turns.
3   Front end alignment incorrect (excessive toe-in). Have professionally aligned.

4   Suspension arm bent or twisted.

66 Excessive tire wear on inside edge

1   Inflation pressures incorrect (Chapter 1).
2   Front end alignment incorrect (toe-out). Have professionally aligned.
3   Loose or damaged steering components (Chapter 1).

67 Tire tread worn in one place

1   Tires out of balance. Balance tires professionally.
2   Damaged or buckled wheel. Inspect and replace if necessary.
3   Defective tire.

Safety first!

Regardless of how enthusiastic you may be about getting on with the job at hand, take the time to ensure that your safety is not jeopardized. A moment's lack of attention can result in an accident, as can failure to observe certain simple safety precautions. The possibility of an accident will always exist, and the following points should not be considered a comprehensive list of all dangers. Rather, they are intended to make you aware of the risks and to encourage a safety conscious approach to all work you carry out on your vehicle.

Essential DOs and DON'Ts

DON'T rely on a jack when working under the vehicle. Always use approved jackstands to support the weight of the vehicle and place them under the recommended lift or support points.

DON'T attempt to loosen extremely tight fasteners (i.e. wheel lug nuts) while the vehicle is on a jack — it may fall.

DON'T start the engine without first making sure that the transmission is in Neutral (or Park where applicable) and the parking brake is set.

DON'T remove the radiator cap from a hot cooling system — let it cool or cover it with a cloth and release the pressure gradually.

DON'T attempt to drain the engine oil until you are sure it has cooled to the point that it will not burn you.

DON'T touch any part of the engine or exhaust system until it has cooled sufficiently to avoid burns.

DON'T siphon toxic liquids such as gasoline, antifreeze and brake fluid by mouth, or allow them to remain on your skin.

DON'T inhale brake lining dust — it is potentially hazardous (see *Asbestos* below)

DON'T allow spilled oil or grease to remain on the floor — wipe it up before someone slips on it.

DON'T use loose fitting wrenches or other tools which may slip and cause injury.

DON'T push on wrenches when loosening or tightening nuts or bolts. Always try to pull the wrench toward you. If the situation calls for pushing the wrench away, push with an open hand to avoid scraped knuckles if the wrench should slip.

DON'T attempt to lift a heavy component alone — get someone to help you.

DON'T rush or take unsafe shortcuts to finish a job.

DON'T allow children or animals in or around the vehicle while you are working on it.

DO wear eye protection when using power tools such as a drill, sander, bench grinder, etc. and when working under a vehicle.

DO keep loose clothing and long hair well out of the way of moving parts.

DO make sure that any hoist used has a safe working load rating adequate for the job.

DO get someone to check on you periodically when working alone on a vehicle.

DO carry out work in a logical sequence and make sure that everything is correctly assembled and tightened.

DO keep chemicals and fluids tightly capped and out of the reach of children and pets.

DO remember that your vehicle's safety affects that of yourself and others. If in doubt on any point, get professional advice.

Asbestos

Certain friction, insulating, sealing, and other products — such as brake linings, brake bands, clutch linings, torque converters, gaskets, etc. — contain asbestos. *Extreme care must be taken to avoid inhalation of dust from such products since it is hazardous to health.* If in doubt, assume that they *do* contain asbestos.

Fire

Remember at all times that gasoline is highly flammable. Never smoke or have any kind of open flame around when working on a vehicle. But the risk does not end there. A spark caused by an electrical short circuit, by two metal surfaces contacting each other, or even by static electricity built up in your body under certain conditions, can ignite gasoline vapors, which in a confined space are highly explosive. Do not, under any circumstances, use gasoline for cleaning parts. Use an approved safety solvent.

Always disconnect the battery ground (–) cable *at the battery* before working on any part of the fuel system or electrical system. Never risk spilling fuel on a hot engine or exhaust component.

It is strongly recommended that a fire extinguisher suitable for use on fuel and electrical fires be kept handy in the garage or workshop at all times. Never try to extinguish a fuel or electrical fire with water.

Fumes

Certain fumes are highly toxic and can quickly cause unconsciousness and even death if inhaled to any extent. Gasoline vapor falls into this category, as do the vapors from some cleaning solvents. Any draining or pouring of such volatile fluids should be done in a well ventilated area.

When using cleaning fluids and solvents, read the instructions on the container carefully. Never use materials from unmarked containers.

Never run the engine in an enclosed space, such as a garage. Exhaust fumes contain carbon monoxide, which is extremely poisonous. If you need to run the engine, always do so in the open air, or at least have the rear of the vehicle outside the work area.

If you are fortunate enough to have the use of an inspection pit, never drain or pour gasoline and never run the engine while the vehicle is over the pit. The fumes, being heavier than air, will concentrate in the pit with possibly lethal results.

The battery

Never create a spark or allow a bare light bulb near a battery. They normally give off a certain amount of hydrogen gas, which is highly explosive.

Always disconnect the battery ground (–) cable *at the battery* before working on the fuel or electrical systems.

If possible, loosen the filler caps or cover when charging the battery from an external source (this does not apply to sealed or maintenance-free batteries). Do not charge at an excessive rate or the battery may burst.

Take care when adding water to a non maintenance-free battery and when carrying a battery. The electrolyte, even when diluted, is very corrosive and should not be allowed to contact clothing or skin.

Always wear eye protection when cleaning the battery to prevent the caustic deposits from entering your eyes.

Household current

When using an electric power tool, inspection light, etc., which operates on household current, always make sure that the tool is correctly connected to its plug and that, where necessary, it is properly grounded. Do not use such items in damp conditions and, again, do not create a spark or apply excessive heat in the vicinity of fuel or fuel vapor.

Secondary ignition system voltage

A severe electric shock can result from touching certain parts of the ignition system (such as the spark plug wires) when the engine is running or being cranked, particularly if components are damp or the insulation is defective. In the case of an electronic ignition system, the secondary system voltage is much higher and could prove fatal.

Chapter 1 Tune-up and routine maintenance

Contents

Specifications

Note: Additional specifications and torque settings can be found in each individual Chapter.

Engine oil capacity
Refill (all)	4 qts
With new filter	
1979 and 1980 Pontiac 265/301 engines	4 qts
All others	5 qts

Filters and emission control devices
Crankcase vent filter type	FB59
PCV valve type	
1974 and 1975	CV768C (all)
1976	CV768C (V8), CV770C (V6)
1977 and 1978	CV797C (V6), CV774C (V8)
1979 and 1980	CV792C (VIN codes W-Y), CV774C (VIN codes L-H)
Fuel filter type	
1974 and 1975	GF441 (4bbl 350 V8), GF427 (V6, 2bbl 350 V8)
1976 through 1978	GF470 (V6), GF427 (V8)
1979 and 1980	GF471 (all)
Oil filter type	
1974 through 1976	PF39 (V6), PF24 (V8)
1977 and 1978	PF 40 (V6), PF25 (V8)
1979 and 1980	PF47 (VIN codes W-Y), PF25 (VIN codes L-H), PF40 (V6)

Ignition system
Distributor type	
1974	Mechanical breaker
1975 through 1980	Breakerless, electronic (designated HEI)
Direction of distributor rotation	Clockwise
Breaker point gap (1974)	0.016 in
Dwell angle (1974)	$30° \pm 2°$
Dwell variation	$3°$ max
Firing order	
V8	1-8-4-3-6-5-7-2
V6	1-6-5-4-3-2
Spark plug gap	See tune-up decal in engine compartment or Specifications in Chapter 5

Ignition timing .... See tune-up decal in engine compartment or specifications in Chapter 5

Clutch pedal free-play .... 1.0±0.3 in (measured at center of pad)

Torque specifications	**ft-lb**
Oil pan drain plug	20
Spark plugs	15
Carburetor mounting nuts	12
Fuel inlet nut (fuel filter)	18
Manual transmission fill plug:	
All except Muncie 4-speed	18
Muncie 4-speed	30
Automatic transmission pan bolts	12
Rear axle filler/inspection plug	22
Rear axle cover bolts	27
Brake caliper mounting bolts	35
Wheel nuts:	
1974 through 1975	70
1976 through 1980	80

1   Introduction

This Chapter was designed to help the home mechanic maintain his (or her) car for peak performance, economy, safety and longevity.

On the following pages you will find a maintenance schedule along with sections which deal specifically with each item on the schedule. Included are visual checks, adjustments and item replacements.

Servicing your car using the time/mileage maintenance schedule and the sequenced sections will give you a planned program of maintenance. Keep in mind that it is a full plan, and maintaining only a few items at the specified intervals will not give you the same results.

You will find as you service your car that many of the procedures can, and should, be grouped together, due to the nature of the job at hand. Examples of this are as follows:

If the car is fully raised for a chassis lubrication, for example, this is the ideal time for the following checks: manual transmission fluid, rear axle fluid, exhaust system, suspension, steering and the fuel system.

If the tires and wheels are removed, as during a routine tire rotation, go ahead and check the brakes and wheel bearings at the same time.

If you must borrow or rent a torque wrench, you will do best to service the spark plugs, repack (or replace) the wheel bearings and check the carburetor mounting torque all in the same day to save time and money.

The first step of this or any maintenance plan is to prepare yourself before the actual work begins. Read through the appropriate sections for all work that is to be performed before you begin. Gather together all necessary parts and tools. If it appears you could have a problem during a particular job, don't hesitate to ask advice from your local parts man or dealer service department.

Routine maintenance intervals

Every 250 miles or weekly – whichever comes first

Check the engine oil level (Section 2).
Check the engine coolant level (Section 2).
Check the windshield washer fluid level (Section 2).
Check the battery water level (if equipped with removable vent caps) (Sec 2).
Check the tires and tire pressures (Section 3).
Check the automatic transmission fluid level (Section 2).
Check the power steering fluid level (Section 2).

Every 3750 miles or 6 months – whichever comes first

Change engine oil and filter (Section 4)*.
Lubricate the chassis components (Section 5).
Check the cooling system (Section 6).
Check the exhaust system (Section 7).
Check the suspension and steering components (Section 8).
Check and adjust (if necessary) the engine drive belts (Section 9).
Check the fuel system components (Section 10).
Check the brake master cylinder fluid level (Section 2).
Check the manual transmission fluid level (Section 2).
Check the rear axle fluid level (Section 2).
Replace the (PCV) valve (Section 1).
Replace the air filter and PCV filter (Section 12).

Every 7500 miles or 12 months – whichever comes first

Check the clutch pedal free-play (manual transmission only) (Section 13).
Rotate the tires (Section 14).
Check the Thermo Controlled air cleaner for proper operation (Section 15).
Check and adjust (if necessary) the engine idle speed (Section 16).
Check the EFE system (Section 17).
Replace the fuel filter (Section 18).
Check and adjust (if necessary) the engine ignition timing (Section 19).
Check the operation of the choke (Section 20).
Check the operation of the EGR valve (Section 21).
Change rear axle fluid (if car is used to pull a trailer) (Section 22).

Every 15 000 miles or 12 months – whichever comes first

Replace the spark plugs (Section 24).
Check and repack the front wheel bearings (perform this procedure whenever brakes are relined, regardless of maintenance interval) (Section 25).
Change the automatic transmission fluid and filter (if mainly driven under following conditions: heavy city traffic in hot-climate regions; in hill or mountain areas; frequent trailer pulling (Section 26).
Check the braking system (Section 27).
Check the mounting torque of the carburetor (Section 28).
Check the spark plug wires (Section 29).
Drain, flush and refill the cooling system (Section 30).
Replace the contact points, adjust dwell angle and check the distributor (1974 models only) (Section 31).

Every 30 000 miles or 24 months – whichever comes first

Change the rear axle fluid (if car is used to pull a trailer, change at 7500 miles) (Section 2).

Change the automatic transmission fluid and filter (if driven under abnormal conditions, see 15 000 miles servicing) (Section 26).

Check the ECS emissions system and replace the charcoal canister filter (Section 32).

*Note: *Buick recommends 3000 mile oil/filter change intervals for engines equipped with a turbocharger. It is advisable, where practical, to shorten the interval even more to further protect against turbocharger wear and damage.*

2   Fluid levels check

1   There are a number of components on a vehicle which rely on the use of fluids to perform their job. Through the normal operation of the car, these fluids are used up and must be replenished before damage occurs. See the *Recommended Lubricants* Section for the specific fluid to be used when adding is required. When checking fluid levels it is important that the car is on a level surface.

Engine oil

2   The engine oil level is checked with a dipstick which is located at the side of the engine block. This dipstick travels through a tube and into the oil pan to the bottom of the engine.

3   The oil level should be checked preferably before the car has been driven, or about 15 minutes after the engine has been shut off. If the oil is checked immediately after driving the car, some of the oil will remain in the upper engine components, thus giving an inaccurate reading on the dipstick.

4   Pull the dipstick from its tube and wipe all the oil from the end with a clean rag. Insert the clean dipstick all the way back into the oil pan and pull it out again. Observe the oil at the end of the dipstick (photo). At its highest point, the level should be between the 'Add' and 'Full' marks.

5   It takes approximately 1 quart of oil to raise the level from the 'Add' mark to the 'Full' mark on the dipstick. Do not allow the level to drop below the 'Add' mark as this may cause engine damage due to oil starvation. On the other hand, do not overfill the engine by adding oil above the 'Full' mark as this may result in oil-fouled spark plugs, oil leaks or oil seal failures.

6   Oil is added to the engine after removing a twist-off cap located either on the rocker arm cover or through a raised tube near the front of the engine. The cap should be duly marked 'Engine oil' or similar wording. An oil can spout or funnel will reduce spills as the oil is poured in.

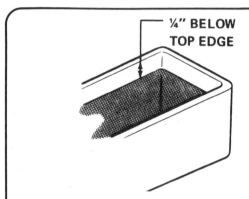

Fig. 1.1 Checking brake fluid in the master cylinder (Sec 2)

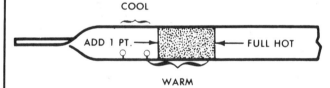

Fig. 1.2 Automatic transmission dipstick and markings (test for fluid level after car has been fully warmed up and with engine running) (Sec 2)

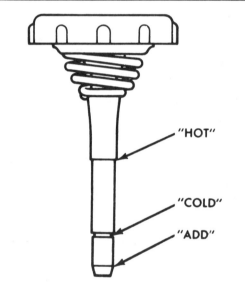

Fig. 1.3 The power steering dipstick is built into the cap (check fluid level with engine running) (Sec 2)

2.4 Checking the oil level at the bottom of the dipstick

2.17 Maintenance-free batteries have an eye which indicates battery condition by changing color

2.18 On conventional batteries, remove the vent caps and check the fluid level (use only distilled water for topping up)

7   Checking the oil level can also be a step towards preventative maintenance. If you find the oil level dropping abnormally, this is an indication of oil leakage or internal engine wear which should be corrected. If there are water droplets in the oil, or it is milky looking, this also indicates component failure and the engine should be checked immediately. The condition of the oil can also be checked along with the level. With the dipstick removed from the engine, take your thumb and index finger and wipe the oil up the dipstick, looking for small dirt particles or engine filings which will cling to the dipstick. This is an indication that the oil should be drained and fresh oil added (Section 4).

Engine coolant

8   Most vehicles are equipped with a pressurized coolant recovery system which makes coolant level checks very easy. A clear or white coolant reservoir attached to the inner fender panel is connected by a hose to the radiator cap. As the engine heats up during operation, coolant is forced from the radiator, through the connecting tube and into the reservoir. As the engine cools, this coolant is automatically drawn back into the radiator to keep the correct level.

9   The coolant level should be checked when the engine is cold. Merely observe the level of fluid in the reservoir, which should be at or near the 'Full cold' mark on the side of the reservoir. If the system is completely cooled, also check the level in the radiator by removing the cap. Some systems also have a 'Full hot' mark to check the level when the engine is hot.

10   If your particular vehicle is not equipped with a coolant recovery system, the level should be checked by removing the radiator cap. However, the cap should not under any circumstances be removed while the system is hot, as escaping steam could cause serious injury. Wait until the engine has completely cooled, then wrap a thick cloth around the cap and turn it to its first stop. If any steam escapes from the cap, allow the engine to cool further. Then remove the cap and check the level in the radiator. It should be about 2 to 3 inches below the bottom of the filler neck.

11   If only a small amount of coolant is required to bring the system up to the proper level, regular water can be used. However, to maintain the proper antifreeze/water mixture in the system, both should be mixed together to replenish a low level. High-quality antifreeze offering protection to -20° should be mixed with water in the proportion specified on the container. Do not allow antifreeze to come in contact with your skin or painted surfaces of the car. Flush contacted areas immediately with plenty of water.

12   On systems with a recovery tank, coolant should be added to the reservoir after removing the cap at the top of the reservoir. Coolant should be added directly into the radiator on systems without a coolant recovery tank.

13   As the coolant level is checked, observe the condition of the coolant. It should be relatively clear. If the fluid is brown or a rust color, this is an indication that the system should be drained, flushed and refilled (Section 29).

14   If the cooling system requires repeated additions to keep the proper level, have the pressure radiator cap checked for proper sealing ability. Also check for leaks in the system (cracked hoses, loose hose connections, leaking gaskets, etc.).

Windshield washer

15   The fluid for the windshield washer system is located in a plastic reservoir. The level inside the reservoir should be maintained at the 'Full' mark.

16   General Motors 'Optikleen' washer solvent or its equivalent should be added through the plastic cap whenever replenishing is required. Do not use plain water alone in this system, especially in cold climates where the water could freeze.

Battery

Note: *There are certain precautions to be taken when working on or near the battery: a) Never expose a battery to open flame or sparks which could ignite the hydrogen gas given off by the battery; b) Wear protective clothing and eye protection to reduce the possibility of the corrosive sulfuric acid solution inside the battery harming you (if the fluid is splashed or spilled, flush the contacted area immediately with plenty of water); c) Remove all metal jewelry which could contact the positive terminal and another grounded metal source, thus causing a short circuit; d) Always keep batteries and battery acid out of the reach of children.*

17   Vehicles equipped with 'Freedom' or maintenance-free batteries require no maintenance as the battery case is sealed and has no removal caps for adding water (photo).

18   If a maintenance-type battery is installed, the caps on the top of the battery should be removed periodically to check for a low water level (photo). This check will be more critical during the warm summer months.

19   Remove each of the caps and add distilled water to bring the level of each cell to the split ring in the filler opening.

20   At the same time the battery water level is checked, the overall condition of the battery and its related components should be inspected. If corrosion is found on the cable ends or battery terminals, remove the cables and clean away all corrosion using a baking soda/water solution or a wire brush cleaning tool designed for this purpose. See Chapter 5 for complete battery care and servicing.

Brake master cylinder

21   The brake master cylinder is located on the left side of the engine compartment firewall and has a cap which must be removed to check the fluid level.

22   Before removing the cap, use a rag to clean all dirt, grease, etc. from around the cap area. If any foreign matter enters the master cylinder with the cap removed, blockage in the brake system lines can occur. Also make sure all painted surfaces around the master cylinder are covered, as brake fluid will ruin paintwork.

23   Release the clip(s) securing the cap to the top of the master cylinder. In most cases, a screwdriver can be used to pry the wire clip(s) free.

24   Carefully lift the cap off the cylinder and observe the fluid level. It should be approximately $\frac{1}{4}$-inch below the top edge of each reservoir.

25   If additional fluid is necessary to bring the level up to the proper height, carefully pour the specified brake fluid into the master cylinder. Be careful not to spill the fluid on painted surfaces. Be sure the specified fluid is used, as mixing different types of brake fluid can cause damage to the system. See Recommended Lubricants or your owner's manual.

26   At this time the fluid and master cylinder can be inspected for contamination. Normally, the braking system will not need periodic draining and refilling, but if rust deposits, dirt particles or water droplets are seen in the fluid, the system should be dismantled, drained and refilled with fresh fluid.

27   Reinstall the master cylinder cap and secure it with the clip(s). Make sure the lid is properly seated to prevent fluid leakage and/or system pressure loss.

28   The brake fluid in the master cylinder will drop slightly as the brake shoes or pads at each wheel wear down during normal operation. If the master cylinder requires repeated replenishing to keep it at the proper level, this is an indication of leakage in the brake system which should be corrected immediately. Check all brake lines and their connections, along with the wheel cylinders and booster (see Chapter 9 for more information).

29   If upon checking the master cylinder fluid level you discover one or both reservoirs empty or nearly empty, the braking system should be bled (Chapter 9). When the fluid level gets low, air can enter the system and should be removed by bleeding the brakes.

Manual transmission

30   Manual shift transmissions do not have a dipstick. The fluid level is checked by removing a plug in the side of the transmission case. Locate this plug and use a rag to clean the plug and the area around it.

31   With the vehicle components cold, remove the plug. If fluid immediately starts leaking out, thread the plug back into the transmission because the fluid level is alright. If there is no fluid leakage, completely remove the plug and place your little finger inside the hole. The fluid level should be just at the bottom of the plug hole.

32   If the transmission needs more fluid, use a syringe to squeeze the appropriate lubricant into the plug hole to bring the fluid up to the proper level.

33   Thread the plug back into the transmission and tighten it securely. Drive the car and check for leaks around the plug.

Automatic transmission

34   The fluid inside the transmission must be at normal operating temperature to get an accurate reading on the dipstick. This is done by driving the car for several miles, making frequent starts and stops to

allow the transmission to shift through all gears.

35 Park the car on a level surface, place the selector lever in 'Park' and leave the engine running at an idle.

36 Remove the transmission dipstick (located on the right side, near the rear of the engine) and wipe all the fluid from the end of the dipstick with a clean rag.

37 Push the dipstick back into the transmission until the cap seats firmly on the dipstick tube. Now remove the dipstick again and observe the fluid on the end. The highest point of fluid should be between the 'Full' mark and $\frac{1}{4}$ inch below the 'Full' mark.

38 If the fluid level is at or below the 'Add' mark on the dipstick, add sufficient fluid to raise the level to the 'Full' mark. One pint of fluid will raise the level from 'Add' to 'Full'. Fluid should be added directly into the dipstick guide tube, using a funnel to prevent spills.

39 It is important that the transmission not be overfilled. Under no circumstances should the fluid level be above the 'Full' mark on the disptick, as this could cause internal damage to the transmission. The best way to prevent overfilling is to add fluid a little at a time, driving the car and checking the level between additions.

40 Use only transmission fluid specified by GM. This information can be found in the Recommended Lubricants Section.

41 The condition of the fluid should also be checked along with the level. If the fluid at the end of the dipstick is a dark reddish-brown color, or if the fluid has a 'burnt' smell, the transmission fluid should be changed with fresh. If you are in doubt about the condition of the fluid, purchase some new fluid and compare the two for color and smell.

Rear axle

42 Like the manual transmission, the rear axle has an inspection and fill plug which must be removed to check the fluid level.

43 Remove the plug which is located either in the removable cover plate or on the side of the differential carrier. Use your little finger to reach inside the rear axle housing to feel the level of the fluid. It should be at the bottom of the plug hole.

44 If this is not the case, add the proper lubricant into the rear axle carrier through the plug hole. A syringe or a small funnel can be used for this.

45 Make certain the correct lubricant is used, as regular and Positraction rear axles require different lubricants. You can ascertain which type of axle you have by reading the stamped number on the axle tube (See Vehicle Identification Numbers at the front of this manual).

46 Tighten the plug securely and check for leaks after the first few miles of driving.

Power steering

47 Unlike manual steering, the power steering system relies on fluid which may, over a period of time, require replenishing.

48 The reservoir for the power steering pump will be located near the front of the engine, and can be mounted on either the left or right side.

49 The power steering fluid level should be checked only after the car has been driven, with the fluid at operating temperature. The front wheels should be pointed straight ahead.

50 With the engine shut off, use a rag to clean the reservoir cap and the areas around the cap. This will help to prevent foreign material from falling into the reservoir when the cap is removed.

51 Twist off the reservoir cap which has a built-in dipstick attached to it. Pull off the cap and clean the fluid at the bottom of the dipstick with a clean rag. Now reinstall the dipstick/cap assembly to get a fluid level reading. Remove the dipstick/cap and observe the fluid level. It should be at the 'Full hot' mark on the dipstick.

52 If additional fluid is required, pour the specified lubricant directly into the reservoir using a funnel to prevent spills.

53 If the reservoir requires frequent fluid additions, all power steering hoses, hose connections, the power steering pump and the steering box should be carefully checked for leaks.

3   Tire and tire pressure checks

1 Periodically inspecting the tires can not only prevent you from being stranded with a flat tire, but can also give you clues as to possible problems with the steering and suspension systems before major damage occurs.

2 Proper tire inflation adds miles to the lifespan of the tires, allows the car to achieve maximum miles per gallon figures, and helps the overall riding comfort of the car.

3 When inspecting the tire, first check the wear on the tread. Irregularities in the tread pattern (cupping, flat spots, more wear on one side than the other) are indications of front end alignment and/or balance problems. If any of these conditions are found you would do best to take the car to a competent repair shop which can correct the problem.

4 Also check the tread area for cuts or punctures. Many times a nail or tack will imbed itself into the tire tread and yet the tire will hold its air pressure for a short time. In most cases, a repair shop or gas station can repair the punctured tire.

5 It is also important to check the sidewalls of the tire, both inside and outside. Check for the rubber being deteriorated, cut or punctured. Also inspect the inboard side of the tire for signs of brake fluid leakage, indicating a thorough brake inspection is needed immediately (Section 26).

6 Incorrect tire pressure cannot be determined merely by looking at the tire. This is especially true for radial tires. A tire pressure gauge must be used. If you do not already have a reliable gauge, it is a good idea to purchase one and keep it in the glove box. Built-in pressure gauges at gas stations are often unreliable. If you are in doubt as to the accuracy of your gauge, many repair shops have 'master' pressure gauges which you can use for comparison purposes.

7 Always check tire inflation when the tires are cold. Cold, in this case, means the car has not been driven more than one mile after sitting for three hours or more. It is normal for the pressure to increase 4 to 8 pounds or more when the tires are hot.

8 Unscrew the valve cap protruding from the wheel or hubcap and firmly press the gauge onto the valve stem. Observe the reading on the gauge and check this figure against the recommended tire pressure listed on the tire placard. This tire placard is usually found attached to the rear portion of the driver's door or on the inside of the glovebox door.

9 Check all tires and add air as necessary to bring all tires up to the recommended pressure levels. Do not forget the spare tire. Be sure to reinstall the valve caps which will keep dirt and moisture out of the valve stem mechanism.

4   Engine oil and filter change

1 Frequent oil changes may be the best form of preventative maintenance available for the home mechanic. When engine oil ages, it gets diluted and contaminated which ultimately leads to premature parts wear.

2 Although some sources recommend oil filter changes every other oil change, we feel that the minimal cost of an oil filter and the relative ease with which it is installed dictates that a new filter be used whenever the oil is changed.

3 The tools necessary for a normal oil and filter change are: a wrench to fit the drain plug at the bottom of the oil pan; an oil filter wrench to remove the old filter; a container with at least a six-quart capacity to drain the old oil into; and a funnel or oil can spout to help pour fresh oil into the engine.

4 In addition, you should have plenty of clean rags and newspapers handy to mop up any spills. Access to the underside of the car is greatly improved if the car can be lifted on a hoist, driven onto ramps or supported by jack stands. Do not work under a car which is supported only by a bumper, hydraulic or scissors-type jack.

5 If this is your first oil change on the car, it is a good idea to crawl underneath and familiarize yourself with the locations of the oil drain plug and the oil filter. Since the engine and exhaust components will be warm during the actual work, it is best to figure out any potential problems before the car and its accessories are hot.

6 Allow the car to warm up to normal operating temperature. If the new oil or any tools are needed, use this warm-up time to gather everything necessary for the job. The correct type of oil to buy for your application can be found in Recommended Lubricants near the front of this manual.

7 With the engine oil warm (warm engine oil will drain better and more built-up sludge will be removed with the oil), raise the vehicle for access beneath. Make sure the car is firmly supported. If jack stands are used they should be placed towards the front of the frame rails which run the length of the car.

8 Move all necessary tools, rags and newspaper under the car. Position the drain pan under the drain plug. Keep in mind that the oil

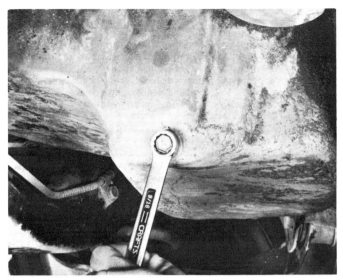

4.9 On certain models, the oil drain plug is located on the side of the pan

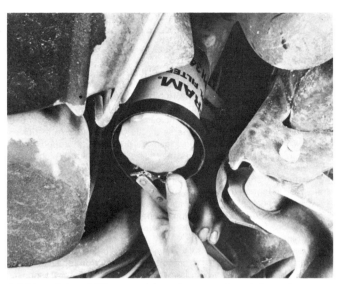

4.14 Install the oil filter wrench over the outer edge of the canister otherwise the canister may collapse and jam

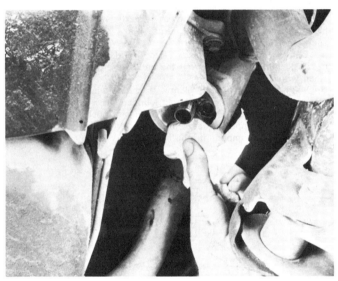

4.18 Clean the filter mounting pedestal and make sure the old rubber gasket has been removed

4.19 A thin coat of engine oil rubbed on the new filter gasket will help ensure a proper seal

4.20 Hand tighten the filter until it contacts the pedestal, then tighten another ½ turn

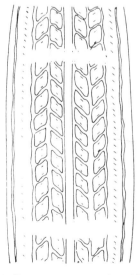

Fig. 1.4 Tread wear indicators run across the width of the tire and show when it is in need of replacement (Sec 3)

will initially flow from the pan with some force, so place the pan accordingly.

9   Being careful not to touch any of the hot exhaust pipe components, use the wrench to remove the drain plug near the bottom of the oil pan (photo). Depending on how hot the oil has become, you may want to wear gloves while unscrewing the plug the final few turns.

10 Allow the old oil to drain into the pan. It may be necessary to move the pan further under the engine as the oil flow reduces to a trickle.

11 After all the oil has drained, clean the drain plug thoroughly with a clean rag. Small metal filings may cling to this plug which could immediately contaminate your new oil.

12 Clean the area around the drain plug opening and reinstall the drain plug. Tighten the plug securely with your wrench. If a torque wrench is available, the torque setting is 20 ft-lb.

13 Move the drain pan in position under the oil filter.

14 Now use the filter wrench to loosen the oil filter (photo). Chain or metal band-type filter wrenches may distort the filter canister, but don't worry too much about this as the filter will be discarded anyway.

15 Sometimes the oil filter is on so tight it cannot be loosened, or it is positioned in an area which is inaccessible with a filter wrench. As a last resort, you can punch a metal bar or long screwdriver directly through the bottom of the canister and use this as a T-bar to turn the filter. If this must be done, be prepared for oil to spurt out of the canister as it is punctured.

16 Completely unscrew the old filter. Be careful, it is full of oil. Empty the old oil inside the filter into the drain pan.

17 Compare the old filter with the new one to make sure they are of the same type.

18 Use a clean rag to remove all oil, dirt and sludge from the area where the oil filter mounts to the engine (photo). Check the old filter to make sure the rubber gasket is not stuck to the engine mounting surface. If this gasket is stuck to the engine (use a flashlight if necessary), remove it.

19 Open one of the cans of new oil and fill the new filter with fresh oil. Also smear a light coat of this fresh oil onto the rubber gasket of the new oil filter (photo).

20 Screw the new filter to the engine following the tightening directions printed on the filter canister or packing box (photo). Most filter manufacturers recommend against using a filter wrench due to possible overtightening or damage to the canister.

21 Remove all tools, rags, etc. from under the car, being careful not to spill the oil in the drain pan. Lower the car off its support devices.

22 Move to the engine compartment and locate the oil filler cap on the engine. In most cases there will be a screw-off cap on the rocker arm cover (at the side of the engine) or a cap at the end of a fill tube at the front of the engine. In any case, the cap will most likely be labeled 'Engine Oil' or something similar.

23 If an oil can spout is used, push the spout into the top of the oil can and pour the fresh oil through the filler opening. A funnel placed into the opening may also be used.

24 Pour about 3 qts. of fresh oil into the engine. Wait a few minutes to allow the oil to drain to the pan, then check the level on the oil dipstick (see Section 2 if necessary). **Note:** *When changing oil (or performing any operation which results in oil drainage or loss) on a turbocharged V6, perform the following steps BEFORE starting the engine:*

(a) *Disconnect the ignition switch connector (pink wire) from the HEI distributor.*

(b) *Crank the engine over several times until the oil light goes out (do not exceed 30 seconds for each cranking interval).*

(c) *Reconnect the pink wire to the distributor, then recheck the oil level. This procedure will ensure that the bearings in the turbocharger are not damaged due to lack of lubrication. If the oil level is at or near the lower 'Add' mark, start the engine and allow the new oil to circulate.*

25 Run the engine for only about a minute and then shut it off. Immediately look under the car and check for leaks at the oil pan drain plug and around the oil filter. If either is leaking, tighten with a bit more force.

26 With the new oil circulated and the filter now completely full, recheck the level on the dipstick and add enough oil to bring the level to the 'Full' mark on the dipstick.

27 During the first few trips after an oil change, make a point to check for leaks and also the oil level.

28 The old oil drained from the engine cannot be reused in its present state and should be disposed of. Oil reclamation centers, auto repair

shops and gas stations will normally accept the oil which can be refined and used again. After the oil has cooled, it can be drained into a suitable container (capped plastic jugs, topped bottles, milk cartons, etc.) for transport to one of these disposal sites. *Do not* dump dirty oil onto the ground. If you do not live near an oil reclamation center properly contained oil will usually be taken by the trash man.

5   Chassis lubrication

1   A grease gun and a cartridge filled with the proper grease (see Recommended Lubricants) are usually the only equipment necessary to lubricate the chassis components. Occasionally on later model vehicles, plugs will be installed rather than grease fittings, in which case grease fittings will have to be purchased and installed.

2   Carefully look over Fig. 1.5 which shows where the various grease fittings are located. A more detailed chart showing both chassis and mechanical lube points is shown under the *Recommended Lubricants* Section at the beginning of this manual. Look under the car to find these components and ascertain if grease fittings or solid plugs are installed. If there are plugs, remove them with the correct wrench and buy grease fittings which will thread into the component. A GM dealer or auto parts store will be able to find replacement fittings. Straight, as well as angled, fittings are available for easy greasing.

3   For easier access under the car, raise the vehicle with a jack and place jack stands under the frame. Make sure the car is firmly supported by the stands.

4   Before you do any greasing, force a little of the grease out the nozzle to remove any dirt from the end of the gun. Wipe the nozzle clean with a rag.

5   With the grease gun, plenty of clean rags and the location diagram, go under the car to begin lubricating the components.

6   Wipe the grease fitting nipple clean and push the nozzle firmly over the fitting nipple. Squeeze the trigger on the grease gun to force grease into the component (photo).

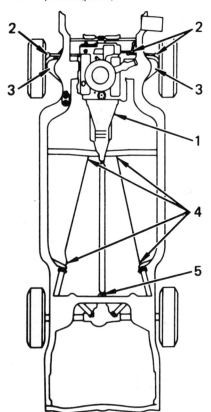

Fig. 1.5 Main chassis lubrication points (Sec 5)

1   *Transmission*
2   *Steering*
3   *Front suspension*
4   *Parking brake cables*
5   *Drive shaft U-joint*

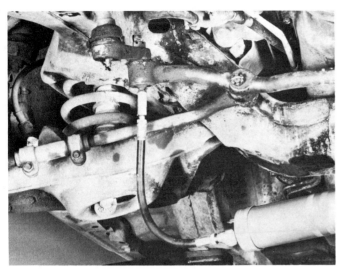

5.6a Pumping grease into one of the steering system grease fittings

5.6b When greasing the balljoints (upper joint is shown here), take care not to over-grease

Note: *The balljoints (one upper and one lower for each wheel) should be lubricated until the rubber reservoir is firm to the touch (photo). Do not pump too much grease into these fittings as this could rupture the reservoir. For all other suspension and steering fittings, continue pumping grease into the nipple until grease seeps out of the joint between the two components. If the grease seeps out around the grease gun nozzle, the nipple is clogged or the nozzle is not fully seated around the fitting nipple. Re-secure the gun nozzle to the fitting and try again. If necessary, replace the fitting.*

7   Wipe the excess grease from the components and the grease fitting. Follow these procedures for the remaining fittings.
8   Check the universal joints on the driveshaft; some have fittings, some are factory sealed. About two pumps is all that is required for grease type universal joints. While you are under the car, clean and lubricate the parking brake cable along with its cable guides and levers. This can be done by smearing some of the chassis grease onto the cable and its related parts with your fingers. Place a few drops of light engine oil on the transmission shifting linkage rods and swivels.
9   Lower the car to the ground for the remaining body lubrication process.
10 Open the hood and smear a little chassis grease on the hood latch mechanism. If the hood has an inside release, have an assistant pull the release knob from inside the car as you lubricate the cable at the latch.
11 Lubricate all the hinges (door, hood, trunk) with a few drops of light engine oil to keep them in proper working order.
12 Finally, the key lock cylinders can be lubricated with spray-on graphite which is available at auto parts stores.

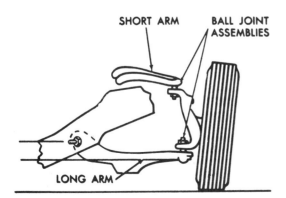

Fig. 1.6 Location of suspension balljoints (Sec 5)

SHORT ARM   BALL JOINT ASSEMBLIES

LONG ARM

6   Cooling system check

1   Many major engine failures can be attributed to a faulty cooling system. If equipped with an automatic transmission, the cooling system also plays an integral role in transmission longevity.
2   The cooling system should be checked with the engine cold. Do this before the car is driven for the day or after it has been shut off for one or two hours.
3   Remove the radiator cap and thoroughly clean the cap (inside and out) with clean water. Also clean the filler neck on the radiator. All traces of corrosion should be removed.
4   Carefully check the upper and lower radiator hoses along with the smaller diameter heater hoses. Inspect their entire length, replacing any hose which is cracked, swollen or shows signs of deterioration. Cracks may become more apparent if the hose is squeezed (photos).
5   Also check that all hose connections are tight. A leak in the cooling system will usually show up as white or rust colored deposits on the areas adjoining the leak.
6   Use compressed air or a soft brush to remove bugs, leaves, etc. from the front of the radiator or air conditioning condensor. Be careful not to damage the delicate cooling fins, or cut yourself on the sharp fins.
7   Finally, have the cap and system tested for proper pressure. If you do not have a pressure tester, most gas stations and repair shops will do this for a minimal charge.

7   Exhaust system check

1   With the exhaust system cold (at least three hours after being driven), check the complete exhaust system from its starting point at the engine to the end of the tailpipe. This is best done on a hoist where full access is available.
2   Check the pipes and their connections for signs of leakage and/or corrosion indicating a potential failure. Check that all brackets and hangers are in good condition and are tight (photo).
3   At the same time, inspect the underside of the body for holes, corrosion, open seams, etc. which may allow exhaust gases to enter the trunk or passenger compartment. Seal all body openings with silicone or body putty.
4   Rattles and other driving noises can often be traced to the exhaust system, especially the mounts and hangers. Try to move the pipes, muffler and catalytic converter (if equipped). If the components can come into contact with the body or driveline parts, secure the exhaust system with new mountings.
5   This is also an ideal time to check the running condition of the engine by inspecting the very end of the tailpipe. The exhaust deposits here are an indication of engine tune. If the pipe is black and sooty

6.4 Check radiator and heater hoses by squeezing

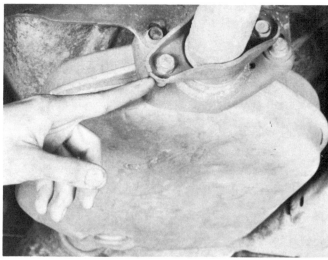

7.2 All exhaust flanges and connections should be checked for leaks

7.5 Black, sooty deposits in the tail pipe end may indicate that tune-up or carburetor adjustment is necessary

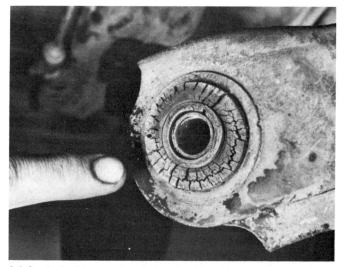

8.6 Cracked rubber bushings in the steering and suspension must be replaced with new ones

(photo), or bright white deposits are found here, the engine is in need of a tune-up including a thorough carburetor inspection and adjustment.

8 Suspension and steering check

1   Whenever the front of the car is raised for service it is a good idea to visually check the suspension and steering components for wear.
2   Indications of a fault in these systems are: excessive play in the steering wheel before the front wheels react; excessive sway around corners or body movement over rough roads; binding at some point as the steering wheel is turned.
3   Before the car is raised for inspection, test the shock absorbers by pushing downward to rock the car at each corner. If you push the car down and it does not come back to a level position within one or two bounces, the shocks are worn and need to be replaced. As this is done, check for squeaks and strange noises from the suspension components. Information on shock absorber and suspension components can be found in Chapter 11.
4   Now raise the front end of the car and support firmly by jack stands placed under the frame rails. Because of the work to be done, make sure the car cannot fall from the stands.
5   Grab the top and bottom of the front tire with your hands and rock

the tire/wheel on its spindle. If there is movement of more than 0.005 in, the wheel bearings should be serviced (see Section 24).
6   Crawl under the car and check for loose bolts, broken or disconnected parts and deteriorated rubber bushings (photo) on all suspension and steering components. Look for grease or fluid leaking from around the steering box. Check the power steering hoses and their connections for leaks. Check the balljoints for wear.
7   Have an assistant turn the steering wheel from side to side and check the steering components for free movement, chafing or binding. If the steering does not react with the movement of the steering wheel, try to determine where the slack is located.

9 Engine drive belt check and adjustment

1   The drive belts, or V-belts as they are sometimes called, at the front of the engine play an important role in the overall operation of the car and its components. Due to their function and material make-up, the belts are prone to failure after a period of time and should be inspected and adjusted periodically to prevent major engine damage.
2   The number of belts used on a particular car depends on the accessories installed. Drive belts are used to turn: the generator (alternator); A.I.R. smog pump; power steering pump; water pump; fan; and air conditioning compressor. Depending on the pulley

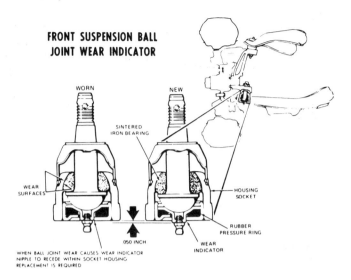

FRONT SUSPENSION BALL JOINT WEAR INDICATOR

WORN

NEW

SINTERED IRON BEARING

WEAR SURFACES

HOUSING SOCKET

RUBBER PRESSURE RING

.050 INCH

WEAR INDICATOR

WHEN BALL JOINT WEAR CAUSES WEAR INDICATOR NIPPLE TO RECEDE WITHIN SOCKET HOUSING REPLACEMENT IS REQUIRED

Fig. 1.7 Location of balljoint wear indicators (Sec 8)

Fig. 1.8 Checking engine drivebelt tension (Sec 9)

7 in (178 mm) to 11 in (280 mm) $\frac{1}{4}$ in (64 mm) deflection
12 in (305 mm) to 16 in (406 mm) $\frac{1}{2}$ in (12.7 mm) deflection

arrangement, a single belt may be used for more than one of these ancillary components.
3   With the engine off, open the hood and locate the various belts at the front of the engine. Using your fingers (and a flashlight if necessary), move along the belts checking for cracks or separation. Also check for fraying and for glazing which gives the belt a shiny appearance. Both sides of the belts should be inspected, which means you will have to twist the belt to check the underside.
4   The tension of each belt is checked by pushing on the belt at a distance halfway between the pulleys. Push firmly with your thumb and see how much the belt moves downward (deflects) (photo). A rule of thumb, so to speak, is that if the distance (pulley center to pulley center) is between 7 inches and 11 inches the belt should deflect $\frac{1}{4}$ inch. If the belt is longer and travels between pulleys spaced 12 inches to 16 inches apart, the belt should deflect $\frac{1}{2}$ in.
5   If it is found necessary to adjust the belt tension, either to make the belt tighter or looser, this is done by moving the belt-driven accessory on its bracket.
6   For each component there will be an adjustment or strap bolt and a pivot bolt. Both bolts must be loosened slightly to enable you to move the component.
7   After the two bolts have been loosened, move the component away from the engine (to tighten the belt) or toward the engine (to loosen the belt) (photo). Hold the accessory in this position and check the belt tension. If it is correct, tighten the two bolts until snug, then recheck the tension. If it is alright, fully tighten the two bolts.
8   It will often be necessary to use some sort of pry bar to move the accessory while the belt is adjusted. If this must be done to gain the proper leverage, be very careful not to damage the component being moved, or the part being pried against.

10 Fuel system check

1   There are certain precautions to take when inspecting or servicing the fuel system components. Work in a well ventilated area and do not allow open flames (cigarettes, appliance pilot lights, etc.) to get near the work area. Mop up spills immediately and do not store fuel-soaked rags where they could ignite.
2   The fuel system is under some amount of pressure, so if any fuel lines are disconnected for servicing, be prepared to catch the fuel as it spurts out. Plug all disconnected fuel lines immediately after disconnection to prevent the tank from emptying itself.
3   The fuel system is most easily checked with the car raised on a hoist where the components under the car are readily visible and accessible.
4   If the smell of gasoline is noticed while driving, or after the car has sat in the sun, the system should be thoroughly inspected immediately.
5   Remove the gas filler cap and check for damage, corrosion and a proper sealing imprint on the gasket. Replace the cap with a new one if necessary.
6   With the car raised, inspect the gas tank and filler neck for punctures, cracks or any damage. The connection between the filler neck and the tank is especially critical. Sometimes a rubber filler neck will leak due to loose clamps or deteriorated rubber; problems a home mechanic can usually rectify.
7   Do not under any circumstances try to repair a fuel tank yourself (except rubber components) unless you have considerable experience. A welding torch or any open flame can easily cause the fuel vapors to explode if the proper precautions are not taken.
8   Carefully check all rubber hoses and metal lines leading away from the fuel tank. Check for loose connections, deteriorated hose, crimped lines or damage of any kind. Follow these lines up to the front of the car, carefully inspecting them all the way. Repair or replace damaged sections as necessary.
9   If a fuel odor is still evident after the inspection, refer to Section 31 on the evaporative emissions system and Section 16 for carburetor adjustment.

11 Positive Crankcase Ventilation (PCV) valve replacement

1   The PCV valve can usually be found pushed into one of the rocker arm covers at the side of the engine. There will be a hose connected to the valve which runs to either the carburetor or the intake manifold.
2   When purchasing a replacement PCV valve, make sure it is for your particular vehicle, model year and engine size.
3   Pull the valve (with the hose attached) from its rubber grommet in the rocker arm cover.
4   Using pliers or a screwdriver, depending on the type of clamp, loosen the clamp at the end of the hose and move the clamp upwards on the PCV hose (photo).
5   Now pull the PCV valve from the end of the hose, noting its installed position and direction.
6   Compare the old valve with the new one to make sure they are the same.
7   Push the new valve into the end of the hose until it is fully seated.
8   Move the hose clamp down the hose and tighten the clamp securely around the end of the hose.
9   Inspect the rubber grommet in the cover for damage and replace it with a new one if faulty.
10   Push the PCV valve and hose securely into the rocker arm cover.
11   More information on the PCV system can be found in Chapter 6.

12 Air filter and PCV filter replacement

1   At the specified intervals, the air filter and PCV filter should be replaced with new ones. A thorough program of preventative maintenance would call for the two filters to be inspected periodically between changes.
2   The air filter is located inside the air cleaner housing on the top of the engine. To remove the filter, unscrew the wing nut at the top of the air cleaner and lift off the top plate (photo). If there are vacuum hoses connected to this plate, note their positions and disconnect them.
3   While the top plate is off, be careful not to drop anything down into the carburetor.

9.7 Adjust belt tension by gently prying on the component while the adjustment bolt is tightened

11.4 Use pliers to release the hose clamp and slide it away from the valve

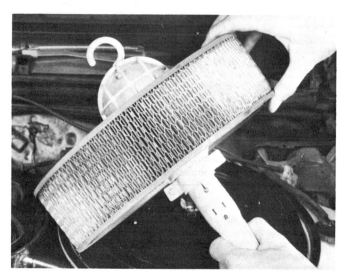

12.5 If light can be easily seen through the filter, it can be reused (if you are in doubt as to the condition of filter, replace it)

12.12 The PCV filter is usually located inside the cleaner housing

4   Lift the air filter out of the housing (photo).
5   To check the filter, hold it up to strong sunlight, or place a flashlight or droplight on the inside of the ring-shaped filter (photo). If you can see light coming through the paper element, the filter is alright. Check all the way around the filter.
6   Wipe the inside of the air cleaner clean with a rag.
7   Place the old filter (if in good condition) or the new filter (if specified interval has elapsed) back into the air cleaner housing. Make sure it seats properly in the bottom of the housing.
8   Connect any disconnected vacuum hoses to the top plate and reinstall the top plate with the wing nut.
9   On nearly all cars the PCV filter is also located inside the air cleaner housing. Remove the top plate as described previously and locate the filter on the side of the housing.
10   Loosen the hose clamp at the end of the PCV hose leading to the filter. Disconnect the hose from the filter.
11   Remove the metal locking clip which secures the filter holder to the air cleaner housing. Pliers can be used for this.
12   Remove the filter and plastic holder from the inside of the air cleaner (photo).
13   Compare the new filter with the old one to make sure they are the same.
14   Place the new filter assembly into position and install the metal locking clip on the outside of the air cleaner.

15   Connect the PCV hose and tighten the clamp around the end of the hose.
16   Reinstall the air cleaner top plate and any vacuum hoses which were disconnected.
17   A few engines will not have the PCV filter at the air cleaner, but rather the filter will be in the PCV hose at some point. To locate the filter, find the hose leading into the side of the air cleaner housing and follow this hose to the filter.
18   Replacing 'in-line' PCV filters is usually a simple matter of disconnecting the hose from the filter and then pushing a replacement filter into the hose.
19   For more information on these filters and the systems they are a part of, see Chapter 4 and Chapter 6.

13 Clutch pedal free travel check

1   If equipped with a manual shift transmission, it is important to have the clutch free play at the proper point. Basically, free play at the clutch pedal is the point at which time the clutch components engage and the car starts moving. When the pedal is pushed all the way to the floor, the clutch parts are disengaged and the car doesn't travel. As the pedal travels away from the floor, the parts engage and the vehicle is set into motion. It is the measured distance which the pedal moves

15.4 Operation of the damper door is checked through the snorkel tube at the end of the air cleaner housing

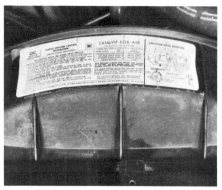

16.3 A typical tune-up decal giving specific information for your particular engine

16.4 The carburetor idle adjustment screw is located on the left side of the carburetor (arrow points to electrically operated idle solenoid)

between these two points which indicates free travel.

2   With the car on a level surface, turn on the engine and allow it to idle. Apply the parking brake to prevent the car from moving.

3   Depress the clutch pedal until it is approximately $\frac{1}{2}$ inch from the floor mat or carpeting.

4   Hold the pedal in this position and move the shift lever between first and reverse gears several times. If this can be done smoothly, the clutch is fully releasing and no adjustment is necessary. If the shift is not smooth, the clutch pedal free play should be adjusted.

5   If adjustment is necessary, refer to Chapter 8 for the step-by-step sequence to follow.

14   Tire rotation

1   The tires should be rotated at the specified intervals and whenever uneven wear is noticed. Since the car will be raised and the tires removed anyway, this is a good time to check the brakes (Section 26) and/or repack the wheel bearings (Section 24). Read over these sections if this is to be done at the same time.

2   The location for each tire in the rotation sequence depends on the type of tire used on your car. Tire type can be determined by reading the raised printing on the sidewall of the tire. The accompanying illustration shows the rotation sequence for each type of tire.

3   See the information in *Jacking and Towing* at the front of this manual for the proper procedures to follow in raising the car and changing a tire; however, if the brakes are to be checked do not apply the parking brake as stated. Make sure the tires are blocked to prevent the car from rolling.

4   Preferably, the entire car should be raised at the same time. This can be done on a hoist or by jacking up each corner of the car and then lowering the car onto jack stands placed under the frame rails. Always use four jack stands and make sure the car is firmly supported all around.

5   After rotation, check and adjust the tire pressures as necessary and be sure to check wheel nut tightness.

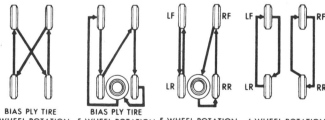

BIAS PLY TIRE
4 WHEEL ROTATION

BIAS PLY TIRE
5 WHEEL ROTATION

5 WHEEL ROTATION

4 WHEEL ROTATION

BIAS-BELTED TIRES   **RADIAL TIRES**

Fig. 1.9 Tire rotation diagram (Sec 14)

15   Thermo controlled air cleaner check

1   All models are equipped with a thermostatically controlled air cleaner which draws air to the carburetor from different locations depending upon engine temperature.

2   This is a simple visual check; however, if access is tight, a small mirror may have to be used.

3   Open the hood and find the vacuum flapper door on the air cleaner assembly. It wil be located inside the long 'snorkel' of the metal air cleaner. Check that the flexible air hose(s) are securely attached and are not damaged.

4   If there is a flexible air duct attached to the end of the snorkel, leading to an area behind the grille, disconnect it at the snorkel. This will enable you to look through the end of the snorkel and see the flapper door inside (photo).

5   The testing should preferably be done when the engine and outside air are cold. Start the engine and look through the snorkel at the flapper door which should move to a closed position. With the door closed, air cannot enter through the end of the snorkel, but rather air enters the air cleaner through the flexible duct attached to the exhaust manifold.

6   As the engine warms up to operating temperature, the door should open to allow air through the snorkel end. Depending on ambient temperature, this may take 10 to 15 minutes. To speed up this check you can reconnect the snorkel air duct, drive the car and then check that the door is fully open.

7   If the thermo controlled air cleaner is not operating properly, see Chapter 6 for more information.

16   Engine idle speed adjustment

1   Engine idle speed is the speed at which the engine operates when no accelerator pedal pressure is applied. This speed is critical to the performance of the engine itself, as well as many engine sub-systems.

2   A hand-held tachometer must be used when adjusting idle speed to get an accurate reading. The exact hook-up for these meters varies with the manufacturer, so follow the particular directions included.

3   Since GM used many different carburetors for their vehicles in the time period covered by this book, and each has its own peculiarities when setting idle speed, it would be impractical to cover all types in this Section. Chapter 4 contains information on each individual carburetor used. The carburetor used on your particular engine can be found in the Specifications Section of Chapter 4. However, all vehicles covered in this manual should have a tune-up decal in the engine compartment, usually placed near the top of the radiator (photo). The printed instructions for setting idle speed can be found on this decal, and should be followed since they are for your particular engine.

4   Basically, for most applications, the idle speed is set by turning an adjustment screw located at the side of the carburetor (photo). This screw changes the linkage, in essence, depressing or letting up on your accelerator pedal. This screw may be on the linkage itself or may be part of the idle stop solenoid. Refer to the tune-up decal or Chapter 4.

5   Once you have found the idle screw, experiment with different

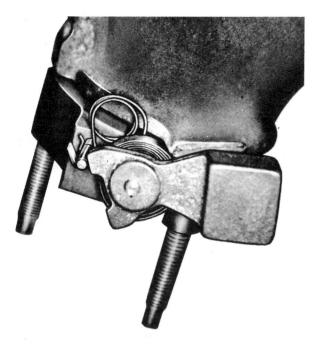

Fig. 1.10 The heat riser valve is at the connection between the exhaust manifold and the exhaust pipe (Sec 17)

2   The heat riser is a valve located inside the right side exhaust pipe, near the junction between exhaust manifold and pipe. It can be identified by an external weight and spring.

3   With the engine and exhaust pipe cold, try moving the weight by hand. It should move freely.

4   Again with the engine cold, start the engine and observe the heat riser. Upon starting, the weight should move to the closed position. As the engine warms to normal operating temperature, the weight should move the valve to the open position, allowing a free flow of exhaust through the tailpipe. Since it could take several minutes for the system to heat up, you could mark the 'cold' weight position, drive the car, and then recheck the weight.

5   The EFE system also blocks off exhaust flow when the engine is cold. However, this system uses more precise temperature sensors and vacuum to open and close the exhaust pipe valve.

6   Locate the EFE actuator which is bolted to a bracket on the right side of the engine (photo). It will have an actuating rod attached to it which will lead down to the valve inside the pipe. In some cases the entire mechanism, including actuator, will be located at the exhaust pipe-to-manifold junction.

7   With the engine cold, have an assistant start the engine as you observe the actuating rod. It should immediately move to close off the valve. Continue observing the rod, which should slowly open the valve as the engine warms. This process may take some time, so you might want to mark the position of the rod when the valve is closed, drive the car to reach normal operating temperature, then open the hood and check that the rod has moved to the open position.

8   Further information and testing procedures can be found in Chapter 6.

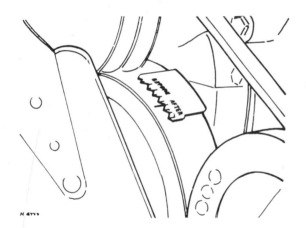
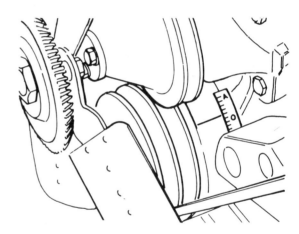

Fig. 1.11 Typical ignition timing marks on the front of the engine (Sec 19)

length screwdrivers until the adjustments can be easily made, without coming into contact with hot or moving engine components.

6   Follow the instructions on the tune-up decal or in Chapter 4, which will probably include disconnecting certain vacuum or electrical connections. To plug a vacuum hose after disconnecting it, insert a properly-sized metal rod into the opening, or thoroughly wrap the open end with tape to prevent any vacuum loss through the hose.

7   If the air cleaner is removed, the vacuum hose to the snorkel should be plugged.

8   Make sure the parking brake is firmly set and the wheels blocked to prevent the car from rolling. This is especially true if the transmission is to be in 'Drive'. An assistant inside the car pushing on the brake pedal is the safest method.

9   For all applications, the engine must be completely warmed-up to operating temperature, which will automatically render the choke fast idle inoperative.

17 EFE system (heat riser) check

1   The heat riser (used on some 1975 models) and the Early Fuel Evaporation (EFE) system both perform the same job, but function in a slightly different manner.

18 Fuel filter replacement

1   On all GM cars, the fuel filter is located inside the fuel inlet to the carburetor (photo). It is made of pleated paper (later models) or bronze (early models). Neither type can be cleaned and reused.

2   This job should be done with the engine cold (after sitting at least three hours). The necessary tools are open end wrenches to fit the fuel line nuts. Flare nut wrenches which wrap around the nut should be used if available. In addition you will need to gather together the replacement filter (make sure it is for your specific vehicle and engine), and clean rags.

3   Remove the air cleaner assembly. If vacuum hoses must be disconnected, make sure you note their positions and/or tag them to help during the reassembly process.

4   Now follow the fuel hose from the fuel pump to the point where it enters the carburetor. The fuel pump is located low on the engine, at the right front. In most cases the fuel line will be metal all the way from the pump to the carburetor.

5   Place some rags under the fuel inlet fittings to catch any fuel as the fittings are disconnected.

6   With the proper size wrench, hold the nut immediately next to the carburetor body. Now loosen the nut-fitting and the end of the metal

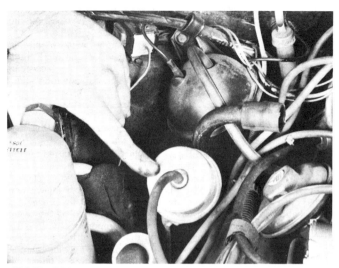

17.6 The EFE actuator is located on the right side of the engine

18.1 The fuel filter is located just inside the fuel inlet

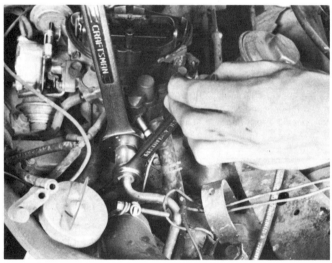

18.6 Use 2 wrenches to loosen the fuel inlet connectors

18.8 Make sure the filter spring is properly positioned

fuel line (photo). A flare nut wrench on this fitting will help prevent slipping and possible damage. However, an open-end wrench should do the job. Make sure the larger nut next to the carburetor is held firmly while the fuel line is disconnected.

7   With the fuel line disconnected, move it slightly for better access to the inlet filter nut. Do not crimp the fuel line.

8   Now unscrew the fuel inlet filter nut which was previously held steady. As this fitting is drawn away from the carburetor body, be careful not to lose the thin washer-type gasket or the spring located behind the fuel filter. Also, pay close attention to how the filter was installed (photo).

9   Compare the old filter with the new one to make sure they are of the same length and design.

10   Reinstall the spring into the carburetor body, after inspecting it for damage or defects.

11   Place the new filter into position behind the spring. If a bronze, cone-shaped filter is used, the smaller end of the cone points away from the carburetor. The later model paper filters will have a rubber gasket and check valve at one end which should point away from the carburetor (photo).

12   Install a new washer-type gasket on the fuel inlet filter nut (a gasket is usually supplied with the new filter) and tighten the nut into the carburetor. Make sure it is not cross-threaded. Tighten securely, but do not over-tighten, as this area can strip easily, causing fuel leaks.

18.11 The rubber gasket end of the paper filter should be installed facing away from the carburetor

13 Hold the fuel inlet nut securely with a wrench while the fuel line is connected. Again, be careful not to cross-thread the connector. Tighten securely.

14 Plug the vacuum hose which leads to the air cleaner snorkel motor so the engine can be run.

15 Start the engine and check carefully for leaks. If the fuel line connector leaks, disconnect it using the above procedures and check for stripped or damaged threads. If the fuel line connector has stripped threads, remove the entire line and have a repair shop install a new fitting. If the threads look alright, purchase some thread sealing tape and tightly wrap the connector threads with the tape. Now reinstall and tighten securely. Inlet repair kits are available at most auto parts stores to overcome leaking at the fuel inlet filter nut.

16 Reinstall the air cleaner assembly, connecting all hoses to their original positions.

19 Ignition timing – adjustment

1 All vehicles are equipped with a tune-up decal inside the engine compartment. This decal gives important ignition timing settings and procedures to be followed specific to that vehicle. If information on the tune-up decal supercedes the information given in this Section, the decal should be followed.

2 At the specified intervals, whenever the contact points have been replaced, the distributor removed or a change made in the fuel type, the ignition timing must be checked and adjusted if necessary.

3 Before attempting to check the timing, make sure the contact point dwell angle is correct (Section 30 1974 models only), and the idle speed is as specified (Section 16).

4 Disconnect the vacuum hose from the distributor and plug the now-open end of the hose with a rubber plug, rod or bolt of the proper size. Make sure the idle speed remains correct; adjust as necessary.

5 Connect a timing light in accordance with the manufacturer's instructions. Generally, the light will be connected to power and ground sources and to the number 1 spark plug in some fashion. The number 1 spark plug is the first one on the right as you are facing the engine from the front.

6 Locate the numbered timing tag on the front cover of the engine. It is just behind the lower crankshaft pulley. Clean it off with solvent if necessary to read the printing and small grooves.

7 Locate the notched groove across the crankshaft pulley. It may be necessary to have an assistant temporarily turn the ignition off and on in short bursts without starting the engine to bring this groove into a position where it can easily be cleaned and marked. Stay clear of all moving engine components if the engine is turned over in this manner.

8 Use white soap-stone, chalk or paint to mark the groove on the crankshaft pulley. Also put a mark on the timing tab in accordance with the number of degrees called for in the Specifications (Chapter 5) or on the tune-up decal inside the engine compartment. Each peak or notch on the timing tab represents 2°. The word 'Before' or the letter 'A' indicates advance and the letter 'O' indicates Top Dead Center (TDC). Thus if your vehicle specifications call for 8° BTDC (Before Top Dead Center), you will make a mark on the timing tab 4 notches 'before' the 'O'.

9 Check that the wiring for the timing light is clear of all moving engine components, then start the engine.

10 Point the flashing timing light at the timing marks, again being careful not to come in contact with moving parts. The marks you made should appear stationary. If the marks are in alignment, the timing is correct. If the marks are not aligned, turn off the engine.

11 Loosen the locknut at the base of the distributor. On GM cars this task is made much easier with a special curved distributor wrench. Loosen the locknut only slightly, just enough to turn the distributor. (See Chapter 5 for further details, if necessary).

12 Now restart the engine and turn the distributor until the timing marks coincide.

13 Shut off the engine and tighten the distributor locknut, being careful not to move the distributor.

14 Start the engine and recheck the timing to make sure the marks are still in alignment.

15 Disconnect the timing light, unplug the distributor vacuum hose and connect the hose to the distributor.

16 Drive the car and listen for 'pinging' noises. These will be most noticable when the engine is hot and under load (climbing a hill, accelerating from a stop). If you hear engine pinging, the ignition timing is too far advanced (Before Top Dead Center). Reconnect the timing light and turn the distributor to move the mark 1° or 2° in the retard direction. Road test the car again for proper operation.

17 To keep 'pinging' at a minimum, yet still allow you to operate the car at the specified timing setting, it is advisable to use gasoline of the same octane at all times. Switching fuel brands and octane levels can decrease performance and economy, and possibly damage the engine.

20 Carburetor choke check

1 The choke only operates when the engine is cold, and thus this check can only be performed before the car has been started for the day.

2 Open the hood and remove the top plate of the air cleaner assembly. It is held in place by a wing-nut at the center. If any vacuum hoses must be disconnected, make sure you tag the hoses for reinstallation to their original positions. Place the top plate and wing nut aside, out of the way of moving engine components.

3 Look at the top of the carburetor at the center of the air cleaner housing. You will notice a flat plate at the carburetor opening (photo).

4 Have an assistant press the accelerator pedal to the floor. The plate should close fully. Start the engine while you observe the plate at the carburetor. Do not position your face directly over the carburetor, as the engine could backfire, causing serious burns. When the engine starts, the choke plate should open slightly.

5 Allow the engine to continue running at an idle speed. As the engine warms up to operating temperature, the plate should slowly open, allowing more cold air to enter through the top of the carburetor.

6 After a few minutes, the choke plate should be fully open to the vertical position.

7 You will notice that the engine speed corresponds with the plate opening. With the plate fully closed, the engine should run at a fast idle speed. As the plate opens, the engine speed will decrease.

8 If during the above checks a fault is detected, refer to Chapter 4 for specific information on adjusting and servicing the choke components.

21 Exhaust Gas Recirculation (EGR) valve check

1 On GM vehicles the EGR valve is located on the intake manifold, adjacent to the carburetor. The majority of the time, when a fault develops in this emissions system it is due to a stuck or corroded EGR valve.

2 With the engine cold to prevent burns, reach under the EGR valve and manually push on the diaphragm (photo). Using moderate pressure, you should be able to press the diaphragm up and down within the housing.

3 If the diaphragm does not move or moves only with much effort, replace the EGR valve with a new one. If you are in doubt about the quality of the valve, go to your local parts store and compare the free movement of your EGR valve with a new valve.

4 Further testing of the EGR system and component replacement procedures can be found in Chapter 6.

22 Rear axle fluid change

1 To change the fluid in the rear axle it is necessary to remove the cover plate on the differential housing. Because of this, purchase a new gasket at the same time the gear lubricant is bought.

2 Move a drain pan (at least 5 pint capacity), rags, newspapers and your wrenches under the rear of the car. With the drain pan under the differential cover, loosen each of the inspection plate bolts.

3 Remove the bolts on the lower half of the plate, but use the upper bolts to keep the cover loosely attached to the differential. Allow the fluid to drain into the drain pan, then completely remove the cover.

4 Using a lint-free rag, clean the inside of the cover and the accessible areas of the differential housing. As this is done, check for chipped gears or metal filings in the fluid indicating the differential should be thoroughly inspected and repaired (see Chapter 8 for more information).

5 Thoroughly clean the gasket mating surface on the cover and the differential housing. Use a gasket scraper or putty knife to remove all traces of the old gasket.

20.3 Once the air cleaner top plate has been removed, the choke plate is clearly visible

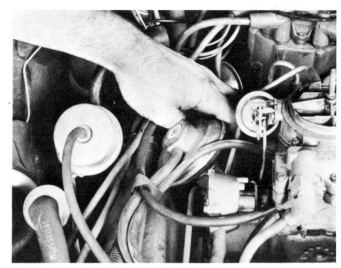

21.2 The EGR valve is a disc-shaped device mounted to the intake manifold, next to the carburetor

6   Smear a thin film of gasket sealant on the cover flange and then press a new gasket into position on the cover. Make sure the bolt holes align properly.

7   Place the cover on the differential housing and install the securing bolts. Tighten the bolts a little at a time, working across the cover in a diagonal fashion until all bolts are tight. If a torque wrench is available, tighten the bolts to the specified torque.

8   Remove the inspection plug on the side of the differential housing (or inspection cover) and fill the housing with the proper lubricant until the level is at the bottom of the plug hole.

9   Securely install the plug.

23 Spark plug replacement

1   The spark plugs are located on each side of the engine on a V8 and may or may not be easily accessible for removal. If the car is equipped with air conditioning or power steering, some of the plugs may be tricky to service in which case special extension or swivel tools will be necessary. Make a survey under the hood to ascertain if special tools will be needed.

2   In most cases the tools necessary for a spark plug replacement job are: a plug wrench or spark plug socket which fits onto a ratchet wrench (this special socket will be insulated inside to protect the porcelain insulator) and a feeler gauge to check and adjust the spark plug gap. If the car is equipped with HEI ignition (1975–1980), a special spark plug wire removal tool is available for separating the wire boot from the spark plug.

3   The best policy to follow when replacing the spark plugs is to purchase the new spark plugs beforehand, adjust them to the proper gap and then replace each plug one at a time. When buying the new spark plugs it is important that the correct plug is purchased for your specific engine. This information can be found in the Specifications Section of Chapter 5, but should be checked against the information found on the tune-up decal located under the hood of your car or in the factory owner's manual. If differences exist between these sources, purchase the spark plug type specified on the tune-up decal as this information was printed for your specific engine.

4   With the new spark plugs at hand, allow the engine to thoroughly cool before attempting the removal. During this cooling time, each of the new spark plugs can be inspected for defects and the gap can be checked.

5   The gap is checked by inserting the proper thickness gauge between the electrodes at the tip of the plug. The gap between these electrodes should be the same as that given in the Specifications or on the tune-up decal. The wire should just touch each of the eletrodes. If the gap is incorrect, use the notched adjuster on the feeler gauge body to bend the curved side electrode slightly until the proper gap is achieved. Also at this time check for cracks in the spark plug body,

indicating the spark plug should be replaced with a new one. If the side electrode is not exactly over the center one, use the notched adjuster to align the two.

6   Cover the fenders of the car to prevent damage to exterior paint.

7   With the engine cool, remove the spark plug wire from one spark plug. Do this by grabbing the boot at the end of the wire, not the wire itself. Sometimes it is necessary to use a twisting motion while the boot and plug wire is pulled free (photo). Using a plug wire removal tool is the easiest and safest method.

8   If compressed air is available, use this to blow any dirt or foreign material away from the spark plug area. A common bicycle pump will also work. The idea here is to eliminate the possibility of material falling into the engine cylinder as the spark plug is replaced.

9   Now place the spark plug wrench or socket over the plug and remove it from the engine by turning in a counter-clockwise motion.

10   Compare the spark plug with those shown on page 169 to get an indication of the overall running condition of the engine.

11   Insert one of the new plugs into the engine, tightening it as much as possible by hand. The spark plug should screw easily into the engine. If it doesn't, change the angle of the spark plug slightly, as chances are the threads are not matched (cross-threaded).

12   Firmly tighten the spark plug with the wrench or socket. It is best to use a torque wrench for this to ensure the plug is seated correctly. The correct torque figure is shown in Specifications.

13   Before pushing the spark plug wire onto the end of the plug, inspect it following the procedures outlined in Section 28.

14   Install the plug wire to the new spark plug, again using a twisting motion on the boot until it is firmly seated on the spark plug. Make sure wire is routed away from the hot exhaust manifold.

15   Follow the above procedures for the remaining spark plugs, replacing each one at a time to prevent mixing up the spark plug wires.

24 Wheel bearing check and repack

1   In most cases, the front wheel bearings will not need servicing until the brake pads are changed. However, these bearings should be checked whenever the front wheels are raised for any reason.

2   With the vehicle securely supported on jack stands, spin the wheel and check for noise, rolling resistance or free play. Now grab the top of the tire with one hand and the bottom of the tire with the other. Move the tire in and out on the spindle. If it moves more than 0.005 in, the bearings should be checked, then repacked with grease or replaced if necessary.

3   To remove the bearings for replacing or repacking, begin by removing the hub cap and wheel.

4   Using an Allen wrench of the proper size, remove the two bolts which secure the disc brake caliper to its support (see Chapter 9).

5   Fabricate a wood block ($1\frac{1}{16}$ inch by $1\frac{1}{16}$ inch by 2 inches in length)

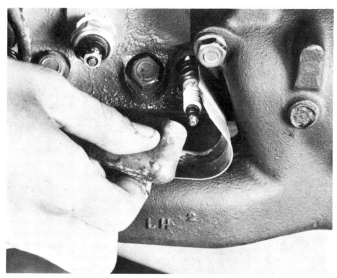

23.7 When removing spark plug wires, grasp the boot – never the wire

24.11 Use a screwdriver to pry out the grease seal for the inner bearing

24.21 The adjusting nut should be tightened only initially with a wrench

25.8 Dropping the rear of the transmission oil pan to drain the fluid

25.12 Inspect the inside of the pan for metal filings and other grit (clean the pan before reinstalling it)

25.14 Installing the new filter

which will be slid between the brake pads to keep them separated. Carefully slide the caliper off the disc and insert the wood block between the pads. Use wire to hang the caliper assembly out of the way. Be careful not to kink or damage the brake hose.

6   Pry the hub grease cap off the hub using a screwdriver. This cap is located at the center of the hub.

7   Use needle-nose pliers to straighten the bent ends of the cotter pin and then pull the cotter pin out of the locking nut. Discard the cotter pin, as a new one should be used on reassembly.

8   Remove the spindle nut and its washer from the end of the spindle.

9   Pull the hub assembly outward slightly and then push it back into its original position. This should force the outer bearing off the spindle enough so that it can be removed with your fingers. Remove the outer bearing, noting how it is installed on the end of the spindle.

10   Now the hub assembly can be pulled off the spindle.

11   On the rear side of the hub, use a screwdriver to pry out the inner bearing lip seal (photo). As this is done, note the direction in which the seal is installed.

12   The inner bearing can now be removed from the hub, again noting how it is installed.

13   Use clean parts solvent to remove all traces of the old grease from the bearings, hub and spindle. A small brush may prove useful; however, make sure no bristles from the brush embed themselves inside the bearing rollers. Allow the parts to air dry.

14   Carefully inspect the bearings for cracks, heat discoloration, bent rollers, etc. Check the bearing races inside the hub for cracks, scoring or uneven surfaces. If the bearing races are in need of replacement, this job is best left to a repair shop which can press the new races into position.

15   Use an approved high temperature front wheel bearing grease to pack the bearings. Work the grease fully into the bearings, forcing the grease between the rollers, cone and cage.

16   Apply a thin coat of grease to the spindle at the outer bearing seat, inner bearing seat, shoulder and seal seat.

17   Put a small quantity of grease inboard of each bearing race inside the hub. Using your finger, form a dam at these points to provide extra grease availability and to keep thinned grease from flowing out of the bearing.

18   Place the grease-packed inner bearing into the rear of the hub and put a little more grease outboard of the bearing.

19   Place a new seal over the inner bearing and tap the seal with a flat plate and a hammer until it is flush with the hub.

20   Carefully place the hub assembly onto the spindle and push the grease-packed outer bearing into position.

21   Install the washer and spindle nut. Tighten the nut only slightly (12 ft-lbs of torque) (photo).

22   In a forward direction, spin the hub to seat the bearings and remove any grease or burrs which could cause excessive bearing play

later.

23   Put a little grease outboard of the outer bearing to provide extra grease availability.

24   Now check that the spindle nut is still tight (12 ft-lbs).

25   Loosen the spindle nut until it is just loose, no more.

26   Using your hand (not a wrench of any kind), tighten the nut until it is snug. Install a new cotter pin through the hole in the spindle and spindle nut. If the nut slits do not line up, loosen the nut slightly until they do. From the hand-tight position the nut should not be loosened any more than one-half flat to install the cotter pin.

27   Bend the ends of the new cotter pin until they are flat against the nut. Cut off any extra length which could interfere with the dust cap.

28   Install the dust cap, tapping it into place with a rubber mallet.

29   Place the brake caliper near the rotor and carefully remove the wood block spacers. Slide the caliper over the rotor. Tighten the caliper mounting bolts to the specified torque. Chapter 9 will give full details on the disc brake caliper assembly.

30   Install the tire/wheel assembly to the hub and tighten the mounting nuts.

31   Grab the top and bottom of the tire and check the bearings in the same manner as described at the beginning of this Section.

32   Lower the vehicle to the ground and fully tighten the wheel nuts. Install the hub cap, using a rubber mallet to fully seat it.

25 Automatic transmission fluid change

1   At the specified time intervals, the transmission fluid should be changed and the filter replaced with a new one. Since there is no drain plug, the transmission oil pan must be removed from the bottom of the transmission to drain the fluid.

2   Before any draining, purchase the specified transmission fluid (see *Recommended Lubricants* and a new filter. The necessary gaskets should be included with the filter; if not, purchase an oil pan gasket and a strainer-to-valve body gasket.

3   Other tools necessary for this job include: jack stands to support the vehicle in a raised position; wrench to remove the oil pan bolts; standard screwdriver; drain pan capable of holding at least 8 pints; newspapers and clean rags.

4   The fluid should be drained immediately after the car has been driven. This will remove any built-up sediment better than if the fluid were cold. Because of this, it may be wise to wear protective gloves (fluid temperature can exceed 350° in a hot transmission).

5   After the car has been driven to warm up the fluid, raise the vehicle and place it on jack stands for access underneath. Make sure it is firmly supported by the four stands placed on the frame rails.

6   Move the necessary equipment under the car, being careful not to touch any of the hot exhaust components.

7   Place the drain pan under the transmission oil pan and remove the

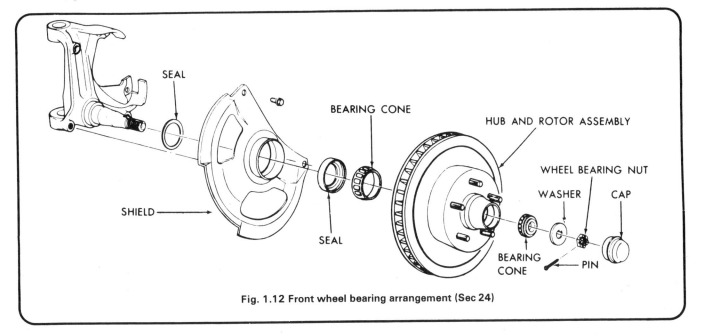

Fig. 1.12 Front wheel bearing arrangement (Sec 24)

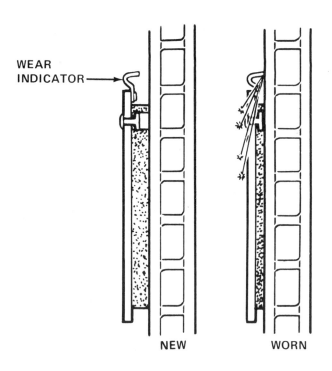

Fig. 1.13 Front disc brake wear indicator (Sec 26)

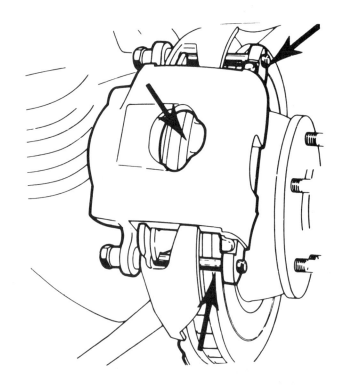

Fig. 1.14 Disc pad wear indicator points (Sec 26)

oil pan bolts along the rear and sides of the pan. Loosen, but do not remove, the bolts at the front of the pan.

8   Carefully pry the pan downward at the rear, allowing the hot fluid to drain into the drain pan (photo). If necessary, use a screwdriver to break the gasket seal at the rear of the pan; however, do not damage the pan or transmission in the process.

9   Support the pan and remove the remaining bolts at the front of the pan. Lower the pan and drain the remaining fluid into the drain receptacle. As this is done, check the fluid for metal filings which may be an indication of internal failure.

10 Now visible on the bottom of the transmission is the filter/strainer held in place by two screws.

11 Remove the two screws, the filter and its gasket.

12 Thoroughly clean the transmission oil pan with solvent. Inspect for metal filings or foreign matter (photo). Dry with compressed air if available. It is important that all remaining gasket material be removed from the oil pan mounting flange. Use a gasket scraper or putty knife for this.

13 Clean the filter mounting surface on the valve body. Again, this surface should be smooth and free of any leftover gasket material.

14 Place the new filter in position, with a new gasket between it and the transmission valve body. Install the two mounting screws and tighten securely (photo).

15 Apply a bead of gasket sealant around the oil pan mounting surface, with the sealant to the inside of the bolt holes. Press the new gasket into place on the pan, making sure all bolt holes line up.

16 Lift the pan up to the bottom of the transmission and install the mounting bolts. Tighten the bolts in a diagonal fashion, working around the pan. Using a torque wrench, tighten the bolts to the specified torque.

17 Lower the car off its jack stands.

18 Open the hood and remove the transmission fluid dipstick from its guide tube.

19 Since fluid capacities vary between the various transmission types, it is best to add a little fluid at a time, continually checking the level with the dipstick. Allow the fluid time to drain into the pan. Add fluid until the level just registers on the end of the dipstick. In most cases, a good starting point will be 4 to 5 pints added to the transmission through the filler tube (use a funnel to prevent spills).

20 With the selector lever in 'Park', apply the parking brake and start the engine without depressing the accelerator pedal (if possible). Do not race the engine at a high speed; run at slow idle only.

21 Depress the brake pedal and shift the transmission through each gear. Place the selector back into 'Park' and check the level on the dipstick (with the engine still idling). Look under the car for leaks around the transmission oil pan mating surface.

22 Add more fluid through the dipstick tube until the level on the dipstick is $\frac{1}{4}$ inch below the 'Add' mark on the dipstick. Do not allow the fluid level to go above this point, as the transmission would then be overfull, necessitating the removal of the pan to drain the excess fluid.

23 Push the dipstick firmly back into its tube and drive the car to reach normal operating temperature (15 miles of highway driving or its equivalent in the city). Park the car on a level surface and check the fluid level on the dipstick with the engine idling and the transmission in 'Park'. The level should now be at the 'Full Hot' mark on the dipstick. If not, add more fluid as necessary to bring the level up to this point. Again, do not overfill.

26 Brakes check

1   The brakes should be inspected every time the wheels are removed or whenever a fault is suspected. Indications of a potential braking system fault are: the car pulls to one side when brake pedal is depressed; noises coming from the brakes when they are applied; excessive brake pedal travel; pulsating pedal; and leakage of fluid, usually seen on the inside of the tire or wheel.

Disc brakes

2   Disc brakes can be visually checked without the need to remove any parts except the wheels.

3   Raise the vehicle and place securely on jack stands. Remove the front wheels (See *Jacking and Towing* at the front of this manual if necessary).

4   Now visible is the disc brake caliper which contains the pads. There is an outer brake pad and an inner pad. Both should be inspected.

5   Most later model vehicles come equipped with a 'wear sensor' attached to the inner pad. This is a small, bent piece of metal which is visible from the inboard side of the brake caliper. When the pads wear to a danger limit, the metal sensor rubs against the disc and makes a screeching sound.

26.13 Use a hammer and cold chisel to remove the lanced knock-out plug on the face of the drum

26.16 Check that all springs are in good condition

26.17 Leaks often occur at the wheel cylinder located at the top of the brake shoe junction

26.19 Inspect the inside surface of the drum for scoring, hot spots, cracks, etc

6   Inspect the pad thickness by looking at each end of the caliper and through the cut-out inspection hole in the caliper body. If the wear sensor clip is very close to the rotor, or the lining material is $\frac{1}{32}$ in or less in thickness, the pads should be replaced. Keep in mind that the lining material is riveted or bonded to a metal backing shoe and the metal portion is not included in this measuring.

7   Since it will be difficult, if not impossible, to measure the exact thickness of the remaining lining material, if you are in doubt as to the pad quality, remove the pads for further inspection or replacement. See Chapter 9 for disc brake pad replacement.

8   Before installing the wheels, check for any leakage around the brake hose connections leading to the caliper or damage (cracking, splitting, etc.) to the brake hose. Replace the hose or fittings as necessary, referring to Chapter 9.

9   Also check the condition of the disc for scoring, gouging or burnt spots. If these conditions exist, the hub/rotor assembly should be removed for servicing (Chapter 9).

Drum brakes (rear)

10   Raise the vehicle and support firmly on jack stands. Block the front tires to prevent the car from rolling; however, do not apply the parking brake as this will lock the drums into place.

11   Remove the wheels, referring to *Jacking and Towing* at the front of this manual if necessary.

12   Mark the hub so it can be reinstalled in the same place. Use a scribe, chalk, etc. on drum and center hub and backing plate.

13   Pull the brake drum off the axle and brake assembly. If this proves difficult, make sure the parking brake is released, then squirt some penetrating oil around the center hub area. Allow the oil to soak in and try again to pull the drum off. Then, if the drum cannot be pulled off, the brake shoes will have to be adjusted inward. This is done by first removing the lanced cutout in the drum or backing plate with a hammer and chisel (photo). With this lanced area punched in, rotate the drum until the opening lines up with the adjuster wheel. Pull the lever off the sprocket and then use a small screwdriver to turn the sprocket wheel which will move the linings away from the drums.

14   With the drum removed, carefully brush away any accumulations of dirt and dust. Do not blow this out with compressed air or in any similar fashion. Make an effort not to inhale this dust as it contains asbestos and is harmful to your health.

15   Observe the thickness of the lining material on both the front and rear brake shoes. If the material has worn away to within $\frac{1}{32}$ in of the recessed rivets or metal backing, the shoes should be replaced. If the linings look worn, but you are unable to determine their exact thickness, compare them with a new set at the auto parts store. The shoes should also be replaced if they are cracked, glazed (shiny surface), or wet with brake fluid.

16   Check that all the brake assembly springs are connected and in

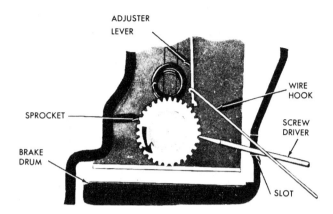

Fig. 1.15 Use a screwdriver and a wire hook (through the access hole) to retract the brake shoes (Sec 26)

good condition (photo).

17 Check the brake components for any signs of fluid leakage. With your finger, carefully pry back the rubber cups on the wheel cylinder located at the top of the brake shoes (photo). Any leakage is an indication that the wheel cylinders should be overhauled immediately (Chapter 9). Also check fluid hoses and connections for signs of leakage.

18 Wipe the inside of the drum with a clean rag, and denatured alcohol. Again, be careful not to breathe the dangerous asbestos dust.

19 Check the inside of the drum for cracks, scores, deep scratches or 'hard spots' which will appear as small discolorations (photo). If these imperfections cannot be removed with fine emery cloth, the drum must be taken to a machine shop equipped to turn the drums.

20 If after the inspection process all parts are in good working condition, reinstall the brake drum (using a metal plug if the lanced knock-out was removed). Install the wheel and lower the car to the ground.

Parking brake

21 The easiest way to check the operation of the parking brake is to park the car on a steep hill, with the parking brake set and the transmission in 'Neutral'. If the parking brake cannot prevent the car from rolling, it is in need of adjustment (see Chapter 9).

27 Carburetor mounting torque

1 The carburetor is attached to the top of the intake manifold by four nuts. These fasteners can sometimes work loose through normal engine operation and cause a vacuum leak.

2 To properly tighten the carburetor mounting nuts, a torque wrench is necessary. If you do not own one, they can usually be rented on a daily basis.

3 Remove the air cleaner assembly, tagging each hose to be disconnected with a piece of numbered tape to make reassembly easier.

4 Locate the mounting nuts at the base of the carburetor. Decide what special tools or adapters will be necessary, if any, to tighten the nuts with a properly sized socket and the torque wrench.

5 Tighten the nuts to a torque of about 12 ft-lbs. Do not overtighten the nuts, as this may cause the threads to strip.

6 If you suspect a vacuum leak exists at the bottom of the carburetor, get a length of spare hose about the diameter of fuel hose. Start the engine and place one end of the hose next to your ear as you probe around the base of the carburetor with the other end. You will be able to hear a hissing sound if a leak exists. A soapy water solution brushed around the suspect area can also be used to pinpoint pressure leaks.

7 If, after the nuts are properly tightened, a vacuum leak still exists, the carburetor must be removed and a new gasket used. See Chapter 4 for more information.

8 After tightening nuts, reinstall the air cleaner, connecting all hoses to their original positions.

28 Spark plug wires check

1 The spark plug wires should be checked at the recommended intervals or whenever new spark plugs are installed.

2 The wires should be inspected one at a time to prevent mixing up the order which is essential for proper engine operation.

3 Disconnect the plug wire from the spark plug. A removal tool can be used for this, or you can grab the rubber boot, twist slightly and then pull the wire free. Do not pull on the wire itself, only on the rubber boot.

4 Inspect inside the boot for corrosion which will look like a white, crusty powder. Later models use a conductive white grease which should not be mistaken for corrosion.

5 Now push the wire and boot back onto the end of the spark plug. It should be a tight fit on the plug end. If not, remove the wire and use a pair of pliers to carefully crimp the metal connector inside the wire boot until the fit is secure.

6 Now using a clean rag, clean the wire its entire length. Remove all built-up dirt and grease. As this is done, inspect for burns, cracks or any other form of damage. Bend the wires in several places to ensure the conductive inside wire has not hardened.

7 Disconnect the wire at the distributor (again, pulling and twisting only on the rubber boot). Check for corrosion and a tight fit in the same manner as the spark plug end. If equipped with HEI ignition (1975 and later), the distributor boots are connected to a circular retaining ring. Release the locking tabs, turn the ring upside-down and check all wire boots at the same time.

8 Reinstall the wire boot (or retaining ring) onto the top of the distributor.

9 Check the remaining spark plug wires in the same way, making sure they are securely fastened at the distributor and spark plug.

10 A visual check of the spark plug wires can also be made. In a darkened garage (make sure there is ventilation), start the engine and observe each plug wire. Be careful not to come into contact with any moving engine parts. If there is a break or fault in the wire, you will be able to see arcing or a small spark at the damaged area.

11 If it is decided the spark plug wires are in need of replacement, purchase a new set for your specific engine model. Wire sets can be purchased which are pre-cut to the proper size and with the rubber boots already installed. HEI ignition systems (1975–1980) use a different type of plug wire from conventional systems. Remove and replace each wire individually to prevent mix-ups in the firing sequence.

29 Cooling system servicing (draining, flushing and refilling)

1 Periodically, the cooling system should be drained, flushed and refilled. This is to replenish the antifreeze mixture and prevent rust and corrosion which can impair the performance of the cooling system and ultimately cause engine damage.

2 At the same time the cooling system is serviced, all hoses and the fill cap should be inspected and replaced if faulty (see Section 6).

3 As antifreeze is a poisonous solution, take care not to spill any of the cooling mixture on the vehicle's paint or your own skin. If this happens, rinse immediately with plenty of clear water. Also, it is advisable to consult your local authorities about the dumping of antifreeze before draining the cooling system. In many areas reclamation centers have been set up to collect automobile oil and drained antifreeze/water mixtures rather than allowing these liquids to be added to the sewage and water facilities.

4 With the engine cold, remove the radiator pressure fill cap.

5 Move a large container under the radiator to catch the water/antifreeze mixture as it is drained.

6 Drain the radiator. Most models are equipped with a drain plug at the bottom of the radiator which can be opened using a wrench to hold the fitting while the petcock is turned to the open position. If this drain has excessive corrosion and cannot be turned easily, or the radiator is not equipped with a drain, disconnect the lower radiator hose to allow the coolant to drain. Be careful that none of the solution is splashed on your skin or in your eyes.

7 If accessible, remove the two engine drain plugs (photo). There is one plug on each side of the engine, about halfway back and on the lower edge near the oil pan rail. These will allow the coolant to drain from the engine itself.

29.7 Engine drain plugs are located on each side of the engine block

30.6 The rotor is attached to the counterweights with 2 screws (remove the screws and lift off the rotor)

30.8 Loosen the 2 screws that secure the contact point assembly to the mounting plate (1974)

30.9 Disconnect the primary wires from the points (1974)

30.11 The condenser is held in place by a single screw

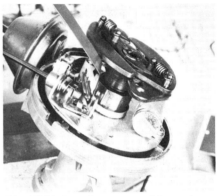

30.19 With the points separated, insert the proper feeler gauge between them and turn the adjusting screw (1974)

30.21 Inspect the rotor contacts for scorching, pitting or wear

30.23 Check the distributor cap contacts for wear and deposits

30.31 With the inspection window open, the point dwell can be adjusted with an Allen wrench (1974)

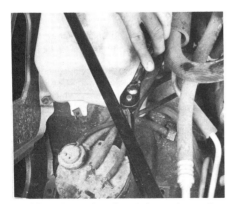

31.4 The charcoal canister is located near the front of the engine compartment (note the hoses attached to the top)

31.5 Remove the filter from the canister bottom

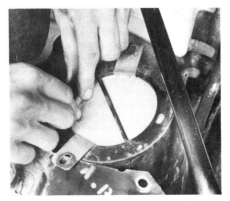

31.6 Make sure the new filter is properly seated around canister surface

8   On systems with an expansion reservoir, disconnect the overflow pipe and remove the reservoir. Flush it out with clean water.

9   Place a cold water hose (a common garden hose is fine) in the radiator filler neck at the top of the radiator and flush the system until the water runs clean at all drain points.

10 In severe cases of contamination or clogging of the radiator, remove it (see Chapter 3) and reverse flush it. This involves simply inserting the cold pressure hose in the bottom radiator outlet to allow the clear water to run against the normal flow, draining through the top. A radiator repair shop should be consulted if further cleaning or repair is necessary.

11 Where the coolant is regularly drained and the system refilled with the correct antifreeze/inhibitor mixture there should be no need to employ chemical cleaners or descalers.

12 To refill the system, reconnect the radiator hoses and install the drain plugs securely in the engine. Special thread sealing tape (available at auto parts stores) should be used on the drain plugs going into the engine block. Install the expansion reservoir and the overflow hose where applicable.

13 On vehicles without an expansion reservoir, refill the system through the radiator filler cap until the water level is about three inches below the filler neck.

14 On vehicles with an expansion reservoir, fill the radiator to the base of the filler neck and then add more coolant to the expansion reservoir so that it reaches the 'FULL COLD' mark.

15 Run the engine until normal operating temperature is reached and with the engine idling, add coolant up to the correct level (see Section 2), then fit the radiator cap so that the arrows are in alignment with the overflow pipe. Install the reservoir cap.

16 Always refill the system with a mixture of high quality antifreeze and water in the proportion called for on the antifreeze container or in your owner's manual. Chapter 3 also contains information on anti-freeze mixtures.

17 Keep a close watch on the coolant level and the various cooling hoses during the first few miles of driving. Tighten the hose clamps and/or add more coolant mixture as necessary.

---

30 Point replacement, dwell angle adjustment and distributor check (1974 models only)

---

1   Although the contact points can be cleaned and dressed with a fine-cut contact file, it may be a false economy for the home mechanic to attempt this. Due to the inaccessibility of the distributor components, it is more practical to merely replace the contact points during tune-ups.

2   The contact point set and condenser are replaced as one complete assembly. Point alignment and spring tension are factory set and require no further adjustment.

3   Whenever distributor servicing is required, as in contact point replacement, it is a good idea to use magnetized tools to prevent screws or nuts from falling down into the distributor body, requiring distributor disassembly to retrieve.

Contact point replacement

4   Remove the distributor cap by placing a screwdriver on the slotted head of the latch. Press down on the latch and give a $\frac{1}{4}$ turn to release the curved section at the bottom of the latch.

5   With both latches disengaged from the distributor body, place the cap (with the spark plug wires still attached) out of the way. Use a length of wire or tape if necessary.

6   Remove the rotor, which is now visible at the top of the distributor shaft. In most cases the rotor is held in place with two screws. On some models, the rotor is merely pushed onto the shaft and can simply be lifted away. Place the rotor in a safe place where it cannot be damaged (photo).

7   If equipped with a radio frequency interference shield (RFI), remove the attaching screws and the two-piece shield to gain access to the contact points.

8   Loosen the two screws which secure the contact point set assembly to the breaker plate (photo). Do not completely remove these screws, as most point sets have slots at these locations. Slide the point set off the breaker plate.

9   Disconnect the primary and condenser wire leads at the point set (photo). These wires may be attached with a small nut (which should

be loosened, but not removed) a small standard screw, or by a quick-disconnect terminal which rquires the tangs to be pressed together to un-lock.

10 The contact breaker point assembly can now be removed completely from the engine compartment.

11 The condenser can now be removed from the breaker plate. Loosen the mounting strap screw and slide the condenser out of the bracket, or completely remove the condenser and strap depending on the exact attachment (photo).

12 Before installing the new points and condenser, clean all lubricant, dirt, etc. from the breaker plate and the rotating cam surface of the distributor shaft.

13 Fully lubricate the center cam with the grease supplied with the new points.

14 Check the cam lubricator wick mounted on the breaker plate. The wick can be rotated to provide lubrication if it is still in good condition, but if in doubt replace the wick with a new one to provide adequate lubrication to the cam surface. It is removed by squeezing the base of the retainer together with long-nosed pliers and then lifting the unit out of the breaker plate. It is important that the cam lubricator wick be adjusted so the end of the wick just touches the cam lobes.

15 Place the new condenser into position and tighten its retaining screw.

16 Slide the new contact point set onto the breaker plate and tighten the two attaching screws.

17 Connect the primary and condenser electrical leads to the new point assembly. Make sure the leads are postioned the same as they were on removal.

18 Although the final gap between the contact points will be adjusted later (dwell angle), it is best to get an initial gap to start the engine. With the points in position and tightened to the breaker plate, see that the points rubbing block is resting on one of the high points of the center cam. To move the center cam, have an assistant just click the ignition key in short bursts. If equipped with a manual transmission, place the shifter in gear and rock the car back and forth.

19 With the rubbing block on a cam high point (points fully open), place a blade-type feeler gauge between the contacts. The gap should be 0.016 in. If not correct, use an Allen wrench to turn the points set socket which will open and close the gap (photo).

20 Install the RFI shield, if applicable.

21 Before installing the rotor, inspect it for cracks or damage. Carefully check the condition of the metal contact at the top of the rotor for excessive burning or pitting (photo). If in doubt as to its quality, replace it with a new one.

22 Install the rotor. Both types are keyed to go onto the shaft only one way. Rotors having attaching screws will have raised pegs on the bottom. Make sure the rotor is firmly seated.

23 Before installing the distributor cap, inspect it for cracks or damage. Closely examine the contacts on the inside of the cap for excessive corrosion or damage (photo). Slight scoring is normal. If in doubt as to the quality of the cap, replace it with a new one as described in Chapter 5.

24 Install the distributor cap, locking the two latches under the distributor body.

25 Start the engine and check the dwell angle and the ignition timing (Section 19).

Point dwell angle adjustment

26 Whenever new contact points are installed or original points are cleaned, the dwell angle should be checked and adjusted to proper specifications.

27 Setting the dwell angle on GM cars is actually very easy; however, a dwell meter must be used for precise adjustment. Combination tach/dwell meters are common tune-up instruments which can be purchased at a reasonable cost. An approximate setting can be achieved without a meter.

28 Connect the dwell meter following the manufacturer's instructions.

29 Start the engine and allow to run at idle until it has reached normal operating temperature. The engine must be fully warmed to achieve an accurate reading. Turn off the engine.

30 Raise the metal 'window' on the outside of the distributor cap. Prop it in the up position, using tape if necessary.

31 Just inside this window is the adjustment screw for the contact points. Insert an Allen wrench of the proper size into the adjustment

screw socket (photo).

32 Start the engine and turn the adjusting screw as required to obtain the specified dwell reading on the meter. Dwell angle specifications are given at the beginning of Chapter 5 as well as on the tune-up decal located inside your engine compartment. If there is a discrepancy between the sources, assume the tune-up decal is correct. Remove your hand from the Allen wrench and recheck the reading.

33 Remove the Allen wrench and close the window fully. Turn off the engine and disconnect the dwell meter.

34 If you simply cannot buy, borrow or rent a dwell meter, you can get an approximate dwell setting without using a meter by the following method.

35 Start the engine and allow to idle until it has reached normal operating temperature.

36 Raise the metal window on the side of the distributor cap and insert the proper size Allen wrench into the point adjustment screw socket.

37 Turn the Allen wrench clockwise until the engine begins to misfire. Then turn the screw one half turn counter-clockwise.

38 Remove the Allen wrench and fully close the window. As soon as possible have the dwell angle checked and/or adjusted with a dwell meter. This will ensure optimum performance.

31 Evaporative Control System (ECS) filter replacement

1 The function of the ECS emissions system is to draw fuel vapors from the tank and carburetor, store them in a charcoal canister, and then burn these fumes during normal engine operation.

2 The filter at the bottom of the charcoal canister should be replaced at the specified intervals. If, however, a fuel odor is detected, the canister, filter and system hoses should immediately be inspected for fault.

3 To replace the filter, locate the canister at the front of the engine compartment. It will have between 3 and 6 hoses running out the top of it.

4 Remove the two bolts which secure the bottom of the canister to the body sheet metal (photo).

5 Turn the canister upside-down and pull the old filter from the bottom of the canister (photo). If you cannot turn the canister enough for this due to the short length of the hoses, the hoses must be duly marked with pieces of tape and then disconnected from the top.

6 Push the new filter into the bottom of the canister, making sure it is seated all the way around (photo).

7 Place the canister back into position and tighten the two mounting bolts. Connect the various hoses if disconnected.

8 The ECS system is explained in more detail in Chapter 6.

Chapter 2 Part A V8 engine

Contents

Specifications

1974 through 1978 Buick 350 CID and 455 CID V8 engines (VIN codes H, J, R, U, V)
All dimensions in inches unless otherwise noted

General

Bore and stroke
350	3.800 x 3.850
455	4.3125 x 3.900

Compression ratio
1974	8.5:1
1975	8.1:1
1976 through 1978	8.0:1
Firing order	1–8–4–3–6–5–7–2

Cylinder numbers
Right bank, front to rear	2–4–6–8
Left bank, front to rear	1–3–5–7

Pistons and pistons rings

Clearance in cylinder
350	0.0008 to 0.0020
455	0.0007 to 0.0013

Pin diameter
350	0.9391 to 0.9394
455	0.9991 to 0.9994

Pin length
350
1974 through 1977	3.060
1978	2.900
455	3.520

Pin press fit in rod
350	0.0007 to 0.0017
455	0.0006 to 0.00016

Piston ring end gap (350)
 No. 1 .... 0.010 to 0.020
 No. 2 .... 0.010 to 0.020
Piston ring end gap (455)
 No. 1 .... 0.013 to 0.023
 2 .... 0.013 to 0.023
Oil ring end gap (all) .... 0.015 to 0.035

Connecting rods

Bearing length
 350
  1974 through 1977 .... 0.737
  1978 .... 0.654
 455 .... 0.820
Bearing oil clearance
 1974 .... 0.0002 to 0.0023
 1975 through 1978 .... 0.0005 to 0.0026
Rod end play (total for two)
 1974
  350 .... 0.006 to 0.020
  455 .... 0.005 to 0.019
 1975 through 1978 .... 0.006 to 0.027

Valves

Valve lifter mechanism .... Hydraulic
Diameter of head
 Intake
  350 .... 1.880 to 1.870
  455 .... 2.005 to 1.995
 Exhaust (1974)
  350 .... 1.505 to 1.495
  455 .... 1.625
 Exhaust (1975 through 1978) .... 1.555 to 1.545
Diameter of stem
 Intake .... 0.3730 to 0.3720
 Exhaust .... 0.3723 to 0.3730
Valve seat angle
 Intake .... 45°
 Exhaust .... 45°

Crankshaft

Main bearing journal diameter
 350 .... 3.0000
 455 .... 3.2500
Crankpin journal diameter
 350 .... 2.0000
 455 .... 2.249 to 2.250
Main bearing-to-journal clearance
 350 .... 0.0004 to 0.0015
 455 .... 0.0007 to 0.0018
End play .... 0.003 to 0.009

Camshaft

Journal diameter (all) .... 1.785 to 1.786
Journal-to-bearing clearance
 No. 1 .... 0.0005 to 0.0025
 Nos. 2, 3, 4 and 5 .... 0.0005 to 0.0035

Oil pump pressure

350 .... 37 lbs @ 2600 rpm
455 .... 40 lbs @ 2400 rpm

Torque specifications   ft-lb

Carburetor-to-intake manifold 15
Connecting rod nuts
 350 40
 455 45
Main bearing cap bolts
 1974 through 1976 115
 1977 and 1978 100
Cylinder head bolts
 350 80
 455 100
Distributor hold down clamp 13
Exhaust manifold-to-head
 1974 through 1976 28
 1977 and 1978 25
Fan pulley 20
Fan pulley-to-harmonic balancer
 1974 through 1976 23
 1977 and 1978 20

Filter assembly-to-pump cover

1974 through 1976	13
1977 and 1978	20
Flywheel-to-crankshaft	60
Fuel pump mounting bolts	20

Harmonic balancer-to-crankshaft

350

1974 through 1976	150
1977	175
1978	225
455	200
Intake manifold-to-head	45

Motor mount-to-block

1974 through 1976	63
1977 and 1978	55
Oil gallery plugs	25
Oil pan-to-block	14
Oil pan drain plug	30
Oil pressure switch-to-block	23
Oil pump cover-to-timing chain cover	10
Oil pump pressure regulator retainer	35
Rocker arm cover-to-head	4
Rocker arm shaft-to-head	30
Starter motor-to-block	35
Thermostat housing-to-intake manifold	20
Timing chain cover-to-block	29
Water pump cover-to-timing chain cover	7

1977 through 1980 Chevrolet 305 CID and 350 CID V8 engines (VIN codes L, U, H)
All dimensions in inches unless otherwise noted

General

Bore and stroke

305	3.736 x 3.480
350	4.000 x 3.480
Compression ratio (all)	8.5:1
Firing order	1–8–4–3–6–5–7–2

Cylinder numbers

Right bank, front to rear	2–4–6–8
Left bank, front to rear	1–3–5–7

Pistons and piston rings

Clearance in cylinder	0.0027 max

Ring-to-groove side clearance

Top ring

1977 and 1978	0.0012 to 0.0042
1979 and 1980	0.0012 to 0.0032

2nd ring

1977 and 1978	0.0012 to 0.0042
1979	0.0012 to 0.0027
1980	0.0012 to 0.0032
Oil control ring (all)	0.005 max

Ring end gap

Top ring (all)

1977/1978/1980	0.010 to 0.030
1979	0.010 to 0.020

2nd ring (305)

1977/1978/1980	0.010 to 0.035
1979	0.010 to 0.025

2nd ring (350)

1977/1978/1980	0.013 to 0.035
1979	0.013 to 0.025

Oil control ring (all)

1977 and 1978	0.015 to 0.065
1979	0.015 to 0.055
1980	0.010 to 0.035
Piston pin diameter (all)	0.9270 to 0.9273
Pin clearance in piston	0.0025 to 0.0010
Pin interference fit in rod	0.0008 to 0.0016

Crankshaft

Main journal diameters

No. 1	2.4484 to 2.4493
Nos. 2, 3, 4	2.4481 to 2.4490
No. 5	2.4479 to 2.4488
Journal taper	0.001 max
Journal out-of-round	0.001 max

Main bearing oil clearance
  No. 1 .... 0.0015
  Nos. 2, 3, 4 .... 0.0025
  No. 5 .... 0.0035
Crankpin diameter
  1977 through 197 .... 2.099 to 2.100
  1980 .... 2.0986 to 2.0998
Crankpin taper .... 0.001 max
Crankpin out-of-round .... 0.001 max
Rod bearing oil clearance .... 0.0035 max
Rod side clearance
  1977 through 1979 .... 0.008 to 0.014
  1980 .... 0.006 to 0.014
Crankshaft endplay .... 0.002 to 0.006

Camshaft
Lobe lift (intake)
  305 .... 0.2485
  350 .... 0.2600
Lobe lift (exhaust) 0.2733
Camshaft journal diameter .... 1.8682 to 1.8692
Camshaft runout .... 0.0015 max
Camshaft endplay .... 0.004 to 0.014

Valves
Valve lifter mechanism .... Hydraulic
Valve lash .... $\frac{3}{4}$ turn down from zero
Valve face angle .... 45°
Valve seat angle .... 46°
Valve seat width
  Intake .... $\frac{1}{32}$ to $\frac{1}{16}$
  Exhaust .... $\frac{1}{16}$ to $\frac{3}{32}$
Valve seat runout .... 0.002 max
Valve stem-to-guide clearance
  Intake .... 0.0010 to 0.0037
  Exhaust .... 0.0010 to 0.0047
Valve spring free length
  Intake 2.030
  Exhaust 1.910
Installed spring height .... $1\frac{23}{32}$
Damper free length 1.860

Torque specifications   ft-lb
Front cover 7
Flywheel housing cover 7
Oil filter bypass valve 7
Oil pan (to crankcase) 7
Oil pump cover 7
Rocker arm cover 4
Camshaft sprocket 20
Oil pan (to crankcase) 12
Clutch pressure plate 35
Distributor clamp 20
Flywheel housing 30
Manifold (exhaust) 20
Manifold (intake) 30
Water outlet 30
Water pump 30
Connecting rod cap 45
Cylinder head 65
Main bearing cap 70
Oil pump 65
Flywheel 60
Harmonic balancer 60
Temperature sending unit 20
Oil filter 25
Oil pan drain plug 20

1977 Oldsmobile 350 CID and 403 CID V8 engines (VIN codes R, K)
All dimensions in inches unless otherwise noted

General
Bore and stroke
  350 .... 4.057 x 3.385
  403 .... 4.351 x 3.385
Compression ratio 8.5:1
Firing order 1-8-4-3-6-5-7-2
Cylinder numbers
  Right bank, front to rear 2-4-6-8
  Left bank, front to rear 1-3-5-7

Pistons and piston rings

Nominal outside diameter	
350	4.057
403	4.351
Clearance at thrust surface	0.001 to 0.002
Piston pin diameter	0.9803 to 0.9807
Ring gap (top and 2nd)	0.010 to 0.023
Oil ring gap	0.015 to 0.055
Ring-to-groove side clearance	
Top	0.002 to 0.004
2nd	0.002 to 0.004

Camshaft

Journal diameters	
No. 1	2.0365 to 2.0357
No. 2	2.0165 to 2.0157
No. 3	1.9965 to 1.9957
No. 4	1.9765 to 1.9757
No. 5	1.9565 to 1.9557
Journal-to-bearing clearance	0.0020 to 0.0058
End clearance	0.011 to 0.077

Crankshaft

Main journal diameters	
No. 1	2.4998 to 2.4988
Nos. 2 through 5	2.4995 to 2.4985
Main bearing oil clearance	
Nos. 1 through 4	0.0005 to 0.0021
No. 5	0.0015 to 0.0031
Endplay	0.0035 to 0.0135

Valves

Head diameter (intake)	
350	1.880 to 1.870
403	2.000 to 1.990
Head diameter (exhaust)	1.497 to 1.507
Stem diameter	
Intake	0.3425 to 0.3432
Exhaust	0.3420 to 0.3427
Stem-to-guide clearance	
Intake	0.0010 to 0.0027
Exhaust	0.0015 to 0.0032
Valve face angle	
Intake	44°
Exhaust	30°
Valve seat angle	
Intake	45°
Exhaust	31°
Pushrod length	8.265

Torque specifications

	ft-lb
Crankshaft bearing cap bolts nos. 1, 2, 3 and 4	80
Crankshaft bearing no. 5	120
Flywheel-to-crankshaft (with automatic transmission)	60
Flywheel-to-crankshaft (with manual transmission)	90
Oil pump-to-bearing cap bolts	35
Oil pump cover-to-pump bolts	8
Rocker arm pivot bolt-to-head	25
Valve cover bolts	Fully driven, seated, not stripped
Oil pan bolts	10
Oil pan drain plug	30
Crankshaft balancer-to-crankshaft bolt	200 to 310
Oil filter element-to-base	20
Oil filter assembly-to-cylinder block bolts	35
Front cover-to-cylinder block bolts	35
Fan driven pulley-to-hub bolts	20
Fan driving pulley-to-balancer bolts	20
Water pump-to-front cover bolts	13
Water outlet-to-manifold bolts	20
Intake manifold-to-cylinder head bolts	40
Exhaust manifold-to-cylinder head bolts	25
Carburetor-to-intake manifold bolts	10
Engine mount-to-cylinder block bolts	75
Engine mount-to-frame mount	50
Starter-to-cylinder block bolts	35
Starter brace-to-cylinder block bolts	25
Starter brace-to-starter bolt	15
Starter brace-to-starter stud	8

Distributor clamp-to-cylinder block bolt 17
Spark plugs 25
Cylinder head bolts 130
Connecting rod nuts 42

1979 and 1980 Pontiac 265 CID and 301 CID V8 engines (VIN codes S, W, Y)
All dimensions in inches unless otherwise noted

General

Bore and stroke
    265 .... 3.75 x 3.00
    301 .... 4.00 x 3.00
Compression ratio 8.2:1
Firing order 1–8–4–3–6–5–7–2
Cylinder numbers
    Right bank, front to rear 2–4–6–8
    Left bank, front to rear 1–3–5–7

Pistons and piston rings

Measurement taken at .... Top of skirt
Clearance in cylinder
    265 .... 0.0017 to 0.0025
    301 .... 0.0025 to 0.0033
(**Note**: *Cylinder block and pistons must be at 70° to 80°F at time of fitting pistons to cylinder*)
Ring end gap
    Upper .... 0.010 to 0.020
    Lower .... 0.010 to 0.020
Side clearance .... 0.0015 to 0.0035
Oil ring gap 0.035
Oil ring side clearance .... 0.0015 to 0.0035

Piston pin

Diameter (265, 301) .... 0.938 to 0.942
Length (265, 301) 3.00
Fit in piston (301 engine) .... 0.0002 to 0.0004
Fit in piston (265) .... 0.0003 to 0.0005
Fit in rod .... Press

Connecting rods

Weight (265, 301) .... 21.9 oz
Length (center to center) (265, 301) 6.050
Bearing oil clearance .... 0.0005 to 0.0025
Endplay on crankshaft
    (Total for two) (265, 301) .... 0.006 to 0.022

Valves

Diameter of head
    Intake (265 engine) 1.60
    Intake (301 engine) 1.72
    Exhaust (265 engine) 1.38
    Exhaust (301 engine) 1.50
Overall length
    Intake (265 engine) 5.119
    Intake (301 engine) 5.0785
    Exhaust (265) 5.120
    Exhaust (301) 5.0785
Diameter of stem 0.3425
Stem to guide clearance
    Intake (265, 301) .... 0.0010 to 0.0027
    Top exhaust (265, 301) .... 0.0010 to 0.0027
    Bottom exhaust (265, 301) .... 0.0020 to 0.0037
Valve seat angle
    Intake (265, 301) .... 46°
    Exhaust (265, 301) .... 46°
Valve face angle
    Intake (265, 301) .... 45°
    Exhaust (265, 301) .... 45°

Crankshaft

Crankshaft endplay .... 0.003 to 0.009
Journal diameter (265, 301) 3.00
Main bearing oil clearance (all) .... 0.0002 to 0.0017
Crankpin diameter (265, 301) 2.000

Camshaft

Bearing diameter (all) 1.900

Valve system

Valve lifter
    Type .... Hydraulic
    Leak-down rate (all) .... 12 to 90 sec @ 50 lb load
    Plunger travel (for gaging purposes) 0.125

Pushrod length (265, 301) 8.12

Oil pump
Pressure (265, 301) ....   35 to 40 psi @ 2600 rpm

Torque specifications

	ft-lb
Bolt—main bearing cap-to-block	70
Bolt—rear main bearing cap-to-block	100
Bolt—cylinder head	95
Bolt—flywheel-to-crankshaft	95
Nut—connecting rod bearing cap	35
Bolt—oil pan-to-block	12
Bolt—oil pump-to-block	30
Bolt—harmonic balancer-to-crankshaft	160
Bolt—exhaust manifold-to-head	35
Bolt—intake manifold-to-head	40
Bolt—camshaft-to-sprocket	40
Nut—rocker arm-to-stud	20
Stud—rocker arm	50
Spark plug	15
Bolt—rocker cover	6
Bolt—timing gear cover	30

1 General description and engine identification

1   Up until 1977, all engines in Buick automobiles were manufactured by Buick. However, since that time, Buick automobiles come
equipped with various engines supplied by Oldsmobile, Chevrolet, and
Pontiac divisions of General Motors.
2   A check of the Vehicle Identification Number (VIN) will quickly
determine from which GM plant your car's engine originated. The VIN
is stamped onto a small metal plate that is affixed to the car's
dashboard. The number gives information concerning the engine, the
year of the car, and so on. This metal tag is located on the dashboard
in the left hand corner (driver's side), up against the windshield. The
fifth digit of the VIN is the number that tells the origin of the engine.
The letters C, A, G, J, V, X and the numbers 2, 3 are Buick codes.
Letters R, K are Oldsmobile and S, W, Y are Pontiac. Chevrolet codes
are the letters L, H, U. There are two exceptions to this rule. If your
Buick has an R code or an H code and was built before 1975 or 1978,
respectively, the engine was manufactured by Buick.
3   Most of the V8 engines offered in Buick cars are small block
engines. That is, they are either 265, 301, 305, or 350 CID (cubic inch
displacement) motors. A big block 455 CID V8 was available in 1974
and, in 1977, Buick also offered a 403 CID V8.
4   There are some differences between the various makes of engines
but overall, repair and maintenance procedures are nearly identical.
Where differences occur, they will be noted. A check of the specifications chart at the beginning of this Chapter will alert the home
mechanic to any differences in the various tolerances.

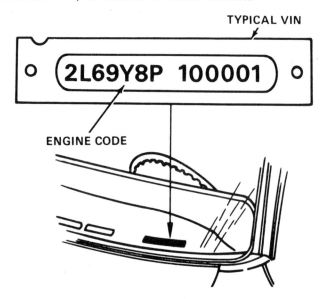

TYPICAL VIN

2L69Y8P 100001

ENGINE CODE

Fig. 2.1 Location of VIN and engine code letter (Sec 1)

2 Engine repair operations – general notes

The following engine removal operations can be performed with
the engine installed and still bolted to its mounts:

1   Removal of the intake and exhaust manifolds
2   Removal of the valve mechanism
3   Removal of the cylinder heads
*4   Removal of the torsional damper, crankcase front cover
(timing cover), front oil seal, timing chain and timing chain
sprockets*
*5   Removal of the flywheel (with the transmission previously
removed)*
6   Removal of the camshaft

The following engine removal operations can be performed with
the engine installed but raised slightly off its mounts:

1   Removal of the oil pan
2   Removal of the oil pump
3   Removal of the rear main oil seal
*4   Removal of the pistons, connecting rods and associated
bearings*
5   Removal of the engine mounts

The following engine removal operations can be performed only
after the engine has been completely removed from the vehicle:

1   Removal of the crankshaft
2   Removal of the main and camshaft bearings

Whenever engine work is required there are some basic steps
which the home mechanic should perform before any work is begun.
These preliminary steps will help prevent delays during the operation.
They are as follows:

*a)   Read through the appropriate Sections in this manual to get
an understanding of the processes involved, tools necessary
and replacement parts which will be needed.*
*b)   Contact your local GM dealer or automotive parts store to
check on replacement parts availability and cost. In many
cases, a decision must be made beforehand whether to
simply remove the faulty component and replace it with a
new or rebuilt unit or to overhaul the existing part.*
*c)   If the vehicle is equipped with air conditioning, it is imperative
that a qualified specialist de-pressurize the system if this is
required to perform the necessary engine repair work. The
home mechanic should never disconnect any of the air
conditioning system while it is still pressurized, as this can
cause serious personal injury as well as possibly damage the
air conditioning system. Ascertain if de-pressurization is
necessary while the vehicle is still operational.*

3 Engine – removal and installation methods and precautions

1   The engine can be removed complete with transmission or
independently, leaving the transmission in the vehicle. Unless heavy
duty lifting equipment is available, the removal of the engine on its

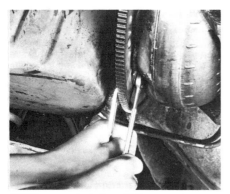

4.25 Remove the bolts which secure the torque converter to the engine drive plate (flvwheel)

5.18a Remove the transmission mounting bolts at the rear crossmember

5.18b The bolts which mount the crossmember to the frame are accessible through holes in the frame rails

5.20 When the transmission is removed with the engine, position the lifting chains so that the assembly hangs at a steep angle

5.22 Disconnect the speedometer cable from the transmission housing

5.26 Remove the shift linkage from the side of the transmission

own is to be recommended particularly if an automatic transmission is installed as the combined weight of both units will be certainly more than one person can handle.

2   During the removal operations, make sure that any jacks used are supplemented with axle-stands before attempting to work under the vehicle.

3   Do not smoke if fuel has been spilled and mop up fuel and oil spillages as quickly as possible.

4   If the vehicle is equipped with air conditioning, *never disconnect any of the system lines.* If the belt-driven compressor can be unbolted and moved to one side of the engine compartment to provide room to service components, this is permissible. If sufficient clearance is not obtainable then the system must be discharged by your dealer or a competent refrigeration engineer and subsequently recharged once the engine work is complete.

5   If air conditioning is fitted, avoid damage to the condenser which is mounted just ahead of the radiator.

4   Engine – removal (without transmission)

1   If the vehicle is equipped with air conditioning, the car should be driven to a GM dealer or refrigeration specialist to have the system depressurized. The air conditioning system cannot be simply unbolted and laid aside for engine removal. Do not attempt to disconnect any of the air conditioning system while it is under pressure as serious damage to the system, as well as to yourself, can occur.

2   Remove the hood. Scribe the hood hinges and brackets to ease alignment when reinstalling. Refer to Chapter 12 for the correct procedure to follow for this job. Set the hood in a safe place where it will not be damaged.

3   Disconnect the battery cables at the battery.

4   Remove the air cleaner assembly and set aside. Make sure to identify all hoses with pieces of tape to make reassembly easier.

5   Drain the radiator and engine block, referring to Chapter 1, if necessary.

6   Disconnect the radiator hoses and transmission fluid cooler lines

(if equipped) and remove the radiator and shroud (see Chapter 3).

7   Remove the fan and fan pulley at the front of the water pump.

8   Disconnect the wiring at the alternator. Mark the wires with coded pieces of tape to help identify them upon reassembly.

9   Disconnect the wires at the temperature switch. Disconnect the ground strap running between the right cylinder head and the firewall.

10   Disconnect the wires at the oil pressure switch or the fluid fitting if a mechanical oil pressure gauge is fitted. The oil pressure port is at the extreme rear of the engine.

11   Disconnect the wiring at the ignition coil. 1974 models have the coil mounted at the rear, adjacent to the distributor. 1975 and later models have the coil inside the distributor cap, in which case the electrical coupler at the distributor will be disconnected. In either case, identify the disconnected wires with coded strips of tape.

12   Disconnect the accelerator linkage where it is supported at the intake manifold.

13   Disconnect the fuel line (from the gas tank) where it attaches to the fuel pump. Have an empty can and some rags handy to catch excess fuel in the system. Plug the hose to keep dirt out of the system and to prevent later fuel drainage.

14   Disconnect the fuel vapor hoses which run from the emission system charcoal canister to the engine. This canister, in most cases, is located in the engine compartment just behind the grille.

15   Disconnect the vacuum hose for the power brake booster (if equipped with power brakes). This vacuum hose runs to the intake manifold, where it should be disconnected.

16   Remove the bolts which attach the power steering bracket to the engine (if equipped with power steering). Leave the hoses connected and use a length of stiff wire (a coat hanger will work well) to tie the pump assembly against the inner fender panel. Make sure it is clear of the engine and will not be damaged.

17   On air conditioned cars, disconnect the compressor ground wire from mounting bracket and remove electrical connector from the compressor clutch. Next, remove the air conditioner compressor and related components.

18   The removal of the distributor and carburetor at this time is optional. Many people remove these components before engine

removal due to the fact that they can be damaged as the engine assembly is lifted free of the vehicle. If it is decided that they be removed, refer to the appropriate Chapters (Chapter 5 and Chapter 4), for the removal sequence. Be sure to cover the openings in the intake manifold to prevent articles from dropping into the recesses.

19 Raise the vehicle and support firmly on jack stands.

20 Drain the oil from the oil pan (Chapter 1).

21 Disconnect the exhaust pipes at the flanges on each exhaust manifold. Penetrating oil may have to be used to loosen frozen nuts.

22 Disconnect the wires at the starter solenoid, marking each with a piece of tape to identify each for reassembly.

23 Remove the starter/solenoid assembly.

24 Remove the flywheel splash shield (manual transmission) or converter housing cover (automatic transmission) as applicable.

25 On vehicles equipped with an automatic transmission remove the converter-to-flywheel bolts. This is done by working through the opening gained by the removal of the cover previously removed. It will be necessary to turn the engine by the bolt at the center of the torsional damper to bring each of the bolts into view. Mark the relative position of the converter to the flywheel with a scribe so it can be reinstalled in the same position. Use a long screwdriver in the teeth of the flywheel to prevent movement as the bolts are loosened (photo).

26 Lower the vehicle.

27 Move back into the engine compartment and make a last check that all wires and hoses are disconnected from the engine assembly and that all peripheral accessories have enough clearance.

28 Attach the hoist lifting chains to the lifting 'eyes' mounted to the engine. There is one bracket at the front of the engine and one at the rear, diagonally opposite. Make sure the chain is looped properly through the engine brackets and secured with strong nuts and bolts through the chain loops. The hook on the hoist should be over the center of the engine with the lengths of chain at equal distances so as to lift the engine straight up.

29 Raise the engine hoist until all slack is out of the chains. Do not lift any further at this time.

30 Remove the through-bolt at each engine mount.

31 Remove the bolts which attach the rear of the engine to the transmission bellhousing.

32 Support the transmission using a jack with wood blocks as cushioners. While under the vehicle, check that all components are clear of the engine assembly.

33 Raise the engine slightly and then pull forward to clear the clutch shaft (manual transmission). Where an automatic transmission is installed, keep the torque converter pushed well to the rear to ensure retaining the engagement of the converter tangs with the oil pump inside the transmission.

34 Carefully lift the engine straight up and out of the engine compartment, continually checking clearances around the engine. Be particularly careful that the engine does not hit the brake master cylinder, firewall, power steering pump (which is wired to the fender well) or the body nosepiece as it is rolled free of the vehicle.

35 The transmission should remain supported by the floor jack or wood blocks while the engine is out of place.

---

5 Engine – removal (with transmission)

1 If the transmission is in need of repairs at the same time as the engine, it is wise to remove both units together. The body and frame construction of the Regal/Century does allow these components to be removed as a single unit, however, be forewarned that extra weight will be involved. Make sure the lifting hoist is capable of handling the extra weight and if at all possible have at least one assistant on hand to help in the procedure.

2 Initially follow the sequence outlined in Section 4, paragraphs 1 through 18.

Manual transmission

3 If equipped with a floor shift, remove the shift lever knob, and on 4-speed models the spring and T-handle.

4 Working under the car, disconnect the speedometer cable by loosening the collar with pliers, then pulling the collar and inner cable out of the transmission. Tie or tape the end of the cable out of the way.

5 Disconnect the electrical wiring at the back-up lamp switch and the TCS switch (1974 models only). Identify these wires with coded pieces of tape to help during reassembly.

6 Disconnect the shift rods from the transmission side cover. Note

the position of each and duly mark with tape to help during the reassembly process.

7 On floorshift models, remove the backdrive rod at the bellcrank and the shift control assembly from its support. The shifter assembly can then be carefully lowered and removed from under the vehicle.

8 On some later models it will be necessary to remove the catalytic converter which is supported at the transmission. (Refer to Chapter 6).

9 Disconnect the clutch linkage at the cross-shaft then remove the cross-shaft at the frame bracket. Disconnect the driveshaft

10 Drain the oil from the engine (Chapter 1).

11 Disconnect the exhaust pipes at the manifold flanges on either side of the engine.

12 On some models equipped with a cross-over exhaust pipe, it will be necessary to remove this cross-over pipe.

13 Disconnect the wiring at the starter solenoid, marking each wire with a coded strip of tape. Remove the starter motor/solenoid.

14 Make a final check under the vehicle that all wiring and peripheral components are disconnected from the transmission and that all accessories are clear of the transmission. Move to the engine compartment and do the same.

15 Position a movable jack (floor jack or transmission jack) under the transmission oil pan using a block of wood as an insulator. Take the weight of the transmission on the jack.

16 Attach the hoist lifting chains to the lifting 'eyes' of the engine. There is one bracket at the front of the engine and one at the rear, diagonally opposite. Make sure the chain is looped properly through the engine brackets and secured with strong bolts and nuts through the chain loops. The hook on the lifting hoist should be at the center of the engine. Position the chains so the engine/transmission unit will be at a steep angle, the front being higher than the rear.

17 Raise the hoist until all slack is removed from the chains. Do not lift any further at this time.

18 Under the car, remove the transmission-to-crossmember bolts and the crossmember-to-frame bolts. Raise the transmission slightly and slide the crossmember to the rear until it can be removed (photos).

19 Remove the through-bolt at each engine mount.

20 Carefully raise the engine and lower the transmission at the same time. Do this a little at a time, checking clearances as you go. If the lifting chains are positioned properly, the engine/transmission unit will hang at a very steep angle. If it is necessary to re-position the lifting chains, carefully lower the engine back onto its mounts, with the floor jack still supporting the transmission (photo).

21 As the assembly is rolled out of the engine compartment, it may be necessary to lift the transmission slightly to clear the front body nosepiece.

Automatic transmission

22 Working under the car, disconnect the speedometer cable. Do this by loosening the collar with pliers, then pulling the inner cable and collar out of the transmission (photo).

23 Disconnect the oil cooler lines at the transmission and then completely remove these lines. Plug the ends to prevent dirt from entering the system.

24 Disconnect the vacuum line at the vacuum modulator.

25 Disconnect the electrical wiring at the transmission, depending on the model year.

26 Disconnect the shift control linkage at the transmission (photo).

27 Remove the driveshaft (see Chapter 8).

28 Insert a plug into the rear of the transmission to prevent fluid loss as the engine/transmission assembly is tilted upon removal. A plastic bag secured with wire or tape will generally suffice.

29 On some later models it will be necessary to remove the catalytic converter (see Chapter 6).

30 Drain the oil from the engine (Chapter 1).

31 Disconnect the exhaust pipes at the manifold flanges on either side of the engine. If equipped with an exhaust cross-over pipe, remove it.

32 Disconnect the wiring at the starter solenoid, marking each wire with a coded strip of tape. Remove the starter/solenoid from the engine.

33 Make a final check that all wiring and peripheral components are disconnected and clear of the transmission. Move to the engine compartment and do the same.

Note: *The remainder of the removal process is the same as for the manual transmission. Follow previously described steps 15 through 21.*

6 Engine/transmission removed – separation and reconnection

Manual transmission

1   Extract the screws and remove the cover plate from the lower front face of the clutch bellhousing.
2   Unscrew and remove the bolts which hold the bellhousing to the engine.
3   Support the weight of the transmission and withdraw it in a straight line so that the clutch disc is not damaged while the main drive gear is still engaged in its splined hub.
4   Refer to Chapter 8 for the following clutch component processes.
5   Unscrew each of the clutch cover bolts a turn at a time until all spring pressure is relieved.
6   Withdraw the clutch assembly from the face of the flywheel taking care not to let the clutch disc drop.
7   Reconnecting the transmission to the engine is the reverse of the separation procedure but if the clutch has been removed, the disc must be centralized.

Automatic transmission

8   Remove the cover plate from the lower front face of the converter housing.
9   Unscrew each of the driveplate to torque converter bolts. The crankshaft will have to be turned to bring the bolts into view. Mark the relative position of the driveplate to the torque converter. The driveplate can be held still for bolt removal by jamming the teeth of the starter ring gear with a large screwdriver.
10 Support the transmission on blocks and then remove the converter bellhousing to engine bolts.
11 Using either a hoist or a floor jack, withdraw the engine from the transmission. While carrying out this operation, keep the torque converter pressed rearwards in full engagement with the oil pump of the transmission.
12 Reconnection is a reversal of separation but align the mating marks on the torque converter and driveplate and tighten all the bolts to the specified torque.

7 Engine – installation (without transmission)

1   Lift the engine with a hoist off the engine stand. The chains should be positioned as on removal, with the engine sitting level.
2   Lower the engine into place inside the engine compartment, closely watching clearances. On manual transmissions, carefully guide the engine onto the transmission input shaft. The two components should be at the same angle, with the shaft sliding easily into the engine.
3   Install the engine mount through-bolts and the bellhousing bolts. Torque-tighten to specifications.
4   Install the remaining engine components in the reverse order of removal, referring to Section 4 as necessary.
5   Fill the cooling system with the proper coolant and water mixture (Chapter 3).
6   Fill the engine with the correct grade of engine oil (Chapter 1).
7   Check the transmission fluid level, adding fluid as necessary.
8   Connect the positive battery cable, followed by the negative cable. If sparks or arcing occurs as the negative cable is connected to the battery, check that all electrical accessories are turned off (check dome light first). If arcing still occurs, check that all electrical wiring is connected properly to the engine and transmission.
9   See Section 48 for the starting up sequence.

8 Engine – installation (with transmission)

1   With the transmission connected to the engine as described in Section 7, attach the lifting chains to the engine in the same fashion as on removal.
2   Tilt and lower the engine/transmission unit into the engine compartment, guiding the engine mounts correctly onto the frame mounts, and at the same time raising the transmission into the correct position.
3   Install the engine mount through-bolts and the rear transmission

crossmember. Tighten all bolts to specification.
4   Install the remaining components in the reverse order of removal. See Section 5.
5   Adjust the clutch, if equipped, as described in Chapter 8.
6   Fill the cooling system with the proper coolant and water mixture (Chapter 3).
7   Fill the engine with correct grade of engine oil (Chapter 1).
8   Check the fluid level in the transmission and add fluid as necessary.
9   Connect the positive battery cable, followed by the negative cable. If sparks or arcing occurs as the negative cable is connected to the battery, check that all electrical accessories are turned off (check interior dome lights first). If arcing still occurs, check that all electrical wiring is connected properly to the engine and transmission.
10 See Section 48 for the starting-up sequence.

9 Engine mounts – replacement with engine in vehicle

1   If on inspection, the flexible mounts have become hard or are split or separated from their metal backing, they must be replaced. This operation may be carried out with the engine/transmission still in the vehicle. See Section 23 for the proper way to raise the engine while it is still inside the car.

Front mounts

2   Remove the through-bolt and nut.
3   Raise the engine slightly using a hoist or jack with wood block under the oil pan at forward edge, then remove the mount and bracket assembly from the frame.
4   Install the new mount, the through-bolt and nut, then tighten all the bolts to the specified torque.

Rear mount

5   Remove the bolts going through the mount and into the transmission. Then raise the transmission slightly using a jack.
6   Remove the mount along with any shims, spacers or brackets.
7   Install the new mount, lower the transmission and align the bolts.
8   Tighten all the bolts to the specified torque.

10 Engine – dismantling (general)

1   It is best to mount the engine on a dismantling stand but if one is not available, then stand the engine on a strong bench so as to be at

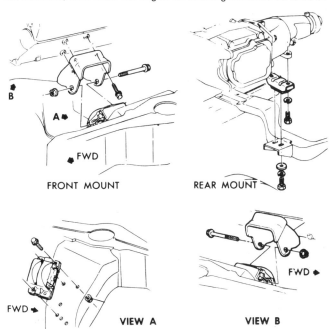

Fig. 2.2 Engine mounts at side of engine and transmission – typical (Sec 9)

11.12 A pair of vise-grip pliers will be useful when removing the oil dipstick tube

12.33 Pontiac-manufactured engines use a bolt to mate the intake manifold to the front cover

13.14 The spark plug heat shields are held in place by bolts located under the exhaust manifold

a comfortable working height.

2   During the dismantling process the greatest care should be taken to keep the exposed parts free from dirt. As an aid to achieving this, it is a sound scheme to thoroughly clean down the outside of the engine, removing all traces of oil and dirt.

3   Use a water soluble grease solvent. The latter compound will make the job easier, as, after the solvent has been applied and allowed to stand for a time, a vigorous jet of water will wash off the solvent and all the grease and filth. If the dirt is thick and deeply embedded, work the solvent into it with a wire brush.

4   Finally wipe down the exterior of the engine with a rag and only then, when it is quite clean should the dismantling process begin. As the engine is stripped, clean each part in a bath of parts cleaner.

5   Never immerse parts which have internal oilways in solvent (such as the crankshaft) but wipe them carefully with a solvent soaked rag. Probe the oilways with a length of wire and if an air line is available, blow the oilways through to clean them.

6   Be extremely careful using combustible cleaning agents near an open flame or inside an enclosed work area. Fumes can ignite from a lighted cigarette or a hot water heater pilot light. Wipe up any fuel or cleaner spills immediately, and do not store greasy or solvent-soaked rags where they can ignite.

7   Re-use of old engine gaskets is false economy and can give rise to oil and water leaks, if nothing worse. To avoid the possibility of trouble after the engine has been reassembled, *always* use new gaskets throughout.

8   Do not throw the old gaskets away as it sometimes happens that an immediate replacement cannot be found and the old gasket is then very useful as a template. Hang up the old gaskets as they are removed on a suitable hook or nail.

9   Wherever possible, replace nuts, bolts and washers finger-tight from wherever they were removed. This helps avoid later loss and mix-ups. If they cannot be replaced then lay them out in such a fashion that it is clear from where they came.

11 Engine – major overhaul dismantling sequence

1   The Sections in this Chapter deal with removal, installation, overhaul and inspection of the various engine components. Reference should be made to appropriate Chapters for removing and servicing the ancillary engine accessories. These parts include the alternator, air pump, carburetor, etc.

2   If the engine is removed from the vehicle for a major overhaul, the entire engine should be stripped of its components. The exact order in which the engine parts are removed is to some degree a matter of personal preference, however, the following sequence can be used as a guide.

   a) *Air Injection Reactor System complete with brackets (Refer to Chapter 6).*
   b) *Alternator (Chapter 5).*
   c) *Accessory drive belts and pulleys (if not previously removed during engine removal).*
   d) *Water pump and related hoses (Chapter 3).*
   e) *Fuel pump and fuel pump push rod (Chapter 4).*

   f) *Distributor with cap and spark plug wires (Chapter 5).*
   g) *Carburetor and fuel lines (Chapter 4).*
   h) *Oil filter (Chapter 1) (photo).*
   i) *Clutch pressure plate and disc (Chapter 8).*
   j) *Oil dipstick and dipstick tube.*
   k) *Spark plugs (Chapter 1).*

3   With these components removed, the general engine sub-assemblies can be removed, serviced and installed using the following Sections in this Chapter.

4   At the appropriate times, refer to Section 37 which deals with general inspection procedures and Section 42 describing the engine reassembly steps.

5   If at any time during the dismantling procedure damage is found to any of the major engine components (cylinder heads, cylinder block, crankshaft, etc.), consider the possibility of purchasing new or rebuilt assemblies as described in Section 38. This decision will in most cases alter your particular rebuilding sequence as dismantling, inspection and assembly will not be required.

12 Intake manifold – removal and installation

Note: *If the vehicle is equipped with air conditioning, carefully examine the routing of the A/C hoses and the mounting of the compressor. Depending on the exact system used, you may be able to remove the intake manifold without disconnecting the A/C system. If you are in doubt, take the car to a certified dealer or refrigeration specialist to have the system de-pressurised. Do not, under any circumstances, disconnect the A/C hoses while the system is under pressure.*

1974 (All)

1   Disconnect the negative cable from the battery, then drain the coolant from the radiator.

2   Remove the air cleaner assembly, then disconnect the coolant temperature indicator wire from the sending unit.

3   Unhook the throttle linkage and disconnect the fuel line from the carburetor (plug the line to prevent fuel leaks and contamination).

4   Remove the bolts that attach the manifold to the engine, then carefully lift the manifold off.

5   Thoroughly clean the mating surfaces of the block, cylinder heads and intake manifold. Make sure that all traces of the old gaskets and gasket sealer are removed. Be sure to use new gaskets and seals during reassembly.

6   Apply a thin coat of RTV gasket sealer to the ends of the new rubber manifold seals, then lay them in position at the front and rear of the block. Make sure they fit snugly against the block and the leads.

7   Apply a thin coat of RTV gasket sealer around the coolant passages in the new manifold-to-head gaskets (both sides), then carefully position the gaskets on the heads. Make sure thay are properly mated with and sealed against the rubber seals (RTV must be used in this area or leaks will occur).

8   Carefully set the intake manifold in place and install the bolts. Make sure that the gaskets are properly positioned after the manifold is installed.

9   Gradually tighten the bolts to the specified torque, working from the center to the ends in a criss-cross pattern.
10   The remainder of the installation procedure is basically the reverse of removal. Once the procedure is complete, start the engine and check for leaks.

1975 through 1977 Buick 350 engine (VIN codes H and J)

11   Disconnect the negative cable from the battery, then drain the coolant from the radiator.
12   Remove the air cleaner assembly, then disconnect:

 a) The upper radiator hose and heater hose at the intake manifold
 b) Accelerator linkage at the carburetor, the linkage bracket at the manifold and the linkage return springs
 c) Cruise control chain (if so equipped)
 d) Booster vacuum line at the manifold
 e) Fuel line at the carburetor (plug the line to prevent fuel leaks and contamination)
 f) Transmission vacuum modulator line
 g) Idle stop solenoid wire (if so equipped)
 h) Distributor wires
 i) Coolant temperature sending unit wire
 j) All vacuum hoses (tag them to ease reassembly)
 k) Coolant by-pass hose at manifold

13   Remove the bolts that attach the manifold to the engine, then carefully lift the manifold off.
14   Refer to steps 5 through 10 for the remainder of the procedure.

1977 Oldsmobile 350/403 engines (VIN codes R and K)

15   The intake manifold removal and installation procedures for these engines is identical to the procedures for the 1975 through 1977 Buick 350 engines. Refer to steps 11 through 14, but note that the EGR valve must be removed before the intake manifold is removed and replaced after the intake manifold is replaced. Also, dip the attaching bolts in engine oil prior to installation and tighten them first to 15 ft-lb, then to 40 ft-lb.

1977 through 1980 Chevrolet 305/350 engines (VIN codes U, H and L)

16   Disconnect the negative cable from the battery, then drain the coolant from the radiator.

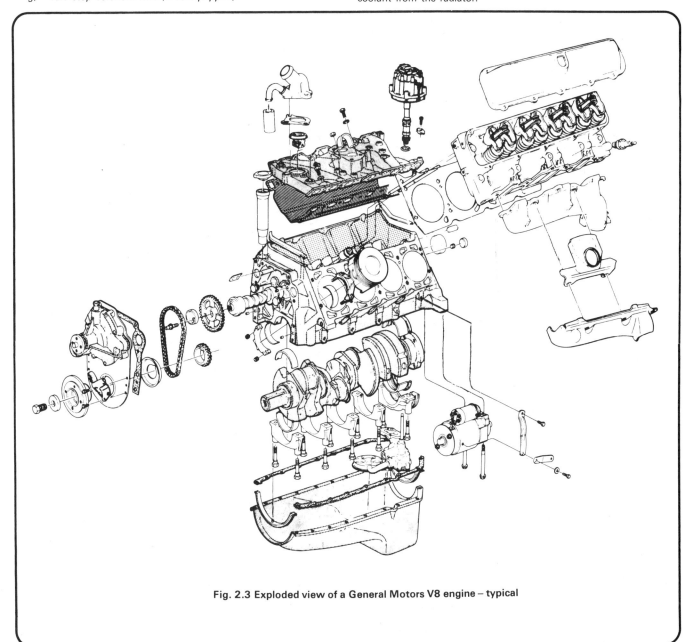

Fig. 2.3 Exploded view of a General Motors V8 engine – typical

17 Remove the air cleaner assembly, then disconnect:

    a)   *The upper radiator hose and the heater hose at the intake manifold*

    b)   *Accelerator linkage and fuel line at the carburetor (plug the line to prevent fuel leaks and contamination)*

    c)   *Crankcase vent hoses*

    d)   *Vacuum hose at distributor*

    e)   *Air cleaner bracket, accelerator return spring and bracket and accelerator bellcrank (as required)*

    f)   *Alternator upper mounting bracket*

18 Remove the distributor cap and tie it out of the way, then mark the distributor body opposite the rotor. Remove the distributor clamp and pull the distributor out of the engine (do not crank the engine over with the distributor removed).

19 Remove the bolts that attach the manifold to the engine, then carefully lift off the manifold.

20 Refer to steps 5 through 10 for the remainder of the procedure. Note that some engines do not use a rubber front and rear seal. Where this is the case, apply a $\frac{3}{16}$ in bead of RTV gasket sealer to the engine block front and rear ridge and extend the bead $\frac{1}{2}$ in up each cylinder head to seal and hold the side gaskets.

21 The distributor must be replaced with the rotor pointing at the mark that was made on the distributor body (it may take more than one try to get everything aligned). Refer to Chapter 5 if problems are encountered during distributor installation.

1979 and 1980 Pontiac 265/301 engines (VIN codes S, W and Y)

Note: *On engines with VIN code Y, the EGR valve must be removed before the intake manifold.*

22 Disconnect the negative cable from the battery, then drain the coolant from the radiator.

23 Remove the air cleaner assembly, then disconnect the closed ventilation hose, the air cleaner vacuum hose and the hot air duct.

24 Remove the water outlet fitting bolts, then pull the fitting off the manifold and position it out of the way (with the radiator hose still attached).

25 Disconnect all emission control vacuum hoses and electrical leads (tag them to ease reassembly), then remove the spark plug wires from the brackets.

26 Remove the power brake vacuum hose (if so equipped) and pull the vacuum hoses off the carburetor (tag them, also). Disconnect the crankcase vent hose.

27 Disconnect the fuel line from the carburetor (plug it to prevent fuel leaks and contamination).

28 Disconnect the throttle cable from the carburetor and the manifold.

29 Remove the bolts that attach the manifold to the engine, then carefully lift the manifold off.

30 Thoroughly clean the mating surfaces of the manifold, cylinder heads and timing chain cover. Be sure to use new gaskets and new O-rings.

31 Position the new gaskets on the cylinder heads and hold them in place with the plastic retainers.

32 Position a new O-ring seal in the timing chain cover, then carefully set the manifold in place. Install the bolts, but do not tighten them.

33 Tighten the timing chain cover-to-manifold bolt (photo) until the metal surfaces contact each other (15 ft-lb), then tighten the remaining manifold bolts to the specified torque.

34 The remainder of the installation procedure is basically the reverse of removal.

---

13 Exhaust manifolds – removal and installation

Note: *Always disconnect the negative cable from the battery before attempting to remove the exhaust manifolds.*

1974 through 1976 (all) and 1977 Buick 350 engine (VIN codes H and J)

1 Raise the front of the vehicle and support it securely on jackstands.

2 Disconnect the forward exhaust pipe from both manifolds, then loosen the clamp and slide it forward out of the catalytic convertor or

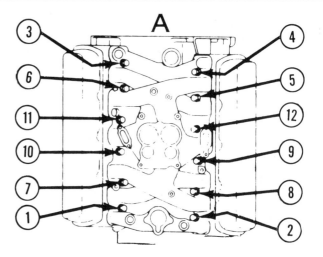

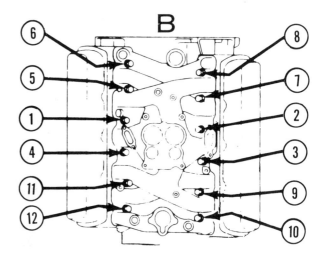

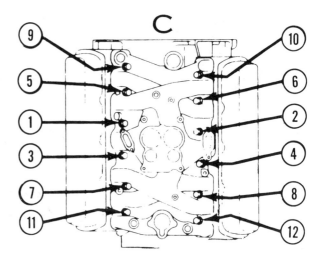

Fig. 2.4 Intake manifold bolt tightening sequence (Sec 12)

    A   *Oldsmobile*
    B   *Chevrolet and Pontiac*
    C   *Buick*

14.13 To keep each pushrod in its original position, use a cardboard box with holes punched in it

15.5 A valve lock being drawn away from the valve stem

15.6 Remove the seal from the stem of the valve (Chevrolet and Pontiac engines)

exhaust pipe. Penetrating oil may be required to loosen the nuts. If the engine is equipped with an AIR emission control system, refer to Chapter 6 and disconnect the tubes from the exhaust manifolds.

3　If the vehicle is equipped with a manual transmission, the equalizer shaft must also be removed.

4　Remove the exhaust manifold-to-cylinder head bolts, then lower the manifold and remove it from beneath the car. Repeat the procedure for the remaining manifold.

5　Installation is basically the reverse of removal. Be sure to thoroughly clean the mating surfaces of the cylinder heads and manifolds and use new gaskets. Also, use a torque wrench to tighten the manifold bolts.

1977 Oldsmobile 350/403 engines (VIN codes R and K)

6　Raise the vehicle and support it securely on jackstands.

7　Remove the crossover pipe, then disconnect the exhaust pipe from the right manifold. Note the locations of the bolt springs and the pipe seal.

8　To improve access, remove the right front wheel, then take out the lower right engine mount bolt. Using a suitable jack, raise the right side of the engine slightly, then remove the exhaust manifold-to-cylinder head bolts. Lower the manifold and remove it from beneath the car.

9　To remove the left side manifold, remove the air cleaner assembly and the hot air shroud, then disconnect the lower alternator bracket.

10　Remove the crossover pipe (if not already done), then lower the vehicle to the ground.

11　Remove the manifold-to-cylinder head bolts and lift out the manifold from above.

12　Installation is basically the reverse of removal. Be sure to thoroughly clean the mating surfaces of the cylinder heads and manifolds and use new gaskets. Also, use a torque wrench to tighten the manifold bolts.

1977 through 1980 Chevrolet 305/350 engines (VIN codes U, H and L)

13　Remove the air cleaner assembly and the carburetor heat stove pipe.

14　Grasp the spark plug wires at the boots and carefully pull them off of the plugs, then remove the wiring heat shields(photo).

15　Disconnect the exhaust pipes from the manifolds and hang the pipes from pieces of wire attached to the frame.

16　Remove the end bolts, then the center bolts, and lift the manifolds away from the engine.

17　Installation is basically the reverse of removal. Note that if a new right side manifold is being installed, the carburetor heat stove must be transferred to the new manifold. Be sure to thoroughly clean the mating surfaces of the cylinder heads and manifolds and use new gaskets. Also, use a torque wrench to tighten the manifold bolts (start with the center bolts and work out to the end bolts). When connecting the pipes to the manifolds, use new gaskets.

1979 and 1980 Pontiac 265/301 engines (VIN codes S, Y, and W)

18　Raise the vehicle and set it on jackstands, then disconnect the

exhaust pipe from the manifolds. Lower the vehicle.

19　Remove the right side manifold-to-cylinder head bolts, then lift out the manifold. **Note:** *It may be necessary to loosen the bolts on the opposite manifold to gain clearance.*

20　To remove the left side manifold, first remove the carburetor air pre-heater shroud. Raise the vehicle, remove the manifold-to-cylinder head bolts and remove the manifold from beneath the car. **Note:** *It may be necessary to loosen the bolts on the opposite manifold to gain clearance.*

21　Installation is basically the reverse of removal. Be sure to thoroughly clean the mating surfaces of the cylinder heads and manifolds and use new gaskets. Since the end holes of the gaskets are slotted, the manifolds can be positioned and the end bolts installed loosely before slipping the gaskets into place. Also, use a torque wrench to tighten the manifold bolts.

14　Cylinder heads – removal

1　**Note:** *If the engine has been removed from the car, disregard the following steps which do not apply.*

2　If equipped with air conditioning, the vehicle should be taken to a certified dealer or refrigeration specialist for de-pressurization. Under no circumstances should you disconnect any of the hoses while the system is under pressure.

3　Remove the intake manifold referring to Section 12.

4　Remove the exhaust manifolds referring to Section 13.

5　Remove the lower mounting bolt for the alternator and lay the alternator aside while the lower bracket is removed.

6　If equipped with air conditioning, remove the A/C compressor and forward mounting bracket. Make sure all hoses and fittings are plugged to prevent dirt from entering the system.

7　If equipped with power steering, remove the pump from its bracket and use wire to keep the pump out of the way. Do not disconnect the hoses.

8　If not done previously, drain the engine block of its coolant. Drain plugs are located on each side of the block for this. By raising the rear of the car about 24 inches the block will drain sufficiently without removing these plugs.

9　Remove the rocker arm cover (valve cover) attaching bolts. Lift the cover off the cylinder head. To break the gasket seal it may be necessary to strike the front of the cover with your hand or a rubber mallet. Do not pry on the sealing surfaces.

10　It is important that each of the valve mechanism components be kept separate once removed so they can be reinstalled in their original positions. A cardboard box or rack, numbered according to engine cylinders, can be used for this.

11　Remove each of the rocker arm nuts (Chevrolet and Pontiac engines), or bolts (Olds engines). Place them at their correct location on the cardboard box or rack. Buick rocker arms and shafts can be removed as a unit once the retaining bolts are removed.

12　Remove each rocker arm assembly, placing each component on the numbered box or rack. Buick rocker arms are held in place on the shaft with plastic retainers which can be pried out of place with pliers. Small piece of the retainer may break off inside the rocker arm shafts; be sure to remove them during the cleaning process.

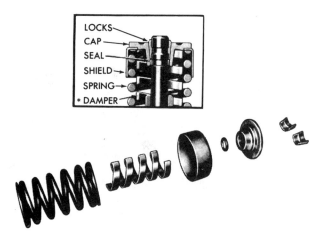

Fig. 2.5 Valve train components – typical (Sec 15)

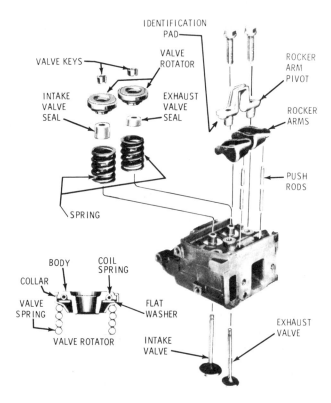

Fig. 2.7 Valve components used on Oldsmobile engines (Sec 15)

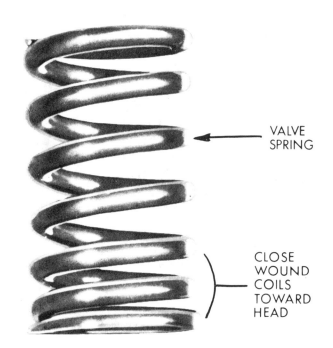

Fig. 2.6 Install the valve springs with the closely wound coils next to the head (Sec 15)

Fig. 2.8 Oversize valve identification (Sec 17)

13 Punch holes in the cardboard box or rack, then lift each of the push rods from the cylinder heads. Place each push rod in its appropriate punched hole (photo).

14 Loosen each of the cylinder head attaching bolts one turn at a time until they can be removed. Note the length of each bolt as it is removed for reinstallation.

15 Disconnect the engine ground strap attached to the rear of one cylinder head.

16 With the help of an assistant, lift the heads free of the engine. Be careful, they are heavy. If the head is stuck to the engine block, do not attempt to pry it free as this may ruin the sealing surfaces. Instead, use a hammer and a block of wood, tapping upwards at each end.

17 Place the heads on wood blocks to prevent damage. Refer to the following Sections covering overhaul, inspection and installation procedures.

15 Cylinder head – dismantling

1 **Note:** *New and rebuilt cylinder heads are commonly available for GM engines at dealerships and auto parts stores. Due to the fact that some specialized tools are necessary for the dismantling and inspection of the heads, and replacement parts may not be readily available, it may be more practical and economical for the home mechanic to purchase replacement heads and install them referring to Section 21.*

2 Another alternative at this point is to take the cylinder heads complete to a competent automotive machine shop or GM dealership for the overhaul process. This is especially true for Buick and Oldsmobile engines where a precise valve stem height is required.

3 If the complete engine is being overhauled at the same time, it may be wise to refer to Section 38 before a decision is made.

4 If it is decided to overhaul the cylinder heads, read through the following Sections first to gain an understanding of the steps involved and the tools and replacement parts necessary for the job. Proceed as follows.

5 Using a valve spring compressor (available at tool or auto parts stores), compress each of the valve springs and remove the valve locking keys. Work on one valve at a time, removing the keys, then releasing the spring and removing the spring cap (rotator), spring shield (if equipped), spring and spring damper. Place these components together on the numbered box or rack used during cylinder head removal. All valve mechanism components must be kept separate so they can be returned to their original positions (photo). On Oldsmobile and Buick engines, remove the old valve stem seals from the guides.

6 Remove the oil seals from the stem of each valve (Chevrolet and Pontiac engines). New seals should be used upon reassembly (photo).

7 Remove any spring shims used at the bottom of the valve spring.

8 Remove each valve, in turn, and place them in the numbered box or rack to complete the valve mechanism removal. Place the valve components in an area where they will not be mixed up.

16 Cylinder head – cleaning

1 Clean all carbon from the combustion chambers and valve ports. GM tool J-8089 is designed for this purpose, however most auto parts stores will carry this cleaning attachment which is connected to a common hand drill motor.

2 Thoroughly clean the valve guides. GM tool J-8101 is available for this, as are many similar devices found at auto parts stores.

3 Use parts cleaner to remove all sludge and dirt from the rocker arm assemblies, push rods and valve components. Work on one set of components at a time, returning each set to its numbered location on your box or rack.

4 A buffing wheel should be used to remove all carbon deposits from the valves. Do not mix up the order of the valves while cleaning them.

5 Clean all carbon deposits from the head gasket mating surface. Be careful not to stratch this sealing surface.

6 Clean the threads on all cylinder head attaching bolts thoroughly.

17 Cylinder head – inspection

1 Carefully inspect the head for cracks around and inside the exhaust ports, combustion chambers or external cracks to the water chamber.

2 Check the valve stem-to-bore clearance using a dial indicator. One at a time, place a valve in its installed position, with the valve head slightly (about $\frac{1}{16}$ in.) off its seat. Now attach a dial indicator to the head with the indicator point just touching the valve stem where it exits the cylinder head. Grab the top of the valve and move it from side to side, noting the movement on the dial indicator. If valve stem clearance exceeds the specifications, an oversize valve must be used, after reaming the valve guide. This is a job for your dealer or machine shop. Excessive clearance will cause excessive oil consumption; insufficient clearance will result in noisy operation and may cause the valve to stick, resulting in harsh engine operation.

3 Inspect each of the valve springs and its damper. Replace any spring which is deformed, cracked or broken.

4 Check the valve spring tension using GM tool J-8056. The springs are compressed to a specified height and then the tension required for this is measured. This is done without the dampers. If not within 10 lbs of the specified load, the spring should be replaced with a new one.

5 Inspect the rocker arm bolts or studs (Chevrolet and Pontiac engines) for wear or damage. On Buick engines, check the rocker arm bores and the shafts for wear. On Oldsmobile engines, check the curved portions of the pivots for wear.

6 Check the push rods for warping by rolling each on a clean, flat piece of glass. Any push rod which is not perfectly straight and free from damage should be replaced with a new one.

7 Check the cylinder head for warpage. Do this by placing a straightedge across the length of the head and measuring any gaps between the straightedge and the head surface with a feeler gauge. This should be done at three points across the head gasket surface, and also in a diagonal fashion across this surface.

8 If warpage exceeds 0.006 in at any point when a straightedge which spans the entire head is used, the cylinder head should be resurfaced. Using a straightedge with a span of 6 inches, the warpage should not exceed 0.003 in. Cylinder head resurfacing is a job for a professional automotive machine shop. Also note that if a cylinder head is resurfaced, the intake manifold position will be slightly altered, requiring the manifold to be resurfaced a proportionate amount.

18 Valves and valve seats – inspection and valve grinding

1 Examine the heads of the valves for pitting and burning, especially the heads of the exhaust valves. The valves and seatings should be examined at the same time. If the pitting on valve and seat is very slight the marks can be removed by grinding the seats and valves together with coarse, and then fine, valve grinding paste.

2 Valve grinding is carried out as follows: smear a trace of coarse carborundum paste on the seat face and apply a suction grinder tool to the valve head. With a semi-rotary motion, grind the valve head to its seat, lifting the valve occasionally to redistribute the grinding paste. When a dull matt even surface finish is produced on both the valve seat and the valve, wipe off the paste and repeat the process with fine carborundum paste, lifting and turning the valve to redistribute the paste as before. A light spring placed under the valve head will greatly ease this operation. When a smooth unbroken ring of light grey matt finish is produced, on both valve and valve seat faces, the grinding operation is completed.

3 Where the valve or seat shows signs of bad pitting or burning, then the valve should be refaced by your dealer and the seat recut. If the refacing of the valve will reduce the edge of the valve head (seat width) to less than that given in the Specifications, replace the valve (photo).

4 Scrape away all carbon from the valve head and the valve stem. Carefully clean away every trace of grinding compound, taking great care to leave none in the ports or in the valve guides. Clean the valves and valve seats with a solvent soaked rag then with a clean rag, and finally, if an air line is available, blow the valves, valve guides and valve ports clean.

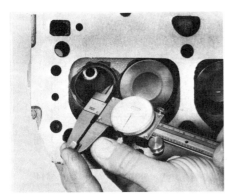
18.3 Measure the valve seat inside the cylinder head

20.6 Use a lifter removal tool to pull the lifter from its engine bore

20.9 If the bottom of the lifter has collapsed or is scratched or nicked replace it with a new one

19 Cylinder head – assembly

1   Make sure all valve mechanism components are perfectly clean and free from carbon and dirt. The bare cylinder head should also be clean and free from abrasive agents which may have been used for valve grinding, reaming, etc.

2   Insert a valve in the proper port. On *Buick and Oldsmobile* engines, push a new seal fully over the valve stem, seating it in the cylinder-head.

3   Assemble the valve spring assembly for that cylinder.

4   Using the valve spring compressor, compress the assembly over the valve stem and hold in this position.

5   On *Chevrolet and Pontiac* engines, install a new oil seal in the lower groove of the valve stem. Make sure it is flat and not twisted.

6   Install the valve locks and release the compressor. Make sure the lock seats properly in the upper groove of the valve stem.

7   On *Oldsmobile and Buick* engines, whenever a new valve is installed or the valves are serviced the valve stem height must be checked. Since this procedure requires a number of special tools, it should be done by a GM dealer service department or a reliable auto repair shop.

20 Valve lifter – removal, inspection, installation

Checking

1   Hydraulic valve lifters are normally very reliable in operation and do not require repeated adjustment.

2   A noisy valve lifter is best traced when the engine is idling. Place a length of hose or tubing near the position of each intake and exhaust valve while listening at the other end of the tube. Another method is to remove the rocker cover (valve cover) and with the engine idling, place a finger on each of the valve spring retainers in turn. If a valve lifter is faulty in operation, it will be evident from the shock felt from the retainer as the valve seats.

3   Provided adjustment is correct, the most likely cause of a noisy lifter is due to a piece of dirt being trapped between the plunger and lifter body.

Removal

4   Remove the intake manifold (Section 12).

5   Remove the valve cover and lift each push rod out of the cylinder block (see Section 14 for details).

6   To pull the lifters out of their bores a special tool can be purchased or a sharp scribe can be positioned at the top of the lifter and used to force the lifter upwards. Do not use pliers or other tools on the outside of the lifter body. Stuck lifters can sometimes be worked free by squirting carburetor cleaner around the body and then working the lifter up and down (photo).

7   Be sure to keep all lifters separated and identified so they can be installed in the same locations.

Inspection

8   After cleaning the lifters (one at a time to prevent mixing up the order), inspect for nicks, gouges, etc. Any damage at all is cause for replacement.

9   Check the bottom of the lifter (that which rides against the camshaft) for scratches or nicks. The lifters should be replaced if the bottom shows a concave condition, with the lifter body collapsing due to wear (photo).

Installation

10   When installing the lifter, make sure thay are liberally coated with 'Molykote' or its equivalent.

11   If the original lifters are reused, they must be installed into their appropriate bores.

12   Install the valve components, valve cover and intake manifold referring to the appropriate Sections

21 Cylinder heads – installation

1   If not already done, thoroughly clean the gasket surfaces on both the cylinder heads and the engine block.

2   To get the proper torque readings, the threads of the attaching bolts must be free of dirt. This also goes for the threaded holes in the engine block. Run a tap through these threaded holes to ensure they are clean.

3   Ascertain which type of head gasket you are using. Engines using steel head gaskets require a thin, even coat of sealer on both sides. No sealer of any kind should be used with composition steel/asbestos gaskets.

4   Place the gasket in place over the engine block dowel pins with the bead up (some gaskets will be marked 'This side up'). Oldsmobile head gaskets are marked with a contrasting color stripe, which must face 'up'.

5   Carefully lower the cylinder head onto the engine, over the dowel pins and the gaskets. Be careful not to move the gasket while doing this.

6   Coat the threads of the cylinder head attaching bolts with clean engine oil (Buick, Oldsmobile and Pontiac engines), or a sealing compound (Chevrolet engines) and install each finger-tight. Do not tighten any of the bolts at this time.

7   Tighten each of the bolts, a little at a time, in the sequence shown. Continue tightening in this sequence until the proper torque reading is obtained. As a final check, work around the head in a logical front-to-rear sequence to make sure none of the bolts have been left out of the sequence.

8   Install the exhaust manifolds as described in Section 13.

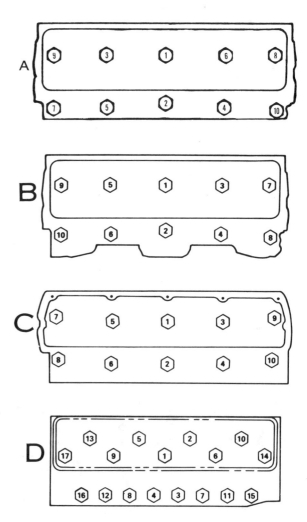

Fig. 2.9 Cylinder head bolt tightening sequence (Sec 21)

A	Buick	C	Oldsmobile
B	Pontiac	D	Chevrolet

21.11a Place some grease on the top of each valve before installing the rocker arms

21.11b Add a small amount of grease to the rocker balls before installation

22.3 Tighten the rocker arm and at the same time check for movement of the pushrod (lash)

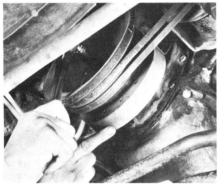

23.11 By turning the torsional damper bolt until the timing mark is at the bottom, the front crankshaft throw will be in an "up" position

23.12 Remove the engine mount thru-bolt

23.15 A wood block placed between the engine mount sections

23.18 Tilt the oil pan down (as shown) at the rear to clear the front crossmember

23.21a The front oil pan seal (Chevrolet engine) has an indentation which fits into the side gasket

23.21b Sealant is applied at the area where the front gasket meets the side gasket

9   Install each of the valve lifters (if removed) into its proper bore. 'Molykote' or its equivalent should be used as a coating on each lifter.
10   Place a small amount of 'Molykote' or its equivalent on each end of the push rods and install each in its original position. Make sure the push rods are seated properly in the lifter cavity.
11   Place each of the rocker arm assemblies back into its original position. Note that on Buick engines the rocker arms and shafts must be installed as a unit. Be sure to use new plastic retainers when assembling the rocker arms on the shafts. The retainers should be seated in the shaft holes using a drift punch with a flat tip at least $\frac{1}{2}$ in in diameter. Tilt the rocker arm towards the pushrods and locate the top of each pushrod in its rocker arm seat. Draw down the shaft assembly by tightening the retaining bolts a little at a time (be sure to tighten them to the specified torque).
12   Adjust the valves as described in Section 22.
13   Install the rocker arm covers (valve covers). Early models use a gasket to seal, while newer models use RTV sealant instead of a gasket. If, when removed, the cover has a gasket, purchase a new gasket and place it into position on the cleaned cylinder head. Tighten the attaching bolts to specifications. If no gasket was used, apply a bead of RTV sealer (or its equivalent) around the entire sealing surface of the cylinder head. This bead should be $\frac{1}{8}$ inch wide. When going around bolt holes always go round the inboard side of the holes. Install the cover while the sealer is still wet and torque the bolts to specifications.
14   Install the intake manifold with new gaskets as described in Section 12.
15   Install the remaining engine components as described in Section 14. Fill the radiator with coolant, start the engine and check for leaks. Adjust the ignition timing and valves as required. Be sure to recheck the coolant level once the engine has warmed up to operating temperature.

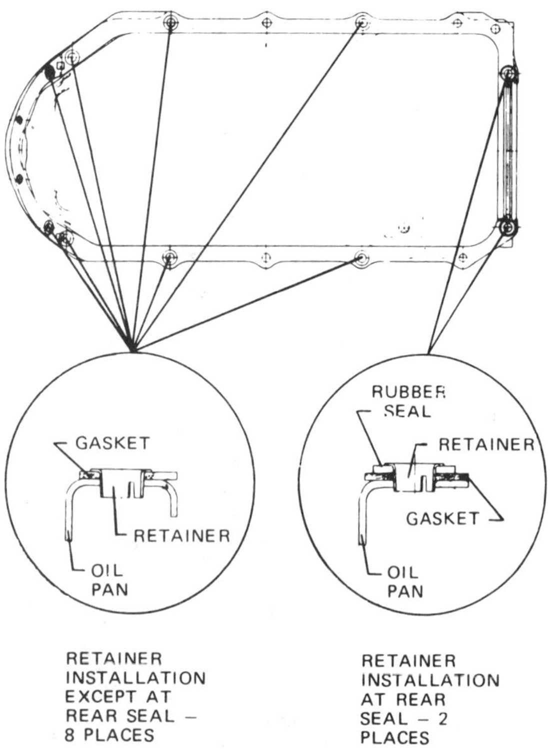

TOP VIEW OF OIL PAN

RETAINER
INSTALLATION
EXCEPT AT
REAR SEAL –
8 PLACES

RETAINER
INSTALLATION
AT REAR
SEAL – 2
PLACES

Fig. 2.10 Oil pan gasket retaining clips are used on some engines
(Sec 23)

22 Valve lash – adjustment

Chevrolet engines

1   If the work is being carried out with the engine in the vehicle, the following preliminary operations must be performed:

  a) Remove the air cleaner
  b) Disconnect the rocker cover vent hoses and wiring
  c) Remove the rocker covers

Note: Viewed from the radiator end of the engine, cylinders on the right are numbered 1-3-5-7 and on the left 2-4-6-8, from front to rear.

2   Rotate the crankshaft until the mark on the torsional damper aligns with the center or O-marking on the timing indicator. If No.1 cylinder valves are moving, the engine is in No. 6 cylinder firing position and the crankshaft must be rotated 360°. If No. 1 cylinder valves are not moving, the piston is at top-dead-center (TDC) which is correct.

3   Back-off the rocker arm stud adjusting nut on No. 1 intake and exhaust valves in turn, until there is play in the pushrod; tighten the nut to *just* eliminate play then tighten the nut one complete turn (photo).

Note: Experience has shown that it is sometimes difficult to determine the position where play is just eliminated during lash adjustment. This can be simplified by the use of a 0.0015 feeler gauge between the rocker and valve stem.

4   With the engine in the No. 1 firing position, as determined in paragraph 2, also adjust the exhaust valves of cylinders 3, 4 and 8 and the intake valves of cylinders 2, 5 and 7.

5   Rotate the crankshaft through 360° to align the torsional damper mark once more, then repeat paragraph 1 for exhaust valves 2, 5, 6 and 7, and intake valves 3, 4, 6 and 8.

6   Clean the gasket surfaces of the cylinder head and rocker arm cover with solvent and wipe dry with a lint-free cloth.

7   Using a new gasket, install the rocker arm cover and torque tighten the bolts to the specified value.

All other engines

8   These valves cannot be adjusted. If the clearance is excessive in the valve train, check that the pivot bolt is tightened to the proper torque specification (or the nylon retainer is seated). Then inspect for worn components.

23 Oil pan – removal and installation

With engine installed in vehicle

1   Disconnect the negative battery cable.
2   Remove the air cleaner assembly and set aside.
3   Remove the distributor cap to prevent breakage as the engine is raised.
4   Unbolt the radiator shroud from the radiator support and hang the shroud over the cooling fan.
5   Remove the oil dipstick and dipstick tube.
6   Raise the car and support firmly on jack stands.
7   Drain the engine oil into a suitable container.
8   Disconnect the exhaust crossover pipe at the exhaust manifold flanges. Lower the exhaust pipes and suspend them from the frame with wire.
9   If equipped with an automatic transmission, remove the converter underpan.
10   Remove the starter (Chapter 5) and the flywheel cover.
11   Use a bolt at the center of the torsional damper to rotate the engine until the timing marks indicate the number 1 cylinder is at Top Dead Center. This will move the forward crankshaft throw upward, providing clearance at the front of the oil pan (photo).
12   Remove the through bolt at each engine mount (photo).
13   At this time the engine must be raised slightly to enable the oil pan to slide clear of the crossmember. The preferred method is to use an engine hoist or 'cherry picker'. Hook up the lifting chains as described in Section 4.
14   An alternative method can be used if extreme care is exercised. Use a floor jack and a block of wood placed under the oil pan. The wood block should spread the load across the oil pan, preventing damage or collapse of the oil pan metal. The oil pump pickup and screen is very close to the oil pan bottom, so any collapsing of the pan may damage the pickup or prevent the oil pump from drawing oil properly.
15   With either method, raise the engine slowly until wood blocks can be placed between the frame front crossmember and the engine block. The blocks should be approximately 3 inches thick. Check clearances all around the engine as it is raised. Pay particular attention to the distributor and the cooling fan (photo).
16   Lower the engine onto the wood blocks. Make sure it is firmly supported. If a hoist is being used, keep the lifting chains secured to the engine.
17   Remove the oil pan bolts. Note the different sizes used and their locations.
18   Remove the oil pan by tilting it downwards at the rear and then working the front clear of the crossmember (photo). It may be necessary to use a rubber mallet to break the seal.
19   Before installing, thoroughly clean the gasket sealing surfaces on the engine block and on the oil pan. All sealer and gasket material must be removed.
20   Apply a thin film of sealer to the new side gaskets and fit them to the engine block. All bolt holes should line up properly.
21   Again using sealer, install the front and rear seals to the engine. Make sure the ends butt with the ends of the side gaskets (photos).
22   Lift the pan into position and install all bolts finger-tight. There is no specific order for torquing the bolts; however it is a good policy to tighten the end bolts first.
23   Lower the engine onto its mounts and install the through bolts. Torque-tighten these to specifications.
24   Follow the removal steps in a reverse order. Fill the engine with the correct grade and quantity of oil, start the engine and check for leaks.

With engine removed from vehicle

25   Most of the above steps will not be required if the engine has been removed from the car.
26   The pan can be simply unbolted and removed from the engine

block as described in paragraphs 17 and 18.
27 Follow paragraphs 19 through 22 for installing the oil pan to the engine block.

24 Oil pump – removal, inspection and installation (1974 through 1977 Buick 350/455 engines)

Removal

1 Unscrew and remove the oil filter.
2 Remove the screws attaching the oil pump cover assembly to the timing chain cover. Remove the cover assembly and slide out the oil pump gear.

Inspection

3 Wash off the gears with a proper solution and inspect for wear, scoring etc. Replace any unserviceable gears with new ones.
4 Unscrew the oil pressure relief valve cap, spring and valve. Do not remove the oil filter by-pass valve and spring as they are staked in place.
5 Wash the parts thoroughly in the proper solvent and inspect the relief valve for wear and scoring. Check to make sure that the relief valve spring is not collapsed or worn on its side. Any relief valve spring which is questionable should be replaced with a new one.
6 Check the relief valve in its bore in the cover. It should be an easy slip-fit only, and any side shake can be felt is too much. The valve and/or cover should be replaced with a new one in this case.
7 The filter by-pass valve should be flat and free of nicks, cracks or warping and scratches.
8 Lubricate the pressure relief valve and spring and install it in the bore of the oil pump case. Install the cap and gasket and torque-tighten to specifications.
9 Insert the oil pump gear and shaft into the oil pump body section of the timing chain cover to check the gear end clearance and side clearance as follows:

 a) *Place a straightedge over the gears and measure the clearance between the straightedge and gasket surface. This will be the end clearance and should be between 0.002 – 0.006 in. If less than 0.002, measure the gears and pocket to determine which is out of specification.*
 b) *Check the oil pump side clearance. Clearance should be between 0.0025 – 0.0050 in. If clearance is greater than 0.0050, measure the gears and pocket to determine which is out of specifications.*
 c) *Place a straightedge across the oil pump cover face to check for flatness. Insert a feeler gauge between the straightedge and the pump cover. Replace the cover with a new one if the clearance is 0.001 in or more.*

10 If all clearances are satisfactory, remove the gears and pack the pocket full of petroleum jelly. Do not use chassis lube.

Installation

11 Re-install the gears, making sure that petroleum jelly is forced into every cavity of the gear pocket and between the teeth of the gears. The pump may not prime itself when the engine is started if the pump is not packed with the petroleum jelly.
12 Install the pump cover assembly screws and tighten them alternately and evenly. Torque-tighten to specifications.
13 Install oil filter and check oil level with the dipstick. Pay close attention to the oil pressure gauge or warning light during the initial start-up and driving period. Shut off the engine and inspect all work if a lack of pressure is indicated.

25 Oil pump – removal, inspection and installation (Chevrolet, Oldsmobile and Pontiac engines – all)

Removal

1 Remove the oil pan as described in Section 23.
2 Remove the bolts securing the oil pump assembly to the rear main bearing cap. Remove the oil pump with its pickup tube and screen as an assembly from the engine block. Once the pump is removed the oil pump driveshaft can be withdrawn from the block. **Note:** *On Olds-*

mobile engines, do not attempt to remove the washers from the driveshaft. Note that the end with the washers fits into the pump.

Inspection

3 In most cases it will be more practical and economical to replace a faulty oil pump with a new or rebuilt unit. If it is decided to overhaul the oil pump, check on internal parts availability before beginning.
4 Remove the the pump cover retaining screws and the pump cover (Oldsmobile engines also have a gasket installed). Index mark the gear teeth to permit reassembly in the same position.
5 Remove the idler gear, drivegear and shaft from the body.
6 Remove the pressure regulator valve retaining pin (Pontiac engines utilize a threaded cap), the regulator valve and the related parts.
7 If necessary, the pick-up screen and pipe assembly can be extracted from the pump body. **Note:** *On Pontiac engines the oil pickup tube/screen assembly should not be disturbed.*
8 Wash all the parts in solvent and thoroughly dry them. Inspect the body for cracks, wear or other damage. Similarly inspect the gears.
9 Check the drive gear shaft for looseness in the pump body, and the inside of the pump cover for wear that would permit oil leakage past the end of the gears.
10 Inspect the pick-up screen and pipe assembly for damage to the screen, pipe or relief grommet.
11 Apply a gasket sealant to the end of the pipe (pick-up screen and pipe assembly) and tap it into the pump body taking care that no damage occurs. If the original press-fit cannot be obtained, a new assembly must be used to prevent air leaks and loss of pressure.
12 Install the pressure regulator valve and related parts.
13 Install the drive gear and shaft in the pump body, followed by the idler gear with the smooth side towards the pump cover opening. **Note:** *On Oldsmobile engines check the gear end clearance by resting a straightedge on the pump body. Try to slip a feeler gauge between the ends of the gears and the straightedge. The clearance should be between 0.0015 to 0.0085 in. If it is not, the pump should be replaced with a new one.* Lubricate the parts with engine oil.
14 Install the cover and torque tighten the screws.
15 Turn the driveshaft to ensure that the pump operates freely.

Installation

16 To install, move the pump assembly into position and align the slot on top end of the driveshaft with the drive tang on the lower end of the distributor. The distributor drives the oil pump so it is essential that these two components mate properly. On Pontiac and Oldsmobile engines the driveshaft fits into the distributor drive gear.
17 Install the securing bolts and torque-tighten to specifications. Pontiac engines require a new gasket between the pump body and the block.
18 Make sure the oil pump screen is parallel with the oil rails. The screen must be in this position to fit into the oil pan properly.

26.7 Use a puller to remove the torsional damper

19 Install the oil pan as described in Section 23. Pay close attention to the oil pressure gauge or warning light during the initial engine start-up period.

26 Torsional damper – removal and installation

1 **Note**: *If the engine has been removed from the car, disregard the following steps which do not apply.*
2 Loosen the alternator, power steering pump and air conditioning compressor (as required) to relieve tension on the drive belts.
3 Remove the cooling fan and the radiator shroud.
4 Remove the drive belts, noting the installed positions of each.
5 Remove the fan pulley from the water pump shaft.
6 Remove the accessory drive pulley from the torsional damper. Then remove the torsional damper retaining bolt at the center.
7 Install a special torsional damper (harmonic balancer) remover to the damper. Draw the damper off the crankshaft, being careful not to drop it as it breaks free. **A common gear puller should not be used to draw the damper as this may separate the outer portion of the damper from the inner hub. Only a puller which bolts to the inner hub should be used.**
8 Before installing the torsional damper, coat the front cover seal

area (on damper) with engine oil.
9 Place the damper in position over the key on the crankshaft. Make sure the damper keyway lines up with the key.
10 Using a torsional damper installer (GM tool J-23523 or equivalent), draw the damper onto the crankshaft. This tool distributes the draw evenly around the inner hub.
11 Remove the installation tool and install the torsional damper center retaining bolt. Torque to specifications.
12 Follow the removal procedure in the reverse order for the remaining components.
13 Adjust the tension of the various belts by referring to Chapter 1.

27 Oil seal (front cover) – replacement

With front cover installed on engine
1 With the torsional damper removed (Section 26), pry the old seal out of the crankcase front cover with a large screwdriver. On Oldsmobile engines it will probably be necessary to use a special oil seal removal tool. Be careful not to damage the front surface of the crankshaft.

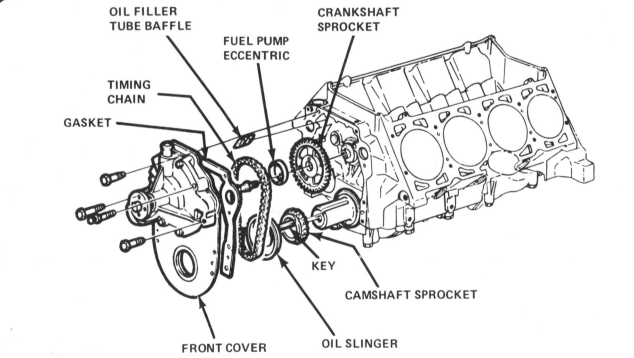

Fig. 2.11 Front cover assembly – Oldsmobile engines (Sec 28)

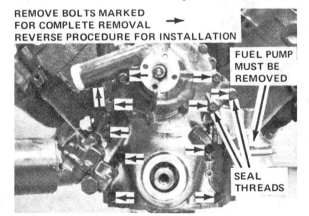

Fig. 2.12 Front cover removal and installation details – 350 CID Buick engines (Sec 28)

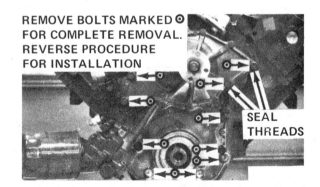

Fig. 2.13 Front cover removal and installation details – 455 CID Buick engines (Sec 28)

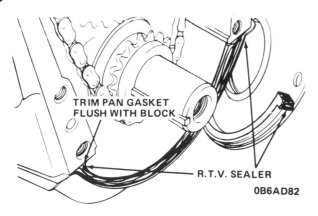

Fig. 2.14 On Oldsmobile engines, trim the oil pan gasket as shown before installing the front cover (Sec 28)

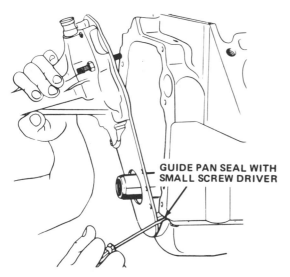

Fig. 2.16 Guide the oil pan seal into place with a small screwdriver – Oldsmobile engines (Sec 28)

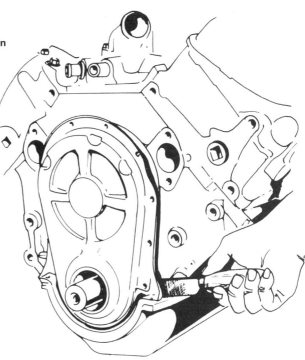

Fig. 2.15 Trimming the oil pan seal – Oldsmobile engines (Sec 28)

Fig. 2.17 Use a sharp knife to trim any protruding oil pan gasket material – Chevrolet engines (Sec 28)

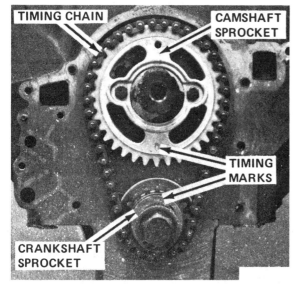

Fig. 2.18 Correct timing mark alignment – Buick engines (Sec 29)

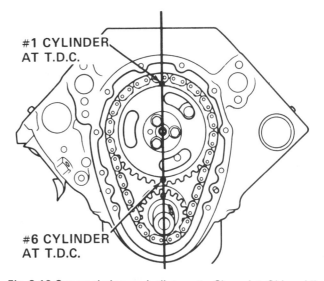

Fig. 2.19 Correct timing mark alignment – Chevrolet, Oldsmobile and Pontiac engines (Sec 29)

2   Apply sealer around the outside diameter of the seal and place the new seal into position with the open end of the seal (seal 'lip') toward the inside of the cover.

3   Drive the seal into the cover until it is fully seated. GM tools are available for this purpose. These tools are designed to exert even pressure around the circumference of the seal as it is hammered into place. A section of large diameter pipe or a large socket could also be used.

4   Take care not to distort the front cover.

With front cover removed from engine

5   This method is preferred, as the cover can be supported as the new seal is driven into place, preventing the possibility of cover distortion.

6   Remove the crankcase front cover as described in Section 28.

7   Pry the old seal out of its bore with a large screwdriver.

8   Support the inside of the cover, around the seal area and install the new seal in the same fashion as described above.

---

28 Crankcase front cover – removal and installation

Removal (all engines)

1   **Note**: *If the engine has been removed from the vehicle, disregard any of the following steps which do not apply.*

2   Disconnect the negative battery cable. *If equipped with a Buick engine*, remove the alternator and brackets as well as the distributor (Chapter 5).

3   Drain the cooling system and disconnect the radiator hoses, heater hose (where applicable) and the small by-pass hose *(except Chevrolet engine)*.

4   *If equipped with an Oldsmobile engine*, remove the top radiator support, the fan shroud and the radiator (Chapter 3).

5   Remove all belts, the fan and fan pulley, the crankshaft drive pulley and the torsional damper (harmonic balancer).

6   *If equipped with a Chevrolet engine*, remove the water pump (Chapter 3). *If equipped with a Pontiac or Buick engine*, remove the fuel pump.

7   Remove the nuts and bolts that attach the cover to the engine, then pull the cover free. Pontiac and Buick engines have bolts attaching the oil pan to the cover (Pontiac engies also have a bolt that threads into the intake manifold).

8   Using vise-grip pliers, pull the dowel pins (if equipped) out of the engine block. Grind a chamfer on one end of each pin. Thoroughly clean all gasket mating surfaces (do not allow the old gasket material to fall into the oil pan), then wipe them with a cloth soaked in solvent.

Installation (Oldsmobile engines)

9   Cut off the excess gasket material at the front of the oil pan until it is flush with the engine block.

10 Using a razor knife, trim about $\frac{1}{8}$-in from each end of the new front pan seal.

11 Install a new gasket to the engine block and a new front seal on the cover. Use RTV gasket sealant on these gaskets and also at the junction of the cover, block and oil pan.

12 Tilt the cover into place and press downward to compress the lower pan seal. Rotate the cover back and forth and guide the pan seal into the cavity using a small screwdriver.

13 Apply engine oil to the bolt threads and loosely install 2 of the bolts to hold the cover in place.

14 Install the dowel pins, chamfered end first, into the engine block.

15 Install the water pump with a new gasket (if removed from cover).

16 Tighten all bolts to the proper torque specifications an install all components in the reverse order of removal. Apply lubricant to the front hub seal before installing the crankshaft hub.

Installation (Chevrolet engines)

17 Ensure that all gasket surfaces are clean and free of excess gasket material.

18 Use a sharp knife to trim any protruding gasket material at the front of the oil pan.

19 Apply a $\frac{1}{8}$-in bead of RTV gasket sealer to the joint formed at the oil pan and engine block, as well as the front lip of the oil pan.

20 Coat the cover gasket with a non-setting sealant, position it on the cover then loosely install the cover. First install the top 4 bolts loosely,

then install $2\frac{1}{4}$ in − 20 x $\frac{1}{2}$ in screws at the lower cover holes. Apply a bead of sealer on the bottom of the cover then install the cover, tightening the screws alternately and evenly and at the same time aligning the dowel pins.

21 Remove the $2\frac{1}{4}$ in − 20 x $\frac{1}{2}$ in screws and install the remaining cover bolts. Torque all cover bolts to the proper specifications.

22 Install the water pump using new gaskets.

23 Follow the removal steps in the reverse order for the remaining components.

Installation (Pontiac engines)

24 Remove the O-ring seal from the recess in the intake manifold water recirculation passage. Inspect it carefully for re-use.

25 Transfer the water pump to the new cover, if used.

26 If a new fuel pump eccentric and bushing are to be installed at this time, remove the camshaft retainer bolt and the washer, eccentric and bushing. When installing, index the tang on the eccentric with the hole in the camshaft sprocket.

27 Position a new gasket over the studs against the engine block. If the oil pan gasket was damaged during removal, new front portions should be cemented in place on the oil pan flanges.

28 Install the O-ring into the intake manifold passage.

29 Place the cover in position over the indexing studs and secure with the bolts and nuts. Install the oil pan-to-timing cover screws after the other fasteners are installed.

30 Install the remaining components in the reverse order of disassembly referring to the appropriate Sections in this Chapter or other Chapters.

Installation (Buick engines)

31 Before re-installing, remove the oil pump cover and pack petroleum jelly around the oil pump gears so that there is no air space left inside the pump. If this is not done, the pump may ''lose its prime'' and not begin pumping oil immediately when the engine is started.

32 Re-install the pump cover, using a new gasket, and torque the bolts to specifications.

33 Make sure that the gasket surface of the block and timing chain cover are smooth and clean and install a new gasket on the cover.

34 Lubricate the harmonic balancer shaft where it will go through the timing chain cover seal so that the seal will not be damaged when the engine is first started.

35 Using the dowel pins on the block, engage the dowel holes in the cover and position the cover against the block.

36 Apply sealer to the bolt threads (see illustration) and tighten the bolts to specifications.

37 Install the harmonic balancer, bolt and washer. Use a screwdriver or other such tool to lock the flex plate or flywheel starter teeth and tighten the harmonic balancer bolt to the specified torque.

---

29 Timing chain and sprockets – removal and installation

1   **Note**: *If the engine has been removed from the vehicle, disregard the following steps which do not apply.*

2   Remove the torsional damper and front cover as described in previous Sections. *On Oldsmobile and Pontiac engines*, remove the fuel pump drive eccentric by unscrewing the bolt from the end of the camshaft (photo). Some Buick engines have a distributor drive gear mounted in front of the fuel pump eccentric (when removing them, note how they are aligned with each other and the camshaft). *On Buick and Oldsmobile engines*, slide the oil slinger off of the end of the crankshaft.

3   To facilitate installation (if the engine is not being totally disassembled), turn the crankshaft until the marks on the camshaft and crankshaft sprockets are perfectly aligned, opposite each other. DO NOT attempt to remove either sprocket or the chain until this is done. Also, do not turn the camshaft or the crankshaft after the sprockets are removed.

4   *On Chevrolet engines and 455 CID Buick engines*, remove the bolts that attach the sprocket to the end of the camshaft. Also, on 455 CID Buick engines, the oil pan must be removed in order to slide the sprocket off of the crankshaft.

5   Generally speaking, the camshaft sprocket, the crankshaft sprocket and the timing chain can be slipped off the shafts together. If resistance is encountered, it may be necessary to use 2 large screwdrivers to carefully pry the sprockets off of the shafts. If extreme

29.2 Removing fuel pump drive eccentric (Pontiac engine shown)

29.5 When using a puller to draw the crankshaft gear off the crankshaft, be careful not to damage the threads on the end of the crankshaft

30.8 Removing the camshaft thrust plate (Pontiac engine)

30.9 When pulling the camshaft from the engine, support it near the block (as shown) and pull slowly so the bearings are not damaged

32.2 With the piston at the bottom of its travel, a ridge reamer is used to remove the ridge or built-up carbon from the top of the cylinder

32.5 Pieces of rubber hose pushed over the rod bolts will protect the crankshaft and cylinders

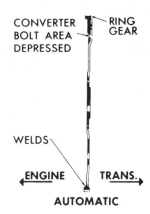

Fig. 2.20 Drive plate (automatic transmission) installed position (Sec 33)

resistance is encountered (which may happen with the crankshaft sprocket), a gear puller will be required. It should be noted that on Oldsmobile engines, the key that indexes the sprocket to the crankshaft must be removed before sliding or pulling the sprocket off of the shaft.

6   If the crankshaft and the camshaft are not disturbed while the timing chain and sprockets are out of place, then installation can begin with step 9. If the engine is completely dismantled, or if the crankshaft or camshaft are disturbed while the timing chain is off, then the No. 1 piston must be positioned at TDC before the timing chain and sprockets are installed.

7   Align the hole in the camshaft sprocket with the dowel pin in the end of the camshaft, then slip the socket onto the end of the camshaft. *On Buick engines,* turn the camshaft until the timing mark on the sprocket is pointed straight down. **Note:** *On Chevrolet, Pontiac and Oldsmobile engines, with the No. 1 piston at TDC, the timing mark on the camshaft sprocket must be pointed straight up.*

8   Slip the crankshaft sprocket onto the end of the crankshaft (make sure the key and keyway are properly aligned), then turn the crankshaft until the timing mark on the sprocket is pointed straight up (all engines).

9   Next, remove the camshaft sprocket from the camshaft and lay the chain over it. Slip the other end of the chain over the camshaft sprocket (try to keep the timing marks aligned as this is done) and reinstall the camshaft sprocket. When the sprockets are properly installed, the timing marks on the sprockets will be perfectly aligned, opposite each other (except on Chevrolet, Pontiac and Oldsmobile engines; refer to the accompanying illustrations and step 7).

10 On Chevrolet engines and 455 CID Buick engines, install the bolts that attach the sprocket to the camshaft, then recheck the alignment of the timing marks. *On Oldsmobile engines,* install the crankshaft key after the sprocket is in place (use a brass hammer to seat the key in the keyway).

11 The rest of the installation procedure is basically the reverse of removal. *On Pontiac engines,* the camshaft should extend through the sprocket so that the hole in the fuel pump drive eccentric will locate on the end of the shaft. Install the eccentric and index the tangs on the eccentric with the small hole in the sprocket hub. On 350 CID Buick engines, make sure the oil groove in the eccentric faces out.

12 Be sure to tighten the crankshaft and camshaft sprocket retaining bolts to the specified torque.

30 Camshaft – removal and installation

1   **Note:** *If the engine has been removed from the car, disregard the following steps which do not apply. Since this procedure requires air conditioning disconnection, take the car to a dealer or specialist for A/C de-pressurization.*

2   Remove the intake manifold as described in Section 12.

3   Remove the push rods from the lifters. In order to do this, the rocker covers must be removed, and the rocker arm assemblies loosened or removed. Further information on this can be found in Section 14.

4   Remove the valve lifters, keeping each separate so they can be

replaced in their original positions. Refer to Section 20 for removal information.

5   Remove the front grille (Chapter 12).

6   Remove the radiator, shroud, air conditioning condenser and hood catch support as necessary to provide clearance for the camshaft as it is drawn from the engine.

7   Remove the fuel pump and fuel pump push rod (Chevrolet engines only) (Chapter 4).

8   Remove the torsional damper (Section 26), the crankcase front cover (Section 28) and the camshaft sprocket/timing chain (Section 29). Install two $\frac{5}{16}$ in – 18x4 in bolts into the camshaft bolt holes (if equipped) to be used as grips to pull on the camshaft. Note that Pontiac engines have a thrust plate (photo) installed in front of the camshaft (remove the 2 bolts that attach the plate to the engine block).

9   Carefully draw the camshaft out of the engine block. Do this very slowly to avoid damage to the camshaft bearings as the journals pass through the bearing surfaces. Always support the camshaft with one hand near the engine block (photo).

10 Before installing the camshaft, coat each of the lobes and journals liberally with 'Molykote' or its equivalent.

11 Slide the camshaft into the engine block, again taking extra care not to damage the bearings.

12 Install the remaining components in the reverse order of removal, referring to the appropriate Sections where necessary.

13 Adjust the valve lash as described in Section 22.

31 Camshaft and bearings – inspection and servicing

1   Examine the bearing surfaces and the surfaces of the cam lobes. Surface scratches, if very shallow, can be removed by rubbing with a fine emery cloth or an oilstone. Any deep scoring will necessitate a new camshaft.

2   If the bearings are worn, they can be extracted using a suitable tool (GM tool set No. J-6098 is designed for this purpose). **Note:** *It will be necessary to drive out the camshaft rear plug from the block.*

3   New bearings are installed using the same tool set, but it is necessary to align the cam bearing oil holes following the manufacturer's instructions supplied with the installation/removal tool.

32 Pistons, connecting rods and bearings – removal

1   Remove the oil pan, oil pump and cylinder heads as described previously in this Chapter.

2   Before the piston assemblies can be forced up through the top of the engine block, a ridge reamer should be used to remove the ridge and/or carbon deposits at the top of each cylinder (photo). Working on one cylinder at a time, turn the engine so the piston is at the bottom of its stroke. Then place a rag on top of the piston to catch the cuttings. After the ridge is removed, crank the engine until the piston is at the top of the cylinder and remove the cloth and cuttings. Failure to remove this ridge may cause damage to the piston rings, pistons or cylinder walls.

3   Inspect the connecting rods and connecting rod caps for cylinder identification. If these components are not plainly marked, identify each using a small punch to make the appropriate number of indentations (left bank – 1, 3, 5, 7, right bank – 2, 4, 6, 8).

4   Working in sequence, remove the nuts on the connecting rod stud and lift the cap (with bearing inside) off the crankshaft. Place the connecting rod cap and bearing on a clean work surface marked cylinder 1, 2, 3, etc.

5   Push a piece of rubber or plastic tubing over the connecting rod studs to completely cover the studs. This is important as these studs could easily damage the crankshaft or cylinder wall when the piston assembly is removed (photo).

6   Push the piston/connecting rod assembly out through the top of the cylinder. Place the piston with its connecting rod next to its rod cap on the sequenced work area.

7   Repeat these procedures for the remaining seven cylinders turning the crankshaft as necessary to gain access to the connecting rod nuts. Reuse the rubber or plastic tubing for each assembly.

8   Remove the bearings from the connecting rods and the connecting rod caps. This is easily done with a small screwdriver. If the engine has many miles, it is false economy to reuse the bearings, but if they are

33.2 Use a center punch to hold the flywheel in place while the bolts are loosened

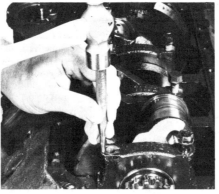

35.3 Use a center punch to put small marks on the bearing caps to identify each for reassembly in its original position

35.7 Gently pry the main bearings loose from the engine block

Fig. 2.21 Removing crankshaft rear oil seal upper half (neoprene type seal) with engine in car (Sec 36)

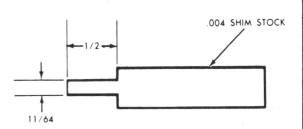

Fig. 2.22 Neoprene type crankshaft rear oil seal installation tool (Sec 36)

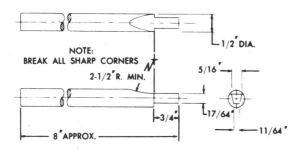

Fig. 2.24 Packing tool fabrication details – braided fabric type crankshaft rear oil seal (Sec 36)

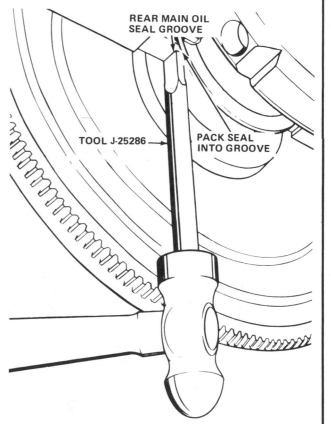

Fig. 2.23 Packing upper half of braided fabric type crankshaft rear oil seal into block (Sec 36)

to be reinstalled place them in a numbered rack.

9   If a piston ring expanding tool is available, use this to remove each of the rings from the piston. An alternative method is to expand the ring just enough to clear the lands of the piston body. Then place strips of tin (about $\frac{1}{4}$ in. wide) under the ring at equal distances around the piston. Using a slight twisting motion, 'walk' the ring up the piston and off the top.

10 Place the rings, in their 'installed' order adjacent to the piston/connecting rod on your numbered work area.

11 Separating the connecting rod from the piston requires the removal of the piston pin. This job is best left to a dealer or automotive machine shop equipped with the proper support tools and an arbor press.

12 Do not take the time to clean and inspect the piston/rod assemblies at this time as they may have to be replaced with new units depending on the condition of the cylinder block and/or crankshaft.

33 Flywheel – removal and installation

1   The flywheel may be unbolted from the crankshaft rear flange after the removal of the transmission and in the case of a manual transmission, unbolting the clutch housing and clutch (refer to Chapters 7 and 8).

2   To prevent the crankshaft from turning as the bolts are loosened, place a block of wood between one of the crankshaft throws and the side of the engine block. An alignment tool pushed through the flywheel and against the engine block will also work (photo).

3   Before installing the flywheel, clean the mating surfaces of the flywheel and the crankshaft.

4   With manual transmissions, install the flywheel by aligning the dowel hole in the crankshaft with the dowel hole in the flywheel.

5   With automatic transmissions, install the flywheel with the torque converter attaching pads toward the transmission.

6   Tighten the bolts a little at a time until the proper torque specification is attained. It is a good idea to use a thread sealing agent (like Locktite) on the bolt threads. Again, use a block of wood or a centerpunch tool against the block to prevent the flywheel from turning as the bolts are tightened.

34 Flywheel and starter ring gear – inspection

1   Examine the starter ring gear for broken or chipped teeth. If evident, the flywheel must be replaced with a new one.

2   On manual transmission versions, examine for scoring on the clutch friction face. Light scoring may be dressed out using emery cloth, but where there is deep scoring the flywheel must be replaced with a new one or clutch damage will soon occur.

3   On automatic transmission models, examine the converter securing bolt holes for elongation.

4   Replace the driveplate complete if either the starter ring gear is worn or the mounting bolt holes are elongated.

35 Crankshaft, main bearings and oil seals – removal

1   The crankshaft and main bearings should only be removed with the engine removed from the car.

2   The engine should be completely stripped of its components as described in the previous Sections of this Chapter.

3   Check that each of the 5 main bearing caps is marked in respect to its location in the engine block. If not, use a punch to make small indentations in the same fashion as for the connecting rods and caps (photo). The main bearing caps must be reinstalled in their original positions.

4   Unbolt the main bearing caps, and lift each cap and its corresponding bearing off the crankshaft. Place all main bearing caps and bearings on a workspace numbered to correspond with the position of the caps in the engine block.

5   Lift the crankshaft from the engine block. Be careful not to damage it in any way.

6   Remove the two halves of the rear main bearing oil seal.

7   Remove the main bearings from the cylinder block and the main bearing caps, keeping them separated as to their positions (photo).

8   The crankshaft gear at the front of the crank can be removed by using a special puller designed for this purpose.

36 Rear main oil seal – replacement (engine in car)

1   *Always replace both halves of the rear main oil seal as a unit. While the replacement of this seal is much easier with the engine removed from the car, as in a total engine rebuild, the job can be done with the engine in place.*

2   Remove the oil pan and oil pump as described prevously in this Chapter.

3   Remove the rear main bearing cap from the engine.

Chevrolet engines (neoprene type seal)

4   Using a screwdriver, pry the lower half of the oil seal from the bearing cap.

5   To remove the upper half of the seal, use a small hammer and a brass pin punch to roll the seal around the crankshaft journal. Tap one end of the seal with the hammer and punch (be careful not to strike the crankshaft) until the other end of the seal protrudes enough to pull the seal out with a pair of pliers.

6   Clean all sealant and foreign material from the cylinder bearing cap and case. Do not use an abrasive cleaner for this.

7   Inspect components for nicks, scratches or burrs at all sealing surfaces.

8   Coat the seal lips of the new seal with light engine oil. Do not get oil on the seal mating ends.

9   Included in the purchase of the rear main oil seal should be a small plastic installation tool. If not included, make your own by cutting an old feeler gauge blade.

10 Position the narrow end of this installation tool between the crankshaft and the seal seat. The idea is to protect the new seal from being damaged by the sharp edge of the seal seat.

36.13 Installing the lower half of the neoprene type rear main bearing seal in the bearing cap (note the installation tool)

36.14 Sealant should be used where the rear main cap touches the engine block

37.7 Measuring the cylinder diameter

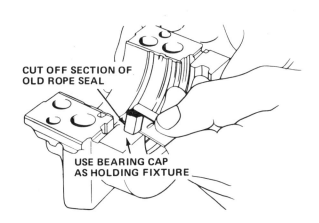

CUT OFF SECTION OF
OLD ROPE SEAL

USE BEARING CAP
AS HOLDING FIXTURE

Fig. 2.25 Use the bearing cap as a holding fixture when cutting short sections off the old seal (Sec 36)

11 Raise the new upper half of the seal into position with the seal lips facing towards the front of the engine. Push the seal onto its seat, using the installation tool as a protector against the seal contacting the sharp edge.

12 Roll the seal around the crankshaft, all the time using the tool as a 'shoehorn' for protection. When both ends of the seal are flush with the engine block, remove the installation tool being careful not to withdraw the seal as well.

13 Install the lower half of the oil seal in the bearing cap, again using the installation tool to protect the seal against the sharp edge (photo). Make sure the seal is firmly seated, then withdraw the installation tools.

14 Smear a bit of sealant to the bearing cap areas immediately adjacent to the seal ends (photo).

15 Install the bearing cap (with seal) and torque the attaching bolts to about 10-12 ft. lb only. Now tap the end of the crankshaft first rearward, then forward to line up the thrust surfaces. Retorque the bearing cap bolts to the proper specification.

Buick, Oldsmobile and Pontiac engines (braided fabric type seal)

16 With the oil pan, oil pump and main bearing cap removed (see previous Sections), insert the special GM seal packing tool or equivalent brass punch against the seal. Drive the old seal into its groove until it is packed tight at each end.

17 Measure the amount which the seal was driven upwards, then add $\frac{1}{16}$-in. Cut 2 pieces that length from the old seal taken from the bearing cap. Use the bearing cap as a guide when cutting.

18 Place a drop of sealant on each end of these seal pieces and then pack them into the upper groove to fill the gap made previously.

19 Trim the remaining material perfectly flush with the block. Be careful not to harm the bearing surface.

20 Install a new rope seal into the main bearing cap groove and push firmly all around using a hammer handle or special GM tool. Make sure the seal is firmly seated, then trim the ends flush with the bearing cap mating surface.

21 Install cap and remaining components in reverse order, tightening all parts to specifications.

37 Cylinder block – inspection

1 It is important that the cylinder block be inspected carefully and as described. The cylinder block was designed to operate with exacting tolerances, and if the engine is reassembled without first properly inspecting the block, all work and cost involved in the rebuild may be for nothing.

2 Clean the cylinder block as necessary to remove built-up sludge and grime. Clean all excess gasket material from the sealing surfaces.

3 Inspect the cylinder block for cracks in the cylinder walls, water jacket, valve lifter bores and main bearing webs. Use a flashlight where necessary. In most cases, cracks will require that a new engine block

be purchased.

4 The cylinder bores must be examined for taper, ovality, scoring and scratches. These checks are important for proper operation of the pistons and piston rings.

5 Scoring and scratches can usually be seen with the naked eye and felt with the fingers. If they are deep, the engine block may have to be replaced with a new one. If the imperfections are slight, a qualified machine shop should be able to hone or bore the cylinders to a larger size.

6 There are two indicators for excessive wear of the cylinders. First, if the vehicle was emitting blue smoke from the exhaust system before engine dismantling. This blue smoke is caused by oil seeping past the piston rings due to the wear of the cylinder walls. Second, the thickness of the ridge at the top of the cylinder (which may have been removed during piston removal) can give an indication about overall cylinder wear.

7 Using an internal-type dial gauge, measure each bore at three different points (photo). Take a measurement near the top of the bore and then near the bottom of the bore. Finally, measure at the center. Jot down all measurements to determine the taper of the cylinder (slightly larger at the top than the bottom or vice versa).

8 An out of round condition can be found in a similar fashion, except measure the cylinder first parallel with the engine centerline and then turn the dial gauge until it is perpendicular with the centerline (180 degrees from first measurement).

9 Where the cylinder bores are worn beyond the permitted tolerances as shown in the Specifications Section, the block will have to be replaced with a new one, honed or bored.

10 A final check of the cylinder block would include an inspection for warpage. This is done with a straightedge and feeler gauges in the same manner as for the cylinder heads. The tolerances described in Section 17 also apply to the cylinder block. If warpage is slight, a machine shop can resurface the block.

38 Engine – rebuilding alternatives

1 At this point in the engine rebuilding process the home mechanic is faced with a number of options for completing the overhaul. The decision to replace the cylinder block, piston/rod assemblies and crankshaft depend on a number of factors with the number one consideration being the condition of the cylinder block. Other considerations are: cost, competent machine shop facilities, parts availability, time available to complete the project and experience.

2 Some of the rebuilding alternatives are as follows:

Individual parts – If the inspection procedures prove that the engine block and most engine components are in reusable condition, this may be the most economical alternative. The block, crankshaft and piston/rod assemblies should all be inspected carefully. Even if the block shows little wear, the cylinder bores should be honed and the camshaft bearings replaced with new ones; both jobs for a machine shop.

Master kit (crankshaft kit) – This rebuild package usually consists of a reground crankshaft and a matched set of pistons and connecting rods. The pistons will come already installed with new piston pins to the connecting rods. Piston rings and the necessary bearings may or may not be included in the kit. These kits are commonly available for standard cylinder bores, as well as for engine blocks which have been bored to a regular oversize.

Short block – A short block consists of a cylinder block with a crankshaft and piston/rod assemblies already installed. All new bearings are incorporated and all clearances will be within tolerances. Depending on where the short block is purchased, a guarantee may be included. The existing camshaft, valve mechanism, cylinder heads and ancillary parts can be bolted to this short block with little or no machine shop work necessary for the engine overhaul.

Long block – A long block, called a 'Target' engine by GM dealerships consists of a short block plus oil pump, oil pan, cylinder heads, valve covers, camshaft and valve mechanism, camshaft gear, timing chain and crankcase front cover. All components are installed with new bearings, seals and gaskets incorporated throughout. The installation of manifolds and ancillary parts is all that is necessary. Some form of guarantee is usually included with purchase.

3 Give careful thought to which method is best for your situation and discuss the alternatives with local machine shop owners, parts dealers or GM dealership partsmen.

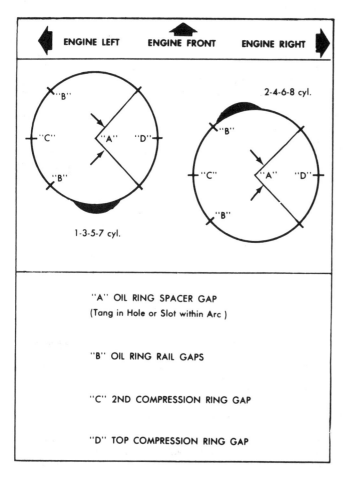

ENGINE LEFT   ENGINE FRONT   ENGINE RIGHT

2-4-6-8 cyl.

1-3-5-7 cyl.

"A" OIL RING SPACER GAP

(Tang in Hole or Slot within Arc)

"B" OIL RING RAIL GAPS

"C" 2ND COMPRESSION RING GAP

"D" TOP COMPRESSION RING GAP

Fig. 2.26 Piston ring gap positions (Sec 41)

39 Crankshaft and bearings – inspection and servicing

1   Examine the crankpin and main journal surfaces for scoring, scratches or corrosion. If evident, then the crankshaft will have to be reground professionally.
2   Using a micrometer, measure each journal and crankpin at several different points for ovality (photo). If this is found to be more than 0.001 inch then the crankshaft must be reground. Undersize bearings are available to suit the recommended reground diameter, but normally your GM dealer will supply the correct matching bearings with the reconditioned crankshaft.
3   After a high mileage, the main bearings and the connecting rod bearings may have worn to give an excessive running clearance. The correct running clearance for the different journals is given in the Specifications. The clearance is best checked using a product such as 'Plastigage' having refitted the original bearings and caps and tightened the cap bolts to the torque values listed in Specifications. *Never attempt to correct excessive running clearance by filing the caps but always fit new shell bearings, having first checked the crankshaft journals and crankpins for ovality and to establish whether their diameters are of standard or reground sizes.*
4   Checking the connecting rod bearings is carried out in a similar manner to that described for the main bearings. The correct running clearance is given in the Specifications.
5   It is good practice to check the running clearance of rod and main bearings even if new bearings are installed. The use of 'Plastigage' is described in Section 43.
6   The crankshaft endplay should be checked by forcing the crankshaft to the extreme front position, then using a feeler gauge at the front end of the rear main bearing. Refer to the Specifications for the permissible clearance. This procedure is detailed in Section 45.
7   The connecting rod side-clearance should be measured with a

feeler gauge between the connecting rod caps. If the side clearance is outside the specified tolerance, replace the rod assembly. This procedure is detailed in Section 44.

40 Piston and connecting rod assemblies – cleaning and inspection

1   In most cases where the engine has seen high mileage, the original pistons will have to be replaced with new ones. This is because the cylinders will have to be bored to a larger size to compensate for normal wear. If however the cylinder walls require only a slight finish honing, the old pistons may be reused if they are in good condition.
2   Wash the connecting rods and pistons in a cleaning solvent and dry with compressed air, if available.
3   Don't use a wire brush or any abrasive cleaning tools on any part of the piston.
4   Clean the ring grooves of the piston with a groove cleaner tool and make sure the oil ring holes and slots are clean (photo).
5   Check the rods for twist and bending and inspect the rods for nicks or cracks. If any of the above items are found, the rod must be replaced with a new one.
6   Inspect the piston for cracked ring lands, skirts or pin bosses. Check for worn or wavy ring lands, scuffed or damaged skirts and eroded areas at the top of the piston. Replace any pistons that are damaged or show signs of excessive wear.
7   Inspect the ring grooves for nicks which may cause the rings to hang up.
8   With the piston still connected to the connecting rod, swivel the rod back and forth and noting the degree of difficulty. Compare all piston/rod assemblies. If the rods seem loose on the piston pins, and move with little or no drag, the piston pins have worn and the piston pin must be replaced.
9   If the cylinder block is in need of any machine work, even finish honing, chances are that the machinist will want the pistons on hand to check piston-to-bore clearance as the cylinder walls are cut. This measurement is critical and should be left to the machine shop.

41 Pistons and piston rings – assembly

1   The piston should be attached to its appropriate connecting rod. As mentioned previously, this is a job for a professional equipped with the proper supports and an arbor press.
2   The new piston rings should be comparable in size to the piston being used.
3   The installation of the piston rings on the piston is critical to the overall performance of the rebuilt engine.
4   Measure the ring end gap of each ring before it is installed in the piston. This is done as follows:

   a) *Arrange the piston rings into sets for each piston. The set will contain a top ring, 2nd ring and a three-piece oil control ring (two rails and a spacer).*
   b) *Slip a top ring into the appropriate cylinder bore. Push the ring into the cylinder bore at the bottom of ring travel. Push the ring down into position with the top of a piston to make sure the ring is square with the cylinder wall (photo).*
   c) *Using a feeler gauge, measure the gap between the ends of the ring (photo). If the gap is less than specified (see Specifications), remove the ring and try another top ring for fit.*
   d) *Check all top rings in the same manner and if necessary use a fine file to remove a slight amount of material from the ends of the ring(s). If inadequate end gap is used, the rings will break during operation.*
   e) *Measure the end gap of each 2nd ring and oil control ring as described above.*

5   Check the fit of each piston ring into its groove by holding the ring next to the piston and then placing the outer surface of the ring into its respective groove. Roll the ring entirely around the piston and check for any binding. If the binding is due to a distorted ring, replace the ring with a new one. Perform this check for the top and 2nd rings of each piston.
6   Install the piston rings as follows:

39.2 Measuring a crankshaft journal

40.4 Cleaning the piston ring grooves with a special tool made especially for this purpose

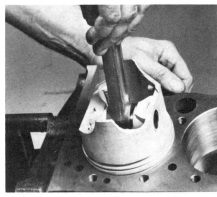

41.4a Use the top of a piston to push the piston ring into its bore for measuring the end gap

41.4b Measure the piston ring end gap with a feeler gauge

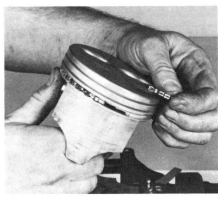

41.6a Installing the oil ring spacer

41.6b A piston ring expanding tool eases ring removal and installation

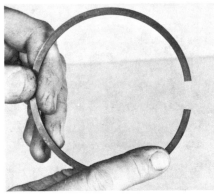

41.6c Most piston rings will be marked with a small dimple to indicate the top side

41.7 Use a feeler gauge to measure the clearance between piston ring and piston ring groove

42.2A Use a hammer and a center punch to push the freeze plug into the block

42.2b Pliers are then used to pull the freeze plug out of the engine block

42.2c A special installation tool (a suitably sized socket or a block of softwood can also be used) is used to force the new plugs into the bores

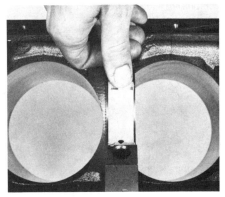

43.4 Installing a main bearing half into the engine block

43.7 Tightening a main bearing cap bolt with a torque wrench

43.8 The flattened Plastigage is then measured using the scale printed on the package

43.11 Put a length of Plastigage on the crankshaft journal (arrow) and install the rod cap and bearing on top of it

44.2 A feeler gauge is used to measure connecting rod side clearance once the piston/rod assemblies are installed

45.9 Measuring crankshaft end-play with a feeler gauge between the rear cap and rear throw

46.7 Most pistons will be marked (as shown) in some way to indicate installation toward the front of the engine

46.8a With the piston ring compressor around the piston, it is sometimes necessary to tap the compressor lightly to seat the rings

46.8b A wood hammer handle can be used to push the piston/connecting rod assembly into the engine block

46.10 Tightening a connecting rod nut with a torque wrench

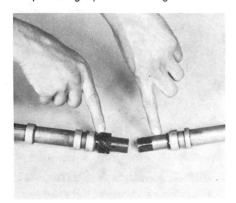

47.6 The pre-oiling tool (right) has the gear and the advance weights ground off

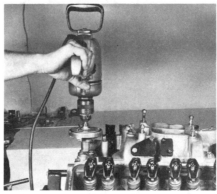

47.7 A common drill motor connects to the modified distributor to turn the oil pump

47.8 Oil and/or assembly grease will spurt from the rocker arms to indicate that the lubrication system is functioning properly

a) Study the accompanying illustration to understand exactly where each ring gap should be located in relation to the piston and other rings. The location of each ring gap is important.

b) If a piston ring expander tool is available, use this to install the rings. If not, small lengths of tin can be used to prevent the rings from entering the wrong groove (see Section 32 on piston ring removal).

c) Install the bottom oil ring spacer in its groove and insert the anti-rotation tang in the oil hole (photo). Hold the spacer ends butted and install the lower steel oil ring rail with the gap properly located. Install the upper steel oil ring rail and properly set its gap. Flex or squeeze the oil ring assembly to make sure it is free in the groove. If not, dress the groove with a file or replace the oil control ring assembly as necessary.

d) Install the 2nd ring (photo) and properly locate its gap. Note that the rings are marked with a dimple to indicate which side should face up (photo).

e) Install the top ring with gap properly positioned.

f) Repeat the above procedures for all piston assemblies.

7   Proper clearance of the piston rings in their grooves is very important. Clearance between the ring and its groove is checked with a blade feeler gauge, sliding the appropriately sized feeler gauge (see Specifications) between the top of the ring and the inside of the groove (photo). Rotate the feeler blade all the way around the piston, checking for proper clearance. Replace rings or clean and dress the groove as necessary for proper clearance.

42 Engine assembly – general information

1   Before assembling any parts to the engine block, the block should have all necessary machine work completed and the engine block should be thoroughly cleaned. If machine work was performed, chances are that the block was hot-tanked afterward to remove all traces of the machined cuttings.

2   The oil galleys and water passages of the block should also be thoroughly clean and free from dirt or machining leftovers. It's good practice to install new freeze plugs in the engine whenever it is stripped for a total overhaul. These plugs are difficult to replace once the engine has been assembled and installed. If the engine was sent out for machine work and hot-tanking, it may be best to let the machine shop remove and install new plugs. If they are to be done at home, proceed as follows:

a) Use a hammer and punch to press one side of the plug into the block (photo).

b) Use pliers to pry the old freeze plug out of its recess (photo).

c) Place a suitable replacement plug into position and hammer into place until flush with the engine block. Special installation tools are available for pressing the plug in place, however a suitable sized socket will work fine (photo).

3   Clean and examine all bolts, nuts and fasteners. Replace any that are damaged.

4   Clean and cover all engine components to keep dirt and dust away from them until they can be installed.

5   Have assembly grease and an oil can filled with engine oil handy to lubricate parts as they are installed.

6   Lay out all necessary tools and a reliable torque wrench on a clean work table for easy retrieval.

7   New gaskets and seals must be used throughout. These are commonly available together in a master rebuild gasket set.

8   In almost all cases, parts to be replaced during a major overhaul include: camshaft bearings, connecting rod bearings, main bearings, piston rings, timing chain, spark plugs and oil filter. These are in addition to any parts found damaged or excessively worn during dismantling or the various inspection processes.

43 Main bearings and rod bearings – checking clearance

1   **Note:** *There are three precautions to take when working with Plastigage. These are:*

a) Plastigage is soluble in oil, so all oil and grease should be removed from the crankshaft and bearing surfaces while the testing is done.

b) Do not rotate the crankshaft while the Plastigage is installed in the engine as this may cause damage to the crankshaft or bearing surfaces.

c) Remove all traces of the Plastigage when testing is complete. Be very careful not to harm the crankshaft or bearing surfaces as the Plastigage is removed. Do not use sharp tools or abrasive cleaners, instead, remove the used Plastigage with your fingernail or a blunt wood stick.

2   Whenever an engine is overhauled the bearing clearances should be checked. This should be done for reused bearings as well as for new bearings.

3   The procedure is basically the same for both the main bearings and the connecting rod bearings.

4   With the crankshaft set into the engine block, install the main bearings into the engine block and the main bearing caps (photo).

5   Remove all oil, grime and foreign materials from the crankshaft and bearing surfaces.

6   Place a piece of Plastigage (available at most auto supply shops) along the length of each main bearing journal on the crankshaft.

7   Install each main bearing cap and tighten the attaching bolts to specifications (photo). The arrow on each cap should face toward the front of the engine.

8   Now remove each bearing cap and measure the width of the Plastigage strip which will have flattened out when the caps were tightened. A scale is provided on the Plastigage envelope for measuring the width of the Plastigage strip, and thus, bearing clearance (photo).

9   If the Plastigage is flattened more at the ends than in the middle, or vice versa, this is an indication of journal taper which·can be checked in the Specifications Section.

10   To test for an out of round condition, remove all traces of the Plastigage (be careful not to damage the crankshaft or bearing surfaces) and rotate the crankshaft 90 degrees. With the crankshaft rotated to this point, use the Plastigage to check the clearances again. Compare these measurements with those taken previously to arrive at eccentricity or out of round.

11   To check connecting rod bearing clearances, install each piston/rod assembly (Section 46) and use the Plastigage as described above (photo).

12   Connecting rod side clearance (Section 44) can also be checked at this time.

13   If the bearings have shown to be within all tolerances, they may be installed following the steps outlined in the appropriate sections.

14   If not within specifications, the bearings should be replaced with the correctly sized bearings. Upper and lower bearings should always be replaced as a unit.

44 Connecting rod side clearance – checking

1   Side clearance can be checked with the piston/rod assemblies temporarily installed for bearing clearance checking.

2   With the piston/rod assemblies installed and the bearing caps tightened to specifications, use a screwdriver to spread the rods apart then insert feeler gauges (photo) to check the clearance between the sides of the connecting rods.

3   If the clearance at this point is below the minimum tolerance, the rod may be machined for more clearance at this area.

4   If the clearance is too excessive, a new rod must be used or the crankshaft must be reground or replaced with a new one.

45 Crankshaft, main bearings and oil seal – installation

1   **Note:** *If a new or reground crankshaft is being installed, or if the original crankshaft has been reground, make sure the correct bearings are being used.*

2   Install the rear main bearing oil seal. The upper half of the seal should be positioned on its cylinder block seat and the lower half on the rear main bearing cap. Install neoprene type seals (Chevrolet engines) with the lips toward the front of the engine. Where two lips are incorporated, install lip with helix towards the front of the engine. Use the protector installation tool when installing the neoprene seal halves. (See Section 36 for use of installation tool and further information) **Note:** *If installing fabric type seals (used on Buick,*

Oldsmobile and Pontiac engines), refer to Section 93, Chapter 2B, for the procedure to follow.

3   Lubricate the seal lips with engine oil.

4   Install the main bearings in the cylinder block and main bearing caps. Lubricate the bearing surfaces with engine oil.

5   Lower the crankshaft into position, being careful not to damage the bearing surfaces.

6   Apply a thin coat of brush-on sealer to the block mating surface and the corresponding surface of the bearing cap. Do not allow sealer to get on the crankshaft or seal (see Section 36).

7   Install the main bearing caps (with bearings) over the crankshaft and onto the cylinder block. The arrows should point toward the front of the engine.

8   Lubricate the cap bolts and install but do not tighten. Using a hammer and a block of wood, tap the shaft back and forth to align the center main bearing. Hold the crankshaft to the front while the No. 3 cap bolts are tightened. Then tighten remaining cap bolts.

9   To measure crankshaft end play, force the crankshaft as far forwards as it will go and use a feeler gauge to measure the gap between the front of the rear main bearing and the crankshaft thrust surface (photo).

10   Install the flywheel as described in Section 33 to ease in engine rotation during reassembly.

---

46 Pistons, connecting rods and bearings – installation

1   With the pistons complete with piston rings and connecting rods, they can be installed in the engine.

2   Make sure the cylinder bores are perfectly clean. Wipe the cylinder walls several times with a light engine oil and a clean, lint-free cloth.

3   Lubricate the connecting rod bearings and install them into their appropriate rod and rod cap.

4   Lightly coat the pistons, rings and cylinder walls with light engine oil.

5   Install a length of rubber or plastic tubing over the connecting rod studs on one rod assembly. This will prevent the threaded bolts from possibly damaging the cylinder wall or crankshaft journal as the piston/rod assembly is pushed into place.

6   Check that all the piston ring gaps are positioned properly (see Section 41).

7   Check that the piston/rod assembly is properly positioned. Most pistons will be marked with an 'F' or a drilled out area indicating the piston should be installed with these marks toward the front of the engine (photo). The rod bearing tang slots should be towards the outside of the engine block once installed.

8   Place a piston ring compressor around the piston, with the base of the compressor flush with the cylinder block (photo). Tighten the compressor until the rings are flush with the piston surface and then push the piston assembly into the bore. A wooden hammer handle can be used to tap the top of the piston slightly (photo). Hold the ring compressor solidly against the cylinder block until all rings are inside the bore. Continue pushing until the connecting rod is near its installed position.

9   Ensure that all bearing surfaces and the crankshaft journal are coated with engine oil and remove the tubing protector pieces. Install the connecting rod bearing cap (with bearing) to the connecting rod.

10   Torque the nuts to specification (photo).

11   Repeat this procedure for all cylinders, using the rubber or plastic tubing on each assembly to prevent damage as the pistons are pushed into place. Rotate the crankshaft as necessary to make the connecting rod nuts accessible for tightening.

---

47 Engine – final assembling and pre-oiling after overhaul

1   After the crankshaft, piston/rod assemblies and the various associated bearings have been installed in the engine block, the remainder of the components (cylinder heads, oil pump, camshaft, etc.) can be installed following the installation procedures located in the various sections of this Chapter.

2   Follow the engine disassembly sequence in the reverse order of installation, using new gaskets where necessary.

3   Adjust the valve lash as described in Section 22 (Chevrolet engines only).

4   After a major overhaul it is a good idea to pre-oil the engine before it is installed and initially started. This will tell you if there are any faults in the oiling system at a time when corrections can be made easily and without major damage. Pre-oiling the engine will also allow the parts to be lubricated thoroughly in a normal fashion, but without heavy loads placed upon them.

5   The engine should be assembled completely with the exception of the distributor and the valve covers.

6   A modified distributor will be needed for this job. This pre-oil tool is a distributor body with the bottom gear ground off and the counterweight assembly removed from the top of the shaft (photo).

7   Place the pre-oiler into the distributor shaft access hole at the rear of the intake manifold and make sure the bottom of the shaft mates with the oil pump. Clamp the modified distributor into place just as you would an ordinary distributor. Now attach an electric drill motor to the top of the shaft (photo).

8   With the oil filter installed, all oil galley-ways plugged (oil pressure sending unit at rear of block) and the crankcase full of oil as shown on the dipstick, rotate the pre-oiler with the drill. Make sure the rotation is in a clockwise direction. Soon, oil should start to flow from the rocker arms, signifying that the oil pump and oiling system is functioning properly (photo). It may take 2 to 3 minutes for the oil to flow to each rocker arm. Allow the oil to circulate throughout the engine for a few minutes.

9   Check for oil leaks at all locations and correct as necessary.

10   Remove the pre-oiler and install the normal distributor and valve covers.

---

48 Engine start-up after major repair or overhaul

1   With the engine in place in the vehicle and all components connected, make a final check that all pipes and wiring have been connected and that no rags or tools have been left in the engine compartment.

2   Connect the negative battery cable. If it sparks or arcs, power is being drawn from someplace and all accessories and wiring should be checked.

3   Fill the cooling system with the proper mixture and amount of coolant (Chapter 3).

4   Fill the crankcase with the correct quantity and grade of oil (Chapter 1).

5   Check the tension of all drive belts (Chapter 1).

6   Remove the high tension wire from the center tower of the distributor cap (1974) or the 'BAT' wire connection from the HEI distributor (1975 – 1980) to prevent the engine from starting. Now crank the engine over for about 15 to 30 seconds. This will allow the oil pump to distribute oil and the fuel pump to start pumping fuel to the carburetor.

7   Now connect the high tension lead at the distributor and start the engine. Immediately check all gauges and warning lights for proper readings and check for leaks of coolant or oil.

8   If the engine does not start immediately, check to make sure fuel is reaching the carburetor. This may take a while.

9   After allowing the engine to run for a few minutes at low speed, turn it off and check the oil and coolant levels.

10   Start the engine again and check the ignition timing, emission control settings and carburetor idle speeds (Chapter 1).

11   Run the vehicle easily during the first 500 to 1000 miles (break-in period) then check the torque settings on all major engine components, particularly the cylinder heads. Tighten any bolts which may have loosened.

Chapter 2 Part B V6 engine

Refer to Chapter 13 for specifications and information applicable to later models

Contents

Specifications

Engine – general
Type .... V6 water cooled, overhead valve
Firing order 1-6-5-4-3-2

Engine availability
1975 and 1976 models
Displacement (cu in)   VIN code
231 C

1977
Displacement (cu in)
231 C
231 .... A

1978
Displacement (cu in)
196 C
231 .... A
*231 .... G
*231 3

1979
Displacement (cu in)
196 C
231 .... A
*231 3

1980
Displacement (cu in)
231 .... A
*231 3

*Turbocharged - see Chapter 2C

General engine dimensions

Engine displacement	196 and 231 cu in
Stroke (in)	3.400
Cylinder bore (diameter) (in)	3.800 (196, 3.500)
Out-of-round (in) (max)	0.0005 max
Taper (max) (in)	0.0005

Engine specifications

All dimensions given in inches

Pistons and piston rings

Piston clearance in bore (measured at skirt top)	0.0008 to 0.0020
Piston ring clearance in groove	
Top	0.003 to 0.005
2nd	0.010 to 0.020
Oil	0.0035 max
Piston ring end gap	
Top	0.010 to 0.020
2nd	0.010 to 0.020
Oil control	0.015 to 0.035
Piston pin diameter	0.9391 to 0.9394
Clearance in piston	0.0004 to 0.0007
Interference fit in rod	0.0007 to 0.0017

Crankshaft

Main journal diameters	
All (except 1975)	2.4995 (1975, 1.785)
Main bearing running clearance	
1975 thru 1978	0.0004 to 0.0015
1979 and 1980	0.0003 to 0.0018
Crankshaft endplay	0.004 to 0.008
Crankpin diameter	
1977 and 1978	2.0000
1979 and 1980	2.2495 to 2.2487
Crankpin out-of-round	0.0015 max
Rod bearing running clearance	0.0005 to 0.0026
Rod side clearance	0.006 to 0.027

Camshaft

Journal diameter	1.785 to 1.786
Journal clearance	
No 1	0.0005 to 0.0025
Nos, 2, 3, 4	0.0005 to 0.0035

Valve system

Rocker arm ratio	1.55:1
Valve lash	One turn down from zero
Valve face angle	45°
Valve seat angle	45°
Valve seat width	
(Intake)	1/32 to 1/16
(Exhaust)	1/16 to 3/32
Valve stem clearance	
(Intake)	0.0015 to 0.0032
(Exhaust)	0.0015 to 0.0032
Valve lifter diameter	0.8420 to 0.8427
Valve lifter clearance in bore	0.0008 to 0.0025

Engine lubrication

Oil pump type	Gear type driven from distributor shaft meshed to camshaft helical gear
Oil filter element	Disposable cartridge type AC PF40
Crankcase oil capacity	
Without oil filter change	4 US qts
With oil filter change	5 US qts
Crankcase vent filter – all	AC FB59
Crankcase (PCV) valve	AC CV770C

Torque specifications (all engines)

	1975 and 1976 ft-lb	1977 thru 1980 ft-lb
Cylinder head bolts	30	80
Rod bearing bolts	40	40
Main bearing bolts	115	100
Crankshaft bolts	175	175
Flywheel-to-crankshaft bolts	60	60
Intake manifold	45	45
Exhaust manifold	25	25
Spark plugs	20	20
Camshaft sprocket	22	22
Water pump	7	7
Rocker arm shaft-to-cylinder head	30	30

Rocker arm cover-to-cylinder head	4	4
Oil drain plug	30	30
Oil pump-to-block or timing cover	10	10
Torsional damper-to-crankshaft	175	175
Oil pan-to-cylinder block	15	14
Special movable timing chain dampener bolt	12	12
Oil filter	20	20
Bellhousing	35	25
Flywheel housing cover	10	10
Oil pump regulator retainer	35	35
Oil pressure switch-to-cylinder block	23	23
Thermostat housing-to-intake manifold	20	13
Automatic transmission-to-cylinder block	35	35
Distributor hold-down clamp	12	13
Fuel pump	20	20
Oil galley plugs	25	25

49 General information

Beginning in 1975, Buick began using the 231 CID V6 engine as the workhorse motor in the Century/Regal line. Made of cast iron, the 231 V6 is a 90° vee with rocker-operated overhead valves. Lubrication is by standard pump system similar to that in the V8 engines.

In 1978 and 1979, Buick also added the 196 CID V6 engine to its lineup. With the exception of the cylinder bore size, the 196 V6 is almost identical to the 231 motor.

As many of the service operations of the V6 engines are very similar to those of the V8 engines, this Chapter will deal with service specifications and procedures that are different from the V8 line. Proper notations will refer the reader back to the Chapter 2A whenever servicing requirements are similar to those outlined in Chapter 2A.

Information specific to the turbocharged V6 engines can be found in Chapter 2C.

50 Engine identification

1 The type of engine in your vehicle can be determined by consulting the Vehicle Identification Number (VIN). The fifth figure in the number code identifies the engine type. The VIN is located on the top of the dashboard and can be read through the windshield.

51 Engine – repair operations (general notes)

1 Refer to Section 2 of Part A for a listing of the operations which can be performed with the engine bolted in place, slightly raised off its mounts and completely removed.
2 This Section also contains information and guidelines to follow during engine servicing.

52 Engine – removal and installation methods and precautions

1 The method of V6 engine removal depends on the type of transmission installed. If the car is equipped with an automatic transmission, the engine should be removed by itself, leaving the transmission in place. If the car is equipped with a manual transmission, it is recommended that the transmission be removed with the engine.
2 During the removal operations, make sure that any jacks used are supplemented with axle-stands before attempting to work under the vehicle.
3 Do not smoke if fuel has been spilled and mop up fuel and oil spillages as quickly as possible.
4 If the vehicle is equipped with air conditioning, *never disconnect any of the system lines.* If the belt-driven compressor can be unbolted and moved to one side of the engine compartment to provide room to service components, this is permissible. If sufficient clearance is not obtainable then the system must be discharged by your dealer or a competent refrigeration engineer and subsequently recharged once the engine work is complete.
5 If air conditioning is fitted, avoid damage to the condenser which is mounted just ahead of the radiator.

53 Engine – removal

Note: *If the vehicle is equipped with an automatic transmission, the engine should be removed by itself. Make sure the transmission is fully supported while the engine is out of the vehicle. If the car is equipped with a manual transmission, General Motors recommends that the engine and transmission be removed together as a single unit.*
1 If the vehicle is equipped with air conditioning, the car should be driven to a dealer or air conditioning shop to have the system depressurized. The air conditioning system cannot simply be unbolted and laid aside for engine removal. Do not attempt to disconnect any of the air conditioning system while it is under pressure. Ths could result in serious physical injury as well as damage to the system.
2 Remove the hood. Scribe marks around the hood hinge and hinge bracket for ease of re-installation.
3 Disconnect the battery ground cable at the engine.
4 Drain the coolant from the engine and radiator and remove the upper radiator shroud assembly.
5 Remove the air cleaner and mark all hoses to it with tape for easier reassembly.
6 Remove the fan, fan pulleys and drivebelts.
7 Disconnect the radiator, heater and transmission cooler (if applicable) from the engine and fasten them out of the way.
8 Disconnect the fuel pump hoses and plug them to keep out dirt and prevent later fuel drainage.
9 Disconnect the vacuum supply hose from the carburetor to the vacuum manifold. If the vehicle is equipped with power brakes, disconnect the vacuum modulator and power brake vacuum hoses at the engine.
10 Disconnect the fuel vapor hoses which run to the emissions system charcoal canister. Label with tape for easy re-installation.
11 Disconnect the throttle control cable at the carburetor.
12 Disconnect the generator, oil and coolant sending unit switch connections at the engine, marking the wires with tape for ease of re-installation. Remove the generator (Chapter 5).
13 Disconnect the engine-to-body ground straps at the engine.
14 Raise the vehicle and support it firmly on jack stands.
15 Remove the starter solenoid wires and mark with tape. Disconnect the solenoid wires and cable shield (if so equipped) from the starter. Remove the starter motor/solenoid assembly (Chapter 5).
16 Disconnect the exhaust pipes from the exhaust manifolds.
17 Remove the lower flywheel (manual transmission) or converter (automatic transmission) cover.
18 *On automatic transmission cars,* remove the bolts attaching the flywheel to the converter. Scribe a chalk mark on the flywheel and the converter for ease in reassembly alignment.
19 Loosen the transmission-to-engine attaching bolts *on automatic transmission vehicles.* On manual transmission cars, disconnect the driveshaft. shaft linkage, clutch equalizer shaft, speedometer cable and transmission mount bolts. Wrap a plastic bag around the rear of the transmission to prevent fluid loss.
21 Drain the oil from the engine oil pan.
22 *On cars with automatic transmission,* lower the vehicle and support the transmission.
23 Check to make certain that wiring harnesses, vacuum hoses, etc., are disconnected from the engine and that there is enough clearance around the engine.
24 Attach a lifting device to the engine and raise the engine just

enough to take the slack out of the lifting chain. Remove the engine mount through-bolts.

25 Remove the bolts which attach the rear of the engine to the transmission bellhousing *on automatic transmission cars. On vehicles with manual transmission,* remove the transmission-to-crossmember bolts and the crossmember-to-frame bolts. Raise the transmission slightly and slide the crossmember to the rear until it can be removed.

26 *On automatic transmission vehicles,* raise the engine slightly and keep the torque converter pushed well to the rear to ensure the engagement of the converter tangs with the oil pump in the transmission. Carefully lift the engine straight up and out of the engine compartment, making sure that it does not hit the brake master cylinder, firewall, power steering pump or body nosepiece as it is removed.

27 *On manual transmission cars,* raise the engine as you lower the transmission. Do this slowly and carefully, checking clearances as you go. The engine/transmission unit will be at a steep angle to clear the engine compartment and the transmission may have to be lifted slightly so that it doesn't hit the front body nosepiece.

54 Engine installation – with transmission (manual)

1 With the transmission attached to the engine, attach the lifting device to the engine.

2 Tilt the engine/transmission unit at an angle and lower it into the engine compartment and guide the engine mounts onto the frame while raising the transmission into the proper position.

3 Install the engine mount front and rear through-bolts.

4 Install the remaining components in reverse order of removal (see previous Section).

5 Adjust the clutch as described in Chapter 8.

6 Fill the engine cooling system with proper coolant.

7 Fill the engine with the proper grade of oil.

8 Check the fluid level in the transmission and add fluid as necessary.

9 Connect the battery positive cable, followed by the negative cable. If sparks or arcing occur as the negative cable is connected to the battery, check that all electrical accessories are turned off and that wiring is properly connected to the engine and transmission.

10 See Chapter 2A for the starting-up sequence.

55 Engine installation – without transmission (automatic)

1 Position the lifting device so that the engine is sitting level.

2 Slowly lower the engine into the engine compartment until the engine and transmission are engaged and the scribe marks on the flywheel and converter are aligned. It may be necessary to raise and lower the jack supporting the transmission to fit the engine mount through-bolts into position.

3 Install the engine mount through-bolts and torque-tighten to specifications.

4 Raise the car and install the bolts attaching the transmission to the engine and tighten to torque specifications. Install the flywheel cover and torque-tighten.

5 Connect the cross-over pipe to the exhaust manifold and torque-tighten to specifications.

6 Connect the starter cables to the starter and the cable shield to the engine block.

7 Connect the fuel lines to the fuel pump.

8 Reposition the power steering pump into the pump brackets and tighten the bolts.

9 Install the fan, fan pulleys, belts and shroud assembly. Adjust the fan belt tension (Chapter 1).

10 Re-install the air cleaner and hoses using the coded tapes as a guide.

11 Fill the cooling system to the proper level (Chapter 1).

12 Fill the engine with the proper grade of oil and check the trransmission fluid level, adding fluid as necessary.

13 Re-install the hood, using the scribed marks on the hinges for alignment (Chapter 12).

14 Connect the battery positive cable, followed by the negative cable. If sparks or arcing occur as the negative cable is connected to the battery, check that all electrical accessories are turned off and that wiring is connected properly to the engine and transmission.

15 See Chapter 2A for the starting-up sequence.

56 Engine mounts – inspection and replacement

Front mount – inspection

1 Raise the engine slightly to place a slight tension on the rubber

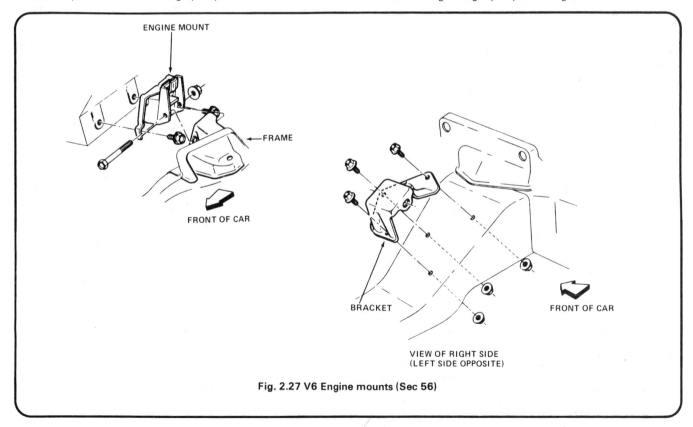

Fig. 2.27 V6 Engine mounts (Sec 56)

mount. This can be done by using a hoist (cherry picker) or with a jack and bracket placed under the forward edge of the oil pan. Inspect the mount for:
  a) Heat cracks on the hard rubber surface.
  b) Rubber separating from the metal plate at the mount.
  c) Rubber split through the center.

Rear mount – inspection

2   Raise the vehicle on a hoist and push up and down on the transmission tailshaft while observing the transmission mount. If the rubber separates from the metal plate of the mount or the tailshaft moves up and down (meaning that the mount is bottomed out), replace the mount. If there is movement between the mount's metal plate and attaching point, tighten the bolts or screws which attach the mount to the transmission or crossmember.

Front mount – replacement

3   Remove the tension on the mount by raising the engine slightly and then remove the engine mount-to-engine block bolts. Remove the engine mount through-bolt.
4   Remove the mount.
5   Install the new mount, through-bolts and nuts.
6   Install the engine mount-to-engine block bolts. Torque-tighten to specifications.

Rear mount – replacement

7   Raise the engine to relieve weight from the engine mounts.
8   Remove the bolts attaching the crossmember to the mount.
9   Remove the mount-to-transmission bolts.
10 Remove the engine mount.
11 Install the new mount on the transmission. While lowering the transmission onto the mount, align and start the crossmember-to-mount bolts. Torque-tighten bolts.

57 Engine – dismantling (general)

1   Refer to Section 10 of Chapter 2 Part A for valuable information concerning major engine servicing or overhaul.

58 Engine – major overhaul dismantling sequence

1   Refer to Section 11 of Chapter 2 Part A which gives a basic guideline to follow when dismantling an engine for overhaul.

59 Intake manifold – removal and installation

1   Disconnect the battery ground cable.
2   Drain the radiator and remove the air cleaner.
3   Disconnect the upper radiator hose and heater hose at the manifold.
4   Disconnect the accelerator linkage at the carburetor, the linkage bracket at the manifold and cruise control chain (if applicable).
5   Disconnect:
  a) The booster vacuum pipe at the manifold.
  b) Fuel line at the carburetor. Plug the line and catch any spillage.
  c) The transmission vacuum modulator line (if applicable).
  d) Idle stop solenoid (if applicable).
  e) Distributor wires. Mark each wire with pieces of tape for ease of reassembly.
  f) The temperature sending unit wire.
  g) Vacuum hoses from the distributor, TVS and EFE valvepipe at the carburetor. Mark hoses with pieces of tape for ease of reassembly.
  h) Coolant by-pass hose at the manifold.
6   Remove the distributor cap, mark the rotor position and remove the rotor to gain access to the left intake manifold "six-lobed socket" head bolt.
7   Remove the "six-lobed socket" head bolt with GM tool J-24394

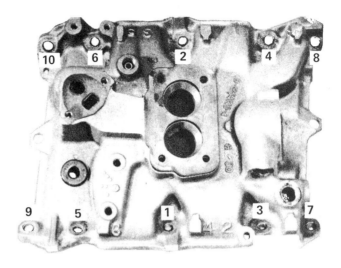

Fig. 2.28 Intake manifold bolt tightening sequence (Sec 59)

or equivalent.
8   Remove the accelerator linkage springs and compressor top bracket (if applicable).
9   Remove the remaining intake manifold bolts (there are 10).
10 Lift the intake manifold, complete with carburetor, from the engine. Do not pry on the mating edges to break the seals as this may cause damage.
11 If the intake manifold is to be replaced with a new one, transfer the following accessories:
  a) Carburetor and carburetor attaching bolts.
  b) Temperature and/or oil sending unit.
  c) Water outlet and thermostat (use a new gasket).
  d) EGR valve (use a new gasket).
  e) Heater hose and water pump hose adapter fittings.
  f) Carburetor choke assembly.
12 Before installing the manifold, cover the engine cavity with lint-free rags and clean the engine block, cylinder heads and manifold gasket surfaces. All old gasket material and sealing compound must be removed before installation. Be sure that all dirt, gasket remains, etc. are removed from the engine cavity.
13 Place the new intake manifold gasket and rubber manifold seal in position at the front and rear rails of the cylinder block. Make sure that the pointed end of the seal fits snugly against the block and head. Before installing the manifold seals, apply RTV or equivalent sealant to the ends of the seals.
14 Install the one-piece manifold gasket and carefully set the manifold in place, locating it on the engine block dowel pins.
15 Install the manifold-to-cylinder head attaching bolts. Referring to the accompanying Figure, gradually tighten the No. 1 and No. 2 bolts until snug. Install the rest of the bolts in the sequence shown. Tighten the bolts to the torque specifications.
16 Connect and/or re-install the components in the reverse order of removal.
17 Connect the battery cable.
18 Close the drain plug and refill the cooling system (Chapter 1).
19 Start the engine and check for leaks. Adjust the ignition timing and carburetor idle as necessary.

60 Exhaust manifold – removal and installation

1   Raise the vehicle and support it on stands.
2   Disconnect the battery ground cable.
3   Remove the crossover pipe and hang it from the frame with wire.
4   Remove the spark plug wires from spark plugs (mark with tape).
5   Disconnect the EFE pipe.
6   Remove the exhaust manifold bolts and the manifold.

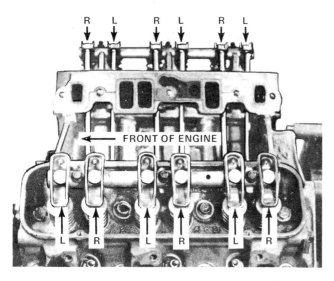

Fig. 2.29 Positioning of service rocker arms on shaft (Sec 62)

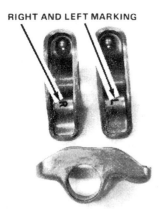

Fig. 2.30 Service rocker arm identification (Sec 62)

7   Before installing the manifold, clean all old gasket material from the mating surfaces on the cylinder head and manifold.
8   Place the new gasket into position on the cylinder head using a thin film of sealer to secure it in place.
9   Install the manifold and torque-tighten the center bolts first, then the end bolts.
10 Install the remaining components in the reverse order of removal. Use a new gasket or packing at the crossover pipe flange.
11 Start the engine and check for exhaust leaks.

61 Cylinder heads – removal

1   On vehicles equipped with AIR, disconnect the rubber hose at the injection tubing check valve. If this is done, the tubing will not have to be removed from the exhaust manifold.
2   Remove the intake manifold, referring to Section 59.
3   Drain the coolant from the engine.
4   When removing the right cylinder head:
   a) Loosen and remove all drivebelts.
   b) Tag with tape, then remove generator wires.
   c) On vehicles equipped with air conditioning, remove the compressor from the mounting bracket and position it out of the way with the hoses connected. Then remove the generator, complete with bracket.
5   When removing the left cylinder head:
   a) Remove the oil dipstick rod and tube.
   b) Remove the power steering gear pump complete with mounting bracket and move it out of the way with the hoses attached, if applicable.

6   Marking their position with pieces of tape, disconnect the wires from the spark plugs. Remove the spark plug wire clips from the rocker arm cover studs.
7   Remove exhaust manifold and bolts, referring to Section 60.
8   Carefully clean the dirt and grease from the cylinder head, valve cover and surrounding area to avoid getting grit and foreign matter into the engine. This is extremely important as dirt can damage the hydraulic valve lifters.
9   Remove the rocker arm cover attaching bolts (photo). Lift the rocker arm cover off the cylinder head. It may be necessary to break the gasket seal by striking the front of the cover with the heel of your hand or a rubber mallet. Do not pry on the sealing surfaces.
10 Whenever the pushrods, lifters or other valve mechanism components are removed, they should be kept separate and in order so that they can be re-installed in their original position. A numbered rack or piece of cardboard with holes punched in it can be used for this.
11 Remove the bolts holding the rocker arm shaft assembly to the cylinder head and lift off the assembly. Remove the pushrods and place them in the numbered rack or cardboard.
12 Loosen the cylinder head bolts a little at a time and remove. Keep track of bolt length and location.
13 Lift the cylinder head off the engine. If the head is stuck to the engine, don't try to pry it free, as this may damage the sealing surfaces. Instead, use a hammer and block of wood, tapping upwards at each end.
14 Set the cylinder head on wood blocks to prevent damage.
15 At this point, you are faced with the decision to overhaul the cylinder heads yourself or to exchange the heads for new or rebuilt units which are commonly available at GM dealers or auto parts stores. Another alternative is to take the cylinder heads complete to a competent machine shop or GM dealer for the overhaul process.
16 If the complete engine is being overhauled at the same time, it may be wise to refer to Section 38 of Part A which deals with rebuilding alternatives.
17 If it is decided to overhaul the cylinder heads, read through the following Sections to gain an undrstanding of the steps involved and the tools and replacement parts which will be necessary.

62 Rocker arm assemblies – removal and installation

1   Remove the rocker arm and shaft assembly from the cylinder head as described in Section 61.
2   Place the assembly on wood blocks on a clean surface.
3   Remove the nylon rocker arm retainers by prying them out using pliers.
4   Remove the rocker arms, clean them in a suitable solution and inspect for wear. Remove the retainer pieces from inside the rocker arm shaft.
5   Lubricating all parts with engine oil, assemble them on the rocker arm shaft. It isn't necessary to re-install the rocker arms in their original location, but they do have to go on in the proper sequence. They are stamped right (R) or left (L) to aid in their correct positioning on the rocker shaft.
6   Center each rocker on the $\frac{1}{4}$ in hole in the shaft. Install new nylon rocker arm retainers in the $\frac{1}{4}$ in holes, using a $\frac{1}{2}$ in drift.
7   Place the rocker arm assembly on the cylinder head. Re-install the bolts attaching the rocker arm assembly. Tighten all bolts to torque specifications.

63 Valves and guides– removal, service and installation

Note: *The valve mechanism for the 231 cu in V6 engine varies from most GM engines in that there is no valve lash adjustment provision. If the valve seat on the cylinder head and/or the valve face are ground, this will probably alter the height of the valve stem above the head surface. GM recommends that if the valve and seat have been refinished enough to allow the end of the valve stem to rise approximately 0.050 in above the normal position, the end of the valve stem should be ground down to bring it to its natural height.*
1   Remove the cylinder head and place on a clean surface.
2   Using a suitable spring compressor, such as GM tool J-8062, compress the valve spring and remove the valve spring cap key. Release the tool and remove the spring and cap.
3   Remove the valve seals from the valves and discard the seals.

Remove the valves and place them in numerical order in a block of wood or piece of cardboard for installation in their original location.

4   At this point in the overhaul process the cylinder head should be thoroughly cleaned and inspected for damage. Sections 16 and 17 of Part A outline these operations and should be followed for all V6 engines.

5   The valves should be inspected for signs of pitting, burned spots or poor seating. Depending on condition, they should either be reground or replaced. A valve should be discarded if re-grinding to true-up the face results in a sharp edge, as this will cause it to run hot. Correct valve face angle is 45°.

6   If the valve stem has too much clearance in its guide, it should be replaced with an oversized valve. This operation is best left to your dealer or a machine shop.

7   The valve seats should be trued-up to 45°, another job for your dealer or a machine shop.

8   After trueing, the valves can be lightly lap-ground to the seats. This is done by applying a trace of coarse carborundum paste on the seat face and using a suction cup grinding tool to lightly rotate the valve in a semi-circular motion. Lift the valve occasionally to re-distribute the paste. When a dull matte, even finish is produced, wipe off the paste and repeat the process with a fine carborundum paste. When a smooth, even ring of grey matte finish results, the process is finished. Carefully clean away any trace of grinding compound. New valves should never be lap-ground as this will destroy the plating on their surfaces.

9   Lubricate the valve stems and guides with engine oil and re-install the valves.

10 Install new intake valve seals. Do not install exhaust valve guide seals.

11 Start the valve seal carefully over the valve stem, pushing the seal down until it touches the top of the guide. Using an installation tool such as GM tool J-22509, push the seal over the valve guide until the upper inside surface of the seal touches the top of the guide. Compress the springs only enough to install the keepers, as excess compression can cause the spring retainer to damage the valve seal.

12 Install the intake and exhaust valve springs.

13 Re-install the valve spring, cap and cap retainer.

14 Install the cylinder head.

64 Cylinder heads – installation

1   Thoroughly clean off the engine block surface, making certain that no foreign material, dirt or gasket pieces have fallen into the engine cylinder bores, bolt holes or valve lifter area. Clean out the bolt holes with an air hose if available.

2   Install the new head gasket, bead side down toward the cylinder block, using the dowel pins in the block to locate and hold it in place. Be careful not to kink or damage the surface of the gasket.

3   Clean the gasket surface of the cylinder head and carefully set it in place on the engine block dowel pins.

4   Use a heavy-body thread sealer on the head bolts because they pass through the engine coolant. Make sure the torque wrench is accurate because uneven tightening can distort the cylinder bores, causing compression loss and excessive oil consumption.

5   Install the head bolts and tighten them a little at a time about three times around in the sequence shown in the accompanying figure. Give the bolts a final torque in the same sequence. Tighten to torque specifications.

6   Install the exhaust manifolds on the heads. Tighten to torque specifications.

7   Wipe the rocker arm shaft and the bosses of the cylinder head with a clean, lint-free cloth and make sure that everything is clean.

8   Remove the pushrods from their numbered rack or cardboard and install them in their proper position.

9   Locate each pushrod in its rocker arm seat by tilting the rocker arm toward the pushrod.

10 Tighten the rocker arm shaft assembly bolts a little at a time. Torque-tighten to specifications.

11 Install the spark plug wires on the rocker arm cover studs and connect the wires using the pieces of tape as a guide.

12 Install the intake manifold as described in Section 59.

13 Install all components removed during cylinder head removal and tighten all drivebelts.

14 Refill the engine with coolant, start the engine and check for leaks.

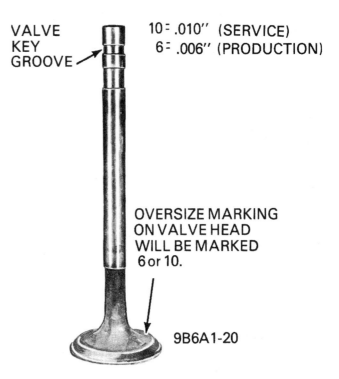

Fig. 2.31 Oversize valve identification (Sec 63)

VALVE KEY GROOVE

10 = .010'' (SERVICE)
6 = .006'' (PRODUCTION)

OVERSIZE MARKING ON VALVE HEAD WILL BE MARKED 6 or 10.

9B6A1-20

Fig. 2.32 Cylinder head bolt tightening sequence (Sec 64)

After the engine has been warmed up, recheck the cylinder head bolt torque.

15 Install the rocker arm cover and new gasket. Torque-tighten the rocker arm cover bolts to specifications.

65 Valve lifters – removal, inspection and installation

1   The valve lifters used on all V6 engines are of the hydraulic type. Information concerning the removal, inspection and installation of the valve lifters can be found in Section 20 of Part A.

66 Valve lash – adjustment

1   The valve lash on 231 cu in V6 engines cannot be adjusted due to the design of the valve mechanism. See Section 63 for more information.

67 Oil pan – removal and installation

1   Disconnect the negative battery cable.
2   Raise the car and support it firmly on jack stands.
3   Drain the engine oil into a suitable container.
4   Remove the automatic transmission flex plate lower cover.
5   Disconnect the exhaust crossover pipe at the manifolds.
6   Remove the oil pan attaching bolts and remove the oil pan.
7   Clean the pan thoroughly wth the proper solvent. Check the gasket
surfaces on the block and pan to make sure that they are clean,
smooth and free of old gasket material.
8   Apply sealer to the new oil pan gasket in several places and install
it on the pan, making certain that the bolt holes line up.
9   Install the oil pan and pan bolts. Torque-tighten the bolts to
specifications.

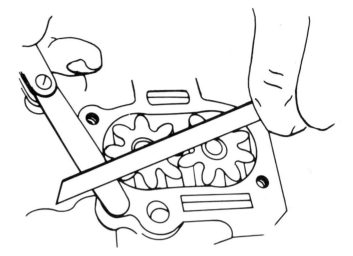

Fig. 2.33 Checking oil pump end clearance (Sec 68)

68 Oil pump – removal, dismantling and inspection

1   Unscrew and remove the oil filter.
2   Remove the screws attaching the oil pump cover assembly to the
timing chain cover. Remove the cover assembly and slide out the oil
pump gear.
3   Wash off the gears with a proper solution and inspect for wear,
scoring etc. Replace any unserviceable gears with new ones.
4   Unscrew the oil pressure relief valve cap, spring and valve. Do not
remove the oil filter by-pass valve and spring as they are staked in
place.
5   Wash the parts thoroughly in the proper solvent and inspect the
relief valve for wear and scoring. Check to make sure that the relief
valve spring is not collapsed or worn on its side. Any relief valve spring
which is questionable should be replaced with a new one.
6   Check the relief valve in its bore in the cover. It should be an easy
slip-fit only, and any side shake which can be felt is too much. The
valve and/or cover should be replaced with a new one in this case.
7   The filter by-pass valve should be flat and free of nicks, cracks or
warping and scratches.

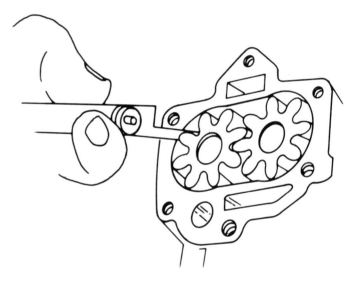

Fig. 2.34 Measuring oil pump side clearance (Sec 68)

69 Oil pump – installation

1   Lubricate the pressure relief valve and spring and install it in the
bore of the oil pump case. Install the cap and gasket and torque-
tighten to specifications.
2   Insert the oil pump gear and shaft into the oil pump body section
of the timing chain cover to check the gear end clearance and side
clearance as follows:

    a)   *Place a straightedge over the gears and measure the*
    clearance between the straightedge and gasket surface. This
    will be the end clearance and should be between 0.002 and
    0.006 in. If less than 0.002, measure the gears and pocket to
    determine which is out of specification.

    b)   *Check the oil pump side clearance. Clearance should be*
    between 0.0025 and 0.0050 in. If clearance is greater than
    0.0050, measure the gears and pocket to determine which is
    out of specifications.

    c)   *Place a straightedge across the oil pump cover face to check*
    for flatness. Insert a feeler gauge between the straightedge
    and the pump cover. Replace the cover with a new one if the
    clearance is 0.001 in or more.

3   If all clearances are satisfactory, remove the gears and pack the
pocket full of petroleum jelly. Do not use chassis lube.
4   Re-install the gears, making sure that petroleum jelly is forced into
every cavity of the gear pocket and between the teeth of the gears. The
pump may not prime itself when the engine is started if the pump is
not packed with the petroleum jelly.
5   Install the pump cover assembly screws and tighten them alternately and evenly. Torque-tighten to specifications.
6   Install oil filter and check oil level with the dipstick. Pay close
attention to the oil pressure gauge or warning light during the initial
start-up and driving period. Shut off the engine and inspect all work if
a lack of oil pressure is indicated.

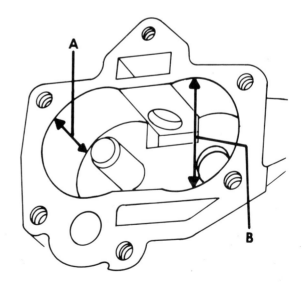

Fig. 2.35 Measuring the gear pocket for wear (A = 0.8697 to
0.8677 in; B = 1.674 to 1.671 in) (Sec 68)

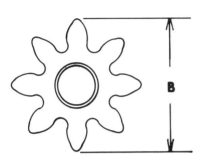

Fig. 2.36 Measuring gears for wear (A = 0.8735 to 0.8720 in; B = 1.666 to 1.664 in) (Sec 68)

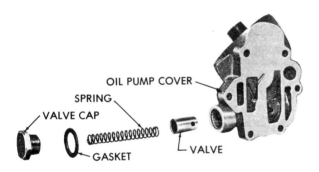

Fig. 2.37 Oil pump cover and pressure relief valve components (Sec 68)

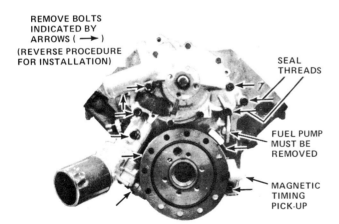

Fig. 2.38 Timing chain cover removal and installation (Sec 72)

70 Oil pump pipe and screen assembly – removal and installation

1   Remove the oil pan (Section 67).
2   Remove the bolts attaching the oil pump pipe and screen assembly to the cylinder block.
3   Clean the screen and housing thoroughly in the proper solvent solution. Blow dry with compressed air if possible.
4   Check to make sure that the oil pump flange gasket surface is smooth and free of dirt and old gasket material.
5   Install the old pipe pickup assembly using a new gasket and tighten the bolts to specifications.
6   Install the oil pan and tighten the bolts to specifications.

71 Torsional damper – removal and installation

1   The torsional damper on V6 engines is basically the same as on V8 engines. Refer to Section 26 of Chapter 2 Part 2A for the removal and installation procedures; however be sure to use the torque specifications given for V6.

72 Timing chain cover – removal and installation

1   Drain the radiator.
2   Disconnect the upper and lower radiator hoses and heater return hose at the water pump.
3   Remove the fan, fan pulleys and belts.
4   Disconnect the fuel lines, plug them and remove the fuel pump.
5   Remove the generator and brackets.
6   Remove the distributor. If the timing chain and sprockets are not going to be disturbed, mark the position of the distributor rotor so that it can be re-installed in the same position.
7   Loosen the front clamp on the thermostat by-pass hose and slide it rearward.
8   Remove the harmonic balancer (torsional damper) bolt and washer and remove the harmonic balancer (Section 71).
9   Remove the bolts attaching the timing chain cover to the cylinder block.
10   Remove the two bolts which attach the oil pan to the timing chain cover.
11   Remove the timing chain cover.
12   Thoroughly clean the timing chain cover, making sure that all old gasket material is removed and that the surface is not damaged.
13   Before re-installing, remove the oil pump cover and pack petroleum jelly around the oil pump gears so that there is no air space left inside the pump. If this is not done, the pump may "lose its prime" and not begin pumping oil immediately when the engine is started.
14   Re-install the pump cover, using a new gasket. Torque bolts to specifications.
15   Make sure that the gasket surface of the block and timing chain cover are smooth and clean and install a new gasket on the cover.
16   Lubricate the harmonic balancer shaft where it will go through the timing chain cover seal so that the seal will not be damaged when the engine is first started.
17   Using the dowel pins on the block, engage the dowel holes in the cover and position the cover against the block.
18   Apply sealer to the bolt threads and tighten the bolts to specifications.
19   Install the harmonic balancer, bolt and washer. Use a screwdriver or other such tool to lock the flex plate or flywheel starter teeth and torque-tighten the harmonic balancer bolt to specifications.

73 Timing chain and sprockets – removal and installation

1   Remove the timing chain cover.
2   Temporarily install the harmonic balancer bolt and washer in the end of the crankshaft.
3   Turn the crankshaft so that the sprocket timing marks are positioned toward each other. Remove the harmonic bolt and washer without changing the position of the sprockets; a sharp tap on the wrench handle will accomplish this.
4   Remove the front crankshaft oil slinger.

5   Remove the camshaft sprocket bolts.
6   Remove the oil pan.
7   Use 2 large screwdrivers to carefully pry first the camshaft sprocket, then the crankshaft sprocket forward alternately until the camshaft sprocket is free. Remove the camshaft sprocket and chain and complete working the crankshaft sprocket off the crankshaft.
8   If the chain is not stretched and parts are to be re-used, clean the timing chain, sprockets and crankshaft oil slinger thoroughly in the proper solvent.
9   *If the engine was not rotated* while the chain and sprockets were off, install the sprockets and chain with the timing marks perfectly in-line; exactly as they were on removal. Then proceed to step 13.
10   *If the engine was rotated*, temporarily install the sprockets and turn the crankshaft until the number one piston is at Top Dead Center and the camshaft O mark is straight down and on the centerline of both shafts.
11   Remove the sprockets and assemble the timing chain on both sprockets. slide the chain assembly onto the shafts with the 'O' marks together and in line with the sprocket hubs.
12   Assemble the oil slinger on the crankshaft with the inside diameter against the sprocket (concave side toward the front of the engine).
13   Install the camshaft sprocket bolts. Torque-tighten to specifications.
14   Install the oil pan using a new gasket.
15   Install the timing chain cover.

74 Crankshaft front oil seal – replacement

1   Remove the timing chain cover (see Section 72).
2   Using a punch, drive out the old oil seal and shedder. Drive from the front toward the rear of the timing chain cover.
3   Coil the new oil seal packing around the opening so that the ends of the packing are at the top. Drive in the new shedder, using a punch. In at least 3 places, stake the shedder in place with the punch.
4   By rotating the handle of a hammer or equivalent tool, size the packing until the balancer hub can be inserted through the opening.
5   Re-install the timing chain cover.

75 Camshaft – removal and installation

1   Drain the cooling system.
2   Remove the radiator, fan, pulleys, belts and water pump.
3   If the vehicle is equipped with air conditioning, unbolt the condensor and position it out of the way. If it is necessary to disconnect any hoses, have the system discharged by your dealer or qualified specialist.
4   Remove the grille. Refer to Chapter 12.
5   Remove the intake manifold, referring to Section 59.
6   Remove the rocker arm covers, rocker arm and shaft assemblies, pushrods and valve lifters referring to the appropriate Sections.
7   Remove the fuel pump and distributor. Plug the fuel lines to prevent drainage.
8   Remove the harmonic balancer (torsional damper), timing chain cover, timing chain and sprockets, referring to the proper Sections. Align the timing marks on the sprockets before removal to avoid burring of the camshaft journals by the crankshaft during removal.
9   Keeping them in the proper order for re-installation, remove the valve lifters (Section 65).
10   Slide the camshaft forward, out of the bearing bores. Be extremely careful during this operation to avoid damaging the bearings and bearing surfaces.
11   Lubricate the camshaft lobes with heavy oil to ease re-installation.
12   After making sure that the camshaft timing marks are aligned, re-install, in reverse order, all of the components which were removed, using new gaskets. Refer to the appropriate Sections on the installation of the timing chain and sprockets and timing chain cover.

76 Pistons, connecting rods and bearings – removal

1   Refer to Section 32 of Part A for this procedure.

77 Manual transmission flywheel – removal and installation

1   Remove the transmission and clutch. Refer to Chapters 7 and 8. Mark the clutch cover and flywheel so that the clutch can be re-installed in the original position.
2   Remove the bolts holding the flywheel to the crankshaft flange. Remove the flywheel. The bolt holes in the flywheel are unevenly spaced so that the flywheel will always be installed in the correct position.
3   When re-installing the flywheel, make sure that the crankshaft flange is free of burrs which could cause run-out and vibration. Torque the bolts to the proper specifications.

78 Automatic transmission flex plate – removal, inspection and installation

1   Remove the transmission. Refer to Chapter 7.
2   Remove the 6 bolts attaching the flywheel to the crankshaft flange. The bolt holes are spaced unevenly so that the flex plate will always be installed in the correct position.
3   Inspect the flex plate and if it is cracked, replace it with a new one.
4   Inspect the crankshaft flange and flex plate for burrs. Any burrs or nicks should be removed with a mill file.
5   Install the flex plate and torque tighten the bolts to proper specifications.
6   By mounting a dial indicator on the engine block, flex plate run-out can be checked at 3 attaching bosses. Crankshaft end play should be held in one direction during the check and flex plate run-out should not exceed .015-in.
7   If run-out is in excess of .015-in, tap the high side of the flex plate with a mallet or similar tool to correct. If this doesn't correct the condition, remove the flex plate and check the flywheel flange for burrs.

79 Crankshaft, main bearings and oil seals – removal

1   The procedures to follow for all V6 engines are quite similar to those found in Section 35 of Part A. Refer to Section 35 for procedures and illustrations.

80 Cylinder block – inspection

1   The cylinder block must be stripped of all parts and thoroughly cleaned and inspected to determine if it is within specifications. Rebuilding an engine when the block is out of tolerance is a waste of time and money.
2   Visually inspect the cylinder block for cracks in the bores, water jackets, lifter bores and main bearing webs. In most cases, cracks will require replacement of the block.
3   Examine the cylinder bores for taper, out of round, scoring and scratches. If the bores are in good condition, honing should be all that is necessary. Deep scratches or scoring will require reboring and the fitting of oversized pistons. Honing and reboring should be left to your dealer or a machine shop because of the special equipment required.
4   Bore taper can be determined by measuring the bore with an internal-type gauge at the top, middle and bottom. The degree of taper will be revealed by the differences in measurements from the top to bottom of the bore.
5   Out-of-round can be found in the same manner, except that the bore should be measured parallel with the engine centerline and then at a point 180 degrees from the first measurement.
6   If the cylinder bores are worn beyond specifications the block will have to be replaced, honed or bored. Blue smoke from the tailpipe and excessive ridging of the cylinder bores is an indication of a worn block.
7   A warped block can be determined by using a straight-edge and dial indicator as described in Section 17 of Part 2A.

81 Engine – rebuilding alternatives

1   Refer to Section 38 of Part A for valuable information concerning the overhaul possibilities available to the home mechanic.

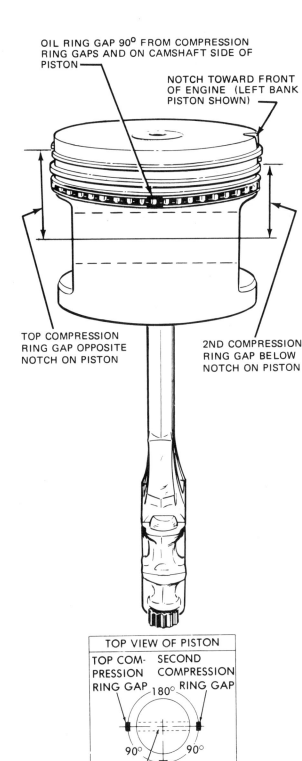

OIL RING GAP 90° FROM COMPRESSION RING GAPS AND ON CAMSHAFT SIDE OF PISTON

NOTCH TOWARD FRONT OF ENGINE (LEFT BANK PISTON SHOWN)

TOP COMPRESSION RING GAP OPPOSITE NOTCH ON PISTON

2ND COMPRESSION RING GAP BELOW NOTCH ON PISTON

TOP VIEW OF PISTON

TOP COM-PRESSION RING GAP

SECOND COMPRESSION RING GAP

180°

90°   90°

PISTON PIN   OIL RING GAP

CAMSHAFT

Fig. 2.39 Piston ring gap positioning (Sec 84)

82 Crankshaft and bearings – inspection and servicing

1   Refer to Section 39 of Part A for these procedures; however make sure that all the clearance specifications are taken from the V6 specifications tables.

83 Piston and connecting rod assemblies – cleaning and inspection

1   Refer to Section 40 of Part A for these procedures.

84 Piston and piston rings – assembly

1   Refer to Section 41 of Part A for this procedure; however, position the pistons rings as shown in the accompanying figure.

85 Engine assembly – general information

1   Refer to Section 42 of Part A.

86 Main bearings and rod bearings – checking clearances

1   Refer to Section 43 of Part A; however, use the specifications listed for V6 engines.

87 Connecting rod side clearance – checking

1   Refer to Section 44 of Part A; however, use the clearance listed in Specifications for V6 engines.

88 Crankshaft, main bearings and oil seals – installation

1   Refer to Section 45 of Part A; however use the specifications listed for V6 engines. Follow the steps outlined in Section 93 for installing the braided fabric oil seal.

89 Pistons, connecting rods and bearings – installation

1   Refer to Section 46 of Part A.

90 Engine – final assembling and pre-oiling

1   Refer to Section 47 of Part A; however, disregard the valve lash adjustment step as this cannot be accomplished on the 231 engine.

91 Engine start-up after major repair or overhaul

1   Refer to Section 48 of Part A.

92 Rear main bearing upper oil seal – repair

1   Although the crankshaft must be removed to install a new braided fabric seal, the existing upper seal can be repaired with the crankshaft in place.
2   Remove the oil pan (Section 67).
3   Using GM tool J21526-2, drive the old seal gently back into its groove, packing it tight. It will pack in to a depth of $\frac{1}{4}$-in to $\frac{3}{4}$-in.
4   Repeat the procedure on the other end of the seal.
5   Measure the amount that the seal was driven up in the groove on one side and add $\frac{1}{16}$-in. Remove the old seal from the main bearing cap. Use the main bearing cap as a fixture and cut off a piece of the old seal to the predetermined length. Repeat this process for the other side.
6   Install GM tool J-21526-1 onto the cylinder block.

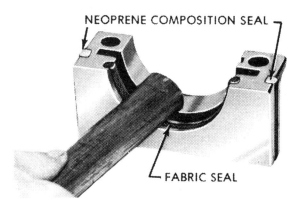

Fig. 2.40 Installing rear main bearing oil seal (Sec 93)

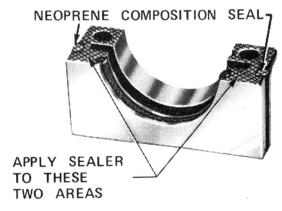

Fig. 2.41 Sealer applied to split line (Sec 93)

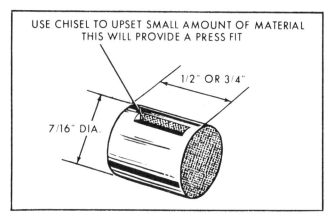

Fig. 2.42 Harmonic balancer weight (Sec 94)

7   Using the packing tool (J-21526-2), work the short pieces of previously cut seal into the guide tool (J-21526-1) and pack them into the cylinder block groove. The guide and packing tools have been machined to provide a built-in stop. Repeat this procedure on both sides. Using oil on the pieces of packing will ease installation.
8   Remove the guide tool.
9   Install a new seal in the main bearing cap and install the cap.
10   Torque tighten to specifications.
11   Install the oil pan.

93   Rear main bearing oil seal – replacement

1   Braided fabric seals pressed into grooves formed in the crankcase and rear bearing cap are used to seal against oil leakage around the crankshaft. The crankshaft must be removed for this operation.
2   Remove the oil pan (Section 67).
3   Remove the bearing caps and the crankshaft.
4   Remove the old oil seal and place a new seal in the groove with both ends projecting above the parting surface of the cap.
5   Use a handle of a hammer or similar tool to force the seal into the groove by rubbing down until the seal projects above the groove not more than $\frac{1}{16}$-in. Cut the ends of the seal flush with the surface of the cap with a single-edged razor blade.
6   Soak the neoprene seals which go into the grooves in the sides of the bearing cap in kerosene for 1 to 2 minutes.
7   Install the neoprene seals in the groove between the bearing cap and the crankcase. The seals are slightly undersize and swell in the presence of heat and oil. They are slightly longer than the groove in the bearing cap and must not be cut to fit.
8   Apply a small amount of RTV sealer at the joint where the bearing cap meets the crankcase to help eliminate oil leakage. A very thin coat is all that is necessary.
9   Install the bearing cap in the crankcase. Force the seals up into the bearing cap with a blunt instrument to be sure of a good seal at the upper parting line between the cap and case.
10   Install oil pan and torque-tighten bolts to specifications.

94   Harmonic balancer – balancing procedure

1   The harmonic balancer can be checked for vibration and balanced to eliminate any vibration.
2   Determine the engine speed at which a vibration occurs by using a tachometer.
3   Place a small amount of body putty or similar material on the inside surface of the fan driving pulley. Run the engine at the speed during which the vibration occurred and note if it persists.
4   Use varying amounts of putty and repeat the procedure until the vibration is decreased.
5   When the vibration is considerably decreased or eliminated, mark the hole drilled in the balancer which is nearest to the putty.
6   Cut a piece of $\frac{7}{16}$-in iron rod to approximately a $\frac{1}{2}$-in length. Using a chisel, upset a small amount of material on the side of the rod piece (see accompanying Figure).
7   Install the rod piece in the previously marked hole.
8   If necessary, install additional pieces of rod in the balancer until the vibration is gone.

95   Automatic transmission flex plate – balacncing procedures

1   Manual transmission flywheels are balanced at the factory and no attempt should be made to balance them. The automatic transmission flex plate can be balanced by use of balance clips available from the dealer parts department.
2   If the flex plate is found to be out of balance:
3   Raise the car and remove the lower flex plate cover. Mark the flex plate at 4 locations 90° apart.
4   Install one clip at one of the mcarked locations. With the transmission in 'Neutral', run the engine and note any vibratcion.
5   If the vibration increases, remove the clip and relocate it 180° from its original location.
6   If the vibration decreases, install another clip next to the original one.
7   If no change is noted in the vibration, movce the clip 90° and run the engine again.
8   Repeat this procedure until a reduction in the vibration is noted. By mcoving the clips in small increments, fine adjustments can be made until the vibration is gone.
9   Make sure that the tangs on the clips are properly set in the flex plate so that they will not shift at high speeds.

Chapter 2 Part C Turbocharger

Refer to Chapter 13 for specifications and information applicable to later models

Contents

Specifications

	ft-lb	Nm
Exhaust outlet pipe-to-elbow assembly	14	19
Elbow assembly-to-compressor housing	15	19.5
Exhaust inlet pipe-to-turbine housing	14	19
Exhaust inlet pipe-to-right manifold	14	19
Oil feed pipe-to-fitting (both ends)	13	17
Oil feed pipe fitting-to-CHRA	7	10
CHRA-to-turbine housing	15	19.5
CHRA backplate-to-compressor housing	13	17.5
Compressor housing-to-plenum	20	27
Compressor housing-to-intake manifold	35	47
Oil drain-to-CHRA	15	20
EGR valve-to-EGR manifold	15	20
EGR valve manifold-to-intake manifold	15	20
EGR valve manifold-to-plenum	15	20
ESC detonation sensor-to-intake manifold	14	19
Carburetor-to-plenum	21	28
Plenum front bracket-to-intake manifold	20	27
Plenum front bracket-to-plenum	21	28
TVBV/PECV-to-intake manifold	25	34
Turbine housing bracket-to-intake manifold	20	27
Turbine housing bracket-to-turbine housing	18	24
Power brake vacuum line-to-plenum	10	14
Plenum side support bracket-to-plenum	21	28
Linkage bracket-to-plenum	20	27
Fuel line-to-carburetor	20	27

1 Turbocharger – general information

Turbocharging offers a way of raising the horsepower and torque output of an engine without the power-robbing belts, drives, and gears of a supercharger. The turbocharger, a snail-shaped device that mounts on the 231 V6 engine between the carburetor and the exhaust manifold, is capable of increasing horsepower by approximately 35% and torque by about 25%. This increase in power is not constant, however. The unit works on an as needed basis.

An Electronic Spark Control (ESC) computer controls exactly when the turbocharger works and when it doesn't. This unit senses engine rpms (through a pickup in the HEI distributor) and engine detonation (via a detonation sensor on the manifold). When the unit determines that additional power is needed, it sends a signal to the turbo and additional boost is gained. When boost is not required, the control center makes sure that the engine remains normally aspirated.

The turbocharger is made up of two turbine wheels mounted to a common shaft. Each wheel is enclosed by a shroud which directs air flow. One shroud connects to the exhaust manifold. This is the turbine unit. The other shroud is linked to the carburetor and the intake manifold. This unit is the compressor. The units work as follows:

Compression of fuel and air in the combustion chamber of an engine is not just a mechanical action of the piston; when fuel/air mixtures are compressed, they gain heat and pressure due to the heat gain. When this pressurized gas is routed through a small exhaust port and down a narrow exhaust pipe, it gains velocity. Directing this pressurized exhaust into the turbine unit provides power for the turbine. The snail-shaped shroud (housing) keeps the gases tightly compressed but allows them to expand and cool as they leave the chamber. The change in heat and velocity is what powers the turbine wheel.

The compressor wheel is driven by the turbine. Fuel and air are compressed as they enter the unit. A charge of compressed gases exits the compressor and enters each cylinder where it produces more power.

Turbine speeds can reach upwards of 50 000 rpm during normal operation of the engine. Since engine speed determines both the speed of the turbine and the size of the charge, it is necessary that the turbocharging system has some built-in safety devices to prevent damage to the motor and the turbo. A wastegate is installed to control speed and pressure in the turbine.

The open wastegate allows escaping exhaust gas to by-pass the turbine. This has the effect of slowing the turbine and compressor wheels.

2   Turbocharger – IMPORTANT CAUTIONS

Note: *Because of the critical nature of the working conditions required for repairs to be effectively performed on the turbocharger, it is recommended that such repairs be left to a Buick dealer or other qualified repair shop.*
1   *Driven by superheated exhaust gases and routinely operating at extremely high temperatures, the turbocharger castings retain engine heat for a very long time.* **Caution:** *It is very important to let the car engine cool for a period of at least three hours after the engine has been run. Even then, it is prudent to wear heavy gloves when handling the turbo unit to prevent serious burns.*
2   The high-speed operation of the turbo dictates that bearing life is dependent upon a constant flow of clean engine oil. Careful attention should always be paid to the condition of the oil lines and to the tightness of their fittings. Overtightening will cause deformation and will lead to leaks.
3   Always change the engine oil and filter after any time that the turbo unit is removed.
4   When dismantling the turbo, take care that no bearings, washers, nuts or screws fall into the turbine. In a unit that operates at speeds up to 50 000 rpms, even a small amount of grit entering the turbo can cause severe damage to both the turbo and the engine. If an object is suspected of falling into the turbine or one of the passageways, flush the object out. After all servicing is done on the unit, flush all passageways out with clean oil. The best defense against dirt, is to work on the turbo only after the engine has been steam cleaned.
5   Cover all inlets and pipes while the unit is dismantled. Account for every nut screw, bolt and washer before and after the unit is reassembled. Don't try to rush your repair work. This will only lead to mistakes that could be very costly.
6   Be exceptionally careful when dismantling the turbocharger. Take special care not to bend, scratch or nick the compressor or turbine wheels. Even minor scratches on the blades can result in an imbalance that will result in failure of the unit.
7   Before disassembly of the turbocharger, scribe the center housing rotating assembly where it bolts up to the compressor and the turbine. The unit should be reassembled in the same basic position that it was in before disassembly.
8   If any sealer is found at any point in turbo disassembly (between the center housing rotating assembly backplate and the compressor housing, for example), it should be replaced when the unit is put back together.

3   Detonation sensor – removal and installation

Note: *Read Section 2 before proceeding.*
1   The detonation sensor is a very sensitive device. Do NOT use an impact wrench on it. Do NOT overtorque it. Never apply any side pressure to the sensor. Use a deep socket for removing the sensor.
2   Squeeze the sides of the connector where it joins the sensor and gently pull straight up on the connector. Don't pull on the wire. Use a socket and remove the unit.
3   When installing the new sensor, take special care not to bang or drop the unit. Use a deep socket to install the sensor and tighten it to the specified torque.

4   Electronic spark control – testing

Note: *Read Section 2 before proceeding.*
1   As mentioned in the general description, the Electronic Spark Control (ESC) monitors engine rpm and detonation and controls the

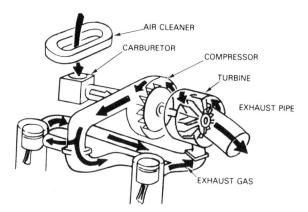

Fig. 2.43 Principle of operation for the turbocharger

function of the turbo through these readings.

Poor Engine Performance And Detonation
2   If the car suffers from poor engine performance or detonation and you suspect the turbo and its control unit, the following test procedure will isolate the problem.
3   First, check the engine coolant for proper level and correct mixture. Inspect all vacuum hoses for leaks, cracks, and proper connections.
4   Check the engine's initial timing and compare it with the specification sticker under the hood. Make sure that you reconnect the vacuum advance hose after completing the timing check.
5   Inspect the detonation sensor wire. Make sure it is properly affixed to the sensor. Make sure that the wire does not touch or is routed close to the spark plug wires and the distributor.
6   Check detonation sensor for proper installation.
7   Turn on the ignition switch. Using a voltmeter, check the light blue wire and the black wire across the ESC relay. On 1980 models, take the reading from terminals F and K at the ESC unit for voltage. Look at the illustration of the ESC controller to find the exact locations of the wires. The controller is located inside the passenger compartment.
8   On 1978 and 1979 models, the ESC relay must be replaced if there is no voltage. On the 1980 model, the open circuit between terminal F on the 10-pin connector and the ignition switch must be repaired if there is under 7.0 volts.
9   Start the engine and let it run until the radiator top is warm. Make sure that the air conditioner is turned off.
10 Hook up a tachometer and timing light; set the fast idle cam on "high step". Engine rpms must be above 1800 rpm to continue with the test.
11 Take a short steel rod (a small wrench or a socket extension will do) and tap the intake manifold in the area of the detonation sensor with medium to heavy taps. Do this fairly rapidly and do NOT tap the sensor unit.
12 Watch the tachometer while tapping. Engine rpms should drop at least 200 to 500 rpm. Timing should also retard by about 20°. Stop tapping. Rpms should return to the fast idle setting within about 20 seconds. If they do, proceed to step 15.
13 If engine revs do not drop off, check the connection from the detonation sensor to the turbo control center. Again, check the installation of the sensor. It should be firmly bolted into place. If it is not, tighten it to the specified torque.
14 Disconnect the detonation sensor connector at the firewall and connect an ohmmeter to the sensor side of the connector. Connect the ohmmeter positive lead to the terminal attached to the center conductor of the sensor lead. Connect the negative lead to a ground. If resistance is not 175 to 375 ohms, replace the detonation sensor with a new one. If the problem remains after the detonation sensor is replaced, unplug the 10-pin connector from the ESC controller. Connect a jumper wire between pins A and B in the harness side of the connector. Unplug the detonation sensor wiring harness connector at the firewall and check for continuity between the terminals of the connector (main harness side). If no continuity exists, repair or replace the wires between the firewall connector and the ESC connector. If continuity does exist, repair or replace the wires between the sensor

and the firewall connector. If the problem still persists, the ESC controller is defective and must be replaced with a new one.

15 If engine rpm dropped back to the fast idle setting in Step 12, disconnect the 4-wire connector that runs from the ESC unit to the distributor.

16 Take a jumper wire and connect pin number 4 to socket number 2 on the connector that is on the distributor side of the harness. (On 1980 models, jump-wire pin A and pin C on the distributor side of the harness).

17 Unhook the connector from the distributor cap and connect the 3-way connector from GM tool J-24642 ignition tester (or a suitable commercial ignition tester) to the HEI module wiring harness. Connect the tester's ground clip to a suitable ground.

18 Connect the battery clip of the tester to the battery negative terminal and connect the red battery clip to the positive battery terminal.

19 Next, take a voltmeter and connect it to the two-way connector (it is on the outside of the distributor). Hook the voltmeter's negative wire to the brown lead and its positive wire to the red wire. Set the voltmeter at 10 volts or at the setting closest to 10 volts and turn on the ignition. The voltmeter should read zero volts.

20 Press the test button and hold it down. The voltmeter should still read zero. If you get a voltage reading, the HEI module is malfunctioning and should be replaced.

21 Disconnect the voltmeter and crank the motor. Hold down the test button while the engine is cranking. A red light should come on momentarily and be followed by a constant green light. If the red light stays on and is not followed by a green light. take the distributor to an authorized GM service center.

22 After the distributor has been checked and repaired (if necessary), remove the jumper and tester and reconnect the ESC unit.

Engine turns over but will not start (1978 and 1979 models)

23 Steps 3 and 4 of this section must be performed before continuing with this sub-section.

24 Check for spark at the spark plug.

25 If there is no spark at the plug, take a voltmeter and hook it up between the light blue wire and the black wire (across the ESC relay).

26 If there is voltage, it means that the ESC relay is faulty and needs replacement. If there is no voltage, turn on the ignition and hook a volt meter between the battery terminal on the distributor, and ground.

27 Note the reading on the meter. If it is under 7.0 volts, the problem is not in the ESC unit. You probably have a short circuit between the battery terminal on the distributor and the ignition switch.

28 Install a voltmeter between terminal A on the engine harness side of the two-wire connector from the ESC box to engine wiring harness. If the reading is under 7.0 volts, check for a short between terminal A and the ignition switch.

29 If the meter reads 7.0 volts or higher, disconnect the 4-pin connector that hooks up the ESC unit and the distributor. Jump wire socket number 2 to pin number 4 on the distributor side of the connector. Turn over the engine and check for spark at the spark plug. If there is spark at the plug, the ESC controller is defective and should be replaced.

30 If there is no spark, check the distributor as outlined in Steps 16 through 22 in this Section.

Engine turns over but will not start (1980 models)

31 Do the service tests outlined in Steps 3 and 4 of this Section.

32 See if the number 2 spark plug is getting spark at the electrode. If the spark plug is operating correctly, check under the troubleshooting section of this manual for other causes of the problem.

33 If there is no spark at the plug, check to see that the 10-pin connector at the ESC box has a good connection. The ESC box is located under the dashboard.

34 Attach a voltmeter from the F pin to the K pin on the connector at the ESC box. If the voltage is under 7.0 volts, there is a short circuit between the F terminal and the ignition. If the problem persists once the short has been repaired, go on to the next step.

35 If the voltage is 7.0 volts or over (or if Step 34 didn't solve the problem), disconnect the 4-pin connector that runs to the distributor

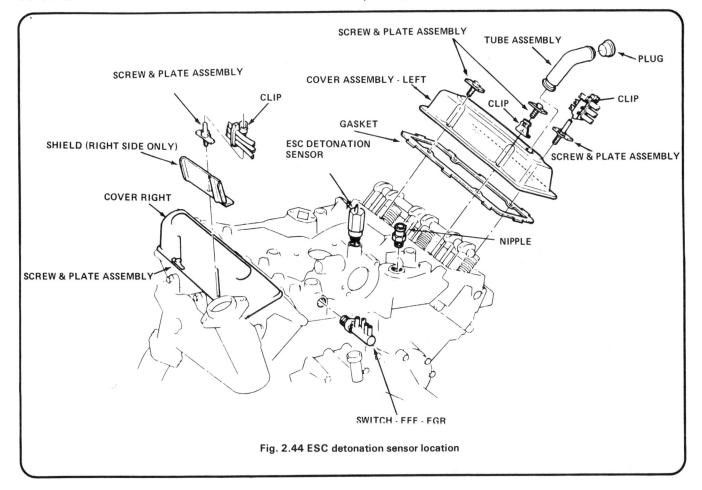

Fig. 2.44 ESC detonation sensor location

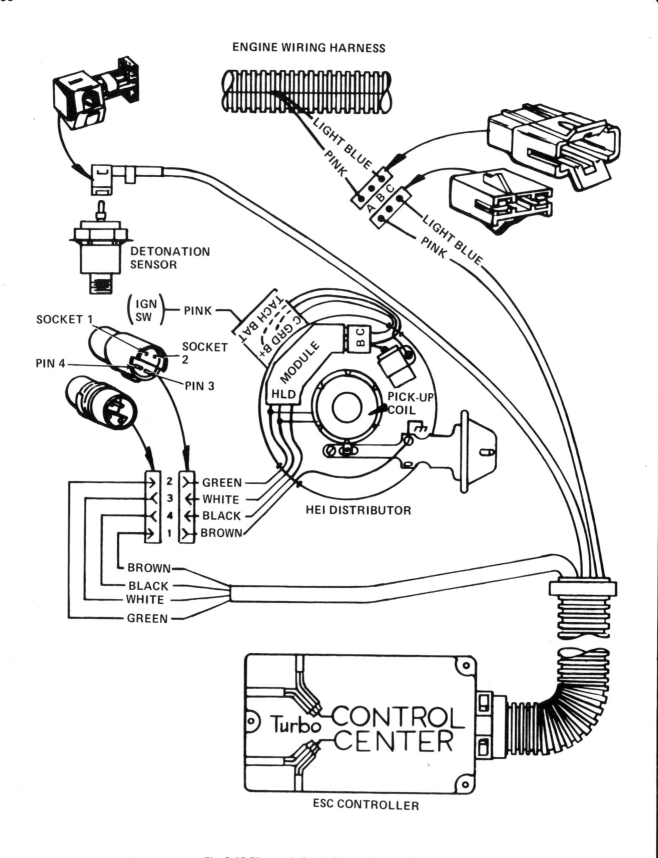

ENGINE WIRING HARNESS

LIGHT BLUE

PINK

LIGHT BLUE

PINK

DETONATION
SENSOR

IGN
SW

PINK

SOCKET 1

SOCKET
2

PIN 4

PIN 3

TACH BAT

C GRD B+

MODULE

B C

HLD

PICK-UP
COIL

2 GREEN
3 WHITE
4 BLACK
1 BROWN

HEI DISTRIBUTOR

BROWN
BLACK
WHITE
GREEN

Turbo CONTROL
CENTER

ESC CONTROLLER

Fig. 2.45 Electronic Spark Control System (1978 and 79)

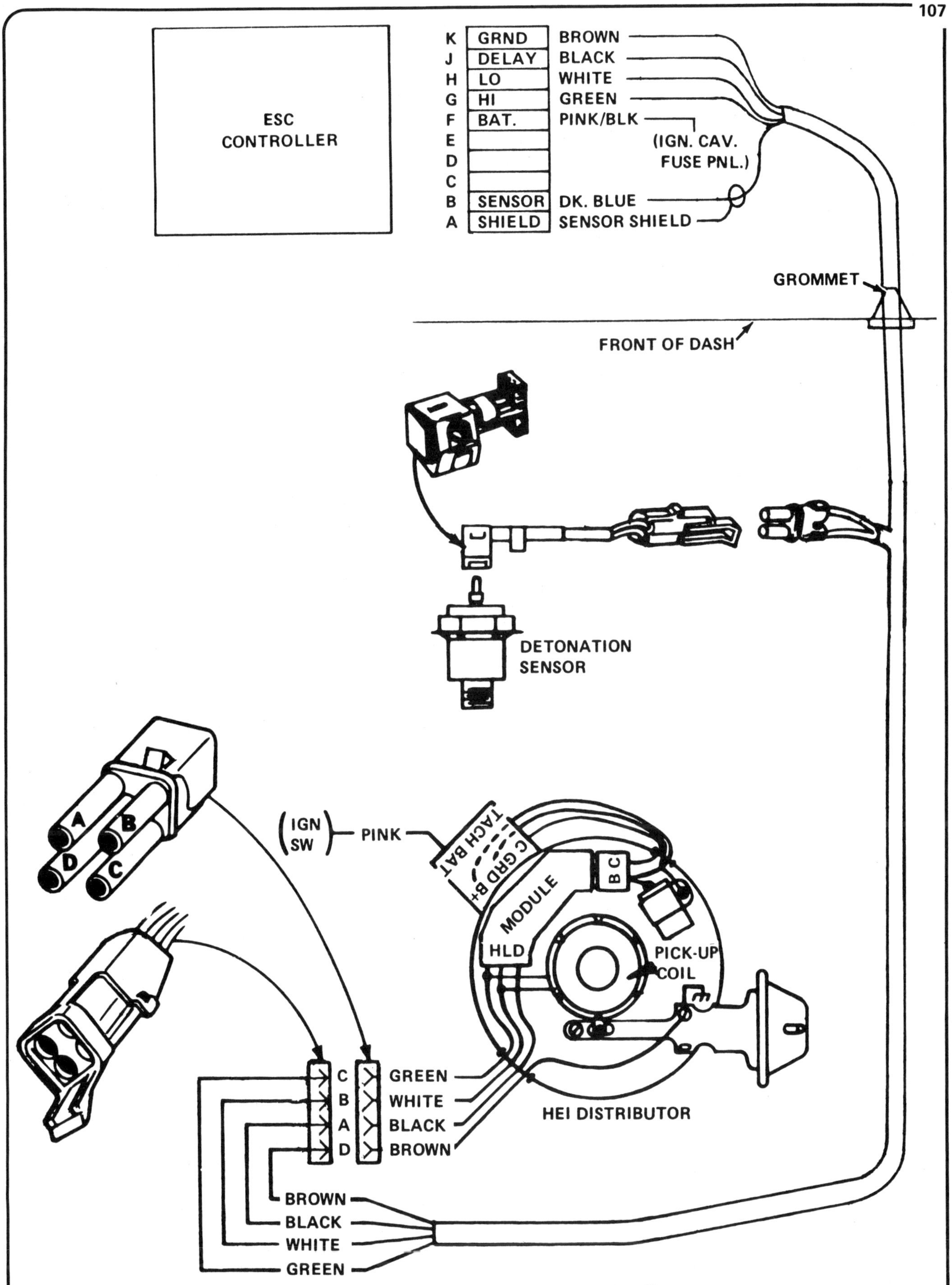

ESC
CONTROLLER

K	GRND	BROWN
J	DELAY	BLACK
H	LO	WHITE
G	HI	GREEN
F	BAT.	PINK/BLK
E		
D		
C		
B	SENSOR	DK. BLUE
A	SHIELD	SENSOR SHIELD

(IGN. CAV.
FUSE PNL.)

GROMMET

FRONT OF DASH

DETONATION
SENSOR

A B
D C

$\left(\begin{matrix} IGN \\ SW \end{matrix}\right)$ — PINK

TACH BAT
C GRD B+

B C

MODULE

HLD

PICK-UP
COIL

C GREEN
B WHITE
A BLACK
D BROWN

HEI DISTRIBUTOR

BROWN
BLACK
WHITE
GREEN

Fig. 2.46 Electronic Spark Control System (1980)

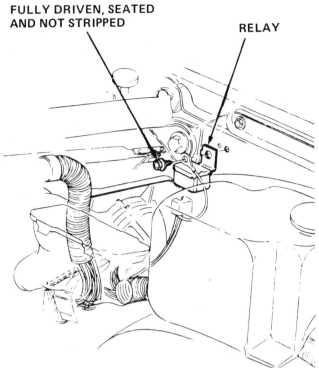

FULLY DRIVEN, SEATED
AND NOT STRIPPED

RELAY

Fig. 2.47 Electronic Spark Control relay switch

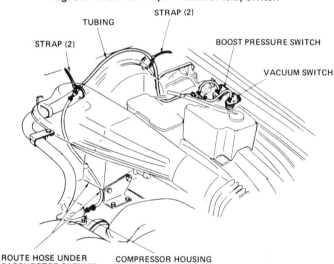

STRAP (2)

TUBING

STRAP (2)

BOOST PRESSURE SWITCH

VACUUM SWITCH

ROUTE HOSE UNDER
CARBURETOR PLENUM

COMPRESSOR HOUSING

Fig. 2.48 Boost gauge switches

and disconnect the 10-pin connector from the ESC unit. Use a continuity tester and check the wiring at pins G, H, J, K. Repair any shorts. Retest. If the trouble remains, proceed to the next step.
36   If the 10-pin connector checks out OK, jump wire pin A and pin C on the distributor side of the harness connector. Try to start the engine. The engine should start and run at idle. DO NOT let the engine race or give it throttle.
37   If the engine will run, the ESC box is defective. If the engine will not run, check the distributor as outlined in Steps 17 through 22. Leave the A pin and C pin jumped. Repair the distributor as necessary. Replace the ESC box if the problem persists.

---

5   Wastegate actuator boost pressure – testing

Note: *Read Section 2 before proceeding.*
1   Inspect all connections for proper hookup and check hoses for leaks and cracks.
2   Disconnect the hose that runs from the actuator to the compressor housing at the actuator. Attach a hand-operated vacuum pump with

gauge and apply 8 psi to the actuator. Somewhere between 7.5 and 8.5 psi, the actuator rod should move 0.008 inch and actuate the wastegate linkage.
3   If it does not work as outlined, replace the actuator and calibrate the linkage for 8 psi by crimping the threads on the rod once it has been turned for the correct setting. Reconnect the vacuum hose.

---

6   Wastegate actuator assembly – removal and installation

Note: *Read Section 2 before proceeding.*
1   Disconnect the 2 hoses from unit and remove retaining clip from the actuator assembly rod.
2   Remove the 2 bolts that hold the actuator to the compressor.
3   Installation is in the reverse procedure.

---

7   Turbocharger vacuum bleed valve (TVBV) (2-bbl carburetor engines) – testing (1978)

Note: *Read Section 2 before proceeding.*
1   The TVBV is located on the intake manifold, in front of and just between the turbocharger and the carburetor.
2   Inspect the valve and its hoses for cracks, splits and for proper hook-up. Replace any hoses that are defective.
3   Unhook the vacuum hose that runs to the power enrichment port on the carburetor and plug the end. Install a manometer into the distributor vacuum hose between the TVBV and the distributor. Use a "T" valve to do this. Start the motor and let it idle. There should not be more than 14 inch H_2O difference on the manometer scale.
4   Now install (via a "T" valve) the manometer into the vacuum hose that runs from the Thermac sensor (see Chapter 6 Emissions for details on the Thermac) to the TVBV and the vacuum hose to the TVBV to the hot air door activator. The engine should be started and the reading should be the same as in Step 3. If not, there may not be sufficient vacuum at the hot air door because the engine has not warmed up enough. Try connecting the manifold vacuum to the input port and redo the test.
5   Remove the vacuum hose from the EGR valve and plug it. "T" one hose from the manometer into the vacuum hose that runs from the EGR signal port to the TVBV. (Again, check Chapter 6, Emissions, for information on the EGR valve). "T" the other manometer hose into the vacuum hose that runs from the TVBV to the EGR-EFE switch. Start the motor and give the car some throttle. The reading should be as in Step 3; 14 inch H_2O difference.
6   Unhook all TVBV hoses at the valve. Make sure the hoses are all properly connected at their opposite ends. Connect one hose of the manometer to the TVBV center vent port and the other side of the manometer to atmosphere.
7   Start the engine and let it idle. There should be no pressure differential. If there is, or if any of the previous tests did not turn out properly, replace the TVBV unit and reinstall all hoses.

---

8   Power enrichment control valve (PECV) (4-bbl carburetor engines) – testing (1978)

Note: *Read Section 2 before proceeding.*
1   On 231 CID turbocharged V6 engines with 4-bbl carburetors there is a Power Enrichment Control Valve (PECV) instead of a TVBV. This unit is in the same location as the TVBV and looks much the same; however testing procedures are a bit different.
2   Carefully check to make sure that all hoses are properly attached and that there are no cracks in the valve or the hoses.
3   Connect one hose of the manometer (via a "T") into the input (center) port vacuum hose between the "T" and the PECV. Connect the other manometer hose directly to the output port vacuum hose. Start the motor and let it run at idle. There should be no more than 12 inch H_2O difference.
4   Disconnect the hoses from the PECV and plug the vacuum source hose. Hook one hose of the manometer to the vent port and hook the manometer's other hose to atmosphere. Run the engine at idle. The reading on the manometer should show no pressure difference.
5   The PECV unit should be replaced if any of the above tests is considered a failure. Install the new unit and replace all hoses in the proper locations.

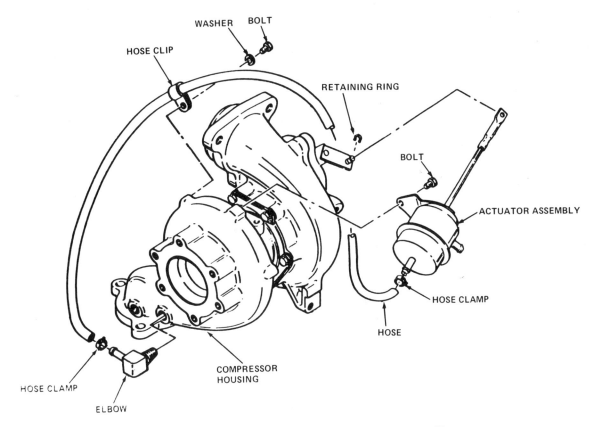

WASHER BOLT

HOSE CLIP

RETAINING RING

BOLT

ACTUATOR ASSEMBLY

HOSE CLAMP

HOSE

COMPRESSOR HOUSING

HOSE CLAMP

ELBOW

Fig. 2.49 Turbocharger with wastegate actuator assembly

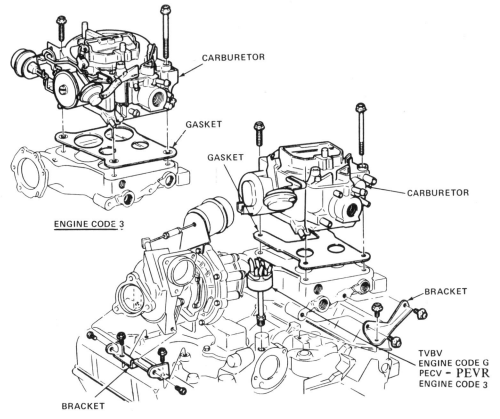

CARBURETOR

GASKET

GASKET

CARBURETOR

ENGINE CODE 3

BRACKET

TVBV
ENGINE CODE G
PECV - PEVR
ENGINE CODE 3

BRACKET

Fig. 2.50 TVBV/PECV/PEVR installation and carburetor-to-plenum hookup

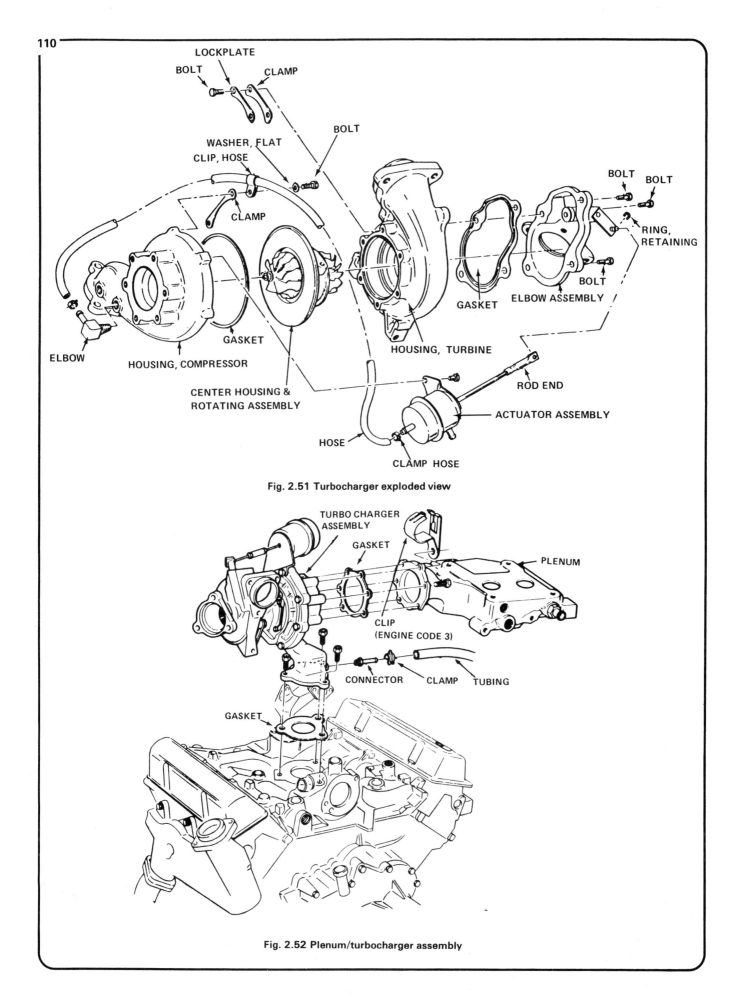

Fig. 2.51 Turbocharger exploded view

Fig. 2.52 Plenum/turbocharger assembly

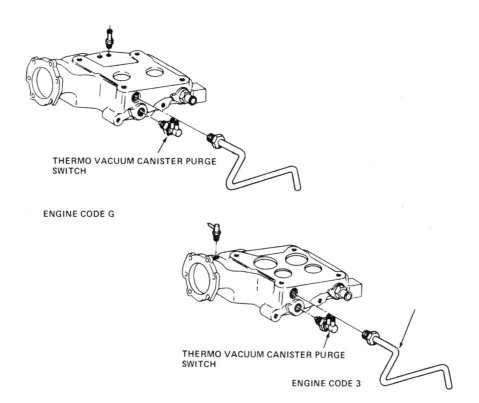

THERMO VACUUM CANISTER PURGE
SWITCH

ENGINE CODE G

THERMO VACUUM CANISTER PURGE
SWITCH

ENGINE CODE 3

Fig. 2.53 Plenum fittings (typical)

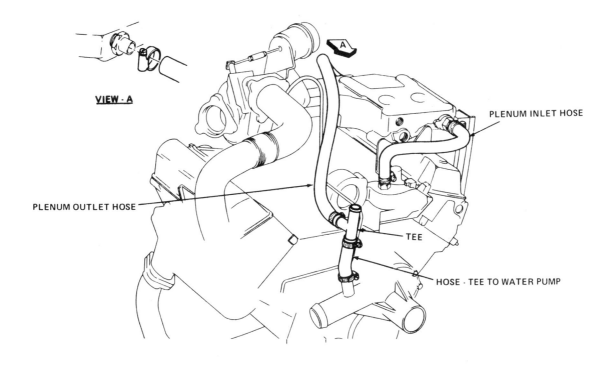

VIEW - A

PLENUM INLET HOSE

PLENUM OUTLET HOSE

TEE

HOSE - TEE TO WATER PUMP

Fig. 2.54 Plenum coolant hose hookup

9 Power enrichment vacuum regulator (PEVR) – testing (1979 and 1980)

Note: *Read Section 2 before proceeding.*

1   The power enrichment vacuum regulator is located in front of and between the turbocharger and the carburetor and threads into the intake manifold.

2   Check the PEVR and hoses for proper installation, cracks and other damage.

3   Connect 1 hose from a manometer (GM special tool number J-23951) between the yellow-striped input hose and the input port (use a 'T' fitting). Connect the remaining manometer hose directly to the PEVR output port.

4   Start the engine and allow it to idle while observing the manometer. There should be no more than a 14 inch H_2O difference. If there is, replace the PEVR with a new one.

5   If the preceding test proves inconclusive, remove the PEVR from the intake manifold and plug the manifold port on the valve, then reconnect the hoses to the PEVR.

6   Connect a pressure/vacuum gauge to the PEVR output hose (use a 'T' fitting), then start the engine and allow it to idle. The gauge reading should be 7 to 9 in Hg (vacuum).

7   Using a hand operated vacuum/pressure pump, apply 3 psi to the manifold signal port of the PEVR. The gauge reading at the output hose should now be 1.4 to 2.6 in Hg. If it is difficult to measure such a low level of vacuum with the gauge in use, apply at least 5 psi to the manifold signal port and check for a gauge reading of zero at the output hose.

8   If the PEVR does not check out as indicated, replace it with a new one.

10 Turbocharger – removal and installation

Note: *Read Section 2 before proceeding.*

1   Disconnect the exhaust outlet and inlet pipes at the turbo.

2   Unhook the oil pipe from the CHRA (Center Housing Rotating Assembly). Wipe up any spilled oil with a rag.

3   Undo the nut that attaches the air intake elbow to the carburetor, then remove the elbow from the carburetor. Leave it attached to the flex tube.

4   Unhook the throttle, detent and cruise linkages from the carburetor. Disconnect the linkage bracket at the plenum. The plenum is the mixing box located underneath the carburetor. Take care not to lose any clips, screws or nuts.

5   Remove the 2 bolts that attach the plenum to the side bracket.

6·   Unhook the fuel line from the carburetor and plug the end. Take care to disconnect any necessary vacuum hoses and mop up any spilled fuel.

7   Empty the cooling system and disconnect the coolant hoses at the front and rear of the plenum. Unhook the power brake vacuum line.

8   Unhook the power vacuum at the plenum and disconnect the front bracket on the plenum by removing the bolt that attaches the bracket to the intake manifold. Leave the plenum attached to the bracket.

9   Remove the 2 bolts that attach the turbine housing to the bracket on the intake manifold and unbolt the 2 bolts that hold the EGR valve manifold to the plenum. Loosen the bolts that attach the EGR valve manifold to the intake manifold.

10   Next, loosen the clamp that attaches the hose from the AIR by-pass pipe to the check valve and remove the hose from the pipe.

11   Unbolt the three bolts that hold the compressor housing to the manifold and remove the turbocharger assembly. The actuator will be attached to the turbo. The turbo will still be attached to the carburetor and the plenum. Unhook any hoses still connected to the turbo assembly.

12   Now, unbolt the turbo/actuator assembly from the carburetor and plenum.

13   Take out the oil drain from the center housing rotating assembly and let any oil in the unit drain out.

14   Assembly and installation of the unit is the exact reverse procedure. However, before the turbocharger is made totally operational, it is a good idea to change the engine oil and filter. This will ensure a constant supply of clean oil to the unit (see special note in Sec. 4 of Chapter 1).

11 Plenum – replacement

1   Steps 1 through 12 in the previous section cover removal of the plenum. If, however, you intend to replace the unit it will be necessary to transfer all fittings and hoses to the new unit. Check back to Step 3 for listing of the parts that belong on the plenum. Installation of the plenum is covered in the previous Section. Reverse the turbo removal procedure.

12 EGR valve manifold – removal and installation

Note: *Read Section 2 before proceeding.*

1   There are 6 bolts to unfasten in order to remove the EGR valve manifold; 2 attach the EGR valve to the valve manifold, 2 attach the valve manifold to the plenum, and 2 attach the valve manifold to the intake manifold. More information on the EGR is in Chapter 6.

2   Unbolt these bolts and unhook the vacuum line that runs to the EGR valve.

3   When installing, first loosely install the bolts that attach the valve manifold to the intake manifold. Next, loosely install the bolts that attach the valve manifold to the plenum.

4   Tighten the valve manifold-to-intake manifold bolts, then tighten the valve manifold-to-plenum bolts.

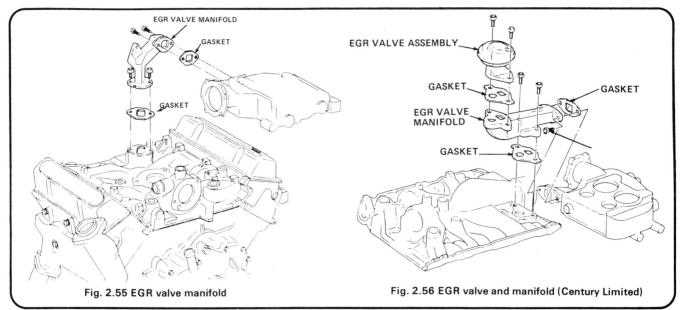

Fig. 2.55 EGR valve manifold   Fig. 2.56 EGR valve and manifold (Century Limited)

5   Bolt up the EGR valve to the valve manifold and install the vacuum line.

13 Turbocharger elbow assembly – removal and installation

1   Jack up the car and block the rear wheels. Set the parking brake.
2   Unbolt the turbo exhaust outlet from the catalytic converter.
3   Lower the car.
4   Remove the clip that attaches the wastegate linkage to the actuator rod and disconnect the turbocharger exhaust outlet from the elbow assembly.
5   Take off the bolts that attach the elbow assembly to the turbine housing.
6   Installation is the reverse procedure.

14 Turbocharger – disassembly and inspection

Note: *Read Section 2 before proceeding.*
1   Removal of the turbocharger is covered in Section 9. If the actuator is still connected to the turbo (you might have taken it off in Section 6), it will be necessary to unbolt the 2 bolts that hold the actuator to the turbo and disconnect the hose that runs from compressor housing to the actuator at the housing.
2   Spin the compressor wheel in the Center Housing Rotating Assembly (CHRA) gently. If there is any binding, replace the CHRA.
3   Unbolt the drain from the CHRA and inspect for carbon build-up coking and oil sludging. If debris and dirt are minor, clean the area with a commercial solvent cleaner. DO NOT use gasoline or other fuels. If the unit is severely plugged, replace it.
4   Inspect the CHRA compressor wheel for signs of oil leakage. If there is leakage, replace the CHRA.
5   With the turbo on a bench, unbolt the 6 bolts and 3 clamps that hold the compressor housing to the turbine housing. Be careful not to bang the CHRA when taking the compressor off the turbine.
6   Look at the CHRA wheels carefully. If there are any broken blades or scratches or other damage, replace the CHRA.
7   If the CHRA is being replaced, lubricate all fitting surfaces and the center shaft with clean engine oil. Carefully install the unit into the turbine housing and using all the bolts and clamps, bolt the turbocharger back together.
8   If the CHRA unit seems OK and you wish to install it back into the turbocharger assembly, take the turbo to your Buick dealer or competent machine shop and have the journal bearings inspected for proper clearance.

Chapter 3 Cooling system

Contents

Specifications

System type	Pressurized, with thermostatic control and pump and fan assistance
Pressure cap setting	15 lb/in^2
Thermostat type	Wax pellet
Thermostat rating	
1974	190°F
1975	190°F
1976	195°F
1977 (except California)	195°F
1977 California engines	180°F
1978 through 1980	195°F
Water pump	Centrifugal vane impeller
Radiator type	Crossflow
Cooling fan	Automatic fluid-clutch fan
Coolant capacity	**US quarts**
1974 w/350 CID engine	17.2 with a/c or Heavy Duty Cooling (HDC) 17.6
w/455 CID	19.4 with a/c or HDC 19.9
1975 w/231 CID	15.3 with a/c or HDC 15.5
w/350 CID	16.9 with a/c or HDC 17.2
1976 w/231 CID	15.5 with a/c 15.4
w/350 CID	16.9 with a/c or HDC 18.7
1977 w/231 CID	12.8 with a/c 12.7
w/350 CID	14.8 with a/c or HDC 16.4
w/403 CID	16.4 with a/c or HDC 18.0
1978 w/231 CID	13.0 with a/c or HDC 13.2
w/305-350 CID	19.2 with a/c or HDC 19.6
1979 w/231 CID	14.5 with 4-bbl carb/HDC 16.4
w/301 CID	17.6 w/4-bbl and a/c-HDC 17.9
w/350 CID	16.4 with a/c or HDC 17.9
1980 w/231 CID (3.8 liter)	13.0 with a/c or HDC 13.8
w/301 CID (4.9 liter)	17.6 with a/c or HDC 18.1
w/305 CID (5.0 liter)	17.6 with a/c or HDC 18.1

Torque specifications	ft-lb	Nm
Pump cover-to-timing chain cover	7	9
Fan pulley	20	27
Thermostat housing-to-intake manifold	20	27
Fan shroud-to-upper radiator mounting	10	13
Alternator bracket-to-w/pump timing chain cover	20	27

1 General information

The engine cooling system is of the pressurized type with pump and fan assistance. It comprises a radiator, flow and return water hoses, water pump, thermostat and vehicle interior heater.

The system is pressurized by means of a spring-loaded radiator filler cap which prevents premature boiling by increasing the boiling point of the coolant. If the coolant temperature goes above this increased boiling point, the extra pressure in the system forces the radiator cap internal spring-loaded valve off its seat and exposes the overflow pipe down which displaced coolant escapes.

It is important to check that the radiator cap is in good condition and that the spring behind the sealing washer has not weakened or corroded. Most service stations have a machine for testing that the cap operates at the specified pressure.

On vehicles built after 1974, a coolant recovery system is provided. This consists of a plastic reservoir into which the coolant which normally escapes down the overflow pipe is retained. When the engine cools and the coolant contracts, coolant is drawn back into the radiator and thus maintains the system at full capacity.

This is a continuous process and provided the level in the reservoir is correctly maintained, no topping-up of the radiator or cooling system will be necessary.

The cooling system functions in the following manner. The water pump discharges engine coolant to each bank of cylinders; this flows from the front of each bank around each cylinder and towards the rear of the block. Passages in the block and cylinder head direct coolant around the inlet and exhaust ports and around the exhaust valve guide inserts. A metered amount of coolant is also diverted to cool the spark plug region.

When the thermostat is closed, coolant is re-directed through a small passage in the front right-hand cylinder head and block to a mating hole in the bottom of the water pump runner. At normal running temperature, the thermostat is open and coolant is directed from the intake manifold through the coolant outlet and thermostat to the radiator.

The radiator is of the crossflow type. Hot engine coolant enters the radiator at the top left-hand side, is cooled by the inrush of cold air through the core (this is created by the fan and ram-effect of air, resulting from forward motion of the vehicle) and returns to the engine via the outlet at the right-hand side.

Later models are fitted with a fluid-type fan coupling. This is a sealed unit, thermostatically controlled which 'slips' the fan blades according to engine temperature and speed, to avoid overcooling with consequent loss of fuel economy.

2 Coolant level

1 **Note**: *If the radiator cap has to be removed when the engine is hot, rotate the cap slowly counterclockwise to the detent and allow the residual pressure to escape. Do not press the cap down until all hissing has stopped and take extreme care that the hands are not scalded.*
2 The level of the coolant in the expansion reservoir should be maintained at the 'FULL HOT' mark. Any checking and topping-up should be carried out with the engine and cooling system at normal operating temperature.

3 Antifreeze and inhibiting solutions

It is recommended that the cooling system is filled with a water/ethylene glycol based antifreeze solution which will give protection down to at least − 20°F at all times. This provides protection against corrosion and increases the coolant boiling point. When handling antifreeze, take care that it is not spilled on the vehicle paintwork, since it will invariably cause damage if not removed immediately.

The cooling system should be drained, flushed and refilled every alternate Fall. The use of antifreeze solutions for periods of longer than two years is likely to cause damage and encourage the formation of rust and scale due to the corrosion inhibitors gradually losing their efficiency.

Before adding antifreeze to the system, check all hose connections and check the tightness of the cylinder head bolts as such solutions are searching.

The exact mixture of antifreeze to water which you should use depends upon the prevailing weather conditions. The mixture should contain at least 50 percent antifreeze, offering protection to −34°F. Under no circumstances should the mixture contain more than 70 percent antifreeze.

4 Automatic fan clutch

Designed to vary the speed of the fan in relation to the temperature of the engine, fan clutches permit the use of a high-delivery fan that ensures excellent cooling ability at reduced engine speeds. Use of this type of cooling apparatus eliminates overcooling, power loss at high engine speeds and excessive noise, and also helps to improve fuel mileage.

Basically, the automatic fan clutch has two modes of operation, engaged and disengaged. The fan only operates when engine temperature demands extra cooling. At high speed or when the engine is cold, the fan clutch disengages the fan and the fan does not operate. The fan clutch is controlled by a bimetallic, thermostatic control coil located on the front of the fan/fan clutch assembly. As engine temperature rises, silicone fluid held in reservoir in the clutch is released into the fan clutch pump. The silicone fills grooves in the clutch housing and the resultant friction causes the fan to engage. As engine temperature drops, the silicone is pumped back into the reservoir and the fan stops working.

5 Fan clutch − troubleshooting

The fan clutch unit is not designed to be repaired. If it is found that the unit is malfunctioning, it should be replaced. Attempts to repair the fan clutch or straighten fan blades will result in a change of balance and/or durability and should not be tried.

Looseness − Up to $\frac{1}{4}$ in lateral movement in the fan clutch assembly when the fan is operating is normal and is not cause for replacement.

Noise − Excessive fan noise will generally occur at engine speeds over 2500 rpm if the clutch is locked up due to internal failure. If the fan cannot be turned by hand or there is a grinding sound as the fan is rotated by hand, the unit should be replaced. There is often, however, noise when the fan is first engaged after motor start-up and when the clutch is engaged for maximum cooling effort. These two conditions are inherent in the normal operation of the unit.

Silicone leak − Small fluid leaks occasionally occur around the bimetallic coil and the bearing assembly. As long as the leak is not excessive, service is not necessary.

Engine overheating − If a persistent problem with overheating develops replacement of the fan clutch may be necessary. However, before replacement of the unit is effected the cooling system should be checked for radiator fluid loss and possible leak. The fan belt should be tested for the proper tension and the thermostat and all hoses should also be checked. The fan clutch can be tested by the following procedure: start with a cold engine to ensure disengagement of clutch. Run the motor and immediately check for excessive freewheeling. To do this spin the fan by hand; if the unit revolves more than 5 complete turns it should be replaced.

6 Thermostat − removal and installation

1 The thermostat is basically a restriction valve which is actuated by a thermostatic element. It is mounted inside a housing on the engine and is designed to open and close at predetermined temperatures to allow coolant to warm-up the engine or cool it.
2 To remove the thermostat for replacement or testing, begin by disconnecting the negative battery cable.
3 Remove the air cleaner for better working access.
4 Drain the coolant into a suitable container for disposal. See Chapter 1 for more information on this. It is not necessary to drain the coolant from the engine.
5 Disconnect the upper radiator hose from the thermostat housing (photo).
6 Remove the thermostat housing bolts and the housing from the engine (photo). On some models, the alternator mounting bracket will

6.5 Disconnecting the upper radiator hose from the thermostat housing

6.6 As the housing is lifted away from the engine, the thermostat becomes visible

6.7 Lift the thermostat out of its bore, noting how it is installed

have to be disconnected first, as this bracket is attached to the housing mounting stud. Also, late model vehicles may have a TVS switch installed in the thermostat housing. If this is the case, disconnect each of the vacuum hoses on the switch (noting their installed positions) and then unscrew the switch from the housing.

7   After lifting the thermostat housing from the engine, the thermostat will be visible and can be removed from the engine (photo). Note how the thermostat sits in the recess, as it must be replaced in this same position.

8   Before installation, use a gasket scraper or putty knife to carefully remove all traces of the old gasket on the thermostat housing and the engine sealing surface. Do not allow the gasket particles to drop down into the intake manifold.

9   Place a $\frac{1}{8}$-in bead of RTV or equivalent sealer around the sealing surface on the engine and place the thermostat into its recess.

10   Immediately place the thermostat housing with sealer and a new gasket into position and torque-tighten the attaching bolts.

11   Where applicable, install the alternator brace and/or the TVS switch and vacuum hoses.

12   Connect the upper radiator hose and tighten the hose clamp securely.

13   Connect the negative battery cable and fill the radiator with the proper amount of antifreeze and water (see Chapter 1).

14   With the radiator cap removed, start the engine and run, until the upper radiator hose becomes hot. When this hose is hot, the thermostat should be in the open position. At this point, add more coolant if necessary to reach the top of the filler neck.

15   Install the radiator cap, making sure the arrows are aligned with the overflow hose.

7   Thermostat – testing

1   The only way to test the operation of the thermostat is by removing the unit from the engine. Usually it is easier and more economical to replace the suspect unit. However, testing the thermostat will help you to determine whether it is the source of an overheating problem. To test, first remove the thermostat as described in Section 5.

2   Inspect the thermostat for excessive corrosion or other damage. Replace it if either of these conditions is present.

3   Place the thermostat in hot water. The water must be 25 degrees hotter than the temperature designation stamped on the unit. A kitchen meat thermometer will test the temperature of the water nicely. Make sure that the water is agitated to ensure even heating of the thermostat, thermometer and water. The valve should fully open.

4   Now remove the thermostat from the water (using a piece of bent wire) and place it in water that is 10 degrees F below the temperature designation of the thermostat. The thermostat valve should close fully.

8   Radiator – removal and installation

1   Disconnect the negative battery cable.

2   Drain the radiator referring to Chapter 1.

3   Disconnect the radiator upper and lower hoses and the automatic

transmission cooling lines if applicable (photo).

4   Disconnect the radiator shroud and hang it over the fan (photos) The shroud is attached with screws going into the radiator with clips or staples across the bottom.

5   Remove the upper metal panel at the top of the radiator (photo).

6   Lift the radiator straight up and out of the engine compartment. Be careful not to scratch the paint on the front nosepiece. If coolant drips on any body paint, immediately wash it off with clear water as the antifreeze solution can damage the finish.

7   With the radiator removed, it can be inspected for leaks or damage. If in need of repairs, have a professional radiator shop or dealer perform the work as special welding techniques are required.

8   Bugs and dirt can be cleaned from the radiator by using compressed air and a soft brush. Do not bend the cooling fins as this is done.

9   Inspect the rubber mounting pads which the radiator sits on and replace as necessary (photos).

10   Lift the radiator into position making sure it is seated in the mounting pads.

11   Install the upper panel, shroud and hoses in the reverse order of removal.

12   Connect the negative battery cable and fill the radiator as described in Chapter 1.

13   Start the engine and check for leaks. Allow the engine to reach normal operating temperature (upper radiator hose hot) and add coolant until the level reaches the bottom of the filler neck.

14   Install cap with arrows aligned with the overflow tube.

9   Water pump – testing

Note: *A failure in the water pump can cause serious engine damage due to overheating. The pump will not be able to circulate cooled water through the engine. There are three ways in which to check the operation of the water pump while it is still installed on the engine. If the pump is suspect, it should be replaced with a new or factory-rebuilt unit.*

1   With the engine warmed up to normal operating temperature, squeeze the upper radiator hose. If the water pump is working properly, a pressure surge should be felt as the hose is released.

2   Water pumps are equipped with 'weep' or vent holes (photo). If a failure occurs to the bladder of the pump, small amounts of water will leak from these 'weep' holes. In most cases it will be necessary to use a flashlight from under the car to see evidence of leakage from this point in the pump body.

3   If the water pump shaft bearings fail there may be a squealing sound at the front of the engine while it is running. Shaft wear can be felt if the water pump pulley is forced up and down. Do not mistake drive belt slippage, which also causes a squealing sound, for water pump failure.

10   Water pump – removal and installation

Note: *It is not economical or practical to overhaul a water pump. If failure occurs, a new or rebuilt unit should be purchased to replace the*

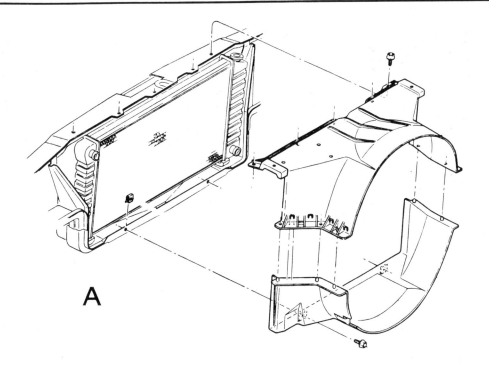

A

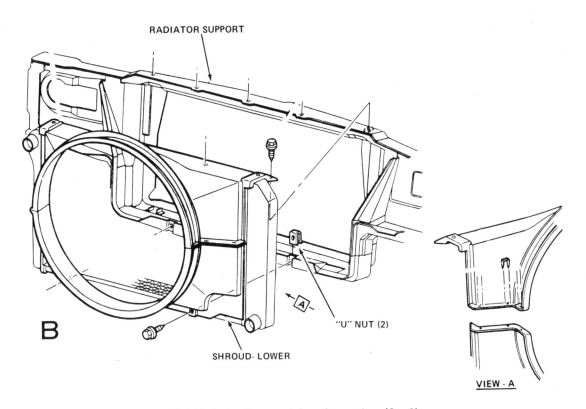

RADIATOR SUPPORT

B

SHROUD- LOWER

"U" NUT (2)

VIEW - A

Fig. 3.1 Typical radiator and shroud mountings (Sec 8)

A   Buick engines   B   Chevrolet engines

8.4a Screws secure the fan shroud to the radiator

8.4b With the shroud disconnected, hang it over the fan, away from the radiator

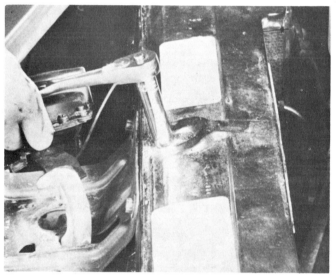

8.5 The radiator top panel is secured by bolts across the top

8.9a One of the upper rubber mounting pads

8.9b A lower mounting pad and its location to radiator

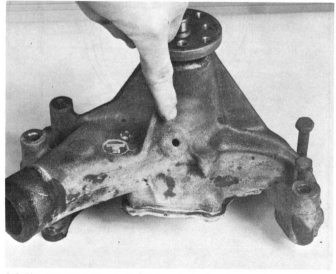

9.2 The "weep" hole out of which water leaks when the internal bladder has failed

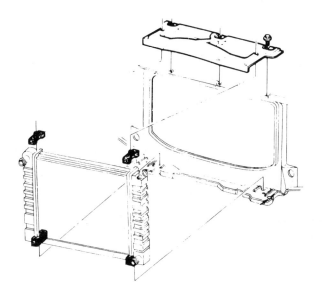

Fig. 3.2 Radiator mountings (Sec 8)

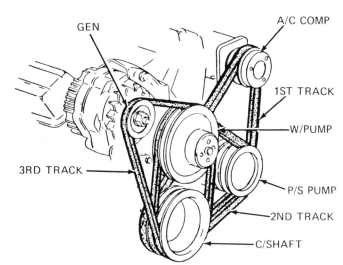

Fig. 3.3 Typical drivebelt routings (Sec 8)

faulty water pump.

1 Disconnect the negative battery cable.

2 Drain the radiator, referring to Chapter 1 if necessary.

3 Reaching inside the radiator shroud, remove the bolts which secure the fan to the water pump hub. Remove the fan and spacer (if equipped). A thermostatic fan clutch must remain in the 'in-car' position.

4 Remove the bolts which secure the radiator shroud to the radiator and lift the shroud up and out of the engine compartment (refer to Section 8).

5 Loosen the two mounting bolts for the alternator. There is an adjusting strap bolt located in the slotted bracket and a long pivot bolt under the alternator.

6 Push the alternator inward to relieve tension on the drive belt and then remove the drive belt from the alternator and water pump pulleys.

7 Remove the water pump pulley from the hub.

8 Completely remove the alternator strap bolt and pivot the alternator away from the water pump. Then lift the mounting bracket off the engine (photo).

9 Disconnect the wiring at the rear of the alternator using identifying pieces of tape if necessary to help in reinstallation.

10 Remove the alternator pivot bolt and lift the alternator off the engine (photo).

11 Loosen the two mounting bolts for the AIR pump. Completely remove the bracket which is attached to the water pump, then pivot the AIR pump away from the engine (photo). On some models, the AIR pump pulley must first be removed from the pump to gain access to the bracket bolts.

12 If equipped with power steering, loosen the adjusting bolt and completely remove the pivot bolt which passes through the water pump (photo). Swing the pump away from the engine as far as possible without crimping the hoses.

13 Disconnect the lower radiator hose, heater hose and by-pass hose (if equipped) from the water pump housing (photo).

14 Remove the remaining bolts which secure the water pump to the front of the engine block. Lift the water pump away from the engine and out of the engine compartment (photos).

15 If installing a new or rebuilt water pump, transfer the heater hose fitting from the old pump to the new one (photo).

16 Clean the gasket surfaces of the engine of all excess gasket material using a gasket scraper or putty knife (photos).

17 Use a thin coat of gasket sealer on the new gaskets and install to the new pump. Place the pump into position on the engine and secure with the bolts. Do not torque-tighten these bolts until the power steering pump bracket and air pump brackets have been installed, as these brackets are secured with the water pump bolts.

18 Install the engine components in the reverse order of removal, tightening the appropriate fasteners to torque specifications.

19 Adjust all drivebelts to the proper tension (see Chapter 1).

20 Connect the negative battery cable and fill the radiator with a mixture of ethylene glycol antifreeze and water in a 50/50 mixture. Start the engine and allow to idle until the upper radiator hose gets hot. Check for leaks. With engine hot, fill with more coolant mixture until the level is at the bottom of the filler neck. Install radiator cap and check coolant level periodically over the next few miles of driving.

11 Water temperature sender – fault diagnosis and replacement

1 The indicator system is composed of a lamp mounted on the instrument panel and a sender unit which is located on the left-hand cylinder head.

2 In the event of an unusual indication or a fault developing, check the coolant level in the system and then ensure that the connecting wiring between the gauge and the sender unit is secure.

3 When the ignition switch is turned on and the starter motor is turning, the indicator lamp should be illuminated (overheated engine indication). If the lamp is not on, the bulb may be burned out, the ignition switch may be faulty or the circuit may be open.

4 As soon as the engine starts, the lamp should go out and remain so unless the engine overheats. Failure of the lamp to go out may be due to the wiring being grounded between the lamp and the sender unit, a defective temperature sender unit or a faulty ignition switch.

5 If the sender unit is to be replaced it is simply unscrewed from the left-hand cylinder head and a replacement installed. There will be some coolant spillage, so check the level after the replacement has been installed.

12 Heater components – removal and installation

Blower assembly

1 If only the blower motor is to be replaced, simply disconnect the wiring and remove the screws attaching the motor to the case.

2 To remove the case, drain the radiator and disconnect the heater hoses (inside the engine compartment) where they attach to the case at the firewall.

3 Disconnect all electrical connections and remove all screws attaching the assembly to the firewall. The case and the heater core can now be removed.

4 Upon installation, be sure to make an air-tight seal around the case.

Control head

5 Remove the trim plate by pulling rearward and unsnapping from

10.10 Lifting the alternator off the engine

10.11 This bracket for the air pump mounts to the water pump and must be removed (not all models)

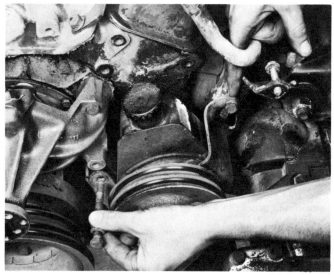

10.12 The long pivot bolt for the power steering pump also mounts to the water pump

10.13a Disconnecting the lower radiator hose from the water pump (Chevrolet only)

10.13b Disconnecting the heater hose from the top of the water pump

10.14a The water pump as it attaches to the front cover assembly (non-Chevrolet engines)

10.14b The water pump removed from the front cover showing the rear side

10.15 If a replacement pump is used, transfer all hose fittings from the old pump to the new pump

10.16a The gasket surfaces must be perfectly clean before the replacement water pump is installed (Chevrolet engine shown)

10.16b Cleaning the gasket surface of the front cover (non-Chevrolet engines)

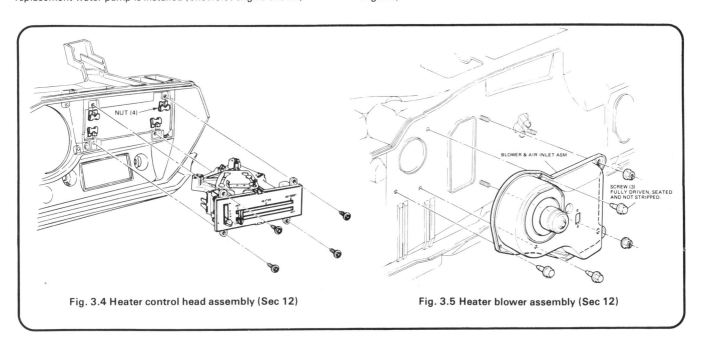

Fig. 3.4 Heater control head assembly (Sec 12)

Fig. 3.5 Heater blower assembly (Sec 12)

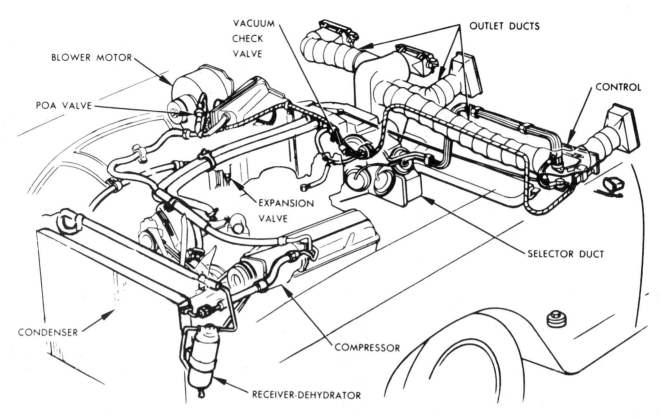

BLOWER MOTOR

POA VALVE

VACUUM
CHECK
VALVE

OUTLET DUCTS

CONTROL

EXPANSION
VALVE

SELECTOR DUCT

CONDENSER

COMPRESSOR

RECEIVER-DEHYDRATOR

Fig. 3.6 Typical air conditioning system components (Sec 13)

the instrument panel.

6   Remove the 4 screws which secure the control head.

7   Pull the head away from dash slightly, then disconnect all the wiring and cables making note of their installed positions.

8   Install in the reverse order.

13 Air conditioner – general description

1   Three types of systems may be encountered. The Four-Season System in which both the heating and cooling functions are performed by the one system. Air entering the vehicle passes through the cooling unit (evaporator) and then around the heating unit, following the 'reheat' principle.

2   The evaporator cools the air passing through it and, by means of its built-in thermostatic switch, controls the operation of the compressor.

3   The system operates by air (outside or recirculated) entering the evaporator core by the action of the blower, where it receives maximum cooling if the controls are set for cooling. When the air leaves the evaporator, it enters the heater/air conditioner duct assembly and by means of a manually controlled deflector, it either passes through or bypasses the heater core in the correct proportions to provide the desired vehicle interior temperature.

4   Distribution of this air is then regulated by a vacuum actuated deflector and passes through the various outlets according to requirements.

5   When, during the cooling operation, the air temperature is cooled too low for comfort, it is warmed to the required level by the heater. When the controls are set to 'HEATING ONLY', the evaporator will cease to function and ambient air will be warmed by the heater in a similar manner to that just described.

6   The main units of the system comprise the evaporator, an engine driven compressor and the condenser.

7   In view of the toxic nature of the chemicals and gases employed in the system, no part of the system should be disconnected by the home mechanic. Due to the need for specialized evacuating and charging equipment, such work should be left to your GM dealer or a refrigeration specialist.

8   The Comfortron System is essentially the same as the Four Season System except that it is fully automatic in operation.

9   The GM Air Conditioner is a dealer installed unit and operates independently of the vehicle heater using only recirculated air.

14 Air conditioner – checks and maintenance

1   Regularly inspect the fins of the condenser (located ahead of the radiator) and if necessary brush away leaves and bugs.

2   Clean the evaporator drain tubes free of dirt.

3   Check the condition of the system hoses and if there is any sign of deterioration or hardening, have them replaced by your dealer.

4   At similar intervals, check and adjust the compressor drivebelt as described in Chapter 1.

Chapter 4 Fuel and exhaust systems

Refer to Chapter 13 for specifications and information applicable to later models

Contents

Specifications

1974

General

Fuel tank capacity	22 gals
Fuel pump pressure	
350 CID engine	3 psi min
455 CID engine	$4\frac{1}{2}$ psi min
Fuel pump volume	1 pt in 30 sec. or less

2GV carburetor

Float level	15/32 in
Float drop adjustment	1 9/32 in
Pump rod adjustment	1 15/32 in
Choke tang adjustment	0.080 in
Choke unloader adjustment	0.180 in
Vacuum break adjustment (350)	
Primary	0.140 in
Secondary	0.120
Vacuum break adjustment (455)	
Primary	0.160 in
Secondary	0.120 in

Idle speed
    Solenoid de-energized .... 500 rpm in 'D'
    Solenoid energized .... 650 rpm in 'D'
Idle mixture .... see tune-up decal inside engine compartment

4MV carburetor
Float level
    455 CID engine .... 13/32 in
    350 CID engine .... 15/32 in
Pump rod location
    455 CID engine .... Inner
    350 CID engine .... Outer
Pump adjustment
    455 CID engine .... $\frac{1}{4}$ in
    350 CID engine .... 0.306 in
Choke rod adjustment .... 0.130 in
Vacuum break adjustment (455)
    Primary .... 0.215 in
    Secondary .... 0.160 in
Vacuum break adjustment (350)
    Primary .... 0.170 in
    Secondary .... 0.150 in
Air valve dash pot .... 0.150 in
Secondary opening adjustment .... 0.070 in
Secondary closing adjustment .... 0.020 in
Air valve spring wind-up
    455 CID engine .... $\frac{7}{16}$ turn
350 CID engine .... $\frac{11}{16}$ turn
Idle speed .... see tune-up decal inside engine compartment
Idle mixture .... see tune-up decal inside engine compartment

1975

General
Fuel tank capacity .... 22 gals
Fuel pump pressure .... 3 psi min
Fuel pump volume .... 1 pint in 30 sec or less

2GC carburetor
Float level
    231 CID engine .... 13/32 in
    350 CID engine .... 15/32 in
Float drop adjustment .... 1 9/32 in
Pump rod adjustment .... 1$\frac{3}{4}$ in
Choke tang adjustment .... 0.080 in
Choke unloader adjustment
    231 CID engine .... 0.140 in
    350 CID engine .... 0.180 in
Vacuum break adjustment (231)
    Primary .... 0.120 in
    Secondary .... 0.120 in
Vacuum break adjustment (350)
    Primary .... 0.140 in
    Secondary .... 0.120 in
Idle speed .... see tune-up decal inside engine compartment
Idle mixture .... see tune-up decal inside engine compartment

4MC carburetor
Float level .... $\frac{5}{16}$ in
Choke cover setting .... 1 notch rich
Pump rod location .... outer hole
Pump rod adjustment .... 15/32 in
Choke rod adjustment .... 0.095 in
Vacuum break adjustment (sedans)
    Primary .... 0.130 in
    Secondary .... 0.150 in
Vacuum break adjustment (wagons)
    Primary .... 0.145 in
    Secondary .... 0.130 in
Air valve dash pot adjustment .... 0.015 in
Secondary opening adjustment .... center of slot
Secondary closing adjustment .... 0.020 in
Air valve spring adjustment .... $\frac{3}{4}$ turn
Choke unloader .... 0.240 in

1976

General
Fuel tank capacity .... 22 gals
Fuel pump pressure .... 3 psi min
Fuel pump volume .... 1 pint in 30 sec or less

2GC carburetor

Float level	
231 CID engine	$\frac{7}{16}$ in
350 CID engine	15/32 in
Float drop adjustment	1 5/32 in
Pump rod adjustment	
231 CID engine	1 19/32
350 CID engine	1 11/32 in
Intermediate choke rod adjustment	0.120 in
Choke cover setting	1 notch rich
Fast idle cam (choke rod)	0.080 in
Vacuum break adjustment (231)	
Primary	0.120 in
Secondary	0.100 in
Vacuum break adjustment (350)	
Primary	0.140 in
Secondary	0.100 in
Choke unloader adjustment	
231 cu in	0.140 in
350 cu in	0.180 in

4MC carburetor

Float level	$\frac{5}{16}$ in
Pump rod location	outer hole
Pump rod adjustment	$\frac{3}{8}$ in
Choke coil lever adjustment	0.120 in
Choke rod (fast idle cam) adjustment	0.095 in
Air valve dash pot adjustment	0.015 in
Vacuum break adjustment	
Primary	0.130 in
Secondary	0.130 in
Choke cover setting	Index
Choke unloader adjustment	0.250 in
Secondary throttle valve locknut adjustment	0.015 in
Secondary closing adjustment	0.020 in
Secondary opening adjustment	center of slot
Air valve spring adjustment	$\frac{3}{4}$ turn

1977

General

Fuel tank capacity	22 gals
Fuel pump pressure	
231 CID engine	3 psi
305 CID engine	7.5 to 9.0 psi
350 CID engine (code H,J)	3 psi
350 CID engine (code R)	5.5 to 6.5 psi
350 CID engine (code L)	7.5 to 9.0 psi
403 CID engine	5.5 to 6.5 psi
Fuel pump volume	1 pint in 30 sec or less

2GC-2GE carburetors

Note: *See carburetor identification for model numbers used below*

Float level	
All 2GC except below	19/32 in
17057140	15/32 in
All 2GE	$\frac{7}{16}$ in
Float drop adjustment	
All except below	1 5/32 in
17057108 & 17057110	1 9/32 in
Pump rod adjustment	
All 26C except below	1 2/32 in
17057140	$1\frac{9}{16}$ in
All 26E except below	1 17/32 in
17057141	$1\frac{1}{2}$ in
17057145	$1\frac{1}{2}$ in
17057147	$1\frac{1}{2}$ in
17057445 – 448	$1\frac{1}{2}$ in
Choke coil lever adjustment	0.120 in
Automatic choke coil adjustment	
All 2GC except below	Index
17057140	1 notch rich
All 2GE	1 notch rich
Choke rod (fast idle) adjustment	
All 2GC except below	0.260 in
17057140	0.080 in
All 2GE	0.080 in
Vacuum break (throttle lever side)	
All 2GC	0.140 in

All 2GE except below	0.110 in
17057143 – 17057144	0.130 in
17057446 – 17057448	0.130 in
Vacuum break (choke side)	
All 2GC except below	0.130 in
17057110	0.160 in
17057140	0.100 in
All 2GE except below	0.040 in
17057143 – 17057144	0.100 in
17057180 – 17057182	0.060 in
17057445 – 17057446	0.110 in
17057447	0.100 in
17057448	0.110 in
Choke unloader adjustment	
All 2GC	0.325 in
All 2GE	0.140 in
Idle speed	see tune-up decal inside engine compartment
Idle mixture	see tune-up decal inside engine compartment

M4MC carburetor

Float adjustment	
All except below	15/32 in
17057241	$\frac{5}{16}$
17057248	$\frac{5}{16}$
17057250	13/32 in
17057253	13/32 in
17057255	13/32 in
17057256	13/32 in
17057258	13/32 in
17057550	13/32 in
17057553	13/32 in
Pump adjustment	
All except below	9/32 in (inner hole)
17057582	9/32 in (outer hole)
17057584	9/32 in (outer hole)
17057241	$\frac{3}{8}$ in (outer hole)
17057248	$\frac{3}{8}$ in (outer hole)
Choke coil lever adjustment	0.120 in
Fast idle adjustment	3 turns
Choke rod (fast idle cam)	
All except below	0.100 in
17057202	0.325 in
17057204	0.325 in
17057502	0.325 in
17057504	0.325 in
17057582	0.325 in
17057584	0.325 in
17057241	0.095 in
17057248	0.095 in
Air valve rod adjustment	
All except below	0.015 in
17057250	0.030 in
17057253	0.030 in
17057255	0.030 in
17057256	0.030 in
17057258	0.030 in
17057550	0.030 in
17057553	0.030 in
Front vacuum break adjustment	
All except below	0.135 in
17057248	0.130 in
17057258	0.215 in
17057550	0.215 in
17057553	0.215 in
17057202	0.160 in
17057204	0.215 in
17057502	0.165 in
17057504	0.230 in
17057582	0.180 in
17057584	0.245 in
Rear vacuum break adjustment	
All except below	0.180 in
17057258	0.225 in
17057550	0.225 in
17057553	0.225 in
17057248	0.110 in

Automatic choke coil adjustment
  All except below .... 2 notches rich
  17057241 .... 1 notch rich
  17057248 .... Index
  17057202 .... 2 notches lean
  17057204 .... 2 notches lean
  17057502 .... 2 notches lean
  17057504 .... 2 notches lean
  17057582 .... 2 notches lean
  17057584 .... 2 notches lean
Unloader adjustment
  All except below .... 0.220 in
  17057241 .... 0.240 in
  17057248 .... 0.240 in
  17057204 .... 0.280 in
  17057502 .... 0.280 in
  17057504 .... 0.280 in
  17057582 .... 0.280 in
  17057584 .... 0.280 in
Secondary lockout adjustment .... 0.015 in
Secondary closing adjustment .... 0.020 in
Secondary opening adjustment .... center of slot
Air valve spring adjustment
  All except below .... $\frac{1}{2}$ turn
  17057204 .... $\frac{7}{8}$ turn
  17057502 .... $\frac{7}{8}$ turn
  17057504 .... $\frac{7}{8}$ turn
  17057582 .... $\frac{7}{8}$ turn
  17057584 .... $\frac{7}{8}$ turn
  17057241 .... $\frac{3}{4}$ turn
  17057248 .... $\frac{3}{4}$ turn

1978

M2MC carburetor
Float level
  All M2MC .... 11/32 in
  All M2ME .... $\frac{1}{4}$ in
Pump adjustment
  All M2MC .... $\frac{1}{4}$ in (outer hole)
  All M2ME except below .... 9/32 in (inner hole)
  17058496 .... $\frac{3}{8}$ in (outer hole)
Choke coil lever adjustment (all) .... 0.120 in
Fast idle adjustment (bench setting) .... see text
Choke rod (fast idle cam) adjustment – angle gauge method
  All M2MC .... 23.5°
  All M2ME except below .... 14.5°
  17058496 .... 15°
Front vacuum break adjustment – angle gauge method
All M2MC .... 26°
  All M2ME except below .... 21°
  17058496 .... 24°
Rear vacuum break adjustment – angle gauge method
  All M2MC .... 36°
  All M2ME except below .... 19°
  17058496 .... 34°
Automatic choke coil adjustment – angle gauge method
  All M2ME .... 2 notches lean
  All M2ME .... 1 notch rich
Unloader adjustment – angle gauge method
  All M2MC .... 35°
  All M2ME except below .... 50°
  17058496 .... 38°
A/C idle speed adjustment (on car) .... see tune-up decal in engine compartment
Fast idle adjustment (on car) .... see tune-up decal in engine compartment
2GC-2GE carburetors
Float level
  2GC 17058104, 17058105 .... 15/32 in
  2GC 17058108 .... 19/32 in
  2GC 17058110 .... 19/32 in
  2GC 17058112 .... 19/32 in
  2GC 17058114 .... 19/32 in
  2GC 17058126 .... 19/32 in
  2GC 17058128 .... 19/32 in
  2GC 17058404, 17058405 .... $\frac{1}{2}$ in
  2GC 17058408 .... 21/32 in
  2GC 17058410 .... 21/32 in

2GC 17058412	21/32 in
2GC 17058414	21/32 in
2GE all	$\frac{7}{16}$ in
Float drop adjustment	
All 2GC	1 9/32 in
All 2GE	1 5/32 in
Pump rod adjustment	
All 2GE except below	1 19/32 in
17058143, 17058448	$1\frac{9}{16}$ in
17058144, 17058188	$1\frac{5}{8}$ in
Choke coil lever adjustment	
2GC all	0.120 in
2GE all	0.120 in
Automatic choke coil adjustment	
2GC 17058104	Index
2GC 17058105	Index
2GC 17058108	Index
2GC 17058110	Index
2GC 17058112	Index
2GC 17058114	Index
2GC 17058126	Index
2GC 17058128	Index
2GC 17058404	$\frac{1}{2}$ notch lean
2GC 17058405	$\frac{1}{2}$ notch lean
2GC 17058408	$\frac{1}{2}$ notch lean
2GC 17058410	$\frac{1}{2}$ notch lean
2GC 17058412	$\frac{1}{2}$ notch lean
2GC 17058414	$\frac{1}{2}$ notch lean
All 2GE	1 notch rich
Choke rod (fast idle cam) adjustment	
All 2GC	0.260 in
All 2GE	0.080 in
Vacuum break adjustment (throttle lever side)	
All 2GE except below	0.110 in
17058141, 17058147, 17058444, 17058448	0.140 in
17058446	0.130 in
17058447	0.150 in
17058188	0.120 in
Vacuum break adjustment (choke side)	
2GC 17058104	0.130 reset to 0.160 at first tune-up
2GC 17058105	0.130 reset to 0.160 at first tune-up
2GC 17058108	0.130 reset to 0.160 at first tune-up
2GC 17058110	0.130 reset to 0.160 at first tune-up
2GC 17058114	0.130 reset to 0.160 at first tune-up
17058126, 17058128	0.130 reset to 0.150 at first tune-up
17058404	0.140 reset to 0.160 at first tune-up
17058405	0.140 reset to 0.160 at first tune-up
17058408	0.140 reset to 0.160 at first tune-up
17058410	0.140 reset to 0.160 at first tune-up
17058412	0.140 reset to 0.160 at first tune-up
17058414	0.140 reset to 0.160 at first tune-up
All 2GE except below	0.080 in
17058140	0.020 in
17058144, 17058145	0.060 in
17058141, 17058147, 17058448	0.100 in
17058446, 17058447	0.110 in
17058185, 17058187, 17058188	0.050 in
Choke unloader adjustment	
All 2GC	0.325 in
All 2GE except below	0.140 in
17058145	0.160 in
17058148, 17058149	0.150 in
Idle speed adjustment – without solenoid	see tune-up decal in engine compartment
Idle speed adjustment – with solenoid	see tune-up decal in engine compartment
A/C idle speed adjustment	see tune-up decal in engine compartment

M4MC-M4ME carburetors

Float levels	
All M4ME	7/32 in
All M4MC except below	15/32 in
17058241	$\frac{5}{16}$ in
17058250	1 3/32 in
17058253	1 3/32 in
17058257	1 3/32 in
17058258	1 3/32 in
17058550	1 3/32 in

Pump adjustment
    All M4ME .... 9/32 in (inner hole)
    All M4MC except below .... 9/32 in (inner hole)
    17058241 .... $\frac{3}{8}$ in (outer hole)
Choke coil lever adjustment (all) .... 0.120 in
Fast idle adjustment (bench setting)
    M4ME .... see text
    M4MC .... see text
Choke rod (fast idle cam) adjustment – angle gauge method
    All M4ME .... 14.5°
    All M4MC except below .... 46°
    17058241 .... 18°
    17058250 .... 18°
    17058253 .... 18°
    17058254 .... 19°
    17058257 .... 19°
    17058258 .... 19°
    17058550 .... 19°
    17058553 .... 19°
    17058559 .... 19°
Air valve rod adjustment
    All M4ME .... 0.015 in
    All M4MC except below .... 0.015 in
    17058250 .... 0.030 in
    17058253 .... 0.030 in
    17058254 .... 0.030 in
    17058257 .... 0.030 in
    17058258 .... 0.030 in
    17058550 .... 0.030 in
    17058553 .... 0.030 in
    17058559 .... 0.030 in
Front vacuum break adjustment – angle gauge method
    All M4ME .... 21°
    M4MC
    17058241 .... 21.5°
    17058250, 17058253 .... 23°
    17058254 .... 24°
    17058257 .... 24°
    17058258 .... 24°
    17058550 .... 24°
    17058553 .... 24°
    17058559 .... 25°
    1705828, 17058582, 17058584 .... 30°
    17058502, 17058504 .... 28°
    17058282 .... 27°
    17058284 .... 27°
    17058202 .... 27°
    17058204 .... 27°
Rear vacuum break adjustment – angle gauge method
    All M4ME .... 21°
    All M4MC except below .... 36.5°
    17058241 .... 19°
    17058250, 17058253 .... 30.5°
Automatic choke coil adjustment (M4MC)
    All M4MC except below .... 2 notches rich
    17058254, 17058559 .... 3 notches rich
    17058228 .... 2 notches lean
    17058502 .... 2 notches lean
    17058504 .... 2 notches lean
    17058582 .... 2 notches lean
    17058584 .... 2 notches lean
    17058202 .... 2 notches lean
    17058204 .... 2 notches lean
    17058282 .... Index
    17058284 .... Index
Automatic choke coil adjustment (all M4ME) .... Index
Unloader adjustment – angle gauge method
    All M4ME .... 38°
    All M4MC except below .... 42°
    17058250 .... 35°
    17058253 .... 35°
    17058254 .... 35°
    17058257 .... 35°
    17058258 .... 35°
    17058550 .... 35°

17058553	35°
17058241	38°
17058559	36.5°
Secondary lockout adjustment (all)	0.015 in
Secondary closing adjustment (all)	0.020 in
Secondary opening adjustment	see Figure
Air valve spring adjustment	
All M4ME	$\frac{3}{4}$ turn
All M4MC except below	$\frac{1}{2}$ turn
17058241	$\frac{3}{4}$ turn
17058582	$\frac{7}{8}$ turn
17058584	$\frac{7}{8}$ turn
17058282	$\frac{7}{8}$ turn
17058284	$\frac{7}{8}$ turn
17058202	$\frac{7}{8}$ turn
17058204	$\frac{7}{8}$ turn
17058502	$\frac{7}{8}$ turn
17058504	$\frac{7}{8}$ turn
17058228	1 turn
Idle speed adjustment – without solenoid	see tune-up decal in engine compartment
Idle speed adjustment with solenoid	see tune-up decal in engine compartment

1979

M2MC – M2ME carburetors

Float level
M2MC

17059134	15/32 in
17059136	15/32 in

M2ME

17059193	13/32 in
17059194	11/32 in
17059190	11/32 in
17059191	11/32 in
17059491	11/32 in
17059492	11/32 in
17059196	11/32 in
17059498	11/32 in
17059180	11/32 in
17059184	11/32 in

Pump adjustment
M2MC

17059134	$\frac{1}{4}$ in
17059136	$\frac{1}{4}$ in

M2ME

17059180	$\frac{1}{4}$ in (inner hole)
17059184	$\frac{1}{4}$ in (inner hole)
17059190	$\frac{1}{4}$ in (inner hole)
17059193	$\frac{1}{4}$ in (inner hole)
17059194	$\frac{1}{4}$ in (inner hole)
17059196	$\frac{1}{4}$ in (inner hole)
17059191	9/32 in (inner hole)
17059491	9/32 in (inner hole)
17059492	9/32 in (inner hole)
17059498	9/32 in (inner hole)
Choke coil lever adjustment	0.120 in

Fast idle cam – angle gauge method
M2MC

17059134	38°
17059136	38°

M2ME

17059193	24.5°
17059194	24.5°
17059190	24.5°
17059191	24.5°
17059491	24.5°
17059492	24.5°
17059196	24.5°
17059498	24.5°
17059180	24.5°
17059184	24.5°

Front vacuum adjustment – angle gauge method
M2MC

17059134	27°
17059136	27°

M2ME

17059193	19°
17059194	19°

17059191	19°
17059180	19°
17059190	19°
17059184	19°
17059491	23°
17059492	23°
17059196	23°
17059498	23°

Rear vacuum break adjustment – angle gauge method
M2ME

17059193	17°
17059194	17°
17059191	17°
17059180	17°
17059190	17°
17059184	17°
17059491	21°
17059492	21°
17059196	21°
17059498	21°

Automatic choke adjustment
M2MC

17059134	1 notch lean (CW)
17059136	1 notch lean (CW)

M2ME

17059491	1 notch rich (CCW)
17059492	1 notch rich (CCW)
17059196	1 notch rich (CCW)
17059193	2 notches rich (CCW)
17059194	2 notches rich (CCW)
17059498	2 notches rich (CCW)
17059191	2 notches rich (CCW)
17059180	2 notches rich (CCW)
17059190	2 notches rich (CCW)
17059184	2 notches rich (CCW)

Unloader adjustment – angle gauge method
M2MC

17059134	38°
17059136	38°

M2ME

17059193	35°
17059194	35°
17059184	35°
17059180	38°
17059190	38°
17059191	38°
17059491	42°
17059492	42°
17059498	42°
17059196	42°

A/C idle speed adjustment	refer to specifications decal
Fast idle adjustment	refer to specifications decal

M4ME – M4MC carburetors
Float level
M4ME

17059240	7/32 in
17059243	7/32 in
17059540	7/32 in
17059543	7/32 in
17059242	7/32 in

M4MC

17059553	13/32 in
17059555	13/32 in
17059250	13/32 in
17059253	13/32 in
10759272	15/32 in
10759208	15/32 in
10759209	15/32 in
10759210	15/32 in
10759211	15/32 in
10759228	15/32 in
10759241	5/16 in
10759247	5/16 in

Pump adjustment
M4ME

17059240	9/32 in (inner hole)

17059243	9/32 in (inner hole)
17059540	9/32 in (inner hole)
17059543	9/32 in (inner hole)
17059242	9/32 in (inner hole)

M4MC

17059553	9/32 in (inner hole)
17059555	9/32 in (inner hole)
17059250	9/32 in (inner hole)
17059253	9/32 in (inner hole)
17059208	9/32 in (inner hole)
17059209	9/32 in (inner hole)
17059210	9/32 in (inner hole)
17059211	9/32 in (inner hole)
17059228	9/32 in (inner hole)
17059241	$\frac{9}{16}$ in (outer hole)
17059247	$\frac{9}{16}$ in (outer hole)
17059272	$\frac{9}{16}$ in (outer hole)
Choke coil adjustment	0.120 in

Fast idle cam relation adjustment – angle gauge method

M4ME

17059240	14.5°
17059243	14.5°
17059540	14.5°
17059543	14.5°
17059242	14.5°

M4MC

17059272	14.5°
17059241	18°
17059247	18°
17059250	18°
17059253	18°
17059553	19°
17059555	19°
17059210	38°
17059211	38°
17059228	38°
17059208	46°
17059209	46°

Air valve rod adjustment – plug gauge method

M4ME – M4MC

17059250	0.030 in
17059253	0.030 in
17059210	0.030 in
17059211	0.030 in
17059228	0.030 in
17059272	0.030 in
All others	0.015 in

Front vacuum break adjustment – angle gauge method

M4ME

17059242	13°
17059240	21°
17059243	21°
17059540	21°
17059543	21°

M4MC

17059247	20°
17059241	21.5°
17059250	23°
17059253	23°
17059553	24°
17059272	24°
17059555	26°
17059210	27°
17059211	27°
17059228	27°

Rear vacuum break adjustment – angle gauge method

M4ME

17059242	13°
17059240	21°
17059243	21°
17059540	23°
17059543	23°

M4MC

17059247	19°
17059241	20.5°
17059208	23°

17059209	23°
17059210	23°
17059211	23°
17059228	23°
17059553	36.5°
17059555	36.5°
17059250	36.5°
17059253	36.5°

Automatic choke coil adjustment
M4ME

17959242	1 notch rich (CCW)
17059240	1 notch rich (CCW)
17059243	1 notch rich (CCW)
17059540	1 notch rich (CCW)
17059543	1 notch rich (CCW)
17059553	2 notches rich (CCW)
17059555	2 notches rich (CCW)
17059250	2 notches rich (CCW)
17059253	2 notches rich (CCW)
17059228	1 notch lean (CW)
17059208	1 notch lean (CW)
17059209	1 notch lean (CW)
17059210	1 notch lean (CW)
17059211	2 notches lean (CW)
17059241	1 notch rich (CCW)
17059247	1 notch rich (CCW)
17059272	2 notches rich (CCW)

Unloader adjustment – angle gauge method
M4ME

17059240	30°
17059243	30°
17059242	30°
17059540	38°
17059543	38°

M4MC

17059553	35°
17059555	35°
17059250	35°
17059253	35°
17059272	35°
17059210	38°
17059211	38°
17059228	38°
17059241	38°
17059247	38°
17059208	42°
17059209	42°

Secondary lockout adjustment	0.015 in
Secondary closing adjustment	0.020 in

E2ME – E2MC carburetors
Float level

17059496	$\frac{5}{16}$ in

Pump adjustment

17059496	$\frac{3}{8}$ in

Choke coil adjustment – plug gauge method

17059496	0.120 in

Fast idle cam – angle gauge method

17059496	24.5°

Front vacuum break adjustment – angle gauge method

17059496	21°
Rear vacuum break adjustment – angle gauge method	30°
Automatic choke coil adjustment	2 notches rich (CCW)
Unloader adjustment – angle gauge method	38°

Air valve spring
M4ME

17059240	$\frac{3}{4}$ turn
17059243	$\frac{3}{4}$ turn
17059540	$\frac{3}{4}$ turn
17059543	$\frac{3}{4}$ turn
17059242	$\frac{3}{4}$ turn

M4MC

17059553	$\frac{1}{2}$ turn
17059555	$\frac{1}{2}$ turn
17059250	$\frac{1}{2}$ turn
17059253	$\frac{1}{2}$ turn
17059208	$\frac{7}{8}$ turn

17059209	$\frac{7}{8}$ turn
17059210	1 turn
17059211	1 turn
17059228	1 turn
17059241	$\frac{3}{4}$ turn
17059247	$\frac{3}{4}$ turn
17059272	$\frac{5}{8}$ turn

1980

E2ME – E2MC carburetors

Choke coil lever adjustment – plug gauge method	0.120 in
Float level	
E2ME	
17080496	$\frac{5}{16}$ in
17080498	$\frac{5}{16}$ in
17080490	$\frac{5}{16}$ in
17080492	$\frac{5}{16}$ in
17080491	$\frac{5}{16}$ in
E2MC	
17080160	$\frac{5}{16}$ in
17080191	11/32 in
17080190	9/32 in
17080195	9/32 in
17080197	9/32 in
17080192	9/32 in
Pump rod adjustment	
E2ME	
17080496	$\frac{3}{8}$ in
17080498	$\frac{3}{8}$ in
17080490	$\frac{3}{8}$ in
17080492	$\frac{3}{8}$ in
17080491	$\frac{3}{8}$ in
E2MC	
17080160	$\frac{1}{4}$ in
17080191	$\frac{1}{4}$ in
17080190	$\frac{1}{4}$ in
17080195	$\frac{1}{4}$ in
17080197	$\frac{1}{4}$ in
17080192	$\frac{1}{4}$ in
Choke rod cam adjustment – angle gauge method	
E2ME	
17080496	24.5°
17080498	24.5°
17080490	24.5°
17080492	24.5°
17080491	24.5°
E2MC	
17080190	24.5°
17080191	24.5°
17080195	24.5°
17080197	24.5°
17080192	24.5°
17080160	14.5°
Vacuum break adjustment	
E2ME	
17080496	38°
17080498	38°
17080490	38°
17080492	38°
17080491	35°
E2MC	
17080190	20°
17080191	18°
17080195	14°
17080197	14°
17080192	20°
17080160	33.5°
Unloader adjustment – angle gauge method	
E2ME	38°
E2MC	38°
17080160	37.5°
all others	38°
Choke setting	tamper proof

E4ME – E4MC carburetors
Float level

E4ME
17080540	$\frac{3}{8}$ in
17080542	$\frac{3}{8}$ in
17080543	$\frac{3}{8}$ in
17080502	$\frac{1}{2}$ in
17080504	$\frac{1}{2}$ in
17080553	15/32 in
17080554	15/32 in
others	N/A

E4MC
17080241	$\frac{7}{16}$ in
17080249	$\frac{7}{16}$ in
17080244	$\frac{5}{16}$ in
17080242	13/32 in
17080240	$\frac{3}{16}$ in
17080243	$\frac{3}{16}$ in
17080271	15/32 in
17080270	15/32 in
17080272	15/32 in

Pump rod location
E4ME
17080540	tamper resistant
17080542	tamper resistant
17080543	tamper resistant
17080502	tamper resistant
17080504	tamper resistant

E4MC
17080241	inner
17080249	inner
17080244	inner
17080242	inner
17080240	inner
17080243	inner
17080253	inner
17080259	inner
17080270	outer
17080271	outer
17080272	outer

Pump rod setting
E4MC
17080241	9/32 in
17080249	9/32 in
17080244	9/32 in
17080242	9/32 in
17080240	9/32 in
17080243	9/32 in
17080253	9/32 in
17080259	9/32 in
17080270	$\frac{3}{8}$ in
17080271	$\frac{3}{8}$ in
17080272	$\frac{3}{8}$ in

E4ME
17080253	9/32 in
17080254	9/32 in
others	tamper resistant
Air valve rod	0.025 in

Choke rod cam adjustment – angle gauge method
E4ME
17080540	14.5°
17080542	14.5°
17080543	14.5°
17080553	17°
17080554	17°

E4MC
17080241	18°
17080249	18°
17080244	24.5°
17080242	14.5°
17080240	14.5°
17080272	14.5°
17080243	14.5°
17080270	14.5°
17080253	17°
17080259	17°
17080271	20°

Front vacuum break adjustment – angle gauge method
E4MC

17080241	23°
17080249	23°
17080272	23°
17080244	18°
17080242	15°
17080240	16°
17080243	16°
17080593	19°
17080540	19°
17080542	19°
17080253	26°
17080259	26°
17080270	26°
17080273	23°

E4ME

17080540	19°
17080542	19°
17080543	19°
17080502	24°
17080504	24°
17080553	25°
17080554	25°

Rear vacuum break adjustment – angle gauge method
E4MC

17080241	20.5°
17080249	20.5°
17080244	14°
17080242	18°
17080240	16°
17080243	16°
17080253	34°
17080259	34°
17080270	34°
17080271	34°
17080272	29.5°

E4ME

17080540	23°
17080542	13°
17080543	23°
17080502	30°
17080504	30°
17080553	35°
17080554	34°

Air valve windup
E4ME

17080540	$\frac{9}{16}$ turn
17080542	$\frac{9}{16}$ turn
17080543	$\frac{9}{16}$ turn
17080502	$\frac{7}{8}$ turn
17080504	$\frac{7}{8}$ turn
17080553	$\frac{1}{2}$ turn
17080554	$\frac{1}{2}$ turn

E4MC

17080241	$\frac{3}{4}$ turn
17080249	$\frac{3}{4}$ turn
17080244	$\frac{5}{8}$ turn
17080242	$\frac{9}{16}$ turn
17080240	$\frac{9}{16}$ turn
17080243	$\frac{9}{16}$ turn
17080253	$\frac{1}{2}$ turn
17080259	$\frac{1}{2}$ turn
17080270	$\frac{5}{8}$ turn
17080271	$\frac{5}{8}$ turn
17080272	$\frac{5}{8}$ turn

1   General description

The fuel system of all models comprises a rear fuel tank, a mechanically operated fuel pump, a carburetor and an air cleaner.

The carburetor may be of dual or four barrel type depending upon the engine capacity and the date of production of the vehicle.

All models are equipped with some form of emission control equipment. The later the date of the vehicle, the more complex and sophisticated do the carburetor and the emission control system become.

2   Air cleaner – servicing

Non-temperature-controlled type (paper element)
1   At the intervals specified in Chapter 1, unscrew the wing nut on top of the air cleaner cover and remove the cover.

2   Remove the cleaner element and discard it, then wipe clean the interior of the casing, insert a new element and install the cover.

Temperature-controlled (thermostatic) air cleaner (TAC)

3   If a plain paper air cleaner element is used, replace it as described in paragraphs 1 and 2 of this Section.

4   If a Polywrap element is used, remove the Polywrap band from the paper element and discard the element. If the band is in good undamaged condition, rinse it clean in kerosene and squeeze it dry. Dip the band in clean engine oil and gently squeeze out the excess. Install the band to a new paper element and reassemble.

5   Any malfunction in the temperature-controlled air cleaner should first be checked out by starting the engine (cold) and observing the position of the deflector flap valve, using a mirror to look up the intake nozzle of the cleaner. This should be closed to cold air but open to warm air. Conversely, once the engine has warmed up, the flap should be open to cold and closed to warm. Both tests are carried out with the engine idling.

6   The vacuum unit can be removed from the air cleaner by drilling out the two spotwelds to remove the retaining strap. The new vacuum unit repair pack will contain the necessary sheet metal screws to hold the retaining strap in position when reassembling.

7   The sensor can be removed by prying up the tabs on the sensor retaining clip.

3   Fuel pump – description and testing

1   The fuel pump is a sealed type and is actuated from the engine camshaft. A pushrod is used between the camshaft and the pump rocker. Fuel pumps on 231 V6 engines are driven directly from the camshaft eccentric without pushrod.

2   No servicing can be carried out as the unit is sealed, but if the pump is suspected of being faulty, carry out the following test.

3   Verify that gas is in the fuel tank. Disconnect the primary wire which runs between the coil and the distributor to prevent the engine firing when the starter motor is actuated. (1974 models only). For 1975 through 1980 models, disconnect the distributor wiring marked 'BAT'.

4   Disconnect the fuel inlet pipe from the carburetor and place its open end in a container.

5   Operate the starter motor and check that well-defined spurts of fuel are being ejected from the open end of the pipe. If so, the pump is operating correctly; if not, replace the pump as described in the following section.

4   Fuel pump – removal and installation

1   To remove the pump, remove the fuel inlet and outlet pipes. Use two wrenches to prevent damage to the pump and connections (photo).

2   Remove the fuel pump mounting bolts, the pump, and the gasket (photo).

3   If the pushrod is to be removed (Chevrolet engines only), first remove the pipe plug or the pump adapter and gasket, as appropriate (photo).

4   When installing, first install the pushrod using the gasket sealant on the pipe plug or gasket (where applicable). Retain the pushrod in position using heavy grease (photo).

5   Install the pump using a new gasket. On Oldsmobile, Pontiac and Buick engines, insert the fuel pump into position and ensure that its rocker arm contacts the camshaft (photo). Use gasket sealant on the screw threads (photos).

7   Connect the fuel pipes, start the engine and check for leaks.

5   Fuel filter – replacement

1   See Chapter 1 for the step-by-step procedure.

6   Fuel tank – removal and installation

1   The fuel tank located between the frame rails and behind the rear axle is held in place by two steel straps. These straps are hinged at either the front or the rear end (with a bolt through the hinge) and secured at the opposite end with a bolt and nut assembly.

2   Disconnect the battery before performing any servicing operations involving the fuel supply.

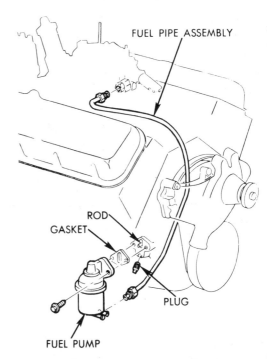

Fig. 4.1 Chevrolet engine fuel pump location (on Oldsmobile engines the pump is attached to the right side of the timing chain cover; on Buick and Pontiac engines it is on the left side)

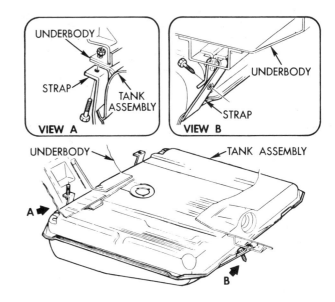

Fig. 4.2 Fuel tank installation – typical (Sec 6)

3   Disconnect the fuel gauge wiring to the top of the tank. On early models, the wire should be disconnected from inside the trunk and then fed through the trunk floorpan with the rubber grommet pushed out of place.

4   Raise the vehicle for access underneath the car.

5   Drain all fuel from the tank into a clean container. Since there are no drain on some models, it is necessary to siphon the fuel through the filler neck, or drain the fuel through the fuel feed line running to the carburetor. Do not start the siphoning process with your mouth as serious personal injury could result. Also make sure that no open flames, lighted cigarettes or sparks are in the area as they could ignite the fuel vapor.

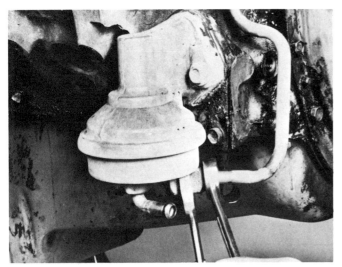

4.1 Removing fuel lines

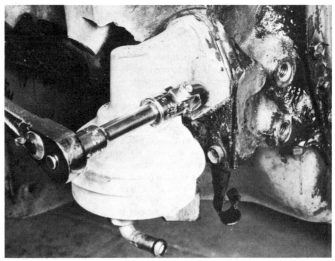

4.2 Removing mounting bolts

4.3 Removing fuel pump pushrod (Chevrolet engines)

4.4 Use heavy grease to retain pushrod during reassembly (Chevrolet engines)

6   Disconnect the fuel hose and/or vapor return hose at the top of the tank.

7   Remove the gauge ground wire attached to the underbody.

8   Disconnect the filler neck at the tank.

9   Support the bottom of the tank using an adjustable jack and a piece of wood to spread the load.

10   Remove the tank strap bolts and carefully lower the tank checking that all connections are free of the tank as it is lowered. Read the following section for important repair and storage information.

11   Installation is a reversal of the removal process. Make sure all electrical connections are clean and properly installed and all hoses are tightened securely to the tank.

7   Fuel tank – repairs and storage

1   Any repairs to the fuel tank or filler neck should be carried out by a professional who has experience in this critical and potentially dangerous work. Even after cleaning and flushing of the fuel system, explosive fumes can remain and ignite during the repairing of the tank.

2   If the fuel tank is removed from the vehicle, it should not be placed in any area where sparks, or open flames could ignite the fumes coming out of the tank. Be especially careful inside garages where a water heater is located as the pilot light of the heater could cause an explosion.

4.5 On Buick, Oldsmobile and Pontiac engines, make sure the rocker arm (arrow) contacts the drive eccentric properly (Pontiac engine shown)

8 Carburetors – description

1   Reference should be made to the Specifications Section of this Chapter for the general application of the different types of carburetors installed during the production run of vehicles covered by this manual. It is emphasized that the information given is not intended to identify a particular carburetor with a specific vehicle, and the actual carburetor fitted to your engine should be checked out by recording the number stamped on the unit, and checking it with your partsman. It is very important not to use an incorrect unit, nor to modify the jets or internal components by substituting parts with different manufacturer's part numbers from those originally used.

2   All units have automatic chokes, either stove (hot air) heated from the manifold, or electrically heated.

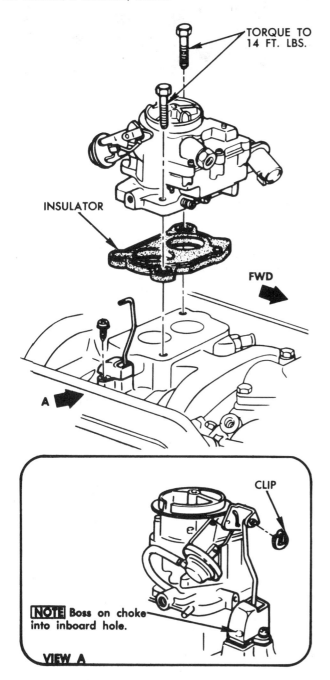

Fig. 4.3 Mechanical type automatic choke – typical (Sec 8)

3   Depending upon engine capacity, the carburetor may be of dual or four-barrel downdraft type.

4   Overhaul of a worn carburetor is not difficult, but always obtain a repair kit in advance, which will contain all the necessary gaskets and replaceable items.

5   If a carburetor has seen considerable use, and is obviously well worn, it will probably be more economical to replace it with a new, or factory reconditioned unit.

Rochester 2G series carburetor

6   This carburetor is a dual barrel, side bowl design.

7   Units fitted to manual and automatic transmission vehicles are similar but vary in calibration.

8   The main metering jets are of a fixed type, calibration being accomplished through a system of air bleeds.

9   A power enrichment valve assembly is incorporated by which power mixtures are controlled by air velocity past the boost venturi according to engine demands.

10 On later model vehicles, an electrically-operated throttle closing solenoid (controlled through the ignition switch) is used to ensure that the throttle valve closes fully after the ignition is switched off, to prevent running-on (dieseling).

11 The choke is automatic and is operated by an exhaust manifold heated coil.

Rochester 4MV (Quadrajet) series carburetor

12 This is a downdraft two stage unit. The primary side uses a triple venturi system. The secondary side has two large bores and one metering system which supplements the primary main metering system and receives fuel from a common float chamber.

Rochester M4MC (Quadrajet) series carburetor

13 This is also downdraft two stage unit and is very similar to the 4 MV unit.

Rochester E2 – E4 series

The E2ME, E4ME and E4MC 2 and 4 barrel carburetors are designed for use with the C-4 (Computer Controlled Catalytic System). The 2-barrel has a triple venturi stackup while the 4-barrel has a TPS (Throttle Position Sensor) designed to assure precise and economical fuel metering.

Rochester M2ME – M2MC Series

The M2 series carburetors are 2-barrel, single stage affairs of downdraft design for use with V8 and turbocharged V6 motors. Its primary side is of the M4MC design.

9 Carburetors – removal and installation

1   Remove the air cleaner.

2   Disconnect the fuel and vacuum pipes from the carburetor.

3   Disconnect the choke rod or electrical wire (M4ME and M2ME carburetors).

4   Disconnect the accelerator linkage.

5   Disconnect the throttle valve linkage or downshift cable (automatic transmission).

6   Remove all hoses and electrical connections, making **very careful note** of where they were removed from. Tags or coded pieces of tape will help.

7   Remove the carburetor attaching nuts and/or bolts.

8   Lift away the carburetor.

9   Remove the gasket and/or insulator.

10 Installation is the reverse of the removal procedure, but the following points should be noted:

   a)   *By filling the carburetor bowl with fuel, the initial start-up will be easier and less drain on the battery will occur.*

   b)   *New gaskets should be used.*

   c)   *Idle speed and mixture settings should be checked, and adjusted if necessary.*

10 Carburetor (Rochester 2GV) – idle adjustment

1   Idle speed adjustment must be carried out after the engine has fully warmed up. The air cleaner must be fitted, except where

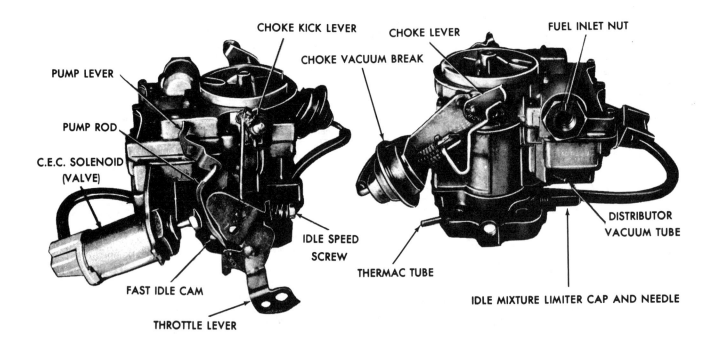

PUMP LEVER

PUMP ROD

C.E.C. SOLENOID (VALVE)

CHOKE KICK LEVER

CHOKE VACUUM BREAK

CHOKE LEVER

FUEL INLET NUT

IDLE SPEED SCREW

FAST IDLE CAM

THROTTLE LEVER

THERMAC TUBE

DISTRIBUTOR VACUUM TUBE

IDLE MIXTURE LIMITER CAP AND NEEDLE

Fig. 4.4 Rochester 2GV carburetor (Sec 10)

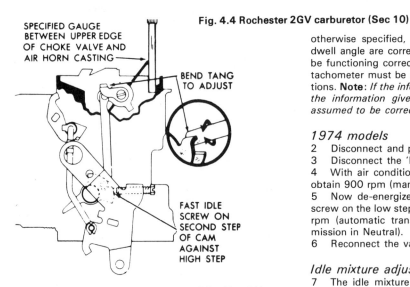

SPECIFIED GAUGE BETWEEN UPPER EDGE OF CHOKE VALVE AND AIR HORN CASTING

BEND TANG TO ADJUST

FAST IDLE SCREW ON SECOND STEP OF CAM AGAINST HIGH STEP

Fig. 4.5 Choke rod adjustment diagram – 2GV (Sec 11)

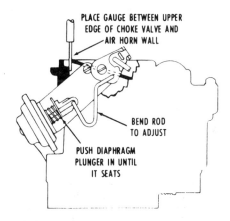

PLACE GAUGE BETWEEN UPPER EDGE OF CHOKE VALVE AND AIR HORN WALL

BEND ROD TO ADJUST

PUSH DIAPHRAGM PLUNGER IN UNTIL IT SEATS

Fig. 4.6 Vacuum break adjustment diagram – 2GV (Sec 12)

otherwise specified, and it is essential that the ignition timing and dwell angle are correctly set. All emission control systems must also be functioning correctly. In order to check engine speed, an external tachometer must be connected, following the manufacturer's instructions. **Note:** *If the information given on the decal label has superseded the information given in Specifications, the decal label should be assumed to be correct.*

1974 models
2   Disconnect and plug the distributor vacuum pipe.
3   Disconnect the 'Fuel Tank' line from the vapor canister.
4   With air conditioning off, adjust the idle stop solenoid screw to obtain 900 rpm (manual in Neutral) or 600 rpm (automatic in Drive).
5   Now de-energize the idle stop solenoid and with the idle cam screw on the low step of the cam, adjust the cam screw to obtain 400 rpm (automatic transmission in Drive) or 500 rpm (manual transmission in Neutral).
6   Reconnect the vacuum and fuel tank lines.

Idle mixture adjustment
7   The idle mixture screws are fitted with limiter caps as already described and any minor adjustment should be restricted to turning the screws within the extent of their travel ($\frac{1}{2}$ to $\frac{3}{4}$ turn clockwise). Turning the screws in leans the mixture.
8   If after overhaul or replacement of carburetor internal components, it is essential to adjust the mixture screws, carry out the following operations:
9   Disconnect the fuel tank vent hose from the vapor canister.
10 Disconnect and plug the distributor vacuum line.
11 Switch off the air conditioning (if fitted).
12 Set transmission in Neutral (manual) or Drive (automatic).
13 Using a pair of pliers break off the tabs on the mixture screw limiter cap.
14 Refer to Specifications and set the engine idle speed to the initial idle speed (lean drop method) given in Specifications Section.
15 Now turn out the mixture screws equally until maximum idle speed is achieved. Readjust the initial speed to that given in the Specifications.
16 Now turn both mixture screws in equally until the final idle speed is obtained as given in the Specifications Section.
17 Reconnect the hoses and fit new limiter caps with the cap stops at the fully rich (backed out) position.
18 An alternative method of setting the idle mixture adjustment is to

connect a CO meter (exhaust gas analyzer) in accordance with the maker's instructions and then turn the mixture screws in or out until the CO level is within the maximum shown in the Specifications Section, consistent with smooth idling.

11 Carburetor (Rochester 2GV) – choke rod adjustment

Note: *The following adjustment will normally only be required after overhaul or repair of the carburetor.*
1   Turn the idle stop screw in until it just touches the bottom step of the fast idle cam, then screw it in exactly one full turn.
2   Position the idle screw so that it is on the second stop of the fast idle cam against the shoulder of the high step.
3   Hold the choke valve plate towards the closed position (using a rubber band to keep it in place) and check the gap between the upper edge of the choke valve plate and the inside wall of the air horn.
4   Adjust to the specified gap, if necessary, by bending the tang on the upper choke lever. The setting should provide the specified fast idle speeds.

12 Carburetor (Rochester 2GV) – choke vacuum break adjustment

1   Remove the air cleaner and plug the air cleaner sensor vacuum take-off port in the carburetor.
2   Using an external suction source, apply suction to the vacuum break diaphragm until the plunger is fully seated.
3   With the diaphragm fully seated, push the choke valve towards the closed position and place a gauge of the specified thickness between the air horn and the choke blade.
4   Bend the vacuum break rod if necessary to obtain the specified dimension (see Specifications Section).

13 Carburetor (Rochester 2GV) – choke unloader adjustment

1   Hold the throttle valve plates in the fully open position.
2   Hold the choke valve plate towards the closed position using a rubber band to keep it in place.
3   Check the gap between the upper edge of the choke valve plate and the inside wall of the air horn.
4   Bend the tang on the throttle lever to adjust the gap to the specified value, if necessary, as given in Specifications Section.

14 Carburetor (Rochester 2GV) – choke coil rod adjustment

1   Hold the choke valve plate fully open.
2   Disconnect the thermostatic coil rod from the upper lever and push down on the rod as far as it will go. The top of the rod should be level with the bottom of the hole in the choke lever.
3   Adjust if necessary by bending the rod.

15 Carburetor (Rochester 2GV) – accelerator pump adjustment

1   Unscrew the idle speed screw.
2   Close both throttle valve plates completely and measure from the top surface of the air horn ring to the top of the pump rod.
3   Bend the rod to obtain the specified dimension.

16 Carburetor (Rochester 2GV) – overhaul

1   When a carburetor develops faults after a considerable mileage, it is usually more economical to replace the complete unit, rather than to completely dismantle it and replace individual components. Where, however, it is decided to strip and rebuild the unit, first obtain a repair kit which will contain all the necessary gaskets and other needed items, and proceed in the following sequence.
2   Bend back the lockwasher tabs then remove the idle stop solenoid (where applicable) from the carburetor.
3   Remove the choke lever from the vacuum break diaphragm link

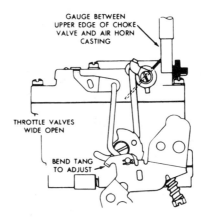

Fig. 4.7 Choke unloader adjustment diagram – 2GV (Sec 13)

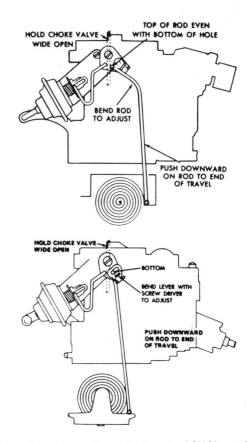

Fig. 4.8 Choke coil rod adjustment – 2GV (Sec 14)

and the vacuum break link from the diaphragm plunger. The diaphragm plunger stem spring need not be removed.
4   Disconnect the vacuum break hose from the tube then remove the diaphragm from the air horn by unscrewing two retaining screws.
5   Remove the fuel inlet filter nut, filter, spring and two gaskets.
6   Remove the pump rod from the throttle lever after removing the retaining clip. Rotate the upper pump lever counter-clockwise, then remove the pump rod from the lever by aligning the rod 'pip' with the lever notch.
7   Remove the fast idle cam retaining screw, rotate the cam and remove it from the rod.
8   Hold the choke open, rotate the upper end of the choke rod towards the pump lever and remove the rod from the upper choke lever.

Fig. 4.9 2GV carburetor air horn – exploded view (Sec 15)

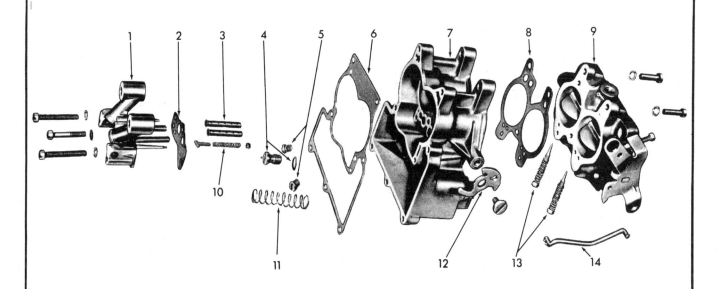

Fig. 4.10 Exploded view of 2GV carburetor bowl and throttle body (Sec 16)

1 Cluster assembly	7 Bowl assembly	11 Accelerator pump spring
2 Gasket	8 Throttle body to bowl gasket	12 Fast idle cam
3 Splash shield (main well)		13 Idle mixture screws
4 Power valve assembly	9 Throttle body assembly	14 Choke rod
5 Main jets	10 Pump discharge check assembly	
6 Air horn gasket		

9   Remove the air horn from the float bowl (8 screws).

10   Remove the float hinge pin, float, splash shield and float needle.

11   Unscrew the float needle seat and remove the gasket.

12   Remove the air horn to float bowl gasket.

13   Depress the power piston shaft, and allow the spring to snap sharply and eject the piston from the casting.

14   Remove the inner pump lever retaining screw then remove the outer pump lever and plastic washer from the air horn. Place the plunger in gasoline to prevent the rubber from drying out.

15   Rotate the pump plunger stem out of the hole in the inner lever if it is required to remove it. Do not bend the tang on the inner lever.

16   If the choke shaft or the valve need replacement, remove the two staked screws, remove the valve, then remove the shaft and lever from the air horn.

17   Remove the pump plunger return spring from the pump well, followed by the inlet check ball (where applicable).

18   Remove the pump inlet screen from the bottom of the float bowl (where applicable).

19   Unscrew the main jets, power valve and gaskets.

20   Remove the cluster and gasket (3 screws and washers). Note the fiber washer on the center screw.

21   Remove the pump discharge spring retainer, the spring and the check ball.

22   Remove the throttle body to bowl attaching screws. Remove the body and gasket.

23   Further dismantling is not recommended. If it is essential to remove the idle mixture needles, pry out the plastic limiter caps, then count the number of turns to bottom the needles and fit replacements in exactly the same position. New limiter caps should be fitted after running adjustments have been made.

24   Clean all metal parts in a suitable cold solvent. Do not immerse rubber parts, plastic parts, the vacuum break assembly, or the idle stop solenoid, or permanent damage will result. Do not probe the jets, but blow them through with clean, dry compressed air. Examine all fixed and moving parts for cracks, distortion, wear and other damage; replace as necessary. Discard all gaskets and fuel inlet filter.

25   Assembly is essentially the reverse of the removal procedure, but the following points should be noted:

   a)   If new idle mixture screws are used, and the original setting was not noted, install the screws finger-tight to seat them, then back-off 4 full turns.

   b)   When installing the choke valve on the seat, the letters 'RP' face upward. Ensure that there is 0.020 inch clearance

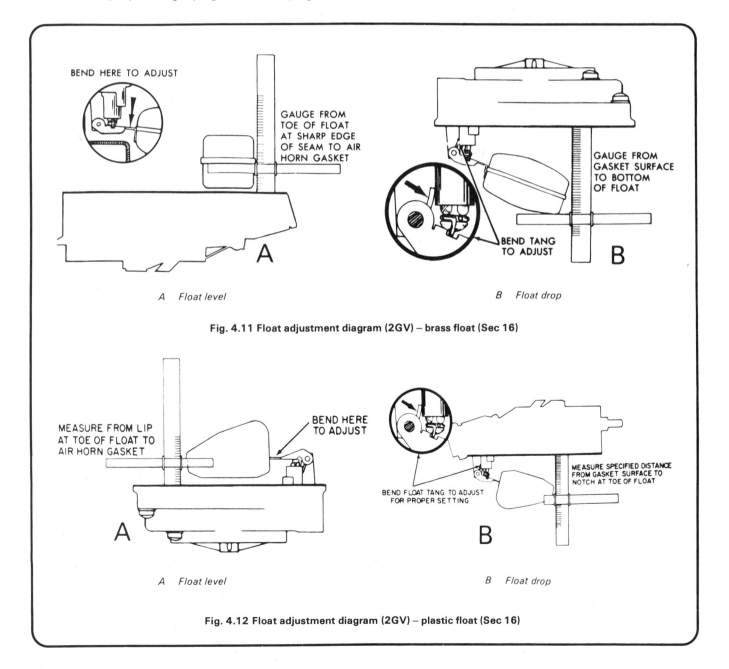

A   Float level   B   Float drop

Fig. 4.11 Float adjustment diagram (2GV) – brass float (Sec 16)

A   Float level   B   Float drop

Fig. 4.12 Float adjustment diagram (2GV) – plastic float (Sec 16)

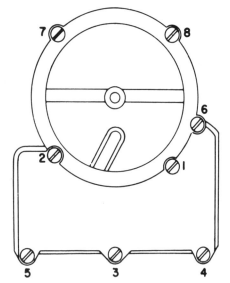

Fig. 4.13 Air horn tightening sequence (Sec 16)

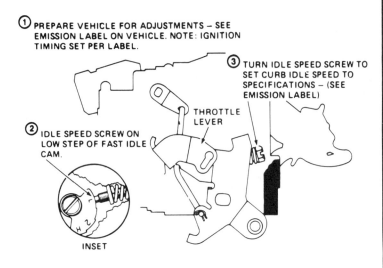

① PREPARE VEHICLE FOR ADJUSTMENTS – SEE EMISSION LABEL ON VEHICLE. NOTE: IGNITION TIMING SET PER LABEL.

③ TURN IDLE SPEED SCREW TO SET CURB IDLE SPEED TO SPECIFICATIONS – (SEE EMISSION LABEL)

THROTTLE LEVER

② IDLE SPEED SCREW ON LOW STEP OF FAST IDLE CAM.

INSET

Fig. 4.15 Idle adjustment diagram for 2GC carburetor without solenoid (Sec 17)

AIR HORN

ACCELERATOR PUMP ROD

FUEL INLET NUT

THROTTLE LEVER

IDLE MIXTURE SCREW

FAST IDLE CAM

CHOKE COIL HOUSING

CANISTER PURGE TUBE

CHOKE HEAT INLET

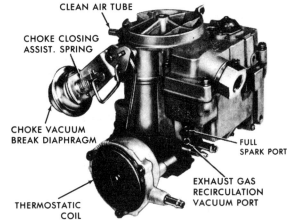

CLEAN AIR TUBE

CHOKE CLOSING ASSIST. SPRING

CHOKE VACUUM BREAK DIAPHRAGM

FULL SPARK PORT

EXHAUST GAS RECIRCULATION VACUUM PORT

THERMOSTATIC COIL

Fig. 4.14 Rochester 2GC carburetor (Sec 17)

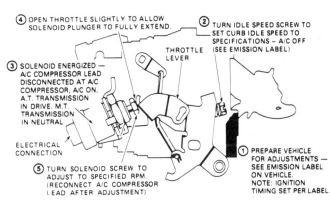

④ OPEN THROTTLE SLIGHTLY TO ALLOW SOLENOID PLUNGER TO FULLY EXTEND.

② TURN IDLE SPEED SCREW TO SET CURB IDLE SPEED TO SPECIFICATIONS – A/C OFF (SEE EMISSION LABEL)

THROTTLE LEVER

③ SOLENOID ENERGIZED – A/C COMPRESSOR LEAD DISCONNECTED AT A/C COMPRESSOR, A/C ON, A.T. TRANSMISSION IN DRIVE. M.T. TRANSMISSION IN NEUTRAL

ELECTRICAL CONNECTION

⑤ TURN SOLENOID SCREW TO ADJUST TO SPECIFIED RPM. (RECONNECT A/C COMPRESSOR LEAD AFTER ADJUSTMENT)

① PREPARE VEHICLE FOR ADJUSTMENTS – SEE EMISSION LABEL ON VEHICLE. NOTE: IGNITION TIMING SET PER LABEL.

Fig. 4.16 Idle speed adjustment diagram for 2GC carburetor with solenoid (Sec 17)

⑤ BEND ROD HERE TO ADJUST (SEE INSET)

④ EDGE OF COIL LEVER MUST LINE UP WITH EDGE OF 120" PLUG GAUGE IN HOLE INSIDE CHOKE HOUSING

③ CLOSE CHOKE VALVE BY PUSHING UP ON LEVER

① REMOVE THERMOSTATIC COVER. COIL ASSEMBLY. AND INSIDE BAFFLE PLATE

② PLACE LOW IDLE SPEED SCREW ON HIGHEST STEP OF FAST IDLE CAM

Fig. 4.17 Choke coil lever adjustment diagram – 2GC carburetor (Sec 19)

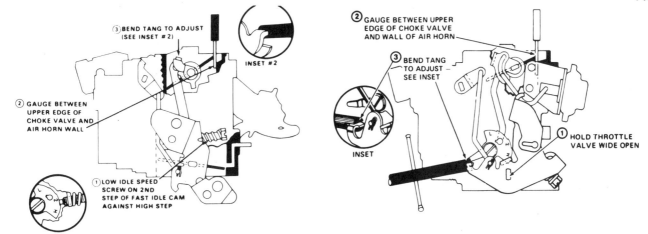

Fig. 4.18 Fast idle cam adjustment diagram – 2GC carburetor (Sec 20)

Fig. 4.19 Choke unloader adjustment diagram – 2GC carburetor (Sec 21)

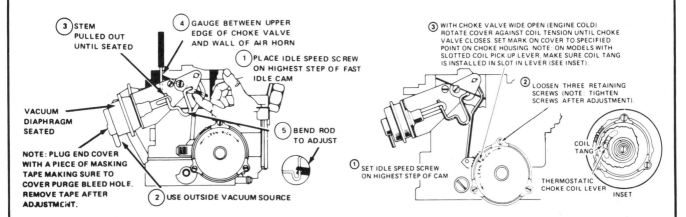

Fig. 4.20 Choke vacuum break adjustment diagram – 2GC carburetor (Sec 22)

Fig. 4.21 Automatic choke coil adjustment diagram – 2GC carburetor (Sec 23)

Fig. 4.22 Removing vacuum break lever – 2GC carburetor (Sec 23)

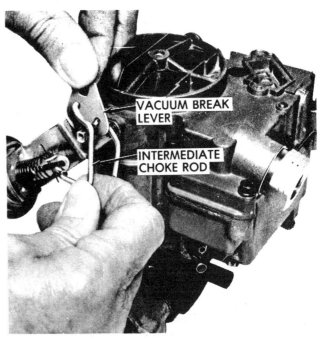

Fig. 4.23 Removing intermediate choke rod – 2GC carburetor (Sec 24)

between the choke kick lever on the air horn before tightening the choke valve screws.

c) *Brass float: With the air horn inverted and the air horn gasket installed, measure the distance from the gasket to the edge of the float seam at the outer edge of the float pontoon. Adjust the float level to the specified dimension by bending the float arm. With the air horn assembly upright and float freely suspended, measure from the gasket to the bottom of the float pontoon. Adjust the float drop to the specified dimension by bending the tang adjacent to the float needle.*

d) *Plastic float: Refer to the procedure for the brass float, but note that for float level and float drop, the dimension is taken from the lip at the toe of the float in both instances.*

e) *Install and tighten the air horn screws evenly in the order shown.*

f) *After reassembly, carry out all the settings and adjustments listed previously in this Chapter.*

17 Carburetor (Rochester 2GC-2GE) – idle adjustment

Note: *If the information given on the decal label has superseded the information given in the Specifications, the decal label should be assumed to be correct.*

Idle speed – 1975 models

1   Have the engine at normal operating temperature with the ignition settings correct.
2   Disconnect the fuel tank hose from the vapor canister.
3   Connect a tachometer to the engine and switch the air conditioning off.
4   Turn the idle speed screw until the engine is running at the speeds specified in Specifications Section with manual transmission in Neutral and automatic transmission in Drive.

Idle mixture – 1975 models

5   The mixture screws are fitted with limiter caps which restrict their movement between $\frac{1}{2}$ and $\frac{3}{4}$ turn lean. Any adjustment should be kept to this but where the carburetor has been overhauled or new components fitted then the caps should be broken off and the following operations carried out.
6   Have the engine at normal operating temperature with air conditioning off and a tachometer connected to the engine.
7   Disconnect the fuel tank hose from the vapor canister.
8   Adjust the idle speed screw until the initial idle speed (see Specifications Section) is obtained.
9   Now unscrew the mixture screws equally until maximum idle speed is achieved. Readjust the idle speed screw again to obtain initial idle speed.
10 Screw in the mixture screws equally until final idle speed (lean drop) is obtained.

Idle speed – 1976 and later models

11 Have the engine at normal operating temperature with ignition settings correct and emission control systems operating correctly.
12 Set the idle speed screw on the low step of the fast idle cam.
13 Turn the idle speed screw to set the curb (initial idle speed) to specification (see Specifications Section or vehicle decal).
14 *Where a solenoid is fitted to the carburetor*, carry out the operations described in paragraphs 11 and 13 and then with (i) the solenoid energized, (ii) the lead disconnected from the air conditioner compressor, (iii) the air conditioner on, open the throttle to allow the solenoid plunger to extend fully. Turn the solenoid hexagonal headed bolt until the idle speed is 700 rpm (manual) or 650 rpm (automatic). Reconnect the compressor lead on completion.
15 2GC carburetors are fitted with a solenoid when the vehicle is equipped with automatic transmission or air conditioning.

Idle mixture – 1976 and later models

16 Refer to paragraphs 5 to 10 of this Section.

18 Carburetor (Rochester 2GC-2GE) – accelerator pump rod adjustment

1   The procedure is as for 2GV carburetor (Section 15).

19 Carburetor (Rochester 2GC-2GE) – choke coil lever adjustment

1   Remove three screws and retainers and remove the thermostatic coil cover, gasket and inside baffle plate assembly.
2   Place the idle speed screw on the highest step of the fast idle cam.
3   Close the choke valve by pushing up on the intermediate choke lever.
4   The edge of the coil lever inside the choke housing must align with the edge of the gauge.
5   If necessary, bend the choke rod to adjust.

20 Carburetor (Rochester 2GC-2GE) – fast idle cam adjustment

1   Place the idle speed screw on the second step of the cam, against the high step.
2   Check the dimension between the upper edge of the choke valve and the air horn wall.
3   If adjustment is necessary to obtain the specified dimension, bend the choke lever tang.

21 Carburetor (Rochester 2GC-2GE) – choke unloader adjustment

1   Hold the throttle valve open with the fingers.
2   Using a suitable gauge, check that the clearance between the edge of the choke valve plate and the air horn wall is as specified (see Specifications Section).
3   If necessary, bend the tang to adjust.

22 Carburetor (Rochester 2GC-2GE) – vacuum break adjustment

1   Using a separate source of suction, such as the mouth or a small hand pump, seat the vacuum break diaphragm.
2   Cover the vacuum break bleed hole with a piece of masking tape.
3   Place the idle speed screw on the high step of the fast cam idle.
4   Hold the choke coil lever inside the choke housing towards the closed choke position.
5   Check the dimension between the upper edge of the choke valve and the air horn wall. If adjustment is required to obtain the specified dimension (see Specifications Section) bend the vacuum break rod.
6   Remove the masking tape on the vacuum unit bleed hole and reconnect the vacuum hose.

23 Carburetor (Rochester 2GC-2GE) – automatic choke coil adjustment

1   Place the idle speed screw on the highest step of the fast idle cam.
2   Loosen the choke coil cover retaining screws.
3   Rotate the cover against the coil tension until the choke begins to close. Continue rotating until the index mark aligns with the specified point on the choke housing, which is between the center and $\frac{1}{2}$ notch lean.
4   Tighten the choke cover retaining screws.

24 Carburetor (Rochester 2GC-2GE) – overhaul

Note: *When a carburetor develops faults after a considerable mileage, it is usually more economical to replace the complete unit rather than to completely dismantle it and replace individual components. However, if it is decided to strip and rebuild the unit, first obtain a repair kit which will contain all the necessary gaskets and other needed items, and proceed in the following sequence. Steps 24 through 27 are not applicable to the 2GE carburetor, as it has an electrically controlled choke mechanism that cannot be serviced.*

1   If the carburetor is fitted with a solenoid (automatic transmission or air conditioning) this should be removed before dismantling the carburetor. To do this, bend back the lockwasher tabs and unscrew the

Fig. 4.24 Removing power piston – 2GC carburetor (Sec 24)

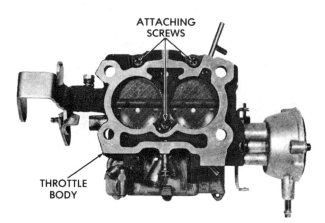

Fig. 4.25 Throttle body attaching screws – 2GC carburetor (Sec 24)

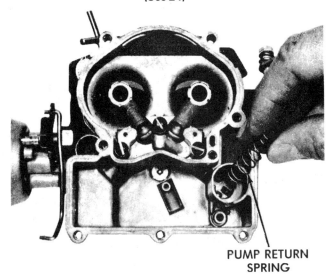

Fig. 4.26 Removing pump return spring – 2GC carburetor (Sec 24)

large nut which holds the solenoid to the bracket. Avoid immersion of the solenoid in cleaning solvent.

2 Remove the fuel inlet filter nut, gasket, filter and spring.

3 Disconnect the lower end of the pump rod from the throttle lever.

4 Remove the upper end of the pump rod from the pump lever.

5 Remove the vacuum break diaphragm hose.

6 Remove the vacuum break diaphragm assembly (2 screws) and disconnect it from the lever on the end of the choke shaft.

7 Remove the vacuum break lever from the end of the choke shaft (1 screw), then remove the intermediate choke rod from the vacuum break lever on the coil housing.

8 Remove the fast idle cam retaining screw, then remove the cam from the end of the choke rod. The upper end of the rod cannot be removed until the air horn has been removed from the float bowl.

9 Remove the 8 air horn attaching screws and lockwashers, then lift off the air horn.

10 Remove the float hinge pin and lift off the float. The float needle and pull clip (where applicable) can now be removed from the float arm.

11 Unscrew the float needle seat and remove the gasket.

12 Depress the power piston and release it to allow it to snap free.

13 Remove the pump plunger assembly and inner pump lever from the shaft by loosening the set screws on the inner lever.

14 If the pump assembly is to be overhauled, break off the flattened end of the pump plunger stem; the service pump uses a grooved pump plunger stem and retaining clip. After removng the inner pump lever and pump assembly, remove the outer lever and shaft assembly from the air horn. Remove the plastic washer from the pump plunger shaft.

15 Remove the gasket from the air horn.

16 Remove the fuel inlet baffle (next to the needle seat).

17 Taking care not to bend the choke shaft, remove the choke valve. The retaining screws may need to be suitably dressed to permit removal.

18 Remove the choke valve shaft. Remove the fast idle cam rod and lever from the shaft.

19 Remove the pump plunger return spring from the float bowl pump well, then invert the bolt and remove the aluminium ball.

20 Remove the main metering jets, power valve and gasket from inside the float bowl.

21 Remove the three screws which retain the venturi cluster; remove the cluster and gasket.

22 Use needle-nosed pliers to remove the pump discharge spring retainer, then remove the spring and check ball from the discharge passage.

23 Remove the three large throttle body to bowl attaching screws and lockwashers. Remove the throttle body and gasket.

24 Remove the thermostatic choke coil cover (3 screws and retainers) and gasket from the choke housing. Do not remove the cap baffle from beneath the coil cover.

25 Remove the choke housing baffle plate.

26 From inside the choke housing, remove the 2 attaching screws; remove the housing and gasket.

27 Remove the screw from the end of the intermediate choke shaft, then remove the choke lever from the shaft. Remove the inner choke coil lever and shaft assembly from the choke housing, followed by the rubber dust seal.

28 Further dismantling is not recommended, particularly with regard to the throttle valves or shaft since it may be impossible to reassemble the valves correctly in relation to the idle discharge orifices. If it is essential to remove the idle mixture needles, break off the plastic limiter caps then count the number of turns to bottom the needles and fit replacements in exactly the same position. New limiter caps should be fitted after running adjustments have been made.

29 Clean all metal parts in a suitable cold solvent. Do not immerse rubber parts, plastic parts, diaphragm assemblies or pump plungers, as permanent damage will result. Do not probe the jets, but blow through with clean, dry compressed air. Examine all fixed and moving parts for cracks, distortion, wear and other damage; replace as necessary. Discard all gaskets and the fuel inlet filter.

30 Assembly is essentially the reverse of the removal procedure, but the following points should be noted:

a) If new idle mixture screws were used, and the original setting was not noted, install the screws finger-tight to seat them, then back off 4 full turns.

b) When installing the rubber dust seal in the choke housing cavity, the seal lip faces towards the carburetor after the housing is installed.

c) *Before installing the choke cover coil and baffle plate assembly, carry out the choke coil lever adjustment (Section 19).*

d) *When installing the choke coil and cover assembly, the end of the coil must be below the plastic tang on the inner choke housing lever. At this stage carry out the automatic choke coil adjustment (Section 23).*

e) *When installing the venturi cluster, ensure that a gasket is fitted on the center screw.*

f) *Install the choke valve with the letters 'RP' or the part number, facing upwards.*

g) *Carry out float level and float drop checks as specified for the 2GV carburetor in Section 16 for plastic floats.*

h) *Install and tighten the air horn screws as shown for 2GV carburetors.*

j) *After reassembly, carry out the relevant settings and adjustments listed previously in this Chapter.*

25 Carburetor (M2M series) – idle adjustment

1   Idle speed adjustment must be carried out after the engine has fully warmed up. The air cleaner must be fitted, except where otherwise specified, and it is essential that the ignition timing and dwell angle are correctly set. All emission control systems must also be functioning correctly. In order to check engine speed, an external tachometer must be connected, following the manufacturer's instructions. **Note:** *if the information given on the decal label has superseded the information given in Specifications, the decal label should be assumed to be correct.*

2   Disconnect the electrical lead from the idle speed solenoid (if so equipped).

3   Adjust the base idle speed screw to the rpm specified on the emission label. The shift selector on automatic transmissions should be in Drive, and manual transmissions should be in Neutral.

4   The idle mixture screws have been preset at the factory and sealed. The only time the mixture screws will need adjusting is in the

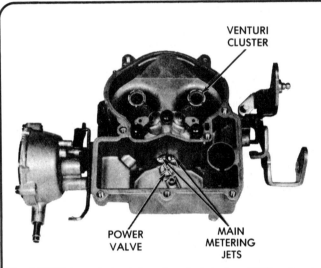

Fig. 4.27 Main metering jets and venturi cluster – 2GC carburetor (Sec 24)

Fig. 4.28 Removing pump discharge retainer – 2GC carburetor (Sec 24)

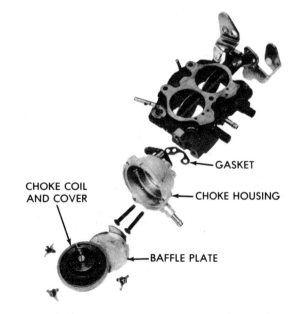

Fig. 4.29 Choke housing assembly – 2GC carburetor (Sec 24)

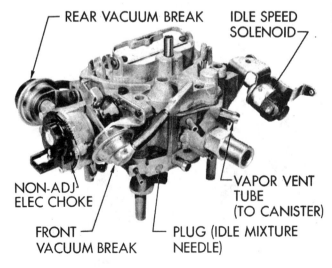

Fig. 4.30 Typical M2ME carburetor (Sec 25)

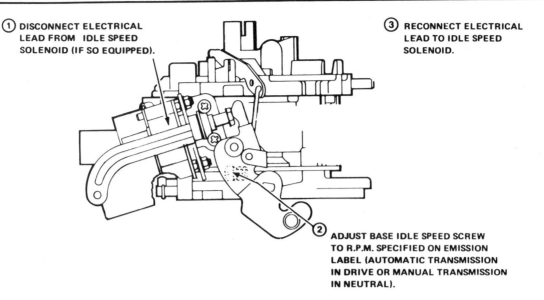

① DISCONNECT ELECTRICAL LEAD FROM IDLE SPEED SOLENOID (IF SO EQUIPPED).

③ RECONNECT ELECTRICAL LEAD TO IDLE SPEED SOLENOID.

② ADJUST BASE IDLE SPEED SCREW TO R.P.M. SPECIFIED ON EMISSION LABEL (AUTOMATIC TRANSMISSION IN DRIVE OR MANUAL TRANSMISSION IN NEUTRAL).

Fig. 4.31 Idle adjustment diagram – M2ME (Sec 25)

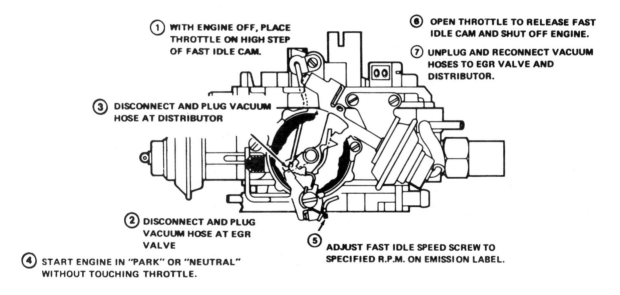

① WITH ENGINE OFF, PLACE THROTTLE ON HIGH STEP OF FAST IDLE CAM.

⑥ OPEN THROTTLE TO RELEASE FAST IDLE CAM AND SHUT OFF ENGINE.

⑦ UNPLUG AND RECONNECT VACUUM HOSES TO EGR VALVE AND DISTRIBUTOR.

③ DISCONNECT AND PLUG VACUUM HOSE AT DISTRIBUTOR

② DISCONNECT AND PLUG VACUUM HOSE AT EGR VALVE

⑤ ADJUST FAST IDLE SPEED SCREW TO SPECIFIED R.P.M. ON EMISSION LABEL.

④ START ENGINE IN "PARK" OR "NEUTRAL" WITHOUT TOUCHING THROTTLE.

Fig. 4.32 Fast idle adjustment diagram – M2ME (Sec 26)

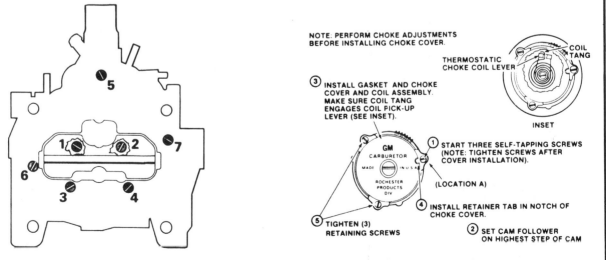

NOTE: PERFORM CHOKE ADJUSTMENTS BEFORE INSTALLING CHOKE COVER.

THERMOSTATIC CHOKE COIL LEVER

COIL TANG

INSET

③ INSTALL GASKET AND CHOKE COVER AND COIL ASSEMBLY. MAKE SURE COIL TANG ENGAGES COIL PICK-UP LEVER (SEE INSET).

① START THREE SELF-TAPPING SCREWS (NOTE: TIGHTEN SCREWS AFTER COVER INSTALLATION).

(LOCATION A)

④ INSTALL RETAINER TAB IN NOTCH OF CHOKE COVER.

⑤ TIGHTEN (3) RETAINING SCREWS

② SET CAM FOLLOWER ON HIGHEST STEP OF CAM

GM CARBURETOR MADE IN U S A ROCHESTER PRODUCTS DIV

Fig. 4.33 Air horn screw tightening diagram – M2ME (Sec 27)

Fig. 4.34 Choke cover installation – M2ME (Sec 27)

case of a major carburetor overhaul, throttle body replacement or in the case of a high emissions reading by official inspections. Because the mixture screws are sealed, an artificial enrichment procedure using propane gas is required to check the mixture. Adjusting the mixture by any other means may be a violation of law.

26 Carburetor (M2M series) – fast idle adjustment

1   With the engine turned off, place the throttle on the high step of the fast idle cam.
2   Disconnect and plug the vacuum hose at the EGR valve.
3   Disconnect and plug the vacuum hose at the distributor.
4   Start the engine in 'Park' or 'Neutral' without touching the accelerator pedal.
5   Adjust the fast idle speed screw to the rpm specified on the emission decal.
6   Open the throttle to release the fast idle cam and turn off the engine.
7   Unplug and reconnect the vacuum hoses to the EGR valve and distributor.

27 Carburetor (M2M series) – overhaul

1   When a carburetor develops faults after a considerable mileage, it is usually more economical to replace the complete unit, rather than to completely dismantle it and replace individual components. Where, however, it is decided to strip and rebuild the unit, first obtain a repair kit which will contain all the necessary gaskets and other needed items and proceed in the following sequence.
2   Remove the solenoid (if equipped) from the float bowl. Screws secure the solenoid and bracket assembly. Do not immerse the solenoid in any type of carburetor cleaner.
3   Remove the choke lever at the top of the carburetor by removing the retaining screw. Then rotate the choke lever to remove the choke rod from its slot in the lever.
4   To remove the choke rod from the lower lever, hold the lower lever outward and twist the choke rod in a counterclockwise direction.
5   Note the position of the accelerator pump rod on its lever. Then remove the pump lever by driving the pivot pin inwards slightly until the lever can be removed from the air horn.
6   Remove the seven screws which attach the top air horn assembly to the bowl. Two of them are countersunk near the center of the carburetor. Lift the air horn straight up and off the float bowl.
7   From the air horn assembly, remove the vacuum break hose followed by the vacuum break control and bracket assembly. Do not immerse the vacuum break assembly in carburetor cleaner.
8   Lift the air horn gasket from the top of the float bowl assembly being careful not to distort the spring holding the main metering rods in place.
9   Remove the pump plunger from the pump well. Following the plunger from the well will be the plunger return spring.
10 Remove the power piston and metering rods from the well. Do this by pressing down on the piston and releasing it quickly with a snap. This procedure may have to be repeated many times. Do not remove the piston with pliers on the metering rod hanger. The A.P.T. metering rod adjustment screw is pre-set and should not be changed. If float bowl replacement is necessary the new float bowl will be supplied with a new A.P.T. metering screw.
11 Remove the metering rods from the power piston by disconnecting the spring from the top of each rod. Rotate the rod to remove from the hangar.
12 Remove the plastic filler block over the float valve.
13 Remove the float assembly and float needle by pulling up on the retaining pin. Also remove the needle, seat and gasket.
14 Remove the main metering jets only if necessary to replace.
15 Remove the pump discharge check ball retainer and check ball.
16 Remove the pump well fill slot baffle.
17 The choke cover is held in place with rivets to discourage tampering. It is removed by drilling out the rivet heads with a 0.159-in drill bit.
18 Remove the choke assembly retainers, cover gasket and choke cover assembly from the main housing. Do not remove the baffle beneath the choke cover coil.
19 The choke housing can be removed from the float bowl by

removing the retaining screw inside the housing.
20 Remove the rear vacuum break rod from the intermediate choke lever.
21 To remove the intermediate choke shaft, remove the retaining screw inside the choke housing and the coil lever from the flats on the shaft. Slide the intermediate shaft outward and remove the fast idle cam from the shaft.
22 Remove the cup seal from the float bowl insert. Do not remove the cup seal from the float bowl insert. Do not remove the insert itself.
23 Turn the float bowl upside down and remove the choke lever from inside the cavity.
24 From the float bowl assembly, remove the fuel inlet nut, gasket, check valve filter and spring.
25 The throttle body can be separated from the float bowl by removing the attaching screws.
26 Remove the pump rod from the throttle lever.
27 Do not remove the plugs covering the idle mixture needles unless it is necessary to replace the mixture screws. The mixture passages should clean with normal soaking and air pressure.
28 Clean all metal parts in a suitable cold solvent. Do not immerse rubber parts, plastic parts, the vacuum break assembly or the idle stop solenoid. Do not probe the jets, but blow them through with clean, dry compressed air. Examine all fixed and moving parts for cracks, distortion, wear and other damage. Replace parts as necessary. Discard all gaskets and the fuel inlet filter.
29 Assembly is essentially the reverse of the removal procedure, but the following points should be noted:

a)   Do not install the choke coil cover assembly until the inside coil lever is adjusted. With the fast idle cam follower on the high step, push up on the coil tang until the choke valve is closed. Insert a 0.120-inch plug gauge and bend the choke rod near the lever until the lower edge of the lever just contacts the plug gauge.

b)   With the float bowl components assembled, adjust the float level. Hold down the float retainer firmly and push the float down tightly against the needle. Measure from the top of the float bowl (without gasket) to the top of the float, about $\frac{3}{16}$ in back from the toe. Bend the float arm as necessary.

c)   Tighten the seven air horn attaching screws evenly in the sequence given.

28 Carburetor (E2M-E4M series) – idle speed adjustment

1   The procedure for setting idle speed on the E2ME carburetor is the same as that for the M2ME. Refer to Section 25.

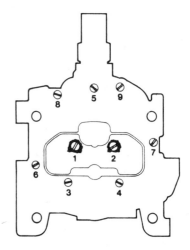

Fig. 4.35 Air horn screw tightening diagram – E2ME (Sec 30)

29 Carburetor (E2M-E4M series) – fast idle adjustment

1   The procedure for adjusting the fast idle on the E2ME is the same as that for the M2ME. Refer to Section 26.

30 Carburetor (E2M-E2M series) – overhaul

1   When a carburetor develops faults after a considerable mileage, it is usually more economical to replace the complete unit, rather than to completely dismantle it and replace individual components. Where, however, it is decided to strip and rebuild the unit, first obtain a repair kit which will contain all the necessary gaskets and other needed items, and proceed in the following sequence:

2   Remove the screws holding the wide open throttle and idle solenoid and bracket assembly to the float bowl. Do not immerse

these parts in carburetor cleaner.

3   Remove the upper choke lever from the end of the shaft by removing the retaining screw and rotating the lever.

4   Remove the choke rod from the lower lever inside the float bowl casting. Do this by holding the lever outward and twisting the rod counterclockwise.

5   Use a drift to drive the pump lever pivot pin inward until the lever can be removed from the air horn. Note the position of the accelerator pump rod in the lever and then remove the pump lever from the pump rod.

6   Remove the vacuum break hose from the tube on the float bowl.

7   Remove the nine (eleven on the E4ME-E4MC) air horn attaching screws. Two of them are countersunk near the center of the carburetor. Lift the air horn straight up and off the float bowl.

8   From the air horn assembly, remove the vacuum break control with its bracket. Do not immerse this in carburetor cleaner.

9   Remove the pump plunger stem seal (and a throttle position

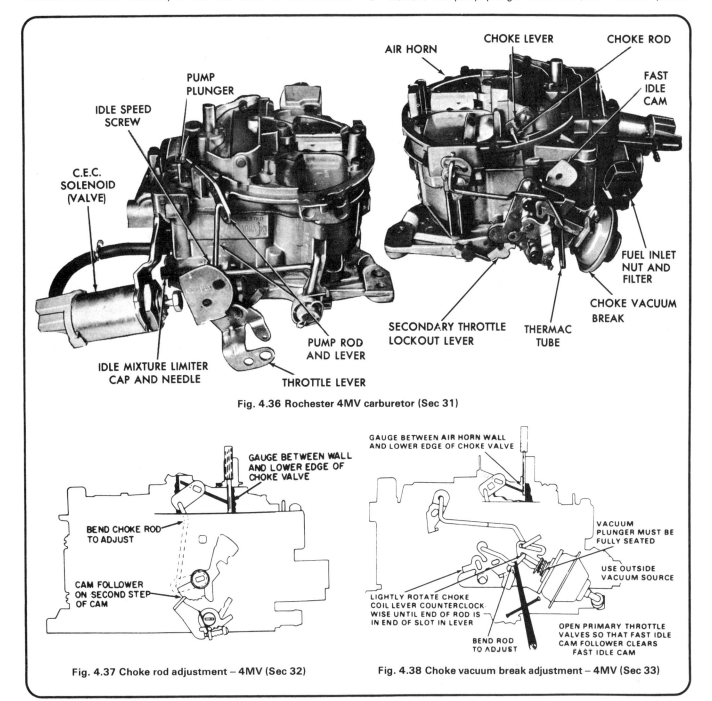

Fig. 4.36 Rochester 4MV carburetor (Sec 31)

Fig. 4.37 Choke rod adjustment – 4MV (Sec 32)

Fig. 4.38 Choke vacuum break adjustment – 4MV (Sec 33)

sensor (TPS) on the E4ME-MC by inverting the air horn and using a small screwdriver to remove the staking. Remove and discard the retainer and seal. Use care when prying seal to avoid damage to the air horn casting.

10 The air horn assembly includes an idle air bleed valve which is pre-set at the factory. The air valve and seals should not be removed from the air horn unless replacement is necessary. The air horn assembly should not be immersed or cleaned in carburetor cleaner in the normal manner as this may damage the O-rings which seal the idle air bleed valve.

11 Holding down on the pump plunger stem, raise the corner of the air horn gasket still attached to the float bowl and remove the pump plunger from its well.

12 Remove the solenoid metering rod plunger by lifting straight up.

13 Remove the rubber seal from around the mixture control solenoid plunger.

14 Remove the air horn gasket from the float bowl.

15 Remove the pump return spring from the well.

16 Remove the plastic filler block over the float valve.

17 Carefully lift out each metering rod assembly. Make sure the return spring comes with the assembly.

18 Remove the mixture control solenoid from the float bowl. Do this by first removing the two attaching screws. Do not remove the solenoid connector at this time. Turn the mixture control screw counterclockwise and remove the screw. Carefully lift the solenoid and connector assembly from the float bowl. The solenoid and connector are serviced as an assembly only.

19 Remove the plastic insert from the cavity in the float bowl under the solenoid connector.

20 Remove the solenoid screw tension spring next to the float hanger clip.

21 Remove the float assembly and float needle by pulling up on the retaining clip. Remove the needle and seat.

22 Remove the large mixture control solenoid spring from the bottom of the float bowl.

23 Remove the main metering jets, if necessary.

24 Remove the pump discharge check ball retainer and check ball.

25 Remove the pump well fill slot baffle, if necessary for replacement.

26 Remove the rear vacuum break control, along with its attaching bracket. Do not immerse this in carburetor cleaner.

27 The non-adjustable choke is designed to be a permanent fixture. Rivets are used to secure the cover. If disassembly is necessary, see the overhaul instructions for the M2ME, as the choke mechanisms are the same.

28 Remove the fuel inlet nut, gasket, check valve filter assembly and spring from the float bowl.

29 Remove the four throttle body attaching screws and remove the throttle body assembly.

30 Remove the pump rod from the throttle lever by rotating the rod until the tang aligns with the slot in the lever.

31 Do not remove the plugs covering the idle mixture needles unless they must be replaced, which is not common in a standard overhaul.

32 Clean all metal parts in a suitable cold solvent. Do not immerse rubber parts, plastic parts, the vacuum break assembly, wide-open throttle switch, solenoid or air horn assembly. Do not probe the jets, but blow them through with clean, dry compressed air. Examine all fixed and moving parts for cracks, distortion, wear and other damage. Replace parts as necessary. Discard all gaskets and the fuel filter.

33 Assembly is essentially the reverse of the removal procedure, but the following points should be noted:

   a) *To make the float level adjustment, hold the float retaining clip firmly in place and push down lightly on the float arm. Measure from the top of the float bowl casting (without gasket) to the top of the float about $\frac{3}{16}$ in back from the toe. Bend the float arm as necessary for adjustment.*

   b) *Tighten the nine air horn attaching screws securely in the sequence given.*

31 Carburetor (Rochester 4MV) – idle adjustment

Note: *If the information given on the decal label has superseded the information given in the Specifications, the decal label should be assumed to be correct.*

1974 (350 and 455 CID engines)

1 Disconnect the distributor vacuum line from the distributor and plug the lines. Connect a tachometer to the engine.

2 Disconnect the fuel tank line from the vapor canister.

3 Switch the air conditioning off.

4 With the engine at the normal operating temperature, adjust the idle stop solenoid screw to obtain 650 rpm (manual transmission in neutral) or 600 rpm (automatic transmission in Drive).

5 Place a fast idle cam follower on the second step of the cam and adjust the fast idle to 1350 rpm (manual) or 1500 rpm (automatic in Park).

6 The mixture screws fitted to these vehicles have limiter caps which restrict their movement to between $\frac{1}{2}$ and $\frac{3}{4}$ turn lean. Any adjustment should be confined to this but where the carburetor has been overhauled or new components fitted, then the cap should be broken off and the following operations carried out.

7 Have the engine at the normal operating temperature with the air conditioning off and a tachometer connected.

8 Disconnect the fuel tank hose from the vapor canister.

9 Adjust the idle speed screw until the initial idle speed (see Specifications Section) is obtained.

10 Now unscrew the mixture screws equally until maximum idle speed is achieved. Readjust the idle speed screw again to obtain the initial idle speed.

11 Screw in the mixture screws equally until the final idle speed (lean drop) is obtained (see Specifications Section).

12 If an Air Injection Reactor System is fitted, now turn the mixture screws $\frac{1}{4}$ turn out equally.

13 If the carburetor is fitted with a solenoid, the final idle speed should be adjusted to complete the turning procedure by de-energizing the solenoid and turning the solenoid Allen screw to attain 450 rpm.

14 An alternative method of adjusting the mixture is to connect a CO meter (exhaust gas analyzer) in accordance with the maker's instructions and adjust the screws equally until the emission level is within the maximum permitted (see Specifications Section).

15 Install new limiter caps to the mixture screws so that any travel will be in the lean direction (screw in) only.

1975 through 1980

16 The operations are similar to those described in the preceding paragraphs 1 through 14 except refer to Specifications Sections for initial, final and fast idle settings.

32 Carburetor (Rochester 4MV) – choke rod adjustment

1 Place the cam follower on the second step of the fast idle cam and against the high step.

2 Rotate the choke valve towards the closed position by turning the external lever counterclockwise.

3 Check that the dimension between the lower edge of the choke valve and the air horn wall (at the lever end) is as specified. Bend the choke rod if adjustment is required.

33 Carburetor (Rochester 4MV) – choke vacuum break adjustment

1 Using an external source of suction, seat the choke vacuum break diaphragm.

2 Open the throttle slightly so that the cam follower clears the fast idle cam steps, then rotate the vacuum break lever towards the closed direction. Ensure that the vacuum break rod is in the outer end of the slot in the diaphragm plunger. A rubber band can be used to hold the vacuum break lever in position.

3 Measure the distance from the lower edge of the choke valve to the air horn wall. Check this against the figure shown in Specifications Section and if adjustment is needed, bend the link rod.

34 Carburetor (Rochester 4MV) – choke coil rod adjustment

1 Rotate the choke coil lever counterclockwise to fully close the choke.

2 With the coil rod disconnected and the cover removed, push down

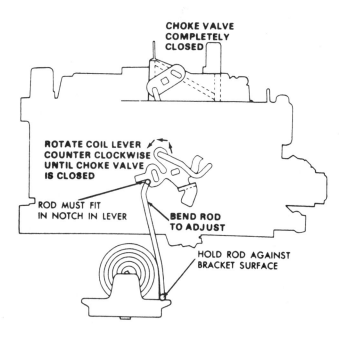

Fig. 4.39 Choke coil rod adjustment 4MV (Sec 34)

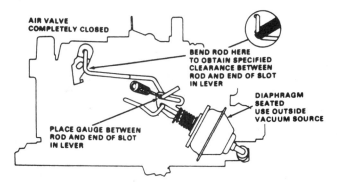

Fig. 4.40 Air valve dashpot adjustment 4MV (Sec 35)

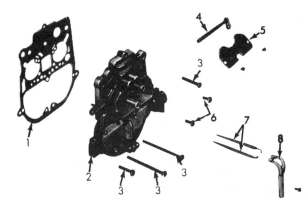

Fig. 4.41 Exploded view of air horn – 4MV (Sec 36)

on the rod until it contacts the bracket surface.

3   The coil rod must fit in the choke lever notch; bend the rod to adjust if necessary.

4   Install the choke coil cover.

5   Install the coil rod in the choke coil lever slot and install the retaining clip.

6   Check that the choke operates freely over its full range of travel.

35 Carburetor (Rochester 4MV) – air valve dashpot adjustment

1   Seat the choke vacuum break diaphragm using an outside source of suction, then measure the dimension between the end of the slot in the vacuum break plunger lever and the air valve when the air valve is fully closed.

2   If adjustment is necessary, bend the rod at the air valve end.

36 Carburetor (Rochester 4MV) – overhaul

1   When a carburetor develops faults after a considerable mileage, it is usually more economical to replace the complete unit rather than to completely dismantle it and replace individual components. However, if it is decided to strip and rebuild the unit, first obtain a repair kit which will contain all the necessary gaskets and other needed items, and proceed in the following sequence.

2   Bend back the lockwasher tabs, then remove the idle stop solenoid.

3   Remove the larger idle stop solenoid bracket screw from the float bowl.

4   Remove the clip from the upper end of the choke rod, disconnect the rod from the upper choke shaft lever and remove the rod from the lower lever in the bowl.

5   Drive the pump lever pivot inwards to remove the roll pin then remove the pump lever from the air horn and pump rod.

6   Remove 2 long screws, 5 short screws and 2 countersunk head screws retaining the air horn to the float bowl.

7   Remove the vacuum break hose, and the diaphragm unit from the bracket.

8   Disconnect the choke assist spring.

9   Remove the metering rod hanger and secondary rods after removing the small screw at the top of the hanger.

10   Lift off the air horn, but leave the gasket in position. Do not attempt to remove the air bleed tubes or accelerating well tubes.

11   If the choke valve is to be replaced, remove the valve attaching screws, then measure the valve and shaft.

12   The air valves and air valve shaft are calibrated and should not be removed. A shaft spring repair kit is available, and contains all the necessary instructions, if these parts require replacement.

13   Remove the pump plunger from the well.

14   Carefully remove the air horn gasket.

15   Remove the pump return spring from the pump well.

16   Remove the plastic filler over the float valve.

17   Press the power piston down and release it to remove it. Remove the spring from the well. Note the power piston plastic retainer which is used for ease of assembly.

18   Remove the metering rods from the power piston by disconnecting the spring from the top of each rod, then rotating the rod to remove it from the hanger.

19   Remove the float assembly by pulling up on the retaining pin until it can be removed, then sliding the float towards the front of the bowl to carefully disengage the needle pull clip.

20   Remove the pull clip and the fuel inlet needle, then unscrew the needle seat and remove the gasket.

21   Unscrew the primary metering jets; do not attempt to remove the secondary metering jets.

22   Remove the discharge ball retainer and the check ball.

23   Remove the baffle from the secondary side of the bowl.

24   Remove the choke assembly after removing the retaining screw on the side of the bowl. Remove the secondary locknut lever from the cast boss on the bowl.

25   Remove the fast idle cam and the choke assembly.

26   Remove the intermediate choke rod and actuating lever from the float bowl.

27   Remove the fuel inlet filter nut, gasket, filter and spring.

28   Remove the throttle body to bowl screws. Remove the throttle body.

29 Remove the throttle body to bowl insulator gaskets.

30 Remove the pump rod from the throttle lever by rotating the rod out of the primary lever.

31 Further dismantling is not recommended. If it is essential to remove the idle mixture needles, pry out the plastic limiter caps then count the number of turns to bottom the needles and fit replacements in exactly the same position. New limiter caps should be fitted after running adjustments have been made (see Section 31).

32 Clean all metal parts in a suitable cold solvent. Do not immerse rubber parts, plastic parts, the vacuum break assembly or the idle stop solenoid, or permanent damage will result. Do not probe the jets, but blow them through with clean dry compressed air. Examine all fixed and moving parts for cracks, distortion, wear and other damage; replace as necessary. Discard all gaskets and the fuel inlet filter.

33 Assembly is essentially the reverse of the removal procedure, but the following points should be noted:

a) If new idle mixture screws are used, and the original setting was not noted, install the screws finger-tight to seat them, then back off 4 full turns (see Section 31).

b) Having installed the float, measure from the top of the float bowl gasket surface (gasket not fitted) to the top of the float at a point $\frac{3}{16}$ in from the toe. Bend the float up, or down, to obtain the specified dimension.

c) Tighten the air horn retaining screws in the sequence shown.

d) When connecting the pump lever to the upper pump rod, install the rod in the inner hole.

e) After reassembly, carry out all the relevant settings and adjustments listed previously in this chapter.

37 Carburetor (Rochester M4MC/M4MCA/M4ME) — idle adjustment

Note: *If the information given on the decal label has superseded the information given in Specifications, the decal labels should be assumed to be correct. In 1978 General Motors changed the design of the carburetor idle mixture screw so that backing out the screw will not appreciably richen the mixture. Idle mixture adjustment is carried out with special propane enrichment equipment, a procedure best left to a dealer.*

1975 thru 1977

1 Have the engine at normal operating temperature, air cleaner in position and air conditioning off. Connect a reliable tachometer to the engine.

2 Disconnect the fuel tank hose from the vapor canister.

3 Disconnect the lead from the idle stop solenoid.

4 With automatic in Drive or manual in Neutral, turn the idle speed screw to obtain the curb (final) idle speed shown in the Specifications Section.

5 Reconnect the solenoid, crack open the throttle slightly to extend the solenoid plunger.

6 Now turn the solenoid plunger screw to set the curb (initial) idle speed shown in Specifications Section.

7 Remove the tachometer and reconnect the fuel tank hose.

8 The idle mixture screws are pre-set and fitted with limiter caps which allow them to be turned about one turn lean to rectify uneven idling. If after carburetor overhaul or replacement of components, the

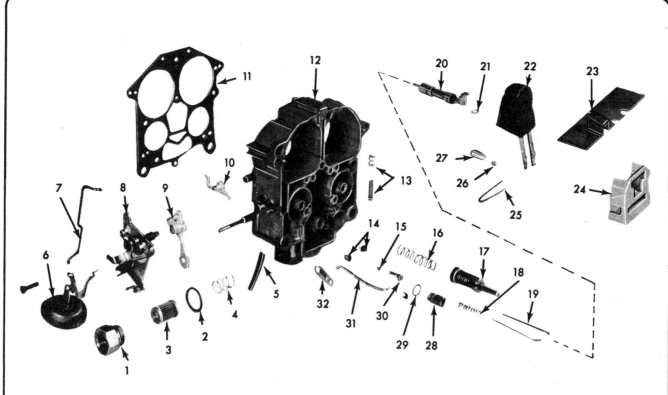

Fig. 4.42 Exploded view of float bowl – 4MV (Sec 36)

1	Fuel inlet nut	9	Fast idle cam
2	Gasket	10	Secondary throttle lockout
3	Fuel filter	11	Gasket
4	Fuel filter spring	12	Float bowl assembly
5	Vacuum break hose	13	Idle speed screw
6	Vacuum diaphragm	14	Primary jets
7	Air valve dashpot	15	Pump discharge ball
8	Choke control bracket	16	Pump return spring

17	Accelerator pump	25	Float hinge pin
18	Power piston spring	26	Float needle pull clip
19	Primary metering rods	27	Float needle
20	Power piston	28	Float needle seat
21	Metering rod retainer	29	Needle seat gasket
22	Float	30	Discharge ball retainer
23	Secondary air baffle	31	Choke rod
24	Float bowl insert	32	Choke lever

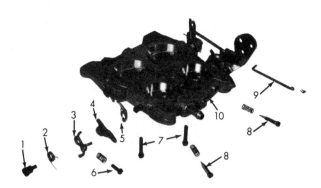

Fig. 4.43 Exploded view of the throttle body – 4MV (Sec 36)

1 Shouldered retaining screw
2 Torsion spring
3 Fast idle adjusting lever
4 Fast idle cam lever
5 Choke unloader lever
6 Fast idle screw
7 Screws
8 Idle mixture needle
9 Accelerator pump rod
10 Throttle body assembly

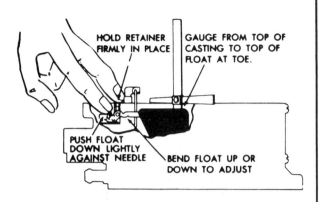

Fig. 4.44 Float adjustment diagram – 4MV (Sec 36)

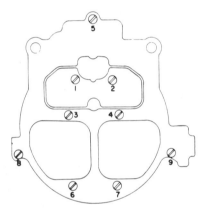

Fig. 4.45 Air horn screw tightening sequence – 4MV (Sec 36)

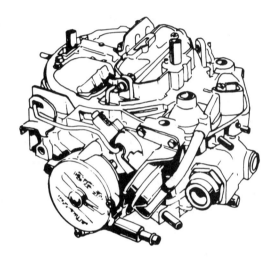

Fig. 4.46 Rochester M4MC Quadrajet carburetor

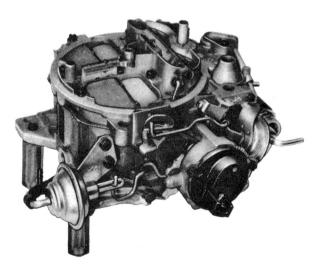

Fig. 4.47 Rochester M4ME carburetor

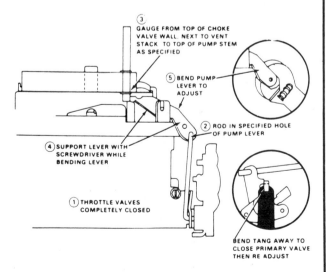

Fig. 4.48 Pump rod adjustment diagram M4MC/M4MCA

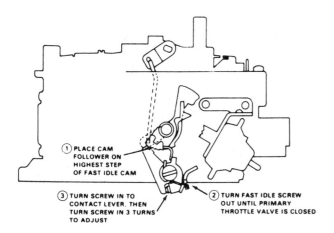

Fig. 4.49 Fast idle adjustment diagram – M4M series (Sec 39)

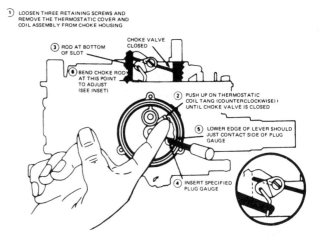

Fig. 4.50 Choke coil level adjustment diagram – M4M series
(Sec 40)

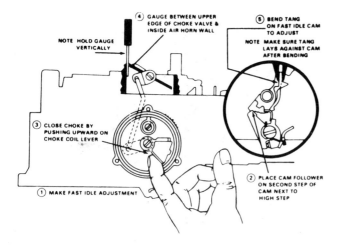

Fig. 4.51 Choke rod (fast idle cam) adjustment diagram – M4M
series (Sec 41)

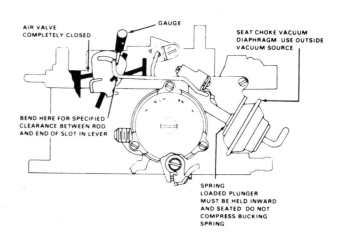

Fig. 4.52 Air valve dashpot adjustment – M4M series (Sec 42)

mixture must be adjusted beyond the limit of travel of the caps, carry out the following operations:

9   Repeat the procedure described in paragraphs 1 and 2.

10 Break off the cap on the mixture screws.

11 Set the idle speed to the curb (initial) figure using the solenoid plunger.

12 Unscrew each of the mixture screws equally until the highest idle speed is achieved. Reduce the speed if necessary to curb (initial) specifications using the solenoid plunger.

13 Now screw in each of the mixture screws equally until the curb (final) idle speed is obtained.

14 Reconnect the fuel tank hose and switch off the engine.

38 Carburetor (Rochester M4M series) – accelerator pump rod adjustment

1   With the fast idle cam follower off the steps of the fast idle cam, back out the idle speed screw until the throttle valves are completely closed in the bore. Make sure that the secondary actuating rod is not restricting movement; bend the secondary closing tang if necessary then readjust it after pump adjustment.

2   Place the pump rod in the inner hole in the lever.

3   Measure from the top of the choke valve wall (next to the vent stack) to the top of the pump stem.

4   If necessary, adjust to obtain the specified dimension (see

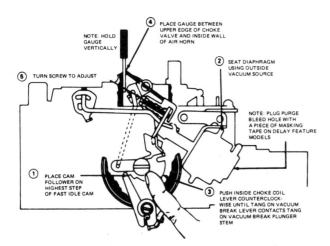

Fig. 4.53 Front vacuum break adjustment diagram – M4M series
(Sec 43)

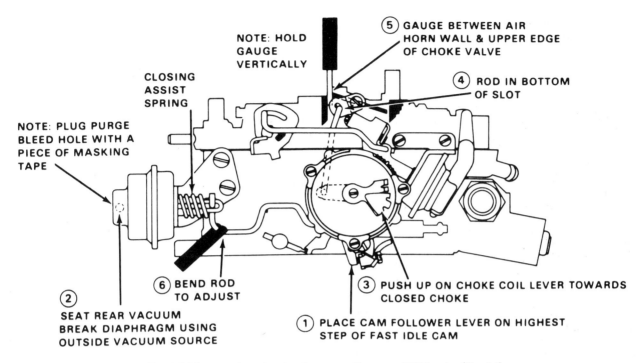

NOTE: HOLD GAUGE VERTICALLY

⑤ GAUGE BETWEEN AIR HORN WALL & UPPER EDGE OF CHOKE VALVE

④ ROD IN BOTTOM OF SLOT

CLOSING ASSIST SPRING

NOTE: PLUG PURGE BLEED HOLE WITH A PIECE OF MASKING TAPE

⑥ BEND ROD TO ADJUST

② SEAT REAR VACUUM BREAK DIAPHRAGM USING OUTSIDE VACUUM SOURCE

③ PUSH UP ON CHOKE COIL LEVER TOWARDS CLOSED CHOKE

① PLACE CAM FOLLOWER LEVER ON HIGHEST STEP OF FAST IDLE CAM

Fig. 4.54 Rear vacuum break adjustment diagram – M4M series (Sec 44)

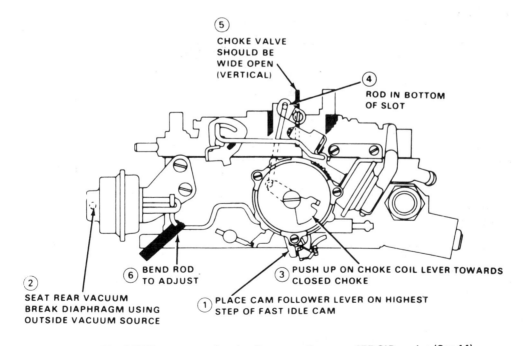

⑤ CHOKE VALVE SHOULD BE WIDE OPEN (VERTICAL)

④ ROD IN BOTTOM OF SLOT

⑥ BEND ROD TO ADJUST

② SEAT REAR VACUUM BREAK DIAPHRAGM USING OUTSIDE VACUUM SOURCE

③ PUSH UP ON CHOKE COIL LEVER TOWARDS CLOSED CHOKE

① PLACE CAM FOLLOWER LEVER ON HIGHEST STEP OF FAST IDLE CAM

Fig. 4.55 Rear vacuum break adjustment diagram – 455 CID engine (Sec 44)

Specifications Section) by bending the lever while supporting it with a screwdriver.
5   Adjust the idle speed.

39 Carburetor (Rochester M4M Series) – fast idle adjustment

Carburetor removed
1   Place the cam follower lever on the highest step of the fast idle cam.
2   Turn the fast idle screw out until the primary throttle valves are closed.
3   Turn in the fast idle screw to contact the lever then screw in a further 3 full turns.

Carburetor in vehicle
4   Connect a tachometer to the engine which should be at the normal operating temperature.
5   Place the transmission in Park or Neutral.
6   Disconnect and plug the vacuum hose at the EGR valve.
7   Position the cam follower on the highest step of the fast idle cam.
8   Turn the fast idle screw to achieve the specified fast idle (see Specifications Section).
9   Remake the original connections, remove the tachometer and switch off the engine.

40 Carburetor (Rochester M4M Series) – choke coil lever adjustment

1   Loosen the 3 retaining screws and remove the cover and coil assembly from the choke housing.
2   Push up on the thermostatic coil tang (counterclockwise) until the choke valve is closed.
3   Check that the choke rod is at the bottom of the slot in the choke lever.
4   Insert a plug gauge (an unmarked drill shank is suitable) of the specified size in the hole in the choke housing.
5   The lower edge of the choke coil lever should just contact the side of the plug gauge.
6   If necessary, bend the choke rod at the point shown.

41 Carburetor (Rochester M4M Series) – fast idle cam (choke rod) adjustment

Note: *Always adjust choke coil lever before carrying out the following operations.*
1   Turn the fast idle screw in until it contacts the fast idle cam follower lever, then turn in 3 full turns more.
2   Place the lever on the second step of the fast idle cam against the rise of the high step.
3   Push upwards on the choke coil lever inside the housing to close the choke valve.
4   Measure between the upper edge of the choke valve and the air horn wall.
5   If necessary, bend the tang on the fast idle cam to adjust, but ensure that the tang lies against the cam after bending
6   Re-check the fast idle adjustment.

42 Carburetor (Rochester M4M Series) – air valve dashpot adjustment

1   Using an external source of suction, seat the front vacuum break diaphragm. Suction from the mouth or a small hand pump is normally adequate.
2   Ensure that the air valves are completely closed then measure between the air valve dashpot and the end of the slot in the air valve lever. This dimension should be 0.015 in.
3   Bend the air valve dashpot rod at the point shown, if adjustment is necessary.

43 Carburetor (Rochester M4M Series) – front vacuum break adjustment

1   Loosen the 3 retaining screws and remove the choke coil cover and coil assembly from the choke housing.

2   Place the cam follower lever on the highest step of the fast idle cam.
3   Using an outside source of suction, seat the diaphragm unit.
4   Push up on the inside choke coil lever until the tang on the vacuum break lever contacts the tang on the plunger.
5   Measure between the upper edge of the choke valve and the inside of the air horn wall.
6   Turn the adjustment screw on the vacuum break plunger to obtain the specified dimension.
7   Install the vacuum hose on completion.

44 Carburetor (Rochester M4M Series) – rear vacuum break adjustment

350 and 403 CID engines
1   Initially follow the procedure of Paragraphs 1 thru 3 in the previous Section, but additionally plug the bleed hose in the end cover of the vacuum break unit using adhesive tape.
2   Push up on the choke coil lever inside the choke housing towards the closed choke position.
3   With the choke rod in the bottom of the slot in the choke lever, measure between the upper edge of the choke valve and the air horn wall.
4   If necessary, bend the vacuum break rod at the point shown to obtain the specified dimension.
5   On completion, remove the adhesive tape and install the vacuum hose.

455 CID engine
6   Loosen the thermostatic cover screws and remove the cover and coil from the choke housing.
7   Place the cam follower lever on the highest step of the fast idle cam.
8   Seat the rear vacuum diaphragm using an external vacuum source (mouth or hand pump).
9   Push up on the choke coil lever inside the choke housing (towards closed choke) until the step is pulled out and seated with the spring compressed.
10 With the choke rod in bottom of the slot in the choke lever, measure between the upper edge of the choke valve plate and the air horn wall. The dimensions should be as specified in the Specifications Section at the beginning of this Chapter.
11 Where necessary, bend the vacuum break rod at the point indicated.
12 Remake the original vacuum hose connection and install the coil assembly and cover.

45 Carburetor (Rochester M4MC and M4MCA) – automatic choke coil adjustment

1   With the hot air heater type of choke, install the choke coil and cover assembly with a gasket between the cover and housing. The tang in the coil must be installed in the slot inside the choke coil lever pick-up arm.
2   Place the fast idle cam follower on the highest step of the fast idle cam then rotate the cover counterclockwise until the choke just closes.
3   Align the index mark on the cover with the specified point (2 notches lean) on the choke housing then tighten the retaining screws.

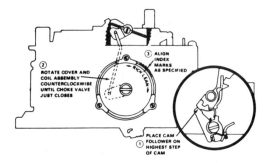

Fig. 4.56 Automatic choke coil adjustment diagram –
M4MC/M4MCA only (Sec 45)

46 Carburetor (Rochester M4ME) – automatic choke coil adjustment

1   With this type of electrically heated automatic choke, make sure that with the coil assembly inside the choke housing, the coil tang contacts the bottom side of the inner face of the choke coil lever pick-up arm.
2   Position the fast idle cam follower on the high step of the cam.
3   Rotate the cover and coil assembly counterclockwise until the choke valve just closes.
4   Align the index marks (center) and install the cover and screws.
Note: *The ground contact for the electrically heated choke is through a metal plate at the rear of the choke assembly. Do not install a gasket between the cover and housing or this will interrupt the circuit.*

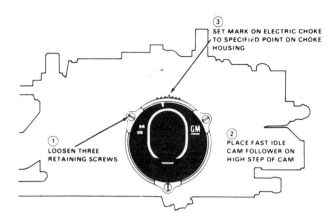

Fig. 4.57 Automatic choke coil adjustment – M4ME only (Sec 46)

47 Carburetor (Rochester M4M Series) – unloader adjustment

1   Adjust the choke coil, as described in the previous section.
2   Hold the throttle valves wide open and the chokes fully closed. A rubber band can be used on the tang of the intermediate choke lever if the engine is warm.
3   Measure between the upper edge of the choke valve and the air horn wall.
4   If adjustment is necessary, bend the tang on the fast idle lever to obtain the specified dimension. Ensure that the tang on the fast idle cam lever contacts the center point of the fast idle cam after adjustment.

48 Carburetor (Rochester M4M Series) – secondary throttle valve lock-out adjustment

Lock-out lever clearance
1   Hold the choke valves and secondary lock-out valves closed then measure the clearance between the lock-out pin and lock-out lever.
2   If adjustment is necessary, bend the lock-out pin to obtain the specified clearance (0.015 inch).

Opening clearance
3   Push down on the tail of the fast idle cam to hold the choke wide open.
4   Hold the secondary throttle valve partly open then measure between the end of the lock-out pin and the toe of the lock-out lever. (This should be 0.015 inch).
5   If adjustment is necessary, file the end of the lock-out pin but ensure that no burrs remain afterwards.

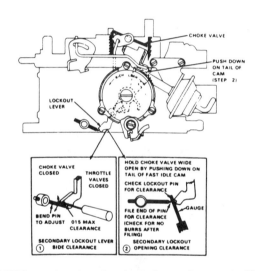

Fig. 4.58 Secondary throttle valve lockout adjustment – M4M series (Sec 48)

49 Carburetor (Rochester M4M Series) – secondary closing adjustment

1   Adjust the engine idle speed, as described previously in this Chapter.
2   Hold the choke valve wide open with the cam follower lever off the steps of the fast idle cam.
3   Measure the clearance between the slot in the secondary throttle valve pick-up lever and the secondary actuating rod.
4   If adjustment is necessary, bend the secondary tang on the primary throttle lever to obtain the specified clearance (0.020 inch).

50 Carburetor (Rochester M4M Series) – secondary opening adjustment

1   Lightly open the primary throttle lever until the link just contacts the tang on the secondary lever.
2   Bend the tang on the secondary lever, if necessary, to position the link in the center of the secondary lever slot.

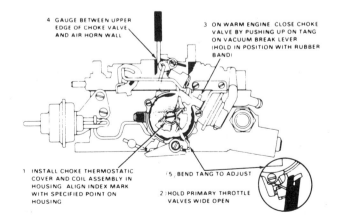

Fig. 4.59 Choke unloader adjustment diagram – M4M series (Sec 47)

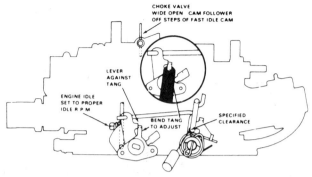

Fig. 4.60 Secondary closing adjustment diagram – M4M series (Sec 49)

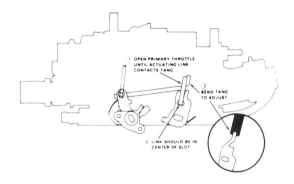

Fig. 4.61 Secondary opening adjustment – M4M series (Sec 50)

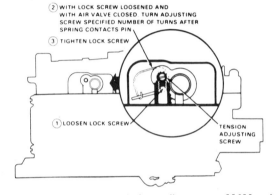

Fig. 4.62 Air valve spring wind-up adjustment – M4M series (Sec 51)

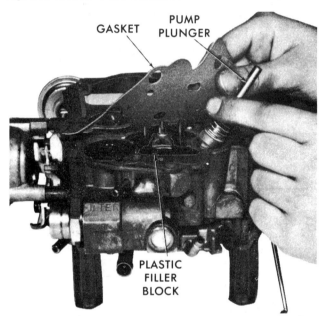

Fig. 4.63 Removing pump plunger – M4M series (Sec 52)

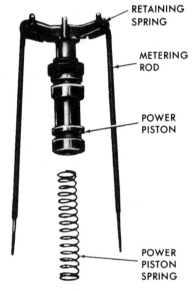

Fig. 4.64 Power piston and metering rods – M4M series (Sec 52)

51 Carburetor (Rochester M4M Series) – air valve spring wind-up adjustment

1   Remove the front vacuum break diaphragm unit and the air valve dashpot rod.

2   Using a suitable hexagonal wrench loosen the lock screw then turn the tension adjusting screw counterclockwise until the air valve is partly open.

3   Hold the air valve closed then turn the tension adjusting screw clockwise the specified number of turns after the spring contacts the pin (Air Valve Spring Wind-up, see Specifications Section).

4   Tighten the lockscrew and install the air valve dashpot rod, and the front vacuum break diaphragm unit and bracket.

Fig. 4.65 Float bowl jets – M4M series (Sec 52)

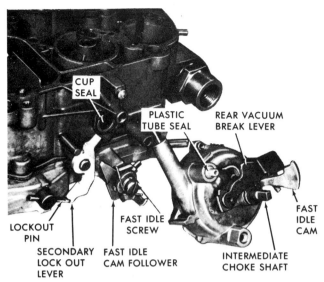

Fig. 4.66 Choke housing assembly – M4M series (Sec 52)

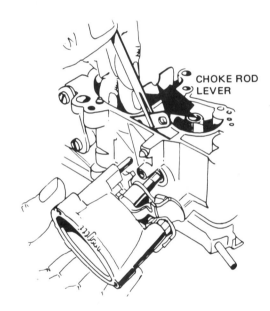

Fig. 4.67 Connecting choke rod lever – M4M series (Sec 52)

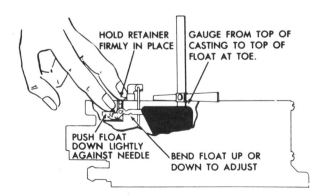

Fig. 4.68 Float level adjustment diagram – M4M series (Sec 52)

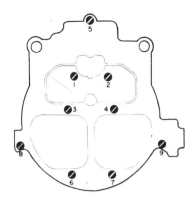

Fig. 4.69 Air horn screw-tightening sequence – M4M series (Sec 52)

52 Carburetor (Rochester M4M Series) – overhaul

1   When a carburetor fault develops after a considerable mileage, it is usually more economical to replace the complete unit rather than to completely dismantle it and replace individual components. However, if it is decided to strip and rebuild the unit, first obtain a repair kit which will contain all the necessary gaskets and other needed items, and proceed in the following manner.

2   If the carburetor has an idle stop solenoid, remove the bracket retaining screws and lift away the solenoid and bracket assembly.

3   Remove the upper choke lever from the end of the choke shaft (1 screw) then rotate the lever to remove it, and disengage it from the choke rod.

4   Remove the choke rod from the lower lever inside the float bowl by holding the lever outwards with a small screwdriver and twisting the rod counterclockwise.

5   Remove the vacuum hose from the front vacuum break unit.

6   Remove the small screw at the top of the metering rod hanger, and remove the secondary metering rods and hanger.

7   Using a suitable drift, drive the small pump lever pivot roll pin inwards to permit removal of the lever.

8   Remove 2 long screws, 5 short screws and 2 countersunk head air horn screws to detach the float bowl. Remove the secondary air baffle deflector (where applicable) from beneath the 2 center air horn screws.

9   Remove the float bowl but leave the gasket in position at this stage. Do not attempt to remove the small tubes protruding from the air horn.

10 Remove the front vacuum break bracket screws and lift off the unit. Detach the air valve dashpot rod from the diaphragm assembly and the air valve lever.

11 If considered necessary, remove the staked choke valve attaching screws then remove the choke valve and shaft from the air horn. Do not remove the air valve and the air valve shaft. The air valve closing spring or center plastic cam can be replaced by following the instructions in the appropriate repair kit.

12 Remove the air horn gasket from the float bowl taking care not to distort the springs holding the main metering rods.

13 Remove the pump plunger and pump return spring from the pump well.

14 Depress the power piston stem and allow it to snap free, withdrawing the metering rods with it. Remove the power piston spring from the well.

15 Taking care to prevent distortion, remove the metering rods from the power piston by disconnecting the tension springs then rotating the rods.

16 Remove the plastic filler block over the float valve then remove the float assembly and needle by pulling up on the pin. Remove the needle seat and gasket.

17 Remove the 2 cover screws and carefully lift out the metering rod and filler spool (metering rod and aneroid on M4MCA carburetors) from the float bowl. **Note:** *The adjustable part throttle (APT) metering rod assembly is extremely fragile and must not be interfered with. If replacement is necessary, refer to paragraphs 35 thru 44.*

18 Remove the primary main metering jets. Do not attempt to remove the APT metering jet or secondary metering orifice plates.

19 Remove the pump discharge check ball retainer and the ball.
20 Remove the rear vacuum break hose and the bracket retaining screws. Remove the vacuum break rod from the slot in the plunger head.
21 Press down on the fast idle cam and remove the vacuum break rod. Move the end of the rod away from the float bowl, then disengage the rod from the hole in the intermediate lever.
22 Remove the choke cover attaching screws and retainers. Pull off the cover and remove the gasket.
23 Remove the choke housing assembly from the float bowl by removing the retaining screw and washer.
24 Remove the secondary throttle valve lock-out lever from the float bowl.
25 Remove the lower choke lever by inverting the float bowl.
26 Remove the plastic tube seal from the choke housing.
27 If it is necessary to remove the intermediate choke shaft from the choke housing, remove the coil lever retaining screw and withdraw the lever. Slide out the shaft and (if necessary), remove the fast idle cam.
28 Remove the fuel inlet filter nut, gasket and filter from the float bowl.
29 If necessary, remove the pump well fill slot baffle and the secondary air baffle.
30 Remove the throttle body attaching screws and lift off the float bowl. Remove the insulator gasket.
31 Remove the pump rod from the lever on the throttle body.
32 If it is essential to remove the idle mixture needles, pry out the plastic limiter caps then count the number of turns to bottom the needles and fit replacements in exactly the same position. New limiter caps should be fitted after running adjustments have been made.
33 Clean all metal parts in a suitable cold solvent. Do not immerse rubber parts, plastic parts, pump plungers, filler spools or aneroids, or vacuum breaks. If the choke housing is to be immersed, remove the cup seal from inside the choke housing shaft hole. If the bowl is to be immersed remove the cup seal from the plastic insert; do not attempt to remove the plastic insert. Do not probe the jets, but blow through with clean, dry compressed air. Examine all fixed and moving parts for cracks, distortion, wear and other damage; replace as necessary. Discard all gaskets and the fuel inlet filter.
34 Assembly is essentially the reverse of the removal procedure, but the following points should be noted:

    a) If new idle mixture screws were used, and the original setting was not noted, install the screws finger-tight to seat them, then back off 4 full turns.
    b) The lip on the plastic insert cup seal (on the side of the float bowl) faces outward.
    c) The lip on the inside choke housing shaft hole cup seal faces inwards towards the housing.
    d) When installing the assembled choke body, install the choke rod lever into the cavity in the float bowl. Install the plastic tube seal into the housing cavity before installing the housing. Ensure that the intermediate choke shaft engages into the lower choke lever. The choke coil is installed at the last stage of assembly.
    e) Where applicable, the notches on the secondary float bowl air baffle are towards the top, and the top edge of the baffle must be flush with the bowl casting.
    f) To adjust the float, hold the retainer firmly in place and push down lightly against the needle. Measure from the top of the float bowl casting (air horn gasket removed) to a point on the top of the float $\frac{1}{16}$ in back from the toe. Bend the float arm to obtain the specified dimension by pushing on the pontoon.
    g) Tighten the air horn screws in the order shown.
    h) On completion of assembly, adjust the front and rear vacuum breaks, fast idle cam (choke rod), choke coil lever and automatic choke coil.

APT metering rod replacement

35 Replacement of the metering rod must only be carried out if the assembly is damaged or the aneroid has failed.
36 Lightly scribe the cover to record the position of the adjusting screw slot.
37 Remove the cover screws then carefully lift out the rod and cover assembly.
38 Hold the assembly upright then turn the adjusting screw counter-clockwise, counting the number of turns until the metering rod

bottoms in the cover.
39 Remove the E-clip from the threaded end of the rod then turn the rod clockwise until it disengages from the cover.
40 Install the tension spring on the new metering rod assembly and screw the rod and spring assembly into the cover until the assembly bottoms.
41 Turn the adjusting screw clockwise the number of turns noted at paragraph 38.
42 Install the E-clip. **Note:** *It will not matter if the scribed line (paragraph 36) does not align exactly provided that the assembly sequence has been followed.*
43 Carefully install the cover and metering rod assembly onto the float bowl, aligning the tab on the cover assembly with the float bowl slot closest to the fuel inlet nut.
44 Install the cover attaching screws and nut.

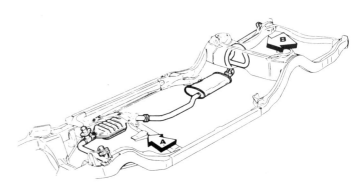

Fig. 4.70 Exhaust system – typical (Sec 53)

53 Exhaust system – general description

1 The exact exhaust system installed will depend on a number of factors, most notably the engine size, geographic area where the car will be driven and the year of production. Typical components of an exhaust system are: the exhaust manifold connected to the engine, a muffler, a catalytic converter (1975 and later) and exhaust pipe to route the gases through the components and out the rear of the car.
2 Information concerning the catalytic converter can be found in Chapter 6 dealing with the emission system.
3 The exhaust system should be periodically checked for leaks which could prove hazardous to persons inside the car. Leaks can be detected by placing your hand along the pipes before the system has warmed up. After driving, the exhaust system can cause injury if touched. A leaking exhaust system can also become apparent by excessive noise during operation.
4 As a general rule, the components of the exhaust system are secured by U-shaped clamps. After removing the clamps, the exhaust pipes (which are of a slightly different diameter) can be pulled away from each other. Due to the high temperatures and exposed location of the exhaust pieces, rust and corrosion can 'freeze' the parts together. Liquid penetrating oils are available to help loosen the connections; however, it is often necessary to cut the parts with a hack saw or cutting torch.
    The later method should be employed only by a person experienced in this work.
5 The exhaust system is often a cause of mysterious rattles and noises heard from inside the car. The rubber-insulated hangers which suspend the system should be checked for deterioration and damage. No exhaust components should come in contact with other vehicle parts.
6 When replacing exhaust system parts, do not tighten the clamp bolts until the complete system has been installed and clearances checked. Then tighten from the front to the rear.

Chapter 5 Engine electrical systems

Refer to Chapter 13 for information applicable to later models

Contents

Specifications

System type	12 volt, negative ground
Battery	Energizer type-lead, acid
Distributor type	
1974	Mechanical contact breaker. Optional High Energy Ignition
1975 through 1980	Breakerless, High Energy Ignition (HEI), electronic
Mechanical distributor contact breaker gap (1974)	
(prior to checking dwell angle)	0.016 in
Dwell angle (1974)	30° ± 2°
Rotation direction of distributor	Clockwise, viewed from the top
Firing order	
V6 engines	1–6–5–4–3–2
V8 engines	1–8–4–3–6–5–7–2
Coil (with mechanical distributor)	
Primary resistance	1.77 to 2.05 Ohms
Secondary resistance	3000 to 20000 Ohms
Resistor	0.43 to 0.68 Ohms
Coil (with HEI distributor)	
Primary resistance	0.41 to 0.51 Ohms
Secondary resistance	3000 to 20000 Ohms
Resistor	0.43 to 0.68 Ohms
Alternator	
Type	Delcotron
Field current	4.0/4.5 amps at 80°F
Output current	varies according to vehicle specifications and particular alternator type
Voltage regulator	Integral with alternator
Starter motor	9 volts
Spark plugs	

Note: *If the spark plug type listed on the tune-up decal (in the engine compartment) differs from the type listed below, the information on the decal should be considered correct.*

	Year and engine	Spark plug	Gap
1974	350	R45TS	0.040 in
	455	R45TS	0.040 in
1975	231	R44SX	0.060 in
	350	R45TSX	0.060 in
1976	231	R44SX	0.060 in
	350	R45TSX	0.060 in
1977	231 (all except Calif)	R46TS	0.040 in
	231 (Calif)	R46TSX	0.060 in
	305	R45TS	0.045 in
	350 (2-bbl carb/automatic)	R46TS	0.040 in
	350 (high altitude/Calif)	R46TSX	0.060 in
	350 (all others)	R45TS	0.045 in
	403	R46SZ	0.060 in
1978	196	R46TSX	0.060 in
	231	R46TSX	0.060 in
	305	R45TS	0.045 in
	350 (4-bbl carb/automatic)	R46SZ	0.060 in
	350 (all others)	R46TSX	0.060 in
1979	196	R45TSX	0.060 in
	231 (49 state manual)	R46TSX	0.060 in
	231 (Calif/high altitude/'E' turbo)	R44TSX	0.060 in
	231 (all others)	R45TSX	0.060 in
	301 (VIN code W)	R45TSX	0.060 in
	301 (VIN code Y)	R46TSX	0.060 in
	305	R45TS	0.045 in
	350 (high altitude)	R45TS	0.045 in
	350 (all others)	R46SZ	0.060 in
1980	231 (low altitude turbo)	R45TS	0.040 in
	231 (all others)	R45TSX	0.060 in
	265	R45TSX	0.060 in
	301	R45TSX	0.060 in
	305	R45TS	0.035 in

Year and engine	Distributor No.	Centrifugal advance crank degrees @ engine rpm	Vacuum advance crank degrees @ in hg	Dwell angle degrees	Ignition timing at engine idle degrees BTDC
1974					
350 CID V8	1112451	0 @ 750 to 1050	BTDC only	28 to 32	4 ($\pm$ 2)
	1112802 HEI				
455 CID V8	1112542		BTDC only	28 to 32	4 ($\pm$ 2)
	1112803 HEI	0 @ 750 to 1050			
455 CID V8 (L-75)	1112521	0 @ 600 to 1050	BTDC only	28 to 32	10 ($\pm$ 2)
455 CID V8 (L-76)	1112520	0 @ 750 to 1050	BTDC only	28 to 32	4 ($\pm$ 2)
1975					
231 CID V6	1110661	0 @ 1000	0 @ 5 to 7	electronic ignition	12
	1110663 (Calif)	10 @ 2000	18 @ 10		
		16 @ 4100			
350 CID V8	1112896	0 @ 750 to 1400	0 @ 6.5 to 8.5	electronic ignition	12
	1112984	4 to 8 @ 2100	10 to 16 @ 11.5		
	1112962	10 to 14 @ 4500			
1976					
231 CID V6	1110668	0 to 4.4 @ 1535	0 to 2 @ 5.3	electronic ignition	12
		12.3 to 16.8 @ 3000	22.5 to 25.5 @ 12.8		
		13.5 to 18 @ 3175			
		11.3 to 18 @ 5000			
	1110661 (Calif)	0 to 4.4 @ 1535			
350 CID V8	1112991	0 to 4.3 @ 1744	0 to 2 @ 6.9	electronic ignition	12
		17.8 to 22 @ 4425	18.5 to 21.5 @ 14.3		
		17.4 to 22 @ 5000			
1977					
231 CID V6	1110694	BTDC timing only	BTDC only	electronic ignition	12
	1110677	BTDC timing only	BTDC only	electronic ignition	12
	1110686 (Calif)	BTDC timing only	BTDC only	electronic ignition	12
305 CID V8	1103239	BTDC timing only	BTDC only	electronic ignition	8
	1103275	BTDC timing only	BTDC only	electronic ignition	8

1978

Engine	Part no.				
196 CID V6	1110695				15
	1110679 (turbo)	BTDC timing only			
	1110731 (Calif)	BTDC timing only			
	1110739 (man trans)	BTDC timing only			
	1110764 (4-bbl carb)	BTDC timing only			
	1110735	BTDC timing only			
305 CID V8	1103281 (high alt)	BTDC timing only	BTDC only	electronic timing	15
	1103282	BTDC timing only			
350 CID V8	1103284 (high alt)	BTDC timing only	BTDC only	electronic ignition	15

1979

Engine	Part no.				
196 CID V6	1110775 (auto trans)	BTDC timing only	BTDC only	electronic ignition	15 @ 600 rpm
	1110770	BTDC timing only	BTDC only	electronic ignition	
231 CID V6	1110766 (high alt)	BTDC timing only	BTDC only	electronic ignition	15 @ 800 / 15 @ 800
	1110779 (auto trans)	BTDC timing only	BTDC only	electronic ignition	15 @ 800
	1110774 (4-bbl carb)	BTDC timing only	BTDC only	electronic ignition	15 @ 600 / a5 @ 800
	1110770	BTDC timing only	BTDC only	electronic ignition	15 @ 650
301 CID V8	1103314 (2-bbl carb)	BTDC timing only	BTDC	electronic ignition	12 @ 650
	1103310 (4-bbl carb)	BTDC timing only	BTDC	electronic ignition	4 @ 600
305 CID V8	1103368	BTDC timing only	BTDC	electronic ignition	20 @ 1100
350 CID V8	1103353 (high alt)	BTDC timing only	BTDC	electronic ignition	8 @ 600

1980

231 CID V6	(high alt)	BTDC timing only	BTDC	electronic ignition	15 @ 550
w/Calif C4 Turbo	(high alt)	BTDC timing only	BTDC	electronic ignition	15 @ 650
301 CID V8	(high alt)	BTDC timing only	BTDC	electronic ignition	12 @ 500
305 CID V8	(high alt)	BTDC timing only	BTDC	electronic ignition	4 @ 550

1 General description – ignition system

In order that the engine can run correctly it is necessary for an electrical spark to ignite the fuel/air mixture in the combustion chamber at exactly the right moment in relation to engine speed and load. The ignition system is based on feeding low tension (LT) voltage from the battery to the coil where it is converted to high tension (HT) voltage. The high tension voltage is powerful enough to jump the spark plug gap in the cylinders many times a second under high compression pressures, providing that the system is in good condition and that all adjustments are correct.

The ignition system fitted to all 1974 cars as standard equipment is the conventional distributor with mechanical contact breaker and coil type. For 1975 and later models a breakerless high energy ignition (HEI) system is standard.

Pre-1975 ignition systems

The ignition system is divided into two circuits: the low tension circuit and the high tension circuit.

The low tension (sometimes known as the primary) circuit consists of the battery lead to the starter motor, lead to the ignition switch, calibrated resistance wire from the ignition switch to the low tension or primary coil winding, and the lead from the low tension coil windings to the contact breaker points and condenser in the distributor.

The high tension circuit consists of the high tension or secondary coil windings, the heavy ignition lead from the center of the coil to the center of the distributor cap, the rotor, and the spark plug leads and spark plugs.

The system functions in the following manner. Low tension voltage is changed in the coil into high tension voltage by the opening and closing of the contact breaker points in the low tension circuit. High tension voltage is then fed via the brush in the center of the distributor cap to the rotor arm of the distributor cap, and each time it

comes in line with one of the 8 segments in the cap, which are connected to the spark plug leads, the opening and closing of the contact breaker points causes the high tension voltage to build up, jump the gap from the rotor arm to the appropriate segment and so, via the spark plug lead to the spark plug, where it finally jumps the spark plug gap before going to ground.

The ignition advance is controlled both mechanically and by a vacuum operated system. The mechanical governor mechanism comprises two weights, which move out from the distributor shaft as the engine speed rises due to centrifugal force. As they move outwards they rotate the cam relative to the distributor shaft, and so advance the spark. The weights are held in position by two light springs and it is the tension of the springs which is largely responsible for correct spark advancement.

The vacuum control consists of a diaphragm, one side of which is connected via a small bore tube to the carburetor, and the other side to the contact breaker plate. Depression in the inlet manifold and carburetor, which varies with engine speed and throttle opening, causes the diaphragm to move, so moving the contact breaker plate, and advancing or retarding the spark. A fine degree of control is achieved by a spring in the vacuum assembly.

On some models, a Transmission Controlled Spark (TCS) system has an effect on vacuum advance. Further information on this system can be found in Chapter 6.

1975 and later ignition systems

Note: *Some Buicks were available with an optional high energy ignition (HEI) system for 1974. If your vehicle is equipped with one, follow the instructions for 1975 and later.*

The high energy ignition (HEI) system is a pulse triggered, transistor controlled, inductive discharge system.

A magnetic pick-up inside the distributor contains a permanent magnet, pole-piece and pick-up coil. A time core, rotating inside the pole piece, induces a voltage in the pick-up coil, and when teeth on the timer and pole piece line up, a signal passes to the electronic module to open the coil primary circuit. The primary circuit current decreases and a high voltage is induced in the coil secondary winding; this is then directed to the spark plugs by the distributor rotor as with the conventional system. A capacitor is fitted to suppress radio interference.

The system features a longer spark duration and the dwell period automatically increases with engine speed. These features are desirable for firing lean and EGR diluted mixtures (refer to Chapter 6).

The ignition coil, somewhat smaller than the coil in a conventional system, and the elctronic module are both housed in the distributor cap. The distributor does not require routine servicing.

Spark advancement is by mechanical and vacuum means, as described for conventional systems. The TCS system is not used.

If the need arises for the vehicle to be cranked remotely using jumper cables from another battery source, the distributor BAT terminal must be disconnected.

2 Battery – maintenance

1   Every week, check the level of the battery electrolyte. The method of doing this depends upon the type of battery. Some batteries have a 'Delco eye' which glows if the level is low. Others have a split ring in the filler opening with which the electrolyte should be level.

2   On later vehicles a 'Freedom' battery is used which does not require topping up.

3   Clean the top of the battery, removing all dirt and moisture (photos). As well as keeping the terminals clean and covered with petroleum jelly, the top of the battery, and especially the top of the cells, should be kept clean and dry. This helps prevent corrosion and ensures that the battery does not become partially discharged by leakage through dampness and dirt. On some models a felt ring is used under the battery terminals. This should be oiled.

4   Once every three months, remove the battery and inspect the battery securing bolts, the battery clamp plate, and battery leads for corrosion (white fluffy deposits on the metal which are brittle to touch). If any corrosion is found, clean off the deposits with an ammonia or soda solution. After cleaning, smear petroleum jelly on the battery terminals and lead connectors. Application of a zinc-base primer and/or underbody paint wil help to prevent recurrence of corrosion on body panel metal.

5   If topping-up the battery becomes excessive and the case has been inspected for cracks that could cause leakage, but none are found, the battery is beng over-charged and the alternator will have to be tested and if necessary serviced as described later in this Chapter.

6   If any doubt exists about the state of charge of a battery, a hydrometer should be used to test it by withdrawing a little electrolyte from each cell in turn.

7   The specific gravity of the electrolyte at the temperature of 80°F (26.7°C) will be approximately 1.270 for a fully charged battery. For every 10°F (5.5°C) that the electrolyte temperature is above that stated, add 0.04 to the specific gravity or subtract 0.04 if the temperature is below that stated.

8   A specific gravity reading of 1.240 with an electrolyte temperature of 80°F (26.7°C) indicates a half-charged battery.

9   With the 'Freedom' type of battery, a charge indicator is built into it which uses a color system to relay the state of charge of the battery.

3 Battery charging

1   In winter time when heavy demand is placed upon the battery, such as when starting from cold, and much electrical equipment is continually in use, it is a good idea to occasionally have the battery fully charged from an external source at the rate of 3.5 to 4 amps.

2   Continue to charge the battery at this rate until no further rise in specific gravity is noted over a four hour period.

3   Alternatively, a trickle charger charging at the rate of 1.5 amps can be safely used overnight.

4   Special rapid boost charges which are claimed to restore the power of the battery in 1 to 2 hours are most dangerous as they can cause serious damage to the battery plates. This type of charge should only be used in a 'crisis' situation.

5   On vehicles equipped with the maintenance-free battery, do not charge the battery if the built-in hydrometer on the top of the battery is a clear or light yellow color. This coloring indicates that the battery needs replacement.

4 Battery – removal and installation

1   The battery is located at the front of the engine compartment. It is held in place by either a hold-down rod running across the top of the battery or a clamp near the bottom of the battery case.

2   As hydrogen gas is produced by the battery, keep open flames or lighted cigarettes away from the battery at all times.

3   Avoid spilling any of the electrolyte battery fluid on the vehicle or yourself. Always keep the battery in the upright position. Any spilled electrolyte should be immediately flushed with large quantities of water. Wear eye protection when working with a battery to prevent serious eye damage from splashed fluid.

4   Always disconnect the negative (–) battery cable first, followed by the positive (+) cable.

5   After the cables are disconnected from the battery, remove the hold-down mechanism, be it a rod or bottom clamp.

6   Carefully lift the battery from its tray and out of the engine compartment.

7   Installation is a reversal of removal, however make sure that the hold-down clamp or rod is securely tightened. Do not over-tighten, however, as this may damage the battery case. The battery posts and cable ends should be cleaned prior to connection.

2.3a Unbolt the cable connector from the terminal and gently pry apart the pinched connector ends

2.3b Use a terminal cleaning brush to clean the battery terminals and cable connectors

5 Condenser (capacitor) – testing, removal and installation (1974)

1 The condenser ensures that when the contact breaker points open, the sparking between them is not excessive to cause severe pitting. The condenser is fitted in parallel and its failure will automatically cause failure of the ignition system as the points will be prevented from interrupting the low tension circuit.

2 Testing for an unserviceable condenser may be done by switching on the ignition and separating the contact points by hand. If this action is accompanied by a blue flash then condenser failure is indicated. Difficult starting, missing of engine after several miles running or badly pitted points are other indications of a faulty condenser.

3 The surest test is by substitution with a new unit.

4 To replace the condenser, remove the distributor cap, rotor and RFI shield.

5 Disconnect the condenser lead and remove the condenser retaining screw. Slide the condenser from the bracket.

6 Installation is the reverse of the removal procedure.

6 Distributor cap – replacement (1974)

Note: *It is imperative that the spark plug wires be installed in the correct order on the distributor cap.*

1 Purchase a replacement distributor cap for the particular model year and engine size.

2 Release the old cap from the distributor body by pushing downward on the slotted latches and then turning the latches $\frac{1}{4}$ turn.

3 Place the new cap next to the old one. Use the metal window and the two latches as reference points to get the new cap in the same relative position.

4 Begin transferring the spark plug wires one at a time from the old cap to the new one. Do not pull on the wire insulation, but rather grab the rubber boot, twist slightly and then pull the plug wire free by the boot.

5 Push the plug wires and boots firmly onto the new distributor cap.

6 Place the new cap and plug wires into position over the top of the distributor and lock it in place by pushing and turning the latches. Make sure the cap is firmly seated.

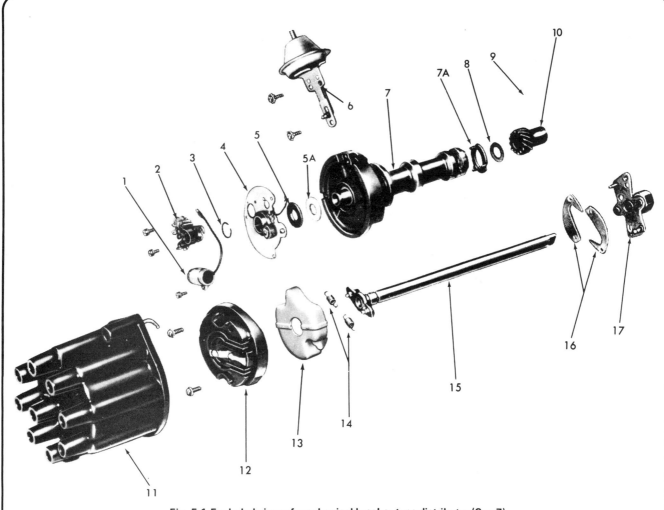

Fig. 5.1 Exploded view of mechanical breaker type distributor (Sec 7)

1 Condenser	6 Vacuum advance unit	11 Cap	16 Advance weight
2 Contact point assembly	7 Housing	12 Rotor	17 Cam weight base
3 Retaining ring	7a Tanged washer	13 Radio frequency	assembly
4 Breaker plate	8 Shim washer	interference shield	
5 Felt washer	9 Drive gear pin	14 Weight springs	
5a Plastic seal	10 Drive gear	15 Mainshaft	

7 Distributor – removal and overhaul (1974)

1 Release the two latches on the distributor cap by pressing them downward with a screwdriver and then turning them $\frac{1}{4}$ turn. Move the cap (with the spark plug wires still attached) out of the way. Use wire or tape if necessary.

2 Disconnect the distributor primary wiring lead from the coil terminal.

3 At this point it is important to mark the position of the rotor and distributor housing for easier reassembly. At the very bottom of the distributor, scribe a mark on the distributor base and another mark in line with the base mark on the engine block. Also note the direction in which the rotor contact is pointed. Make a mark on the distributor housing in-line with the rotor contact strip.

4 Disconnect the vacuum line at the distributor.

5 Note the position of the vacuum advance mechanism (canister from which vacuum hose was just disconnected) relative to the engine.

6 Remove the distributor hold-down bolt and clamp from the base of the distributor.

7 Lift the distributor straight up and out of the engine.

8 Avoid rotating the engine with the distributor removed as the ignition timing will be changed.

9 To disassemble, remove the rotor (2 screws), the advance weight springs and the weights. Where applicable, also remove the radio frequency interference (RFI) shield.

10 Drive out the roll pin retaining the gear to the shaft then pull off the gear and spacers.

11 Ensure that the shaft is not burred, then slide it from the housing.

12 Remove the cam weight base assembly.

13 Remove the screws retaining the vacuum unit and lift off the unit itself.

14 Remove the spring retainer (snap-ring) then remove the breaker plate assembly.

15 Remove the contact points and condenser, followed by the felt washer and plastic seal located beneath the breaker plate.

16 Wipe all components clean with a solvent moistened cloth and examine them for wear, distortion and scoring. Replace parts as necessary. Pay particular attention to the rotor and distributor cap to ensure that they are not cracked.

17 Fill the lubricating cavity in the housing with general purpose grease then fit a new plastic seal and felt washer.

18 Install the vacuum unit, the breaker plate in the housing and the spring retainer on the upper bushing.

19 Lubricate the cam weight base and slide it on the mainshaft; install the weights and springs.

20 Insert the mainshaft in the housing then fit the shims and drive-gear. Install a new roll-pin.

21 Install the contact point set (Chapter 1).

22 Install the rotor, aligning the round and square pilot holes.

23 Install the distributor as described in Section 8.

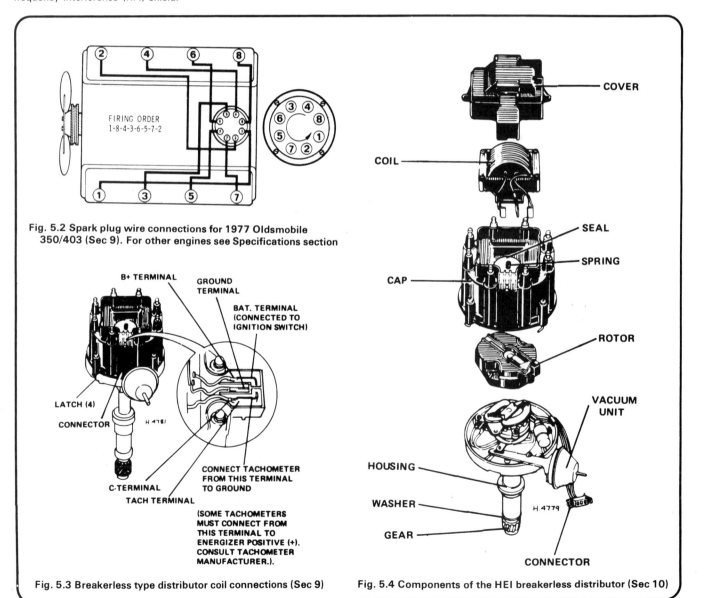

Fig. 5.2 Spark plug wire connections for 1977 Oldsmobile 350/403 (Sec 9). For other engines see Specifications section

FIRING ORDER
1-8-4-3-6-5-7-2

Fig. 5.3 Breakerless type distributor coil connections (Sec 9)

Fig. 5.4 Components of the HEI breakerless distributor (Sec 10)

Measuring plug gap. A feeler gauge of the correct size (see ignition system specifications) should have a slight 'drag' when slid between the electrodes. Adjust gap if necessary

Adjusting plug gap. The plug gap is adjusted by bending the ground electrode inwards, or outwards, as necessary until the correct clearance is obtained. Note the use of the correct tool

Normal. Gray brown deposits, lightly coated core nose. Gap increasing by around 0.001 in (0.025 mm) per 1000 miles (1600 km). Plugs ideally suited to engine, and engine in good condition

Carbon fouling. Dry, black, sooty deposits. Will cause weak spark and eventually misfire. Fault: over-rich fuel mixture. Check: carburetor mixture settings, float level and jet sizes; choke operation and cleanliness of air filter. Plugs can be re-used after cleaning

Oil fouling. Wet, oily deposits. Will cause weak spark and eventually misfire. Fault: worn bores/piston rings or valve guides; sometimes occurs (temporarily) during running-in period. Plugs can be re-used after thorough cleaning

Overheating. Electrodes have glazed appearance, core nose very white – few deposits. Fault: plug overheating. Check: plug value, ignition timing, fuel octane rating (too low) and fuel mixture (too weak). Discard plugs and cure fault immediately

Electrode damage. Electrodes burned away; core nose has burned, glazed appearance. Fault: pre-ignition. Check: as for 'Overheating' but may be more severe. Discard plugs and remedy fault before piston or valve damage occurs

Split core nose (may appear initially as a crack). Damage is self-evident, but cracks will only show after cleaning. Fault: pre-ignition or wrong gap-setting technique. Check: ignition timing, cooling system, fuel octane rating (too low) and fuel mixture (too weak). Discard plugs, rectify fault immediately

8   Distributor – installation (1974)

If engine was not rotated after removal

1   Turn the rotor about $\frac{1}{8}$ turn in a clockwise direction past the mark made on the distributor housing upon removal.
2   Lower the distributor down into the engine, positioning the vacuum advance mechanism in the approximate position as removal. To mesh the gears at the bottom of the distributor it may be necessary to turn the rotor slightly.
3   With the base of the distributor all the way down against the engine block, the rotor should be pointed to the mark made on the distributor housing. If these two marks are not in alignment, repeat the previous steps.
4   Now turn the distributor housing until the scribed marks at the bottom of the distributor are in alignment.
5   Place the clamp into position and tighten the clamp bolt securely.
6   Connect the vacuum hose to the distributor and connect the primary wire to the coil terminal.
7   Install the distributor cap.
8   Check the ignition timing as described in Chapter 1.

If engine was rotated after removal

9   Turn the crankshaft by applying a wrench to the crankshaft pulley bolt at the front of the engine until the number 1 piston is at top-dead-center (TDC). This can be ascertained by removing the number 1 spark plug and feeling the compression being generated. If you are careful not to scratch' the cylinder, you can also use a length of stiff wire to feel the piston come to the top of the cyinder.
10 With the number 1 piston at TDC (as indicated by the timing marks on the front cover), the distributor should be firing this cylinder.
11 Hold the distributor over its recess with the vacuum advance unit in its 'installed' position. It should be pointed towards the front of the right-hand cylinder head.
12 Point the metal contact on the rotor towards the number 1 cylinder and lower the distributor into place.
13 With the distributor fully seated to the engine (it may be necessary to turn the rotor slightly to mesh the gears), the rotor contact should be in-line with the number 1 spark plug wire in the distributor cap. To find out if this is true, temporarily install the cap to the distributor, checking the rotor contact and the number 1 spark plug terminal.
14 Install the clamp and the hold-down bolt at the bottom of the engine. Leave the bolt loose enough to enable you to turn the distributor.
15 Start the engine and adjust the timing as described in Chapter 1.
16 *On 455 CID V8 engines,* there is a punch mark on the drive gear which represents the position of the contact end of the rotor. This enables the distributor to be installed with the cap in place.
17 Once installed, turn the distributor until the contact points are just about to open and tighten the clamp bolt.
18 Tighten all connections and install the distributor cap.
19 Check and adjust the dwell angle and the timing as soon as the engine has been run to normal operating temperature.

9   Distributor – removal and installation (1975 through 1980)

1   The procedures for removing and installing the breakerless distributor are basically the same as for the conventional unit described in Sections 7 and 8. Follow the sequence given in Sections 7 and 8 with the following exceptions:

   a)   *Disconnect the wiring connector on the outside of the distributor.*
   b)   *The spark plug wires are connected to a ring around the top of the distributor cap. This retaining ring can be removed once the latches are disengaged.*
   c)   *Ignore all references to the contact points and setting the dwell angle as this does not apply to the breakerless distributor.*
   d)   *Set the ignition timing after installation.*

10   Distributor (breakerless-type) – overhaul

1   Remove the distributor as previously described.
2   Remove the rotor (2 screws).

Fig. 5.5 Distributor centrifugal advance (Sec 10)

3   Remove the 2 screws retaining the module. Move the module aside and remove the connector from the 'B' and 'C' terminals. (photo).
4   Remove the connections from the 'W' and 'G' terminals.
5   Carefully drive out the roll pin from the drive gear (photo).
6   Remove the gear, shim and tanged washer from the distributor shaft.
7   Ensure that the shaft is not burred, then remove it from the housing.
8   Remove the washer from the upper end of the distributor housing.
9   Remove 3 screws and take out the pole-piece, magnet and pick-up coil (photo).
10 Remove the lock ring, then take out the pick-up coil retainer, shim and felt washer.
11 Remove the vacuum unit (2 screws).
12 Disconnect the capacitor lead and remove the capacitor (1 screw).
13 Disconnect the wiring harness from the distributor housing.
14 Wipe all components clean with a solvent moistened cloth and examine them for wear, distortion and other damage. Replace parts as necessary.
15 To assemble, position the vacuum unit to the housing and secure with the 2 screws.
16 Position the felt washer over the lubricant reservoir at the top of the housing then position the shim on top of the felt washer.
17 Position the pick-up coil retainer to the housing. The vacuum advance arm goes over the actuating pin of the advance mechanism. Secure it with the lock-ring.
18 Install the pick-up coil magnet and pole-piece. Loosely install the 3 screws to retain the pole-piece.
19 Install the washer to the top of the housing. Install the distributor shaft then rotate it and check for equal clearance all round between the shaft projections and pole-piece. Secure the pole-piece when correctly positioned.
20 Install the tanged washer, shim and drivegear. Align the gear and install a new roll pin.
21 Loosely install the capacitor with one screw.
22 Install the connector to the 'B' and 'C' terminals on the module with the tab at the top.
23 Apply silicone grease to the base of the module and secure it with 2 screws. This grease is essential to ensure good heat conduction.
24 Position the wiring harness with the grommet in the housing notch then connect the pink wire to the capacitor stud and the black wire to the capacitor mounting screw. Tighten the screw.
25 Connect the white wire from the pick-up coil to the module 'W' terminal and the green to the 'G' terminal.
26 Install the advance weights, weight retainer (dimple downwards), and springs.
27 Install the rotor and secure with the 2 screws. Ensure that the

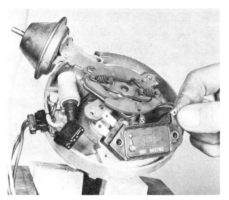

10.3 The electronic module is secured to the inside of the distributor with 2 screws

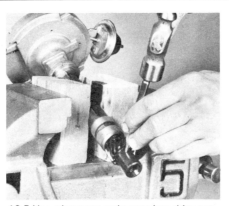

10.5 Use a hammer and a punch to drive out the rollpin from the bottom of the distributor shaft

10.9 The pole-piece and washer removed from the upper end of the distributor body

notch on the side of the rotor engages with the tab on the cam weight base.

28   Install the distributor as previously described.

11 Ignition coil – removal and installation

1974
1   This is a straightforward operation, requiring only the removal of the electrical connections and the two mounting screws. It is a good policy to mark the connections before removal to ensure that they are re-installed correctly.

1975 on
2   Disconnect the battery wire and harness connector from the distributor cap.
3   Remove the coil cover (3 screws) and the coil assembly (4 screws) from the distributor cap.
4   Note the position of each wire, duly marking them if necessary. Remove the coil ground wire then push the leads from the underside of the connectors. Remove the coil from the distributor cap.
5   Installation is the reverse of the removal procedure, but ensure that the leads are connected to their original positions (photo).

12 Spark plugs

1   Properly functioning spark plugs are a necessity if the engine is to perform properly. At the intervals specified in Chapter 1 or your owner's manual, the spark plugs should be replaced with new ones. Removal and installation information can be found in the Tune-up and Basic Maintenance Chapter.
2   It is important to replace spark plugs with new ones of the same heat range and type. A series of numbers and letters are stamped on the spark plug to help identify each variation.
3   The spark plug gap is of considerable importance as, if it is too large or too small the size of the spark and its efficiency will be seriously impaired. To set it, measure the gap with a feeler gauge, and then bend open, or close, the outer plug electrode until the correct gap is achieved. The center electrode should never be bent as this may crack the insulation and cause plug failure, if nothing worse.
4   The condition and appearance of the spark plugs will tell much about the condition and tune of the engine. If the insulator nose of the spark plug is clean and white with no deposits, this is indicative of a weak mixture, or too hot a plug (a hot plug transfers heat away from the electrode slowly – a cold plug transfers it away quickly.
5   If the tip and insulator nose is covered with hard black looking deposits, then this is indicative that the mixture is too rich. Should the plug be black and oily, then it is likely that the engine is fairly worn, as well as the mixture being too rich.
6   If the insulator nose is covered with light tan to greyish brown deposits, then the mixture is correct and it is likely that the engine is in good condition.
7   If there are any traces of long brown tapering stains on the outside of the white portion of the plug, then the plug will have to be replaced with a new one, as this shows that there is a faulty joint between the plug body and the insulator, and compression is being allowed to leak away.

8   Always tighten a spark plug to the specified torque – no tighter.

13 Charging system – general description

The charging system is made up of the alternator, voltage regulator and the battery. These components work together to supply electrical power for the engine ignition, lights, radio, etc.

The alternator is turned by a drive belt at the front of the engine, Thus, when the engine is operating, voltage is generated by the internal components of the alternator to be sent to the battery for storage.

The purpose of the voltage regulator is to limit the alternator voltage to a pre-set value. This prevents power surges, circuit overloads, etc. during peak voltage output. Since 1974, Buick cars have had the voltage regulator built into the alternator housing.

The charging system does not ordinarily require periodic maintenance. The drive belts, electrical wiring and connections should, however, be inspected during normal tune-ups (see Chapter 1).

14 Alternator – maintenance and special precautions

1   The alternator fitted to all models is a Delco-Remy Delcotron.
2   Alternator maintenance consists of occasionally wiping away any dirt or oil which may have collected.
3   Check the tension of the driving belt (refer to Chapter 1, Section 41).
4   No lubrication is required as alternator bearings are grease sealed for the life of the unit.
5   Take extreme care when making circuit connections to a vehicle fitted with an alternator and observe the following. When making connections to the alternator from a battery always match correct polarity. Before using electric-arc welding equipment to repair any part of the vehicle, disconnect the connector from the alternator and disconnect the positive battery terminal. Never start the car with a battery charger connected. Always disconnect both battery leads before using a mains charger. If boosting from another battery, always connect in parallel using heavy cable. It is not recommended that testing of an alternator should be undertaken at home due to the testing equipment required and the possibility of damage occurring during testing. It is best left to automotive electrical specialists.

15 Alternator – removal and installation

1   Disconnect both leads from the battery terminals.
2   Disconnect the leads from the rear face of the alternator, marking them first to ensure correct installation (photo).
3   Loosen the alternator mounting and adjuster link bolts, push the unit in towards the engine as far as possible, and slip off the drivebelts (photos).
4   Remove the mounting bolts and lift the alternator from the engine compartment.
5   Installation is a reversal of removal; however adjust the drivebelt tension. **Note:** *New alternators are not usually supplied with pulleys. The old one should therefore be removed if a new unit is to be purchased. To do this, hold the alternator shaft still with an Allen wrench while the pulley nut is unscrewed.*

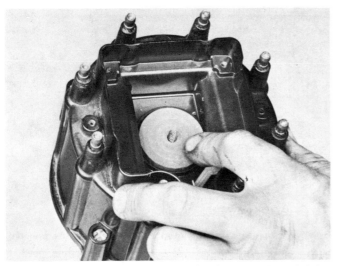

11.5 Before installing a new coil, ensure that the center electrode is in good condition

15.2 Disconnect the wiring from the rear side of the alternator

15.3a The long pivot bolt for the alternator is under the housing

15.3b The adjusting strap bolt is located inside a slotted bracket

16 Alternator – testing

Note: *Due to the fine tolerances and critical nature of the alternator components, it is suggested that the home mechanic take it to a rebuild shop if the following tests point to a defective unit.*

1   A malfunction in the charging circuit will manifest itself in one or more of the following conditions: A faulty alternator dash lamp, an undercharged battery and an overcharged battery.

Alternator indicator lamp – faulty operation

2   Turn on ignition. The indicator lamp should be on. Start the engine. The lamp should go out. If it does, it is operating properly. Proceed to step 14.

3   If the lamp stays on, check the drive belt for proper tension and adjust as necessary. Redo the test. The indicator lamp should go out. If it does, proceed to step 14.

4   If the lamp is still lit, check the 10 amp "gauges" and "trans" fuse in the fuse block. Replace if necessary.

5   Next, connect a voltmeter to the battery terminal on the alternator and to chassis ground. Turn on the ignition. If the meter reads zero voltage, repair the open circuit between the battery terminal on the alternator and the battery or junction block.

6   If the meter reads the approximate voltage of the battery, disconnect the number 1 and 2 connector at the alternator. Connect the voltmeter from the number 1 connector to ground. If zero voltage is registered, repair the open circuit in the number 1 connector wire that runs from the connector to chassis ground.

7   If the voltmeter reads from 2 to 4 volts (approx), reinstall the number 1 and 2 connector wires and disconnect the wires from the battery terminal on the alternator.

8   Now connect the ammeter black lead to the battery terminal wires and the ammeter red lead to the battery terminal connection on the alternator.

9   Reconnect the battery ground strap, turn on *all* accessories and start the motor. Turn the headlights to high beam and make sure the heater blower is also on "high". Record the ammeter reading.

10   If the output reading is within 10 amps of the rating stamped on the alternator frame (casing), check the battery connections and the condition of the battery. A hydrometer can be used to check the battery (see Sec 2).

11   If the meter reading is *not* within 10 amps of the stamped rating, insert a screwdriver into the test hole (located on the rear of the alternator). Be sure that the screwdriver touches the tab and the side of the test hole. **Note**: *Tab is within $\frac{3}{4}$-in of the casting surface. Do not insert screwdriver deeper than 1-inch into frame or severe damage to*

alternator will result. If test hole is not accessible, take the alternator to a shop. Redo the previous test and note the reading.

12 If the reading is within 10 amps of the stamped rating, replace the regulator subsection of the alternator. As mentioned previously, take the unit to a professional.

13 If the output is *not* within 10 amps of the rating, replace the alternator. Again, it is best to have the unit professionally serviced.

14 Turn the ignition switch on. The engine should not be running for this test. The dash lamp should be on. If it is, proceed to "undercharged battery".

15 If the lamp is dimly lit, check the condition, charge, and connections of the battery. Next check the "gauges" and "trans" fuse in the fuse block. Make sure the connections are firm and clean.

16 If the dash lamp is off, disconnect the number 1 and 2 connector wires at the alternator. Ground the number 1 wire but *do not* ground

the number 2 wire. If the lamp remains off, either the bulb is burned out or there is a short in the number 1 wire (between the alternator and the ignition switch).

17 If the lamp came on when you disconnected the number 1 and 2 wires, reconnect them and insert a screwdriver into the test hole on the back of the alternator. *Note the caution mentioned in step 11.*

18 If the lamp remains lit, the regulator section of the alternator is faulty and needs to be replaced. Take the unit to an automotive electric shop.

19 If the lamp remains off, check the number 1 wire and make sure it is making good contact on the terminal. If the lamp still remains off, the alternator needs to be overhauled.

20 Turn off the ignition switch. The lamp should go out and you can proceed to "undercharged battery".

21 If the lamp did not go out, disconnect the number 1 and 2 wires

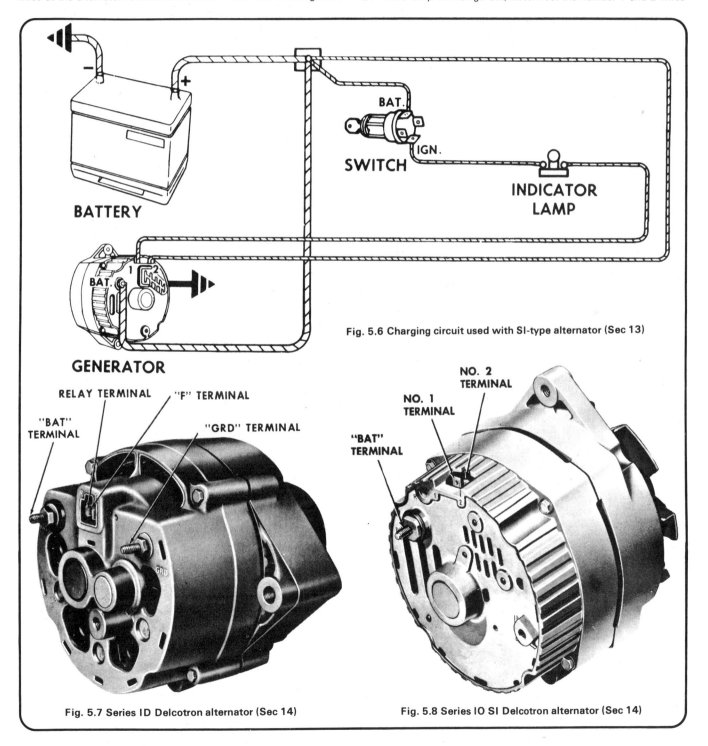

Fig. 5.6 Charging circuit used with SI-type alternator (Sec 13)

Fig. 5.7 Series ID Delcotron alternator (Sec 14)

Fig. 5.8 Series IO SI Delcotron alternator (Sec 14)

at the alternator. If the lamp now goes out, the rectifier bridge in the alternator is faulty and the unit should be professionally serviced.

22 If the lamp remains on, there is a short circuit between the number 1 and 2 connector wires.

Undercharged battery

23 Check to see that the low battery condition has not been caused by leaving accessories or the ignition on.

24 Next, check the drive belt tension and adjust if necessary. See Chapter 1 for this procedure.

25 Using a hydrometer, check the specific gravity of the battery electrolyte.

26 Inspect the wiring for loose connections and open circuits. Make sure that the slip connectors at the alternator are firewall are tight.

27 When all connections are tight and all harness leads connected, attach a voltmeter from: 1) the alternator "BAT" terminal to ground; 2) the alternator number 1 terminal to ground; 3) the alternator number 2 terminal to ground. If the reading on the meter is zero, there is an open circuit between the voltmeter and the battery. Generating alternators have a built-in safety switch which prevents them from operating when there is an open circuit in the harness connected to the number 2 terminal. Frequently, this open circuit will occur at the junction between harness and battery terminal. Check the crimp between the terminal and harness wire.

28 If the system checks out under the previous tests, check the alternator. Disconnect the battery ground cable and introduce an ammeter into the circuit at the "BAT" terminal on the alternator. Reconnect the battery ground.

29 Turn on all accessories, connect an external resistor across the battery and operate the engine at medium speed. Adjust the resistor for maximum output reading.

30 Check the ammeter reading. If it is within 10 amps of the rating (stamped on the case of the alternator) the alternator is not defective. Recheck steps 23 through 27.

31 If the output rating shown on the ammeter is *not* within 10 amps of the stamped rating on the casing, insert a screwdriver into the test hole (re-read step 11 before doing this). If there is no test hole, take the alternator to an automotive electric shop.

32 Again, run the engine at a medium speed and adjust the external resistor as necessary to obtain maximum output. Recheck the ammeter reading. If the output is within 10 amps, it will be necessary to have the field winding and the regulator checked. Take the unit to a qualified professional.

Overcharged battery

33 Overcharging is typified by battery overboiling. As with the two other test sections, battery condition must be ascertained, as outlined in Section 2, by testing the battery electrolyte with a hydrometer.

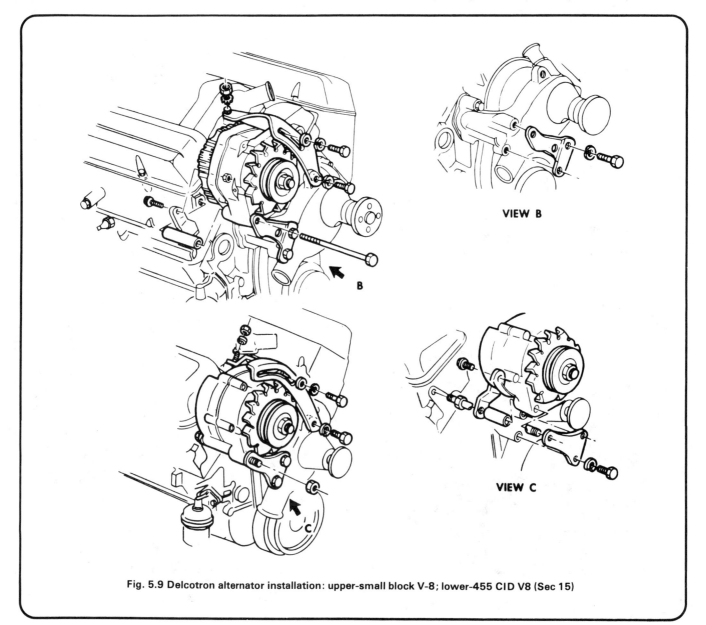

VIEW B

VIEW C

Fig. 5.9 Delcotron alternator installation: upper-small block V-8; lower-455 CID V8 (Sec 15)

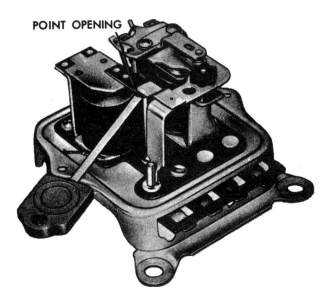

POINT OPENING

Fig. 5.10 Checking field relay point opening (Sec 17)

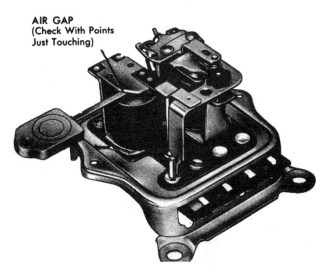

AIR GAP
(Check With Points
Just Touching)

Fig. 5.11 Checking field relay air gap (Sec 17)

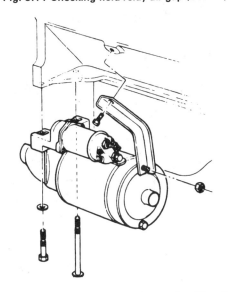

Fig. 5.12 Typical starter motor mounting (Sec 20)

34 If the condition of the battery is found to be good, connect a voltmeter from the number 2 alternator terminal to ground. If the meter is zero, the number 2 wire has an open circuit.

35 If the number 2 leads test out ok, it will be necessary to take the unit to a shop and have the field winding tested for shorts.

17 Starting system – general description

The function of the starting system is to crank the engine. This system is composed of a starting motor, solenoid and battery. The battery supplies the electrical energy to the solenoid which then completes the circuit to the starting motor which does the actual work of cranking the engine.

The solenoid and starting motor are mounted together on a pad at the side of the engine. No periodic lubrication or maintenance is required to the starting system components.

The electrical circuitry of the vehicle is arranged so that the starter motor can only be operated when the clutch pedal is fully depressed (manual transmission) or the transmission selector lever is at 'P' or 'N' (automatic transmission).

18 Starter motor – testing in vehicle

1 If the starter motor does not rotate at all when the switch is operated, check that the speed selector lever is in 'N' or 'P' (automatic transmission) and that the front seat belts are connected (starter interlock system) and also that the clutch pedal is depressed (where applicable).

2 Check that the battery is well charged and all cables, both at the battery and starter solenoid terminals, are secure.

3 If the motor can be heard spinning but the engine is not being cranked, then the overrunning clutch in the starter motor is slipping and the assembly must be removed from the engine and dismantled.

4 If, when the switch is actuated, the starter motor does not operate at all but the solenoid plunger can be heard to move with a loud 'click' then the fault lies in the main solenoid contacts or the starter motor itself.

5 If the solenoid plunger cannot be heard to move when the switch is actuated then the solenoid itself is defective or the solenoid circuit is open.

6 To check out the solenoid, connect a jumper lead between the battery (+) terminal and the terminal on the solenoid to which the purple cable is attached. If the starter motor now operates, the solenoid is OK and the fault must lie in the ignition or neutral start switches or in their interconnecting wiring.

7 If the starter motor still does not operate, remove the starter/solenoid assembly for dismantling, testing and repair.

8 If the starter motor cranks the engine at an abnormally slow speed, first ensure that the battery is fully charged and all terminal connections are tight, also that the engine oil is not too thick a grade and that the resistance is not due to a mechanical fault within the power unit.

9 Run the engine until normal operating temperature is attained, shut it off and disconnect the coil to distributor LT wire or 'BAT' connection on HEI distributors so that the engine will not fire during cranking.

10 Connect a voltmeter positive lead to the starter motor terminal of the solenoid and then connect the negative lead to ground.

11 Actuate the ignition switch and take the voltmeter readings as soon as a steady figure is indicated. Do not allow the starter motor to turn for more than 30 seconds at a time. A reading of 9 volts, or more, with the starter motor turning at normal cranking speed proves it to be in good condition. If the reading is 9 volts, or more, but the cranking speed is slow, then the motor is faulty. If the reading is less than 9 volts and the cranking speed is slow, the solenoid contacts are probably at fault and should be replaced as described later in this Chapter.

19 Starter motor – removal and installation

1 Disconnect the ground cable from the battery.

2 Raise the vehicle to a satisfactory working height.

3 Disconnect the leads at the starter solenoid marking each with a coded piece of tape for easy identification upon reassembly. Temporarily replace each of the securing nuts to the terminals as they have

various thread types which could cause damage to the studs if not properly re-installed.

4   Loosen the starter motor front bracket nut and then remove the two mount bolts.

5   Remove the front bracket bolt, rotate the bracket so that the starter motor can be withdrawn by lowering its front end.

6   Installation is a reversal of removal but tighten the mount bolts first to the specified torque and then tighten the front bracket bolt and nut.

7   Install each of the wires to the solenoid terminals using your identification coding.

20 Starter motor – dismantling and component testing

Note: *Due to the critical nature of the disassembly and testing of the starter motor it may be advisable for the home mechanic to simply purchase a new or factory-rebuilt unit. If it is decided to overhaul the starter, check on the availability of replacement components before proceeding.*

1   Disconnect the starter motor field coil connectors from the solenoid terminals.

2   Unscrew and remove the through bolts.

3   Remove the commutator end-frame, field frame assembly and the armature from the drive housing.

4   Slide the two-section thrust collar off the end of the armature shaft and then using a piece of suitable tube drive the stop/retainer up the armature shaft to expose the snap-ring.

5   Extract the snap-ring from its shaft groove and then slide the stop/retainer and overrunning clutch assembly from the armature shaft.

6   Dismantle the brush components from the field frame.

7   Release the V-shaped springs from the brushholder supports.

8   Remove the brushholder support pin and then lift the complete brush assembly upwards.

9   Disconnect the leads from the brushes if they are worn down to half their original length and they are to be replaced.

10 The starter motor is now completely dismantled except for the field coils. If these are found to be defective during the tests described later in this Section removal of the pole shoe screws is best left to a

service station who will have the necessary pressure driver.

11 Clean all components and replace any obviously worn components.

12 **Note**: *On no account attempt to undercut the insulation between the commutator segments on starter motors having the molded type commutators. On commutators of conventional type, the insulation should be undercut (below the level of the segments) by 1/32 inch. Use an old hacksaw blade to do this and make sure that the undercut is the full width of the insulation and the groove is quite square at the bottom. When the undercutting is completed, brush away all dirt and dust.*

13 Clean the commutator by spinning it while a piece of number '00' sandpaper is wrapped round it. On no account use any other type of abrasive material for this work.

14 If necessary, because the commutator is in such bad shape, it may be turned down in a lathe to provide a new surface. Make sure to undercut the insulation when the turning is completed.

15 *To test the armature for ground:* use a lamp-type circuit tester. Place one lead on the armature core or shaft and the other on a segment of the commutator. If the lamp lights then the armature is grounded and must be replaced.

16 *To test the field coils for open circuit:* place one test probe on the insulated brush and the other on the field connector bar. If the lamp does not light, the coils are open and must be replaced.

17 *To test the field coils for ground:* place one test probe on the connector bar and the other on the grounded brush. If the lamp lights then the field coils are grounded.

18 The overrunning clutch cannot be repaired and if faulty, it must be replaced as a complete assembly.

21 Starter motor – reassembly and adjustment

1   Install the brush assembly to the field frame as follows:

2   Install the brushes to their holders.

3   Assemble the insulated and grounded brushholders together with the V-spring and then locate the unit on its support pin.

4   Push the holders and spring to the bottom of the support and then rotate the spring to engage the V in the support slot.

5   Connect the ground wire to the grounded brush and the field lead

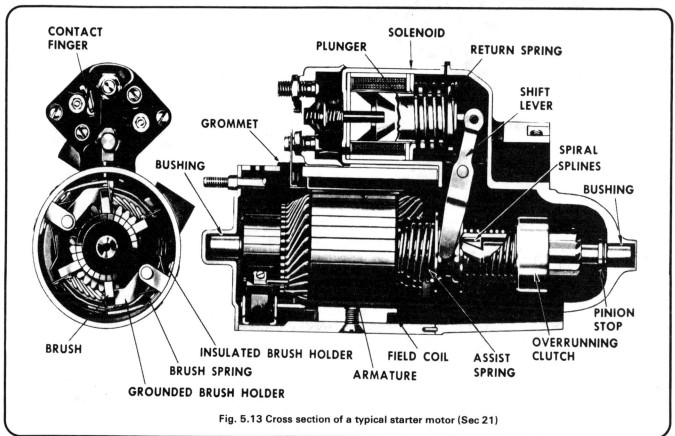

Fig. 5.13 Cross section of a typical starter motor (Sec 21)

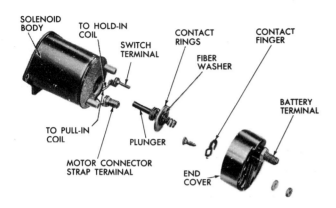

Fig. 5.14 Exploded view of starter motor solenoid (Sec 23)

wire to the insulated brush.

6   Repeat the operations for the second set of brushes.

7   Smear silicone oil onto the drive end of the armature shaft and then slide the clutch assembly (pinion to the front) onto the shaft.

8   Slide the pinion stop/retainer onto the shaft so that its open end is facing away from the pinion.

9   Stand the armature vertically on a piece of wood and then position the snap-ring on the end of the shaft. Using a hammer and a piece of hardwood, drive the snap-ring onto the shaft.

10 Slide the snap-ring down the shaft until it drops into its groove.

11 Install the thrust collar on the shaft so that the shoulder is next to the snap-ring. Using two pairs of pliers, squeeze the thrust collar and stop/retainer together until the snap-ring fully enters the retainer.

12 Lubricate the drive housing bushing with silicone oil and after ensuring that the thrust collar is in position against the snap-ring, slide the armature and clutch assembly into the drive housing so that at the same time, the shift lever engages with the clutch.

13 Position the field frame over the armature and apply sealing compound between the frame and the solenoid case.

14 Position the field frame against the drive housing taking care not to damage the brushes.

15 Lubricate the bushing in the commutator end-frame using silicone oil; place the leather brake washer on the armature shaft and then slide the commutator end-frame onto the shaft.

16 Reconnect the field coil connectors to the MOTOR terminal of the solenoid.

17 Now check the pinion clearance. To do this, connect a 6 volt battery between the solenoid S terminal and ground and at the same time fix a heavy connecting cable between the MOTOR terminal and ground (to prevent any possibility of the starter motor rotating). As the solenoid is energized it will push the pinion forward into its normal cranking position and retain it there. With the fingers, push the pinion away from the stop/retainer in order to eliminate any slack and then check the clearance between the face of the pinion and the face of stop/retainer using a feeler gauge. The clearance should be between 0.010 and 0.140 inch to ensure correct engagement of the pinion with the flywheel (or driveplate – automatic transmission) ring-gear. If the clearance is incorrect, the starter will have to be dismantled again and any worn or distorted components replaced, no adjustment being provided for.

22 Starter motor solenoid – removal, repair and installation

1   After removing the starter/solenoid unit as described in Section 20 disconnect the connector strap from the solenoid MOTOR terminal.

2   Remove the two screws which secure the solenoid housing to the end-frame assembly.

3   Twist the solenoid in a clockwise direction to disengage the flange key and then withdraw the solenoid.

4   Remove the nuts and washers from the solenoid terminals and then unscrew the two solenoid end-cover retaining screws and washers and pull off the end-cover.

5   Unscrew the nut washer from the battery terminal on the end-cover and remove the terminal.

6   Remove the resistor bypass terminal and contactor.

7   Remove the motor connector strap terminal and solder a new terminal in position.

8   Use a new battery terminal and install it to the end-cover. Install the bypass terminal and contactor.

9   Install the end-cover and the remaining terminal nuts.

10 Install the solenoid to the starter motor by first checking that the return spring is in position on the plunger and then insert the solenoid body into the drive housing and turn the body counter clockwise to engage the flange key.

11 Install the two solenoid securing screws and connect the MOTOR connector strap.

Chapter 6 Emissions systems

Contents

Specifications

Torque specifications

	ft-lbs	in-lbs
Diverter valve-to-air pump		90
Air pump mounting bolts	20 to 35	
Air pump pulley bolts	24	
Exhaust manifold		
(inner bolts)	20	
(outer bolts)	30	
Actuator mounting bolts		25
Thermal vacuum switches	15	
Catalytic converter fill plug	28	

1 General information

1 Despite the general bad feelings towards emission controls, they play a necessary and integral role in the overall operation of the internal combustion engine. Your car is designed to operate with its pollution control systems, and disconnecting them or failing to properly maintain the components is illegal, not to mention being potentially harmful to the engine.

2 Through the years as smog standards became more stringent, emission control systems have become more diverse and complex. Where once the anti-pollution devices incorporated were installed as peripheral components to the main engine, later model engines work closely with, and in some cases are even controlled by, the emission control systems. Nearly every system in the make-up of a modern-day automobile is affected in some fashion by the emission systems.

3 This is not to say that the emission systems are particularly difficult for the home mechanic to maintain and service. You can perform general operational checks, and do most (if not all) of the regular maintenance easily and quickly at home with common tune-up and hand tools.

4 While the end result from the various emission systems is to reduce the output of pollutants into the air, (namely hydrocarbons [HC], carbon Monoxide [CO], and oxides of Nitrogen [NOx]) the various systems function independently toward this goal. This is the way in which this chapter is divided.

2 Positive crankcase ventilation (PCV) system

General description

1 The positive crankcase ventilation, or PCV as it is more commonly called, reduces hydrocarbon emissions by circulating fresh air through the crankcase to pick up blow-by gases which are then re-routed through the carburetor or intake manifold to be reburned by the engine.

2 The main components of this simple system are vacuum hoses and a PCV valve which regulate the flow of gases according to engine speed and manifold vacuum.

Positive crankcase ventilation system – checking

3 The PCV system can be checked for proper operation quickly and easily. This system should be checked regularly as carbon and gunk deposited by the blow-by gases will eventually clog the PCV valve and/or system hoses. When the flow of the PCV system is reduced or stopped, common symptoms are rough idling or a reduced engine speed at idle.

4 To check for proper vacuum in the system, remove the top plate of the air cleaner and locate the small PCV filter on the inside of the air cleaner housing.

5 Disconnect the hose leading to this filter. Be careful not to break the moulded fitting on the filter.

6 With the engine idling, place your thumb lightly over the end of the hose. Leave it there for about 30 seconds. You should feel a slight pull or vacuum (photo). The suction may be heard as your thumb is released. This will indicate that air is beong drawn all the way through the system. If a vacuum is felt, the system is functioning properly. Check that the filter inside the air cleaner housing is not clogged or dirty. If in doubt, replace the filter with a new one, which is an inexpensive safeguard.

7 If there is very little vacuum, or none at all, at the end of the hose, the system is clogged and must be inspected further.

8 Shut off the engine and locate the PCV valve. Carefully pull it from its rubber grommet. Shake it and listen for a clicking sound. If the valve does not click freely, replace the valve with a new one.

9 Now start the engine and run it at idle speed with the PCV valve removed. Place your thumb over the end of the valve and feel for a suction (photo). This should be relatively strong vacuum which will be felt immediately.

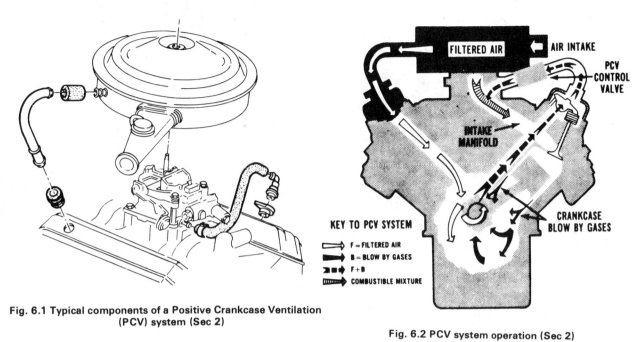

Fig. 6.1 Typical components of a Positive Crankcase Ventilation (PCV) system (Sec 2)

FILTERED AIR → AIR INTAKE

PCV CONTROL VALVE

INTAKE MANIFOLD

CRANKCASE BLOW BY GASES

KEY TO PCV SYSTEM

F = FILTERED AIR
B = BLOW BY GASES
F + B
COMBUSTIBLE MIXTURE

Fig. 6.2 PCV system operation (Sec 2)

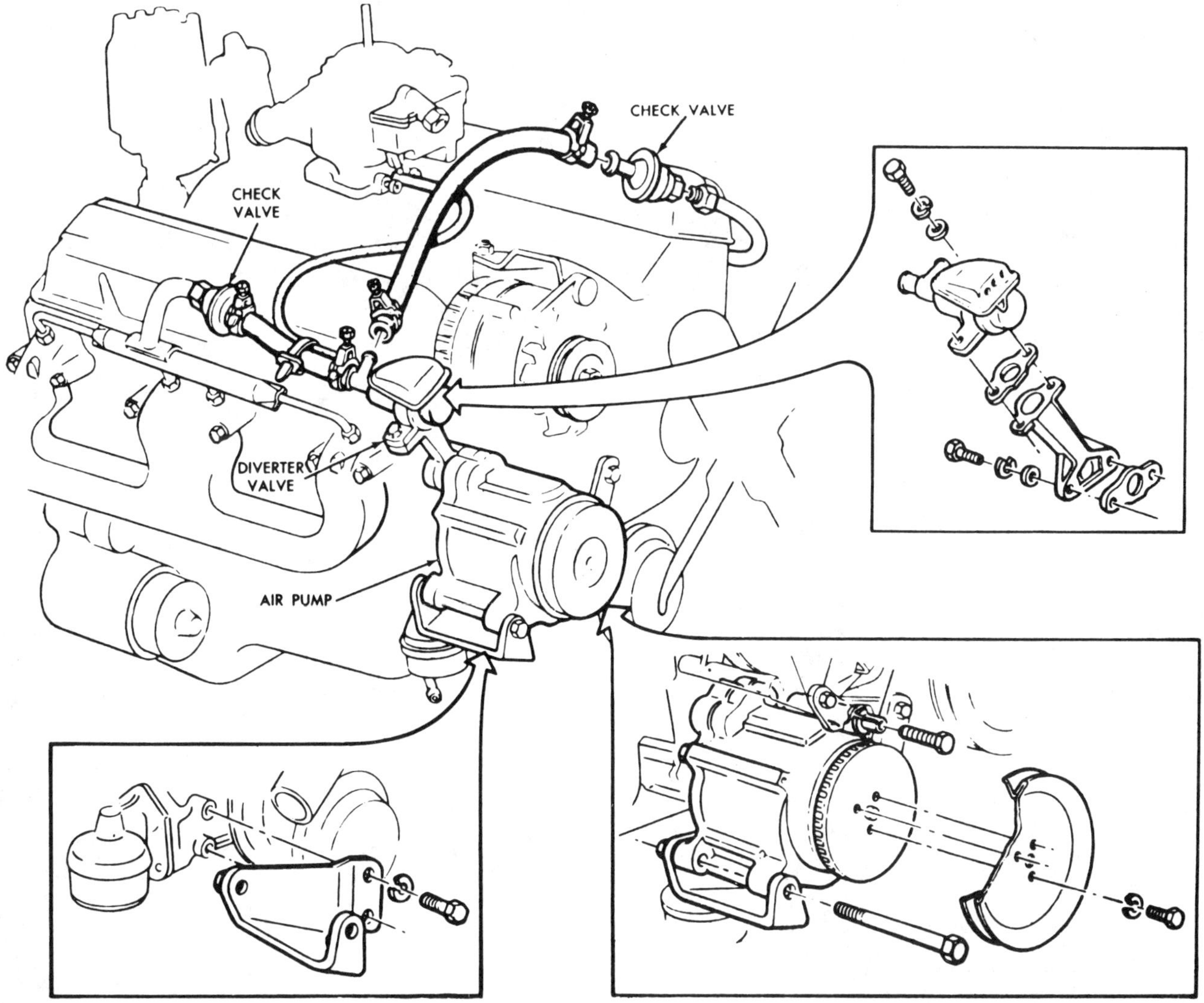

CHECK VALVE

CHECK VALVE

DIVERTER VALVE

AIR PUMP

Fig. 6.3 Typical Air Injection Reactor (AIR) system (Sec 3)

2.6 Checking for vacuum in the PCV hose where it connects to the air cleaner

2.9 Checking for vacuum in the line at the PCV valve

3.7 With the hose disconnected from the check valve, air should be felt with the engine running

3.10 A small diameter hose leads to the diverter valve. This is the vacuum signal hose to be disconnected during testing

3.29 A slightly different type of diverter valve shown here with the air delivery hoses and vacuum hose disconnected

3.36 The air delivery manifold has threaded fittings in the exhaust manifold. Shown is a flare nut wrench which wraps around the fitting to prevent rounding off the flats

10 If little or no vacuum is felt at the PCV valve, turn off the engine and disconnect the vacuum hose from the other end of the valve. Run the engine at idle speed and check for vacuum at the end of the hose just disconnected. No vacuum at this point indicates that the vacuum hose or inlet fitting at the engine is plugged. If it is the hose which is blocked, replace it with a new one or remove it from the engine and blow it out sufficiently with compressed air. A clogged passage at the carburetor or manifold requires that the component be removed and thoroughly cleaned or carbon build-up. A strong vacuum felt going into the PCV valve, but little or no vacuum coming out of the valve, indicates a failure of the PCV valve requiring replacement with a new one.

11 When purchasing a new PCV valve make sure it is the proper one. Each PCV valve is metered for specific engine sizes and model years. An incorrect PCV valve may pull too much or too little vacuum, possibly causing damage to the engine.

12 Information on removing and installing the PCV valve can be found in Chapter 1.

3 Air injection reactor (AIR) system

General description

1 The function of the air injection reactor system is to reduce hydrocarbons in the exhaust. This is done by pumping fresh air directly into the exhaust manifold ports of each engine cylinder. The fresh oxygen-rich air helps combust the unburned hydrocarbons before they are expelled as exhaust.

2 This system operates at all engine speeds and will bypass air only for a short time during deceleration and at high speeds. In these cases the additional fresh air added to the over-rich fuel/air mixture may cause backfiring or popping through the exhaust.

3 This system as it is used on GM engines consists of; the air injection pump (with supporting brackets and drivebelt) at the front of the engine, an air diverter valve attached to the pump housing, the manifold and injection tubes running into each port at the exhaust manifolds, and a check valve for each hose leading from the pump to the injection tubes on either side of the engine. Instead of a diverter valve, the V6 engine uses a bypass valve in conjunction with a vacuum differential valve. On the V6, fresh air is pumped into the rear of the manifold and then to the exhaust ports of the cylinders.

Air injection reactor system – checking

4 Properly installed and adjusted air injection systems are fairly reliable and seldom cause problems. However, a malfunctioning system can cause engine surge, backfiring and over-heated spark plugs. The air pump is the most critical component of this system and the belt at the front of the engine which drives the pump should be your first check. If the belt is cracked or frayed, replace it with a new one. Check the tension of the drive belt by pressing it with your finger. There should be about ½ inch of play in the belt when pushed half-way between the pulleys.

5 The adjusting or replacement procedures for the drivebelt depend on the mounting of the air pump. On some models, a single belt is used for both the air pump and the alternator. If this is the case, loosen the mounting bolt and the adjusting bolt for the alternator and then push against the alternator to tighten the belt. Hold in this position while the two bolts are tightened. The procedure is basically the same for air pumps which use their own belt, except it will be the air pump which will be loosened.

6 To check for proper air delivery from the pump, follow the hoses from the pump to where they meet the injection tube/manifold assembly on each side of the engine. Loosen the clamps and disconnect the hoses.

7 Start the engine and with your fingers or a piece of paper, check that air is flowing out of these hoses (photo). Accelerate the engine and observe the air flow, which should increase in relation to engine speed. If this is the case, the pump is working satisfactorily. If air flow was not present, or did not increase, check for crimps in the hoses, proper drivebelt tension, and for a leaking diverter valve which can be heard with the pump operating.

8 To check the diverter valve, sometimes called the 'gulp' valve or anti-backfire valve, make sure all hoses are connected and start the engine. Locate the muffler on the valve which is a canister unit with holes in it. The V6 bypass valve closely resembles a diverter valve. The vacuum differential valve is located on top of the bypass valve.

9 Being careful not to touch any of the moving engine components, place your hand near the muffler outlet holes and check that no air is escaping with the engine at idle speed. Now have an assistant depress the accelerator pedal to accelerate the engine and then quickly let off the pedal. A momentary blast of air should be felt discharging through the diverter valve muffler. The vacuum differential valve on the V6 (located on top of the bypass valve) is checked in the same way as a diverter valve. The bypass valve is checked by disconnecting and blocking the vacuum source. This should produce a continuous blast of air.

10 If no air discharge was felt, disconnect the smaller vacuum hose at the diverter valve (photo). Place your finger over the end of the hose and again have your assistant depress the accelerator and let it off. As the engine is decelerating, a vacuum should be felt. If vacuum was felt, replace the diverter valve with a new one. If no vacuum was felt, the

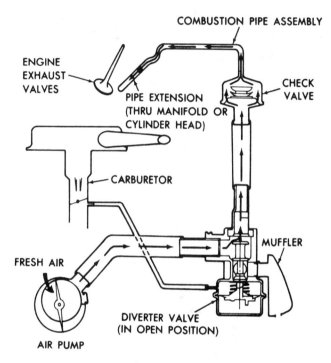

Fig. 6.4 AIR system operation during normal driving (Sec 3)

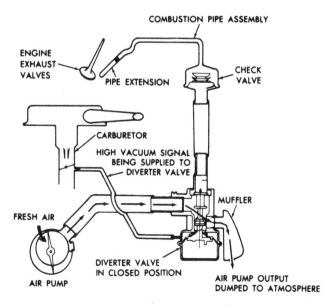

Fig. 6.5 AIR system operating during deceleration and high engine vacuum (Sec 3)

3.38 An exhaust manifold, injection tubes fitted inside the ports and the air delivery manifold

3.44 Two wrenches should be used to loosen the check valve from the manifold

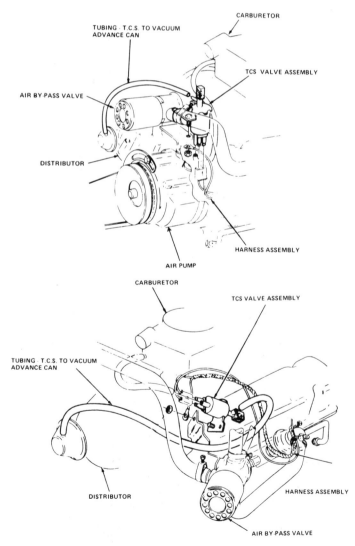

Fig. 6.6 TCS valve and hoses (Sec 4)

vacuum hose or engine vacuum source is plugged, requiring a thorough cleaning to eliminate the problem.

11 To check valves are located on the air manifold assembly and their function is to prevent exhaust gases from flowing back into the air pump. To find out if they are functioning properly, disconnect the two air supply hoses where they attach to the check valves. Start the engine, and being careful not to touch any moving engine components, place your hand over the outlet of the check valve. No exhaust should flow out of the check valve. The valve can be further checked by turning off the engine, allowing it to cool, and orally blowing through the check valve (toward the air manifold). Then attempt to suck back through it. If the valve is allowing you to suck back towards the air pump, it is bad and should be replaced.

12 Another check for this system is for leaks in the hose connection and/or hoses themselves. Leaks can often be detected by sound or feel with the pump in operation. If a leak is suspected, use a soapy water solution to verify this. Pour or sponge the solution of detergent and water on the hoses and connections. With the pump running, bubbles will form if a leak exists. The air delivery hoses are of a special design to withstand engine temperatures, so if they are replaced make sure the new hoses are of the proper standards.

Air pump – removal and installation

13 As mentioned earlier, some air pumps share a common drivebelt with the alternator where others use their own belt. This will affect the removal and installation procedure somewhat.

14 Disconnect the air delivery hoses at the air pump. Note the position of each hose for reassembly.

15 Disconnect the vacuum source hose at the diverter valve.

16 Compress the drivebelt to keep the air pump pulley from turning, and remove the bolts and washers securing the pulley to the pump.

17 To get some slack in the belt, loosen the alternator adjusting bolt and the pivot bolt. Push the alternator inward until the belt and air pump pulley can be removed from the pump.

18 Remove the bolts which secure the air pump to its brackets and then lift the pump and diverter valve assembly from the engine compartment.

19 If the diverter valve is to be installed onto the new air pump, remove the bolts securing it to the pump and separate the two components.

20 Check the pump for evidence that exhaust gas has entered it, indicating a failure of one or both the check valves.

21 Install the diverter valve to the new air pump using a new gasket. Torque the attaching bolts to specifications.

22 Install the air pump to its engine mounting brackets with the attaching bolts loose. The exception to this is on models where the mounting bolts are inaccessible with the pulley installed. In this case, the pump mounting bolts should be fully tightened to specifications at this point.

23 Install the pump pulley with the bolts only hand tight.

24 Place the drive belt into position on the air pump pulley and adjust the belt by gently prying on the alternator until about $\frac{1}{2}$ inch of play is felt in the belt when pushed with your fingers half-way between the pulleys. Tighten the alternator bolts, keeping the belt tension at this point.

25 Keep the pump pulley from turning by compressing the drive belt and torque the pulley bolts to specifications.

26 Connect the hoses to the air pump and diverter valve. Make sure the connections are tight.

27 Tighten the mounting bolts for the pump to specifications.

28 Check the operation of the air pump as outlined previously.

Diverter valve – removal and installation

29 Disconnect the vacuum signal line and air delivery hoses at the diverter valve. Note the position of each for assembly (photo).

30 Remove the bolts which secure the valve to the air pump and remove the diverter valve from the engine compartment.

31 When purchasing a new diverter or bypass valve, keep in mind that although many of the valves are similar in appearance, each is designed to meet particular requirements of various engines. Therefore, be sure to install the correct valve.

32 Install the new diverter valve to the air pump or pump extension with a new gasket. Torque the securing bolts to specification.

33 Connect the air delivery and vacuum source hoses and check the operation of the valve as outlined previously.

Air manifold and injection tubes – removal and installation

34 Due to the high temperatures at this area, the connections at the exhaust manifold may be difficult to loosen. Commercial penetrating oil applied to the threads of the injection tubes may help in the removal procedure.

35 Disconnect the air delivery hoses at the manifold check valves.

36 Loosen the threaded connectors on the exhaust manifold at each exhaust port (photo). Slide the connectors upwards on the injection tubes so the threads are out of the exhaust manifold.

37 Pull the injection tube/air manifold assembly from the engine exhaust manifold and out of the engine compartment. Depending on the model year, injection tube extensions leading inside the engine may come out with the assembly.

38 On models where the extension tubes remain inside the exhaust manifold, they must be pressed out after the exhaust manifold is removed from the engine (photo).

39 If the exhaust manifold was removed from the engine to clean or replace the extensions, reinstall the manifold with extensions to the engine using a new gasket. Torque to the proper specifications.

40 Thread each of the injection tube connectors loosely into the exhaust manifold, using an anti-seize compound on the threads. After each of the connectors is sufficiently started, tighten each securely.

41 Connect the air supply hoses to the check valves.

42 Start the engine and check for leaks as previously described.

Check valve – removal and installation

43 Disconnect the air supply hose at the check valve.

44 Using two wrenches on the flats provided, remove the check valve from the air manifold assembly (photo). Be careful not to bend or twist the delicate manifold or injection tubes as this is done.

45 Installation is a reversal of the removal procedure.

---

4 Transmission controlled vacuum spark advance (TCS) system

General description

1 Designed to eliminate the vacuum advance (at the distributor) under certain driving conditions, the Transmission Controlled Spark (TCS) System is installed only on vehicles equipped with a manual transmission. The system is also known as a Combination Emission Control (CEC) system.

2 It consists of a vacuum advance solenoid (located in the vacuum hose to the distributor), a mechanically operated switch (through the shift linkage) and an electrical harness (connecting the other two units).

3 Normally, the solenoid valve is open, however, it closes off vacuum when electricity flows through the solenoid. A vent directs vacuum from the hose to the distributor advance unit when the valve is closed.

4 The mechanical switch is usually closed but it opens to stop electricity flow to ground when the transmission is shifted to 3rd gear on 3-speed transmissions, 4th gear on 4-speed units, and 4th or 5th gears on 5-speed transmissions. In other words, once the car is moving, there will be no vacuum advance until it is in top gear.

Transmission Controlled Vacuum Spark Advance – checking

5 A malfunctioning TCS system will have either continuous vacuum advance (which will result in the automobile not meeting Federal emission standards) or, no vacuum advance (which will result in poor fuel economy). Check the TCS system as follows:

6 Raise up the car and put jackstands under the rear axle. Make sure that both rear wheels clear the ground. Block the front wheels, then start the engine and put the transmission in neutral.

7 Attach a vacuum gauge to the vacuum advance line at the distributor and position it so that it can be seen from the driver's position. Increase accelerator pressure until the engine speed is 1000 rpm. The vacuum gauge should have a reading of zero.

8 Shift the 3-speed manual into 3rd, the 4-speed manual into 4th,

4.17 The idle solenoid is located on the left side of the carburetor and has an electrical connector attached

4.18 The solenoid has a bolt at one end which contacts the throttle linkage (adjusting this bolt changes the engine idle speed)

and the 5-speed manual into 4th or 5th gear. Check the vacuum gauge reading. It should register a vacuum. If there is no vacuum reading proceed to the following:

9   Connect a test lamp (using a GM 1893 bulb or equivalent) between the two terminals of the TCS solenoid. Shift the transmission into top gear. The test lamp should be off.

10 If the lamp is on, check for a grounded wire between the transmission and the solenoid connection. If the wire is not shorted, replace the transmission switch.

11 Now shift the transmission into the neutral position. The lamp should come on. If the lamp does not light, check for an open circuit. Replace the transmission switch is the circuit is not open.

12 If steps 10 and 11 check out properly and there is still no vacuum as required in step 8, replace the TCS solenoid.

5   Forced air pre-heat system

General description

1   While coming under different names, the end result from this system is the same – to improve engine efficiency and reduce hydrocarbon emissions during the initial warm-up period of the car.

2   There are two different methods used to achieve this goal. First, a thermostatic air cleaner (Thermac) is used to draw warm air from the exhaust manifold directly into the carburetor. Second, some form of exhaust valve is incorporated inside the exhaust pipe to recirculate warm exhaust gases (which are then used to pre-heat the carburetor and choke).

3   It is during the first few miles of driving (depending on outside temperature) when this system has its greatest effect on engine performance and emissions output. Once the engine has reached normal operating temperature, the flapper valves in the exhaust pipe and air cleaner open, allowing for normal engine operation.

4   Because of this cold-engine only function, it is important to periodically check this system to prevent poor engine performance when cold, or over-heating of the fuel mixture once the engine has reached operating temperatures. If either the exhaust heat valve or air cleaner valve sticks in the 'no heat' position, the engine will run poorly, stall and waste gas until it has warmed up on its own. A valve sticking in the 'heat' position causes the engine to run as if it is out of tune due to the constant flow of hot air to the carburetor.

5   The components which make up this system include: a heat valve inside the exhaust pipe on the right side of the engine (called a heat riser on 1974 models), an actuator and thermal vacuum switch (on 1975 through 1980 models to control the heat valve) and a thermostatic air cleaner consisting of a temperature sensor, vacuum diaphragm and heat stove (all models 1974 through 1980). Initial checking procedures can be found in Chapter 1.

Forced air pre-heat system – checking

6   The conventional heat riser, installed on cars built up until 1975, should be checked often for free operation. Because of the high exhaust temperatures and its location (which is open to the elements),

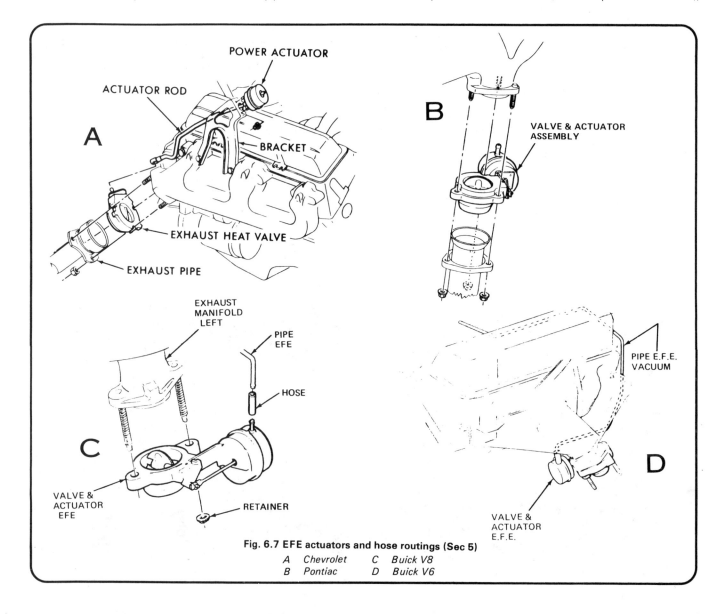

Fig. 6.7 EFE actuators and hose routings (Sec 5)

A   Chevrolet   C   Buick V8
B   Pontiac   D   Buick V6

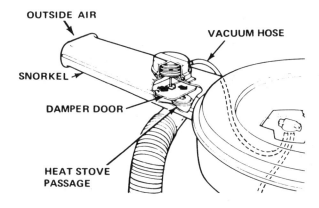

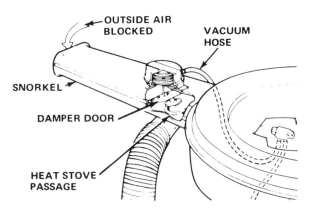

Fig. 6.8 Components and operation of Thermac assembly. Cold engine at top, warmed engine bottom (Sec 5)

corrosion frequently keeps the valve from operating freely.

7   To check the heat riser operation, locate it on the exhaust manifold (it can be identified by an external weight and spring) and with the engine cold, try moving the counter-weight. The valve should move freely (with no binding). Now have an assistant start the engine (still cold) while the counter-weight is observed. The valve should move to the closed position and then slowly open as the engine warms.

8   A stuck or binding heat riser valve often can be loosened by soaking the valve shaft with solvent as the counter-weight is moved back and forth. Light taps with a hammer may be necessary to free a tightly stuck valve. If this proves unsuccessful, the heat riser must be replaced with a new one after disconnecting it from the exhaust pipe.

9   In 1975, General Motors introduced a replacement for the heat riser which they called the Early Fuel Evaporation (EFE) System. This system provides the same function, but uses manifold vacuum to open and close the heat valve.

10   To check this system, locate the actuator and rod assembly which is on a bracket attached to the right (left on V6) exhaust manifold. With the engine cold, have an assistant start the engine. Observe the movement of the actuator rod which leads to the heat valve inside the exhaust pipe. It should immediately operate the valve to the closed position. If this is the case, the system is operating corrrectly.

11   If the actuator rod did not move, disconnect the vacuum hose at the actuator and place your thumb over the open end (photo). With the engine cold and at idle, you should feel a suction at the hose end. If there is vacuum at this point, replace the actuator with a new one.

12   If there is no vacuum in the line, this is an indication that either the hose is crimped or plugged, or the thermal vacuum switch (threaded into the water outlet) is not functioning properly. Replace the hose or switch as necessary.

13   To make sure the EFE system is disengaging once the engine has warmed, continue to observe the actuating rod as the engine reaches normal operating temperature (approximately 180 degrees depending on engine size). The rod should again move, indicating the valve is in the open position.

14   If after the engine has warmed, the valve does not open, pull the vacuum hose at the actuator and check for vacuum with your thumb. If there is no vacuum, replace the actuator. If there is vacuum, replace the TVS switch on the water outlet housing.

Thermac assembly – checking

15   The thermostatic air cleaner components can be quickly and easily checked for proper operation. Routine checking procedures and illustrations can be found in Chapter 1.

16   With the engine off, observe the damper door inside the air cleaner snorkel. If this is difficult because of positioning on V8 engines, use a mirror. The valve should be open, meaning that in this position all air

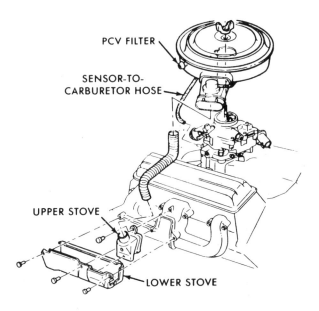

Fig. 6.9 Hoses and mountings of Thermac assembly (Sec 5)

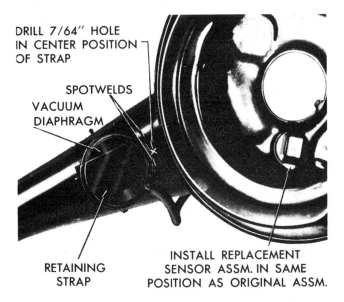

Fig. 6.10 Thermac vacuum diaphragm and sensor replacement (Sec 5)

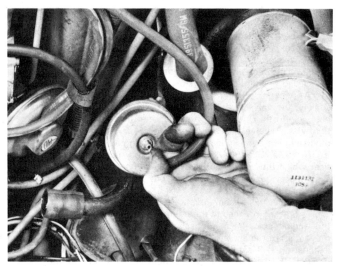

5.11 Checking for vacuum at the hose which leads to the actuator

would flow through the snorkel and none through the exhaust manifold hot-air duct at the underside of the air cleaner housing. Thermal sensors on V6's have a check valve which keeps the damper door closed when the air cleaner is cold and the engine is off.

17 Now have an assistant start the engine and continue to observe the flapper door inside the snorkel. With the engine cold and at idle the damper door should close off all air from the snorkel allowing heated air from the exhaust manifold to enter the air cleaner as intake. As the engine warms to operating temperature the damper door should move, allowing outside air through the snorkel to be included in the mixture. Eventually, the door should recede to the point where most of the incoming air is through the snorkel and not the exhaust manifold passage.

18 If the damper door did not close off snorkel air when the cold engine was first started, disconnect the vacuum hose at the snorkel vacuum motor and place your thumb over the hose end, checking for vacuum. If there is vacuum going to the motor, check that the damper door and link are not frozen or binding within the air cleaner snorkel. Replace the vacuum motor if the hose routing is correct and the damper door moves freely.

19 If there was no vacuum going to the motor in the above test, check the hoses for cracks, crimps or disconnections. If the hoses are clear and in good condition, replace the temperature sensor inside the air cleaner housing.

Actuator and rod assembly – replacement
20 Disconnect the vacuum hose from the actuator.
21 Remove the two nuts which attach the actuator to the bracket.
22 Disconnect the rod from the heat valve and remove the actuator and rod from the engine compartment.
23 Install the actuator and rod in the reverse order, tightening the attaching nuts to specifications.

Exhaust heat valve – replacement
24 Remove the crossover exhaust pipe.
25 Disconnect the actuating rod from the heat valve.
26 Remove the valve from inside the exhaust pipe.
27 Installation is a reversal of removal however, make sure all attaching fasteners are tightened to proper specifications.

Thermal vacuum switch (TVS) – replacement
28 Drain the engine coolant until the fluid level is below the engine water outlet (thermostat) housing. On the V6, the TVS is located on the engine manifold.
29 Disconnect the hoses from the TVS switch making note of their positions for reassembly.
30 Using a suitable wrench, remove the TVS switch.
31 Apply a soft setting sealant uniformly to the threads of the new

TVS switch. Be careful that none of the sealant gets on the sensor end of the switch.
32 Install the switch and tighten to specifications.
33 Connect the vacuum hoses to the switch in their original positions and add coolant as necessary.

Air cleaner vacuum motor – replacement
34 Remove the air cleaner assembly from the engine and disconnect the vacuum hose from the motor.
35 Drill out the two spot welds which secure the vacuum motor retaining strap to the snorkel tube.
36 Remove the motor attaching strap.
37 Lift up the motor, cocking it to one side to unhook the motor linkage at the control damper assembly.
38 To install, drill a 7/64 inch hole in the snorkel tube at the center of the retaining strap.
39 Insert the vacuum motor linkage into the control damper assembly.
40 Using the sheet metal screw supplied with the motor service kit, attach the motor and retaining strap to the snorkel. Make sure the sheet metal screw does not interfere with the operation of the damper door.
41 Connect the vacuum hose to the motor and install the air cleaner assembly.

Air cleaner temperature sensor – replacement
42 Remove the air cleaner from the engine and disconnect the vacuum hoses at the sensor.
43 Carefully note the position of the sensor. The new sensor must be installed in exactly the same position.
44 Pry up the tabs on the sensor retaining clip and remove the sensor and clip from the air cleaner.
45 Install the new sensor with a new gasket in the same position as the old one.
46 Press the retaining clip on the sensor. Do not damage the control mechanism in the center of the sensor.
47 Connect the vacuum hoses and install the air cleaner to the engine.

6 Fuel evaporation system

General description
1 Although the evaporative control system is one of the most complex looking, it is in actuality one of the most basic and trouble-free portions of the emissions network. Its function is to reduce hydrocarbon emissions. Basically, this is a closed fuel system which reroutes wasted fuel back to the gas tank and stores fuel vapors instead of venting them to the atmosphere.
2 Due to its very nature of having few moving parts, the evaporative control system requires no periodic maintenance except for a replacement of the oiled fiberglass filter in the bottom of the charcoal canister at the recommended intervals.
3 A tip-off that this system is not operating properly is the strong smell of fuel vapors or if the engine starves from lack of fuel during acceleration.
4 A pressure vacuum gasoline filler cap must be used, as a standard cap may render the system ineffective and could possibly collapse the fuel tank. Other components which make up this system include: a special gas tank with fill limiters and vent connections, a charcoal canister with integral purge valve and filter which stores vapor from the fuel tank to be burned by the carburetor, a carburetor bowl vent valve and various hoses linking the main components.

Fuel evaporative system – checking
5 As mentioned earlier, this system requires little maintenance, however, if a problem is suspected the system should be inspected.
6 With the engine cold and at room temperature, disconnect the fuel tank line at the charcoal canister. On all models the canister is located inside the engine compartment behind the headlight. Each of the hose connections are duly labeled.
7 As this hose is disconnected, check for the presence of liquid fuel in the line. Fuel in this vapor hose is an indication that the vent controls

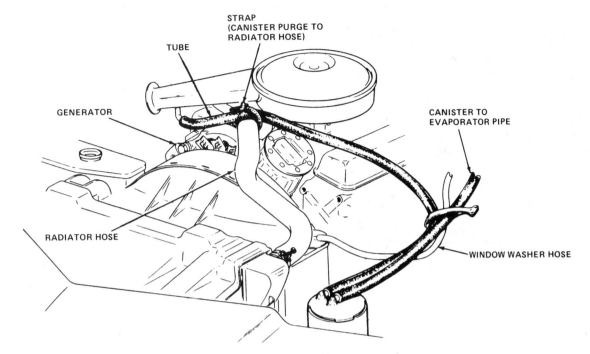

Fig. 6.11 Typical ECS system canister and hose routings (Buick shown) (Sec 6)

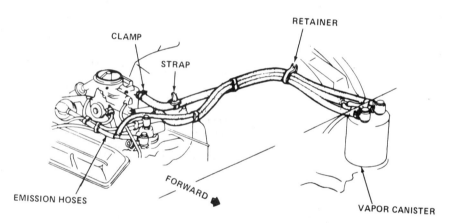

Fig. 6.12 Typical ECS hose routing at engine (Chev. shown) (Sec 6)

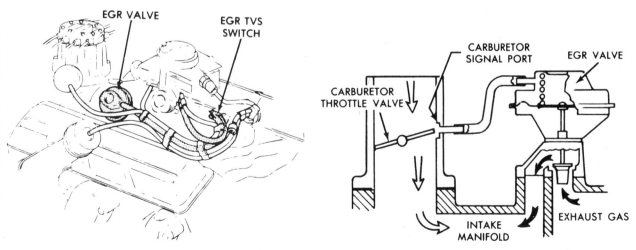

Fig. 6.13 Typical EGR system components and hose routing (Sec 7)

Fig. 6.14 Operation of EGR system (Sec 7)

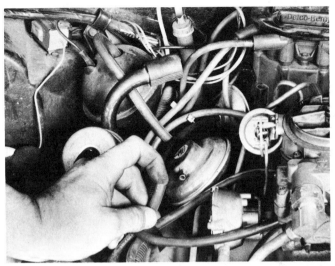

7.13 Checking for vacuum at the end of the hose which attaches to the EGR valve

or pressure-vacuum relief valve in the gas cap are not functioning properly.

8   Hook up a pressure/suction device on the end of the fuel vapor line. Apply 15 psi pressure to the line and observe for excessive loss of pressure.

9   Check for a fuel vapor smell in the engine compartment and around the gas tank.

10 Remove the fuel filler cap and check for pressure in the gas tank.

11 If there is a large loss of pressure or a fuel odor, inspect all lines for leaks or deterioration.

12 With the fuel filler cap removed, apply pressure again and check for obstructions in the vent line.

13 To check the purge valve built into the canister, start the engine, allow it to reach normal operating temperature, and disconnect the vacuum signal line running from the engine to the canister. With your thumb over the end of the hose, raise the engine speed to about 1500 rpm and check for vacuum. If there is no vacuum signal, check the EGR operation as described in this chapter. The vacuum signal for the canister and the EGR valve originate from the same source.

14 The purge line to the charcoal canister functions with the PCV vacuum source, so if there is no vacuum when this hose is disconnected from the canister check the PCV valve vacuum.

Charcoal canister and filter – replacement

15 Chapter 1 contains all information concerning the servicing of the fuel evaporation system, in particular the replacement of the canister filter.

---

7   Exhaust gas recirculation (EGR) system

General description

1   This system is used to reduce oxides of nitrogen (NOx) emitted from the exhaust. Formation of these pollutants takes place at very high temperatures; consequently, it occurs during the peak temperature period of the combustion process. To reduce peak temperatures, and thus the formation of NOx, a small amount of exhaust gas is taken from the exhaust system and recirculated in the combustion cycle.

2   To tap this exhaust supply without an extensive array of pipes and connections in the exhaust system, additional exhaust pasages are cast into the intricate runner system of the intake manifold. Because of this arrangement, most of the EGR routing components are hidden from view under the manifold.

3   Very little maintenance other than occasionally inspecting the vacuum hoses and the EGR valve is required. Two types of EGR valves are used: negative backpressure (1974 - 1979) and positive backpressure (some models 1977 through 1980). Besides the heart of the system – the EGR valve – the only moving part which can wear out

is a thermal vacuum switch (TVS) which controls the vacuum signal to the EGR valve at varying engine temperatures.

4   The EGR system does not recirculate gases when the engine is at idle or during deceleration. The system is also regulated by the thermal vacuum switch which does not allow the system to operate until the engine has reached normal operating temperature.

5   Common engine problems associated with the EGR system are: rough idling or stalling when at idle, rough engine performance upon light throttle application and stalling on deceleration.

Checking

6   Locate the EGR valve. The location varies from year to year, but on most models it is located on the intake manifold adjacent to the right side of the carburetor. The EGR valve is a disc-shaped diaphragm.

7   Place your finger under the EGR valve and push upwards on the diaphragm plate. The diaphragm should move freely from the open to the closed position. If it doesn't, replace the EGR valve.

8   Start the engine and run it at idle speed. Depress the EGR diaphragm with your finger (if the valve or adjacent accessories are hot, wear gloves). When the diaphragm is depressed (you've just closed the valve to recirculate exhaust), the engine should lose speed, stumble, or even stall. If engine speed remained unchanged, the EGR passages should be checked for blockage. To do this, it is necessary to remove the intake manifold. See Chapter 2 for the procedure to follow. Any further checking of the positive backpressure-type EGR valve will require special tools. Any doubtful valve should be replaced, as this is more economical than purchasing special tools. Negative backpressure-type EGR valves can be further checked as follows:

9   Allow the engine to reach its normal operating temperature. Have an assistant depress the accelerator pedal slightly and hold the engine speed constant just above idle.

10 Disconnect the vacuum signal line at the EGR valve and check to see if the diaphragm plate moves downward. It should move downward and be accompanied by an increase in engine speed.

11 Reinstall the vacuum line to the EGR valve. The plate should move upward and be accompanied by a decrease in engine speed.

12 If the diaphragm does not move, check to see if the engine is at normal operating temperature. Repeat the test if you have any doubts.

13 Next, test to see if any vacuum is reaching the EGR valve. With the engine running and the accelerator pedal slightly depressed, remove the vacuum hose at the EGR valve. Place the end of your thumb over the open end of the hose and see if there is any vacuum (photo). If there is vacuum, replace the EGR valve. If there is no vacuum, inspect the hose for cracks, breaks or blockage. If the hose is intact, reinstall it.

14 The EGR system uses a thermal vacuum switch to regulate EGR valve operation in relation to the engine temperature. This vacuum switch opens as the coolant temperature increases, allowing vacuum to reach the EGR valve. The exact temperature at which the vacuum switch opens varies from model year to model year, but is related to the normal operating temperature of the engine. To test the switch, it is best to have the engine hot.

15 Disconnect the vacuum hose at the EGR valve; connect the vacuum gauge to the disconnected end of the hose and start the motor. Note the reading on the gauge while the engine is idling. Next, have an assistant depress the accelerator pedal slightly and note this new reading. Depress the pedal a bit more. The vacuum reading should increase as the gas pedal is depressed.

16 If the gauge does not respond to throttle opening, disconnect the hose which leads from the carburetor to the thermal vacuum switch. Install the vacuum gauge in the vacuum hose end of the switch and repeat the test. If the gauge responds to accelerator opening, the thermal vacuum switch is defective and should be replaced.

17 If the vacuum gauge does not respond to an increase in throttle opening, check for a plugged hose or carburetor orifice.

EGR valve – replacement

18 Disconnect the vacuum hose at the EGR valve.

19 Remove the nuts or bolts which secure the valve to the intake manifold.

20 Lift the EGR valve from the engine.

21 Clean the mounting surfaces of the EGR valve. Remove all traces of gasket material.

22 Place the new EGR valve, with new gasket, on the intake manifold. Install the spacer, if used. Tighten the attaching bolts or nuts.

23 Connect the vacuum signal hose.

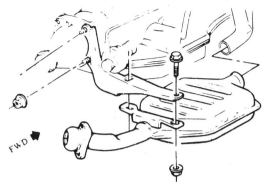

AUTOMATIC TRANSMISSION

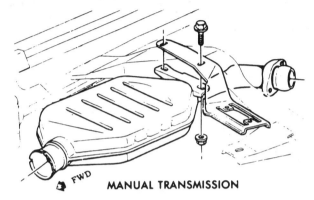

MANUAL TRANSMISSION

Fig. 6.15 Typical installation of a catalytic converter (Sec 8)

Thermal vacuum switch – replacement

24 Drain the engine coolant until the coolant level is beneath the switch.

25 Disconnect the vacuum hoses from the switch, noting their positions for reassembly.

26 Using a suitable wrench, remove the switch.

27 When installing the switch, apply thread sealer to the threads being careful not to allow the sealant to touch the bottom sensor.

28 Install the switch and tighten it to specifications.

8 Catalytic converter

General description

1   The catalytic converter is an emission control device added to the exhaust system to reduce hydrocarbon and carbon monoxide pollutants. This converter contains beads which are coated with a catalytic substance containing platinum and palladium.

2   It is imperative that only unleaded gasoline be used in a vehicle equipped with a catalytic converter. Unleaded fuel reduces combustion chamber deposits, corrosion and prevents lead contamination of the catalyst.

3   Periodic maintenance of the catalytic converter is not required; however, if the car is raised for other service it is advisable to inspect the overall condition of the catalytic converter and related exhaust components.

4   If the catalytic converter has been proven by an official inspection station to be defective, the converter can be replaced with a new one or the coated beads drained and replaced. Physical damage or the use of leaded fuels are the main causes of a malfunctioning catalytic converter.

5   It should be noted that the catalytic converter can reach very high temperatures in operation. Because of this, any work performed to the converter or in the general area where it is located should be done only after the system has sufficiently cooled. Also, caution should be exercised when lifting the vehicle with a hoist as the converter can be damaged if the lifting pads are not properly positioned.

6   There are no functional tests which the home mechanic can make to determine if the catalytic converter is performing its task.

Catalytic converter – replacement

7   While the removal of the catalytic converter will be a rare occurrence, it can be successfully separated from the exhaust system for replacement.

8   Raise the car and support firmly with jack stands. The converter and exhaust system should be cool before proceeding.

9   Disconnect the converter at the front and rear. On most models a flange is used with four bolts and nuts to secure the converter to its mating exhaust pipes. If the fasteners are frozen in place due to the high temperatures and corrosion, apply a penetrating oil liberally and allow to soak in. As a last resort, the fasteners will have to be carefully cut off with a hacksaw.

10 Gently separate the inlet and outlet converter flanges from the exhaust pipes and remove the converter from under the vehicle.

11 Installation is a reversal of the removal process; however, always use new nuts and bolts.

Catalyst – replacement

12 There are two types of catalytic converters now being used on vehicles. The monolith converter has coated rods which cannot be serviced. If failure occurs, the entire converter must be replaced with a new one. The catalyst in bead type converters can be changed by draining and filling the beads through a plug at the bottom of the converter.

13 With specialized equipment, the beads can be replaced with the converter still positioned under the car. This is definitely a job for a dealer who has the equipment and training necessary to perform this operation.

14 Bead replacement is more easily done with the converter removed from the car. Follow the sequence outlined in the preceding paragraphs to do this.

15 With the converter on a suitable work bench, remove the pressed fill plug. This is done by driving a small chisel between the converter shell and the fill plug lip. Deform the lip until pliers can be used to remove the plug. Be careful not to damage the converter shell surface where the plug seals.

16 Once the plug is removed, drain the beads into a suitable container for disposal. Shake the converter vigorously to remove all beads.

17 To fill the catalytic converter with new beads, raise the front of the converter to approximately 45 degrees and pour the beads through the fill hole. Tapping lightly on the converter belt with a hammer as the beads are poured in will help to settle them. Continue tapping and pouring until the converter is full.

18 A special service fill plug will be required to replace the stock one which was removed. This consists of a bridge, bolt and fill plug and is installed as follows:

   a) *Install the bolt into the bridge and put the bridge into the converter opening. Move it back and forth to loosen the beads until the bridge sits flat on the inside of the converter, straight across the opening (bolt centered).*

   b) *Remove the bolt from the bridge and put the washer and fill plug, dished side out, over the bolt.*

   c) *While holding the fill plug and washer against the bolt head, thread the bolt 4 or 5 turns into the bridge.*

   d) *After fill plug has seated against the converter housing, tighten the bolt to 28 ft-lb.*

19 Install the converter, start the engine and check for leaks.

9 Computer command control system (C4)

General description

1   This system, also known as the 'C4' system, first became available on the 1980 models. The computer command control system controls exhaust emissions while retaining drivability by maintaining a continuous interaction between all of the emissions systems. Any malfunction in the computer command system is signaled by a 'Check Engine' light on the dash which goes on and remains lit until the malfunction is corrected.

2   The computer command control system requires special tools for maintenance and repair so any work on it should be left to your dealer

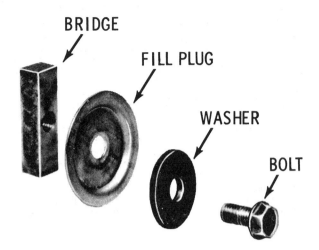

Fig. 6.16 Fill plug components of bead-type catalytic converter (Sec 8)

or a qualified technician. Although complicated, the system can be understood by examining each component and its function.

Electronic control module (ECM)

3   The electronic control module (ECM) is essentially a small on-board computer located under the dash on most vehicles which monitors up to 15 engine/vehicle functions and controls as many as nine different operations. The ECM contains a programmable read only memory (PROM) calibration unit which tailors each ECM's performance to conform to the vehicle. The PROM is programmed with the vehicle's particular design, weight, axle ratio, etc. and cannot be used in another ECM in a car which differs in any way.

4   The ECM receives continuous information from the computer command system and processes it in accordance with PROM instructions. It then sends out electronic signals to the system components, modifying their performance.

Oxygen sensor (OS)

5   The oxygen sensor (OS) is mounted in the exhaust pipe, upstream of the catalytic converter. It monitors the exhaust stream and sends information to the ECM on how much oxygen is present. The oxygen level is determined by how rich or lean the fuel mixture in the carburetor is.

Mixture control solenoid

6   This controls the fuel flow through the carburetor idle and main metering circuits. The solenoid cycles 10 times per second, constantly adjusting the fuel/air mixture. The ECM energizes the solenoid on information it receives from the oxygen sensor to keep emissions within limits.

Coolant sensor

7   This sensor is the coolant stream sends information to the ECM on engine temperature. The ECM can then vary the fuel/air ratio for conditions such as cold start. The ECM can also perform various switching functions on the EGR, EFE and AIR management systems according to engine temperature. This feedback from the coolant sensor to the ECM also is used to vary spark advance and activate the hot temperature light.

Pressure sensors

8   The ECM uses the information from various pressure sensors to adjust engine performance. The sensors are: barometric pressure sensor (BARO), manifold absolute pressure (MAP) sensor and the throttle position sensor (TPS) as well as the abovementioned coolant sensor.

Barometric pressure sensor (BARO)

9   Located in the engine compartment, the barometric pressure sensor provides a voltage to the ECM, indicating ambient air pressure which varies with altitude. Not all vehicles are equipped with this sensor.

Manifold absolute pressure (MAPS)

10   Also located in the engine compartment, the MAPS senses engine vacuum (manifold) pressure. The ECM uses this information to adjust fuel/air mixture and spark timing in accordance with driving conditions.

Throttle position sensor (TPS)

11   Mounted in the carburetor body, the TPS is moved by the accelerator pump and sends a low voltage signal to the ECM when the throttle is closed and a higher voltage when it is opened. The ECM uses this voltage feed to recognize throttle position.

Idle speed control (ISC)

12   The idle speed control maintains low idle without stalling under changing load conditions. The ECM controls the idle speed control motor on the carburetor to adjust the idle.

Electronic spark timing (EST)

13   The high energy ignition (HEI) distributor used with this system has no provision for centrifugal or vacuum advance of spark timing. This is controlled electronically by the ECM except under certain conditions such as cranking the engine.

14   The AIR, EGR, EFE and fuel evaporative systems explained elsewhere in this chapter are also controlled by the ECM in the computer command control system.

Air injection reactor

15   When the engine is cold, the ECM energizes an air switching valve which allows air to flow to the exhaust ports to lower carbon monoxide (CO) and hydrocarbon (HC) levels in the exhaust.

Exhaust gas recirculator (EGR)

16   The ECM controls the ported vacuum to the EGR with a solenoid valve. When the engine is cold the solenoid is energized to block vacuum to the EGR valve until the engine is warm.

Evaporative emission system

17   When the engine is cold or idling, the ECM solenoid blocks vacuum to the valve at the top of the charcoal canister. When the engine is warm and at a specified rpm, the ECM de-energizes the valve, releasing the collected vapors into the intake manifold.

Early fuel evaporation (EFE)

18   The ECM controls a valve which shuts off the system until the engine is warm.

Computer command control system diagnostic circuit check

19   Using the proper equipment, the computer command control system can be used to diagnose malfunctions within itself. The "Check Engine" light can flash trouble codes stored in the ECM "Trouble Code Memory". As stated before, this diagnosis should be left to your dealer or a qualified technician because of the tools required and the fact that ECM programming varies from one model vehicle to another.

Troubleshooting – emission systems

Condition	Possible cause
Engine idles abnormally rough and/or stalls	EGR valve vacuum hoses misrouted Leaking EGR valve EFE valve malfunctioning PCV system clogged or hoses misrouted TCS system malfunctioning
Engine runs rough on light throttle acceleration	Malfunctioning EGR valve EFE valve malfunctioning TCS system malfunctioning
Engine stalls and/or backfires during deceleration	Restriction in EGR vacuum hoses Sticking EGR valve Malfunctioning AIR diverter valve Malfunctioning TCS system
Engine detonation	EGR control valve blocked or air flow restricted Binding EFE (heat riser) valve Malfunctioning or restricted operation of Thermac air cleaner Clogged PCV valve and/or hoses
Engine dieseling on shut-off	TCS idle stop solenoid improperly adjusted Thermac valve sticking
Excessive engine oil consumption	Clogged PCV valve and or hoses
Poor high gear performance	Malfunctioning TCS switch
Fuel odor	Evaporative emission system hoses clogged; hoses disconnected or cracked; charcoal canister filter in need of replacement

Note: *If equipped with C4 system (1980 models), see Section 9*

Chapter 7 Part A Manual transmission

Contents

Specifications

Transmission type .... 3 or 4 forward speeds (all synchromesh) and reverse. Floor or steering column shift.

Application
1975 through 1980 .... 76 mm Saginaw 3-speed
1978 through 1979 .... 76 mm Saginaw 4-speed

Oil capacity
3 speed units .... 3.5 US pts
4 speed units .... 3.5 US pts

Torque specifications
	ft-lbs
3-speed Saginaw	
Clutch gear retainer to case bolts	14
Side cover to case bolts	14
Extension to case bolts	45
Shift lever to shifter shaft bolts	25
Lubrication filler plug	13
Transmission case to clutch housing bolts	53
Crossmember to frame nuts	25
Crossmember to mount bolts	40
Mount to transmission bolts	32
4-speed Saginaw	
Clutch gear retainer to case bolts	15
Side cover to case bolts	15
Extension to case bolts	45
Shift lever to shifter shaft bolts	25
Lubrication filler plug	18
Transmission case to clutch housing bolts	75
Crossmember to frame nuts	25
Crossmember to mount and mount to extension bolts	40
Mount to transmission bolts	32

1 General information

All Buick manual transmissions are of a synchronized, constant-mesh design. These transmissions are fully synchronized in all forward gears. The transmission installed in Buick automobiles are either 3- or 4-speed manual-shift and can be controlled by either a column or a console linkage setup. There is no provision made for periodic oil changing; however, oil level should be checked occasionally and topped up as necessary.

Manual transmissions may be of the three or four-speed type manufactured by Muncie, Saginaw or Warner. Gearshift is by column or floor-mounted lever according to model.

The forward speeds on all versions are of the synchromesh type.

No provision is made for periodic oil changing but the oil level should be checked at the specified intervals and topped up as necessary.

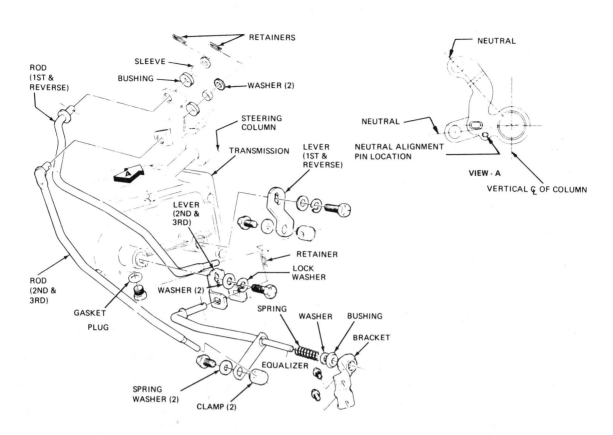

Fig. 7.1 Column shift linkage (3-speed transmission) (Sec 2)

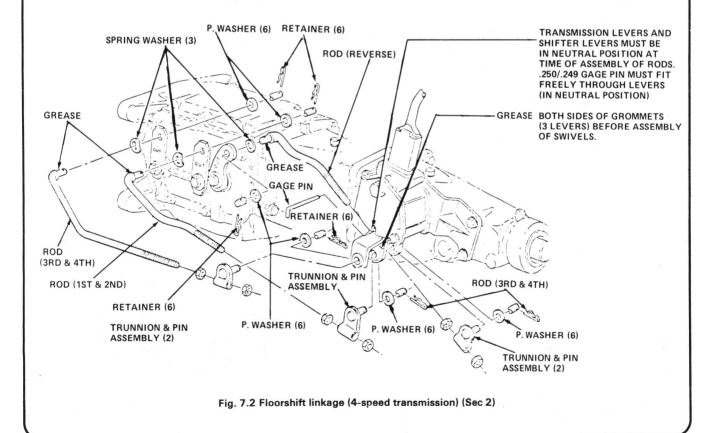

TRANSMISSION LEVERS AND SHIFTER LEVERS MUST BE IN NEUTRAL POSITION AT TIME OF ASSEMBLY OF RODS. .250/.249 GAGE PIN MUST FIT FREELY THROUGH LEVERS (IN NEUTRAL POSITION)

GREASE BOTH SIDES OF GROMMETS (3 LEVERS) BEFORE ASSEMBLY OF SWIVELS.

Fig. 7.2 Floorshift linkage (4-speed transmission) (Sec 2)

2 Shift linkage – adjustment

Column shift

1 Place the shift lever in 'Reverse' and the ignition switch in the 'Lock' position.
2 Raise the vehicle for access beneath, then loosen the shift control swivel locknuts. Pull down slightly on the 1st/Reverse control rod attached to the column lever to remove any slackness, then tighten the locknut at the transmission lever.
3 Unlock the ignition switch and shift the column lever to Neutral. Position the column lower levers in the 'Neutral' position, align the gauge holes in the levers and insert a $\frac{3}{16}$ inch diameter gauge pin.
4 Support the rod and swivel to prevent movement, then tighten the 2nd/3rd shift control rod locknut.
5 Remove the alignment tool from the column lower levers and check the operation. Place the column shift lever in 'Reverse' and check the interlock control. It must not be possible to obtain 'Lock' except in 'Reverse'.
6 Lower the vehicle to the ground.

Floorshift

7 Switch the ignition to 'Off' then raise the vehicle for access beneath.
8 Loosen the swivel locknuts on the shift rods. Check that the rods pass freely through the swivels.
9 Set the shift levers to 'Neutral' at the transmission.
10 Move the shift control lever into the 'Neutral' detent position, align the control assembly levers, and insert the locating gauge into the lever alignment slot.
11 Tighten the shift rod swivel locknuts then remove the gauge.
12 Shift the transmission control lever into 'Reverse' and place the ignition switch in the 'Lock' position. Loosen the locknut at the back drive control rod swivel, then pull the rod down slightly to remove any slack in the column mechanism. Tighten the clevis jam nut.
13 Check the interlock control; the key should move freely to, and from, the 'Lock' position when the adjustment is correct.
14 Check the transmission shift control and readjust if necessary.
15 Lower the vehicle to the ground.

3 Transmission mounts – checking

1 Raise the car for access beneath and support firmly with stands. Make sure the vehicle is secured, as you must jostle the vehicle somewhat to check the mounts.
2 Push upward and pull downward on the transmission extension housing and observe the transmission mount.
3 If the extension can be pushed upwards but cannot be pulled down, this is an indication that the rubber is worn and the mount is bottomed out.
4 If the rubber portion of the mount separates from the metal plate, this also means that the mount should be changed.
5 Check that all of the attaching screws or nuts are tight on the crossmember and the transmission.

4 Floorshift transmission backdrive linkage – adjustment

1 Shift the transmission into 'Reverse' and turn the ignition switch to the 'Lock' position.
2 Raise the vehicle for access beneath.
3 Loosen the backdrive control rod swivel locknut, pull down on the column linkage to remove any slackness, then tighten the clevis jam nut.
4 Check that the ignition key moves freely through the 'Lock' position; readjust if necessary at the bellcrank.
5 Lower the vehicle to the ground.

5 Shift control assembly – removal and installation

Column shift models

1 Refer to Chapter 11 in conjunction with stering column dismantling.

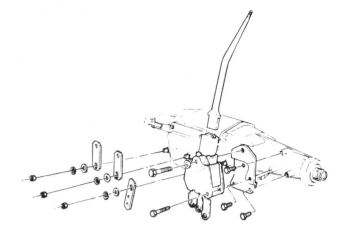

Fig. 7.3 Floorshift control installation – typical (Sec 5)

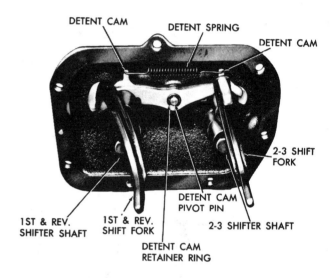

Fig. 7.4 Transmission side cover (3-speed Saginaw) (Sec 7)

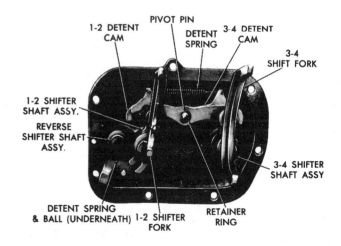

Fig. 7.5 Transmission side cover (4-speed Saginaw) (Sec 8)

6.11 Extension housing oil seal

9.3 Speedometer drive cable at transmission

9.6 Transmission mount-to-crossmember bolt

Floorshift (3- and 4-speed)

2   With the shift lever in the Neutral position, remove the shift lever knob and center console trim plate.
3   Raise the vehicle and support firmly on stands.
4   Disconnect the shift rods from the shift control levers. They are secured with retaining clips. Mark each rod and its appropriate lever for easy reinstallation, and take care not to lose any special washers used.
5   Remove the bolts which secure the shift control unit to its support assembly.
6   Rotate the control assembly and pull it down past the crossmember and remove it from under the vehicle.
7   To reinstall, slide the control assembly up into the rubber boot and position it against the support. Install the retaining bolts.
8   Place the control levers in the Neutral position and insert a $\frac{1}{4}$-inch gauge pin (see Section 2, 'Shift linkage – adjustment').
9   Connect the shift rods to the control levers and install the appropriate washers and retaining pins.
10   Lower the vehicle and check for proper operation. Make the necessary adjustment referring to the proper sections in this chapter.

6   Transmission oil seals – replacement

1   The following oil seals can be replaced without removing the transmission from the car.

Speedometer gear seal

2   Raise the vehicle for access beneath. Set firmly on stands.
3   Disconnect the speedometer cable, remove the lockplate to extension bolt and lockwasher, then remove the lockplate.
4   Insert a screwdriver in the lockplate fitting, and pry the fitting gear and shaft from the extension.
5   Pry out the O-ring.
6   Installation is the reverse of removal, but lubricate the new seal with transmission lubricant and hold the assembly so that the slot in the fitting is towards the lockplate boss on the extension.

Extension oil seal

7   Remove the drive shaft, as described in Chapter 8. Remove any ancillary items necessary to provide additional clearance.
8   Carefully pry out the old seal.
9   Carefully clean the counterbore and examine for any damage.
10   Pre-lubricate between the lips of the new seal with transmission lubricant and coat the outer diameter with a suitable sealant.
11   Carefully install the seal, lips inwards, until the flange seats, ideally a tubular spacer should be used for this job (photo).
12   Reinstall the drive shaft (refer to Chapter 8) and any other ancillary items removed.

7   Transmission side cover (3- speed Saginaw) – overhaul

1   Shift transmission into 'Neutral' and raise the vehicle for access beneath. Set firmly on stands.

2   Disconnect the control rods from the levers on the side of the transmission.
3   Remove the cover assembly from the transmission case and allow the oil to drain.
4   Remove both shift forks from the shifter shaft assemblies and both shifter shaft assemblies from the cover.
5   Pry out shaft O-ring seals if replacement is required.
6   Remove the detent cam spring and pivot retainer C-clip. Remove both detent cams.
7   Inspect all parts for damage and wear, and replace as necessary.
8   With the detent spring tang projecting up over the 2nd/3rd shifter shaft cover opening, install the 1st/Reverse detent cam onto the detent cam pivot pin. With the detent spring tang projecting up over the first and reverse shifter shaft cover hole, install the 2nd/3rd detent cam.
9   Install the C-clip to the pivot shaft and hook the spring into the detent cam notches.
10   Install the shifter shaft assemblies carefully into the cover and the shift forks to the shifter shaft assemblies. Lift up the detent cam to allow the forks to seat properly.
11   Set the shifter levers into the Neutral detent (center position) and position the gasket on the case.
12   Carefully position the side cover, ensuring that the shift forks are aligned with their appropriate mainshaft clutch sliding sleeves.
13   Install and torque tighten the cover bolts to the specified value.
14   Top-up the oil in the transmission and lower the vehicle to the ground.

8   Transmission side cover (4- speed Saginaw) – overhaul

1   Shift the transmission into 'Neutral'.
2   Raise the vehicle for access beneath. Set firmly on stands.
3   Remove the shift levers from the shifter shafts.
4   Remove the cover assembly and allow the oil to drain.

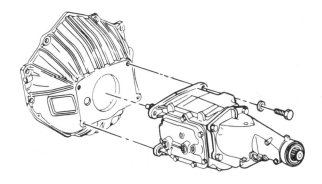

Fig. 7.6 Typical transmission mounting (Sec 9)

5   Remove the outer shifter levers.
6   Remove the shift forks from the shifter shaft assemblies, and the three shifter shaft assemblies from the cover.
7   If necessary, pry out the O-ring on the 1st/2nd and Reverse shafts.
8   Remove the Reverse shifter shaft detent ball and spring.
9   Remove the detent cam spring and the pivot pin C-clip. Mark the cams for identification on reassembly, then remove them.
10   Inspect all the parts for damage and wear and replace as necessary.
11   With the detent spring tang projecting up over the 3rd/4th shifter shaft cover opening, install the 1st/2nd detent cam onto the detent cam pivot pin. With the detent spring tang projecting up over the 1st/2nd shifter shaft cover hole, install the 3rd/4th detent cam.
12   Install the detent cam C-clip to the pivot shaft and hook the spring into the cam notches.
13   Install the 1st/2nd and 3rd/4th shifter shaft assemblies carefully into the cover.
14   Install the shift forks to the shifter shaft assemblies, lifting up on the detent cam to permit the forks to seat.
15   Install the Reverse detent ball and spring, then install the Reverse shifter shaft assembly to the cover.
16   Move the shifter levers into 'Neutral'.
17   Position the cover gasket on the case and carefully position the side cover, ensuring that the shift forks are aligned with their appropriate mainshaft clutch sliding sleeves.
18   Screw in the side cover bolts and tighten to the specified torque.
19   Top-up the transmission oil and then lower the car to the ground.

9   Transmission – removal and installation

1   Remove the shift lever knob, and on 4-speed models the spring and T-handle (not necessary on column shift models)..
2   Raise the vehicle for access beneath.
3   Disconnect the speedometer cable and TCS switch on the transmission (photo).
4   Remove the drive shaft (refer to Chapter 8).
5   Support the engine/transmission by placing a jack and block of wood as an insulator under the oil pan.
6   Remove the transmission mount to crossmember bolts and crossmember to frame attaching bolts. Support the engine and remove the crossmember (photo).
7   Disconnect the shift rods from the transmission and on floorshift models disconnect the backdrive rod at the bellcrank.
8   On floorshift models, remove the bolts attaching the shift control assembly to the support; then carefully pull the unit down until the shift lever clears the rubber boot. Remove the assembly from the vehicle.
9   Remove the transmission to clutch housing upper bolts. Install guide pins in the holes, then remove the lower bolts.

Note: *On some later models it may be necessary to remove the catalytic converter to permit removal of the transmission. (Refer to Chapter 6, for further information).*
10   Lower the supporting jack until the transmission can be withdrawn rearwards and removed.
11   When installing, raise the transmission into position and slide it forwards, guiding the clutch gear into the clutch housing.
12   Install the transmission clutch housing retaining bolts and lockwashers, and torque-tighten to the specified value.
13   Slide the shift lever into the rubber boot and position the shaft control to the support. Install and torque-tighten the retaining bolts.
14   Connect the shift rods to the transmission and torque-tighten the bolts. Connect the backdrive rod to the bellcrank.
15   Raise the engine and position the crossmember. Install and torque-tighten the transmission mount and crossmember retaining bolts.
16   Install the drive shaft (refer to Chapter 8).
17   Connect the speedometer cable and TCS switch wiring.
18   Install the T-handle and spring (4-speed), and the shift knob on floorshift models.
19   Fill the transmission with the correct quantity and grade of lubricant, then lower the vehicle to the ground.

10   3-speed (Saginaw) transmission – overhaul

1   Remove the transmission, drain the oil and remove the side cover assembly (refer to Section 7).
2   Remove the drive-gear bearing retainer and gasket.
3   Remove the drive-gear bearing stem snap-ring, then pull out the gear until a large screwdriver can be used to lever the drive-gear bearing from its location.
4   Remove the speedometer driven gear from the rear extension, then remove the extension retaining bolts.
5   Remove the reverse idler shaft E-ring.
6   Withdraw the drivegear, mainshaft and extension assembly together through the rear casing.
7   From the mainshaft, detach the drive-gear, needle bearings and synchronizer ring.
8   Expand the snap-ring in the rear extension which retains the rear bearing and then withdraw the rear extension.
9   Using a dummy shaft or special tool (J22246) drive the countershaft (complete with Woodruff key) out of the rear of the transmission case. Carefully remove the dummy shaft and extract the countergear, bearings and thrust washers from the interior of the transmission case.
10   Drive the reverse idler shaft out of the rear of the transmission case using a long drift.
11   The mainshaft should only be dismantled if a press or bearing puller is available: otherwise take the assembly to your Buick dealer. Be careful to keep all components separated and in order for easier reassembly.

10.13 Removing 2nd-speed blocker ring and gear from the front end of the mainshaft (Saginaw 3-speed)

10.15 Extracting rear bearing snap-ring (Saginaw 3-speed)

10.32a Putting together the countergear rollers (Saginaw 3-speed)

10.32b Countergear rollers retained with grease (Saginaw 3-speed)

10.32c Countergear needle-roller retaining washer in position (Saginaw 3-speed)

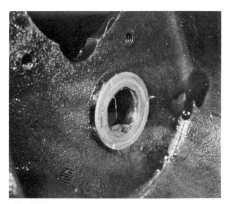

10.32d Countergear thrust washer held in position with grease (Saginaw 3-speed)

10.34 Install the countershaft with the slot to the rear (Saginaw 3-speed)

10.35a Mainshaft rear bearing outer snap-ring in position in the extension housing (Saginaw 3-speed)

10.35b Expanding rear bearing outer snap-ring (Saginaw 3-speed)

10.36 Mainshaft pilot bearings retained with grease (Saginaw 3-speed)

10.38a Installing clutch drive gear, mainshaft and extension (Saginaw 3-speed)

10.38b Countergear anti-lash plate (Saginaw 3-speed)

10.40 Clutch drive gear bearing outer snap-ring (Saginaw 3-speed)

10.41 Installing clutch drivegear bearing shaft snap-ring (Saginaw 3-speed)

10.42 Installing clutch drive gear bearing retainer and gasket (Saginaw 3-speed)

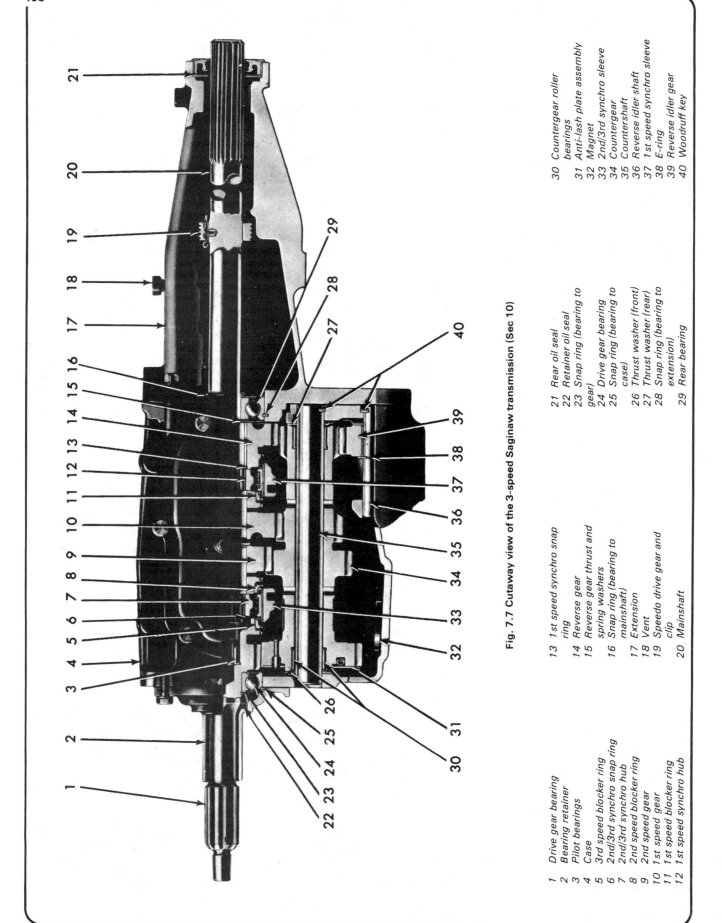

Fig. 7.7 Cutaway view of the 3-speed Saginaw transmission (Sec 10)

1 Drive gear bearing
2 Bearing retainer
3 Pilot bearings
4 Case
5 3rd speed blocker ring
6 2nd/3rd synchro snap ring
7 2nd/3rd synchro hub
8 2nd speed blocker ring
9 2nd speed gear
10 1st speed gear
11 1st speed blocker ring
12 1st speed synchro hub

13 1st speed synchro snap ring
14 Reverse gear
15 Reverse gear thrust and spring washers
16 Snap ring (bearing to mainshaft)
17 Extension
18 Vent
19 Speedo drive gear and clip
20 Mainshaft

21 Rear oil seal
22 Retainer oil seal
23 Snap ring (bearing to gear)
24 Drive gear bearing
25 Snap ring (bearing to case)
26 Thrust washer (front)
27 Thrust washer (rear)
28 Snap ring (bearing to extension)
29 Rear bearing

30 Countergear roller bearings
31 Anti-lash plate assembly
32 Magnet
33 2nd/3rd synchro sleeve
34 Countergear
35 Countershaft
36 Reverse idler shaft
37 1st speed synchro sleeve
38 E-ring
39 Reverse idler gear
40 Woodruff key

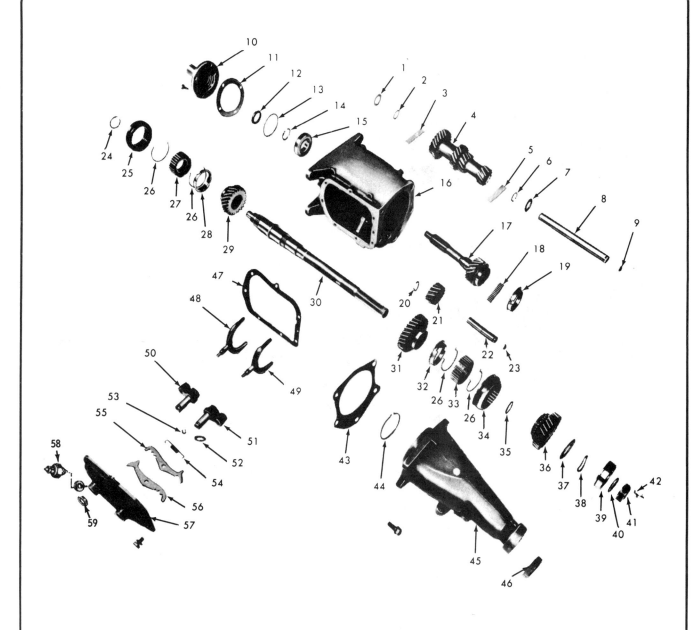

Fig. 7.8 Exploded view of the 3-speed Saginaw transmission (Sec 10)

1	Thrust washer (front)	15	Drive gear bearing
2	Bearing washer	16	Case
3	Needle bearings	17	Drive gear
4	Countergear	18	Pilot bearings
5	Needle bearings	19	3rd speed blocker ring
6	Bearing washer	20	E-ring
7	Thrust washer (rear)	21	Reverse idler gear
8	Countershaft	22	Reverse idler shaft
9	Woodruff key	23	Woodruff key
10	Bearing retainer	24	Snap ring (hub to shaft)
11	Gasket	25	2nd/3rd synchro sleeve
12	Oil seal	26	Synchro key spring
13	Snap ring (bearing to case)	27	2nd/3rd synchro hub assembly
14	Snap ring (bearing to gear)	28	2nd speed blocker ring
		29	2nd speed gear

30	Mainshaft	45	Extension
31	1st speed gear	46	Oil seal
32	1st speed blocker ring	47	Gasket
33	1st/2nd synchro hub assembly	48	2nd/3rd shift fork
34	1st/2nd synchro sleeve	49	1st/reverse shift fork
35	Snap ring (hub to shaft)	50	2nd/3rd shifter shaft assembly
36	Reverse gear	51	1st/reverse shifter shaft assembly
37	Thrust washer	52	O-ring seal
38	Rear bushing	53	E-ring
39	Rear bushing	54	Spring
40	Snap ring (bearing to shaft)	55	2nd/3rd detent cam
41	Speedo drive gear	56	1st/reverse detent cam
42	Retaining clip	57	Side cover
43	Gasket	58	TCS switch and gasket
44	Snap ring (rear bearing to extension)	59	Lip seal

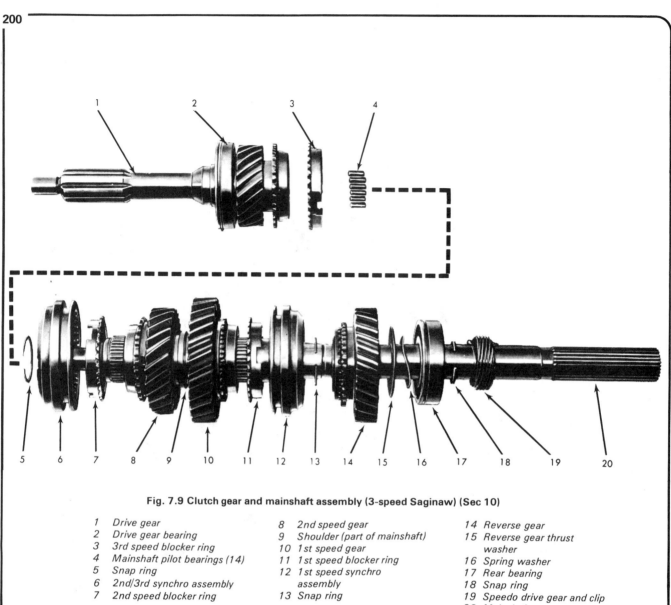

Fig. 7.9 Clutch gear and mainshaft assembly (3-speed Saginaw) (Sec 10)

1	Drive gear	8	2nd speed gear
2	Drive gear bearing	9	Shoulder (part of mainshaft)
3	3rd speed blocker ring	10	1st speed gear
4	Mainshaft pilot bearings (14)	11	1st speed blocker ring
5	Snap ring	12	1st speed synchro assembly
6	2nd/3rd synchro assembly	13	Snap ring
7	2nd speed blocker ring		

14	Reverse gear
15	Reverse gear thrust washer
16	Spring washer
17	Rear bearing
18	Snap ring
19	Speedo drive gear and clip
20	Mainshaft

11.5 Removing speedometer drive gear from mainshaft (Saginaw 4-speed)

11.6 Extracting rear bearing snap-ring from mainshaft (Saginaw 4-speed)

11.7 Removing wave washer, thrustwasher and 1st gear from the mainshaft (Saginaw 4-speed)

11.8a Removing 1st/2nd gear blocker ring (Saginaw 4-speed)

11.8b Extracting 1st/2nd synchro hub snap-ring (Saginaw 4-speed)

11.8c Removing the 1st/2nd synchro sleeve/reverse gear (Saginaw 4-speed)

11.9 Removing 2nd speed blocker ring and gear (Saginaw 4-speed)

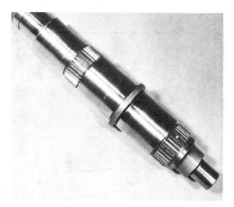

11.11a Mainshaft showing fixed shoulder (Saginaw 4-speed)

11.11b Installing 3rd speed gear to mainshaft (Saginaw 4-speed)

11.12a Installing 3rd/4th gear blocker ring (Saginaw 4-speed)

11.12b Installing the 3rd/4th synchro assembly (Saginaw 4-speed)

11.13 Installing the 3rd/4th synchro hub snap-ring (Saginaw 4-speed)

11.15 Installing the 1st/2nd synchro assembly (Saginaw 4-speed)

11.21 Mainshaft pilot bearings retained with grease (Saginaw 4-speed)

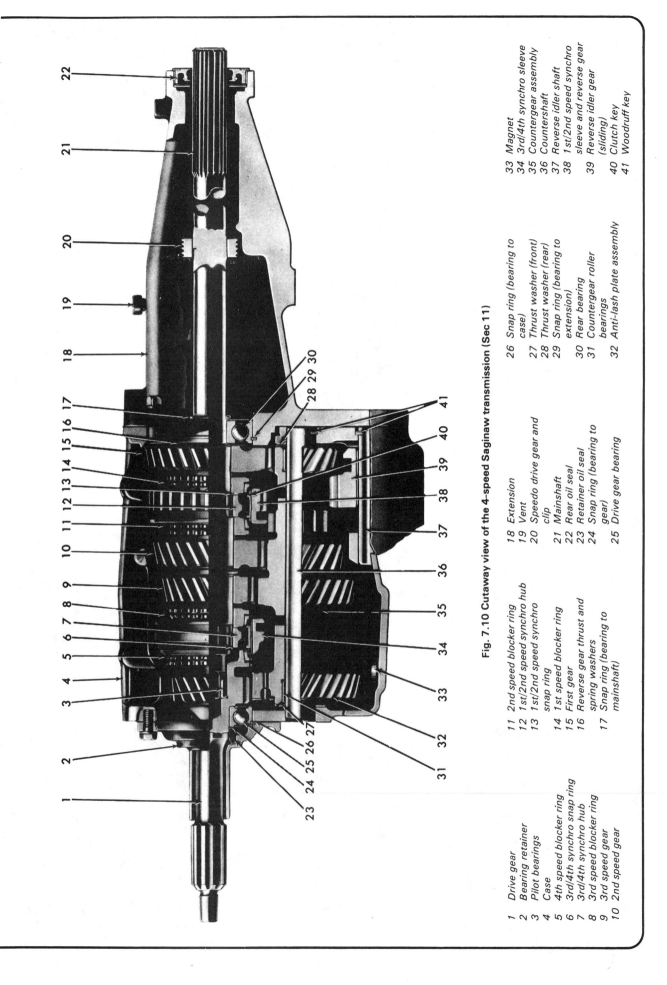

Fig. 7.10 Cutaway view of the 4-speed Saginaw transmission (Sec 11)

1 Drive gear
2 Bearing retainer
3 Pilot bearings
4 Case
5 4th speed blocker ring
6 3rd/4th synchro snap ring
7 3rd/4th synchro hub
8 3rd speed blocker ring
9 3rd speed gear
10 2nd speed gear

11 2nd speed blocker ring
12 1st/2nd speed synchro hub
13 1st/2nd speed synchro
   snap ring
14 1st speed blocker ring
15 First gear
16 Reverse gear thrust and
   spring washers
17 Snap ring (bearing to
   mainshaft)

18 Extension
19 Vent
20 Speedo drive gear and
   clip
21 Mainshaft
22 Rear oil seal
23 Retainer oil seal
24 Snap ring (bearing to
   gear)
25 Drive gear bearing

26 Snap ring (bearing to
   case)
27 Thrust washer (front)
28 Thrust washer (rear)
29 Snap ring (bearing to
   extension)
30 Rear bearing
31 Countergear roller
   bearings
32 Anti-lash plate assembly

33 Magnet
34 3rd/4th synchro sleeve
35 Countergear assembly
36 Countershaft
37 Reverse idler shaft
38 1st/2nd speed synchro
   sleeve and reverse gear
39 Reverse idler gear
   (sliding)
40 Clutch key
41 Woodruff key

12 Remove the 2nd/3rd synchro hub snap-ring from the mainshaft. Do not mix up the synchro unit components; although identical, the components of each unit are matched in production.

13 Remove the synchro unit, 2nd speed blocker ring and 2nd speed gear from the front end of the mainshaft (photo).

14 Depress the speedometer drive-gear retaining clip and remove the gear from the mainshaft.

15 Remove the rear bearing snap-ring from its mainshaft groove (photo).

16 Support the reverse gear and press the mainshaft out of the rear bearing, and snap-ring from the rear end of the mainshaft.

17 Remove 1st/reverse synchro hub snap-ring from the mainshaft and remove the synchro unit.

18 Remove the 1st speed blocker ring and 1st speed gear from the rear end of the mainshaft.

19 Clean all components in solvent and dry thoroughly. Check for wear or chipped teeth. If there has been a history of noisy gearshifts or the synchro facility could easily be 'beaten' then replace the appropriate synchro unit.

20 Extract the oil seal from the rear end of the rear extension and drive in a new one with a tubular drift.

21 Clean the transmission case inside and out and check for cracks, particularly around the bolt holes.

22 Extract the drive-gear bearing retainer seal and drive in a new one.

23 Start rebuilding the transmission by first reassembling the mainshaft. Install 2nd speed gear so that the rear face of the gear butts against the flange on the mainshaft.

24 Fit the blocker ring, followed by the 2nd/3rd synchro assembly (shift fork groove nearer rear end of the mainshaft). Make sure that the notches of the blocker ring align with the keys of the synchro assembly.

25 Fit the snap-ring which retains the synchro hub to the mainshaft.

26 To the rear end of the mainshaft, install the 1st speed gear, followed by the blocker ring.

27 Install the 1st/reverse synchro unit (shift fork groove nearer the front end of the mainshaft), again making sure that the notches of the blocker ring align with the keys of the synchro unit.

28 Install the snap-ring, reverse gear thrust washer and spring washer.

29 Install the mainshaft rear ball bearing with the outer snap-ring groove nearer the front of the shaft.

30 Install the rear bearing shaft snap-ring.

31 Fit the speedometer drive gear and retaining clip.

32 Insert a dummy shaft through the countergear, and stick the roller bearings (27 at each end), needle retainer washers and the transmission case thrust washers, in position using thick grease. Note that

the tangs on the thrust washers are away from the gear faces. **Note:** *If no dummy shaft is available, carefully stick the roller bearings in place, but when installing the shaft (paragraph 34), take care that they are not dislodged (photos).*

33 Install reverse idler gear and shaft with Woodruff key from the rear of the transmission case. Do not install the idler shaft E-ring at this time.

34 Install the countergear assembly from the rear of the transmission case and then insert the countershaft so that it picks up the roller bearings and the thrust washers, at the same time displacing the dummy shaft or tool (if used). The countershaft should be inserted so that its slot is at its rear end when installed (photo).

35 Expand the snap-ring in the rear extension and locate the extension over the rear end of the mainshaft and onto the rear bearing. Make sure that the snap-ring seats in the rear bearing groove (photos).

36 Insert the mainshaft pilot bearings (14 of them) into the clutch gear cavity and then assemble the 3rd speed blocker ring onto the clutch drive gear (photo).

37 Locate the clutch drive gear, pilot bearings and 3rd speed blocker ring over the front of the mainshaft. Do not fit the drive gear bearing at this time; also make sure that the notches in the blocker ring align with the keys in the 2nd/3rd synchro unit.

38 Stick a new gasket (using grease) to the rear face of the transmission case and then, from the rear, insert the combined clutch drive gear mainshaft and rear extension. Make sure that the 2nd/3rd synchro sleeve is pushed fully forward so that the clutch drive gear engages with the countergear anti-lash plate (photos).

39 Install the rear extension to transmission case bolts. Torque tighten to specifications.

40 Fit the outer snap-ring to the clutch drive gear bearing and install the bearing over the drive gear and into the front of the transmission case (photo).

41 Fit the clutch drive gear bearing shaft snap-ring (photo).

42 Install the clutch drive gear bearing retainer and its gasket making sure that the oil return hole is at the bottom (photo).

43 Now install the reverse idler gear E-ring to the shaft.

44 With the synchronizer sleeves in the neutral position, install the side cover, gasket and fork assembly (Section 7). Torque-tighten all the bolts

45 Install the speedometer driven gear in the rear extension.

---

11 4-speed (Saginaw) transmission – overhaul

---

1 Carry out the operations of paragraph 1 thru 9 of Section 10 but note than an E-ring is not fitted to the reverse idler shaft.

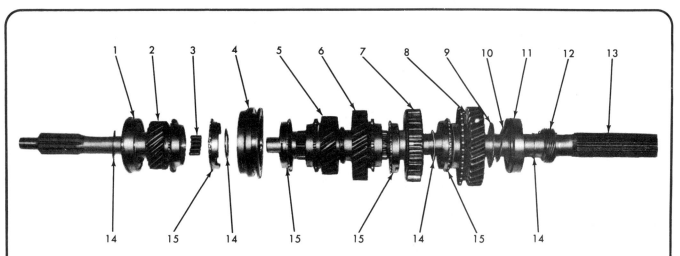

Fig. 7.11 Clutch gear and mainshaft assembly (4-speed Saginaw) (Sec 11)

1 Drive gear bearing	5 3rd speed gear
2 Drive gear	6 2nd speed gear
3 Mainshaft pilot bearings	7 1st/2nd synchro and reverse
4 3rd/4th synchro assembly	gear assembly

8 1st speed gear	12 Speedo drive gear
9 Thrust washer	13 Mainshaft
10 Spring washer	14 Snap ring
11 Rear bearing	15 Synchro blocker ring

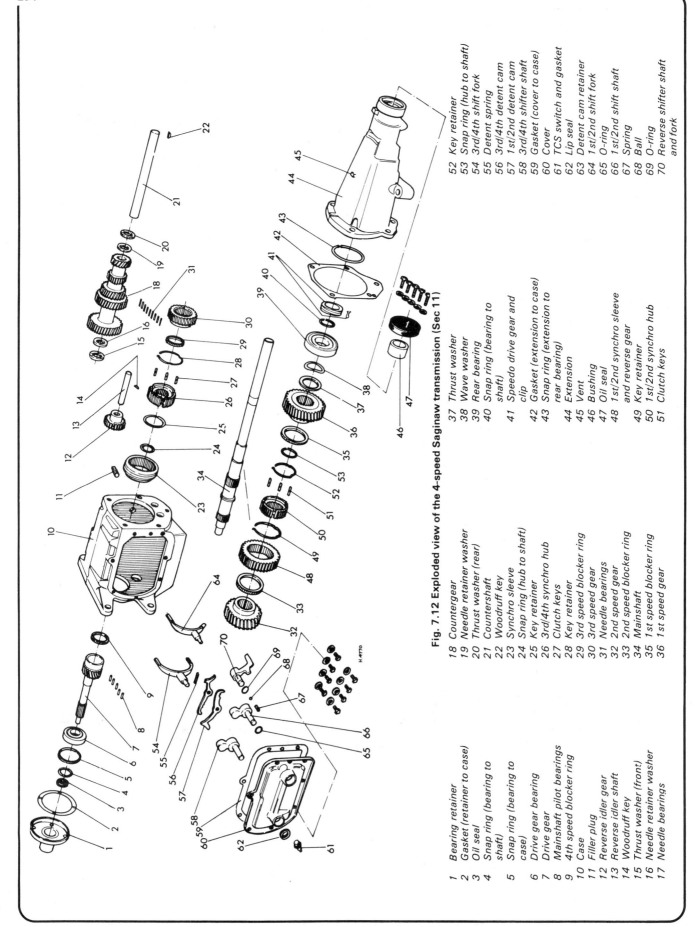

Fig. 7.12 Exploded view of the 4-speed Saginaw transmission (Sec 11)

1 Bearing retainer
2 Gasket (retainer to case)
3 Oil seal
4 Snap ring (bearing to shaft)
5 Snap ring (bearing to case)
6 Drive gear bearing
7 Drive gear
8 Mainshaft pilot bearings
9 4th speed blocker ring
10 Case
11 Filler plug
12 Reverse idler gear
13 Reverse idler shaft
14 Woodruff key
15 Thrust washer (front)
16 Needle retainer washer
17 Needle bearings

18 Countergear
19 Needle retainer washer
20 Thrust washer (rear)
21 Countershaft
22 Woodruff key
23 Synchro sleeve
24 Snap ring (hub to shaft)
25 Key retainer
26 3rd/4th synchro hub
27 Clutch keys
28 Key retainer
29 3rd speed blocker ring
30 3rd speed gear
31 Needle bearings
32 2nd speed gear
33 2nd speed blocker ring
34 Mainshaft
35 1st speed blocker ring
36 1st speed gear

37 Thrust washer
38 Wave washer
39 Rear bearing
40 Snap ring (bearing to shaft)
41 Speedo drive gear and clip
42 Gasket (extension to case)
43 Snap ring (extension to rear bearing)
44 Extension
45 Vent
46 Bushing
47 Oil seal
48 1st/2nd synchro sleeve and reverse gear
49 Key retainer
50 1st/2nd synchro hub
51 Clutch keys

52 Key retainer
53 Snap ring (hub to shaft)
54 3rd/4th shift fork
55 Detent spring
56 3rd/4th detent cam
57 1st/2nd detent cam
58 3rd/4th shifter shaft
59 Gasket (cover to case)
60 Cover
61 TCS switch and gasket
62 Lip seal
63 Detent cam retainer
64 1st/2nd shift fork
65 O-ring
66 1st/2nd shift shaft
67 Spring
68 Ball
69 O-ring
70 Reverse shifter shaft and fork

2   Remove the reverse idler gear stop-ring (where applicable), the use a long drift to drive the reverse idler shaft out of the rear of the transmission case.

3   Remove the 3rd/4th synchro hub snap-ring from the mainshaft. Do not mix up the synchro unit components, which although identical in appearance are matched in production.

4   Remove the synchro unit, 3rd gear blocker ring and 3rd speed gear from the front end of the mainshaft.

5   Depress the speedometer drive-gear retaining clip and remove the gear from the mainshaft (photo).

6   Remove the rear bearing snap-ring from its mainshaft groove (photo).

7   Support 1st gear and press the mainshaft out of the rear bearing. Remove the snap-ring, the rear bearing, the wave washer, thrust washer and 1st gear from the rear end of the mainshaft (photo).

8   Remove the blocker ring and 1st/2nd synchro hub snap-ring from the mainshaft and remove the synchro unit/reverse gear (photos).

9   Remove the 2nd speed blocker ring and 2nd speed gear from the rear end of the mainshaft (photo).

10 Carry out the operations of paragraphs 19 thru 22 of Section 10.

11 Commence rebuilding the transmission by first reassembling the mainshaft. Install 3rd speed gear so that the rear face of the gear butts against the flange on the mainshaft (photos).

12 Install the blocker ring, followed by 3rd/4th synchro assembly (shift fork groove nearer mainshaft flange). Make sure that the notches of the blocker ring align with the keys of the synchro assembly

(photos).

13 Install the snap-ring which retains the synchro hub to the mainshaft (photo).

14 To the rear end of the mainshaft, install the 2nd speed gear followed by the blocker ring.

15 Install the 1st/2nd synchro unit (shift fork groove nearer the front of the mainshaft), again making sure that the notches of the blocker ring align with the keys of the synchro unit. Install the snap-ring and blocker ring (photo).

16 Install 1st gear, the steel thrust washer and the wave washer.

17 Install the mainshaft rear ball bearing with the outer snap-ring groove nearer the front of the shaft.

18 Install the rear bearing shaft snap-ring.

19 Fit the speedometer drive-gear and retaining clip.

20 Carry out the operations of paragraphs 32 thru 35 of Section 10 but ignore the reference to the E-ring.

21 Insert the mainshaft pilot bearings (14 of them) into the clutch cavity and then assemble the 4th speed blocker ring onto the clutch drive-gear (photo).

22 Locate the clutch drive-gear, pilot bearings and 4th speed blocker ring over the front of the mainshaft. Do not fit the drive-gear bearing at this time; also make sure that the notches in the blocker ring align with the keys in the 3rd/4th synchro unit.

23 Carry out the operations of paragraphs 38 thru 42 and paragraph 44 of Section 10. Note that the reference at paragraph 38 to 2nd/3rd synchro sleeve will now be 3rd/4th synchro sleeve.

Chapter 7 Part B Automatic transmission

Refer to Chapter 13 for information applicable to later models

Contents

Specifications

Transmission type .... 3-speed Turbo-Hydra-Matic with hydrokinetic torque converter. Shift control is either a steering column rod or floorshift

Application

1974/1975/1977	Turbo Hydra-Matic 350 and 400
1976	Turbo Hydra-Matic 350
1978/1979	Turbo Hydra-Matic 200 and 350
1980	Turbo Hydra-Matic 200, 250 and 350

Fluid capacities

Turbo Hydra-Matic 200
* Routine fluid change	2.5 US qts
Filling from dry (overhaul)	10.0 US qts

Turbo Hydra-Matic 250
* Routine fluid change	4 US qts
Filling from dry (overhaul)	10.75 US qts

Turbo Hydra-Matic 350
* Routine fluid change	2½ US qts
Filling from dry (overhaul)	10.0 US qts

Turbo Hydra-Matic 400
*Routine fluid change	3.75 US qts
Filling from dry (overhaul)	11 US qts

* The small quantity required at routine fluid changing is due to the fact that the fluid in the torque converter cannot be drained unless dismantled.

Torque specifications

	ft-lb	in-lb
Turbo Hydra-Matic 250 and 350		
Pump cover-to-pump body	17	
Pump assembly-to-case	20	
Valve body and support plate	13	
Parking lock bracket	29	
Oil suction screen		40
Oil pan-to-case	13	
Extension-to-case	25	
Modulator retainer-to-case	12	
Inner selector lever to shaft	25	
Detent valve actuating bracket		52
Converter-to-flexplate bolts	35	
Under pan-to-transmission case		110
Transmission case-to-engine	35	

Oil cooler pipe connectors-to-transmission case or radiator 15
Oil cooler pipe-to-connectors 12
Gearshift bracket-to-frame 15
Gearshift shaft-to-swivel 20
Manual shaft-to-bracket 20
Detent cable-to-transmission 75
Intermediate band adjust nut 15

Turbo Hydra-Matic 400

Pump cover bolts 18
Parking pawl bracket bolts 18
Center support bolts 23
Pump to case attaching bolts 18
Extension housing-to-case attaching bolts 23
Rear servo cover bolts 18
Detent solenoid bolts 8
Control valve body bolts 8
Bottom pan attaching screws 12
Modulator retainer bolt 18
Governor cover bolts 18
Manual lever-to-manual shaft nut 8
Manual shaft-to-inside detent lever 18
Linkage swivel clamp nut 43
Converter dust shield screws 93
Transmission-to-engine mounting bolts 35
Converter-to-flexplate bolts 32
Rear mount-to-transmission bolts 40
Rear mount-to-cross-member bolt 40
Cross-member mounting bolts 25
Line pressure take-off plug 13
Strainer retainer bolt 10
Oil cooler pipe connectors-to-transmission case or radiator 11
Oil cooler pipe-to-connector 10
Gearshift bracket-to-frame 15
Gearshift shaft-to-swivel 20
Manual shaft-to-bracket 20
Downshift switch-to-bracket 30

Turbo Hydra-Matic 200

Pump cover bolts 18
Pump-to-case bolts 18
Parking pawl bracket bolts 18
Control valve body bolts 9
Oil screen retaining bolts 9
Oil pan bolts 12
Torque converter-to-flexplate bolts 35
Transmission-to-engine bolts 25
Converter dust shield screws 8
Speedometer driven gear bolts. 8
Fluid cooler line-to-transmission 25
Fluid cooler line-to-radiator 20
Linkage swivel clamp nut 30
Converter bracket-to-adapter 13
Transmission rear support bolts 40
Rear mounting-to-support bolts 21
Support center nut 33
Adapter-to-transmission bolts 33

1   General information

Buick Turbo Hydra-Matic transmissions are fully automatic 3-speed units. These units contain a 3-element hydrokinectic torque converter coupling that is capable of torque multiplication in an infinitely variable ratio between approximately 2:1 and 1:1.

In view of the fact that special tools and equipment are needed to carry out overhaul operations on any of the units mentioned in this Chapter, it is recommended that the owner take the unit to a transmission repair shop. Work performed in a shop is generally done at relatively low cost, is guaranteed, and done quickly. Therefore, information in this chapter will be restricted to maintenance and adjustment procedures; also, the removal and installation of the transmission. This will enable the home mechanic to install the rebuilt, or new, unit at quite a saving over a professional shop.

2   Identification

Besides checking the transmission serial number, there is a quick way to determine which type of automatic transmissions a particular vehicle is fitted with. Read the following transmission oil pan descriptions and see the accompanying illustration to identify the various models.

Turbo Hydra-Matic 200/250/350

This transmission is a two-piece design with a downshift cable running from the accelerator to the right side of the transmission case. The oil pan is square-shaped with one corner angled.

Turbo Hydra-Matic 400

The case of the 400 is also two-piece, but the downshifting is electrically controlled from a switch at the carburettor to the left side of the transmission. The oil pan shape elongated and irregular.

3 Extension housing oil seal – replacement

1   This operation can be carried out without removing the transmission from the vehicle.
2   Place the vehicle over a pit or jack it up to gain access to the transmission. Support the vehicle with jack stands.
3   Disconnect the drive shaft from the transmission as described in Chapter 8.
4   Pry out the defective seal using a screwdriver or chisel as a lever.
5   Apply jointing compound to the outer edge of the new seal and drive it into position using a piece of tubing as a drift.
6   Install the driveshaft and check the fluid level in the transmission unit.

4 Column shift linkage – checking and adjustment

1   To adjust the selector linkage it will first be necessary to release the control clamp and set the transmission lever and the shift lever in the neutral detent.
2   Assemble the clamp spring washer and screw to the equalizer lever and control rod.
3   Hold clamp flush against rod. Take care that no pressure in any direction is exerted on the rod or equalizer lever while you are tightening the clamp screw.
4   Tighten the screw to the specified torque.

5 Floorshift linkage – adjustment

1   Loosen the cable hookup at the transmission lever.
2   Position the floorshift lever in the 'Park' detent.

3   Set the transmission lever into the 'Park' position.
4   Move pin to give a 'free pin' fit in the transmission lever and tighten to 23 ft-lbs.

6 Turbo Hydra-Matic 250 and 350 – downshift (detent) cable replacement

1   Install a new seal on the transmission end of the new cable and lubricate the outer edge with transmission fluid.
2   Connect the cable to the transmission rod, then fasten the cable housing to the transmission and tighten the bolt securely.
3   Attach the cable to the filler tube with the clip. Note that on the 250 transmission, the cable should be routed in front of the tube.
4   Slip the other end of the cable through the engine bracket and attach it to the throttle lever on the carburetor. Make sure the locking tangs expand and lock the cable fitting to the bracket.
5   On 350 transmissions, ensure that the 'snap lock' button is in the disengaged position (the cable should be free to slide through the 'snap lock' fitting). Next, open the throttle lever on the carburetor to the wide open position, then push the 'snap lock' button to the engaged position (flush with the outside of the fitting).
6   On 250 transmission, attach the cable to the bracket with the retainer slot in a vertical position. When the throttle lever is opened completely, the cable length will be automatically and permanently adjusted.

7 Turbo Hydra-Matic 400 – downshift (detent) switch adjustment

1   The switch is mounted on the accelerator pedal bracket as shown in the accompanying illustration.
2   Initial adjustment is made by pushing the switch plunger as far as possible. Final adjustment will occur automatically the first time the accelerator pedal is fully depressed.

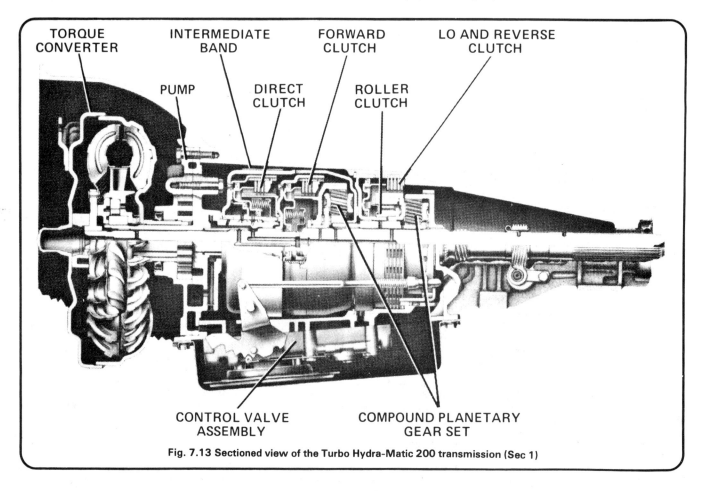

Fig. 7.13 Sectioned view of the Turbo Hydra-Matic 200 transmission (Sec 1)

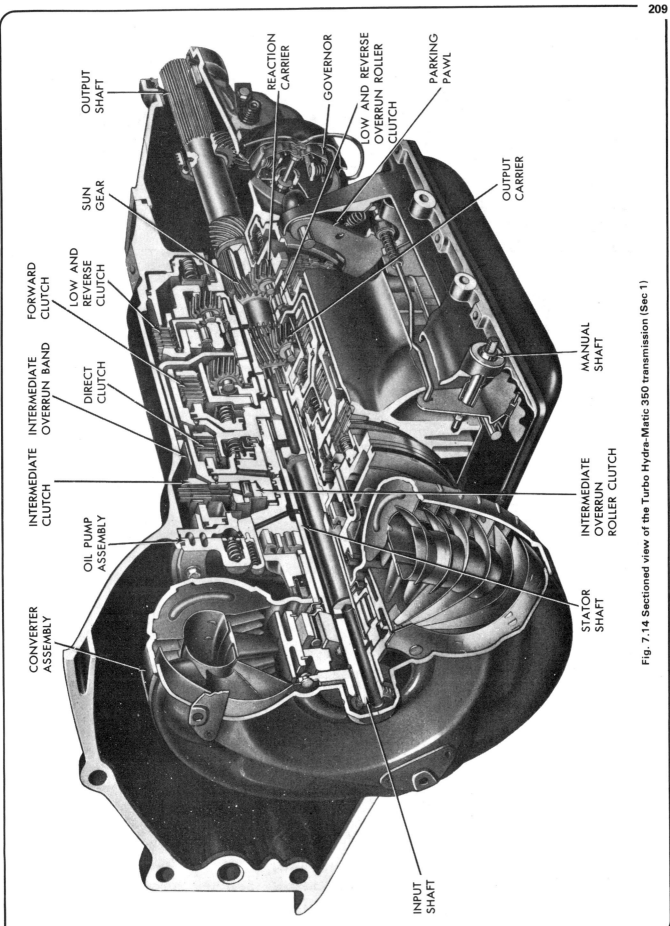

OUTPUT SHAFT

REACTION CARRIER

GOVERNOR

LOW AND REVERSE OVERRUN ROLLER CLUTCH

PARKING PAWL

SUN GEAR

OUTPUT CARRIER

FORWARD CLUTCH

LOW AND REVERSE CLUTCH

INTERMEDIATE OVERRUN BAND

DIRECT CLUTCH

INTERMEDIATE CLUTCH

OIL PUMP ASSEMBLY

CONVERTER ASSEMBLY

MANUAL SHAFT

INTERMEDIATE OVERRUN ROLLER CLUTCH

STATOR SHAFT

INPUT SHAFT

Fig. 7.14 Sectioned view of the Turbo Hydra-Matic 350 transmission (Sec 1)

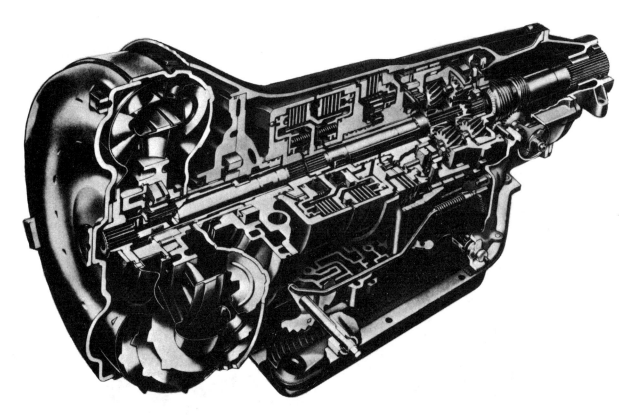

Fig. 7.15 Sectioned view of the Turbo Hydra-Matic 400 transmission (Sec 1)

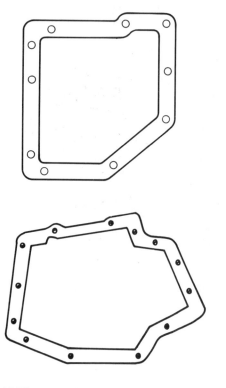

Fig. 7.16 The transmission oilpan shape can sometimes be used
for identification purposes
*(Top: GM Turbo Hydra-Matic 200/250/350; Bottom: GM Turbo
Hydra-Matic 400) (Sec 2)*

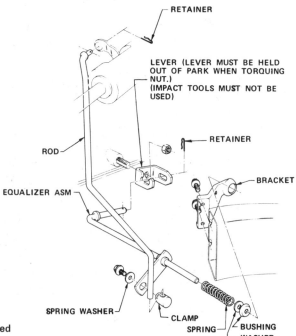

RETAINER

LEVER (LEVER MUST BE HELD
OUT OF PARK WHEN TORQUING
NUT.)
(IMPACT TOOLS MUST NOT BE
USED)

ROD

RETAINER

EQUALIZER ASM

BRACKET

SPRING WASHER

CLAMP

SPRING

BUSHING

WASHER

Fig. 7.17 Typical steering column linkage set-up (Sec 4)

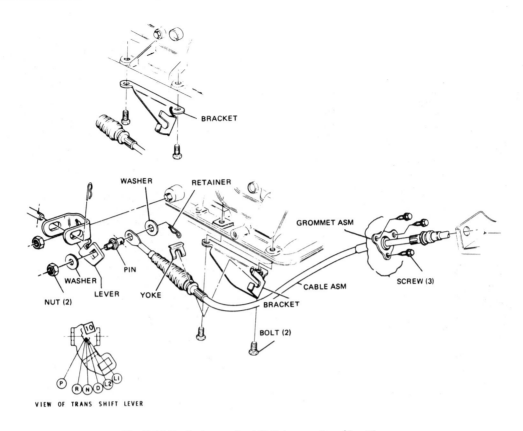

Fig. 7.18 Typical console shift linkage set-up (Sec 5)

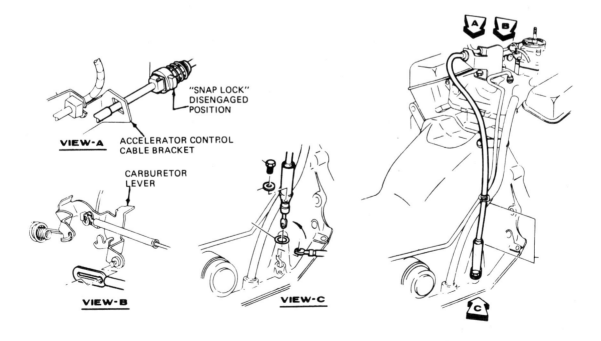

Fig. 7.19 250/350 Turbo Hydra-Matic downshift detent cable installation details (Sec 6)

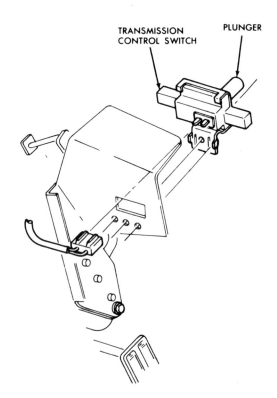

TRANSMISSION
CONTROL SWITCH   PLUNGER

**Fig. 7.20 Downshift detent switch (Turbo Hydra-Matic 400)
(Sec 7)**

8   Turbo Hydra-Matic 200 – T.V. cable replacement

The procedure for T.V. cable replacement is identical to the
procedure for Turbo Hydra-Matic 350 downshift detent cable replacement (refer to Section 6, steps 1 through 5). Note that the cable
should be routed in front of the transmission filler tube.

9   Turbo Hydra-Matic transmission – combined neutral start/back-up lamp/seat belt warning switch adjustment

Column shift

1   If a new switch is being installed, set the shift lever against the
'Neutral' gate by rotating the lower lever on the shift tube in a
counterclockwise direction as viewed from the driver's seat.
2   Locate the switch actuating tang in the shifter tube slot and then
tighten the securing screws.
3   Connect the wiring harness and switch on the ignition and check
that the starter motor will actuate.
4   If the switch operates correctly, move the shift lever out of neutral
which will cause the alignment pin (fitted during production of the
switch) to shear.
5   If an old switch is being installed or readjusted, use a pin (0.093
to 0.097 in diameter) to align the hole in the switch with the actuating
tang. Insert the pin to a depth of $\frac{1}{4}$ inch. Remove the pin before moving
the shift lever out of neutral.

Floor shift

6   This is similar to the procedure just described for column shift
except that the shift lever should be set in 'Park' not 'Neutral'.
7   Access to the switch is obtained after removal of the trim plate
and shift control assembly.

10 Turbo Hydra-Matic transmission – removal and installation

1   Disconnect the battery ground cable and release the parking
brake.
2   Raise the vehicle on a hoist or place it over an inspection pit.
3   Disconnect the speedometer cable, detent cable, electrical leads,
modulator vacuum line and oil cooler pipes, as appropriate.
4   Disconnect the shift control linkage.
5   Disconnect the driveshaft (Chapter 8).
6   Support the transmission with a suitable jack, and disconnect the
rear mount from the frame crossmember.
7   Remove the two bolts at each end of the crossmember then
remove the crossmember.
8   Remove the converter underpan.
9   Loosen the exhaust downpipe bolts at the manifold and unscrew
them about $\frac{1}{4}$ inch.
10   Mark the relationship of the flexplate to the torque converter and
then unscrew the connecting bolts. These are accessible through the
front of the torque converter housing but will have to be brought into
view one at a time by applying a wrench to the torsional damper
center bolt.
11   Lower the transmission as far as possible without causing any
engine or transmission components to come into contact with the
engine compartment firewall.
12   Remove the transmission to engine connecting bolts and remove
the oil filler tube at the transmission.
13   Raise the transmission to its normal position, support the engine
with the jack and slide the transmission rearwards from the engine.
Keep the rear of the transmission downwards so that the converter
does not fall off.
14   Installation is the reverse of the removal procedure, but additionally ensure that the weld nuts on the converter are flush with the
flexplate and that the converter rotates freely in this position. Tighten
all bolts finger-tight before torque-tightening to the specified value.

Chapter 8 Driveline

Contents

Specifications

Clutch
Clutch type	Single dry plate, diaphragm spring
Clutch actuation	Mechanical by rod
Clutch pedal free-play (measured at center of pedal pad)	1.00 ± .3 in
Clutch throwout (release) bearing type	Grease sealed ball

Driveshaft
Driveshaft type	Open, single section, tubular steel with two universal joints and one slip joint

Rear axle
Rear axle type	Salisbury, semi-floating with cast carrier having overhung hypoid pinion and ring gear. Optional Positraction (limited slip) axle available on all models
Rear axle ring gear diameter	Varies between $7\frac{1}{2}$, $8\frac{1}{2}$, $8\frac{3}{4}$-inches

Lubricant capacity
Light duty axle	4.25 pints
Heavy duty axle	5.4 pints

B and O type axles (see Section 17, this Chapter)
Axleshaft endplay	0.001 to 0.018 (1974 through 1977) 0.001 to 0.020 (1978 through 1980)
Pinion bearing pre-load:	
New	20 to 25 lb-in
Used	10 to 15 lb-in

Torque specifications
Clutch
	ft-lb
Clutch pressure plate bolts	35
Transmission case to clutch bellhousing bolts	53
Clutch bellhousing to engine bolts	53
Clutch release to fork-ball	40
Clutch adjustment locknut	10

Driveshaft
Universal joint to companion flange	15

Rear axle

	1974 through 1977 ft-lb	1975 through 1980 ft-lb
Differential carrier cover bolts	30	80
Ring gear bolts	85	
Differential bearing cap bolts	60	
Oil filler plug	20	
Differential pinion lock	20	12

1   General description – clutch

All models are fitted with a single dry plate, diaphragm spring-type clutch. Operation is by means of a pendant foot pedal and rod linkage. The unit comprises a pressure plate assembly which contains the pressure plate, diaphragm spring and fulcrum rings. The assembly is bolted to the rear face of the flywheel.

The driven plate (friction disc) is free to slide along the gearbox input shaft and it is held in place between the flywheel and pressure plate faces by the pressure exerted by the diaphragm spring. The friction lining material is riveted to the driven plate which incorporates a spring-cushioned hub designed to absorb transmission rotational shocks and to assist in ensuring smooth take-offs.

The circular diaphragm spring assembly is mounted on shouldered pins and held in place in the cover by fulcrum rings. The spring itself is held in place by spring steel clips.

Depressing the clutch pedal pushes the throwout-bearing, mounted on its hub retainer, forward to bear against the fingers of the diaphragm spring. This action causes the diaphragm spring outer edge to deflect and so move the pressure plate rearwards to disengage the pressure plate from the driven plate.

When the clutch pedal is released, the diaphragm spring forces the pressure plate into contact with the friction linings of the driven plate and at the same time pushes the drive plate fractionally forward on its splines to ensure full engagement with the flywheel. The driven plate is now firmly sandwiched between the pressure plate and the flywheel and so the drive is taken up.

2   Clutch – adjustment

1   The free-play at the clutch pedal should be approximately 1 inch.
2   There is only one linkage adjustment to compensate for all normal clutch wear.
3   To check for correct adjustment, apply the parking brake, block the front wheels and start the engine. Hold the clutch pedal approximately $\frac{1}{2}$ inch from the floor and move the shift lever between 'First' and 'Reverse' gears several times. If the shift is not smooth, clutch adjustment is necessary.
4   Raise the car to permit access to the clutch linkage under the car. Place firmly on jack stands.
5   Disconnect the return spring at the clutch fork.
6   Rotate the clutch lever and shaft assembly until the clutch pedal

is firmly against the rubber bumper on the dashboard brace. If in doubt about this, have an assistant check from inside the car.
7   Push the outer end of the clutch fork rearward until the release bearing lightly contacts the pressure plate fingers.
8   Keep the fork in this position while the pushrod is removed from its holes in the shaft. Now place the rod in the gauge hole of the shaft, directly above the normal operating hole (see accompanying illustration).
9   With the push rod in the gauge hole, loosen the locking nut and turn the rod to increase its length. Increase the length of the rod until all lash is removed from the system.
10   Remove the rod from the gauge hole and return it to the lower operating hole in the shaft. Install the retainer and then carefully tighten the nut, being sure the length of the rod is not changed.
11   Connect the return spring and check the pedal free-play as described previously. Lower the vehicle, then check for correct operation and free travel.

3   Clutch pedal – removal and installation

1   Disconnect the return spring for the clutch pedal.
2   Disconnect the clutch pedal push rod where it meets the pedal arm. This is held in place at the top of the pedal with a lock pin.
3   Disconnect the electrical coupler for the neutral start switch. Then remove the switch from the top of the clutch pedal.
4   The pivot shaft which runs through the clutch and brake pedals must now be removed. It is held in place with a retaining nut on one end. Remove the nut and slide the shaft until it clears the pedal support. Now insert a dummy shaft in the support to hold the brake pedal components in place while the pivot shaft is removed.
5   Remove the pivot shaft, pedal arm and bushings.
6   Inspect all parts and replace as necessary. Do not clean the nylon bushings with cleaning agent, simply wipe them clean with a cloth. Lubricate the bushings and all moving parts.
7   To reinstall the pedal, push the bushings into place and then the pivot shaft and pedal arm.
8   Install the retaining nut to the end of the shaft.
9   Install the neutral start switch and connect its wiring coupler.
10   Connect the push rod to the pedal arm. Make sure it is securely fastened.
11   Connect the return spring and check for free travel. Adjust the components as required.

4   Clutch cross-shaft – removal and installation

1   Remove the linkage return and lower linkage springs. Disconnect the clutch pedal and fork push rods from their respective cross-shaft levers.
2   Loosen the outboard ball stud nut and slide the stud out of the slot in the bracket.
3   Move the cross-shaft outboard far enough to clear the inboard ball stud, then lift it out and remove it from the vehicle.
4   Check the ball stud seats on the cross-shaft, the engine bracket ball stud assembly and the anti-rattle spring for damage and wear; replace parts as necessary.
5   When installing, reverse the removal procedure. Lubricate the ball studs and seat with graphite grease on assembly and finally adjust the clutch (Section 2).

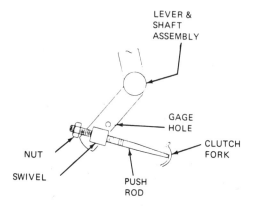

Fig. 8.1 Clutch adjustment diagram (Sec 2)

LEVER &
SHAFT
ASSEMBLY

GAGE
HOLE

CLUTCH
FORK

NUT

SWIVEL

PUSH
ROD

5   Clutch – removal, servicing and installation

1   Access to the clutch is normally obtained by removing the transmission, leaving the engine in the car. If, of course, the engine is

being removed for major overhaul, then the opportunity should always be taken to check the clutch assembly for wear at the same time.

2   Disconnect the clutch fork pushrod and spring then remove the clutch housing from the engine cylinder block.

3   Slide the clutch fork from the ball stud and remove the fork from the dust boot.

4   If necessary, the ball stud can be removed from the clutch housing by unscrewing (photo).

5   If there are no alignment marks on the clutch cover (an X-mark or white-painted letter) scribe or center-punch marks for indexing purposes during installation.

6   Unscrew the bolts securing the pressure plate and cover assembly one turn at a time in a diagonal sequence to prevent distortion of the clutch cover.

7   With all the bolts and lockwashers removed, carefully lift the clutch away from the flywheel taking care that the driven plate does not fall or become damaged.

8   It is not practicable to dismantle the pressure plate assembly and the term 'dismantling' is usually used for simply fitting a new clutch driven plate and pressure plate (if necessary).

9   If a new clutch driven plate is being fitted, replace the throwout bearing at the same time. This will preclude having to replace it at a later date when wear on the clutch lining is still very small.

10 If the pressure plate assembly requires replacement, an exchange unit must be purchased. This will have been accurately set up and balanced to very fine limits.

11 Examine the clutch plate friction linings for wear and loose rivets, and the disc for rim distortion, cracks, broken hub springs, and worn splines. The surface of the friction linings may be highly glazed, but as long at the clutch material pattern can be clearly seen this is

satisfactory. Compare the amount of lining wear with a new clutch disc at the stores in your local service station. If worn, the driven plate must be replaced.

12 Check the machined faces of the flywheel and the pressure plate. If either are grooved they should be machined until smooth, or replaced.

13 If the pressure plate is cracked or split, it is essential that an exchange unit is fitted; also if the pressure of the diaphragm spring is suspect, this should be checked and replaced if necessary.

14 Check the throwout bearing for smoothness of operation. There should be no harshness or slackness in it. It should spin reasonably freely bearing in mind it has been pre-packed with grease. If in doubt, replace the bearing with a new one.

15 It is important that no oil or grease gets on the clutch plate friction linings, or the pressure plate and flywheel faces. It is advisable to replace the clutch with clean hands and to wipe down the pressure plate and flywheel faces with a clean dry rag before assembly begins.

16 Place the driven plate against the flywheel making sure that the longer splined boss faces towards the flywheel (thicker torsional spring assembly projection towards the transmission).

17 Install the pressure plate and clutch cover assembly so that the marks made on dismantling are in alignment. Tighten the bolts only finger-tight so that the driven plate is gripped, but can still be slid sideways.

18 The clutch plate must now be aligned so that when the engine and transmission are mated, the clutch shaft splines will pass through the splines in the center of the driven plate hub.

19 Alignment can be carried out quite easily by inserting a round bar or long screwdriver through the hole in the center of the clutch, so that the end of the bar rests in the small hole in the end of the crankshaft

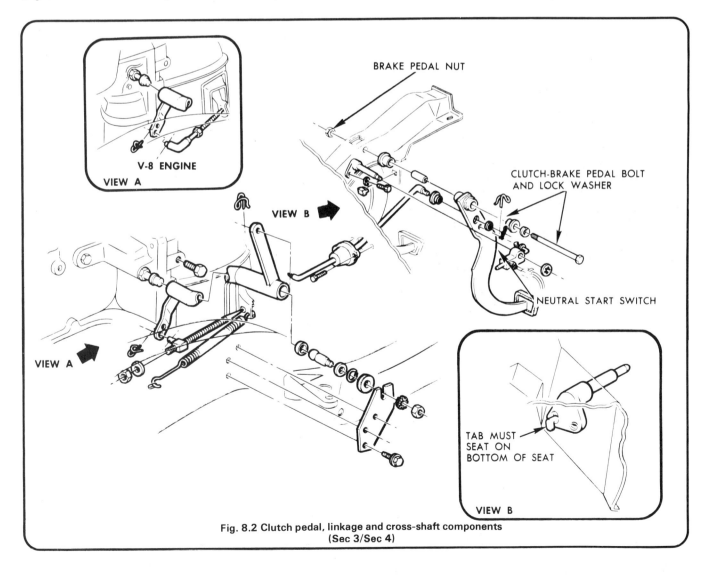

Fig. 8.2 Clutch pedal, linkage and cross-shaft components
(Sec 3/Sec 4)

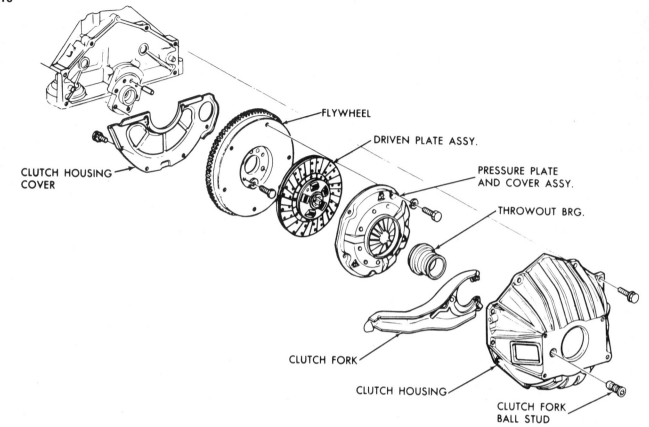

FLYWHEEL

DRIVEN PLATE ASSY.

PRESSURE PLATE
AND COVER ASSY.

THROWOUT BRG.

CLUTCH HOUSING
COVER

CLUTCH FORK

CLUTCH HOUSING

CLUTCH FORK
BALL STUD

Fig. 8.3 Exploded view of clutch components (Sec 5)

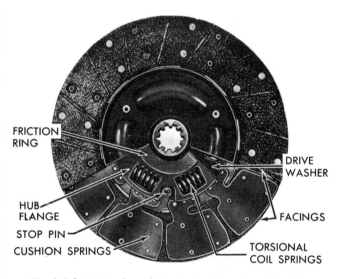

FRICTION
RING

DRIVE
WASHER

HUB
FLANGE

STOP PIN

FACINGS

CUSHION SPRINGS

TORSIONAL
COIL SPRINGS

Fig. 8.4 Cutaway view of the clutch-driven plate (Sec 5)

SWITCH

Tab must seat.

VIEW A

Fig. 8.6 Neutral start switch mounting (Sec 6)

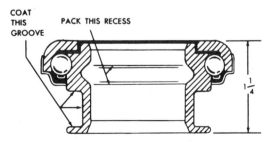

COAT
THIS
GROOVE

PACK THIS RECESS

$1\frac{1}{4}$

Fig. 8.5 Sectional view of the clutch release (throwout) bearing
(Sec 5)

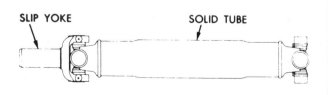

SLIP YOKE

SOLID TUBE

Fig. 8.7 Typical driveshaft (Sec 7)

5.4 Front face of transmission showing the clutch fork ball stud

5.19 Aligning the clutch driven plate using an old drive gear

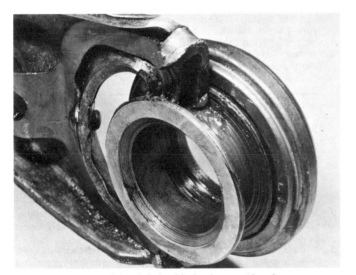

5.24a Engagement of clutch fork with the throwout bearing

5.24b Rear view of the clutch fork and throwout bearing

5.24c Clutch fork and throwout bearing installed

containing the input shaft pilot bushing. Ideally an old clutch drive gear or aligning tool should be used (photo).

20 Using the clutch shaft bearing bushing as a fulcrum, moving the bar sideways or up and down will move the clutch plate in whichever direction is necessary to achieve proper alignment.

21 Alignment is easily judged by removing the bar and viewing the driven plate hub in relation to the hole in the center of the clutch cover plate diaphragm spring. When the hub appears exactly in the center of the hole, all is correct. Alternatively, the clutch shaft will fit the bushing and center of the clutch hub exactly, obviating the need for visual alignment. On pressure plate covers which have cutaway edges, the center plate can be centralized simply by lining up its edges with the edge of the flywheel, just using the fingers.

22 Tighten the clutch cover bolts firmly in a diagonal sequence to ensure that the cover plate is pulled down evenly and without distortion to the flange. Torque the bolts to specifications.

23 Lubricate the clutch fork fingers at the throwout bearing end, and the ball and socket, with a high melting point grease. Also lubricate the throwout bearing collar and groove.

24 Install the clutch fork and dust boot into the clutch housing and install the throwout bearing to the fork (photos).

25 Install the clutch housing.

26 Install the transmission. Refer to Chapter 2 or Chapter 7, as necessary.

10.2 Marking the position of the driveshaft and universal joint components (all parts must be installed in their original positions)

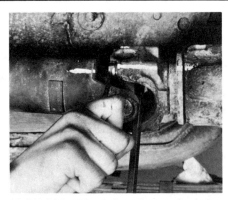

10.3 Hold the driveshaft as the securing bolts are loosened

10.5 When reinstalling, be careful not to damage the seal at the rear of the transmission

27 Connect the fork pushrod and spring, lubricating the spring and pushrod ends.
28 Adjust the shift linkage (Chapter 7) and the clutch linkage (Section 2).

6 Neutral start switch – removal and installation

1   This switch is a safety device intended to prevent the vehicle from being started without the clutch pedal being fully depressed. The small switch mounts to the clutch pedal mounting bracket and is activated by a plastic shaft which is part of the switch.
2   Disconnect the electrical coupler at the switch.
3   Compress the switch actuating shaft retainer and remove the shaft, with the switch attached, from the bracket.
4   To install, slide the switch onto the bracket and make sure the tab is fully seated. Then rotate the switch actuating shaft until it aligns with the hole in the clutch pedal arm and pop the shaft into the hole.
5   Connect the electrical coupler to the switch.
6   The switch is self-aligning, meaning that there is no need for adjustments.

7 General description – driveshaft

The driveshaft is of a one piece tubular steel construction having a universal joint at each end to allow for vertical movement of the rear axle. At the front end of the shaft is a sliding sleeve which engages with the transmission unit splined output shaft.

The universal joint is retained by a nylon material which is injected into a groove in the yoke during manufacture. This latter type of joint can be serviced by the use of a repair kit which utilizes snap-rings inboard of the yoke when the joint is reassembled. Some models may have snap-rings as original equipment.

Some driveshafts incorporate a vibration damper. This item is not serviced separately, and in the event of replacement being necessary, the damper and sleeves are to be replaced as an assembly.

The driveshafts are finely balanced during manufacture and it is recommended that an exchange unit is obtained rather than dismantling the universal joints when wear is evident. However, this is not always possible and provided care is taken to mark each individual yoke in relation to the one opposite, then the balance will usually be maintained. Do not drop the assembly during operations.

8 Universal joints – testing for wear

1   Wear in the needle roller bearings is characterized by vibration in the transmission, 'clonks' on taking up the drive, and in extreme cases of lack of lubrication, metallic squeaking and ultimately grating and shrieking sounds as the bearings break up.
2   It is easy to check if the needle roller bearings are worn with the shaft in position, by trying to turn it with one hand, the other hand holding the rear axle flange when the rear universal joint is being checked, and the front half coupling when the front universal joint is being checked. Any movement between the shaft and the couplings is indicative of considerable wear.
3   A further test for wear is to attempt to lift the shaft and note any movement between the yokes of the joints.
4   If wear is evident, either fit a new driveshaft assembly complete or replace the universal joints, as described later in this Chapter.

9 Driveshaft out-of-balance – correction

1   Vibration of the driveshaft at certain roadspeeds may be caused by any of the following:

   a) Undercoating or mud on the shaft
   b) Loose rear strap attachment bolts
   c) Worn universal joints
   d) Bent or dented driveshaft

2   Vibrations which are thought to be emanating from the drive shaft are sometimes caused by improper tire balance. This should be one of your first checks.
3   If the shaft is in a good, clean, undamaged condition, it is worth disconnecting the rear end attachment straps and turning the shaft 180 degrees to see if an improvement is noticed. Be sure to mark the original position of each component before disassembly so the shaft can be returned to the same location.
4   If the vibration persists after checking for obvious causes and changing the position of the shaft, the entire assembly should be checked out by a professional shop or replaced.

10 Driveshaft – removal and installation

1   Raise the rear of the vehicle and support it securely on blocks or axle-stands.
2   Mark the relationship of the driveshaft to the companion flange on the rear axle pinion (photo).
3   Disconnect the rear universal joint by unscrewing and removing the nuts from the U-bolts or strap retaining bolts, or by removing the flange bolts (photo). Where U-bolts or retaining straps are used, wrap adhesive tape around the bearing cups to prevent them being displaced and the needle rollers dropping out.
4   Lower the rear end of the driveshaft and then withdraw the complete shaft assembly to the rear. The front splined sliding sleeve section will be drawn off the transmission output shaft during the removal operation and a small amount of lubricant may be lost from vehicles equipped with manual transmission.
5   Installation is a reversal of removal but remember to align the shaft to flange mating marks and take care not to damage the transmission extension oil seal with the sliding joint splines (photo).
6   Check the transmission oil level when installation is complete.

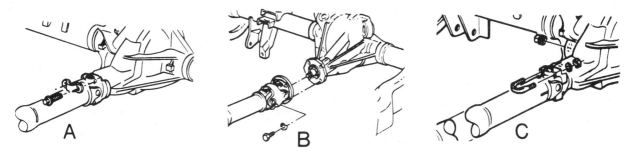

Fig. 8.8 Method of attachment of driveshaft to rear axle (Sec 10)

A   Strap   B   Flange   C   'U' bolt

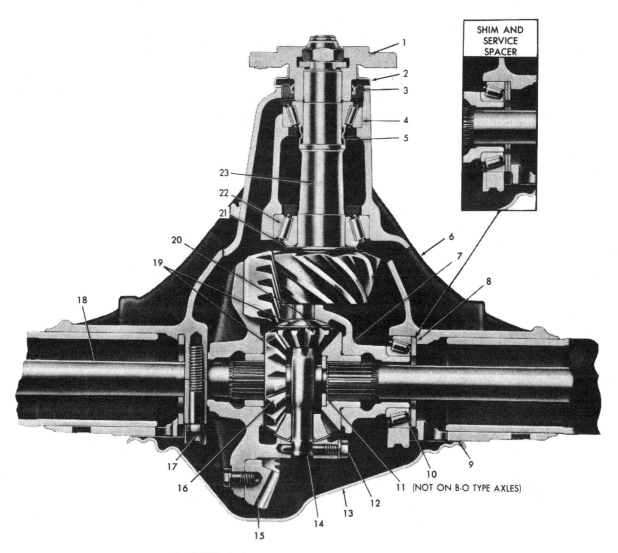

SHIM AND SERVICE SPACER

(NOT ON B-O TYPE AXLES)

Fig. 8.9 Typical rear axle differential cross-section (Sec 12)

1 Companion flange	9 Gasket	17 Bearing cap
2 Deflector	10 Differential bearing	18 Axle shaft
3 Pinion oil seal	11 'C' lock	19 Thrust washer
4 Pinion front bearing	12 Pinion shaft lock bolt	20 Differential pinion
5 Pinion bearing spacer	13 Cover	21 Shim
6 Differential carrier	14 Pinion shaft	22 Pinion rear bearing
7 Differential case	15 Ring gear	23 Drive pinion
8 Shim	16 Side gear	

11 Universal joints – dismantling and reassembly

Cleveland-type joint (snap-ring retainers)

1   Clean away all dirt from the ends of the bearings on the yokes so that the snap-rings can be removed using a pair of snap-ring pliers. If the snap-rings are very tight, tap the end of the bearing cup (inside the snap-ring) to relieve the pressure (photo).

2   Support the trunnion yoke on a short piece of tube or the open end of a socket then use a suitably sized socket to press out the cross (trunnion) by means of a vise (photo).

3   Press the trunnion through as far as possible then grip the bearing cup in the jaws of a vise to fully remove it. Repeat the procedure for the remaining cups.

4   On some models, the slip yoke at the transmission end has a vent hole. When dismantling, ensure that this vent hole is not blocked.

5   A universal joint repair kit will contain a new trunnion, seals, bearings, cups and snap-rings.

6   Start reassembly by packing each of the reservoirs at the trunnion ends with lubricant.

7   Make sure that the dust seals are correctly located on the trunnion so that the cavities in the seals are nearer the trunnion.

8   Using a vise, press one bearing cup into the yoke so that it enters by not more than one quarter-inch.

9   Using a thick grease, stick each of the needle rollers inside the cup.

10 Insert the trunnion into the partially fitted bearing cup taking care not to displace the needle rollers.

11 Stick the needle bearings into the opposite cup and then holding the trunnion in correct alignment, press both cups fully home in the jaws of the vise.

12 Install the new snap-rings.

13 Repeat the operations on the other two bearing cups.

14 In extreme cases of wear or neglect, it is possible that the bearing cup housings in the yoke will have worn so much that the cups are a loose fit in the yokes. In such cases, replace the complete driveshaft assembly.

15 Always check the wear in the sliding sleeve splines and replace the sleeve if worn.

Saginaw-type joint (plastic retainers)

16 Where a Saginaw joint is to be disassembled, the procedure given in the previous section for pressing out the bearing cup is applicable. If the joint has been previously repaired it will be necessary to remove the snap-rings inboard of the yokes; if this is to be the first time that servicing has been carried out, there are no snap-rings to remove, but the pressing operation in the vise will shear the plastic molding material.

17 Having removed the cross (trunnion), remove the remains of the plastic material from the yoke. Use a small punch to remove the material from the injection holes.

18 Reassembly is similar to that given for the Cleveland type joint except that the snap-rings are installed inside the yoke. If difficulty is encountered, strike the yoke firmly with a hammer to assist in seating.

12 General description and identification – rear axle

The rear axle is of hypoid, semi-floating type. The differential carrier is a casting with a pressed steel cover and the axle tubes are of steel construction.

Due to the need for special gauges and equipment and to the fact that individual differential components are no longer supplied (only a complete rear axle unit) the servicing and repair operations should be

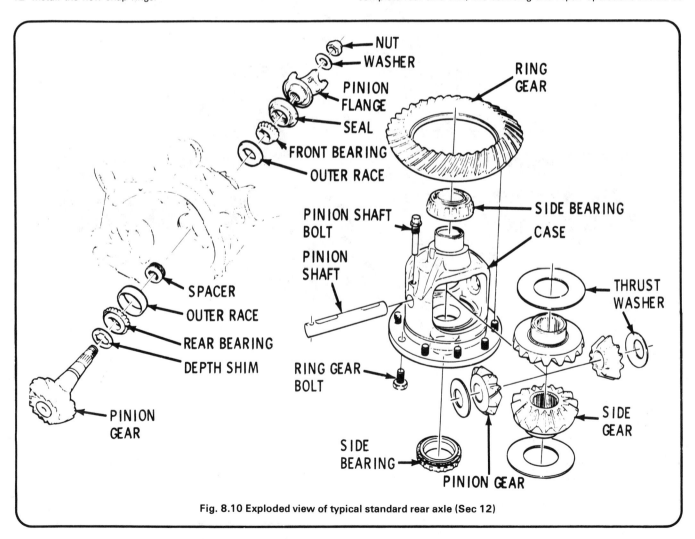

Fig. 8.10 Exploded view of typical standard rear axle (Sec 12)

confined to those described in this chapter.

An optional 'Positraction' (limited slip) differential unit has been available since the earliest models. Basically, the inclusion of clutch cones or plates and springs slow the rotation of the differential case when one wheel is on a firm surface and the other on a slippery one. This slowing action applies additional force to the pinion gears and through the medium of the cone which is splined to the axleshafts, exerts equalizing rotational power to the axleshaft which is driving the wheel under traction.

In order to be able to undertake certain operations, particularly removal of the axleshafts, it is important to know the axle identification number. This is located on the front face of the right-hand axle tube about 3 inches from the differential cover. After the dirt and road grime has been brushed away, the code can be read (photo). A typical General Motors axle code for 1974 and later models will read: 1974 AN B 0852.

The first two letters, in this case AN, are the axle code. By using this axle code and a ratio chart you can determine the gear ratios installed in the axle assembly.

The third letter of the code identifies the manufacturer of the axle. This is important, as axle design varies slightly between manufacturers. This single-letter code will be one of the following: B-Buick, C-Chevrolet (Buffalo), G-Chevrolet gear and axle, K-GM of Canada, M-GM of Canada, O-Oldsmobile or P-Pontiac. Manufacturers code letters B or O, indicate that the wheel bearings are pressed onto the axleshafts whereas all other letters have bearings pressed into the axle tubes and the axleshafts are retained with C-locks.

Following the manufacturer's code letter will be varying numbers which indicate which day of the year that the axle was built. The numbers 1 or 2 following the date code represents day or night shift.

11.1 Removing the snap-rings from the bearing cap surface

11.2 Pressing out the trunnion (cross) using a vise and sockets (one socket should be slightly smaller than the bearing cup and the socket on the other side should be slightly larger)

12.4 The rear axle identification number stamped onto the surface of the right axle tube

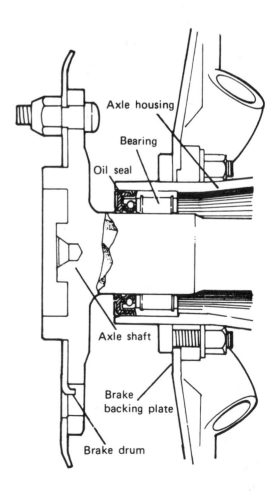

Fig. 8.11 Sectional view of standard (not B and O) rear hub bearing and axleshaft (Sec 13)

13.4 The pinion shaft lock-screw and the pinion shaft being removed from the differential assembly

13.5 The C-lock being withdrawn from the differential

14.2a After the brake components are removed, the oil seal is visible

14.2b The splined end of the axleshaft can be used to pry the seal out of position

13 Axleshaft – removal and installation (except B and O type axles)

1   The following operations apply to rear axles which have the wheel bearings pressed into the ends of the axle casing tubes (third letters of axle code – C, G, K, P, M).
2   Raise the rear of the vehicle and support securely and remove the wheel and brake drum.
3   Unscrew and remove the pressed steel cover from the differential carrier and allow the oil to drain into a suitable container.
4   Unscrew and remove the lock screw from the differential pinion shaft. Remove the pinion shaft (photo).
5   Push the outer (flanged) end of the axleshaft inwards and remove the C-ring from the inner end of the shaft (photo).
6   Withdraw the axleshaft taking care not to damage the oil seal in the end of the axle housing as the splined end of the axleshaft passes through it.
7   Installation is a reversal of removal but tighten the lock screw to the specified torque.
8   Always use a new cover gasket and tighten the cover bolts to the specified torque.
9   Refill the unit with the correct quantity and grade of lubricant.

14.3 The new seal should be driven into place, flush with the axle casing

14 Axleshaft oil seal – replacement (except B and O type axles)

1 Remove the axleshaft as described in the preceding Section.
2 Pry out the old oil seal from the end of the axle casing, using a large screwdriver or the inner end of the axleshaft itself as a lever (photos).
3 Apply high melting point grease to the oil seal recess and tap the seal into position so that the lips are facing inwards and the metal face is visible from the end of the axle housing. When correctly installed, the face of the oil seal should be flush with the end of the axle casing (photo).
4 Installation of the axleshaft is as described in the preceding Section.

15 Axleshaft bearing – replacement (except B and O type axles)

1 Remove the axleshaft (Section 14) and the oil seal (Section 15).
2 A bearing extractor will now be required or a tool made up which will engage behind the bearing.
3 Attach a slide hammer and extract the bearing from the axle casing.

4 Clean out the bearing recess and drive in the new bearing using a piece of tubing *applied against the outer bearing track.* Lubricate the new bearing with gear lubricant. Make sure that the bearing is tapped in to the full depth of its recess and that the numbers on the bearing are visible from the outer end of the casing.
5 Discard the old oil seal and install a new one and install the axleshaft.

16 Axleshaft – removal, overhaul and installation (B and O type)

Note: *Design specifications allow for a maximum of 0.020 (0.018 on 1974-1977), inches of end play on the axle shaft. If shaft end plate is excessive it will be necessary to replace the shaft bearing and seals.*
1 To check for excessive end play, jack up the car and remove the wheel and the brake drum. Attach a dial gauge with its stem against the shaft's end flange. Move the shaft in and out by hand. If the play exceeds the maximum, the shaft bearing is probably worn.
2 To remove the shaft, unbolt the nuts that hold the retaining plates to the brake backing plates. Pull the retainers clear of the backing plates and reinstall 2 opposite nuts (finger-tight) to hold the backing plate in position.
3 Attach a slide hammer to the wheel mounting studs and withdraw the shaft. Do not attempt to pull the shaft by hand, you'll pull the

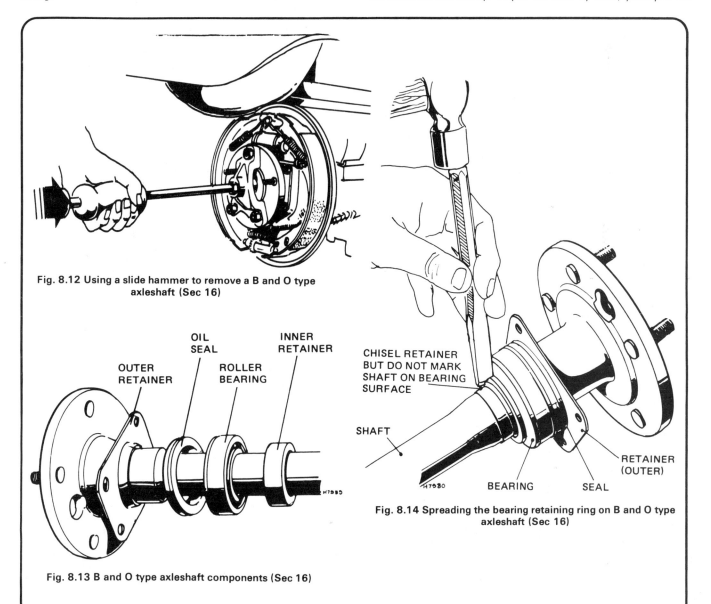

Fig. 8.12 Using a slide hammer to remove a B and O type axleshaft (Sec 16)

OUTER RETAINER   OIL SEAL   ROLLER BEARING   INNER RETAINER

Fig. 8.13 B and O type axleshaft components (Sec 16)

CHISEL RETAINER BUT DO NOT MARK SHAFT ON BEARING SURFACE

SHAFT   BEARING   SEAL   RETAINER (OUTER)

Fig. 8.14 Spreading the bearing retaining ring on B and O type axleshaft (Sec 16)

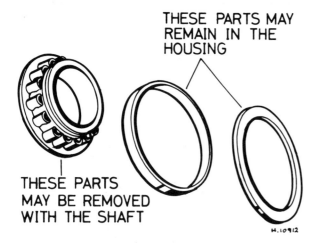

THESE PARTS MAY REMAIN IN THE HOUSING

THESE PARTS MAY BE REMOVED WITH THE SHAFT

H.10912

Fig. 8.15 Axle-bearing components on B and O type axleshaft (Sec 16)

vehicle off the jack stands.

4 Both the shaft bearing and the bearing retainer ring are fitted to the shaft with a heavy press and both must be removed to replace the seal. Tighten the shaft in a vise so that the retainer ring rests on the vise jaws. Using a cold chisel and a hammer, crack the ring in two places. This will spread the ring so that it will slide off the shaft. Take care not to score the shaft. Do not try to torch the ring off as this will ruin the temper of the shaft.

5 Using a suitable press, extract the bearing from the shaft.

6 Remove and discard the seal.

7 Reinstall the retainer plate on the shaft. Put a small amount of grease between the lips of the seal and install the seal. Press on the bearing and the retaining ring against it.

8 Apply gear lubricant to the splines at the inner end of the shaft and put bearing grease on the bearing end and the bearing recess in the axle housing tube.

9 Insert the axleshaft through the housing. You'll be able to feel when the splines on the shaft contact the differential side gears. You may have to turn the shaft back and forth a bit, while pushing, to get it seated. If the shaft cannot be pushed fully into position, use a soft-faced mallet and strike the end flange a couple of times to seat the shaft.

10 Bolt the retainer plate the the backing plate, install the drake drum and wheel.

---

17 Pinion oil seal (all axles) – replacement

1 Place the vehicle over an inspection pit or raise the rear end to provide adequate working clearance.

2 Disconnect the driveshaft as described in Section 10 and tie it to the body sideframe. Do not allow it to slide out of the transmission.

3 Using a torque wrench check the torque required to rotate the pinion and record this for use later.

4 Scribe or dot punch alignment marks on the pinion stem, nut and flange so that they can be refitted in the same relative position.

5 Count the number of threads visible between the end of the nut and the end of the pinion stem and record for use later.

6 A suitable tool must now be used to hold the pinion flange quite still while the self-locking pinion nut is removed. This can easily be made by drilling two holes at the end of a length of flat steel bar and bolting it to the frame.

7 Unscrew and remove the pinion nut.

8 Withdraw the companion flange. If this is tight, use a two or three legged extractor engaged behind the flange. On no account attempt to lever behind the deflector or to hammer on the end of the pinion stem.

9 Pry out the old seal and discard it.

10 Lubricate the lips of a new seal with extreme pressure lithium based grease and tap it into position making sure that it enters the housing squarely and to its full depth.

11 Align the mating marks made before dismantling and install the companion flange. If necessary, use a piece of tubing as a spacer and

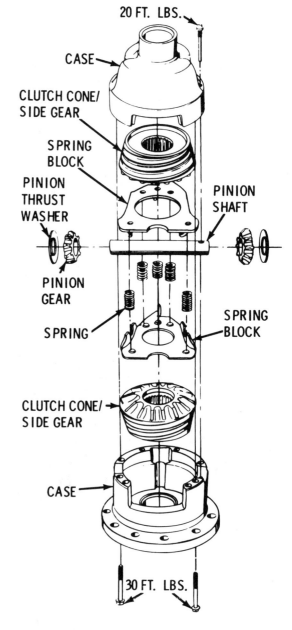

20 FT. LBS.

CASE

CLUTCH CONE/ SIDE GEAR

SPRING BLOCK

PINION THRUST WASHER

PINION SHAFT

PINION GEAR

SPRING

SPRING BLOCK

CLUTCH CONE/ SIDE GEAR

CASE

30 FT. LBS.

Fig. 8.16 Cone-type limited slip differential (Sec 18)

screw on the pinion nut to force the flange fully home on the stem. *On no account, attempt to hammer the flange home.*

12 Smear a non-hardening jointing compound on the ends of the splines which are visible in the center of the companion flange so that any oil seepage will be sealed in.

13 Install the thrust-washer and nut but tighten the nut carefully so that the original number of threads is exposed.

14 Now measure the torque required to rotate the pinion and tighten the nut fractionally until the figure compares with that recorded before dismantling. In order to compensate for the drag of the new oil seal, the nut should be further tightened so that the rotational torque of the pinion exceeds that recorded before dismantling by between 1 and 5 lbf-in. The rotational torque (pinion bearing preload) is normally between 15 and 30 lb-in with new bearings and 10 and 15 lb-in with bearings which have been in service.

15 Reconnect the driveshaft, install the brake drum and wheel and lower the vehicle.

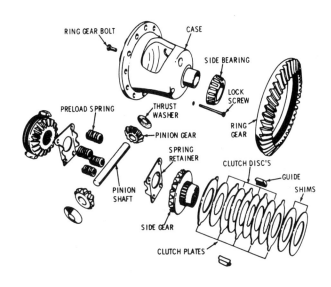

Fig. 8.17 'P' type limited slip rear axle (Sec 18)

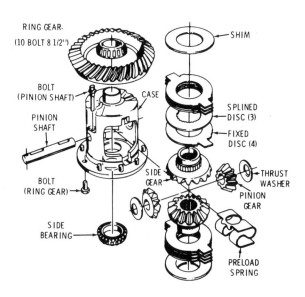

Fig. 8.18 Disc-type limited slip rear axle (Sec 18)

18 Positraction (limited slip) type axles – description, testing and precautions

1   This type of axle incorporates a special type of differential unit. Essentially the device provides more driving force to the wheel with traction when one wheel begins to spin.

2   Two types of assembly are used, one having clutch plates and the other having cones. Some makes of Positraction are not repairable and in the event of a fault occurring or wear developing, the complete assembly must be replaced.

3   An on-vehicle check can be carried out in the following way. If equipped with manual transmission, shift into 'Neutral'.

4   Raise the rear of the vehicle until the wheels are off the ground. Remove one wheel.

5   Using a suitable adaptor connect a torque wrench to the axleshaft flange. Alternatively, a spring balance can be used.

6   Have an assistant hold the wheel still in position on the opposite hub quite firmly to prevent it from rotating, then measure the torque required to start the axleshaft (opposite to the one to which the torque wrench is attached) moving. A minimum of 40 lb-ft should be required for an axle which has seen considerable service and 70 lb-ft for a new, or nearly new assembly.

7   Always use fluid lubricant for topping up a Positraction type axle.

8   Never run the engine when one rear wheel is off the ground as the vehicle may obtain traction through the remaining wheel and jump off the jacks or support stands.

19 Rear axle assembly – removal and installation

1   Raise the rear of the vehicle and support it securely on stands placed under the body frame rails.

2   Position an adjustable floor jack under the differential housing and just take up the weight. Do not raise sufficiently to take the weight of the vehicle from the frame stands.

3   Disconnect the lower shock absorber mountings (Chapter 11).

4   Remove the driveshaft.

5   Remove the rear wheels and brake drums. See Chapter 9 for information if difficulty is experienced in removing the brake drums.

6   Disconnect the hydraulic brake lines from their clips on the axle housing.

7   Unbolt and remove the differential cover, allowing the fluid to drain into a suitable container.

8   Remove the axleshafts as described in Section 13 or Section 16 of this Chapter, depending on type.

9   Depending on axle type, unbolt the brake backing plates, carefully withdraw the brake assemblies and wire them up to the frame without bending the hydraulic pipes or disconnecting them.

10 Remove the leaf springs as described in Chapter 11.

11 Withdraw the axle assembly from under the vehicle.

12 Installation is a reversal of removal but tighten all suspension bolts and nuts to the specified torque (refer to Chapters 9 and 11). Fill the axle assembly with the proper grade and amount of lubricant (see Specifications, this Chapter, and Chapter 1).

Chapter 9 Braking system

Contents

Specifications

System type .... Four wheel hydraulic, dual circuit. All models, 1974 through 1980 have front disc brakes as standard with rear drum brakes. Optional four-wheel disc brakes were available from 1977 through 1980.

Drum size

1974 through 1980 (except 1976)	9.5 x 2 in
1976	11 x 2 in

Refinishing data (drums)

Maximum refinish internal diameter	9.560 in
Wear limit	9.590 in
Maximum out-of-round	0.002 in

Refinishing data (rotors)

	original	refinish	wear limit
Front rotor thickness	1.040 in	0.980 in	0.965 in
Rear rotor thickness	0.974 in	0.921 in	0.9055 in
Maximum thickness variation	0.0005 in		
Maximum runout (warp)	0.004 in		

Torque specifications

	ft-lb	in-lb
Master cylinder-to-dash		
1974 through 1977	24	
1978 through 1980	15	
Master cylinder-to-booster	24	
Booster-to-dash		
1974 through 1977	24	
1978	13	
1979 and 1980	15	
Bleeder valves		
1974 through 1977	5	
1978 through 1980		140
Wheel cylinder-to-flange		15
Caliper mounting bolt	35	
Flexible hose-to-caliper		
1974 through 1976	22	
1977 and 1978	32	
1979 and 1980	18	
Shield-to-steering knuckle		
1974 through 1977	10	
1978 through 1980		120
Brake hose-to-caliper		
1974 through 1977	22	
1978 through 1980	32	

1 General description

The hydraulic system comprises two separate front and rear circuits.

The master cylinder is of tandem type with separate reservoirs for two circuits and in the event of a leak or failure in one hydraulic braking circuit, the other circuit will remain fully operative. A visual warning of circuit failure or air in the system is given by a warning lamp activated by displacement of the piston in the brake distribution (pressure differential warning) switch from its normal 'in balance' position.

The parking brake operates mechanically to the rear brakes only. It is operated by a foot operated pedal to the left of the steering column.

A combination valve is fitted into the hydraulic circuit and provides the following three services:

Metering valve: This prevents the front disc brakes from operating until the rear shoes have contacted the drum.

Failure warning switch: This switch operates if either front or rear brakes fail to operate and a dash warning lamp then operates.

Proportioner: This reduces rear brake system pressure during rapid deceleration, reducing the tendency for rear wheel skidding.

A power brake booster, which utilizes engine manifold vacuum and atmosphere pressure to provide assistance to the hydraulically operated brakes, is available as an option.

All brakes are self adjusting.

2 Maintenance and inspection

1   See Chapter 1 for maintenance and inspection procedures

3 Drum brakes – lining inspection and replacement

1   Jack up the rear of the vehicle and remove the roadwheel. Fully release the parking brake.
2   Mark the position of the brake drum in relation to one of the wheel studs so that the drum can be installed in the same relative attitude.
3   Remove the brake drums. If the brake drums are stuck tight due to severe wear (causing the shoes to be 'locked' in grooves in the drum interior) and cannot be removed by gently tapping with a soft faced hammer or hardwood block, then the lanced area of the brake drum must be chiselled or knocked out. Rotate the drum until the adjuster lever can be released from the sprocket by pulling it outwards with a thin rod inserted through the aperture. The sprocket can then be backed-off to release the drum. **Note:** *If the lanced area in the drum is knocked out, ensure that all metal is removed from the brake compartment. Install a metal hole cover afterwards to prevent contamination of the brakes.*
4   Brush away any accumulations of dust, taking great care not to inhale it as it contains asbestos and is injurious to health.
5   Inspect the thickness of the friction material. If it has worn down to within $\frac{1}{32}$ in of the lining rivets or the metal backing plate of the shoe, then the shoes must be replaced (photo). It is recommended that new or factory exchange shoes are obtained rather than attempt to reline the old ones yourself. Perform work on one brake assembly at a time, using the other side for reference.
6   Unhook the brake shoe pull-back springs from the anchor pin and link end (photos).
7   Remove the actuator return spring, the link, the hold-down pins and the springs (photo).
8   Remove the actuator assembly but do not dismantle unless parts are broken.

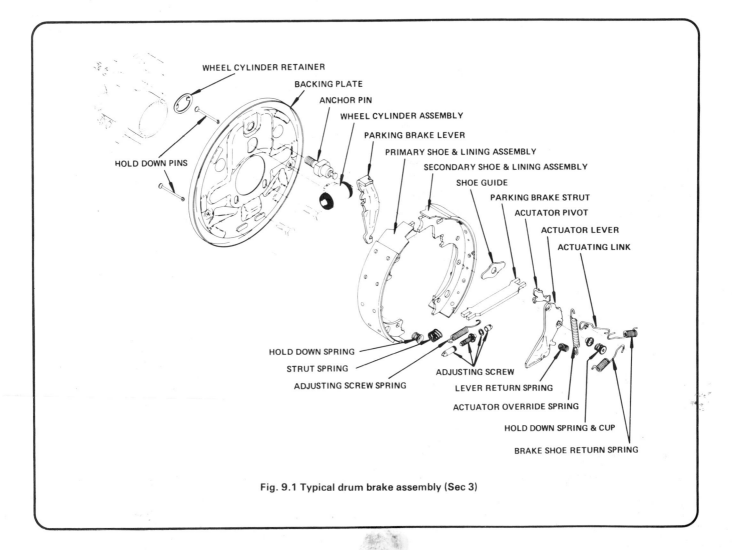

Fig. 9.1 Typical drum brake assembly (Sec 3)

3.5 Measuring the thickness of the brake shoe lining

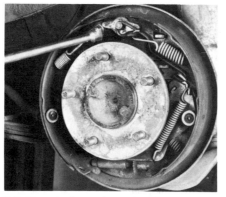

3.6a Use a brake service tool to disconnect the return spring for the primary brake shoe (a screwdriver can be used to pry the spring loose)

3.6b The return spring for the secondary (rear) shoe also has a stiff wire link

3.7 To remove anchor spring assemblies, compress the spring and then turn the end of the pin at the center of the spring

3.9 The primary shoe is held to the secondary shoe by a spring located just behind the adjusting "starwheel"

3.10a Removing the parking brake strut which runs between the shoes, behind the axle flange (pay attention to how it is installed)

3.10b Pliers are used to disconnect the secondary shoe from the parking brake cable

3.14 After lubricating the parking brake cable, pull back the spring and connect the lever

3.15a Grease should be applied to the raised portions of the backing plate to prevent squeaks (these areas contact the brake shoes)

3.15b Grease is also applied to the anchor pin

3.15c The adjustment "starwheel" should be lubricated to ensure easy adjustment

3.19a The actuating spring is located just ahead of the parking brake lever

9   Separate the brake shoes. This is achieved by removing the adjustment screw and spring. If the shoes are to be re-installed, mark the positions in which they are fitted (photo).

10 Remove the parking brake lever from the secondary brake shoe (photos).

11 If there is any sign of hydraulic oil leakage at the wheel cylinders, the cylinder should be replaced or overhauled.

12 Check the flange plate attaching bolts for tightness. Clean any rust and dirt from the shoe contact faces on the flange plate.

13 When installing, ensure that no grease or oil contact the linings and that they are free from nicks and burrs.

14 Lubricate the parking brake cable and the fulcrum end of the parking brake lever with brake lube. Attach the lever to the secondary shoe and ensure that it moves freely (photo).

15 Put a smear of brake lube on the contact point of the pads and flange plate, and the threads of the brake adjusting screw (photos).

16 Connect the brake shoes together with the adjusting screw spring, then place the screw, socket and nut in position. **Note:** *Adjusting screws are marked 'L' or 'R' (left or right side of vehicle). The sprocket (star-wheel) should only be installed next to the secondary shoe and the adjusting screw spring inserted to prevent interference with the sprocket. Ensure that the sprocket lines up with the adjusting hole in the flange plate.*

17 Connect the parking brake cable to the lever.

18 Secure the primary shoe (short lining forward) first with the hold down pin and spring using pliers, and at the same time engage the shoes with the wheel cylinder connecting links.

19 Install the actuator assembly and secondary shoe with the hold down pin and spring using needle-nosed pliers. Position the parking brake strut and strut spring (photo).

20 Install the guide plate over the anchor pin, then install the wire link. The wire link is connected to the actuator assembly first then placed over the anchor pin stud while holding the adjuster assembly fully down (photo).

21 Install the actuator return spring, easing it in place with a screwdriver or similar tool.

22 Hook the pull back springs into the shoes then install the spring from the primary shoe over the anchor pin and then the spring from the secondary shoe over the wire link end (photo).

23 Ensure that the actuating lever functions by moving it by hand, then turn the sprocket back $1\frac{1}{4}$ turns to retract the shoes (photos).

24 Install the drum and roadwheel, ensuring that the drum locating tang is in line with the locating lobe in the hub.

25 Lower the vehicle to the ground.

26 Make numerous forward and reverse stops to finally adjust the brakes, until a satisfactory pedal action results.

4   Disc pads – inspection and replacement

1   At the intervals specified in Chapter 1, remove the front road-wheels and inspect the thickness of the pad material remaining. Check the ends of the outboard shoes by looking in at each end of the caliper. The inboard shoe can be checked by looking down through the inspection hole at the top of the caliper. Pads should be replaced when they are worn down to $\frac{1}{32}$ inch thickness over the rivet heads.

2   In addition to the visual inspection, all models are equipped with an audible warning device which will indicate that the disc pads have worn down to their safe limit. The device is essentially a spring steel tang which emits a squeal by rubbing on the disc when the friction material has worn down to 0.030 in.

3   To replace the disc pads, first check that the brake fluid reservoir is no more than $\frac{1}{3}$ full. Siphon off fluid above this level and discard it. **Note:** *To replace the rear disc pads on a 4-wheel disc system, refer to Section 7 for disc caliper removal.*

4   Raise the front end of the vehicle and remove the wheels. Perform disc pad replacement on one brake brake assembly at a time, using the assembled brake for reference if necessary.

5   Push the piston back into its bore. If necessary a C-clamp can be used but a flat bar will usually do the job. As the piston is depressed to the bottom of the caliper bore, so the fluid in the master cylinder reservoir will rise. Ensure that it does not overflow.

6   Using an Allen key remove the 2 mounting bolts which attach the caliper to the support, then lift off the caliper (photo).

7   Remove the shoes, then position the caliper so that the brake hose will not have to support the caliper weight. If the disc pads are to be

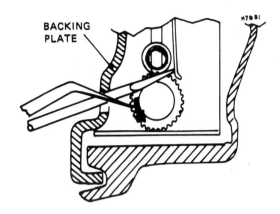

Fig. 9.2 Adjusting brake shoes inward to remove a stuck brake drum (Sec 3)

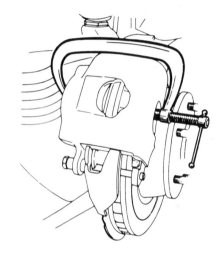

Fig. 9.3 Using a 'C' clamp to depress the caliper piston (Sec 4)

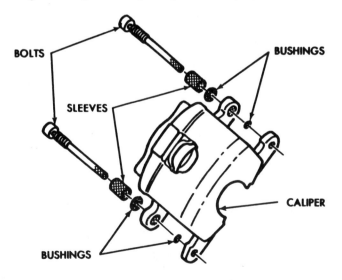

BOLTS

BUSHINGS

SLEEVES

CALIPER

BUSHINGS

▓ LUBRICATE AREAS INDICATED

Fig. 9.4 Caliper lubrication points (Sec 4)

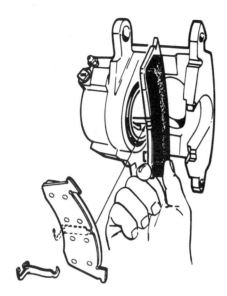

Fig. 9.5 Installing disc shoe support spring (Sec 4)

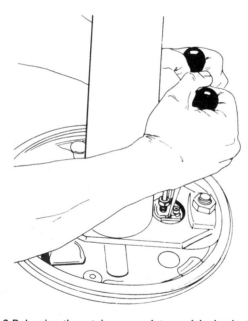

Fig. 9.6 Releasing the retainers on a late-model wheel cylinder (Sec 5)

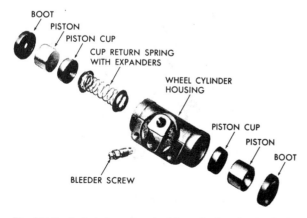

Fig. 9.7 Exploded view of typical drum brake wheel cylinder (Sec 5)

re-installed, mark their position (photo).

8   Remove the shoe support spring from the piston.

9   Remove the 2 sleeves from the inboard ears of the caliper.

10   Remove the 4 rubber bushings from the grooves in each caliper ear (photo).

11   Clean the holes and bushing grooves in the caliper ears.

12   Examine the inside of the caliper for signs of fluid leakage. If evident, the caliper should be overhauled.

13   When installing, ensure that the caliper is clean and that the dust boot is undamaged.

14   Lubricate new sleeves, rubber bushings, bushing grooves and the end of the mounting bolts using Delco Silicone Lube or equivalent.

15   Install the rubber bushings on the caliper ears (photo).

16   Install the sleeves to the inboard ears so that the end towards the shoe is flush with the machine surface of the ear.

17   Install the shoe support spring and inboard shoe in the center off the piston cavity. Push down until the shoe is flat against the caliper.

18   Position the outboard shoe in the caliper with the ears at the top of the shoe over the caliper ears and the tab at the bottom of the shoe engaged in the caliper cutout. If equipped with wear sensor, it will go towards the rear of the caliper (photo).

19   With the shoes installed, lift up the caliper and rest the bottom edge of the outboard lining on the outer edge of the disc to make sure that no clearance exists between the tab at the bottom and the caliper abutment.

20   Position the caliper over the disc, lining up the holes in the caliper ears and mounting bracket.

21   Install the mounting bolts, ensuring that they pass under the retaining ears of the inboard shoe and through the holes in the outboard shoe and caliper ears, then into the mounting bracket.

22   Torque-tighten the mounting bolts to 35 ft-lb.

23   Pump the brake pedal to seat the linings on the disc then bend the upper ears of the outboard shoe until no radial clearance exists between the shoe and the caliper housing.

24   Install the front wheel and lower the vehicle.

25   Service the other side using the same procedures.

26   Add brake fluid to the master cylinder reservoir until it is $\frac{1}{4}$ inch from the top.

26   Pump the brake pedal several times until a satisfactory pedal action is obtained then top up the master cylinder reservoir again (if necessary).

---

5   Wheel cylinder (drum brake) — removal, overhaul and installation

---

1   Raise the vehicle and remove the wheel.

2   Remove the brake drum. See 'Note' in Section 3.

3   Clean around the hydraulic connection to the wheel cylinder then disconnect the line. Plug the end of the line to prevent fluid loss and dirt contamination.

4   Remove the brake shoe pull-back springs.

5   Remove the cylinder-to-flange plate securing screws and disengage the pushrods from the brake shoes. Remove the cylinder (photo). On late models, the cylinder is attached by retainers. Two sharp awls must be used to release the tabs (see Fig. 9.6).

6   Using pliers, remove the boots from the cylinder and discard them.

7   Remove and discard the piston cups.

8   Inspect the cylinder bore and pistons for corrosion and pitting. Discard if pitted, but where there is staining, the surface may be polished with crocus cloth working around the circumference (not along the length).

9   Ensure your hands are clean, dry and free from grease, gasoline, kerosene or cleaning solvents then clean the metal parts in new brake fluid or denatured alcohol.

10   Shake off the surplus fluid for ease of handling.

11   Lubricate the cylinder with clean brake fluid and insert the spring expander assembly.

12   Insert new cups which must be clean and dry and **not** lubricated. The flat surface must be forward to enter ends of the cylinder. Use only the fingers to manipulate the cups.

13   Install the pistons, flat surface uppermost. **Do not** lubricate them before installation.

14   Press new boots into the cylinder counterbores. **Do not** lubricate them before installation.

15   When installing the wheel cylinder, position the wheel cylinder on

Labels on Fig. 9.7:
BOOT
PISTON
PISTON CUP
CUP RETURN SPRING WITH EXPANDERS
WHEEL CYLINDER HOUSING
PISTON CUP
PISTON
BOOT
BLEEDER SCREW

3.19b The parking brake strut has recesses in it to fit in the brake shoe cutouts

3.20 Use the brake tool or a screwdriver to force the wire link over the anchor pin

3.22 The installed position of the primary shoe return spring

3.23a The adjusting mechanism sprocket is specifically designed for either right-hand or left-hand operation. Do not mix from side to side

3.23b The brakes are adjusted by lifting the lever away from the sprocket and turning the adjusting mechanism (the brakes do this automatically when the car goes into 'Reverse')

4.6 An Allen head wrench is needed to remove the caliper mounting bolts from the inboard side

4.7 Once the caliper is removed from the rotor, the pads are easily pulled from the caliper

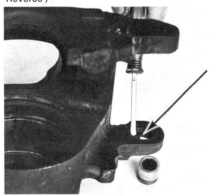

4.10 Rubber sleeves are located inside grooves and can be pried out with a screwdriver for replacement

4.15 Lubricate the caliper bushings and push them into position

4.18 The outboard shoe is installed with its flange in the caliper cutout area

5.5 The two screws which mount the wheel cylinder are located on the inboard side of the backing plate (early models only)

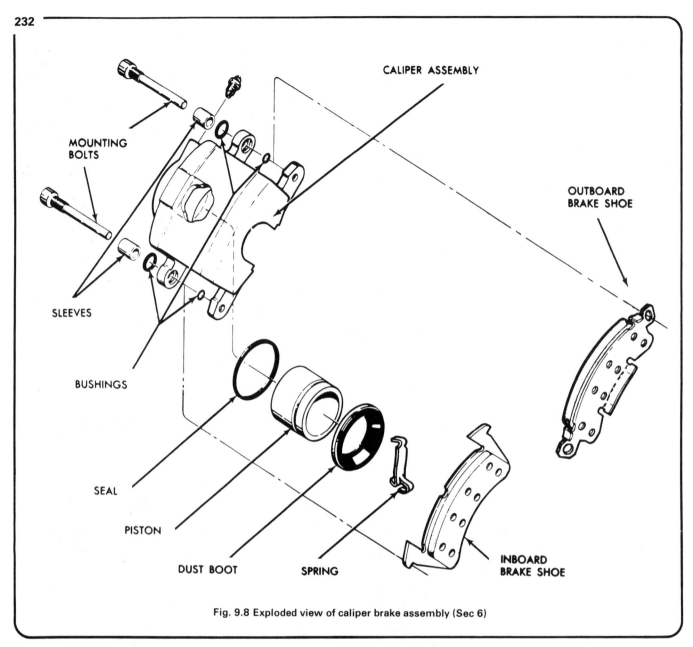

MOUNTING
BOLTS

CALIPER ASSEMBLY

OUTBOARD
BRAKE SHOE

SLEEVES

BUSHINGS

SEAL

PISTON

DUST BOOT

SPRING

INBOARD
BRAKE SHOE

Fig. 9.8 Exploded view of caliper brake assembly (Sec 6)

6.11 The piston boot should be installed in the groove, with the fold
toward the open end of the piston

6.12 Forcing the piston back into the caliper

the brake flange plate and install screws loosely. If equipped with locking tabs instead of mounting screws, follow this procedure:

    a) *Hold the wheel cylinder against the backing plate by inserting a wood block between the cylinder and the axle flange*

    b) *Press a new retaining clip over the wheel cylinder with the tabs away from and horizontal to the backing plate. Use a 1 - $\frac{1}{8}$ in, 12-point socket to firmly lock the retainer. Both tabs should be fully engaged*

16 Install the pushrods and pull-back springs, then connect the hydraulic line to the cylinder, moving the cylinder as necessary to prevent stripping the threads.

17 Tighten the cylinder mounting screws.

18 Install the brake drum and wheel.

19 Bleed the braking system (Section 10) then lower the vehicle to the ground.

6   Disc caliper – overhaul

1   Remove the disc pads as described in Section 4. Disconnect the brake flexible hose from the rigid brake line at the support bracket. Cap the line to prevent loss of fluid.

2   Unbolt and remove the caliper (also as described in Section 4) complete with flexible hose. Unscrew the hose from the caliper noting the copper sealing gaskets which should be replaced with new ones when the hose is reconnected.

3   To disassemble, clean the exterior of the caliper using brake fluid (never use gasoline, kerosene or cleaning solvents) then place the assembly on a clean workbench.

4   Drain the fluid from the caliper and then place a cloth pad between the caliper piston and body then apply air pressue to the fluid inlet hole to free the piston; a small hand pump is adequate. If this method proves unsuccessful at dislodging the piston, hydraulic fluid pressure must be used. With the brake pads removed, reconnect the caliper to the brake line on the vehicle and have an assistant slowly depress the brake pedal. The fluid will force the piston out of its bore. Be careful that the piston is not damaged.

5   Carefully pry the dust boot out of the caliper bore.

6   Using a small piece of wood or plastic, remove the piston seal from its groove in the caliper piston bore. Metal objects may cause bore damage.

7   Remove the caliper bleeder valve, then remove and discard the sleeves and bushings from the caliper ears. Also discard all rubber parts.

8   Clean the remaining parts in brake fluid. Allow them to drain and then shake them vigorously to remove as much fluid as possible.

9   Carefully examine the piston for scoring, nicks and burrs and loss of plating. If surface defects are present, parts must be replaced. Check the caliper bore in a similar way, but light polishing with crocus cloth is permissible to remove light corrosion and stains. Discard the mounting bolts if they are corroded or damaged.

10 When assembling, lubricate the piston bores and seal with clean brake fluid; position the seal in the caliper bore groove.

11 Lubricate the piston with clean brake fluid then assemble a new boot in the piston groove with the fold towards the open end of the piston (photo).

12 Insert the piston squarely into the caliper bore then apply force to bottom the piston in the bore (photo).

13 Position the dust boot in the caliper counterbore then use a suitable drift to drive it into its location (GM tool no J-22904 is available for this purpose). Ensure that the boot is installed below the caliper face and evenly all round.

14 Install the bleeder screw.

15 The remainder of the procedure for installation is the reverse of the removal procedure. Always use new copper gaskets when connecting the brake hose and finally bleed the system of air (Section 10).

7   Disc caliper (rear) – removal

Note: *Steps 6 and 9 are unnecessary if the caliper is being removed for overhaul. These steps can be done when the caliper unit is on the bench.*

1   Drain 2/3 of the fluid from the reserve chamber of the master cylinder for the rear. Be careful not to spill any brake fluid on the

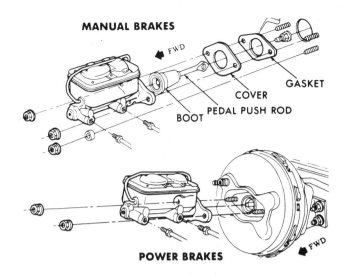

Fig. 9.9 Typical master cylinder mounting (Sec 8)

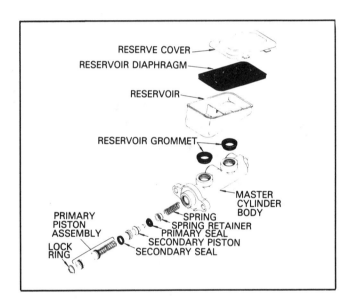

Fig. 9.10 Exploded view of a typical power brake master cylinder (Sec 8)

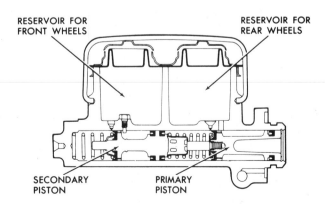

Fig. 9.11 Typical hydraulic system in a master cylinder (Sec 8)

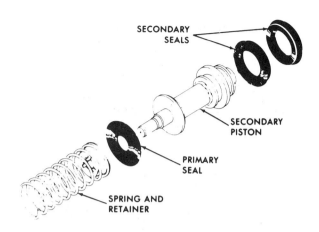

Fig. 9.12 Exploded view of a Delco secondary piston (Sec 8)

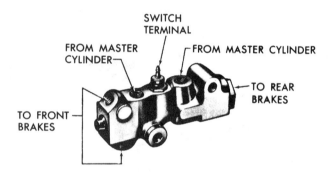

Fig. 9.13 Combination valve and switch (Sec 10)

finished surfaces of the automobile.

2   Jack up the car and remove the rear wheel. Mark the positioning between the wheel and the axle flange. Reinstall one of the wheel nuts–flat side to rotor–to keep the rotor in the proper position.

3   Loosen tension on the parking brake cable at the equalizer bracket. Do this by grasping the cable stud with a pair of vise-type pliers and loosening the nut with a wrench.

4   Remove the cable from the parking brake lever at the wheel.

5   Remove the spring and conduit bracket on rear disc assembly by compressing the prongs.

6   Holding the lever-arm in place, remove the lock nut, lever, lever seal, anti-friction washer, and return spring. Clean away any dirt in the area of the lever seal.

7   Use a "C" clamp with a minimum opening of seven inches; put the firm end of the clamp on the lever-stop and the screw end on the back of the outer lining assembly. Tighten the clamp until the piston bottoms in the unit.

8   Lube the housing surface (located under the lever seal) with silicone. Install a *new* anti-friction washer, *new* lever seal and the lever. Make sure the lever points downward when it is installed on the hex nut.

9   Rotate the lever toward the car's front end and while holding it in this position, install nut and torque to 25 lb-ft. Rotate lever back to original position.

10   Replace the lever return spring and remove "C" clamp.

11   Disconnect the brake line from the caliper and plug the line to prevent fluid loss.

12   Unbolt the caliper and remove it, along with the brake shoes.

13   Once the caliper has been removed from the car, it can be serviced in the same manner as those for the front wheels. Refer to Section 6 for details on this procedure.

8   Master cylinder – removal, overhaul and installation

As many types and sizes of master cylinders were installed on the Regal and Century, it may be wise to take all components with you to the auto parts store for proper fitting.

1   Remove the hydraulic lines at the master cylinder (photo). Collect any fluid spillage with dry cloths and plug the ends of the hydraulic lines to prevent fluid loss or dirt from entering the system.

2   On manual brakes, disconnect the pushrod at the brake pedal inside the car.

3   Unbolt and remove the master cylinder from the firewall or power booster. Be careful that no brake fluid is accidently dripped on any painted surface as it will ruin the finish.

4   Drain all fluid from the master cylinder and place the unit in a vise. Use wood blocks to cushion the jaws of the vise.

5   On manual brakes remove the pushrod retaining ring.

6   Remove the secondary stop bolt from the bottom of the front fluid reservoir (Delco Moraine) or from the base of the master cylinder body (Bendix) (photo).

7   Remove the retaining ring from the groove and take out the primary piston assembly (photo). Following the primary piston out of the bore will be the secondary piston, spring and retainer. A piece of bent stiff wire can be used to draw these assemblies out of the cylinder bore (photo).

Note: *Some models have a removable reservoir which can be pried off the main cylinder body during overhaul.*

8   Examine the inside surface of the master cylinder and the secondary piston. If there is evidence of scoring or 'bright' wear areas, the entire master cylinder should be replaced with a new one.

9   If the components are in good condition, wash in clean hydraulic fluid. Discard all the rubber components and the primary piston. Purchase a rebuild kit which will contain all the necessary parts for the overhaul.

10   Inspect the tube seats which are located in the master cylinder body where the fluid pipes connect. If they appear damaged they should be replaced with new ones which come in the overhaul kit. They are forced out of the body by threading a screw into the tube and then prying outwards (photo). The new ones are forced into place using a spare brake line nut (photo). All parts necessary for this should be included in the rebuild kit.

11   Place the new secondary seals in the grooves of the secondary piston (photo).

12   Assemble the primary seals and seal protector over the end of the secondary piston.

13   Lubricate the cylinder bore and secondary piston with hydraulic fluid (photo). Insert the spring retainer into the spring then place the retainer and spring over the end of the secondary piston (photos). The retainer should locate inside the primary seal lips.

14   With the master cylinder vertical, push the secondary piston into the bore to seat its spring (photo).

15   Coat the seals of the primary piston with brake fluid and fit it into the cylinder bore. Hold it down while the retaining ring is installed in the cylinder groove.

16   Continue to hold the piston down while the stop screw is installed.

17   Install the reservoir diaphragm into the reservoir cover plate making sure it is fully collapsed inside the recessed lid.

18   Install the master cylinder in the reverse order of removal, torque-tightening the attaching nuts to specifications.

19   Fill the master cylinder with fresh brake fluid and bleed the master cylinder and complete hydraulic system as outlined in Section 11.

9   Hydraulic brake hoses – inspection, removal and installation

1   Periodically, examine all hydraulic brake lines, both rigid and flexible, for rusting, chafing and general deterioration. Also check the security of the connections.

2   If the hoses or pipes have to be disconnected, extensive loss of fluid can be avoided if the vent holes in the master cylinder fluid reservoir cap are taped over to create a vacuum.

Drum brakes

3   Using a back-up wrench on the hose fitting, unscrew the connector from the hose fitting.

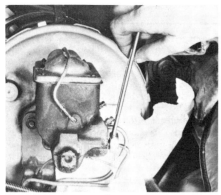

8.1 It is best to use a flare nut wrench to disconnect the hydraulic lines at the master cylinder

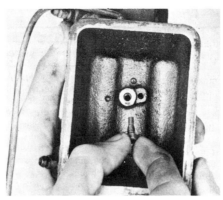

8.6 The stop bolt is located at the bottom of the reservoir

8.7a Depress the piston as the retaining ring is pried free with a screwdriver

8.7b A wire hook can be used to draw out the piston assembly

8.10a After a screw is threaded into the tube seat, two screwdrivers are used to pry the tube seat out of its bore

8.10b A new tube seat being installed

8.11 Fitting the new seals to the secondary piston

8.13a Liberally coat all parts with fresh brake fluid during assembly

8.13b Installing the spring retainer to the end of the spring

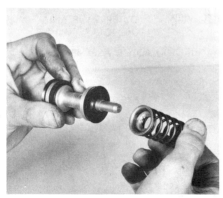

8.13c The spring assembly is then pushed onto the secondary piston assembly

8.14 The piston/spring assembly is then pushed into the master cylinder bore

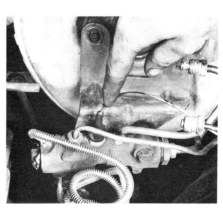

10.1 The combination valve is located just under the master cylinder in most models (the electrical wire is for the dashboard warning light)

4   Remove the U-shaped retainer from the hose fitting, withdraw the hose fitting from the support bracket, turn it out of the wheel cylinder and remove the copper gasket.

5   When installing, use a new copper gasket, moisten the screw threads with brake fluid and torque-tighten to the wheel cylinder.

6   With the weight on the suspension and the wheels 'straight-ahead', insert the female end of the hose through the support bracket, allow it to seek its own position without kinking then install the U-shaped retainer and secure the hose in the bracket.

7   Turn the wheels from lock-to-lock to ensure that the hose does not contact other parts (reposition the female end if necessary).

8   Place the tubular steel connector in the hose fitting and torque-tighten, using a back-up wrench on the hose fitting.

9   Remove the tape from the master cylinder reservoir, top-up with new brake fluid and then bleed the system of air.

Disc brakes

10   To disconnect a rigid line from a flexible hose, unscrew the connector out of the hose end fitting. These connectors are located at the support brackets. Always hold the flexible hose and fitting quite still by using an open-ended wrench.

11   To remove the flexible hose, extract the retainer from the hose and fitting and pull the hose from the support bracket.

12   Remove the hose to caliper bolt, remove the center connector and the hose.

13   Installation is a reversal of removal but always use new copper gaskets in conjunction with the flexible hose end fittings and always let the flexible hose take up its natural curvature; never secure it in a twisted or kinked position.

Rigid lines

14   Rigid lines which need to be replaced can be purchased at many service stations. Take the old pipe as a pattern and make sure that the pipes are fitted with the correct connectors and that the ends are double-flared.

10   Hydraulic system pressure valves and switches

1   On all models a combination distribution block, or combination valve is installed in the hydraulic line (photo). It is located adjacent to the master cylinder or on the inside of the body frame rail and its functions are as follows:

The metering valve holds off full pressure to the front disc brakes until a certain pressure level is reached. This allows the pressure in the rear brake circuit to build up sufficiently to overcome the force of the shoe retracting springs and ensure balanced braking between front and rear wheels.

The warning switch incorporates a piston which normally remains in a central position (in balance) when the front and rear independent hydraulic pressures are equal. In the event of a failure in either circuit, the piston is displaced and completes an electrical circuit through a switch terminal and lights a warning lamp in the vehicle interior.

The proportioning valve limits hydraulic pressure to the rear brakes to prevent them locking before full braking effort is obtained by the front disc brakes.

2   The following tests should be carried out periodically.

Brake warning lamp check

3   Disconnect the electrical lead from the switch terminal and connect the lead to ground.

4   Turn the ignition switch 'ON' and the brake failure warning lamp should light up. If it does not, check for burned out bulb or faulty wiring.

Warning switch operation check

5   The operation of the switch can be checked by switching on the ignition and with the help of an assistant, bleeding first a front caliper and then a rear wheel cylinder as described in the following Section. The warning lamp should light immediately after the bleeder valve is released and heavy pressure applied to the brake foot pedal.

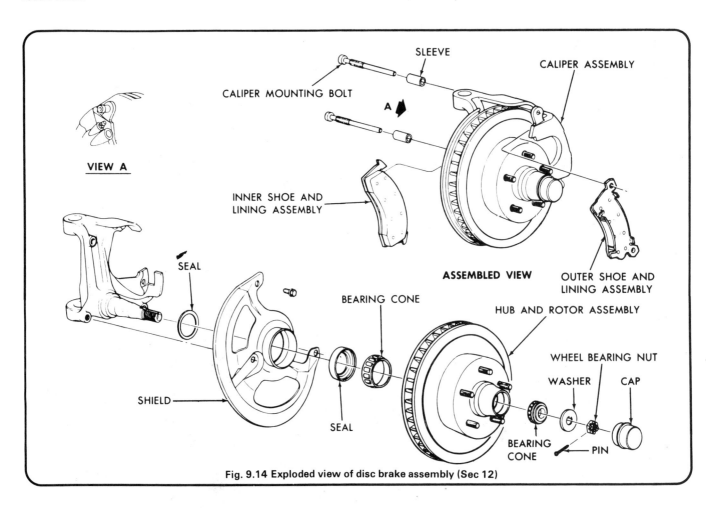

Fig. 9.14 Exploded view of disc brake assembly (Sec 12)

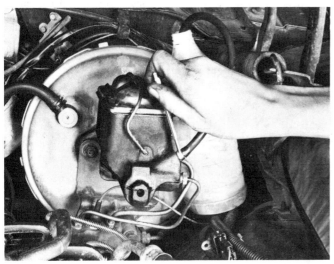

11.4 Most master cylinders are equipped with a bleeder valve (the procedure is the same as for each wheel)

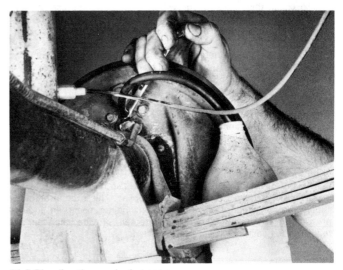

11.5 Bleeding the rear brake system

6   Any fault detected in the switch can only be rectified by replacement of the complete valve/switch assembly.

7   Bleed the hydraulic system (both circuits) on completion as described in the next Section.

11 Hydraulic system – bleeding

Note: *Never allow the hydraulic fluid to come in contact with the paint work of the vehicle as it will ruin the car's finish*

1   Whenever the hydraulic system is disconnected (to remove or install a component) air will enter the fluid lines and bleeding must be carried out. This is not a routine operation and if air enters the system without any repair operations having been carried out, then the cause must be sought and the fault rectified.

2   When applying the foot brake pedal, if the first application causes the pedal to go down further than usual but an immediate second or third application (pumping) reduces the pedal travel and improves the braking effect, this is a sure sign that there is air in the system.

3   Use only clean hydraulic fluid (which has remained unshaken for 24 hours and has been stored in an airtight container) for topping-up the master cylinder reservoirs during the following operations. Make sure that the reservoirs are kept topped-up during the whole of the bleeding operations otherwise air will be drawn into the system and the whole sequence of bleeding will have to be repeated. Where power brakes are fitted, depress the brake pedal several times to destroy any residual vacuum.

4   If the master cylinder is equipped with bleeder valves, do these valves first and then move to the wheel closest to the master cylinder (photo). Proceed to each wheel, working away from the master cylinder.

5   Push a length of hose onto the bleeder valve and then immerse the open end of the hose in a jar containing sufficient brake fluid to keep the end of the hose well covered (photo).

6   Unscrew the bleeder valve $\frac{3}{4}$ turn and have an assistant depress the brake pedal. Just before the pedal reaches the floor, close the bleeder valve and allow the pedal to be released. Bubbles will flow from the tube as air is expelled and the operation must be repeated until the bubbles cease.

7   Repeat the operation on the other front caliper then transfer operations to the rear brakes. At all times remember to maintain the fluid level as stated in paragraph 3.

8   On vehicles equipped with a combination valve the pin in the end of the metering part of the valve must be held in the open position. This can be carried out using the official tool (J 23709) or a similar device clamped under the mounting bolt which should have been temporarily loosened. The pin must be pushed, and held in.

9   If any difficulty is experienced in bleeding the hydraulic system or if the help of an assistant cannot be obtained, a pressure bleeding kit

is a worthwhile investment. If connected in accordance with the makers' instructions, each bleed valve can be opened in turn to allow the system fluid to be pressure ejected until clear of air bubbles without the need to replenish the master cylinder reservoir during the process.

10   If the front or rear hydraulic circuit has been 'broken' beyond the distribution block then only the particular circuit concerned need be bled. If the master cylinder has been removed and replaced or its connecting pipelines, then both circuits must be bled.

12 Disc and drum – inspection and servicing

1   Whenever the disc brake pads are inspected for wear, take the opportunity to check the condition of the disc (rotor) surfaces. Light scoring or grooving is normal but deep grooves or severe erosion are not. Some models have a single deep groove in the rotor called a 'squeal' groove. Do not be fooled into thinking this groove is due to damage.

2   If vibration has been noticed during application of the brake pedal, suspect disc runout.

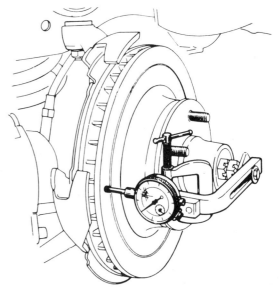

Fig. 9.15 Checking rotor for lateral runout (Sec 12)

3   To check this, a dial gauge will be required or the use of feeler blades between the disc and a fixed point.

4   Turn the disc slowly and check that the runout does not exceed 0.004 in.

5   Sometimes the different wearing characteristics of the disc material may cause it to wear to uneven thickness. Any variation in thickness over 0.0005 in will also cause vibration during brake application.

6   Discs usually have the wear limit and refinish thickness dimensions cast into them.

7   If your dealer cannot refinish a disc to come within the specified tolerances then a new disc must be installed (refer to front suspension, Chapter 11).

8   Whenever a brake drum is removed for lining inspection, check the drum for cracks, scoring or out-of-round.

9   An out-of-round drum will usually give rise to a pulsating feeling of the brake pedal as the brakes are applied. The internal diameter should be checked at several different points using an internal micrometer. Drums can be refinished internally provided the wear and refinish sizes cast into it are not exceeded.

13 Brake pedal – removal and installation

1   Disconnect the battery ground cable.

2   Disconnect the clutch pedal return spring if a manual transmission is fitted.

3   Remove the clip retainer from the pushrod pin which travels through the pedal arm.

4   Remove the nut from the pedal shaft bolt. Slide the shaft out far enough to clear the brake pedal arm.

5   The brake pedal can now be removed, along with the spacer and bushing. The clutch pedal (if equipped) will remain in place.

6   When installing, lubricate the spacer and bushings with brake lube and tighten the pivot nut to specifications.

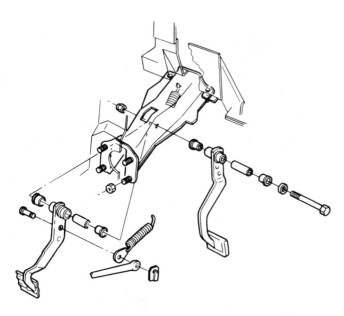

Fig. 9.16 Brake pedal mounting (Sec 13)

14 Stop lamp switch – replacement and adjustment

1   This switch is located on a flange or bracket protruding from the brake pedal support.

2   With the brake pedal in the fully released position, the plunger on the body of the switch should be fully pressed in. When the pedal is pushed in, the plunger releases and sends electrical current to the stop lights at the rear of the car.

3   Electrical contact should be made when the pedal is depressed .38 to .64 inches. If this is not the case, the switch can be adjusted by turning it in or out as required.

4   To replace the switch if it is faulty, disconnect the electrical coupler (two couplers if car is equipped with cruise control) and loosen the switch lock nut until the switch can be unscrewed from the bracket. Installation is a reversal of this procedure.

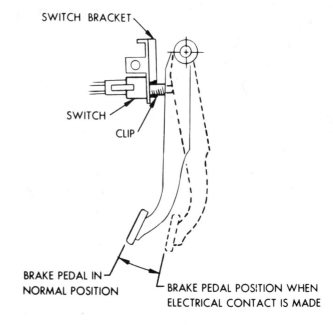

Fig. 9.17 Stoplamp switch (Sec 14)

15 Parking brake – adjustment

1   The adjustment of the parking brake cable may be necessary whenever the rear brake cables have been disconnected or the parking brake cables have stretched due to age and stress.

2   Depress the parking brake pedal exactly two ratchet clicks and then raise the car for access underneath.

3   Tighten the adjusting nut until the left rear tire can just barely be turned in a rearward motion (photo). The tire should be completely locked from moving in a forward rotation.

4   Carefully release the parking brake pedal and check that the tire is able to rotate freely in either direction. It is important that there is no drag on the rear brakes with the pedal released.

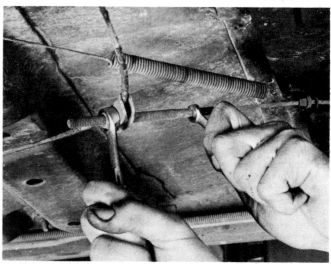

15.3 The parking brake is adjusted from under the car (the threaded rod allows plenty of adjustment)

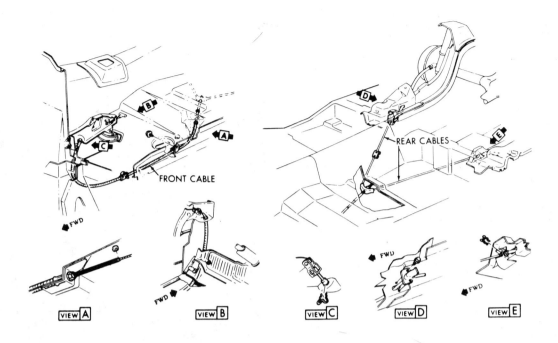

Fig. 9.18 Parking brake assembly (Sec 15)

16 Parking brake pedal – removal and installation

1   Disconnect the battery ground cable and the parking brake warning switch wire.
2   Remove the clip and ball from the clevis (if necessary, the equalizer nut can be slackened).
3   Remove the pedal rear mounting bolt and the nuts from the mounting studs at the front of the dash panel (under the hood).
4   Remove the pedal assembly.
5   Installation is the reverse of the removal procedure, but the nuts and pedal rear mounting bolt must be torque-tightened.

17 Power brake booster – general description

A power brake booster has been an option on all models since its introduction. The booster utilizes vacuum from the engine manifold.
In the event of a fault developing in the booster, enough vacuum is stored to provide sufficient assistance for two or three brake applications and after that the performance of the hydraulic part of the braking system is only affected in so far as the need for higher pedal pressures will be noticed. Alternative types of power brake boosters have been used; these are the Delco-Moraine and the Bendix types. The principle of operation is similar in each case, and the descriptive cycle given in the following paragraph is applicable to both types.
Brakes released: In the 'at rest' condition with the engine running, vacuum is present on both sides of the power piston. Air at atmospheric pressure, entering through the filter behind the push rod, is shut off at the air valve. The floating control valve is held away from the seat in the power piston insert. Any air in the system is drawn through a small passage in the power piston, past the power piston insert valve seat to the insert itself. It then travels through a drilling in the support plate, into the space in front of the power piston then to the intake manifold via a check valve. Vacuum therefore exists on both sides of the power piston which is held against the rear of the housing under spring action.
Brake application: When the pedal is depressed, the push rod carries the air valve away from the floating control valve. The floating control valve will follow until it contacts the raised seat in the power piston insert; vacuum is now shut off to the rear power piston and atmospheric air enters through the filter past the air valve seat and through a passage into the housing at the rear of the power piston. The power piston therefore moves forward to operate the floating piston

assembly of the hydraulic master cylinder. As pressure increases on the end of the master cylinder piston, the hydraulic reaction plate is moved off its seat on the lower piston and contacts the reaction levers. These levers swing on their pivots and bear against the end of the air valve operating rod assembly to provide a feed back (approximately 30% of the master cylinder load) to the pedal. This enables the driver to 'feel' the degree of brake application.
Brake holding: When the desired braking force is achieved the power piston moves forward until the floating control valve again seats on the air valve. The power piston will now remain stationary until there is a change in applied pedal pressure.
Brakes released: When the pedal pressure is released the air valve is forced back to contact the power piston under spring action. As it moves, the floating control valve is pushed off its seat on the power piston insert by the air valve. Atmospheric air is shut off by the air valve seating on the floating control valve. As the floating control cable lifts from its seat, it opens the rear of the power piston to intake manifold vacuum, and the power piston returns to the rear housing.

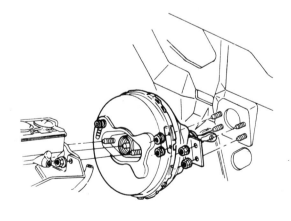

Fig. 9.19 Power brake booster mounting (Sec 17)

The hydraulic pressure in the brake system is released as the floating piston assembly returns to the normal position.

Vacuum failure: In the event of vacuum failure, ie; engine switched off or failure of the vacuum line, application of the brake pedal moves the pedal push rod which in turn contacts the master cylinder push rod and the brakes are applied. This gives a condition as found in the standard braking system, and a correspondingly higher pedal pressure is required.

The power brake unit requires no special maintenance apart from periodic inspection of the hoses and inspection of the air filter beneath the boot at the pedal push rod end.

Dismantling of the power brake unit requires the use of special tools and in the event of a fault developing, it is recommended that a new or factory-exchange unit is fitted rather than attempt to overhaul the original booster.

18 Power brake booster – removal and installation

1   Remove the securing nuts which hold the master cylinder to the power brake unit. Position the master cylinder out of the way, being careful not to strain the hydraulic lines leading to the master cylinder. If there is any doubt as to the flexibility of the fluid lines disconnect them at the cylinder and plug the ends.
2   Disconnect the vacuum hose leading to the front of the power brake booster. Cover the end of the hose.
3   Loosen the four nuts that secure the booster to the firewall. Do not remove these nuts at this time.
4   Inside the car, disconnect the power brake pushrod from the brake pedal. Do not force the pushrod to the side when disconnecting.
5   Now fully remove the four booster mounting nuts and carefully lift the unit out of the engine compartment.

6   When installing, loosely install the four mounting nuts and then connect the pushrod to the brake pedal. Torque-tighten the attaching nuts and reconnect the vacuum hose and master cylinder. If the hydraulic brake fluid lines were disconnected, the master cylinder as well as the entire braking system should be bled to eliminate any air which has entered the system (see Section 11).

18.2 Disconnecting the vacuum hose to the power booster

Chapter 10 Chassis electrical system

Refer to Chapter 13 for information applicable to later models

Contents

Specifications

Wiper motor current

Low speed	6.0 Amps
High speed	4.5 Amps

Light Bulbs

Note: *Bulb numbers are AC brand bulbs (the factory specified replacement bulbs)*

Headlamp	
1974 through 1975	6014
1976 through 1977	
Type 1A	4651
Type 2A	4652
1978 through 1980	6052
Park & directional	
1974 through 1980	1157NA
Side marker lamp	
1974 through 1977	194
1978 through 1980	1157NA
Tail, stop & directional lamp	
1974 through 1980	1157

Back-up lamp
    1974 through 1977 1157
    1978 through 1980
        Regal 1157
        Century 1156
License plate lamp (all) 194
Rear side marker lamp (all) 194
Luggage compartment lamp
    1974 through 1977 89
    1978 through 1980 1003
Speedometer
    1974 through 1977 194
    1978 through 1980 168
Gauges
    1974 through 1977 168
    1978 through 1980 194
Clock
    1974 through 1977 1893
    1978 through 1980 1816
Fuel gauge
    1974 through 1977 194
    1978 through 1980 168
Lights/wiper illumination
    1974 through 1975 161
    1976 through 1977 194
    1978 through 1980 168
High beam indicator (all) 194
Turn signal indicator (all) 194
Telltales (charge, oil pressure, low fuel, brakes, water) 194
Cruise control
    1974 through 1977 1445
    1978 through 1980 161
Turbo lights (1978 through 1980 only) 161
Fasten seatbelt
    1974 through 1977 1893
    1978 through 1980 194
Tailgate ajar (1974 through 1977) 1893
Rear defogger 194
Headlamp "on" (1974 through 1977) 194
Cluster lamps (Oil pressure, fuel economy, brake warning, water temp.)
1974 through 1977 74
Fuel economy (1978 through 1980) 161
Glove box 1891
Radio dial (am – 1974 through 1977) 1893
Radio dial (radio/tape – 1974 through 1977) 564
Radio dial (am/fm and stereo – 1974 through 1977) 216
Radio dial (1978 through 1980) 1893
Ash tray assembly 1445
Map lamp 211-2
Heater/AC
    1974 through 1976 1893
    1977 through 1980 194
Trouble light (under hood) 1004
Stereo indicator 66
Flasher/hazard (1978 through 1980) 562
Vanity mirror 562
Sail Panel lamps (1974 through 1977 Century Custom and Regal
Coupes) .... 211-1 or 212
Dome
    1974 through 1977 .... 211 or 211-1
    1978 through 1980 561
Courtesy
    1974 through 1977 89
    1978 through 1980 906
Dome/reading lamo (all) 212
Reading lamp 1004

1 General description

The electrical system is of the 12 volt, negative ground type.

Power for the lighting system and all electrical accessories is supplied by a lead/acid type battery which is charged by an alternator.

This chapter covers repair and service procedures for the various lighting and electrical components not associated with the engine. Information on the battery, alternator, voltage regulator and starter motor can be found in Chapter 5.

It should be noted that whenever portions of the electrical system are worked on, the negative battery cable should be disconnected to prevent electrical shorts and/or fires.

2 Fuses

1 The electrical circuits of the car are protected by a combination of fuses, circuit breakers and fusible links.

2 The fuse panel or fuse box is located in most models underneath

the dashboard, on the left side of the vehicle. It is easily accessible for fuse inspection or replacement without completely removing the box from its mounting.

3   Each of the fuses is designed to protect a specific circuit, and the various circuits are identified on the fuse panel itself.

4   If an electrical component has failed, your first check should be the fuse. A fuse which has 'blown' can be readily identified by inspecting the element inside the glass tube. If this metal element is broken, the fuse is inoperable and must be replaced with a new one.

5   When removing and installing fuses it is important that metal objects are not used to pry the fuse in or out of the holder. Plastic fuse pullers are available for this purpose.

6   It is also important that the correct fuse be installed. The different electrical circuits need varying amounts of protection, indicated by the amperage rating on the fuse. See the Specifications Section of this Chapter for the correct amperage needs of each circuit.

7   At no time should the fuse be bypassed by using metal or foil. Serious damage to the electrical system could result.

8   If the replacement fuse immediately fails do not replace again until the cause of the problem is isolated and corrected. In most cases this will be a short circuit in the wiring system caused by a broken or deteriorated wire.

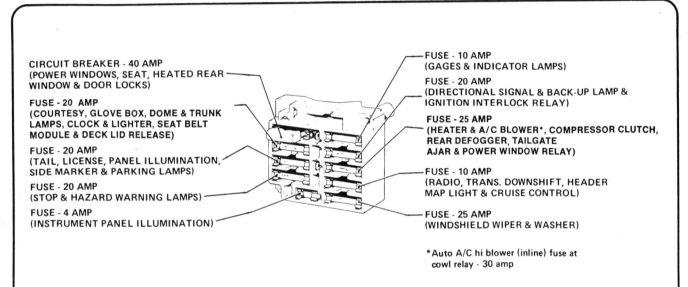

Fig. 10.1 Typical fuse block – 1974 through 1977 (Sec 2)

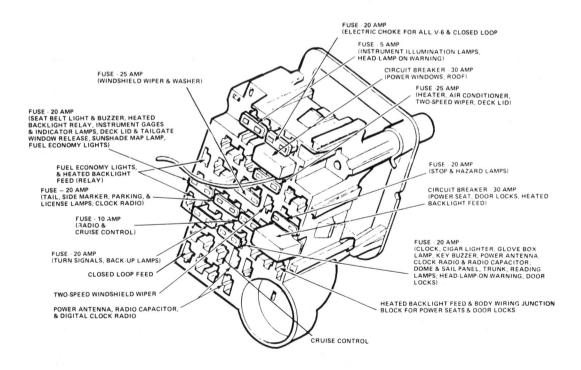

Fig. 10.2 Typical fuse block – 1978 through 1980 (Sec 2)

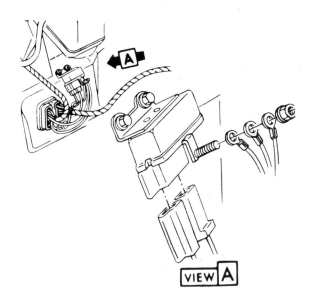

Fig. 10.3 Typical horn relay (Sec 6)

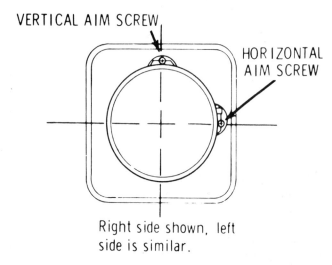

VERTICAL AIM SCREW

HORIZONTAL AIM SCREW

Right side shown, left side is similar.

Fig. 10.4 Adjustment screw locations for headlamp (Sec 8)

3   Fusible links

1   In addition to fuses, the wiring system incorporates fusible links for overload protection. These links are used in circuits which are not ordinarily fused, such as the ignition circuit.
2   Although the fusible links appear to be of a heavier gauge than the wire they are protecting, this appearance is due to the heavy insulation. All fusible links are four wire gauges smaller than the wire they are incorporated into.
3   The exact locations of the four fusible links used may differ slightly but their protective circuits are the same. They are as follows:

a)   *A 14-gauge fusible link protecting the 10-gauge battery charging circuit. This may be located at the 'Bat' terminal of the starter solenoid or as a pigtail lead at the battery positive cable.*
b)   *A 16-gauge link to protect all unfused wiring of 12-gauge or larger. This is located at the horn relay or junction block.*
c)   *A 20-gauge link is used to protect the generator warning light*

and the field circuitry which is of 16-gauge thickness. This link is also located at the junction block. Later models also have another fusible link at the horn relay for this purpose.
d)   *Two fusible links are used to protect the ammeter circuit. They are 20-gauge and located at the junction block and horn relay.*

4   The fusible links cannot be repaired, but rather a new link of the same wire size and Hypalon insulation can be put in its place. This process is as follows:
5   Disconnect the battery ground cable.
6   Disconnect the fusible link from the starter solenoid.
7   Cut the damaged fusible link out of the wiring system. Do this just behind the connector.
8   Strip the insulation from the circuit wiring approximately $\frac{1}{2}$ inch.
9   Position connector on the new fusible link and crimp into place in the wiring circuit.
10   Use rosin core solder at each end of the new link to obtain a good solder joint.
11   Use plenty of electrical tape around the soldered joint. No exposed wiring should show.
12   Connect the fusible link at the starter solenoid. Connect the battery ground cable. Test circuit for proper operation.

4   Circuit breakers

1   A thermo circuit breaker is used to protect the headlight wiring, and is located in the light switch. An electrical overload in the system will cause the lights to go on and off, or in some cases to remain off. If this happens, check the entire headlight wiring system immediately. Once the overload condition is corrected the circuit breaker will function normally.
2   Vehicles equipped with power windows and/or power door locks will also have a circuit breaker for protection of electrical overloads to these circuits. They are located on the bulkhead of the engine compartment.

5   Turn signal and hazard flashers

1   Small canister-shaped flasher units are incorporated into the electrical circuits for the directional signals and hazard warning lights.
2   When the units are functioning properly an audible click can be heard with the circuit in operation. If the turn signals fail on one side only, and the flasher unit cannot be heard, a faulty bulb is indicated. If the flasher click can be heard, a short in the wiring is indicated.
3   If the turn signals fail on both sides, the fault may be due to a blown fuse, faulty flasher unit or switch, or a broken or loose connection. If the fuse has blown, check the wiring for a short before installing a new fuse.
4   The hazard warning lamps are checked in the same manner as paragraph 3 above.
5   The hazard warning flasher unit is located in the fuse box located under the dashboard on the left side. The turn signal flasher may be mounted in the fuse box or under the lower lip of the instrument panel.
6   When replacing either of these flasher units it is important to buy a replacement of the same capacity. Vehicles of model years 1974 – 1977 have 2-lamp turn signal flashers and 4-lamp hazard units. 1978 and later models have 2-lamp turn signal units and 6-lamp hazard flashers. Check the new flasher against the old one to be assured of the proper replacement.

6   Horns – fault testing

1   If the horn proves inoperable, your first check should be the fuse. A blown fuse can be readily identified at the fuse box under the lower left side of the dashboard.
2   If the fuse is in good condition, disconnect the electrical lead at the horn. Run a jumper wire from a 12-volt source (+ battery terminal) to the wiring terminal on the horn. If the horn does not blow, the fault lies in the grounding of the horn or the horn itself.
3   If current is not reaching the horn, indicated by the horn sounding from the above test, there is a failure in the circuit before the horn.
4   In most cases a failure of the horn relay is indicated if the circuit before the horn is at fault. Other checks would include bent metal

contacts on the horn actuator or loose or broken wires in the system.

5   The horn relay is located in the wiring system, usually under the dashboard near the fuse box. When checking or replacing the horn relay be aware that the threaded stud is always hot and shorting of this stud to ground could destroy a fusible link, disabling the vehicle until the link is replaced.

7   Headlight sealed beam unit – removal and installation

1   Whenever replacing the headlight, do not turn the spring-loaded adjusting screws of the headlight, as this will alter the aim.
2   Remove the headlight bezel screws and remove the decorative bezel.
3   Use a cotter pin removal tool or similar device to unhook the spring from the retaining ring.
4   Remove the two screws which secure the retaining ring and withdraw the ring. Support the light as this is done.
5   Pull the sealed beam unit outward slightly and disconnect the electrical connector from the rear of the light. Remove the light from the vehicle.
6   Position the new unit close enough to connect the electrical connector. Make sure that the numbers molded into the lens are at the top.
7   Install the retaining ring with its mounting screws and spring.
8   Install the decorative bezel and check for proper operation. If the adjusting screws were not altered, the new headlight will not need to have the aim adjusted.

8   Headlamps – adjustment

1   Adjustment screws are provided at the front of the lamp to alter the lamp beam in both the horizontal and vertical planes.
2   It is strongly recommended that this work is left to a service station having modern beam setting equipment, any adjustment at home being regarded as a temporary, emergency operation.

9   Bulb replacement – front end

Parking lamp turn signal
All models
1   Remove the screws which secure the lens to the body. Carefully extract the lens, being careful not to damage the fiber gasket (photo).
2   Push in on the bulb and turn it $\frac{1}{4}$ turn counter clockwise. Remove the bulb from the socket (photo).
3   Check that the electrical contacts and wiring are in a useable condition and push the new bulb into place. This is done with a twisting motion.
4   Check the operation of the new bulb and if satisfactory, install the lens covering.
5   The bulb is housed in a metal socket which is located behind the grille. Open the hood, reach in and twist socket out of the rear of the housing.
6   Twist the socket out of the rear of the housing and replace the bulb as described above.

Side marker lamps
All models
7   The bulb is located inside a twist socket at the rear of the housing. Twist the socket on the inner fender panel $\frac{1}{4}$ turn and disengage the socket and bulb from the housing. The old bulb can then be released from the socket and a new one put in its place.

10   Bulb replacement – rear end

1   All the various bulbs for the rear end lighting are accessible from inside the trunk. The bulbs are located inside a metal socket which is secured to the rear of the particular housing.
2   The lamp bulb socket for all the lamps except the license plate is removed by twisting the socket $\frac{1}{4}$ turn. The bulb inside the socket can then be replaced and the socket re-installed (photo).
3   In most cases the license plate sockets must be pried out of the

rear of the housing. Use a screwdriver to carefully lift the socket and bulb out of the hole in the housing. Replace the bulb and then push the socket back into position.

11   Bulb replacement – interior

Center console lamps
1   Pry up the switch assembly from the console and remove the bulb from its socket.
2   The courtesy lamp bulb is accessible after extracting the lens screws and removing the lens.

Automatic floor shift quadrant lamps
3   Remove the quadrant trim plate from the console and withdraw the lamp socket.

Interior (roof) lamp
4   Pinch the sides of the plastic lamp lens together and remove it.
5   The festoon type bulb can now be carefully pried from between the spring contacts.

12   Bulb replacement – instrument panel

1   All of the instrument illumination and telltale bulbs are mounted in twist sockets on the rear of the printed circuit instrument panel.
2   Most of the sockets can be reached without removing the instrument panel. For better access it is recommended that the steering column trim cover be removed from the lower portion of the dashboard. If, with the trim cover removed, the upper bulbs are still inaccessible, then the instrument cluster will have to be removed (See Section 17).

13   Headlamp switch – removal and installation

1   Disconnect the negative cable at the battery.
2   Remove the steering column cover from the bottom of the dashboard for better access.
3   With the headlights in the 'full on' position, reach up under the dashboard and depress the lighting switch shaft retainer while pulling gently on the lighting knob. Remove the shaft and knob assembly.
4   Remove the nut which secures the lighting switch to the carrier.
5   For better access to the switch, remove the screws which secure the instrument cluster carrier and tilt the cluster.
6   Unplug the electrical connector at the switch and remove the switch.
7   Installation is a reversal of removal, however, make sure that all ground connections are refastened and that the switch shaft is fully seated in the switch. The shaft retainer should lock the shaft into place.

14   Cigar lighter assembly – removal and installation

1   Disconnect the negative battery cable at the battery.
2   Reach up under the dashboard and disconnect the electrical connector at the rear of the lighter housing. The lighter housing is located in the ashtray. Pull the ashtray out and down to remove it.
3   Grip the retaining nut at the lighter's rear and turn the socket with your thumb until the nut is loose enough to turn from rear. Remove element from ashtray.
4   When installing make sure the grounding ring is between the lighter housing and the retainer.

15   Speedometer cable – replacement

1   Disconnect the negative battery cable.
2   Reach up under the dashboard and disconnect the speedometer cable casing from the speedometer head. This is done by pressing the retaining spring clip towards the front of the instrument cluster and then pulling back on the speedometer cable casing.
3   Remove the dash panel sealing plug from the casing.

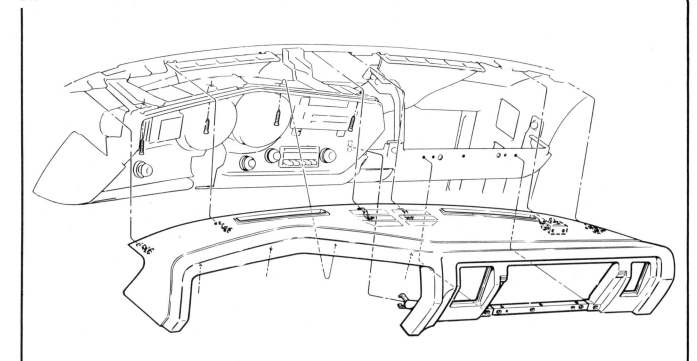

Fig. 10.5 Mounting points for dashboard – typical (Sec 16)

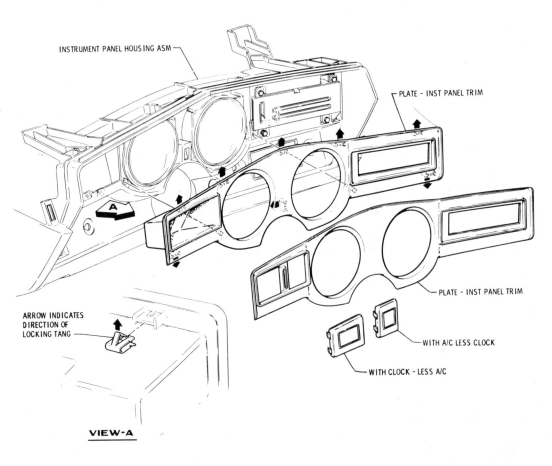

INSTRUMENT PANEL HOUSING ASM

PLATE - INST PANEL TRIM

PLATE - INST PANEL TRIM

WITH A/C LESS CLOCK

WITH CLOCK - LESS A/C

ARROW INDICATES
DIRECTION OF
LOCKING TANG

VIEW-A

Fig. 10.6 Trim plates and tab locations – typical (Sec 16)

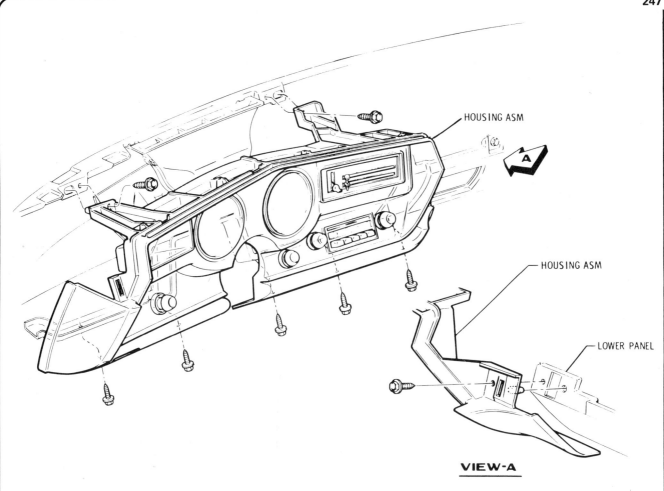

HOUSING ASM

HOUSING ASM

LOWER PANEL

VIEW-A

Fig. 10.7 Instrument panel housing – typical (Sec 16)

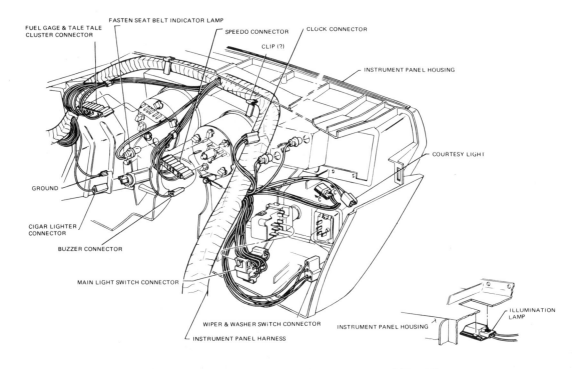

FUEL GAGE & TALE TALE
CLUSTER CONNECTOR

FASTEN SEAT BELT INDICATOR LAMP

SPEEDO CONNECTOR

CLOCK CONNECTOR

CLIP (?)

INSTRUMENT PANEL HOUSING

COURTESY LIGHT

GROUND

CIGAR LIGHTER
CONNECTOR

BUZZER CONNECTOR

MAIN LIGHT SWITCH CONNECTOR

WIPER & WASHER SWITCH CONNECTOR

INSTRUMENT PANEL HARNESS

INSTRUMENT PANEL HOUSING

ILLUMINATION
LAMP

Fig. 10.8 Wiring harness behind instrument panel (Sec 16)

4   Using pliers, pull the old core out of the top of the casing. If the inner cable has broken, it will be necessary to remove the lower piece of cable from under the vehicle. Some models come equipped with a two-piece speedometer cable, while some have a single cable leading all the way from the speedometer head to the transmission. Ascertain which type you have and disconnect the lower end as necessary to pull out the remaining broken piece of inner cable.
5   When installing a new speedometer cable core always lubricate it the entire length with special graphite lubricant designed for this purpose. Do not use oil.
6   Push the core into the casing, using a twisting motion when necessary. Make sure the end of the core is fully engaged in the pinion gear inside the transmission.
7   Reinstall the dash sealing plug and connect the casing to the rear of the instrument cluster. As in removal, push in on the retaining clip and then push the casing fully into the rear of the gauge.
8   Road test the vehicle and check for proper operation of the speedometer.

16 Instrument panel – removal and installation

Note: *Before starting any work on the instrument panel, disconnect the battery ground cable.*

1974 through 1976

1   In order to remove the instrument panel, it is necessary to first remove the glove box and door, the lower trim plates, and the dashboard.
2   Open the glove box door and take out the screws that attach it to the dash. Lift out the door. Now, remove the 2 remaining screws and the box.
3   Unscrew the 2 lower attaching screws and lift out the right lower trim plate.
4   Take out the 4 instrument panel to dashboard screws and unhook the speaker connector from the radio.
5   Lift out the dashboard; try not to damage the edges when removing it from your car. Put the dash panel in an area where it will not be marred.
6   Position the shift lever in "L" (column shift only) and disconnect the shift indicator connector cable.
7   Pry the trim bezel (plate) away from the instrument panel. Use caution; the bezel is easy to break or crack.
8   Disconnect air conditioning/heater cables and mark them with masking tape for correct identification later on.
9   Unhook the speedometer cable from the head, disconnect any wiring connectors, pull all light sockets and mark them for easy identification.
10 Take off the radio control knobs and undo the 8 remaining screws that hold the instrument panel in place.
11 Remove the instrument panel. The radio will drop approximately 1 in. This is normal.
12 If the panel is to be replaced with a new one, it will be necessary to scavenge all necessary clips, knobs, hook ups, and so on from the old panel.
13 Installation is the reverse process. When you install the right trim plate, insert the top of the trim panel into place first and secure the bottom with two screws.

1977 through 1980

1   Follow Steps 1, 2, and 4 (omit step 3) from the previous section (1974 through 1976 Instrument panel removal).
2   Pull on dash assembly to disengage the retaining clips; on the right side, the unit must be pulled down and to the rear to loosen the clip at the top of the glove box.
3   Lift off the dash panel and remove it from the automobile. Put it in a location where it will not be damaged.
4   Follow steps 6, 7, 8, 9, 10, 11 and 12 from the previous section.
5   Installation is the reverse procedure.

17 Gauge printed circuit board – replacement

1   Disconnect the negative battery cable.
2   Remove the instrument panel as described in Section 17.

3   With the instrument cluster on a clean workbench, remove 5 cluster lens screws, lens and the 10 bulbs from the sockets. Take out 1 screw and 6 clips. Lift the printed circuit off the rear of the instrument cluster.
4   Place the new printed circuit into position, securing it with the illumination bulbs and gauge nuts.
5   Reinstall the instrument cluster referring to Section 17.
6   Connect the negative battery cable.

18 Speedometer – removal and installation

1   If the speedometer is being removed along with the instrument panel, follow the steps in Section 17. Make sure that the battery ground cable is disconnected whenever you work on the instrument cluster.
2   Position the shift lever into the "L" position and disconnect the shift indicator cable from the steering column.
3   Carefully pry the trim bezel away from the instrument panel.
4   Remove the 3 screws that hold the speedometer in place, disengage the wire connector and pull speedometer forward.
5   Undo the speedometer cable and lift the speedometer out of the instrument panel.
6   Installation is the exact reverse procedure.

19 Clock – removal and installation

1   Disconnect the battery ground cable.
2   Carefully pry the instrument panel trim bezel away from the panel.
3   Unscrew the 2 retaining screws, pull clock forward and unhook the wire connector. Lift out the clock.
4   Reverse the procedure for installation.

20 Windshield wiper system – general description

A two-speed wiper motor is installed as standard equipment and incorporates the gear train and the self-parking mechanism.
The wiper arms will only park when the motor is operating in low speed.
The drive from the wiper motor to the wiper arms is by means of a crank arm and a strut to the transmission shafts.
On all models, the windshield wiper motor incorporates the drive system for the windshield washers.
Two types of windshield wiper assemblies may be encountered according to vehicle model. On one type, the wiper arms park parallel with and about two inches above the windshield molding while on the other type, the blades park in a depressed position against a step on the windshield lower molding.

21 Washer/wiper switch – removal and installation

1   This switch needs to be removed only when it is to be replaced.
2   Remove headlight switch knob and escutcheon (1979 - 1980). Disconnect negative battery cable and carefully pry away the instrument panel trim plate.
3   Using one or two narrow blade screwdrivers, insert a blade into each of the slots above the switch knobs. Bend the retaining clips down and pull top of switch outward.
4   Disconnect wire and remove switch from panel. Installation is the reverse procedure, except that switch needs only to be pressed directly into opening, not tilted.

22 Windshield wiper arm – removal and installation

1   Make sure that the wiper arms are in the self-parked position, the motor having been switched off in the low speed mode.
2   Note carefully the position of the wiper arm in relation to the windshield lower reveal moulding. Use tape on the windshield to mark the exact location of the wiper arm on the glass.
3   Using a suitable hooked tool or a small screwdriver, pull aside the small spring tang which holds the wiper arm to the splined trans-

mission shaft and at the same time pull the arm from the shaft (photo).
4   Installation is a reversal of removal but do not push the arm fully home on the shaft until the alignment of the arm has been checked. If necessary, the arm can be pulled off again and turned through one or two serrations of the shaft to correct the alignment without the necessity of pulling aside the spring tang.
5   Finally, press the arm fully home on its shaft and then wet the windshield glass and operate the motor on low speed to ensure that the arc of travel is correct.

23 Wiper motor – removal and installation

1   Raise the hood and remove the cowl screen at the base of the windshield.
2   Reaching through the opening, loosen the transmission drive link to crank arm attaching nuts.
3   Remove the transmission drive links from the crank arm of the motor.
4   Disconnect the washer hoses and electrical wiring at the motor.
5   Remove the three bolts which secure the motor to the firewall cowling. Push the crank arm through its mounting hole and then withdraw the motor.
6   Installation is a reversal of removal, however, make sure that the motor is in the 'Park' position.

24 Windshield wiper motor/transmission – servicing

1   The unit has a very long operating life and when it has finally worn so much that dismantling and repair is necessary, consideration should be given to the purchase of a new or reconditioned unit, particularly if the major components require replacement.

25 Washer assembly – removal, servicing and installation

1974

1   The washer pump can be removed independently, leaving the wiper motor in the vehicle. Disconnect the washer hoses and electrical wiring.
2   Remove the washer pump mounting screws and lift off the pump from the wiper motor.
3   Pull off the four lobe washer pump drive cam. This is a press fit and may require prying.
4   Remove the felt washer from the wiper shaft.
5   Remove the ratchet dog retaining screw, then hold the spring loaded solenoid plunger in position and lift the solenoid assembly and ratchet dog off the pump frame. Separate the dog from the mounting plate if necessary.

6   To remove the ratchet wheel, move the spring out of the shaft groove and slide the ratchet wheel off its shaft.
7   To separate the pump and pump actuator plate from the frame, pull the pump housing towards the valve end until the grooves in the housing clear the frame.
8   Reassembly is the reverse of the dismantling procedure.
9   Installation is the reverse of the removal procedure.

1975 through 1980

10 Disconnect the washer hoses from the pump and disconnect the wires from the pump relay.
11 Remove the plastic pump cover.
12 Remove the frame screws and withdraw the pump and frame.
13 Extract the screw and lift the ratchet dog from the mounting plate.
14 Disengage the pawl spring from the pawl and then slide the pawl from the cam follower pin.
15 Pry the ratchet spring out the slot in the shaft, hold the relay armature against the relay coil and slide the ratchet wheel off the shaft.
16 Pry off the retainer and slide the cam off the shaft.
17 Remove the relay armature and spring.
18 Chisel off the four tabs that secure the coil mounting bracket. Remove the relay coil and terminal board.
19 To remove the plastic pump housing, pull it towards the valve end until the grooves in the housing clear the base. Detach the assembly from the cam follower pin. The piston and plastic housing are serviced as an assembly.
20 The valve can be removed from the pump housing after extracting the four screws but make sure to mark the relative position of the valve to the housing before separating.
21 Reassembly is a reversal of dismantling but note that the wiper motor must be in the 'Park' position before assembling the pump and the wiper motor.

26 Modified pulse wiper/washer system – description, removal, dismantling, reassembly, installation

1   This system which is fitted to some models as optional equipment is designed to provide (i) a low speed single wipe cycle delay of up to 10 seconds and (ii) wash/wipe cycle comprising squirts, wiping and switching off in the 'Park' position.
2   To remove the washer pump, first withdraw the complete wiper/washer assembly from the vehicle.
3   Remove the plastic tab from the opening under the terminals and pull the plastic cover from the mounting post.
4   Disconnect the electrical leads and extract the three screws that attach the pump to the wiper transmission.
5   The valve assembly can be removed after extracting the four

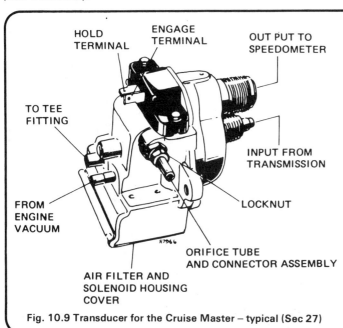

Fig. 10.9 Transducer for the Cruise Master – typical (Sec 27)

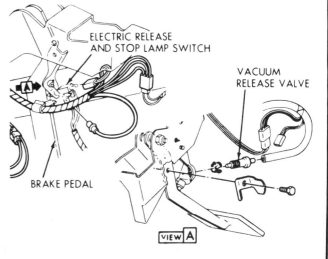

Fig. 10.10 Cruise Master release switches, valve and bracket – typical (Sec 27)

securing screws.

6   Slide the cam from the shaft after first removing the retainer.

7   Remove the pulse relay timing device, holding switch and override switch (one screw) from the washer frame.

8   Disconnect the red and yellow leads from the pulse relay and detach it from the locator pins.

9   Remove the dog spring assembly and the ratchet pawl retaining ring. Disconnect the pawl spring and slide the pawl from the cam follower shaft.

10   Disconnect the relay armature spring and remove the armature.

11   Release the ratchet gear spring from the groove in the shaft and slide the ratchet gear from the shaft.

12   To release the pump housing from its sheet metal hose, pull it towards the valve assembly until the grooves in the plastic pump housing clear the base. Detach the assembly from the cam follower pin.

13   Bend or chisel off the four bent over tabs that secure the coil mounting bracket to its base.

14   Reassembly is a reversal of dismantling but observe the following points.

15   When installing the pulse relay onto the switch base locator pins, rotate the drive cam counter clockwise and secure the complete assembly with the screw. Remember to insert the sealing rings between the housing and valve body.

27 Cruise master – description, adjustment and component replacement

1   This cruising speed control system is optionally available on certain models and allows the driver to maintain a constant highway speed without the necessity of continual adjustment of foot pressure on the accelerator pedal.

2   The system employs a servo unit connected to the intake manifold, a speedometer cable-driven regulator and various switches.

3   An override capability is built in.

4   Any malfunction in the performance of the system should first be checked out by inspecting the fuse, the security of the leads and terminals, and the vacuum pipes and connections.

5   The following adjustments should then be checked and if necessary altered to conform to those specified.

6   The servo operating rod which connects to the carburetor throttle linkage should be adjusted by turning the link on the rod until there is 0.02 to 0.04 inches of free play at the carburetor.

7   *The regulator* can be adjusted by turning the orifice tube in or out *(never remove it as it cannot be re-installed).* If the vehicle cruises below the engagement speed, screw the orifice tube out. If the vehicle cruises above the engagement speed, screw the orifice tube in. Each

$\frac{1}{4}$ turn of the orifice tube will change the cruise speed by about 1 mph. Tighten the locknut after each adjustment.

8   *The brake release switch* contacts must open when the brake pedal is depressed between 0.38 and 0.64 inch measured at the pedal pad.

9   The vacuum valve plunger must clear the pedal arm when the arm is moved $\frac{5}{16}$ inch measured at the switch.

10   *The column mounted engagement switch* is non-adjustable, and is serviced only as part of the complete turn signal lever assembly.

11   Faulty components should be replaced as complete assemblies after disconnecting electrical leads, vacuum hoses and control cables from them as necessary.

28 Power radio antenna – removal and installation

1   Access to the power antenna is through the under side of the right front fender.

2   Lower the antenna mast all the way by turning off the ignition. If the unit has failed in the extended position, it may be necessary to cut off the mast portion of the antenna unit. Do this only if you can't remove the antenna in the extended position. The mast section of the antenna can be replaced without purchasing an entire antenna.

3   Disconnect the negative battery cable.

4   If your car is equipped with an AM/FM/CB combination, unscrew the knob from the antenna top. It will also be necessary to remove the loading coil.

5   Unscrew the 2 attaching screws on the inside top of the fender and disconnect the wiring and lead-in connections at the fender well/motor junction.

6   Apply masking tape to the edges between the door and fender. This will minimize the chance of chipping the paint. Do not leave this tape on the car longer than necessary and don't have the car parked in the sun while performing this operation. If the tape does not remove easily at the procedure end, apply bug and tar remover or turpentine sparingly to the loose edge of the tape. Do not rub the fluid into the paint and wash the area with warm soap and water when you loosen the tape.

7   Open the right door to the halfway position (you are going to remove the screws that attach the fender panel to the door line support). Remove the lowest screw from inside the door. Open the door fully and remove the 3 remaining screws from outside the door.

8   Take out the 3 most rearward screws that attach the fender panel to the wheelhouse.

9   Remove the lower antenna attaching screw (in the fender well).

10   Pull outward on the lower edge of the fender panel just enough to let the antenna unit drop out.

11   Installation is a reverse procedure but you will need the help of an assistant to replace the top 2 antenna attaching screws.

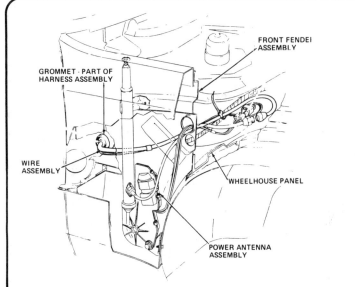

Fig. 10.11 Power antenna mounting – typical (Sec 28)

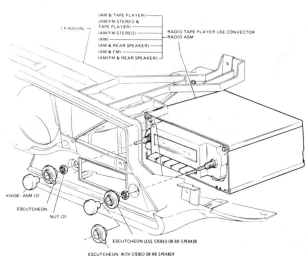

Fig. 10.12 Radio mounting and knobs – typical (Sec 30)

ZONES OF BULB BRILLIANCE

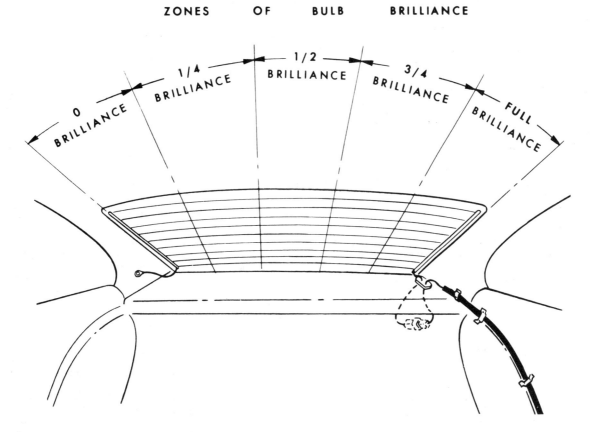

Fig. 10.13 Testing the rear defogger grid pattern with lamp (Sec 32)

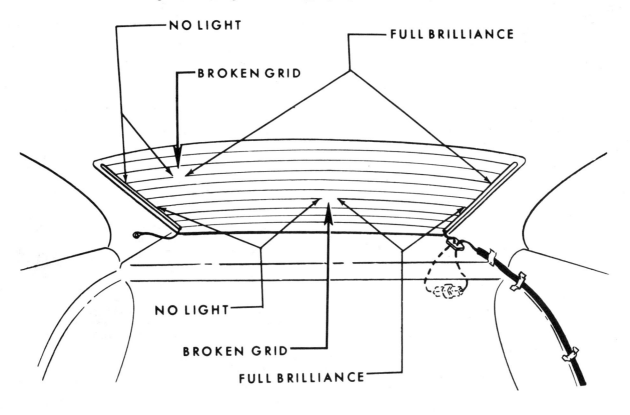

Fig. 10.14 Lamp brilliance with broken defogger lines (Sec 32)

29 Seat belt warning systems

1974 through 1976

1   Before the vehicle can be started, the belts must be fastened *after* the weight of the driver or passenger has been placed on their respective seats.

2   A warning system is actuated if any attempt is made to start the vehicle without the belts having been properly fastened.

3   The warning system will again be actuated if, after the engine has been started and the vehicle is in a forward gear or speed range, the occupied front seat belts are unfastened.

4   Once the engine has been started, the engine can be switched off and subsequently restarted with either or both front seat belts unfastened provided the driver only remains in his seat. Once the driver's weight is removed from his seat then the original starting procedure will again apply.

5   In order to facilitate vehicle maintenance and repair, a mechanic's start position is incorporated in the ignition switch. The engine will then start irrespective of the mode of the front seat belts or whether either front seat is occupied. Whenever the engine is started by this method, the warning buzzer can be terminated if the seat buckle switch is cycled.

6   An anti-bounce device is built into the system to prevent the non-start mode being re-established should a front seat occupant raise his weight from his seat (with seat belt fastened) for a period not exceeding ten seconds.

7   An override relay is incorporated in the system to permit starting the engine in the event of complete system failure. The relay is mounted within the engine compartment and to bring the relay into use, carry out the following operations:

8   Turn the ignition 'ON'.

9   Open the hood and depress and then release the button on the override relay. The engine can now be started and the vehicle driven until such time as the ignition key is turned to the 'OFF' or 'LOCK' position, when the override relay will return to its de-energized position.

1977 through 1980

10   The system used on these later vehicles incorporates a timer-controlled buzzer and warning lamp which operate for a few seconds after the ignition is switched on without the seat belts having been fastened.

11   With this system, the fastening of safety belts is left to the driver and abandons the need for complicated starter interlock and other devices used in earlier systems.

30 Radio – removal and installation

1   Disconnect the negative battery cable.

2   Pull off the radio control knobs and bezels. Disconnect the air duct assembly control, there are 2 screws that attach it to the dash panel.

3   Using a deep socket, remove the control shaft lock nuts now visible at the base of the shafts.

4   Look up under the dashboard, at the rear of the radio unit. Any obstructions, commonly a center air duct or hoses, should be disconnected and removed for access.

5   Remove the screws or nuts securing the rear mounting bracket to the radio.

6   Push the radio forward until the shafts are clear of the dashboard and then lower the unit enough to remove the electrical connections at the rear of the radio. Also disconnect the antenna lead-in cable.

7   Carefully lower the radio unit and remove.

8   Installation is a reversal of the removal operation, however, always attach the speaker wiring harness before applying power to the radio.

31 Power door lock system

1   This optional system incorporates a solenoid actuator inside each door. The solenoid is electrically operated from a control switch on the instrument panel and operates the lock through a linkage. Each actuator has an internal circuit breaker which may require one to three minutes to reset.

2   To remove the solenoid, raise the door window and remove the door panel trim pad as described in Chapter 12.

3   After prying away the water shield, the solenoid can be seen

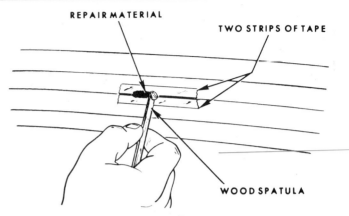

REPAIR MATERIAL

TWO STRIPS OF TAPE

WOOD SPATULA

Fig. 10.15 Repairing window defogger grid (Sec 32)

through the large access hole. The solenoid can be mounted to either the rear door lock pillar or the inner metal door panel.

4   Early models use attaching screws through the door panel and into the solenoid bracket. Later models use rivets to secure the solenoid to the pillar. These must be drilled out using a $\frac{1}{4}$ inch drill bit.

5   Once the securing devices are removed, disconnect the wiring harness at the solenoid and the actuating link held in place with a metal clip. Remove the solenoid from the door cavity.

6   To install, place the solenoid in position and connect the electrical connector and actuating link. If rivets were drilled out, new aluminum rivets ($\frac{1}{4}$ x 0.500'' size) can be used upon reassembly. Optionally, $\frac{1}{4}$ – 20 screws and U nuts can be used.

7   Check the operation of the door locks before installing the water shield and trim panel.

32 Electric grid-type rear defogger – testing and repair

1   This option consists of a rear window with a number of horizontal elements that are baked into the glass surface during the glass forming operation.

2   Small breaks in the element system can be successfully repaired without removing the rear window.

3   To test the grids for proper operation, start the engine and turn on the system.

4   Ground one lead of a test lamp and lightly touch the other prod to each grid line.

5   The brilliance of the test lamp should increase as the probe is moved across the element from right to left. If the test lamp glows brightly at both ends of the grid lines, check for a loose ground wire for the system. All of the grid lines should be checked in at least two places.

6   To repair a break in a grid line it is recommended that a repair kit specifically for this purpose be purchased from a GM dealer. Included in the repair kit will be a decal, a container of silver plastic and hardener, a mixing stick and instructions.

7   To repair a break, first turn off the system and allow it to de-energize for a few minutes.

8   Lightly buff the grid line area with fine steel wool and then thoroughly clean the area with alcohol.

9   Use the decal supplied in the repair kit, or use electrician's tape above and below the area to be repaired. The space between the pieces of tape should be the same as existing grid lines. This can be checked from outside the car. Press the tape tightly against the glass to prevent seepage.

10   Mix the hardener and silver plastic thoroughly.

11   Using the wood spatula, apply the silver plastic mixture between the pieces of tape, overlapping the damaged area slightly on either end.

12   Carefully remove the decal or tape and apply a constant stream of hot air directly to the repaired area. A heat gun set at 500 to 700 degrees Fahrenheit is recommended. Hold the gun asbout 1 inch from the glass for 1 to 2 minutes.

13   If the new grid line appears off color, tincture of iodine can be used to clean the repair and bring it back to the proper color. This mixture should not remain on the repair for more than 30 seconds.

14   Although the defogger is now fully operational, the repaired area should not be disturbed for at least 24 hours.

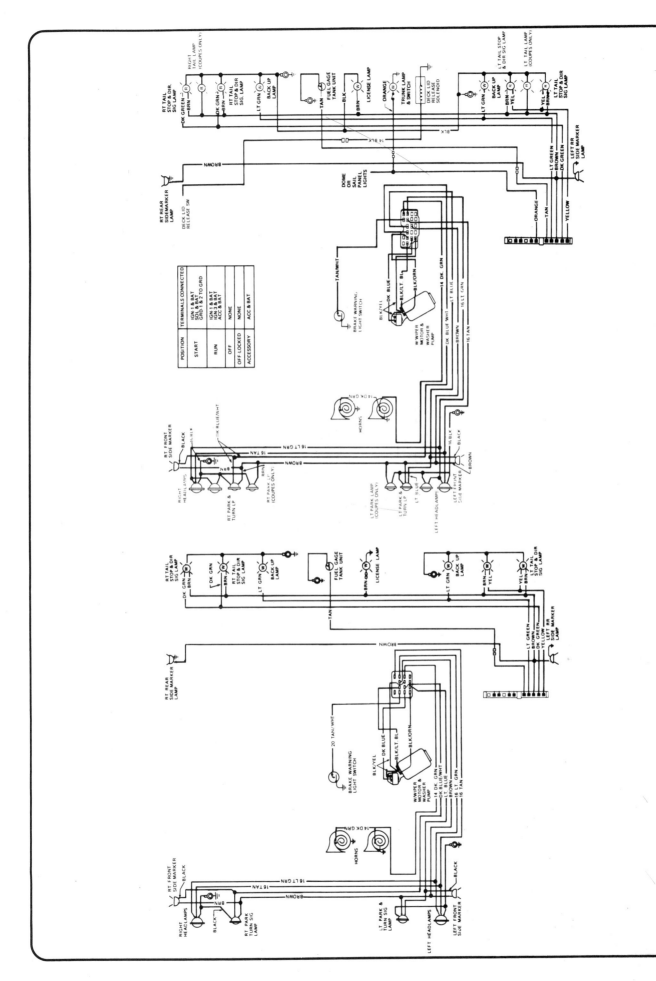

Fig. 10.16 Left: front and rear body wiring diagram (1974 and 1975); Right: front and rear body wiring diagram (1976)

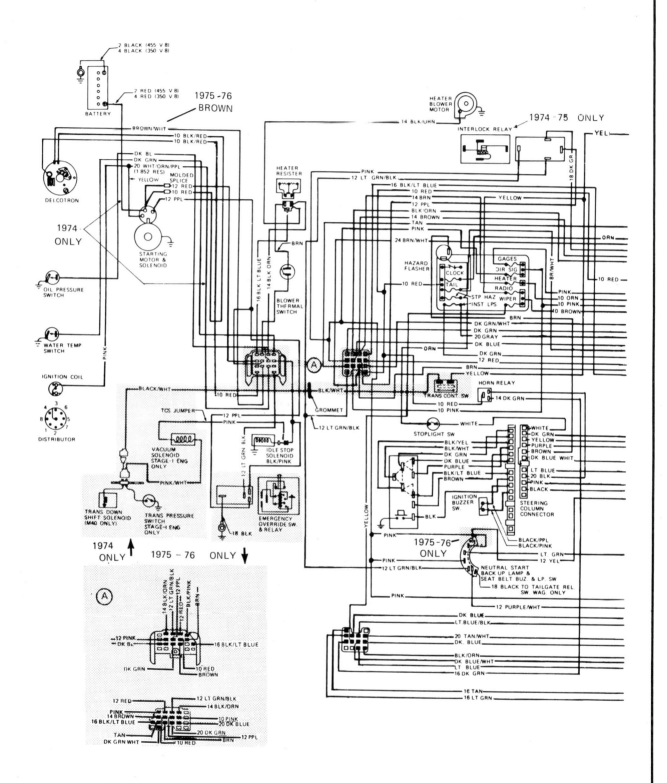

Fig. 10.17 Engine and interior wiring diagram (1974 through 1976)

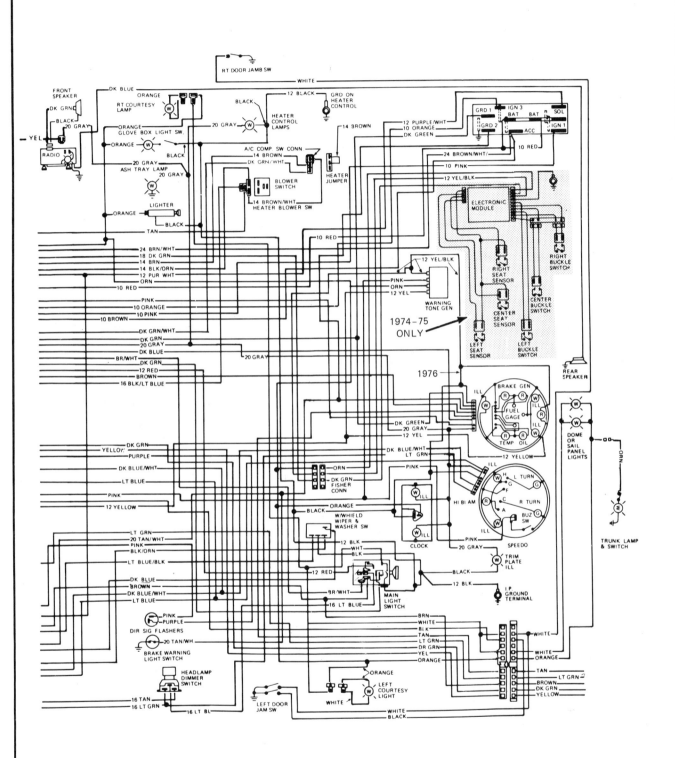

Fig. 10.18 Engine and interior wiring diagram (1974 through 1976 continued)

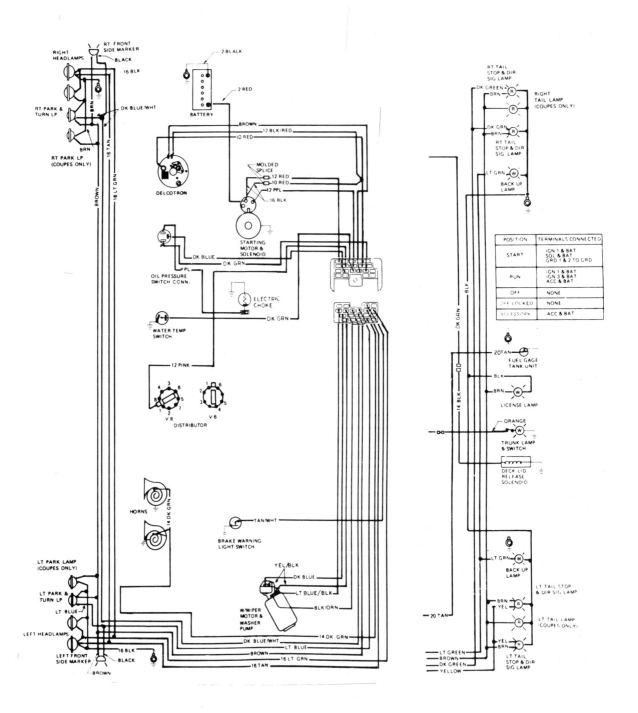

Fig. 10.19 Front and rear body/engine wiring diagram (1977)

POSITION	TERMINALS CONNECTED
START	IGN 1 & BAT SOL & BAT GRD 1 & 2 TO GRD
RUN	IGN 1 & BAT IGN 3 & BAT ACC & BAT
OFF	NONE
OFF LOCKED	NONE
ACCESSORY	ACC & BAT

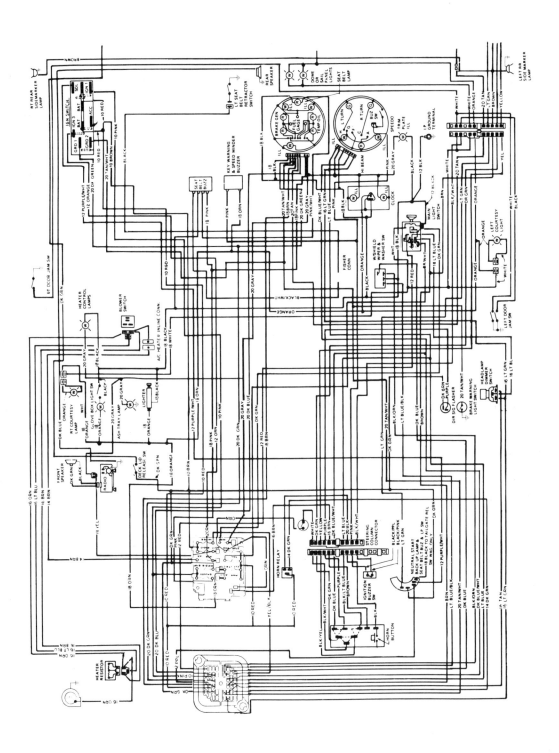

Fig. 10.20 Interior wiring diagram (1977)

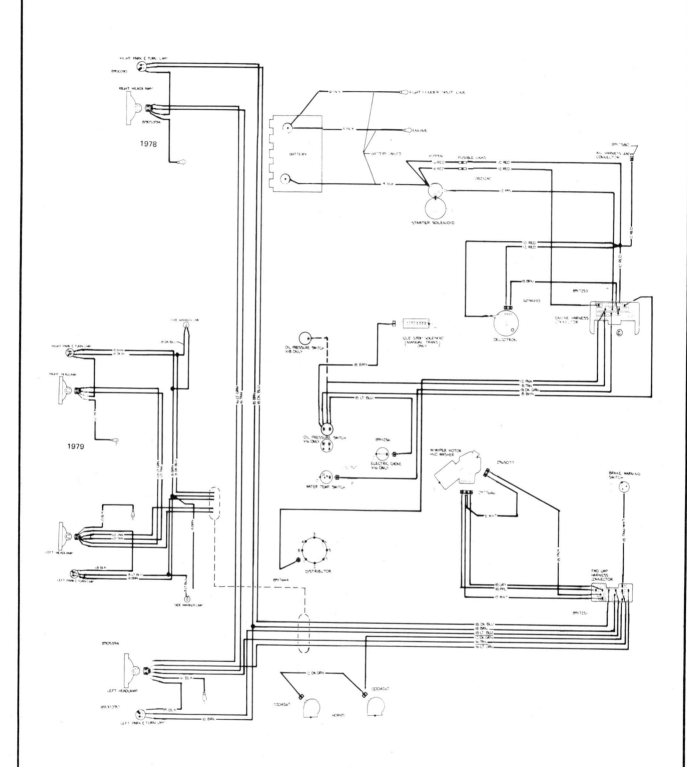

Fig. 10.21 Front body/engine wiring diagram (1978 and 1979)

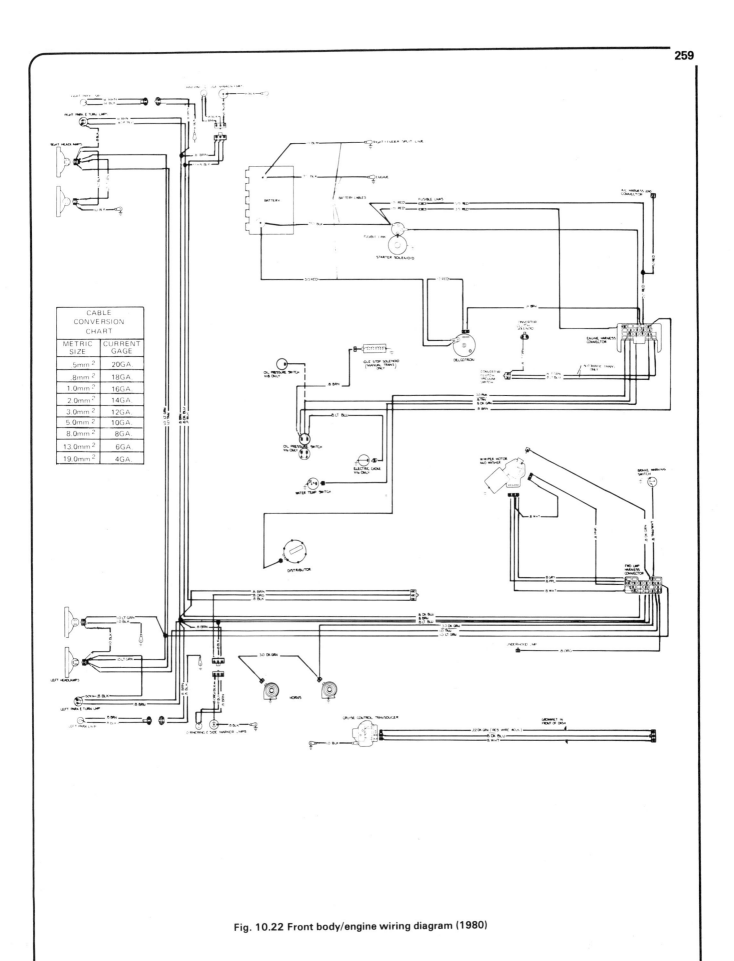

Fig. 10.22 Front body/engine wiring diagram (1980)

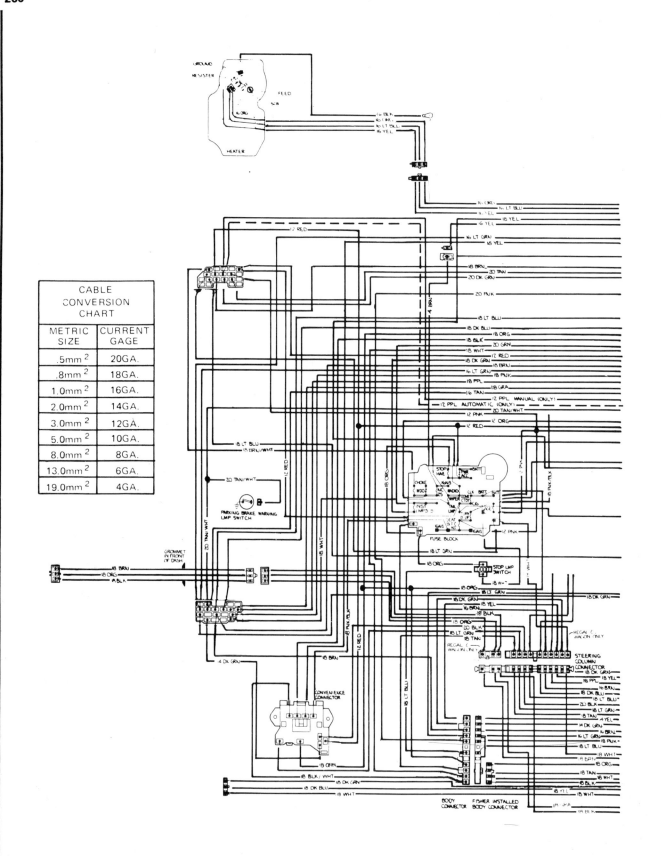

CABLE CONVERSION CHART

METRIC SIZE	CURRENT GAGE
.5mm²	20GA.
.8mm²	18GA.
1.0mm²	16GA.
2.0mm²	14GA.
3.0mm²	12GA.
5.0mm²	10GA.
8.0mm²	8GA.
13.0mm²	6GA.
19.0mm²	4GA.

Fig.10.23 Interior wiring diagram (1978 through 1980)

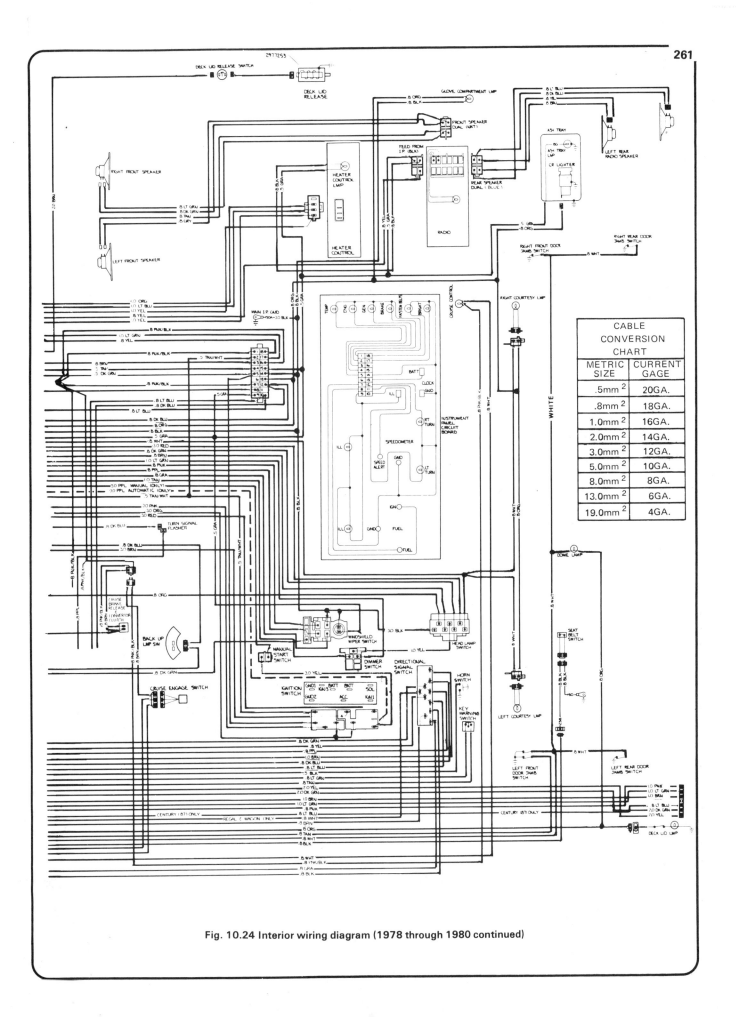

Fig. 10.24 Interior wiring diagram (1978 through 1980 continued)

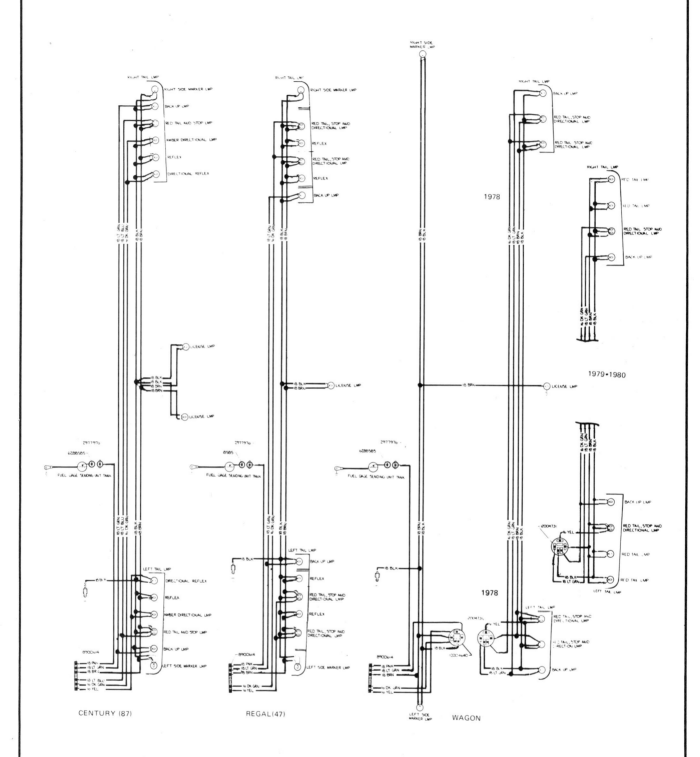

Fig. 10.25 Rear body wiring diagram (1978 through 1980)

Chapter 11 Suspension and steering

Contents

Specifications

Front end alignment specifications

	Caster (in degrees)	Camber (in degrees)	Toe-in (in inches)
1974	-1 to $+1$	$-\frac{1}{4}$ to $+1\frac{1}{4}$ (right side) $+\frac{1}{4}$ to $+1\frac{3}{4}$ (left side)	$\frac{1}{16} \pm \frac{1}{8}$
1975	$+1$ to $+3$	$-\frac{1}{4}$ to $+1\frac{1}{4}$ (right side) $+\frac{1}{4}$ to $+1\frac{3}{4}$ (left side)	$\frac{1}{16} \pm \frac{1}{8}$
1976	$+1$ to $+3$	$-\frac{1}{4}$ to $+1\frac{1}{4}$ (right side) $+\frac{1}{4}$ to $+1\frac{3}{4}$ (left side)	$\frac{1}{16} \pm \frac{1}{8}$
1977	$+1$ to $+3$ (radial tires) 0 to $+2$ (bias tires)	$-\frac{1}{4}$ to $+1\frac{1}{4}$ (right side) $+\frac{1}{4}$ to $+1\frac{3}{4}$ (left side)	$\frac{1}{16} \pm \frac{1}{8}$
1978	0 to $+2$ (manual steering) $+2$ to $+4$ (power steering)	-0.3 to $+1.3$	$\frac{1}{16}$ to $+\frac{1}{4}$
1979	0 to $+2$ (manual steering) $+2$ to $+4$ (power steering)	-0.3 to $+1.3$	$\frac{1}{16}$ to $+\frac{1}{4}$
1980	0 to $+2$ (manual steering) $+2$ to $+4$ (power steering)	-0.3 to $+1.3$	$\frac{1}{16}$ to $+\frac{1}{4}$

Torque specifications
Front suspension
1974 through 1976   ft-lb

Front shock-to-lower control arm	20
Front shock-to-frame	8
Stabilizer bushing-to-frame	24
Upper control arm shaft-to-frame	70
Upper ball joint-to-knuckle	60
Front lower control arm-to-frame	Bolt 130
	Nut 95
Lower ball joint-to-knuckle	90
Stabilizer link-to-lower control arm	12
Idler arm-to-frame	40
Tie rod end-to-steering knuckle	35
Lower control arm bumper	17
Steering arm-to-tie rod end	30 to 40 (45 max.)
Tie rod clamp	19 to 24
Tie rod-to-intermediate rod	30 to 50 (55 max.)
Pitman arm-to-intermediate rod	40 to 50 (55 max.)
Pitman arm-to-steering gear	160 to 210
Idler arm-to-intermediate rod	30 to 40 (45 max.)
Idler arm-to-frame	45 to 55

1977

Stabilizer link nut	13
Stabilizer bar bracket-to-frame bolts and nuts*	24
Shock absorber upper attaching nut	8
Shock absorber-to-control arm bolts	20
Upper control arm-to-frame attaching nuts	75
Lower control arm-to-frame attaching nuts* - front	125
Lower control arm-to-frame attaching nuts* - rear	95
Upper arm bushing nuts - rear*	55
Upper arm bushing nuts - front*	90
Service ball joints-to-upper control arm	8
Lower	70
Upper	50
Splash shield-to-steering bolts	10
Lower control arm	20

1978

Stabilizer link nut	13
Stabilizer bar bracket-to-frame bolts and nuts*	24
Shock absorber upper attaching nut	8
Shock absorber-to-control arm bolts	20
Upper control arm-to-frame attaching nuts	46
Lower control arm-to-frame attaching nuts* - front	61
Lower control arm-to-frame attaching nuts* - rear	61
Upper arm bushing nuts - rear*	55
Upper arm bushing nuts - front*	90
Service ball joints-to-upper control arm	8
Lower	85
Upper	61
Splash shield-to-steering bolts	10
Lower control arm	2

1979 through 1980

Stabilizer link nut	13
Stabilizer bar bracket-to-frame bolts and nuts*	24
Shock absorber upper attaching nut	8
Shock absorber-to-control arm bolts	20
Upper control arm-to-frame attaching nuts	45
Lower control arm-to-frame attaching nuts*	65
Upper arm bushing nuts - rear*	85
Upper arm bushing nuts - front*	85
Service balljoints-to-upper control arm	8
Lower	90
Upper	65
Splash shield to steering knuckle bolts	10
Lower control arm	20

Torque with weight of car on wheels

Rear suspension
1974 through 1976   ft-lb

Rear shock upper mounting bolt	20
Rear shock lower mounting	65
Upper and lower control arm bolt	90
Upper and lower control arm nut	80
Rear prop. shaft "U" joint-to-pinion flange	12 to 20

1977

Shock absorbers
Upper attaching nuts	14
Lower nut	65
Upper attaching belt	20

*Suspension arms
Upper arm-to-frame nuts	80
Upper arm-to-frame bolts	90
Upper arm-to-differential nuts	75
Upper arm-to-differential bolts	85
Lower arm-to-frame nuts	80
Lower arm-to-frame bolts	90
Lower arm-to-differential nuts	75
Lower arm-to-differential bolts	85
Stabilizer shaft to lower control arm nut	55
Stabilizer shaft bracket to control arm belt	22

1978

Shock absorbers
Upper attaching nuts	12
Lower nut	65
Upper attaching bolt	20

*Suspension arms
Upper arm-to-frame nuts	70
Upper arm-to-differential nuts	70
Upper arm-to-differential bolts	85
Lower arm-to-frame nuts	70
Lower arm-to-frame bolts	90
Lower arm-to-differential bolts	90
Stabilizer shaft-to-lower control arm nut	35

1979 through 1980
Wheel nuts (exc. cast alum. wheels)	80
W/cast alum. wheels	90

Shock absorbers
Upper attaching bolts and nuts	20
Lower stud nut	65

*Control arms
Upper arm-to-frame nuts	70
Upper arm-to-frame bolts	70
Upper arm-to-axle housing nuts	70
Upper arm-to-axle housing bolts	70
Lower arm-to-frame nuts	70
Lower arm-to-frame bolts	70
Lower arm-to-axle housing nuts	80
Lower arm-to-axle housing bolts	80
Stabilizer shaft-to-lower control arm nut	35

Torque with weight of car on wheels

Steering

1974 through 1978 (power steering)   ft-lb
Gear housing-to-frame	70
Lower coupling flange-to-worm shaft	30
Steering column coupling-to-steering gear shaft flange	20
Gear side cover-to-housing	45
Pitman arm-to-Pitman shaft	180
Adjuster plug locking	80
Pitman shaft lash adjuster locking	35
Rack - piston nut end	75
Ball return guide retainer	5
Pump discharge part	35
Pump-to-mounting bracket	35
Pump mounting bracket-to-engine	35
Pressure hose-to-pump	35
Pressure hose-to-gear	35
Return hose-to-gear	35

1979 through 1980 (power steering)
Gear to frame bolts	70
High pressure line fitting (at gear)	40
Oil return line fitting (at gear)	40

Pitman shaft
Adjusting screw locknut	32
Adjuster plug locknut	80
Pitman shaft nut	185
Coupling flange bolt	30

1974 through 1979 (manual steering)
Gear housing-to-frame	70
Lower coupling flange-to-worm shaft	30

Gear side cover-to-housing 30
Pitman arm-to-pinion shaft 180
Pitman shaft lash adjuster locking 25
Worm bearing adjuster locking 85
Ball return guide retainer 10

1980 (manual steering)
Gear-to-frame bolts 70
Pitman shaft nut 185
Side cover bolts 30
Pitman shaft adjusting screw locknut 25
Coupling flange-to-gear pinch bolt 30
Clamp-to-ball nut screw 4

Steering linkage
1974 through 1976
Steering arm-to-tie rod end .... 30 to 40 (45 max.)
Tie rod clamp .... 19 to 24
Tie rod-to-intermediate rod .... 30 to 50 (55 max.)
Pitman arm-to-intermediate rod .... 40 to 50 (55 max.)
Pitman arm-to-steering gear .... 160 to 210
Idler arm-to-intermediate rod .... 30 to 40 (45 max.)
Idler arm-to-frame .... 45 to 55

1977 through 1978
Steering arm-to-tie rod end nut* 35
Tie rod clamp nuts 14
Tie rod-to-intermediate rod nut* 40
Pitman arm-to-intermediate rod nut* 45
Pitman arm-to-steering gear nut - P/S 185
Idler arm-to-intermediate rod nut* 35
Idler arm-to-frame nut 50

1979 through 1980
Steering arm-to-tie rod end nut 40
Tie rod clamp nuts 14
Tie rod-to-intermediate rod nut 40
Pitman arm-to-intermediate rod nut 45
Pitman arm-to-steering gear nut - P/S 184
    Manual 184
Idler arm-to-intermediate rod nut* 35
Idler arm-to-frame nut 61

*Do not back off to insert cotter pin, turn to next hole

Steering column

1974 through 1976	**ft-lb**	**in-lb**
Pinch bolt, fabric coupling-to-steering gear	30	
Pinch bolt, demountable flange-to-steering gear	30	
Nuts, fabric coupling	20	
Bolt and nut, pot coupling clamp - 1 in	50	
Bolt and nut, pot coupling clamp - $\frac{5}{8}$ in	35	
Spring retaining screw		35
Support screws		60
Housing screws		
Optional		100
Standard		60
Signal switch mounting screws		25
Shaft lock cover screws		15
Ignitlon switch mounting screws		35
Neutral start mounting switch screws		
Optional		20
Standard		15
Tilt release lever screw		30
Hazard warning knob		5
Steering wheel nut	30	
Signal switch lever screw		15
Shift gate mounting screws		45
Bearing screws (synchro)		90
1977 through 1980		
Steering wheel to shaft	30	
Turn signal switch attaching screws		35
Ignition switch attaching screws		35
Bracket-to-steering column support nuts	25	
Toe-pan-to-dash screws		45
Toe-pan clamp screws		60
Bracket to steering column bolt	30	
Cover (tilt and tilt & telescope)-to-housing screws		100
Clamp-to-steering shaft nut (A-B-C)	55	
Support-to-lock plate (tilt and tilt & telescope) screws		
Flex coupling nuts	20	
Flex coupling-to-shaft bolt	30	

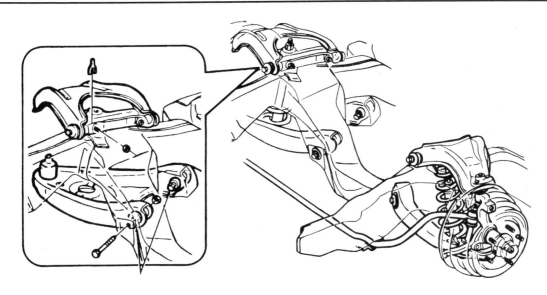

Fig. 11.1 Typical front suspension (Sec 1)

1 General description

The front suspension on all models is of independent type incorporating upper and lower suspension arms, coil springs, hydraulic telescopic shock absorbers and a stabilizer bar.

The rear suspension on all models is of upper and lower control arm type with coil springs and telescopic shock absorbers.

The steering gear is of the recirculating ball type with an energy-absorbing column incorporating an ignition lock. All models can be equipped with power steering or an optional tilt steering column.

Pressed steel wheels are used and bias-ply tires are standard on earlier models with either bias-belted or radial tires on later models.

2 Maintenance and inspection (balljoints)

1　At intervals specified in Chapter 1 check all the steering and suspension joints for wear or deterioration of the rubber bushings or dust excluders. With the help of an assistant check for 'lost' movement between the steering wheel at the front roadwheels which must be due to wear or looseness of the components.

2　Lower suspension arm balljoint wear must be checked in one of the following ways: Check the wear indicators for indication or excessive lower balljoint wear. When new, a dimension of 0.050 inch should exist from the grease nipple fitting to the balljoint cover surface;

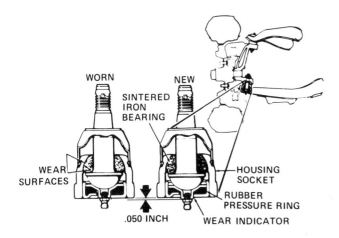

Fig. 11.2 Front suspension balljoint wear indicator (Sec 2)

if the fitting is flush, or has receded inside the cover, the balljoint must be replaced.

3 Front wheel bearings – lubrication, replacement and adjustment

1　See Chapter 1, Section 24 for complete details on servicing the front wheel bearings.

4 Shock absorbers – removal, inspection and installation

Note: *Any sign of oil on the outside of shock absorber bodies will indicate that the seals have started to leak and the units must be replaced as assemblies. Where the shock absorber has failed internally, this is more difficult to detect although rear axle patter or tramp, particularly on uneven road surfaces may provide a clue. When a shock absorber is suspected to have failed, remove it from the vehicle and holding it in a vertical position operate it for the full length of its stroke eight or ten times. Any lack of resistance in either direction will indicate the need for replacement.*

Front shock absorber

1　Raise the front end of the vehicle. Use an open-ended wrench to prevent the upper (squared) end from turning, then remove the upper stem retaining nut, retainer and rubber grommet.

2　Remove the 2 bolts retaining the lower shock absorber pivot to the control arm (photo).

3　Pull the assembly out from the bottom.

4　When installing, fit the lower retainer and rubber grommet in place over the upper stem.

5　Install the shock absorber in the fully extended position up through the lower control arm and spring.

6　Fit the upper rubber grommet, retainer and attaching nut after the shock absorber upper stem has passed through the upper control arm frame bracket.

7　Using an open-ended wrench, hold the upper stem and torque-tighten the retaining nut.

8　Install the bolts at the shock absorber lower pivot, torque tighten, then lower the vehicle.

Rear shock absorber

9　Raise the rear end of the vehicle, and support the rear axle.

10　Remove the lower shock absorber retaining nut, retainer and rubber grommet.

11　Remove the two upper attaching bolts and then remove the shock absorber.

12　When installing, push the lower retainer and rubber grommet into

4.2 Removing the lower bolts for the front shock absorbers

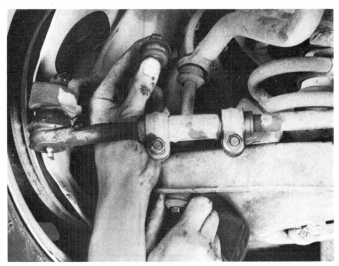

5.1 The ends of the stabilizer bar are secured with a locknut and cushioned with rubber grommets.

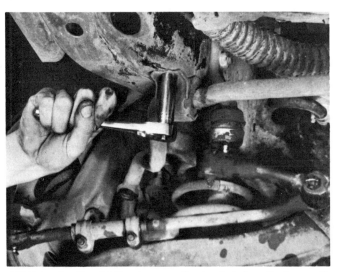

5.2 Removing the stabilizer bar mounting brackets from the frame rails

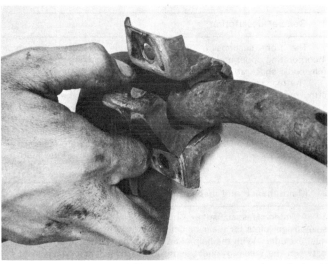

5.5 A rubber insulator is used at each mounting bracket (the slit should go towards the front of the vehicle)

position. Extend the shock absorber to the proper length.
13 Place the shock absorber into position and install the two upper attaching bolts.
14 Push the remaining retainer and grommet into position and install the lower attaching nut.
15 Torque all fasteners and lower the vehicle.

5 Stabilizer bar – removal and installation

Front stabilizer bar
1   Raise the front end of the vehicle then disconnect the stabilizer bar from the lower control arms (photo).
2   Remove the stabilizer bar brackets from the frame then lift away the stabilizer bar (photo).
3   Remove the link bolts, spacers and rubber grommets from the lower control arms or stabilizer bar.
4   Inspect all the parts for damage, wear and deterioration. Fit new parts as necessary.
5   If new frame bushings are required, slide them into position along the stabilizer bar. The slit should be facing the front of the car (photo).
6   When installing, fit the brackets over the bushings and connect them (loosely) to the frame.

7   Ensure that the stabilizer bar is centralized then torque-tighten all the bolts.
8   Lower the vehicle to the ground.

Rear stabilizer bar
9   Raise the rear end of the vehicle and support the rear axle.
10 Remove the stabilizer bar to spring retainer bracket attachment.
11 Remove the stabilizer bar to body bracket bolt and remove the assembly. Make note of any shims used.
12 Fit the bushings onto the stabilizer bar then place the bar in position.
13 Fit the upper retaining bolts and the stabilizer bar to spring attachment. Install bolts loosely at this point.
14 Ensure that the weight of the vehicle is being carried by the rear axle only, then torque-tighten the bolts.
15 Lower the vehicle to the ground.

6 Front coil spring – removal and installation

NOTE: *As the coil spring is under pressure during part of the removal and installation process, proper tools should be used and caution exercised. For added safety, a chain should be used to secure the coil spring to the lower control arm.*

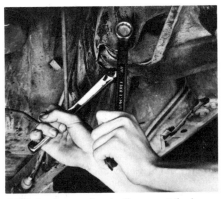

6.7 Using 2 wrenches to disconnect the lower control arm pivot bolt

6.8 Lower the control arm slowly and carefully with the floor jack

7.3 Loosen upper ball stud nut 1 turn

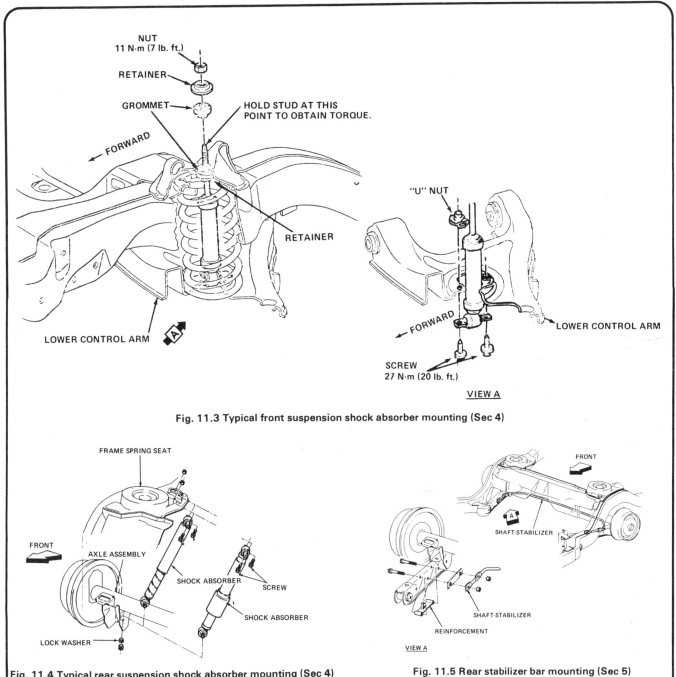

NUT
11 N·m (7 lb. ft.)

RETAINER

GROMMET

HOLD STUD AT THIS
POINT TO OBTAIN TORQUE.

FORWARD

RETAINER

LOWER CONTROL ARM

"U" NUT

FORWARD

LOWER CONTROL ARM

SCREW
27 N·m (20 lb. ft.)

VIEW A

Fig. 11.3 Typical front suspension shock absorber mounting (Sec 4)

FRAME SPRING SEAT

FRONT

AXLE ASSEMBLY

SHOCK ABSORBER

SCREW

SHOCK ABSORBER

LOCK WASHER

Fig. 11.4 Typical rear suspension shock absorber mounting (Sec 4)

FRONT

SHAFT-STABILIZER

SHAFT-STABILIZER

REINFORCEMENT

VIEW A

Fig. 11.5 Rear stabilizer bar mounting (Sec 5)

NOTE Spring to be installed with tape at lowest position. Bottom of spring is coiled helical, and the top is coiled flat with a gripper notch near end of wire.

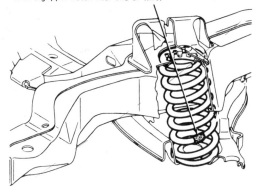

NOTE After assembly, end of spring coil must cover all or part of one inspection drain hole. The other hole must be partly exposed or completely uncovered.

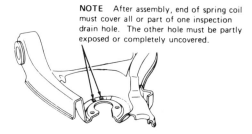

Fig. 11.6 Typical front coil spring mounting (Sec 6)

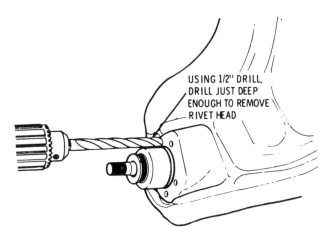

USING 1/2" DRILL DRILL JUST DEEP ENOUGH TO REMOVE RIVET HEAD

Fig. 11.7 Drilling upper balljoint rivet heads for removal (Sec 7)

1 Raise the front end of the vehicle and support firmly with jack stands on the frame. The suspension arms should hang free.
2 Remove the shock absorber (Section 4).
3 Remove the wheel.
4 Disconnect the stabilizer bar from the lower control arm. It can remain intact by the frame brackets.
5 Position a floor jack under the lower control arm. GM dealers have a special adapter for use with floor jacks which cradle the inner bushings.
6 Slowly raise the jack to relieve the tension on the lower control arm pivot bolts. At this point the spring is under pressure. Install a chain around the spring and through the control arm as a safety measure. Check that the floor jack is firmly supporting the control arm and will not slip.
7 With tension off the pivot bolts, remove the rear pivot bolt nut. Remove the forward pivot bolt and nut. It may be necessary to follow

the bolts through the control arm with a hammer and drift (photo).
8 Slowly and carefully lower the floor jack. The control arm should lower with it (photo).
9 Before removing the spring, note the position of the spring in relation to its bottom seat and the identifying tag attached to one of the coils.
10 When all the compression is removed from the spring, remove the safety chain and the spring.
11 During installation, be sure that the coil is properly seated in the lower control arm. The end of the bottom coil should cover all or part of one of the small inspection/drain holes drilled in the control arm. The other hole should be partly or completely uncovered.
12 It is recommended that the safety chain be again used upon installation. With the control arm and spring raised into position, install the pivot bolts and nuts. It is necessary that the front bolt be installed with its head towards the front of the vehicle. The rear bolt can be installed in either direction. Torque-tighten these bolts to specifications before lowering the jack and removing the safety chain.
13 Install the remaining components in the reverse order of disassembly and tighten all fasteners to the proper torque.

7   Front suspension balljoints – removal, inspection and installation

Upper balljoint
1 Raise the front end of the vehicle and remove the wheel.
2 Remove the upper ballstud cotter pin.
3 Loosen the ballstud nut by one turn only (photo).
4 Remove the ballstud nuts.
5 Remove the upper balljoint stud and swing the steering knuckle out of the way.a
6 Raise the uper arm and support it with a block of wood between it and the frame.
7 The balljoint is spring-loaded in its socket to compensate for wear. If there is any lateral play ir if the joint can be turned in its socket with the fingers, the joint should be replaced.
8 If replacement is necessary, use a grinding wheel to remove the rivets, but take care not to damage the control arm or balljoint seat.
9 When installing, fit the balljoint in the control arm and attach with the nuts and bolts provided (nuts at the top). Torque-tighten.
10 Turn the ballstud collar pin hole fore and aft to the length of the car.
11 Remove the wooden blocks used at paragraph 21.
12 Ensure that the tapered hole in the steering knuckle is clean and undamaged then mate the ballstud to it.
13 Install the stud nut and tighten to torque specifications. Tighten the nut further to align the cotterpin holes and then fit a new cotter pin.
14 Install the new lubrication nipple and lubricate the joint.

Lower balljoint
15 Raise the front end of the vehicle.
16 Remove the ballstud cotter pin.
17 Loosen the ballstud nut by one turn only.
18 Press out the balljoint stud using the method described for upper balljoints in paragraph 3.
19 Remove the lower stud nut then pull outwards at the bottom of the tire. At the same time, push the tire and wheel upwards to free the knuckle from the ballstud.
20 Remove the wheel.
21 Raise the upper control arm and place a 2-in x 4-in block of wood between the frame and control arm. If found necessary, remove the tie-rod from the steering knuckle.
22 Using a suitable vise and tubular spacers (GM tools J 9519-7 or J 9519-10 can be used of available) press the lower balljoint out of the control arm.
23 Using a suitable vise and tubular spacers (tools J 9519-9 or J 9519-10) install the replacement balljoint with the air vent in the rubber boot facing inwards.
24 Turn the ballstud cotter pin hole fore and aft to the length of the car.
25 Remove the wooden block used in paragraph 31.
26 Ensure that the tapered hole in the steering knuckle is clean and undamaged then mate the ballstud to it.
27 Install the stud nut and torque-tighten to specifications. Tighten

the nut further and install a new correr pin after aligning the holes.

28 Fit a new lubrication nipple and lubricate the new joint.

29 Replace the wheel (and tie-rod, if removed) and lower the car.

8 Upper suspension control arm – removal, servicing and installation

1 Raise the front end of the vehicle and lower the control arm onto a jack for support.

2 Remove the wheel.

3 Separate the upper control arm ball stud (Section 7).

4 Remove the 2 nuts securing the control arm shaft to the frame bracket. Tape together the shims and ensure that they are eventually installed in the same position.

5 In some cases it will be necessary to remove the upper control arm attaching bolts to provide clearance for removal of the upper control arm assembly. These bolts are splined, and may be removed as follows:

   a) Use a brass drift to tap the bolt gently downwards.
   b) Pry the bolt upwards using a suitable box wrench.
   c) Remove the nut, then use a suitable pry bar and block of wood to pry the bolts from the frame.

6 Remove the upper control arm.

7 If, on inspection, the control arm pivot bushings are worn, their replacement is a job best left to your GM dealer, but if you are to carry out this work without the use of a press, employ a long bolt and suitable tubular spacers for both removal and installation of the bushings.

8 When installing, loosen the endshaft retainer bolts and/or nuts.

9 If removed, position the new control arm attaching bolts loosely in the frame and install the control arm cross-shaft on the attaching bolts.

10 Use a normal free-running nut (not a locknut) to tighten the serrated bolts onto their seats.

11 When the splined bolts are seated, remove the free-running nuts and fit the regular locknuts.

12 Install the shims in their original fitted positions then torque-tighten the nuts. Tighten the thinner shim pack nut first for improved clamping force and torque retention.

13 Install the ball stud through the knuckle, torque-tighten the nut, further tighten to align the cotter pin holes then fit a new cotter pin.

14 Fit the wheel and lower the vehicle to the floor.

15 Torque-tighten the shaft retainer bolts and/or nuts.

9 Lower suspension control arm – removal, servicing and installation

1 Remove the front coil spring (Section 6).

2 Remove the control arm ball stud (Section 7).

3 Remove the control arm from the vehicle.

4 If, on inspection, the control arm pivot bushings are worn, their replacement is best left to your GM dealer but if you are to carry out this work without the use of a press, employ a long bolt and suitable tubular spacers for both removal and installation. **Note:** *It is not essential for the control arm to be removed for bushing replacement except for the front bushings on 1975 and later models.*

5 Installation is the reverse of the removal procedure. Torque-tighten the nuts to the specified torque.

10 Steering knuckle – removal and installation

1 Raise the front end of the vehicle so that the weight is on the springs.

2 Remove the wheels.

3 Remove the disc brake caliper and rotor (Refer to Chapter 9, if necessary). When removing the caliper, use a block of wood to keep the disc pads separated.

4 Remove the splash shield.

5 Hang the caliper assembly from some convenient part of the suspension. Do not let the hydraulic line take the weight.

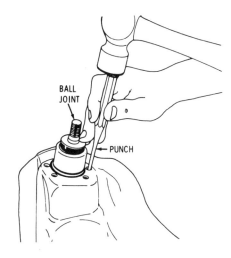

Fig. 11.8 Removing upper balljoint rivets with a punch (Sec 7)

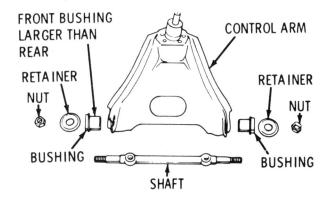

Fig. 11.9 Upper control arm components (Sec 8)

6 Remove the upper and lower ball joint stud cotter pins and disconnect the ball studs from the steering knuckle.

7 Disconnect the tie-rod end from the steering knuckle. This procedure can be found in Section 13.

8 Remove the steering knuckle.

9 When installing, place the steering knuckle into position and insert the upper and lower ball stud.

10 Install the ball stud nuts and torque-tighten to the specified value. Further tighten to align the cotter pin hole and then install a new cotter pin.

11 Connect the tie-rod and tighten to the specified torque.

12 Install the splash shield, hub and rotor.

13 Install the outer bearing, spindle washer and nut. Adjust the bearing as described in Chapter 1.

14 Install the caliper and the wheels. Lower the car to the ground.

11 Rear springs – removal, servicing and installation

1 Raise the car and support it under the frame.

2 Support the rear axle with an adjustable lifting device.

3 On the side from which the spring is to be removed, disconnect the shock absorber at the lower mount. On some models ('74 through '77) disconnect the hydraulic brake line at the axle housing.

4 Disconnect the upper control arm at the axle.

5 Remove stabilizer bar, if applicable.

6 Lower the the jack until the suspension is fully extended. Mark the exact location of the pig-tail on the upper end of the spring and its relation to the frame. Pry the bottom pig tail over the axle retainer and remove the spring and insulator.

7   Installation is the reverse of removal and the spring must be returned to it's exact original location. Bleed the brakes (Chapter 9) on vehicles which required the disconnection of the rear brake lines.

12 Rear suspension control arms – removal, servicing and installation

1   Raise the vehicle and support it so that the rear axle hangs freely.
2   Remove the rear springs as specified in Sec. 11.
3   Use a jack to raise the axle until tension is relieved in the control arm which is to be removed.
4   Extract the control arm pivot bolts and remove the control arms.
5   If the control arm bushings are worn, have your dealer replace them with new ones as a press and special tools are required.
6   Installation is the reverse of removal except that all bolts should not be tightened to specified torque settings until after the vehicle's weight has been lowered onto its suspension.

13 Steering gear and linkage – inspection

1   See Chapter 1, Section 8 for the proper procedures involved in inspecting the steering system.

14 Steering linkage and balljoints – removal and installation

1   The balljoints on the two outer tie-rods and those on the central relay rod are all connected by means of a tapered ball stud located in a tapered hole and secured by a castellated nut and cotter pin.
2   The outer tie-rods are of tubular, internally threaded sleeve type and are secured to the tie-rod ends by clamps and bolts.
3   To remove the balljoint, first raise the front end of the car then remove the ball stud nut. On occasion the tapered studs have been known to simply pull out. More often they are well and truly wedged in position and a gear puller or slotted steel wedges may be driven between the ball unit and the arm to which it is attached. Another method is to place the head of a hammer (or other solid metal article) on one side of the hole in the arm into which the pin is fitted. Then hit it smartly with a hammer on the opposite side. This has the effect of squeezing the taper out and usually works, provided one can get a good swing at it. Always keep the stud nut at the top of the stud threads to protect the threads from damage (photos).
4   Measure the length of exposed thread on each of the tie-rod ends (as a guide to reassembly), release the pinch bolts from the clamps and unscrew the tie-rod end from the tie-rod sleeve (photo).
5   When installing the new tie-rod ends, screw them into the sleeves exactly the same amount as the original ones.
6   Arrange for your dealer to check the toe-in, or follow the

14.3b A puller is then installed in position and tightened against the threaded stud

14.3c With the puller tight, a sharp blow with a hammer will break the connection

14.3a After removing the cotter pin, the locknut is loosened to the end of the threaded stud

14.4 When replacing tie rods, count the number of exposed threads and mark the threaded shaft to enable the new tie rod to be installed in the same position

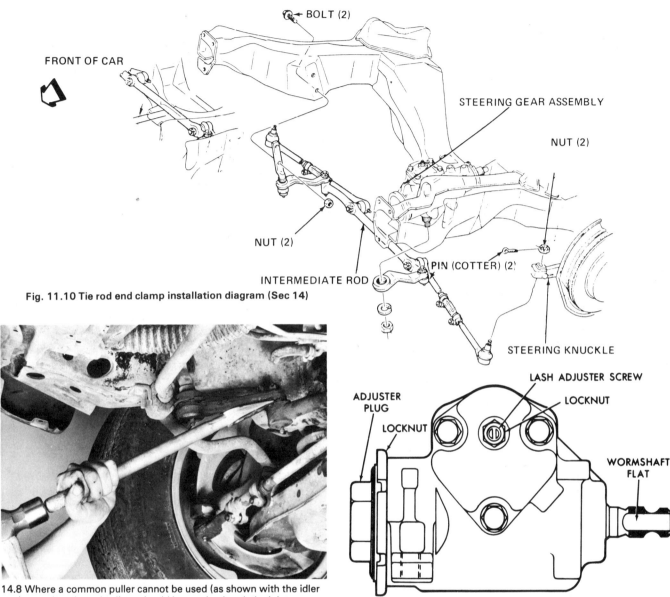

Fig. 11.10 Tie rod end clamp installation diagram (Sec 14)

14.8 Where a common puller cannot be used (as shown with the idler arm), a wedge-shaped splitter should be used to break the joint connection

Fig. 11.11 Typical steering gear adjustment points (Sec 14)

procedure given in Section 33. Pay particular attention to the special instructions for the position of the clamps if you are carrying out this operation yourself.

7   If the balljoints on the central relay rod are worn then the relay rod will have to be replaced as an assembly. Again, the toe-in will have to be checked afterwards (see previous paragraph).

8   If it is necessary to remove the idler arm this is first disconnected at the frame mounting (one nut, washer and bolt), then disconnected at the idler arm end by using the same procedure given for the other steering linkage joints (photo).

15 Manual steering gear – maintenance and adjustment (steering gear in car)

1   The steering gear is normally filled with lubricant for life and unless a severe leak occurs, necessitating a complete overhaul, refilling with lubricant will not be required.

2   In order to rectify conditions of lost motion, slackness and vibration which have been found to be directly attributable to the steering gear, carry out the following operations:

3   Disconnect the ground cable from the battery.

4   Remove the nut from the Pitman arm and then mark the relative position of the arm to the Pitman shaft.

5   Using a suitable extractor remove the Pitman arm.

6   Loosen the adjuster plug locknut on the steering gear and unscrew the adjuster plug one quarter-turn.

7   Remove the horn button or shroud from the steering wheel and then turn the steering wheel in one direction to full lock and then turn the wheel back through one half turn. Now apply a $\frac{3}{4}$ inch socket to the steering wheel center nut and either using a torque wrench or a spring balance check the bearing drag when the wheel is turned through a 90° arc of travel.

8   This drag is the thrust bearing preload and it should be within the specifications listed at the front of this chapter. Tighten or slacken the adjuster plug until the correct preload is obtained and then torque-tighten the adjuster plug locknut.

9   Any jerky or lumpy feeling as the steering wheel is turned will indicate worn or damaged bearings in the steering gear.

10   Now turn the steering wheel gently from one stop to the other counting the number of turns of the steering wheel from lock-to-lock. Now turn the wheel exactly half the number of turns counted so that the steering gear is in the centered position.

11   Loosen the lash adjuster screw locknut and turn the lash adjuster

screw clockwise until all lash has been removed from between the ball nut and the Pitman shaft sector teeth. Torque-tighten the locknut.

12 Now check the 'over-center' preload by taking the highest torque reading obtainable as the wheel is moved through its centered position. The preload should be within the specifications listed at the front of this chapter, **in excess of** the torque stated at paragraph 8 above. Adjust the position of the lash adjuster screw if necessary to achieve this.

13 Install the Pitman arm and horn shroud, and connect the battery ground cable.

16 Steering wheel – removal and installation

Standard models
1 Disconnect the negative battery cable.
2 Remove the screws securing the steering wheel shroud. These are on the underside of the steering wheel towards the dashboard.
3 Lift the steering wheel shroud and horn contact lead assembly from the steering wheel.
4 On 1975 – 1980 models, remove the snap ring from the steering shaft (photo).

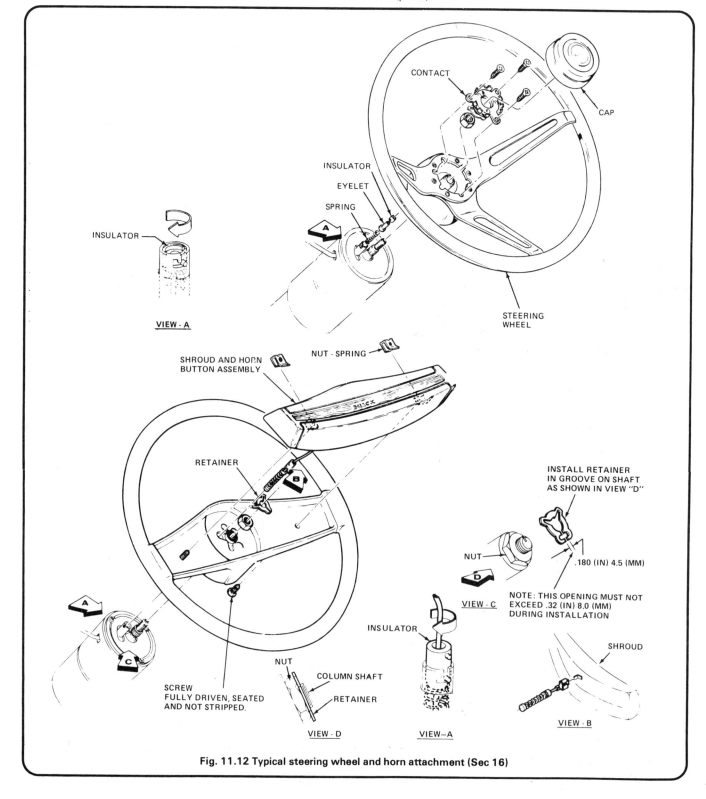

Fig. 11.12 Typical steering wheel and horn attachment (Sec 16)

16.4 Some models may have a retaining clip over the main shaft nut

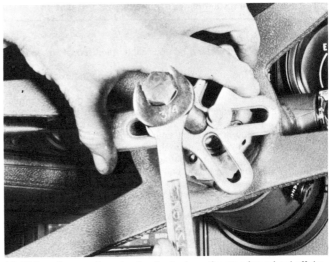

16.17 Install a steering wheel puller to draw the steering wheel off the column

5   Mark the steering wheel and column to enable installation of the wheel in the same position.

6   Remove the steering wheel lock nut from the shaft.

7   Using a steering wheel puller, remove the steering wheel from the column. Threaded holes are provided in the steering wheel to accept the puller anchor screws. Use the lock nut to protect the top threads of the threaded shaft. Do not strike the puller or the end of the column as this may damage components of the collapsible steering column.

8   When installing, set the turn signal lever to the neutral position and set the wheel into position. Use the alignment marks made upon disassembly to correctly position the wheel.

9   Tighten the steering wheel lock nut to the proper specifications. Do not overtighten this nut as this may cause interference problems. Install the snap ring (1975 – 1980 models).

10 Place the shroud onto the wheel, guiding the horn contact lead into the directional signal canceling cam tower.

11 Install the shroud attaching screws and connect the negative battery cable. Check the operation of the horn.

Cushioned steering wheel models
12 Disconnect the negative battery cable.
13 Carefully pry off the horn button cap with a screwdriver (photos).

14 On 1975 – 1980 models, remove the snap ring from the end of the shaft (photo).

15 Remove the steering wheel lock nut.

16 Remove the three screws securing the upper horn insulator and remove the insulator, receiver, belleville spring and shim (if used).

17 Use a steering wheel puller to remove the steering wheel from the column (photo). Threaded holes are provided in the steering wheel for the puller anchor screws. Use the lock nut to protect the top threads of the steering shaft. Do not strike the puller or the end of the column with a hammer as this may damage internal components of the collapsible column.

18 To install, place the turn signal lever in the neutral position and set the wheel onto the steering shaft. Use the alignment marks made upon disassembly to correctly position the steering wheel. Secure with the lock nut, tightening the nut to the proper specifications. Do not overtighten this nut.

19 Install the snap ring (1975 – 1980 models).

20 Install the horn lower insulator, eyelet and spring in the horn contact tower.

21 Install the belleville spring, receiver and horn upper insulator and secure with the three screws.

22 Install the horn button cap and connect the negative battery cable. Check the operation of the horn.

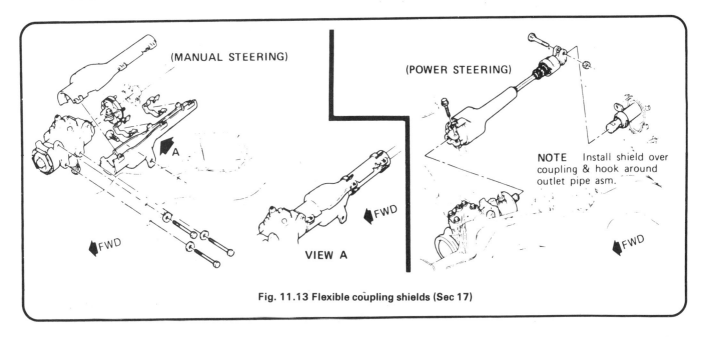

(MANUAL STEERING)

(POWER STEERING)

NOTE   Install shield over coupling & hook around outlet pipe asm.

A

FWD

FWD

VIEW A

FWD

Fig. 11.13 Flexible coupling shields (Sec 17)

17 Steering column couplings – removal and installation

Flexible coupling

1   Disconnect the battery ground cable (and coupling shield if applicable).
2   Remove the intermediate steering shaft flange to flexible coupling retaining bolts.
3   Remove the steering gear to frame bolts; lower the steering gear.
4   Push the intermediate shaft rearwards and rotate it out of the way.
5   Using a suitable 12-point socket wrench, remove the coupling clamp bolt. Remove the flexible coupling.
6   Install the flexible coupling to the steering gear wormshaft splined end, taking care to align the mating flats.
7   Install the coupling clamp bolt and torque tighten, after ensuring that the coupling reinforcement is bottomed on the wormshaft.
8   Install the intermediate shaft to the coupling and loosely install the flange to coupling bolts.
9   Install the steering gear to frame bolts and torque-tighten.
10   Align the flexible coupling pins centrally in the intermediate shaft flange slots then torque-tighten the coupling bolts.
11   Connect the battery ground lead (and the coupling shield, if applicable).

Pot joint coupling

12   Disconnect the battery ground cable (and the coupling shield, if applicable).
13   Remove the intermediate shaft flange to flexible coupling retaining bolts.
14   Remove the pot joint clamping bolt (at the steering shaft).
15   Remove the steering gear to frame bolts; lower the gear.
16   Push the intermediate steering shaft rearwards until it bottoms in the pot joint and clears the flexible coupling alignment pins.
17   Remove the intermediate shaft and pot joints as an assembly.
18   When installing, align the flats on the pot joint and steering shaft then mate them. Install the clamp and bolt, and torque-tighten.
19   Install the intermediate shaft to the flexible coupling and loosely install the coupling bolts.
20   Install the steering gear to the frame bolts and torque-tighten.
21   Align the flexible coupling pins centrally in the intermediate shaft flange slots then torque-tighten the coupling bolts.
22   Connect the battery ground cable (and the coupling shield, if applicable).

18 Pot joint coupling – disassembly and reassembly

1   To disassemble the pot joint, pry off the snap-ring and slide the coupling over the shaft. Remove the bearings and tension spring from the pivot pin. Clean the pin and the end of the shaft then scribe a

location mark on the pin on the same side as the shaft chamber. Support the shaft securely then press out the pin taking care that it is not damaged, or bearing damage may occur. Remove the seal clamp then slide the seal off the end of the shaft.
2   To reassemble the pot joint, first ensure that all the parts are clean then slide the seal onto the shaft so that the lip of the seal is against the shoulder on the shaft. Install the clamp. Press the pin into the shaft, aligning the scribed location marks. Ensure that the pin is centered within 0.012 inch, or binding will result. Liberally grease the inside and outside of the bearings and the inside of the cover then install the tension spring and bearings on the pin. Install the seal into the end of the cover and secure with the snap-ring.

19 Manual steering gear – removal and installation

1   Remove the battery ground cable (and the coupling shield, if applicable).
2   Remove the nuts, lockwashers and bolts at the steering shaft to coupling flange.
3   Remove the Pitman arm lock nut and washer. Mark the position of the Pitman arm in relation to the shaft and remove the Pitman arm with a suitable puller.
4   Remove the screws securing the steering gear to the frame and remove it from the vehicle.
5   When installing, place the gear into position so that the coupling mounts properly on the flanged end of the steering shaft. Secure the gear to the frame, fit the washers and bolts, then torque-tighten.
6   Secure the steering coupling to the flanged end of the column with the lockwashers and nuts. Torque-tighten the nuts.
7   Install the Pitman arm.
8   Connect the battery ground cable (and the coupling shield, if applicable).

20 Pitman shaft seal (manual steering) – replacement (steering gear in car)

1   Remove the Pitman arm.
2   Turn the steering from stop-to-stop and count the exact number of turns. Now rotate the wheel half the number of turns counted so that the steering gear is centered (wormshaft flat at 12 o'clock position).
3   Remove the side cover from the steering gear housing (three screws) and lift the Pitman shaft and side cover from the housing.
4   Pry the seal from the housing using a screwdriver and tap a new one into position using a suitable socket or piece of tube.
5   Remove the lash adjuster screw locknut and detach the side cover from the Pitman shaft by turning the adjuster screw clockwise.
6   Insert the Pitman shaft into the steering gear so that the center tooth of the shaft sector enters the center tooth of the ball nut.
7   Pack the specified grease into the housing and install a new side cover gasket. Install the side cover onto the lash adjuster screw. This is achieved by inserting a small screwdriver through the threaded adjuster hole in the side cover and turning the lash adjuster screw counterclockwise. When the screw bottoms, turn it back ¼ turn.
8   Tighten the side cover bolts to the specified torque.
9   Carry out the adjustments described previously and tighten the lash adjuster screw locknut.
10   Install the Pitman arm.

21 Turn signal switch – removal and installation

1   Disconnect the negative battery cable and remove the steering wheel as detailed in Section 16.
2   Remove the steering column trim cover located at the base of the dashboard.
3   At the end of the steering column, late models have a plastic cover plate which should be pried out of the column using a screwdriver in the slots provided (photo).
4   The lock plate will now have to be removed from the steering column. This is held in place with a snap ring which fits into a groove in the steering shaft. The lock plate must be depressed to relieve pressure on the snap ring. A special U-shaped tool which fits on the shaft should be used to depress the lock plate as the snap ring is removed from its groove (photo).

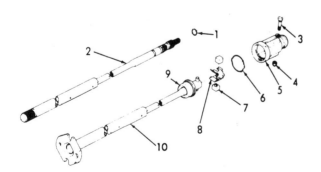

Fig. 11.14 Exploded view of pot joint coupling (Sec 18)

1	Stop ring	6	Snap-ring
2	Upper shaft	7	Bearings
3	Coupling bolt	8	Clip
4	Nut	9	Seal
5	Coupling	10	Lower shaft

21.3 Removing the plastic cover with a screwdriver

21.4 The steering column lock plate is held tightly in place by a snap ring on the center shaft (the plate must be depressed as the snap ring is pried off)

21.8 The turn signal mechanism is held in place with 3 screws and can be drawn off the column once the lever is removed

5   Slide the cancelling cam, upper bearing preload spring and thrust washer off the end of the shaft.
6   Remove the turn signal lever attaching screw and withdraw the turn signal lever from the side of the column.
7   Push in on the hazard warning knob and unscrew the knob from the threaded shaft.
8   Remove the three turn signal assembly mounting screws (photo).
9   Pull the switch wiring connector out of the bracket on the steering column jacket. Tape the connector terminals to prevent damage. Feed the wiring connector up through the column support bracket and pull the switch, wiring harness and connectors out the top of the steering column.
10 Installation is a reversal of removal, however, make sure the wiring harness is in the protector as it is pulled into position. Before installing the thrust washer, upper bearing preload spring and cancelling cam, make sure the switch is in the neutral position and the warning knob is pulled out. Always use a new snap ring on the shaft for the lock plate.

22 Ignition lock cylinder – removal and installation

1974 thru 1978
1   The lock cylinder is located on the upper right-hand side of the steering column. The lock cylinder should only be removed in the 'RUN' position, otherwise damage to the warning buzzer switch may occur.
2   Remove the steering wheel (Section 16) and directional signal switch (Section 21). **Note:** *The directional signal switch need not be fully removed provided that it is pushed rearwards far enough for it to be slipped over the end of the shaft. Do not pull the harness out of the column.*
3   Insert a thin blade or driver into the slot in the turn signal switch housing. Break the housing flash loose and at the same time depress the spring latch at the lower end of the lock cylinder. Holding the latch depressed withdraw the lock cylinder from the housing.
4   The lock cylinder cannot be dismantled; a new one (coded to accept the original key) must be installed in the original cylinder sleeve after the assembly has been dismantled by releasing the cylinder to sleeve staking.
5   To assemble the new lock cylinder to the sleeve, insert the ignition key part way into the lock and then place the wave washer and anti-theft ring onto the lower end of the lock cylinder, making sure that the plastic keeper in the sleeve protrudes.
6   Now align the lock bolt on the cylinder and the tab of the anti-theft washer with the slot in the sleeve. Push the lock cylinder fully onto the sleeve and then insert the ignition key fully and rotate the cylinder clockwise.
7   Rotate the lock counterclockwise to 'LOCK'.
8   Secure the lock assembly in the jaws of a vise suitably protected with wood or cloth. Install the adaptor ring onto the lower end of the cylinder so that the finger of the adaptor is located at the step in the sleeve and the serrated edge of the adaptor can be seen after assembly to the cylinder. The key must also be free to rotate at least 120°.

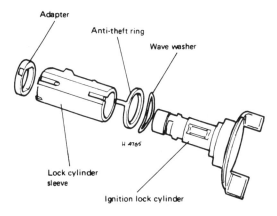

Fig. 11.15 Ignition lock cylinder (Sec 22)

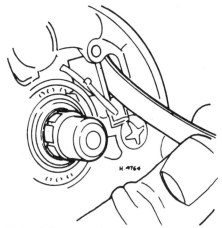

Fig. 11.16 Breaking turn signal housing flash to release lock cylinder (Sec 22)

9   Tap the adaptor onto the cylinder until it is at the bottom of the cylinder flats and the cylinder projects about $\frac{1}{16}$ inch above the adaptor.
10 Using a small punch, stake the lock cylinder over the adaptor ring in four positions just outboard of the four dimples.
11 To install the new lock cylinder/sleeve assembly, hold the sleeve and rotate the lock clockwise against the stop.
12 Insert the cylinder/sleeve assembly into the housing so that the key on the cylinder sleeve is aligned with the housing key way.
13 Insert a 0.070 in diameter drill between the lock bezel and the housing and then rotate the cylinder counterclockwise, maintaining pressure on the cylinder until the drive section mates with the sector.
14 Press in the lock cylinder until the snap-ring engages in the grooves and secures the cylinder in the housing. Remove the drill and check the lock action.
15 Install the turn signal switch and the steering wheel.

1979 thru 1980

16 The lock cylinder should be removed in the 'RUN' position only.
17 Remove the steering wheel (Section 16) and turn signal switch (Section 21). It is not necessary to completely remove the switch. Pull it up and over the end of the steering shaft. Do not pull the wiring harness out of the column.
18 Remove the ignition key warning switch (Section 23).
19 Using a magnetized screwdriver, remove the lock retaining screw. Do not allow this screw to drop down into the column as this will require a complete disassembly of the steering column to retrieve the screw.
20 Pull the lock cylinder out of the side of the steering column.
21 To install, rotate the lock cylinder set and align the cylinder key with the keyway in the steering column housing.
22 Push the lock all the way in and install the retaining screw.
23 Install the remaining components referring to the appropriate Sections.

23 Ignition key warning switch – removal and installation

1   The ignition key warning switch is located within the column housing. It can be removed with or without the ignition lock cylinder.
2   Remove the steering wheel (Section 16).
3   Follow the procedures outlined in Section 21 for removing the turn signal switch, however do not completely remove the switch. Pull the switch over the end of the column shaft. Do not pull the wiring harness out of the steering column.
4   If the ignition lock cylinder is still intact, set the key to the 'ON' position.
5   Use a piece of stiff wire (a paper clip will work fine) to remove the switch. Make a hook at the end of the wire and lip this hooked end into the loop of the clip at the top of the switch. Pull up on the wire and remove the clip and switch together from the steering column. Do not allow the clip to fall down into the column.
6   If the lock cylinder is still in the column, the buzzer switch actuating button (on the lock cylinder) must be depressed before the new warning switch can be installed.

7   Install the switch with the contacts towards the upper end of the steering column and with the formed end of the spring clip at the lower end of the switch. Reinstall the remaining components referring to the appropriate Sections.

24 Ignition switch – removal and installation

1   As a precaution against theft of the vehicle, the ignition switch is located inside the channel section of the brake pedal support and remotely controlled by a rod and rack assembly from the ignition lock cylinder.

1974 thru 1976

2   To remove the ignition switch, the steering column must either be removed or lowered and well supported. There is no need to remove the steering wheel.
3   Before removing the switch (two screws) set it to the 'LOCK' position. If the lock cylinder and actuating rod have already been removed, the 'LOCK' position of the switch can be determined by inserting a screwdriver in the actuating rod slot and then moving the switch slide up until a definite stop is felt and then moving it down one detent.
4   Installation is a reversal of removal but again the switch must be in the 'LOCK' position and the original or identical type securing screws must be used. Longer or thicker screws could cause the collapsible design of the steering column to become inoperative.
5   When installing the steering column, refer to Section 25.

1977 thru 1980

6   On these models, the switch should be set to the 'OFF-UN-LOCKED' position before removal. If the lock cylinder has already been removed, the switch actuating rod should be pulled up until a definite stop is felt and then pushed down two detents.
7   Before installing the switch, set it to the 'OFF-UNLOCK' position and set the gearshift lever in neutral. Setting the switch should be carried out in the following way. Move the switch slider two positions to the right from 'ACCESSORY' to 'OFF/UNLOCK'. Fit the actuator rod into the slider hole and assemble to the steering column using two screws. These screws must be of the original type and only tighten the lower one to 35 in-lb torque.

25 Steering column – removal and installation

1   Disconnect the battery ground cable.
2   Remove the steering wheel.
3   Remove the nuts and washers securing the flanged end of the steering shaft to the flexible couplings. On later models, loosen the front dash mounting plates.
4   Disconnect the transmission control linkage (column shift) or backdrive linkage (floor shift).
5   Disconnect the steering column harness at the connector and the neutral start switch and back-up lamp switch connectors if so equipped.
6   On 1974 models, remove the screws which secure the 2 halves of the floor pan cover, then remove the screws securing the halves and seal to floor pan. Remove the covers.
7   On 1975 thru 1976 vehicles, remove the column plate-to-floor pan screws.
8   For 1977 on, the removal operations are similar to those mentioned above except the intermediate shaft coupling should be separated from the lower end of the steering column by removal of the connecting bolt. Extract the screws which secure the two halves of the floorpan cover and remove the covers.
9   Remove the transmission indicator cable, where applicable.
10 For accessibility, move the front seat to its rearward position.
11 Remove the column bracket-to-instrument panel nuts, then with the help of an assistant, remove the assembly from the vehicle.
12 The following assembly operations must be strictly adhered to in order that the built-in safety design characteristics of the steering column will be able to function properly in an accident.
13 Refer to the accompanying illustration (1979 shown) and assemble the lower dash cover to the seal.
14 Loosely assemble the covers to the column. The dash cover must be able to slide on the mast jacket.

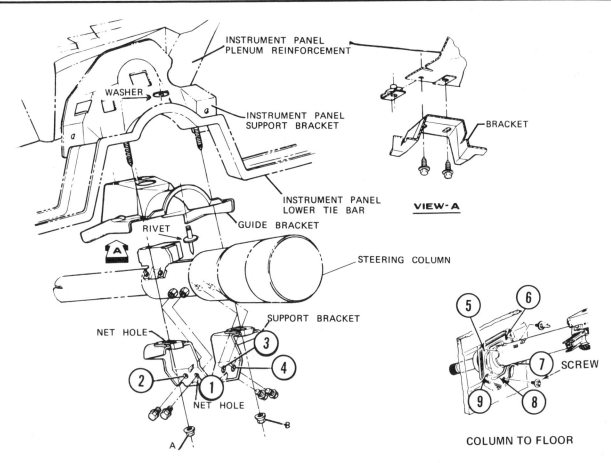

Fig. 11.17 Steering column installation diagram (see text for key) (Sec 25)

15 Attach the bracket to the jacket and install the bolts 1, 2, 3 and 4 in that order.
16 Install the ignition switch connector to the ignition switch.
17 Install the steering column into the vehicle and connect the flange to the flexible coupling. Fit the lockwasher and nuts into place.
18 Fit the nuts (A and B) loosely.
19 Locate the lower cover to the dash by starting screw (9) in its hole.
20 Install the screws in the following order, tightening each one as it is installed: 5, 6, 7, 8, 9.
21 Install and tighten the two cover screws.

26 Steering column (standard version) – disassembly and reassembly

1   Remove the four dash panel bracket-to-steering column screws and retain the bracket so that the mounting capsules will not be damaged.
2   Secure the column in a vise by gripping one set only of the weld nuts.
3   Remove the directional signal switch and lock cylinder, and the ignition key warning switch and the ignition switch as described previously.
4   On column shift models, drive out the upper shift lever pivot pin and remove the shift lever.
5   Remove the upper bearing and thrust washer.
6   Remove the 4 screws which attach the directional signal switch and ignition lock housing to the jacket; remove the housing assembly.
7   Take out the thrust cap from the lower side of the housing.
8   Lift the ignition switch actuating rod and rack assembly together with the shaft lock bolt and spring assembly from the housing.
9   Remove the shift gate.
10 Remove the ignition switch actuator sector through the lock cylinder hole by pushing on the block tooth sector with a rod or punch.
11 Remove the gearshift lever housing and shroud, or the transmission control lock tube housing and shroud, as applicable.

12 Remove the shift lever spring from the gearshift housing, or the lock tube spring, as applicable.
13 Pull the steering shaft from the lower end of the jacket assembly.
14 Remove the back-up switch or neutral safety switch (2 screws).
15 Remove the lower bearing retainer.
16 *Automatics and floorshifts:* Remove the lower bearing retainer, adaptor assembly, shift tube spring and washer. Press out the lower bearing by applying pressure to the outer race then slide out the shift tube assembly.
17 *Column shift (manual transmission):* Remove the lower bearing adaptor, bearing and first/reverse shift lever. Press out the lower bearing by applying pressure to the outer race. Remove 3 screws from the lower end bearing and slide out the shift tube assembly.
18 From the upper end of the mast jacket, remove the gearshift housing lower bearing.
19 Replace any worn components and commence reassembly by applying a thin coating of lithium soap grease to all friction surfaces, and then installing the sector into the turn signal housing. To do this, reach through the lock cylinder hole, place the sector onto the shaft using a blunt tool.
20 Install the shift gate onto the housing.
21 Insert the rack preload spring into the housing from the lower end so that both ends of the spring are attached to the housing.
22 Assemble the locking bolt to the crossover arm on the rack.
23 Insert the rack and lock bolt assembly into the housing (teeth upwards). Align the first tooth on the sector with the first tooth on the rack so that the block teeth will line up when the rack assembly is pushed right in.
24 Install the thrust cup into the housing.
25 Install the gearshift housing lower bearing, aligning the indentations with the projections in the jacket.
26 Install the shift lever spring into the housing.
27 Install the housing and shroud assemblies onto the mast jacket, rotating slightly to ensure proper seating in the bearing.
28 With the shift lever housing in position, and the gearshift housing at 'park', pull the rack downwards and install the directional signal

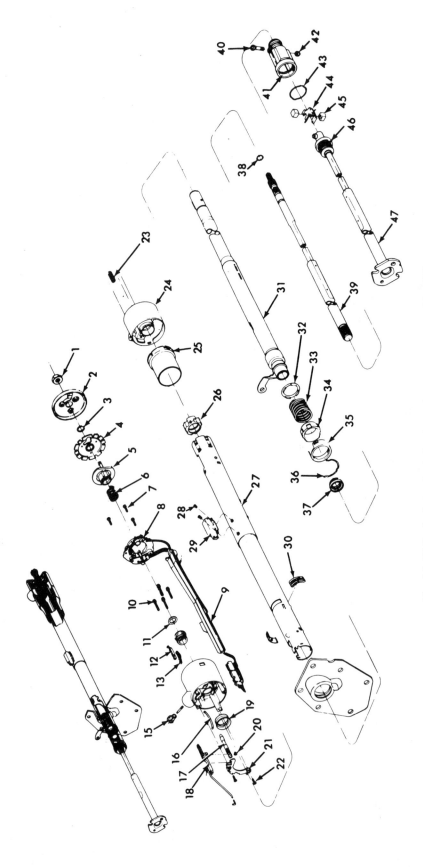

Fig. 11.18 Typical standard steering column components (Sec 26)

1 Shaft nut
2 Cover
3 Lock plate retaining ring
4 Lock plate
5 Cancelling cam
6 Bearing preload spring
7 Turn signal screws
8 Turn signal switch
9 Protector cover
10 Turn signal housing screws

11 Bearing thrust washer
12 Key warning switch
13 Switch clip
14 Turn signal housing
15 Ignition switch sensor
16 Switch pack preload spring
17 Shaft lock bolt
18 Switch rod and rack assembly
19 Thrust cap

20 Shaft lock bolt washer
21 Shift lever detent plate
22 Detent plate screws
23 Shift lever spring
24 Gearshift lever housing
25 Shift shroud
26 Gearshift housing bearing
27 Mast jacket
28 Ignition switch screws
29 Ignition switch

30 Neutral safety or back-up switch retainers
31 Shift tube
32 Thrust spring washer
33 Shift tube thrust spring
34 Lower bearing adapter
35 Lower bearing reinforcement
36 Retainer
37 Lower bearing

38 Shaft stop ring
39 Steering shaft
40 Pot joint bolt
41 Nut
42 Pot joint cover
43 Seal retaining ring
44 Bearing spring
45 Bearing blocks
46 Pot joint seal
47 Intermediate shaft

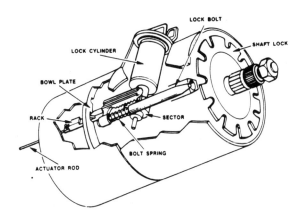

Fig. 11.19 Standard column locking and neutral start systems (Sec 26)

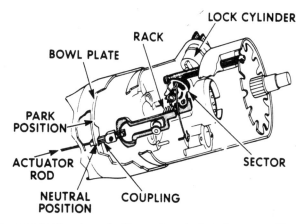

Fig. 11.20 Tilt column locking and neutral start systems (Sec 27)

switch and lock cylinder housing onto the jacket. When seated, install the 4 screws.

29 Press the lower bearing fully into the adaptor assembly.

30 *Automatics and floorshifts:* Assemble the spring, and the lower bearing and adaptor assembly into the bottom of the jacket. Hold the adaptor in place then install the lower bearing reinforcement and retainer. Ensure that the retainer snaps into the slots.

31 *Column shift (manual transmission):* Loosely install the 3 screws in the jacket and shift tube bearing. Assemble the first/reverse lever, and lower bearing and adaptor assembly into the bottom of the jacket. Hold the adaptor in place then install the bearing reinforcement and retainer. Ensure that the retainer snaps into the slots. Place a 0.005 inch shim (feeler) between the first/reverse lever and spacer then turn the upper shift tube bearing down and tighten the 3 screws. Finally remove the shim.

32 Install the neutral safety or back-up switch.

33 Slide the steering shaft into the column then install the upper bearing thrust washer.

34 Install the ignition key warning switch, directional signal switch, lock cylinder assembly and ignition switch, as described previously.

35 Install the shift lever and shift lever pivot pin, then remove the assembly from the vise.

36 Install the 4 dash bracket to column screws and torque-tighten.

27 Steering column (tilt version) – disassembly and reassembly

1 Initially follow the procedure given in paragraphs 1, 2 and 3 for dismantling of the standard version column.

2 Remove the tilt release lever then drive out the shift lever pivot pin and remove the shift lever from the housing.

3 Remove the directional signal housing (3 screws).

4 Install the tilt release lever and move the column to the highest position. Use a suitable screwdriver to remove the tilt lever spring retainer by pressing inwards approximately $\frac{3}{16}$ inch then turning $\frac{1}{8}$ turn (45°) counterclockwise until the ears align with the grooves in the housing.

5 Remove the pot joint to steering shaft clamp bolt then remove the intermediate shaft and pot joint assembly.

6 Push the upper shaft in sufficiently to remove the upper bearing inner race and seat. Pry off the lower bearing retainer and remove the bearing reinforcement, bearing and bearing adaptor assembly from the lower end of the mast jacket.

7 Withdraw the upper bearing housing pivot pins using a suitable nut and bolt (GM tool no J-21854-1 is recommended).

8 Install the tilt release lever and disengage the lock shoes then remove the bearing housing by pulling upwards to extend the rack fully down. Now move the housing to the left to disengage the ignition switch rack from the actuator rod.

9 Remove the steering shaft assembly from the upper end of the column, then the upper bearing seat and inner race.

10 Disassemble the shaft by removing the centering spheres and anti-lash spring.

11 Remove the transmission indicator wire, where applicable.

12 Remove the 4 screws retaining the shaft bearing housing support followed by the housing support. Remove the ignition switch actuator rod.

13 Using a suitable extractor, remove the shift tube (or transmission control lock tube – floorshift) from the lower end of the mast jacket.

14 Remove the bearing housing support lockplate by sliding out of the jacket notches and tipping it down towards the hub at the 12 o'clock position. Slide it under the jacket opening and remove the wave washer.

15 Remove the shift lever housing or lock tube housing from the mast jacket. Remove the shift lever spring by winding it up with pliers, then pulling it out. On floor change models the spring plunger has to be removed.

16 To disassemble the bearing housing, remove the tilt lever opening shield then take out the lock bolt spring by removing the retaining screw and moving the spring clockwise.

17 Remove the snap-ring from the sector driveshaft then use a small punch to lightly tap the driveshaft from the sector. Remove the driveshaft, sector, lockbolt, rack and rack spring.

18 Drive out the tilt release lever then remove the lever and spring. To relieve the load on the release lever, hold the shoes inwards and wedge a block between the top of the shoes (over the slots) and the bearing housing.

19 Drive out the lock shoe retaining pin then the lock shoe springs. **Note**: *With the tilt lever opening on the left and the shoes uppermost, the 4-slot shoe is on the left.*

20 If the bearings are to be replaced, remove the separator and balls. Carefully drive out the race from the housing, followed by the second race.

21 During the assembly procedure, all friction surfaces should be lightly smeared with lithium based grease.

22 Where dismantled, carefully press the bearing into the housing using a suitable sized socket.

23 Install the lockshoe springs, shoes and shoe pin, using a suitable rod (approx. 0.180 inch) for locating purposes.

24 Install the shoe release lever, spring and pin. To relieve the release lever load, hold the shoes inwards and wedge a block between the top of the shoes (over the slots) and bearing housing.

25 Install the sector driveshaft; lightly tap it on until the snap-ring can be installed.

26 Install the lockbolt and engage it with the sector cam surface then install the rack and spring. The block tooth on the rack must engage correctly in the sector. Install the tilt release lever.

27 Install the lockbolt spring. Torque-tighten the retaining screw.

28 Wind up the shift lever spring with pliers and install (push) it onto the housing. On floor shift models the plunger has to be installed.

29 Slide the gearshift lever housing onto the steering mast jacket.

30 Install the wave-washer for the bearing support lockplate.

31 Install the lockplate, working it into the notches in the jacket by tipping towards the housing hub at the 12 o'clock position and sliding it under the jacket opening. The lockplate can then be slid into the notches in the jacket.

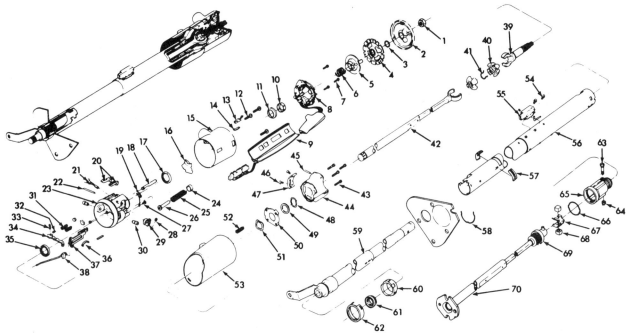

Fig. 11.21 Tilt steering column components (Sec 27)

1   Shaft nut
2   Cover
3   Lock plate retaining ring
4   Lock plate
5   Cancelling cam
6   Bearing preload spring
7   Directional signal screws
8   Directional signal switch
9   Protector cover
10 Upper bearing seat
11 Upper bearing race
12 Turn signal housing
    screws
13 Key warning switch
14 Switch clip
15 Direction signal housing
16 Tilt lever opening
    shield
17 Upper bearing
18 Shaft lock bolt

19 Lock bolt spring
20 Lock shoes
21 Sector shaft
22 Lock shoe pin
23 Bearing housing
24 Tilt lever spring
    retainer
25 Tilt lever spring
26 Tilt lever spring guide
27 Lock bolt spring screw
28 Sector snap ring
29 Sector
30 Bearing housing pivot
    pins
31 Shoe release springs
32 Spring
33 Shoe release lever pin
34 Shoe release lever
35 Lower bearing

36 Ignition switch rack
    spring
37 Ignition switch rack
38 Ignition switch rod
39 Upper steering shaft
40 Centering spheres
41 Centre sphere spring
42 Lower steering shaft
43 Screws
44 Bearing housing support
45 Pin
46 Shift tube index plate
    screws
47 Shift tube index plate
48 Support retaining ring
49 Support thrust washer
50 Support plate lock
51 Support wave washer
52 Gearshift lever spring

53 Gearshift lever housing
54 Ignition switch screws
55 Ignition switch
56 Mast jacket
57 Neutral-safety or
    back-up switch retainers
58 Shift tube
59 Lower bearing adaptor
60 Lower bearing
61 Lower bearing
    reinforcement
62 Retainer
63 Pot joint bolt
64 Nut
65 Pot joint cover
66 Seal retaining ring
67 Bearing spring
68 Bearing blocks
69 Pot joint seal
70 Intermediate shaft

32 Carefully install the shift tube into the lower end of the mast jacket, aligning the keyway in the tube with the key in the shift lever housing. The next part of the operation ideally requires the use of GM tool no J-23073 although by the judicious use of spacers, washers and a long bolt a suitable alternative can be made up. Install the tube as shown and pull the shift tube into the housing by rotating the outer nut. Do not exert any load on the end of the shift tube and ensure that the shift tube lever is aligned with the slotted opening at the lower end of the mast jacket.
33 Install the bearing support thrust washer and retaining ring by pulling the shift lever housing upwards to compress the wave washer.
34 Install the bearing support, aligning the 'V' in the support with the 'V' in the jacket. Insert the support to lockplate screws and torque-tighten.
35 Align the lower bearing adapter with the notches in the jacket then push the adapter into the lower end. Install the lower bearing, bearing reinforcement and retainer, ensuring that the slip is aligned with the slots in the reinforcement, jacket and adapter.
36 Install the centering spheres and anti-lash spring in the upper shaft then install the lower shaft from the same side of the spheres as the spring ends protrude.
37 Install the steering shaft assembly into the shift tube from the upper end, guiding the shaft carefully through the tube and bearing.
38 Install the ignition switch actuator rod through the shift lever housing and insert it in the bearing support slot. Extend the rack

downwards from the housing.
39 Assemble the bearing housing over the steering shaft, engaging the rack over the end of the actuator rod.
40 Install the external release lever then hold the lock shoes in the disengaged position and assemble the bearing housing over the steering shaft until the pivot pin holes align. Now install the pivot pins.
41 Place the bearing housing in the fully up position then install the tilt lever spring guide, spring and spring retainer. Using a suitable screwdriver, push in the retainer and turn clockwise to engage in the housing.
42 Install the upper bearing inner race and seat.
43 Install the tilt lever opening shield.
44 Remove the tilt release lever, install the directional signal housing and torque-tighten the 3 retaining screws.
45 Install the tilt release lever and the shift lever, then drive in the shift lever pin.
46 Install the ignition key warning switch, lock cylinder, directional signal switch and ignition switch, as described previously.
47 Align the grooves across the upper end of the pot joint with the steering shaft flat and assemble the intermediate shaft assembly to the upper shaft. Install the clamp bolt and bolt, and torque-tighten.
48 Install the neutral safety or back-up switch.
49 Install the 4 dash panel bracket to column screws and torque-tighten. **Note:** *Ensure that the slotted openings in the bracket face the upper end of the column.*

28 Power steering – general description

With the optional power steering gear, hydraulic pressure is generated in an engine-driven vane type pump and supplied through hoses to the steering box spool valve. The valve is normally positioned in the neutral mode by a torsion bar but when the steering wheel is turned and force is applied to the steering shaft then the spool moves in relation to the body and allows oil to flow to the appropriate side of the piston nut. The greater the movement of the steering wheel, the greater the hydraulic pressure which is applied and therefore the greater the power assistance given to the drive.

Apart from the procedures given in the following sections, it is recommended that where any major fault develops, rectification is entrusted to a dealer or specialist in power steering systems.

29 Power steering – maintenance and adjustment

1 The fluid level should be checked regularly, as described in Chapter 1.
2 The pump drivebelt tension should be checked regularly, refer to Chapter 1.
3 The over-center adjustment is the only adjustment which can be satisfactorily carried out without removing the steering gear from the vehicle.
4 If the vehicle is equipped with a tilt column, disconnect the column flexible coupling. Using a torque wrench or a spring balance attached to the steering wheel nut obtain and record the steering shaft turning torque. Reconnect the coupling (if installed).
5 Disconnect the Pitman arm from the relay rod.
6 Loosen the Pitman shaft adjusting screw locknut and unscrew the adjuster screw out of the side cover as far as it will go.
7 Disconnect the battery ground cable.
8 Remove the horn button (already carried out on tilt column vehicles).
9 Turn the steering wheel from stop to stop through its full travel and then turn it to its center (wheels straight ahead) position.
10 Now check the combined ball/thrust bearing preload using a (pound/inch) torque wrench on the steering wheel nut and turning it a quarter turn through the center position in both directions. Take the highest reading. On vehicles equipped with a tilt column, subtract the turning torque recorded earlier when the coupling was disconnected.
11 Tighten the Pitman shaft adjusting screw in small increments rechecking the over-center preload between each adjustment until the total gear preload falls within that specified (see Specifications Section).
12 Tighten the adjuster screw locknut, install the Pitman arm, the horn button and reconnect the battery ground cable.

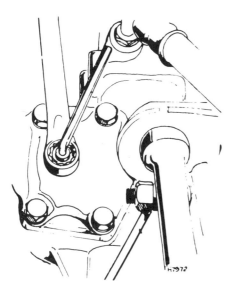

Fig. 11.22 Power steering gear over-center adjustment (Sec 29)

30 Power steering gear – removal and installation

1 The procedure is similar to that described previously for the manual type except that the hydraulic hoses must be disconnected from the steering gear housing.
2 Plug the ends of the hoses and the fluid inlet and outlet holes in the housing.
3 When installation is complete, bleed the system as described in Section 32.

31 Power steering pump – removal and installation

1 Disconnect the hydraulic hoses either from the pump or the steering gear and keep them in the raised position to prevent the fluid draining away until they can be plugged.
2 Remove the pump drive belt by loosening the pump mounts and pushing it in towards the engine.
3 Unscrew and remove the pump mounting bolts and braces and remove the pump.
4 To remove the pump pulley it will almost certainly require the use of a special extractor, the type depending upon the actual pulley fitted. Consult your dealer if the pulley is to be removed.
5 Installation is a reversal of removal but tighten the hose unions to the specified torque and then fill the fluid reservoir.

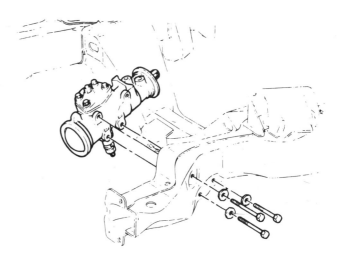

Fig. 11.23 Typical power steering gear mounting (Sec 30)

6 Prime the pump by turning the pulley in the reverse direction to that of normal rotation until air-bubbles cease to emerge from the fluid when observed through the reservoir filler cap.
7 Install the drive belt and tension it as described in Chapter 1.
8 Bleed the system as described in Section 32 of this Chapter.

32 Power steering hydraulic system – bleeding

1 This is not a routine operation and will normally only be required when the system has been dismantled and reassembled.
2 Fill the reservoir to its correct level with fluid of recommended type, and allow it to remain undisturbed for at least 2 minutes.
3 Start the engine and run it for two or three seconds only. Check the reservoir fluid level and top-up if necessary.
4 Repeat the operations described in the preceding paragraph until the fluid level remains constant.
5 Raise the front of the vehicle until the wheels are clear of the ground.
6 Start the engine and increase its speed to about 1500 rpm. Now turn the steering wheel gently from stop-to-stop. Check the reservoir fluid level adding some if necessary.
7 Lower the vehicle to the ground and with the engine still running move the vehicle forward sufficiently to obtain full right lock followed

by full left lock. Re-check the fluid level. If the fluid in the reservoir is extremely foamy, allow the vehicle to stand for a few minutes with the engine switched off and then repeat the previous operations.

8   Air in the power steering system is often indicated by a noisy pump but a low fluid level can also cause this.

33 Front wheel alignment and steering angles

1   Accurate front wheel alignment is essential for good steering and slow tire wear. Before considering the steering angles; check that the tires are correctly inflated, that the front wheels are not buckled, the hub bearings are not worn or incorrectly adjusted and that the steering linkage is in good order, without slackness or wear at the joints.

2   Wheel alignment consists of four factors:

Camber which is the angle at which the front wheels are set from the vertical when viewed from the front of the car. Positive camber is the amount (in degrees) that the wheels are tilted outwards at the top from the vertical.

Caster is the angle between the steering axis and a vertical line when viewed from each side of the car. Positive caster is when the steering axis is inclined rearward.

Steering axis inclination is the angle, when viewed from the front of the car, between the vertical and an imaginary line drawn between the upper and lower suspension control arm balljoints.

Toe-in is the amount by which the distance between the front inside edges of the wheels (measured at hub height) is less than the diametrically opposite distance measured between the rear inside edges of the front wheels.

3   On all other models, the caster and camber angles are set by means of shims inserted between the upper control arm shaft and the frame bracket.

4   Due to the need for special gauges and equipment, it is not advised that camber or caster angles should be adjusted at home.

5   To adjust the toe-in (which should only be done after establishing that caster and camber are correct), obtain or make a toe-in gauge. Once can be made up from a length of tubing, cranked to clear the oil pan and clutch or torque converter housing and having a screw and locknut at one end.

6   Use a gauge to measure the distance between the two inner wheel rims at hub height at the rear of the wheels.

7   Push the vehicle to rotate the wheel through 180° (half a turn) and then measure the distance between the inner wheel rims at hub height at the front of the wheels ('Y').

8   The distance between the two measurements is the toe-in (where the first measurement is larger than the second). Refer to the specifications for the correct value.

9   Toe-in or toe-out can be altered by increasing or decreasing the length of the tie-rods. For 1975 models, the tie-rods must be decreased in length to increase the toe-in; for other models the tie-rod length must be increased to increase the toe-in. Where any adjustment is made, the screwed sleeves should be turned by equal amounts at each side.

10   Where new tie-rods, tie-rod ends or steering components have been installed, always commence adjustment with the overall lengths of the tie-rods exactly equal. Take the measurements from the balljoint centers and have the wheels and steering wheel in the straight-ahead position.

34 Wheels and tires

1   The wheels are of pressed steel type and the tires may be conventional, radial or bias belted. Never mix tires of different construction on the same axle.

2   Check the tire pressures weekly, including the spare, preferably when the tires are cold, first thing in the morning.

3   The wheel nuts should be tightened to the specified torque, and it is an advantage if a smear of grease is applied to the wheel stud threads.

4   Every 7500 miles, the wheels should be moved round the vehicle in order to even out the tire tread wear. To do this, remove each wheel in turn, clean it thoroughly (both sides) and remove any stones which may be embedded in the tread. Check the tread wear pattern which will indicate any mechanical or adjustment faults in the suspension or steering components. Examine the wheel bolt holes for elongation or wear. If such conditions are found, replace the wheel.

5   Replacement of the tires should be carried out when the thickness of the tread pattern is worn to a minimum of $\frac{1}{16}$ inch or the wear indicators (if incorporated) are visible.

6   The method of moving the tires depends on whether the spare (5th) wheel is brought into the rotational pattern, and to the type off construction of the tire. With radial ply tires, move them front to rear on the same side only.

7   The type of tire and inflation pressures are recorded on a sticker located on the vehicle door and the specification varies according to the particular vehicle model and tires fitted. Always adjust the front and rear tire pressures after moving the wheels round as previously described.

8   Have all wheels balanced initially and again half way through the useful life of the tires.

Chapter 12 Bodywork

Contents

1 General description

Buick "A" body cars (Century and Regal) are available in a variety of trim packages. Bodies are based on a 2-door, 4-door and wagon.

Body panels often subject to damage can be replaced by the owner. These panels and parts are: bumpers, grille, front body panel, fenders, inner fender skirts, doors, trunk, and radiator support panel. For major repairs or replacement of parts other than these, it is suggested that the owner contact a competent body repair shop.

2 Maintenance – bodywork and underframe

1 The condition of your vehicle's bodywork is of considerable importance as it is on this that the resale value will mainly depend. It is much more difficult to repair neglected bodywork than to replace mechanical assemblies. The hidden portions of the body, such as the wheel arches, fender skirts, the underframe and the engine compartment are equally important, although obviously not requiring such frequent attention as the immediately visible paint.

2 Once a year or every 12 000 miles it is a sound scheme to visit your local dealer and have the underside of the body steam cleaned. All traces of dirt and oil will be removed and the underside can then be inspected carefully for rust, damaged hydraulic pipes, frayed electrical wiring and similar trouble areas. The front suspension should be greased on completion of this job.

3 At the same time, clean the engine and the engine compartment either using a steam cleaner or a water-soluble cleaner.

4 The wheel arches and fender skirts should be given particular attention as undercoating can easily come away here and stones and dirt thrown up from the wheels can soon cause the paint to chip and flake, and so allow rust to set in. If rust is found, clean down to the bare metal and apply an anti-rust paint.

5 The bodywork should be washed once a week or when dirty. Thoroughly wet the vehicle to soften the dirt and then wash down with a soft sponge and plenty of clean water. If the surplus dirt is not washed off very gently, in time it will wear the paint down.

6 Spots of tar or bitumen coating thrown up from the road surfaces are best removed with a cloth soaked in a cleaner made especially for this purpose.

7 Once every six months, or more frequently depending on the weather conditions, give the bodywork and chrome trim a thoroughly good wax polish. If a chrome cleaner is used to remove rust on any of the vehicle's plated parts, remember that the cleaner can also remove part of the chrome, so use it sparingly.

3 Maintenance – upholstery and carpets

1 Remove the carpets or mats and thoroughly vacuum clean the interior of the vehicle every three months or more frequently if necessary.

2 Beat out the carpets and vacuum clean them if they are very dirty. If the upholstery is soiled apply an upholstery cleaner with a damp sponge and wipe off with a clean dry cloth.

3 Consult you local dealer or auto parts store for cleaners made especially for newer automotive upholstery fabrics. Always test the cleaner in an inconspicuous place.

4 Maintenance – vinyl roof covering

Under no circumstances try to clean any external vinyl roof covering with detergents, caustic soap or spirit cleaners. Plain soap and water is all that is required, with a soft brush to clean dirt that may be ingrained. Wash the covering as frequently as the rest of the vehicle. Application of wax or one of the many vinyl conditioner/cleaners will help retard depletion of the oils in the vinyl and prevent cracking.

5 Minor body damage – repair

See photo sequence on pages 286 and 287.

Repair of minor scratches in the vehicle's bodywork

If the scratch is very superficial, and does not penetrate to the metal of the bodywork, repair is very simple. Lightly rub the area of the scratch with a paintwork renovator, or a very fine cutting paste, to remove loose paint from the scratch and to clear the surrounding bodywork of wax polish. Rinse the area with clean water.

Apply touch-up paint to the scratch using a thin paint brush; continue to apply thin layers of paint until the surface of the paint in the scratch is level with the surrounding paintwork. Allow the new paint at least two weeks to harden: then blend it into the surrounding paintwork by rubbing the paintwork, in the scratch area, with a paintwork renovator or a very fine cutting paste. Finally, apply wax polish.

An alternative to painting over the scratch is to use a paint transfer. Use the same preparation for the affected area, then simply pick a patch of a suitable size to cover the scratch completely. Hold the

This photo sequence illustrates the repair of a dent and damaged paintwork. The procedure for the repair of a hole is similar. Refer to the text for more complete instructions

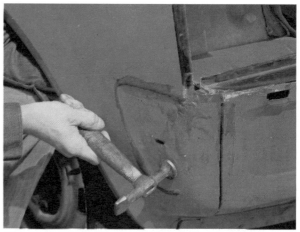

After removing any adjacent body trim, hammer the dent out. The damaged area should then be made slightly concave

Use coarse sandpaper or a sanding disc on a drill motor to remove all paint from the damaged area. Feather the sanded area into the edges of the surrounding paint, using progressively finer grades of sandpaper

The damaged area should be treated with rust remover prior to application of the body filler. In the case of a rust hole, all rusted sheet metal should be cut away

Carefully follow manufacturer's instructions when mixing the body filler so as to have the longest possible working time during application. Rust holes should be covered with fiberglass screen held in place with dabs of body filler prior to repair

Apply the filler with a flexible applicator in thin layers at 20 minute intervals. Use an applicator such as a wood spatula for confined areas. The filler should protrude slightly above the surrounding area

Shape the filler with a surform-type plane. Then, use water and progressively finer grades of sandpaper and a sanding block to wet-sand the area until it is smooth. Feather the edges of the repair area into the surrounding paint.

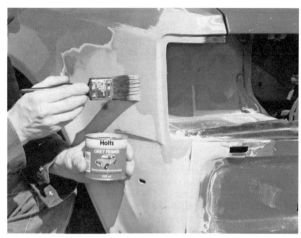

Use spray or brush applied primer to cover the entire repair area so that slight imperfections in the surface will be filled in. Prime at least one inch into the area surrounding the repair. Be careful of over-spray when using spray-type primer

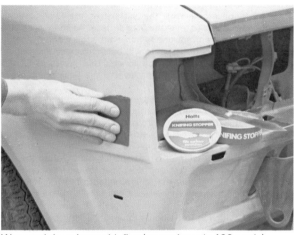

Wet-sand the primer with fine (approximately 400 grade) sandpaper until the area is smooth to the touch and blended into the surrounding paint. Use filler paste on minor imperfections

After the filler paste has dried, use rubbing compound to ensure that the surface of the primer is smooth. Prior to painting, the surface should be wiped down with a tack rag or lint-free cloth soaked in lacquer thinner

Choose a dry, warm, breeze-free area in which to paint and make sure that adjacent areas are protected from over-spray. Shake the spray paint can thoroughly and apply the top coat to the repair area, building it up by applying several coats, working from the center

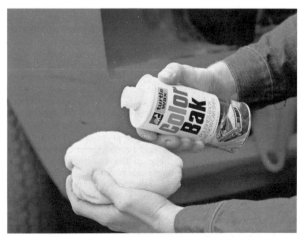

After allowing at least two weeks for the paint to harden, use fine rubbing compound to blend the area into the original paint. Wax can now be applied

patch against the scratch and burnish its backing paper; the paper will adhere to the paintwork, freeing itself from the backing paper at the same time. Polish the affected area to blend the patch into the surrounding paintwork.

Where the scratch has penetrated right through to the metal of the bodywork, causing the metal to rust, a different repair technique is required. Remove any loose rust from the bottom of the scratch with a penknife, then apply rust inhibiting paint to prevent the formation of rust in the future. Using a rubber or nylon applicator fill the scratch with bodystopper paste. If required, this paste can be mixed with cellulose thinners to provide a very thin paste which is ideal for filling narrow scratches. Before the stopper-paste in the scratch hardens, wrap a piece of smooth cotton rag around the top of a finger. Dip the finger in cellulose thinners and then quickly sweep it across the surface of the stopper-paste in the scratch; this will ensure that the surface of the stopper-paste is slightly hollowed. The scratch can now be painted over as described earlier in this Section.

Repair of dents in the vehicle's bodywork

When deep denting of the vehicle's bodywork has taken place, the first task is to pull the dent out, until the affected bodywork almost attains its original shape. There is little point in trying to restore the original shape completely, as the metal in the damaged area will have stretched on impact and cannot be reshaped fully to its original contour. It is better to bring the level of the dent up to a point which is about $\frac{1}{8}$ in (3 mm) below the level of the surrounding bodywork. In cases where the dent is very shallow anyway, it is not worth trying to pull it out at all.

If the underside of the dent is accessible, it can be hammered out gently from behind, using a mallet with a wooden or plastic head. Whilst doing this, hold a suitable block of wood firmly against the impact from the hammer blows and thus prevent a large area of the bodywork from being 'belled-out'.

Should the dent be in a section of the bodywork which has double skin or some other factor making it inaccessible from behind, a different technique is called for. Drill several small holes through the metal inside the area – particularly in the deeper section. Then screw long self-tapping screws into the holes just sufficiently for them to gain a good purchase in the metal. Now the dent can be pulled out by pulling on the protruding heads of the screws with a pair of pliers.

The next stage of the repair is the removal of the paint from the damaged area, and from an inch or so of the surrounding 'sound' bodywork. This is accomplished most easily by using a wire brush or abrasive pad on a power drill, although it can be done just as effectively by hand using sheets of sandpaper. To complete the preparation for filling, score the surface of the bare metal with a screwdriver or the tang of a file, or alternatively, drill small holes in the affected area. This will provide a really good 'key' for the filler paste.

To complete the repair see the Section on filling and re-spraying.

Repair of rust holes or gashes in the vehicle's bodywork

Remove all paint from the affected area and from an inch or so of the surrounding 'sound' bodywork, using an abrasive pad or a wire brush on a power drill. If these are not available a few sheets of sandpaper will do the job just as effectively. With the paint removed you will be able to gauge the severity of the corrosion and therefore decide whether to renew the whole panel (if this is possible) or to repair the affected area. New body panels are not as expensive as most people think and it is often quicker and more satisfactory to fit a new panel than to attempt to repair large areas of corrosion.

Remove all fittings from the affected area except those which will act as a guide to the original shape of the damaged bodywork (eg headlamp shells etc). Then, using tin snips or a hacksaw blade, remove all loose metal and any other metal badly affected by corrosion. Hammer the edges of the hole inwards in order to create a slight depression for the filler paste.

Wire brush the affected area to remove the powdery rust from the surface of the remaining metal. Paint the affected area with rust inhibiting paint; if the back of the rusted area is accessible treat this also.

Before filling can take place it will be necessary to block the hole in some way. This can be achieved by the use of Zinc gauze or Aluminum tape.

Zinc gauze is probably the best material to use for a large hole. Cut a piece to the approximate size and shape of the hole to be filled, then position it in the hole so that its edges are below the level of the surrounding bodywork. It can be retained in position by several blobs of filler paste around its periphery.

Aluminum tape should be used for small or very narrow holes. Pull a piece off the roll and trim it to the approximate size and shape required, then pull off the backing paper (if used) and stick the tape over the hole; it can be overlapped if the thickness of one piece is insufficient. Burnish down the edges of the tape with the handle of a screwdriver or similar, to ensure that the tape is securely attached to the metal underneath.

Having blocked off the hole the affected area must now be filled and sprayed – see Section on bodywork fitting and re-spraying.

Bodywork repairs – filling and re-spraying

Before using this Section, see the Sections on dent, deep scratch, rust holes and gash repairs.

Many types of bodyfiller are available, but generally speaking those proprietary kits which contain a tin of filler paste and a tube of resin hardener are best for this type of repair. A wide, flexible plastic or nylon applicator will be found invaluable for imparting a smooth and well contoured finish to the surface of the filler.

Mix up a little filler on a clean piece of card or board – measure the hardener carefully (follow the maker's instructions on the pack) otherwise the filler will set too rapidly or too slowly.

Using the applicator apply the filler paste to the prepared area; draw the applicator across the surface of the filler to achieve the correct contour and to level the filler surface. As soon as a contour that approximates the correct one is achieved, stop working the paste – if you carry on too long the paste will become sticky and begin to 'pick up' on the applicator. Continue to add thin layers of filler paste at twenty-minute intervals until the level of the filler is just proud of the surrounding bodywork.

Once the filler has hardened, excess can be removed using a metal plane or file. From then on, progressively finer grades of sandpaper should be used, starting with a 40 grade production paper and finishing with 400 grade wet-and-dry paper. Always wrap the sandpaper around a flat rubber, cork or wooden block – otherwise the surface of the filler will not be completely flat. During the smoothing of the filler surface the wet-and-dry paper should be periodically rinsed in water. This will ensure that a very smooth finish is imparted to the filler at the final stage.

At this stage the 'repair area' should be surrounded by a ring of bare metal, which in turn should be encircled by the finely 'feathered' edge of the good paintwork. Rinse the repair area with clean water, until all of the dust produced by the rubbing-down operation has gone.

Spray the whole repair area with a light coat of primer – this will show up any imperfections in the surface of the filler. Repair these imperfections with fresh filler paste or bodystopper, and once more smooth the surface with sandpaper. If bodystopper is used, it can be mixed with cellulose thinners to form a really thin paste which is ideal for filling small holes. Repeat this spray and repair procedure until you are satisfied that the surface of the filler, and the feathered edge of the paintwork are perfect. Clean the repair area with clean water and allow to dry fully.

The repair area is now ready for final spraying. Paint spraying must be carried out in warm, dry, windless and dust free atmosphere. This condition can be created artificially if you have access to a large indoor working area, but if you are forced to work in the open, you will have to pick your day very carefully. If you are working indoors, dousing the floor in the work area with water will help to settle the dust which would otherwise be in the atmosphere. If the repair area is confined to one body panel, mask off the surrounding panels; this will help to minimise the effects of a slight mis-match in paint colours. Bodywork fittings (eg chrome strips, door handles etc) will also need to be masked off. Use genuine masking tape and several thicknesses of newspaper for the masking operations.

Before commencing to spray, agitate the aerosol can thoroughly, then spray a test area (an old tin, or similar) until the technique is mastered. Cover the repair area with a thick coat of primer; the thickness should be built up using several thin layers of paint rather than one thick one. Using 400 grade wet-and-dry paper, rub down the surface of the primer until it is really smooth. While doing this, the work area should be thoroughly doused with water, and the wet-and-dry paper periodically rinsed in water. Allow to dry before spraying on more paint.

Spray on the top coat, again building up the thickness by using several thin layers of paint. Start spraying in the center of the repair

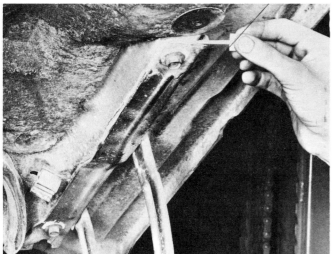

8.3 Use a scribe, felt pen or paint to mark the position of the hinge on the underside of the hood

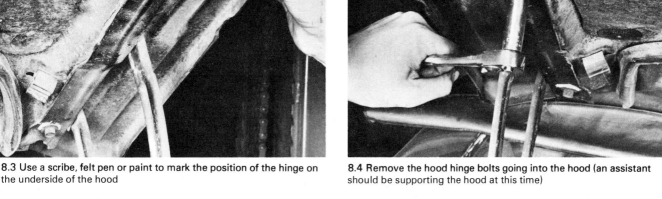

8.4 Remove the hood hinge bolts going into the hood (an assistant should be supporting the hood at this time)

area and then using a circular motion, work outwards until the whole repair area and about 2 inches of the surrounding original paintwork is covered. Remove all masking material 10 to 15 minutes after spraying on the final coat of paint. Allow the new paint at least two weeks to harden, then, using a paintwork renovator or a very fine cutting paste, blend the edges of the paint into the existing paintwork. Finally, apply wax polish.

6   Bodywork and frame repairs – major damage

1   Major damage must be repaired by competent mechanics with the necessary welding and hydraulic straightening equipment.
2   If the damage has been serious it is vital that the frame is checked for correct alignment as otherwise the handling of the vehicle will suffer and many other faults – such as excessive tire wear, and wear in the transmission and steering – may occur.
3   There is a special body jig which most body repair shops have and to ensure that all is correct it is important that this jig be used for all major repair work.

7   Hood – adjustment

1   When the hood is fully closed it should rest squarely on the various rubber bumpers. You should not be able to 'rock' or pivot the hood on the bumpers. Airspace between the hood and fenders should be even (looking from front to rear) on both sides. The hood is attached to the car by 2 hinges. By moving the hood forward/rearward and from side to side on these hinges the fit can be adjusted.
2   By raising or lowering the bumpers (there are 4 adjustable bumpers: 2 on the radiator support and 2 at the rear) it is possible to control the vertical fit of the hood. The bumpers are threaded like bolts and turning them in the desired direction can usually be accomplished by hand. Some bumpers have a setting nut at their base. If this is the case on your car, it will be necessary to loosen this nut before turning the bumpers.
3   When a hood is slightly out of alignment (from left to right) it is often possible to correctly position it without loosening the hinges. This is done by opening the latch and with the hood halfway up, pushing on the edge of the hood in the direction you want the hood to go. Usually 3 or 4 slight pushes will do a better job than one heavy push.
4   Major alignment adjustments to the hood must be made by loosening the hinges. This is done as follows:

   a)   Scribe a line around the entire hinge plate to be repositioned. This will enable you to judge the amount of movement.
   b)   Loosen the appropriate screws on the hood hinge to be

   adjusted and move the hood into the correct alignment. Move the hood only a little at a time. Tighten the hinge screws and carefully lower the hood to check the position.
   c)   Adjust the hood bumpers on the radiator support so that the hood, when closed, is flush with the fender and grille top surfaces.
   d)   The hood catch and lock assembly is adjustable to provide a positive closing of the hood. The hood catch assembly on the radiator support section has slotted mounting holes to allow the catch to be moved into alignment with the hood lock bolt. The lock bolt on the hood can be lengthened or shortened to engage with the catch. When closed properly the hood bumpers should be slightly compressed.

3   The catch and lock assembly, as well as the hinges should be periodically lubricated to prevent sticking or jamming.

8   Hood – removal and installation

1   Raise hood and support it in the extreme 'up' position. A 2x4 can be used for this purpose. Do not bang the radiator with the support material.
2   Place folded towels under the rear corners of the hood to prevent body damage.
3   Scribe a line around each hinge to aid in proper reinstallation (photo).
4   With the help of an assistant, remove the bolts that hold the hood to the hinges (photo). Have an assistant hold the hood while you remove the support.
5   Carefully remove the hood from the car and lean it against the wall. Place towels under the rear corners of the hood to prevent paint chipping.

9   Grille – removal and installation

1974
Radiator grille
1   Disconnect the battery cables and remove battery.
2   Remove the 6 nuts that hold the grille in place and pull grille away from the car.
3   Installation is the exact reverse procedure.
Bumper grille
4   Put car into 'Park' and set emergency brake.
5   Crawl under car and remove the 2 bolts and 1 nut on each of the 4 grille mounting brackets.
6   Remove brackets and pull grille out from behind the bumpers.

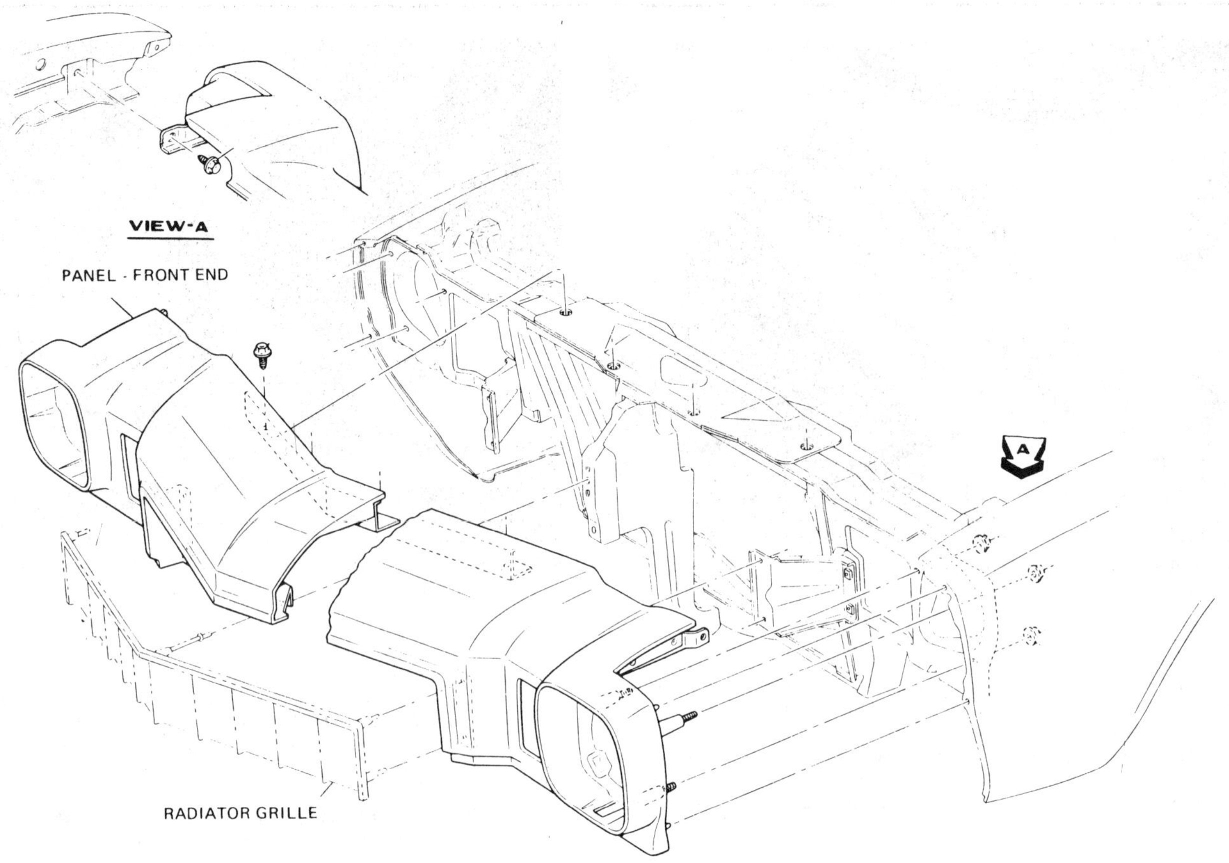

VIEW-A

PANEL - FRONT END

RADIATOR GRILLE

Fig. 12.1 Typical front end body panel – 74 Regal shown (Sec 9)

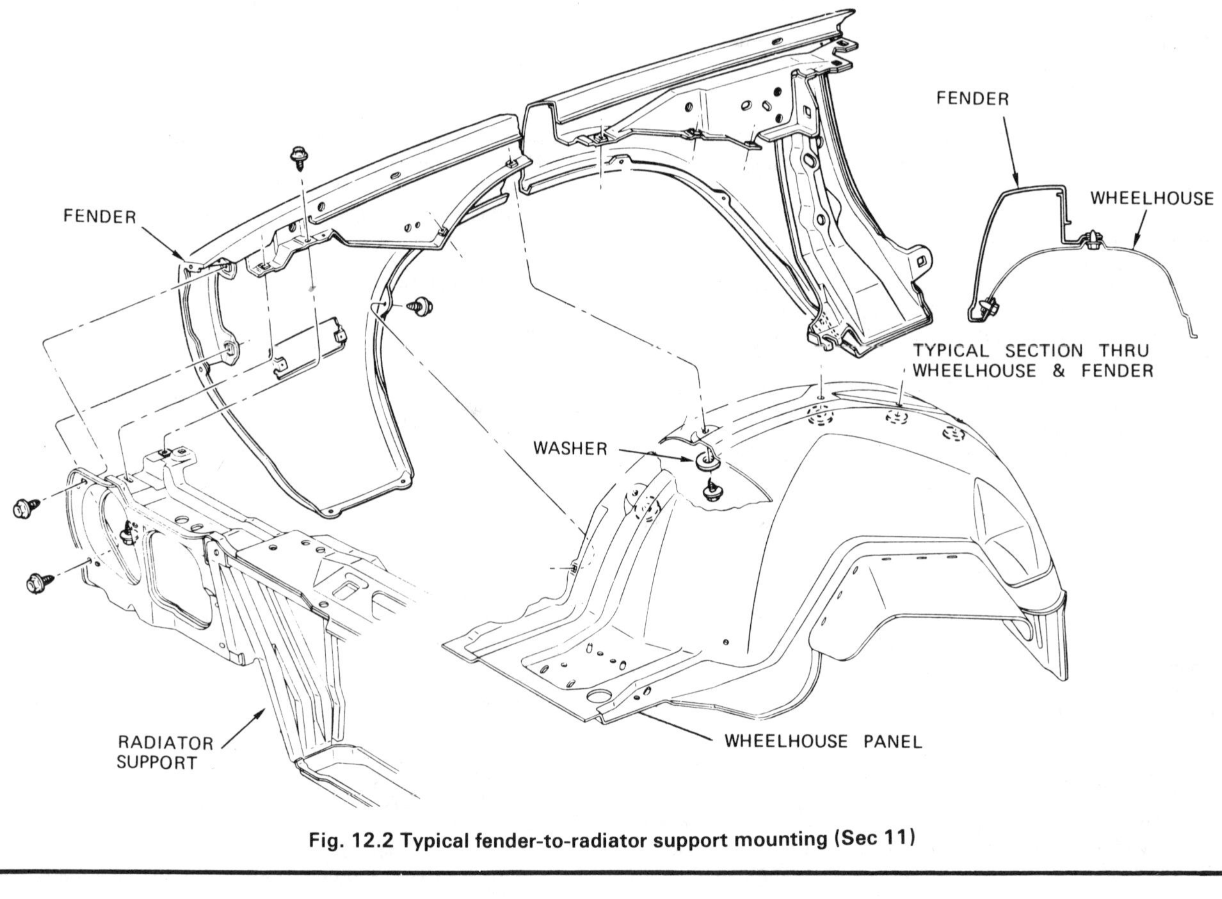

FENDER

FENDER

WHEELHOUSE

TYPICAL SECTION THRU
WHEELHOUSE & FENDER

WASHER

RADIATOR
SUPPORT

WHEELHOUSE PANEL

Fig. 12.2 Typical fender-to-radiator support mounting (Sec 11)

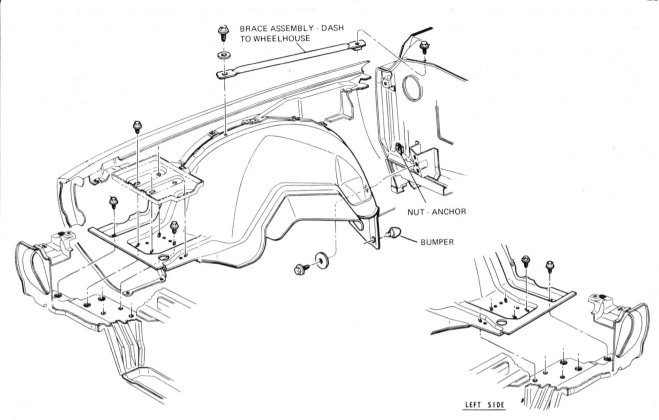

BRACE ASSEMBLY - DASH
TO WHEELHOUSE

NUT - ANCHOR

BUMPER

LEFT SIDE

Fig. 12.3 Typical wheel well mounting (Sec 11)

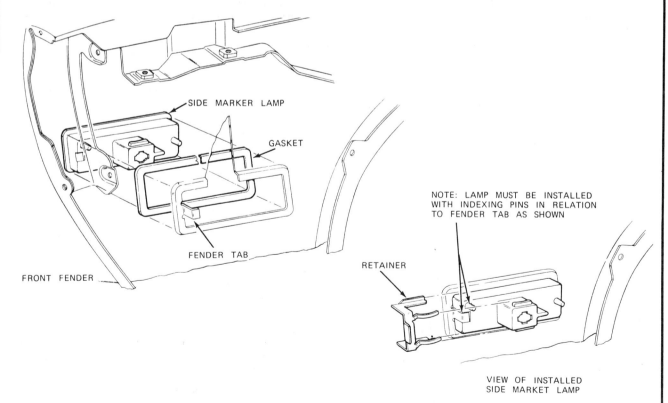

SIDE MARKER LAMP

GASKET

FENDER TAB

FRONT FENDER

NOTE: LAMP MUST BE INSTALLED
WITH INDEXING PINS IN RELATION
TO FENDER TAB AS SHOWN

RETAINER

VIEW OF INSTALLED
SIDE MARKET LAMP

Fig. 12.4 Side marker lamp installation – typical (Sec 11)

7   Installation is the exact reverse procedure.
1975
8   Disconnect battery cables and remove battery (Century only).
9   Unhook parking light wiring at parking light (Century).
10 Undo the nuts that hold the grille in place and pull grille away from car.
11 If the grille is being replaced it will be necessary to scavenge all wiring, lamps and bezels off the old grille (Century).
12 Installation is the exact reverse procedure.
1976
2-door and Wagon
13 Reach behind the grille and remove the 4 front screws and 2 bolts that secure radiator and pull grille away from car. Installation is the reverse procedure.
2-door Century
14 Remove the 8 nuts on the back of each grille panel.
15 Pull grille back from front panel and lift it out from between the radiator and the front panel.
16 Installation is the reverse procedure.
2-door Century replacement grilles
17 The replacement grilles are 6 small insert panels instead of the 2 grille halves.
18 Undo the 2 screws that hold each panel in the front body piece. Pull grilles back and out from between radiator and body panel.
19 Installation is the reverse but you must bend the tabs out to hold the grille in place.
Regal
20 Reach behind the grille and remove the 6 screws that hold the grille in place.
21 Pull the grille away from the car from the outside.
22 Installation is the reverse procedure.
1977
23 Grille removal is the same as for 1976. Grille replacement for the Regal is the same as for the Century replacement grille (1976).
1978
Century
24 Raise hood and unplug headlamp wiring.
25 Undo the 10 nuts and 1 screw that hold the grille and grille bracket to the front body panel.
26 Pull grille away from the car. The headlamp housings may be loose as this is done. Be careful you don't let them fall.
27 Installation is the reverse procedure.
Regal
28 Raise hood and undo the 9 nuts and unhook the 2 tension springs that hold grille in place.
29 Push grille in to clear the mounting studs. Tip grille back at top. Do not bang radiator cooling fins.
30 Push up gently and pull grille out from the bottom.
31 Installation is the reverse procedure.
1979
32 Procedure for grille removal is the same as for 1978.
1980
33 Raise hood and remove the 8 nuts and 2 screws that mount grille to the front body panel.
34 Grille is pulled away from car to remove. It may require some jiggling or tilting as the 1978 Regal grille does.
35 Installation is the reverse procedure.

10 Bumpers – removal and installation

1   Bumper supports and brackets are slotted to allow for alignment and leveling of bumper. Before removal, it is a good idea to scribe around each support and bracket and mark exactly where the bolts line up. This will make installing the bumpers much easier than it would otherwise be.
2   Unless absolutely necessary, leave the energy absorbers on the vehicle when the bumpers are removed.
3   Each bumper has 4 mounting bolts on each of its 2 energy absorbers. Unbolting the bumper from the absorbers frees the bumper.
4   Have an assistant help you take the bumpers off the car. They are heavy and can fall on an unsuspecting mechanic.
5   Bumper trim, guards and chrome facing all bolt through the steel

support brace that runs the length of the bumper. By undoing the numerous bolts through this brace it is possible to completely disassemble the bumper.

11 Front fenders and skirt – removal and installation

1   To protect paint on adjoining panels, it is advisable to mask the panels with tape. Do not apply masking tape to a car that has recently been parked in the sun and do not leave the tape on the car if it is to be parked outside in direct sunlight.
2   Disconnect the negative battery cable. If the right fender is being removed, disconnect both cables and remove the battery.
3   Set the parking brake, block the rear wheels and raise the vehicle. Use a jack stand or similar support to hold the car steady. Remove the wheel.
4   Remove the chrome headlight ring (1974 through 1977).
5   The fender can now be removed by unbolting the 4 fender-to-radiator bolts, the fender brace rod, and the 5 fender-to-body skirt bolts. It is necessary to unbolt the hood hinge and support the hood.
6   Take out the retaining clip for the side marker lamp and remove the fender-to-wheel well panel bolts. Place a towel between the bumper and the fender and walk the fender away and back (towards the car door) from the car.
7   Disconnect and remove all cables, wiring harness clips, washer reservoir, battery tray, etc. from inner skirt. Label all hoses and unconnected wiring for easy identification later on.
8   Remove the wheel well-to-radiator support and any body bolts.
9   The inner skirt can now be lifted clear of the car.
10 Installation is the reverse of removal.

12 Hood latch and lock assemblies – removal and installation

1   To maintain the proper alignment of the catch and lock, open the hood and scribe a line around the lock plate on the hood and the catch plate mechanism on the support brace.
2   Remove the catch plate assembly by removing the screws retaining the catch to the radiator support, center support and tie bar.
3   Remove the screws retaining the lock plate to the inside of the hood.
4   Upon reinstallation, line up the identifying scribe marks on both the catch plate and the lock plate and tighten the attaching screws. For further information on adjusting the hood see Section 7.

13 Trunk lid – removal and installation

1   Open the trunk and place blankets or some form of protective covering around the forward edge of the trunk opening to protect the window and body panel.
2   If a trunk light installed, disconnect the wiring to it.
3   Carefully scribe an outline of the hinge straps on the inner trunk lid. This will enable you to replace the trunk lid in the same location (photo).
4   With the aid of an assistant, remove the four attaching bolts and lift away the trunk lid (photo).
5   Installation is a reversal of the removal process, however make sure the trunk lid is installed in the same location and adjusted properly (see Section 14).

14 Trunk lid – adjustments

1   All adjustments for the trunk to be moved forward, rearward or sideways are done at the hinges. With the four retaining bolts slightly loosened, move the trunk lid to the desired position and tighten the bolts. Move the lid only a little at a time and check that the locking assembly remains in line (Section 16).
2   To adjust the trunk lid in an up or down fashion, and to align properly with the rear quarter panels, shims should be installed between the hinge strap and the trunk lid. Loosen the appropriate securing bolts enought to slide body shims into position and then tighten the bolt(s). Carefully close the trunk lid, checking the alignment of the lock assembly and lid in relation to the quarter panels.

13.3 Like the hood, the trunk hinges should be marked prior to removal

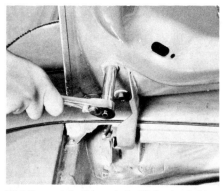

13.4 It may take 2 people to lift the trunk lid away from the body once the bolts have been removed (an assistant should support the trunk lid while you unbolt it)

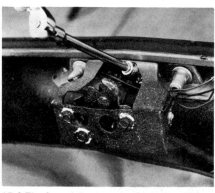

15.2 The 2 retaining nuts for the lock cylinder are accessible from the inside of the trunk

3 Torque rods are incorporated to control the amount of effort needed to operate the trunk lid. The torque rod ends are located in cutout notches adjacent to the hinges. They are adjusted as follows:

  a) *To increase the amount of effort required to raise the trunk lid (which will make the lid easier to close), move the torque rod(s) to a lower adjusting notch.*

  b) *To make the trunk lid rise easier (thus making the lid more difficult to close), reposition the torque rod end(s) to a higher notch.*

To grip the end of the torque rod for adjusting, use a $\frac{1}{4}$ inch pipe. Also, it is not necessary for each side to be adjusted to the same notch position.

15 Trunk lid lock cylinder – removal and installation

1 The lock cylinder is secured to the rear body panel by two lock nuts and washers.
2 Open the trunk lid and remove the two retaining nuts, washers and guards (photo).
3 For best access, lower the chrome bezel on the rear outside panel.
4 Remove the lock cylinder from the lock body.
5 When installing, make sure the lock cylinder shaft engages with the lock.

16 Trunk lid lock assembly – removal, adjusting and installation

1 To remove the lid lock assembly attached to the rear body panel, first remove the lock cylinder as prevously described.
2 Scribe identifying marks around each of the lock attaching bolts and then remove the bolts.
3 Remove the lock assembly from the lock body.
4 The lid lock striker is attached to the inside of the trunk lid, secured by screws. Before removing the screws, and the striker assembly, mark the vertical position of the striker to enable the assembly to be replaced in the same location.
5 Before attempting to adjust the lock striker or lock assembly, it is important that the trunk lid itself is correctly positioned.
6 To check the engagement of the striker to the lock, place a small amount of modeling clay at both sides of the lock bolt. Carefully close the trunk lid. Open the lid and check the impression left in the clay. The depression in the clay should be centered in the lock frame. Where required, the lock frame can be adjusted sideways or the striker up or down to obtain the proper engagement. These adjustments should be performed with the attaching bolts only slightly loosened, and the components should be moved only a little at a time.

17 Door trim panel – removal and installation

1 Remove the window crank handle. This is secured to the regulator shaft with a clip. The trim panel should be pushed away from the base

of the handle to expose the crankshaft and clip. A special forked tool is available to push the clip out of the groove, or you can carefully use a screwdriver (photo).
2 The handle which operates the door latch mechanism is retained with screws. It is first necessary to remove the decorative cover plate (photo). With the screws removed, the remote control rod can be disconnected from the rear of the handle and the handle assembly removed from the door.
3 Remove the inside locking knob by unscrewing it from its shaft.
4 On models equipped with a remote control mirror, remove the control escutcheon from the trim panel and disengage the control cable.
5 On models with an armrest built into the trim panel, remove the screws which are located in the recessed area meant to be used to pull the door shut.
6 If equipped with a separate armrest not intended to be a part of the trim panel, remove the screws which attach it to the trim panel and the inner door skin. The screws are sometimes hidden with decorative plugs which should be carefully pried out to reveal the screw.
7 Depending on the style and year of production, there may or may not be exposed screws securing a portion of the trim panel. If so, remove any exposed screws.
8 Where no screws can be readily seen, chances are that the panel is held in place with retaining clips. To disengage these clips, insert a flat, blunt tool (like a screwdriver blade wrapped with tape) between the metal door skin and the trim panel. Carefully pry the door panel away from the door, keeping the tool close to the clips to prevent damage to the panel. Start at the bottom and work around the door towards the top. The top section is secured at the window channel. Once the retaining clips are pried free, lift the trim panel upwards and away from the door (photo).
9 Before installing the trim panel, check that all the trim retainer clips are in good condition and the water shield is correctly applied to the metal door skin.
10 Engage the top of the trim panel first and then position the panel correctly on the door. The cutout for the window winder can be used as a rough guide.
11 Press the retaining clips into their respective cups or holes in the metal door skin. Pressure can be used by the palm of your hand or a clean rubber mallet.
12 Follow the removal process in the reverse order to install the various components to the door.
13 To install the window crank handle, first install the retaining clip to the handle, then push the handle onto the shaft. Check that the clip is properly seated in the shaft groove.

18 Door lock cylinder – removal and installation

1 Remove the inside door trim as described in Section 17.
2 Raise the window to the full up position and pry the water shield away from the inner door skin to gain access to the rear of the lock cylinder.
3 To help prevent tools or inner door components from falling down to the bottom of the door cavity, place rags or newspapers inside the cavity.

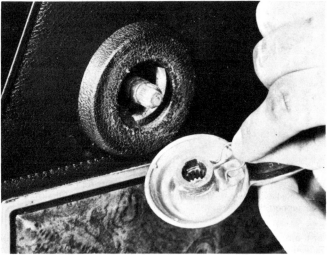

17.1 The window crank is secured to the shaft with a retaining clip which must be removed, by gentle prying, from the shaft (use a screwdriver or a special tool and take care not to tear the door panel)

17.2 Remove any decorative door trim from around the door handle before the trim panel is pried loose

17.8 A screwdriver is used to gently pry the trim panel away from the door

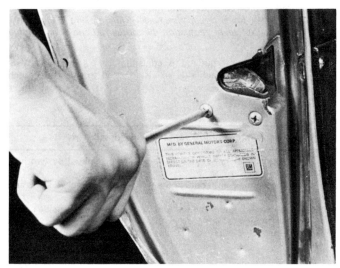

19.5 The attaching screws for the lock are in the door jamb

4   With a screwdriver, slide the lock cylinder retaining clip (on the inboard side of the outer door skin) out of the lock cylinder. Be careful not to damage the outer door skin.
5   With the clip removed, the lock cylinder can be removed from the outside of the door.
6   Installation is a reversal of removal.

19 Door lock assembly – removal and installation

1   Remove the door trim panel as described in Section 17.
2   Pry back the water shield at the rear of the door to gain access to the inside locking assembly.
3   Temporarily install the window crank and roll the window to the full up position.
4   Working through the large access hole in the inner door skin, disconnect the connecting rod at the lock mechanism. This rod is held in place with a gripper clip which is released by rotating it off the rod.
5   Remove the three lock attaching screws located in the door jamb at the rear of the door (photo). Remove the lock assembly through the access hole.
6   Installation is a reversal of removal.

20 Door exterior handle – removal and installation

1   Remove the inside door trim panel and pry back the water shield at the rear of the door.
2   Raise the window to the full up position.
3   From inside the door, remove the two attaching nuts to the exterior handle and remove the handle assembly from the outside of the door. On some later models it will be necessary to first remove the guide bracket for access to the handle nuts. This bracket is held in place with four screws on the door skin.
4   When installing, make sure the handle gasket is in good condition to prevent water leaks. The installation procedure is a reversal of removal.

21 Door window glass – removal and installation

Note: If equipped with power windows, have a dealer or glass specialist perform this procedure.
1   Remove the door trim panel (Section 17).

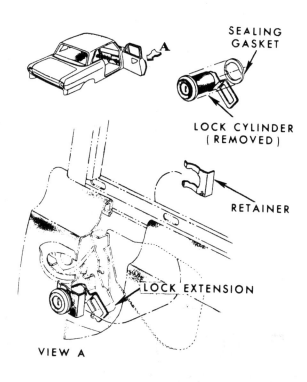

SEALING
GASKET

LOCK CYLINDER
(REMOVED)

RETAINER

LOCK EXTENSION

VIEW A

Fig. 12.5 Front door lock cylinder assembly (Sec 18)

2   Remove the inner water shield.
3   Remove the up-travel stops at the front and rear of the door.
4   Loosen the front and rear belt trim support retainers located at the top of the door in the window channel.
5   Position the window in the three-quarter-down position and remove the lower sash channel to glass attaching nuts through the small access holes in the inner door skin.
6   Lift the window straight up and out of the channel, aligning the rollers with the notches provided in the inner door skin.
7   Installation is a reversal of removal, however, install all attaching screws loosely and adjust the channels, guides and stops as necessary before finally tightening the fasteners.

22 Door window regulator – removal and installation

Note: *If equipped with power windows, have a dealer or glass specialist perform this procedure.*
1   Remove the door inner trim panel and water shield (Section 17).
2   Mark the location and remove the door window and inner panel cam (Section 21).
3   Remove the regulator-to-inner door attaching fasteners. Early models use bolts, while later models have rivets which must be carefully drilled out with a $\frac{1}{4}$-inch drill bit. Remove the regulator through the large access hole.
4   When installing, if rivets were drilled out, U-nuts on the regulator body and $\frac{1}{4}$-20x$\frac{1}{2}$ inch attaching screws should be substituted. Tighten attaching screws or bolts and reverse the removal sequence.

23 Door – removal and installation

1   Disconnect the battery ground cable.
2   Open the door fully and support it on blocks and cloth pads placed under its lower edge.
3   If the vehicle is equipped with power-operated windows, remove the trim panel and disconnect the regulator wiring harness.
4   Prior to removal of doors, scribe round the fitted position of the hinge on the door.
5   Using a cranked wrench, and with an assistant supporting the weight of the door, remove the door hinge retaining bolts.
6   Having removed the door, it is now possible to remove the hinge from the hinge pillar, but again scribe round the fitted position first.
7   Refitting doors and hinges is the reverse of the removal procedure. If necessary the hinge positions may be altered slightly to ensure correct alignment.
Note: *When refitting the door, ensure that the lock striker fork-bolt engages with the striker. If necessary the position of the fork bolt can be adjusted by loosening with a wrench, repositioning, then retightening.*

24 Windshield and back window – removal and installation

1   These operations are best left to specialists as the glass is retained by quick setting adhesive/caulk material which leaves no room for error in application or positioning of the windshield.
2   The rear view mirror support is bonded to the windshield and can only be removed by extremely careful application of heat from an air gun (250° to 350°F) – another job for a specialist.

25 Tailgate – removal and installation

1   Pad the rear bumper with towels. Lower the window fully. Open the tailgate. If your car has a "magic" tailgate, open it in the door position.
2   Reach in behind the access panel and unplug any wiring that goes into the tailgate.
3   Have an assistant support the gate, and using an impact screwdriver, remove the gate from its hinges.
4   Installation is the reverse procedure.

Chapter 13 Supplement: Revisions and information on 1981 and later models

Contents

1   Introduction

This supplement contains specifications and service procedure changes that apply to Buick mid-size rear wheel drive models produced from 1981 through 1987. Also included is information related to previous models that was not available at the time of the original publication of this manual.

Where no differences (or very minor differences) exist between 1981 through 1987 models and earlier models, no information is given. In such instances, the original material included in Chapters 1 through 12 should be used.

2   Specifications

Note: *The following specifications are revisions of or supplementary to those listed at the beginning of each Chapter of this manual. The original specifications apply unless alternative information is included here.*

Engine — 1983 and 1984 V6

General

Displacement . . . .   231 and 252 cu in
Bore and stroke
   231 cu in . . . .   3.800 X 3.400 in
   252 cu in . . . .   3.965 X 3.400 in

Pistons and piston rings

Piston clearance limits (231 cu in)

Non-turbo

Top land	0.046 to 0.056 in
Skirt top	0.0008 to 0.0020 in
Skirt bottom	0.0013 to 0.0035 in

Turbo

Skirt at piston pin centerline	0.0022 to 0.0034 in
Skirt bottom	0.0008 to 0.0026 in

Torque specifications	**Ft-lb**
Engine balancer assembly-to-crankshaft bolt	
1983 and 1984	225
1985 on	200

Turbocharger

Torque specifications	**Ft-lb**
Turbocharger exhaust outlet pipe-to-turbine housing	
Through 1985	15
1986 on	20
Elbow assembly-to-turbine	15
Exhaust inlet pipe	
Through 1985	15
1986 on	23
Oil feed pipe	7
CHRA-to-turbine housing	15
CHRA-to-compressor	13
Throttle body-to-compressor	20
Oil drain-to-compressor	
Through 1984	20
1985 on	22
Wastegate actuator mounting bolt	22
Bracket bolts and nuts	
Through 1985	22
1986 on	20

Engine — 1986 and 1987 V8 (307 cu in Pontiac VIN code Y)

Note: *This engine is virtually identical to the 1977 Oldsmobile 350/403 CID V8 engines covered in Chapter 2. The specifications included here are only those that differ from the specifications for the Olsmobile 350/403 engines in Chapter 2. For all specifications not listed here, refer to Chapter 2, Part A.*

General

Bore and stroke	3.800 X 3.385 in

Pistons and piston rings

Nominal piston outside diameter	3.800 in
Clearance at thrust surface	0.00075 to 0.00175 in
Ring gap (top and 2nd)	0.009 to 0.019 in

Camshaft

Journal diameters

No. 1	2.0365 to 2.0352 in
No. 2	2.0165 to 2.0152 in
No. 3	1.9965 to 1.9952 in
No. 4	1.9765 to 1.9752 in
No. 5	1.9565 to 1.9552 in
End clearance	0.006 to 0.022 in

Valves

Valve face angle

Intake	46°
Exhaust	60°

Valve seat angle

Intake	45°
Exhaust	59°
Pushrod length	7.718 in

Torque specifications	**Ft-lb**
Intake manifold-to-cylinder head bolts	40*
Carburetor-to-intake manifold bolts	12
Cylinder head bolts	125*

* Clean and dip entire bolt in new engine oil before installation and tightening to obtain correct torque reading

Fuel and exhaust systems
Carburetor specifications — Rochester E2ME, E2MC and E2SE
Float level
   Carburetor number .... 5/16 in
     17081191
     17081196
     17082182
     17082184
     17082192
     17082194
     17083190
     17083192
     17084193
     17085190
     17086190
   Carburetor number .... 11/32 in
     17081192
     17081194
     17081197
     17081198
     17081199
     17081496
     17081497
     17084430
     17084431
     17084434
     17084435
   Carburetor number .... 9/32 in
     17084356
     17084357
     17084358
     17084359
     17084633
     17084635
     17084536

Choke rod
   Carburetor number .... 18°
     17081192
     17081194
     17081197
     17081198
     17081199
     17081496
     17081497
     17082184
     17082192
     17082194
     17083190
     17083192
     17084191
     17085190
     17086190
   Carburetor number .... 24.5°
     17081191
     17081196
   Carburetor number .... 22°
     17084356
     17084357
     17084358
     17084359
     17084368
     17084370
   Carburetor number .... 15°
     17084430
     17084431
     17084434
     17084435
   Carburetor number .... 28°
     17084452
     17084453
     17084455
     17084456
     17084458

17084532
17084632
17084633
17084635
17084636

Vacuum break
  Carburetor number . . . .   28° (front) 24° (rear)
  17081191
  17081192
  17081194
  17081196
  17081197
  17081198
  17081199
  17081496
  17081497
  17082182
  17082184
  17082192
  17082194
  17083190
  17083192
  17085190
  17086190

  Carburetor number 17084191 . . . .   28° (front) 25° (rear)

  Carburetor number . . . .   25° (front) 30° (rear)
  17084356
  17084357
  17084358
  17084359
  17084368
  17084370

  Carburetor number . . . .   26° (front) 38° (rear)
  17084430
  17084431
  17084434
  17084435

  Carburetor number . . . .   25° (front) 35° (rear)
  17084452
  17084453
  17084455
  17084456
  17084458
  17084532
  17084632
  17084633
  17084635
  17084636

Choke unloader
  Carburetor number . . . .   38°
  17081191
  17081192
  17081194
  17081196
  17081197
  17081198
  17081199
  17081496
  17081497

  Carburetor number . . . .   32°
  17082182
  17082192
  17082194
  17083190
  17083192
  17085190
  17086190

  Carburetor number 17084191 . . . .   35°

  Carburetor number . . . .   30°
  17084356
  17084357
  17084358
  17084359

Carburetor number . . . .   30° (continued)
    17084368
    17084370

Carburetor number . . . .   42°
    17084430
    17084431
    17084434
    17084435

Carburetor number . . . .   45°
    17084452
    17084453
    17084455
    17084456
    17084458
    17084532
    17084632
    17084633
    17084635
    17084636

Carburetor specifications — Rochester E4MC and E4ME
Float level
    Carburetor number . . . .   5/16 in
        17081242
        17084240
        17084244
        17084246
        17084248

    Carburetor number 17081289 . . . .   13/32 in

    Carburetor number . . . .   9/32 in
        17082244
        17082249
        17082260
        17082264
        17082269

    Carburetor number 17081243 . . . .   1/4 in

    Carburetor number . . . .   3/8 in
        17082245
        17082246
        17082247
        17082248
        17082249
        17082265
        17082266
        17082267
        17082268
        17082269
        17082294
        17082295
        17082298
        17082299

    Carburetor number . . . .   11/32 in
        17086008
        17086077

Choke rod
    Carburetor number . . . .   18°
        17082247
        17082248
        17082267
        17082268
        17082298
        17082299

    Carburetor number . . . .   24.5°
        17081242
        17081243
        17081245
        17081247
        17081248
        17081249
        17081289
        17082244

17082245
17082246
17082247
17082249
17082260
17082264
17082265
17082266
17082269
17082294
17082295
17084240
17084244
17084246
17084248

Carburetor number . . . .   14°
17086008
17086077

Vacuum break
Carburetor number 17081242 . . . .   17° (front) 15° (rear)
Carburetor number 17081243 . . . .   19° (front) 17° (rear)
Carburetor number . . . .   28° (front) 24° (rear)
17081245
17081247
17081248
17081249
17081289

Carburetor number . . . .   21° (front) 16° (rear)
17082244
17082260
17082264

Carburetor number . . . .   26° (front) 26° (rear)
17082245
17082246
17082247
17082248
17082266
17082267
17082268
17082294
17082295
17082298
17082299

Carburetor number . . . .   20° (front) 15° (rear)
17082249
17082269

Carburetor number 17084246 . . . .   22° (front) 24° (rear)
Carburetor number . . . .   24° (front only)
17084240
17084244
17084248
Carburetor number . . . .   25° (front) 43° (rear)
17086008
17086077

Choke unloader
Carburetor number . . . .   38°
17081242
17081243
17081245
17081247
17081248
17081289
17082249
17082269

Carburetor number . . . .   32°
17082246
17082247
17082248
17082260
17082264
17082265
17082266
17082267

Carburetor number	32° (continued)
17082268	
17082294	
17082295	
17082298	
17084240	
17084244	
17084246	
17084248	
Carburetor number	35°
17086008	
17086077	

3 Engine

General information

Later models are equipped with a 252 cu in (4.1 litre) V6 engine as an option. This engine is similar to the V6 engine used in earlier models and service operations are the same. Refer to the beginning of this Chapter for specifications which differ from earlier engines.

Beginning in 1986, a Pontiac V8 was made available as an engine option. It displaces 307 cubic inches and can be identified by the VIN code Y. It is virtually identical to the 1977 Oldsmobile 350/403 CID V8's covered in Chapter 2, Part A, so the service and repair procedures for the Oldsmobile engines should be followed. The only exception is camshaft removal and installation, which is outlined later in this Section. Be sure to refer to the Specifications in this Supplement for the items that differ from the Oldsmobile engines.

Camshaft — removal and installation (307 Pontiac V8 engine only)

Follow the procedure in Chapter 2, Part A, for the Oldsmobile engines, but note that the camshaft on the Pontiac V8 is held in place by a thrust plate, which is attached to the block with two bolts. After the timing chain and sprocket are removed, the thrust plate must be detached before the camshaft is removed.

4 Turbocharger

General information

The turbocharger on 1984 fuel-injected models differs from carburetor-equipped models. Because the turbocharger operation is controlled by the C4 system, described in Chapter 6, on later models, maintenance is confined to checking the connections and linkages for security and damage.

Wastegate actuator assembly — removal and installation

1   Disconnect the vacuum hose at the actuator and remove the clip retaining the actuator rod to the wastegate lever.
2   Remove the two bolts attaching the mounting bracket compressor housing and remove the wastegate actuator.
3   Installation is the reverse of removal.

Turbocharger — removal and installation

4   Disconnect the air inlet tube from the throttle body and unplug the throttle body vacuum harness connector.
5   Disconnect and plug the coolant and heater hoses at the throttle body.
6   Remove the throttle body mounting nuts, carefully separate the throttle body from the engine and set it aside.
7   Disconnect the oil pressure feed line at the turbocharger and plug the openings.
8   Disconnect the exhaust inlet pipe from the exhaust manifold and the turbocharger.
9   Remove the exhaust outlet pipe from the turbocharger.
10 Remove the upper and lower right-side bracket-to-turbocharger nuts.
11 Remove the stabilizer bracket bolt from the left side of the compressor housing and separate the turbocharger from the manifold adapter.
12 Attach the turbocharger mounting and stabilizer brackets to the intake manifold.
13 Install the turbocharger, throttle body and gasket and adapter and

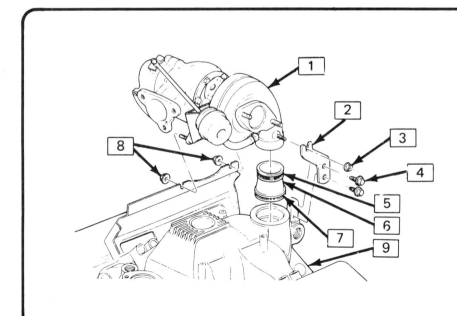

Fig. 13.1 Fuel injection equipped engine turbocharger component layout (Sec 4)

1   *Turbocharger assembly*
2   *Stabilizer bracket*
3   *Nut*
4   *Bolt*
5   *Seal*
6   *Adapter*
7   *Seal*
8   *Nut*
9   *Intake manifold*

seals on the manifold. **Note:** *The threads of all turbocharger and exhaust pipe-to-manifold bolts must be coated with anti-seize compound prior to installation.*

14 Install the turbocharger and throttle body assembly on the mounting bracket and adapter, tightening the bolts to the specified torque.

15 Attach the inlet and outlet pipes to the turbocharger and exhaust manifold.

16 Connect the oil pressure feed line to the turbocharger.

17 Connect the coolant and heater line to the throttle body.

18 Connect the throttle body vacuum harness and air inlet tube.

19 After installation, the TV cable must be adjusted (Section 7) and

the boost pressure checked. Because of the special tools and techniques necessary, the boost pressure check and adjustment should be left to your dealer service department.

Exhaust inlet pipe — removal and installation

20 Remove the nuts retaining the pipe and adapter to the turbocharger.

21 Remove the bolts and separate the pipe from the engine.

22 Carefully clean all traces of gasket material and other foreign material from the flanges and contact surfaces of the pipe and adapter.

23 Coat the threads of the nuts and bolts with anti-seize compound and install the pipe and adapter.

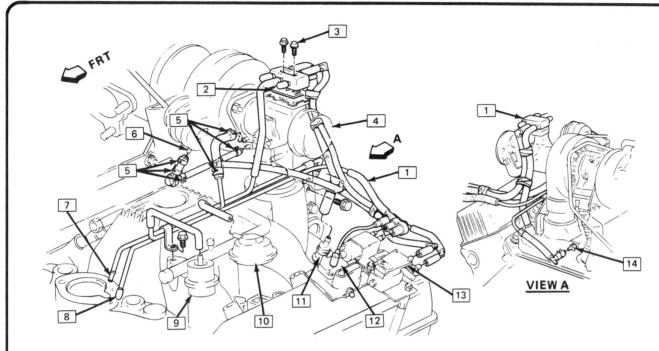

Fig. 13.2 Turbocharger connections (Sec 4)

1 Vacuum/pressure, PCV and purge hoses	5 Clamps	10 EGR valve
2 Gasket	6 Wastegate	11 PCV valve
3 Bolt	7 To fuel vapor canister	12 EGR valve vacuum control
4 Throttle body assembly	8 To water injection bottle	13 Solenoid wastegate valve
	9 Fuel regulator	14 Manifold vacuum pressure

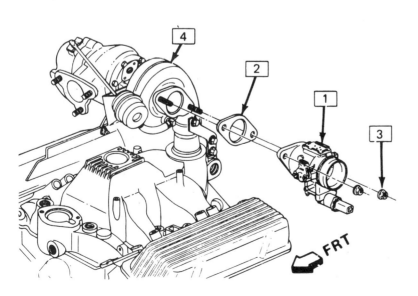

Fig.13.3 Throttle body components (Sec 4)

1 Throttle body
2 Gasket
3 Nut
4 Turbocharger

Wastegate actuator — removal and installation

24 Disconnect the vacuum hose from the actuator.
25 Remove the actuator rod-to-wastegate lever retaining clip.
26 Remove the bolts attaching the mounting bracket to the compressor housing and separate the wastegate actuator from the engine.
27 Place the wastegate actuator in position and install the mounting bolts. Tighten them to the specified torque.
28 Connect the actuator rod to the wastegate lever and install the retaining clip.
29 Connect the vacuum hose to the actuator.

Intercooler — general information

Turbocharged vehicles manufactured after 1985 are equipped with an intercooler. Its function is to reduce the temperature of the compressed fuel/air mixture before it enters the throttle body. The result is increased horsepower output. The intercooler is located behind the radiator. Removal of the device is straight-forward and involves removal of the shroud, loosening of the duct clamps and removal of the mounting bracket bolts.

5 Fuel and exhaust systems

General information

Later models continue to use the E2ME and E2MC 2-barrel and E4ME and E4MC 4-barrel carburetors described in Chapter 4.
In addition, an E2SE 2-barrel carburetor is used on some models. The operation of this carburetor is controlled by the electronic control module (ECM) in conjunction with an oxygen sensor in the exhaust system.
1984 turbocharged models are equipped with port-type fuel injection.

Port-type fuel injection — general information

This system consists of an air intake manifold, the throttle body, the injectors, the fuel rail assembly, an electric fuel pump and attendant plumbing.
Air is drawn through the air cleaner and throttle body and then into the manifold. A mass air flow sensor mounted between the air cleaner and the throttle measures the mass of air passing through the manifold and compensates for temperature and pressure variations. The air is drawn into the cylinders, where the fuel is injected above the intake valves.
While the engine is running, the fuel constantly circulates through the fuel rail, which removes vapors and keeps the fuel cool while maintaining a constant pressure at the injectors of 36 psi.
The operation of the fuel injection system is controlled by the ECM so that it works in conjunction with the rest of the vehicle functions to provide improved driveability and emissions control.
Because the port-type fuel injection system meters fuel and air precisely, it is important to the proper operation of the vehicle that the fuel and air filters be changed at the specified intervals.

Releasing fuel injection system pressure

1 The fuel injection system must be depressurized before any work is done or fuel spray will be released when the line is disconnected.
2 Remove the fuel pump fuse from the fuse block located in the passenger compartment, then start the engine to use up the fuel remaining in the lines.
3 Crank the engine over for approximately three more seconds to make sure all fuel is exhausted, then turn the ignition Off.
4 Reinstall the fuel pump fuse in the fuse block.

Air and fuel filter replacement

5 The fuel and air filters should be replaced every 25000 miles or 25 months, whichever occurs first, or more often when driving in dusty conditions.
6 The fuel filter is located in the engine compartment on the lower left side of the engine and the air filter element is in a housing at the right front corner of the engine.
7 Refer to the accompanying illustration for filter replacement.

Carburetor adjustments

Float level
8 Hold the float retainer firmly in place, push the float down until it lightly contacts the needle and measure the float level with the gauge. The gauging point is 3/16-inch back from the toe of the float as shown in the illustration.
9 On carburetors used with the C4 sytem, the float should be ad-

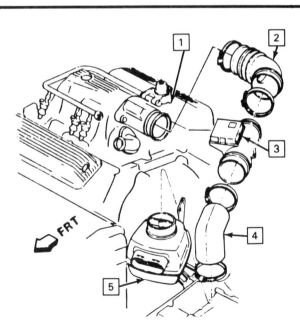

Fig. 13.4 Fuel injection air system (Sec 5)

1 Throttle body assembly
2 Rear air intake duct
3 Mass airflow sensor
4 Air intake duct
5 Air cleaner assembly

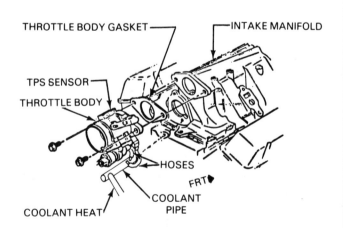

Fig. 13.5 Fuel injection throttle body components (Sec 5)

justed if the height varies from that shown in the Specifications Section of this Chapter by plus-or-minus 1/16-inch.

10 If the level is too high, hold the retainer in place and push down on the center of the float pontoon until the specified setting is obtained.

11 If the level is too low on *non-electronic solenoid* equipped carburetors, remove the power piston, metering rods, plastic filler block and the float. Bend the float arm up to adjust it. Reinstall the parts and visually check the alignment of the float.

12 If the level is too low on *electronic solenoid* equipped carburetors, remove the metering rods and the solenoid connector screw. Count and record for use at the time of reassembly the number of turns necessary to lightly bottom the mixture screw. Back the screw out and remove it, followed by the solenoid, connector and the float. Bend the float up to adjust it. Install the parts and reset the mixture screw to the recorded number of turns.

Choke rod (1981 and 1982)

13 With the choke coil lever and fast idle properly adjusted, install a choke valve measuring gauge such as GM tool J-26701.

14 Rotate the degree scale until it is opposite the pointer.

15 Make sure the choke valve is closed and place a magnet on it as shown in the illustration.

16 Rotate the scale until the bubble is centered and then rotate it until the specified degree is opposite the pointer.

17 Place the cam follower on the second step of the cam and against the rise of the high step.

18 Push up on the choke coil lever or the vacuum break lever to close the choke and hold it in position with a rubber band.

19 Adjust by bending the tang on the fast idle cam until the bubble is centered.

Choke rod (1983 on)

20 Attach a rubber band to the green tang of the intermediate choke shaft as shown in the illustration.

21 Close the choke valve by opening the throttle.

22 Install a choke angle gauge such as GM tool J-26701 and set the

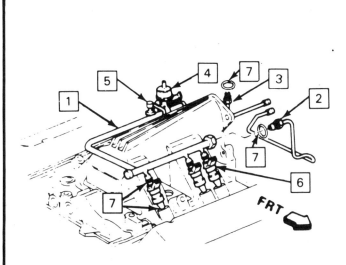

Fig. 13.6 Fuel rail assembly components (Sec 6)

1 Fuel rail
2 Fuel inlet
3 Fuel return
4 Fuel pressure regulator
5 Fuel pressure tap
6 Fuel injector
7 O-ring

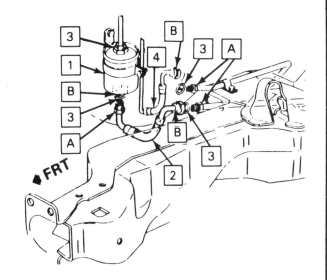

Fig. 13.7 Port-type fuel injection fuel filter replacement (Sec 5)

1 Fuel filter
2 Fuel feed line
3 O-ring
4 Fuel return line
A Tighten to 22 ft-lb
B Use a backup wrench at this point

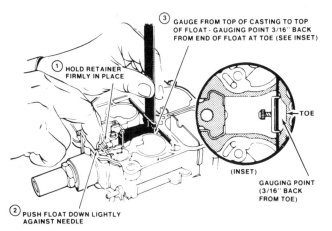

Fig. 13.8 Float level adjustment (Sec 5)

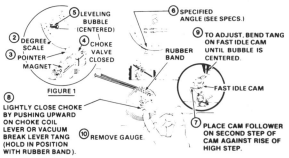

Fig. 13.9 Choke rod adjustment (1981 and 1982) (Sec 5)

angle to specification.

23 Place the cam follower on the second step of the cam, against the high step. If the follower does not contact the cam, turn the fast idle speed screw until it does. the final fast idle adjustment must be made according to the information on the *Emissions Control Information label* under the hood.

24 Bend the fast idle cam tang until the bubble is centered.

Front vacuum break (1981 and 1982)

25 Install the J-26701 gauge and rotate the degree scale until the zero is opposite the pointer.

26 Place the magnet squarely on top of the choke valve and make sure the valve is closed completely.

27 Rotate the gauge until the bubble is centered and then rotate it until the specified degree is opposite the pointer.

28 Seat the diaphragm using a vacuum source or pump. On vacuum delay equipped models, remove the rubber cover over the filter element and plug the small bleed hole with a piece of tape. Remove the tape after adjustment.

29 Hold the choke valve toward the closed position by pushing up on the coil lever or the vacuum break lever tang. Secure it in place with a rubber band.

30 To adjust, remove the vacuum break from the carburetor, place the bracket securely in a vise and grind or file off the weld retaining the adjustment screw cover. Remove the cover, reinstall the vacuum break and adjust it by turning the screw in or out until the gauge bubble is centered.

Front vacuum break (1983 on)

31 Attach a rubber band to the green tang of the intermediate choke shaft and open the throttle to allow the choke valve to close.

32 Install the GM J-26701 gauge tool and set the gauge to the specified angle.

33 Apply at least 18 in Hg of vacuum to retract the vacuum break to the specified adjustment.

34 On 4-barrel carburetors, the air valve rod can sometimes restrict the plunger from retracting completely and it might be necessary to bend the rod slightly . The final rod clearance must be set after the vacuum break adjustment has been made.

35 With the vacuum applied, adjust the screw until the gauge bubble is centered.

Rear vacuum break (1981 and 1982)

36 With the choke coil lever and fast idle correctly adjusted, install the J-26701 gauge tool and rotate the degree scale to zero.

37 Close the choke valve completely and place the magnet squarely on top of the valve.

38 Rotate the gauge until the bubble is centered and then rotate the scale so the specified degree is opposite the pointer.

39 Apply vacuum to seat the vacuum diaphragm.

40 Hold the choke valve toward the closed position while pushing up on the choke coil or vacuum break lever and retain it in position with a rubber band.

41 Adjust by using a 1/8-inch hex head wrench to turn the screw in the rear cover until the gauge bubble is centered. Apply RTV-type sealant over the screw head to maintain the setting.

Rear vacuum break (1983 on)

42 Attach a rubber band to the green tang of the intermediate choke shaft as shown in the illustration.

43 Open the throttle until the choke valve closes.

44 Install the J-26701 angle gauge tool on the carburetor and set the angle to specification.

45 Plug any bleed holes and apply vacuum to the vacuum break plunger.

46 On 4-barrel carburetors it may be necessary to bend the air valve rod slightly at the point indicated in the illustration to allow full travel of the plunger.

47 To center the gauge bubble, either of two methods can be used. With the vacuum applied, use a 1/8-inch hex head wrench to turn the

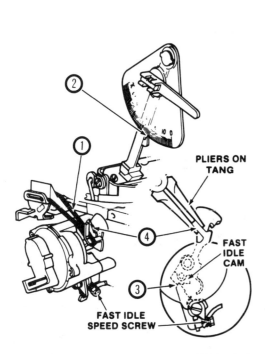

Fig. 13.10   Choke rod adjustment (1983 on) (Sec 5)

1 *Rubber band on the intermediate choke shaft green tang*
2 *Angle gauge set to specification*
3 *Cam follower on the second step, against the high step*
4 *Adjust by bending the fast idle cam tang to center the bubble*

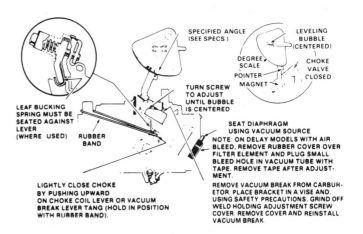

Fig. 13.11   1981 and 1982 front vacuum break adjustment (Sec 5)

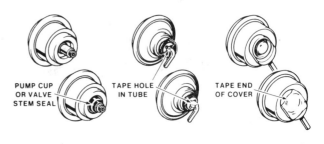

Fig. 13.12   Methods of plugging the vacuum delay air bleed holes (Sec 5)

adjustment screw (A in the illustration). Alternately, support the vacuum break rod at point S and bend the rod (B in the illustration) with the vacuum applied.

Choke unloader

48 Attach a rubber band to the green tang of the intermediate choke shaft as shown in the illustration and open the throttle to allow the choke valve to close.

49 Install the J-26701 gauge tool and set the angle to specification.
50 On 4-barrel carburetors, hold the secondary lockout lever away from the pin as shown in the illustration.
51 Hold the throttle lever in the wide open position and bend the fast idle lever tang until the gauge bubble is centered.

Idle speed adjustment — preparation

52 Prior to idle speed adjustment the engine must be at normal

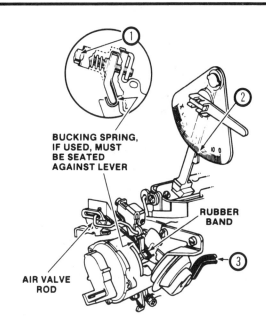

Fig. 13.13   1983 on front vacuum break adjustment
(Sec 5)

1 Adjustment screw
2 Adjustment gauge set
     to specification
3 Vacuum port

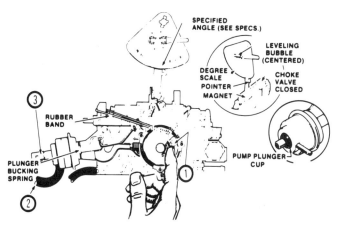

Fig. 13.14   Rear vacuum break adjustment (1981 and 1982)
(Sec 5)

1 Push up lightly to close
     the choke
2 Apply vacuum
3 Adjust here and seal with
     RTV-type sealant after
     adjustment

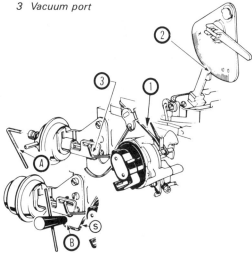

Fig. 13.15   Rear vacuum break adjustment (1983 on)
(Sec 5)

1 Rubber band attached
     to the intermediate
     choke shaft green
     tang
2 Angle gauge set to
     specification
3 Air valve rod

A Adjustment using
     1/8-inch hex wrench
B Adjustment by bending
     the vacuum break
     rod while supporting
     it at point S

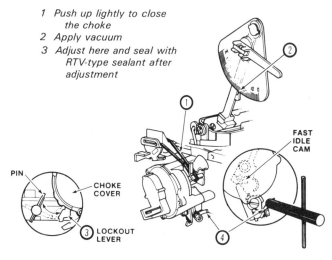

Fig. 13.16   Choke unloader adjustment (Sec 5)

1 Rubber band on
     intermediate shaft
     green tang
2 Angle gauge set to
     specification

3 4-barrel carburetor
     secondary lockout
     lever and pin
4 Adjustment is made by
     bending the fast idle
     lever tang

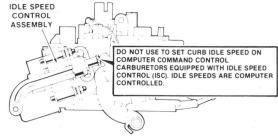

DO NOT USE TO SET CURB IDLE SPEED ON COMPUTER COMMAND CONTROL CARBURETORS EQUIPPED WITH IDLE SPEED CONTROL (ISC). IDLE SPEEDS ARE COMPUTER CONTROLLED.

Fig. 13.17   Idle speed control used on C4 system equipped
carburetors (Sec 5)

Fig. 13.18   Non-solenoid equipped curb idle speed adjustment
(Sec 5)

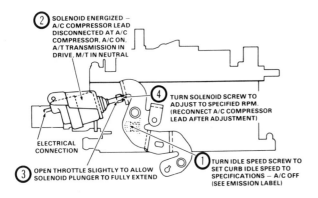

Fig. 13.19   Solenoid equipped curb idle speed adjustment
(Sec 5)

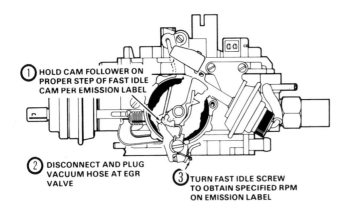

Fig. 13.20   Fast idle speed adjustment (Sec 5)

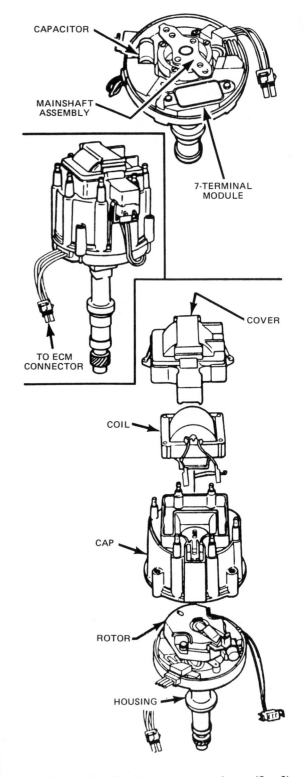

Fig. 13.21   Distributor component layout (Sec 6)

operating temperature and the ignition timing set to the specification on the *Emissions Control Information label*. Connect a tachometer to the engine.

53 Some models equipped with the C4 system use an idle speed control (ISC) assembly mounted on the carburetor and controlled by the ECM to control idle. *Do not attempt to adjust the idle on the idle speed control. Adjustment should be left to your dealer or a properly equipped shop. Also, the ISC should never be unplugged while the ignition is on or the ECM will be destroyed.*

Curb idle speed adjustment (non-solenoid equipped)

54 With the air conditioner Off, adjust the curb idle screw to the specifications on the *Emissions Control Information label* as shown in

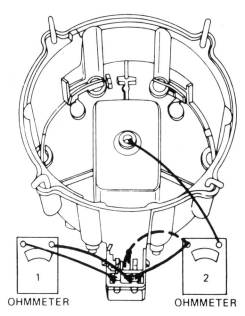

Fig. 13.22   Testing the coil-in-cap coil (Sec 6)

1   With the ohmmeter
    connected, the
    reading should be
    near zero

2   Connect the ohmmeter
    as shown, using the
    High scale (the coil is
    faulty if both
    readings are infinite)

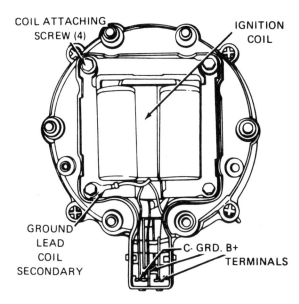

Fig. 13.23   Removal of the coil-in-cap ignition coil (Sec 6)

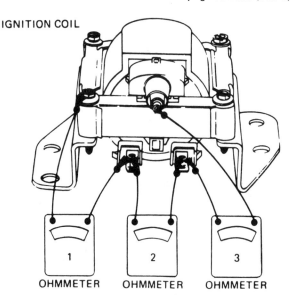

Fig. 13.24   Testing the separately mounted ignition coil
(Sec 6)

1   On the High scale the
    reading should be
    very high (infinite) or
    there is a fault in the
    coil

2   On the Low scale, the
    reading should be

    very low or zero (if it
    is high, the coil is
    faulty)

3   On the High scale, the
    reading should not be
    Infinite (if it is,
    replace the coil)

the illustration.

Curb idle speed adjustment (solenoid equipped)

55   Adjust the curb idle as described in the previous Step.

56   With the air conditioner On, the compressor lead disconnected at the compressor, the solenoid energized and the transmission in Neutral (manual) or Drive (automatic), open the throttle slightly to completely extend the solenoid plunger.

57   Adjust the curb idle to the specified rpm by turning the solenoid screw.

58   Reconnect the air conditioner compressor after adjustment.

Fast idle speed adjustment (non-solenoid equipped)

59   With the transmission in Park (automatic) or Neutral (manual), hold the cam follower on the step specified on the *Emissions Control Information label* as shown in the illustration and turn the fast idle screw to obtain the specified rpm.

Fast idle speed adjustment (solenoid equipped)

60   With the transmission in Park (automatic) or Neutral (manual), hold the cam follower on the step specified on the *Emissions Control Information label*.

61   Disconnect the vacuum hose at the EGR valve and plug it.

62   To obtain the fast idle rpm specified on the label, turn the fast idle screw as shown in the illustration.

---

6   Engine electrical systems

General description — distributor

Most later distributors are not equipped with vacuum advance units as advance is controlled by the electronic control module (ECM).

Some later distributors incorporate a Hall effect switch under the pickup coil.

In addition to the distributor cap mounted ignition coil described in Chapter 5, some later models have a separately mounted coil.

1984 turbocharged models with port-type fuel injection do not have a conventional distributor and use a Computer Controlled Coil Ignition. This system uses a coil pack, ignition module and crankshaft and camshaft sensors to precisely control the spark.

Distributor — overhaul

1   Unplug the electrical connector(s), disengage the latches and remove the distributor cap.

2   Test the ignition coil, referring to the appropriate accompanying illustration.

3   To remove a distributor cap ignition coil, remove the coil cover screws, then lift off the cover, followed by the coil mounting screws. Separate the clip from the cap and remove the coil arc seal. Clean the cap carefully with a soft cloth and inspect it for cracks and damage.

4   On Hall effect switch equipped distributors, test the switch by connecting a 12-volt power supply and voltmeter as shown in the illustrations. Check the polarity markings carefully before making any connections.

5   When the knife blade is not inserted as shown, the voltmeter should read less than 0.5 volts. If the reading is more, the Hall effect switch is faulty and must be replaced with a new one.

6   With the knife blade inserted, the voltmeter should read within 0.5

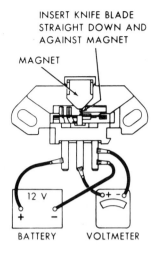

Fig. 13.25   Testing the Hall effect switch (Sec 6)

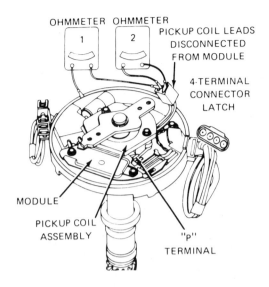

Fig. 13.26   Testing the pickup coil (coil-in-cap distributor)
(Sec 6)

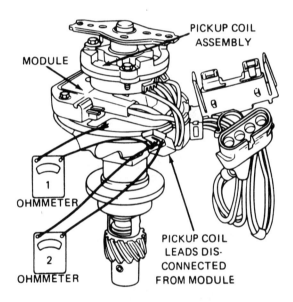

Fig. 13.27   Testing the pickup coil on a distributor with a
separately mounted ignition coil (Sec 6)

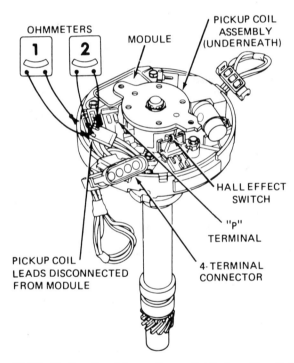

Fig. 13.28   Testing the pickup coil on a distributor with a Hall
effect switch (Sec 6)

volts of battery voltage. Replace the switch with a new one if the reading is more.

7   To test the pickup coil on all models, remove the rotor and pickup leads and connect an ohmmeter as shown in the accompanying illustrations.

8   If the distributor is equipped with a vacuum unit, connect a vacuum source or pump.

9   Apply vacuum to the unit and observe the ohmmeter to make sure the reading remains steady as vacuum is applied. Replace the vacuum unit with a new one if it is inoperative or the ohmmeter reading changes. Make sure that the application of vacuum does not cause the distributor teeth to align (which will cause a normal jump in the ohmmeter reading).

10   With the ohmmeter attached as shown in Step 1 in the illustrations, the reading should be infinite. With the ohmmeter attached as shown in Step 2, the reading should be between 500 and 1500 ohms. Replace the coil with a new one if it fails either test.

11   Place the distributor in a vise using blocks of wood to protect it.

12   Mark the relative positions of the gear and shaft and drive the roll pin out as shown in the illustration. Remove the gear and pull the shaft from the distributor housing.

13   On distributors with the ignition coil mounted in the cap, remove the aluminum shield for access to the pickup coil and module. The

pickup coil can then be lifted out after removing the C-washer. Remove the two screws and lift the module, capacitor and harness assembly from the distributor base. When installing, apply a coat of silicone lubricant under the module.

14   On distributors which use a separately mounted ignition coil, remove the C-washer and lift the pickup coil assembly out. Unplug the harness, remove the screws and separate the module from the base.

15   Wipe the distributor base and module clean with a cloth and inspect it for cracks and damage.

16   Reassembly is the reverse of the disassembly procedure. Be sure to apply a coat of silicone lubricant to the distributor base under the module. After reassembly, spin the distributor shaft to make sure there is no contact by the pickup coil and/or the Hall effect pickup teeth. Loosen and retighten as necessary to eliminate any contact.

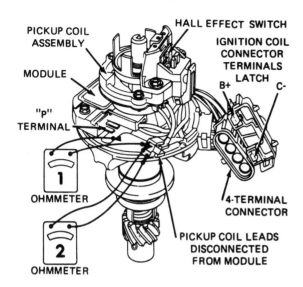

Fig. 13.29 Testing the pickup coil on a Hall effect distributor using a separately mounted ignition coil (Sec 6)

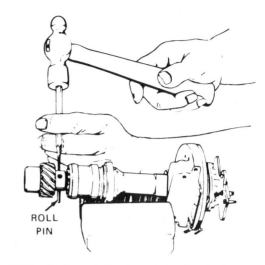

Fig. 13.30 Driving out the pin retaining the distributor gear to the shaft (Sec 6)

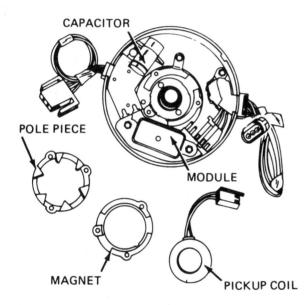

Fig. 13.31 Ignition coil-in-cap distributor component layout (Sec 6)

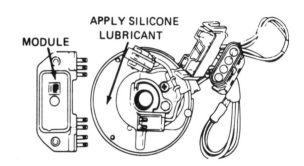

Fig. 13.32 Removal or installation of the module on a distributor with a separately mounted ignition coil (Sec 6)

7 Automatic transmission

Column shift linkage adjustment

1   Place the shift lever in the shift indicator Neutral position.
2   Position the transmission shift lever in the Neutral detent.
3   Referring to the accompanying illustration, install the clamp spring and screw assembly on the equalizer lever and control rod.
4   Hold the clamp flush against the equalizer lever and tighten the clamp screws finger tight. Make sure that no force is exerted in either direction on the rod or the equalizer lever while the screw is being tightened.
5   Tighten the screw to 21 ft-lb.
6   After adjustment the engine should start in the Park and Neutral positions only.

Throttle valve (TV) cable — inspection and adjustment

7   The throttle valve (TV) cable used on some models is connected between the transmission throttle valve and the carburetor. The TV

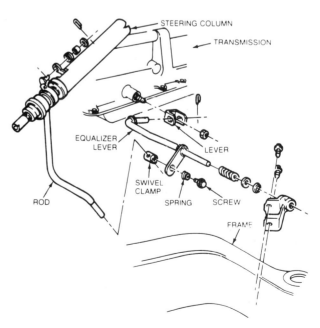

Fig. 13.33 Typical automatic transmission column shift linkage (Sec 7)

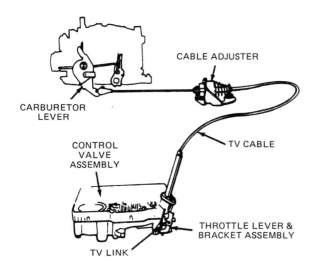

Fig. 13.34 Throttle valve (TV) cable and linkage component layout (Sec 7)

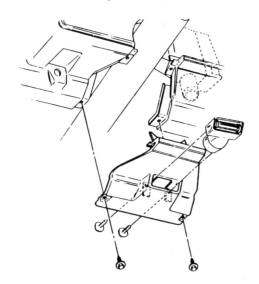

Fig. 13.37 Steering column trim panel installation (Sec 8)

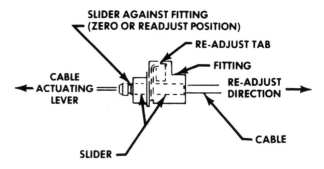

Fig. 13.35 Throttle valve cable adjustment (Sec 7)

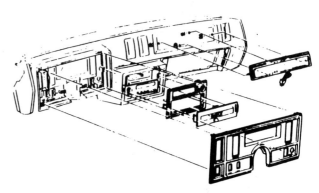

Fig. 13.36 Instrument panel left and center trim panel installation (Sec 8)

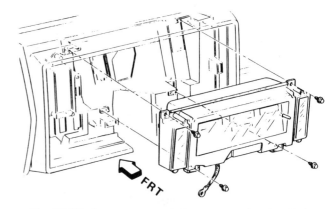

Fig. 13.38 Instrument panel cluster removal or installation (Sec 8)

cable controls the transmission line pressure, shift points, part throttle downshifts and detent downshifts. Symptoms of an improperly adjusted TV cable are early or slipping shifts, failure to downshift and delayed or sharp upshifts.

8   Inspect the entire length of the cable for secure connections, sticking or binding and damaged or bent brackets.

9   With the engine off, depress the re-adjust tab and move the slider back through the fitting, away from the throttle body, until it stops against the fitting. Release the re-adjust tab.

10   Open the throttle to the full throttle stop position and then release it. This will automatically adjust the TV cable.

11   Check the cable for sticking or binding and road test the vehicle to check for proper operation.

8 Chassis electrical system

Instrument cluster housing — removal and installation

1   With the transmission in Low and the tilt wheel (if equipped) all the way down, grasp the left hand trim cover firmly on both sides and remove it by pulling straight out.

2   Remove the four cluster cover-to-instrument panel screws.

3   Disconnect the speedometer cable at the transmission or in the engine compartment (on models with two-piece cables) to gain the necessary slack.

4   Remove the steering column trim cover, disconnect the shift indicator clip and lower the steering column.

5   Pull the cluster forward sufficiently to provide clearance and disconnect the speedometer cable, bulb wiring and digital cluster harness connector and ground strap. With the transmission still in Low, remove the screw retaining the vehicle speed sensor optic head to the speedometer.

6   Lift the housing from the instrument panel.

7   Installation is the reverse of removal.

Wiring diagrams

8   Note that wiring diagrams for later models have been included at the end of this Chapter. The wiring color code for earlier models, included in Chapter 10, is also valid for later models. Due to space limitations we are not able to provide every diagram for each model; however, a representative sampling is included.

313

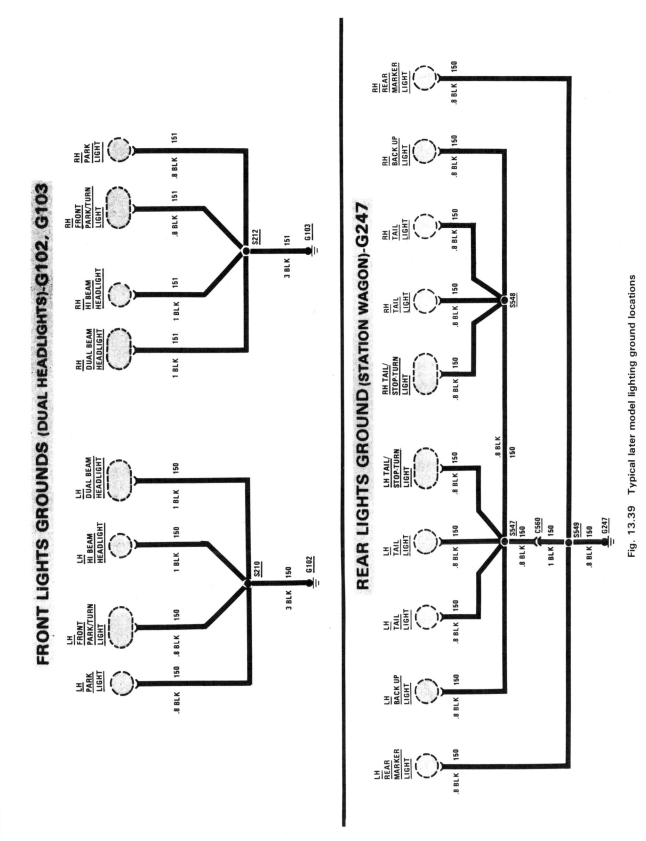

Fig. 13.39 Typical later model lighting ground locations

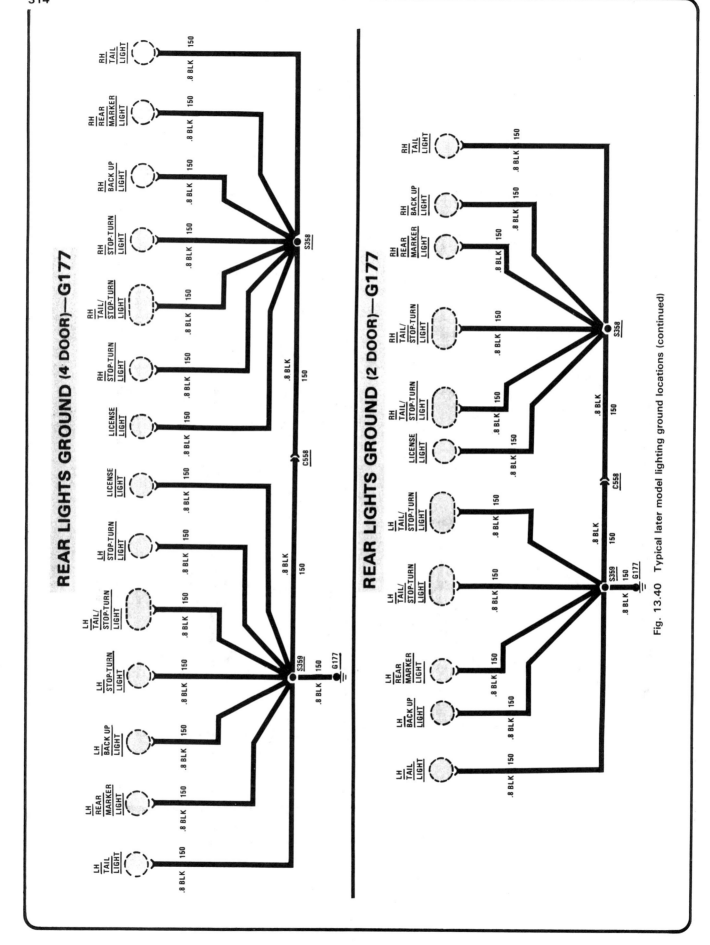

REAR LIGHTS GROUND (4 DOOR)—G177

REAR LIGHTS GROUND (2 DOOR)—G177

Fig. 13.40   Typical later model lighting ground locations (continued)

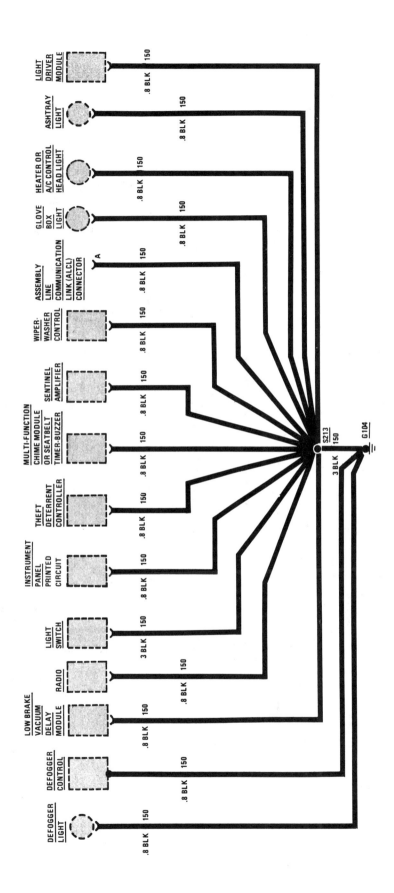

Fig. 13.41 Typical later model instrument panel ground locations

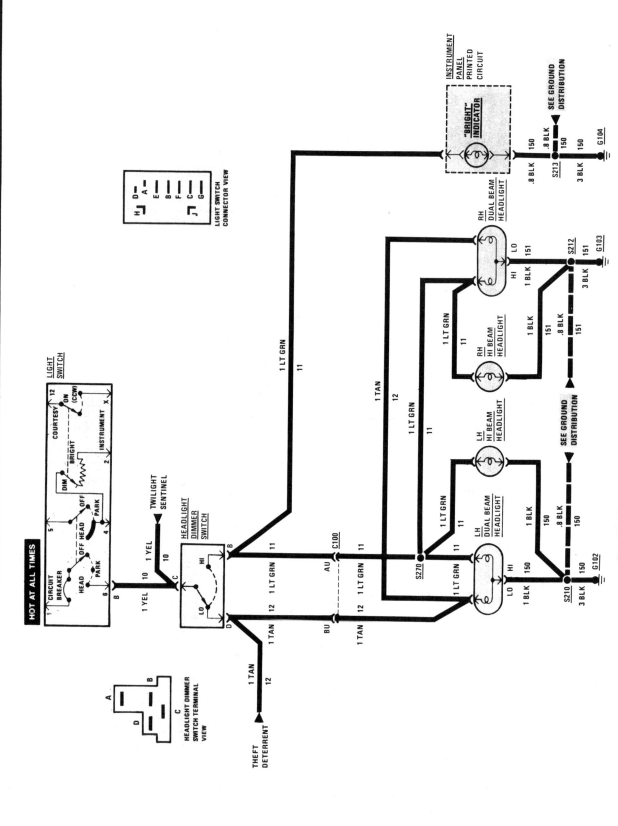

Fig. 13.42 Typical later model headlight wiring diagram

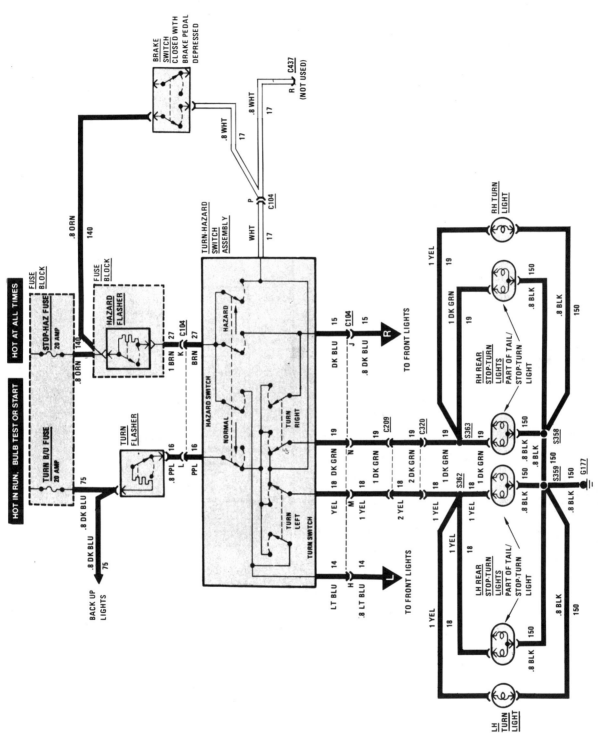

Fig. 13.43 Typical later model turn, stop, front park and marker light wiring diagram (except station wagon)

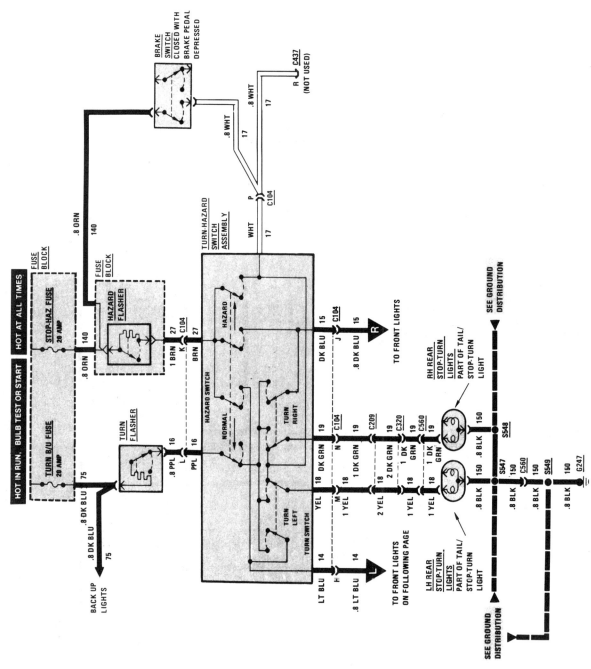

Fig. 13.44   Typical later model station wagon turn, stop, front park and marker light wiring diagram

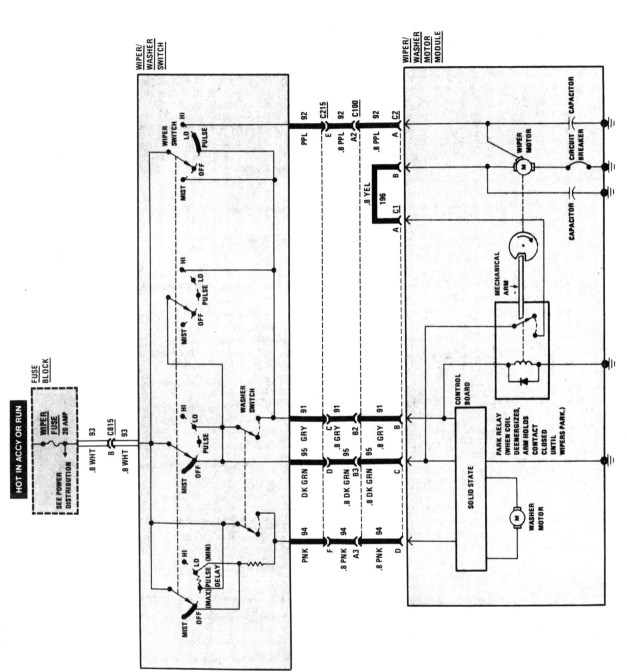

Fig. 13.45 Typical later model wiper/washer wiring diagram

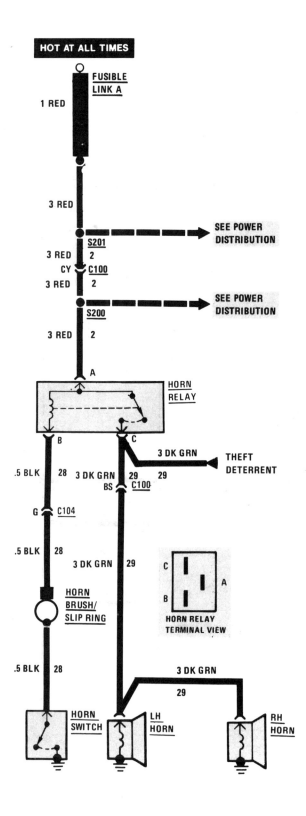

Fig. 13.46 Typical later model horn wiring diagram

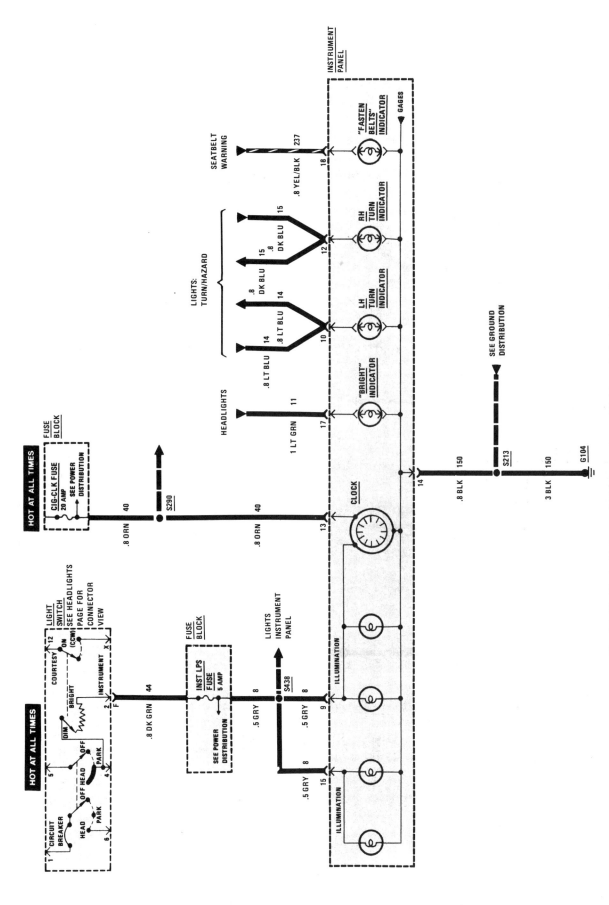

Fig. 13.47 Typical later model instrument panel lights and clock wiring diagram

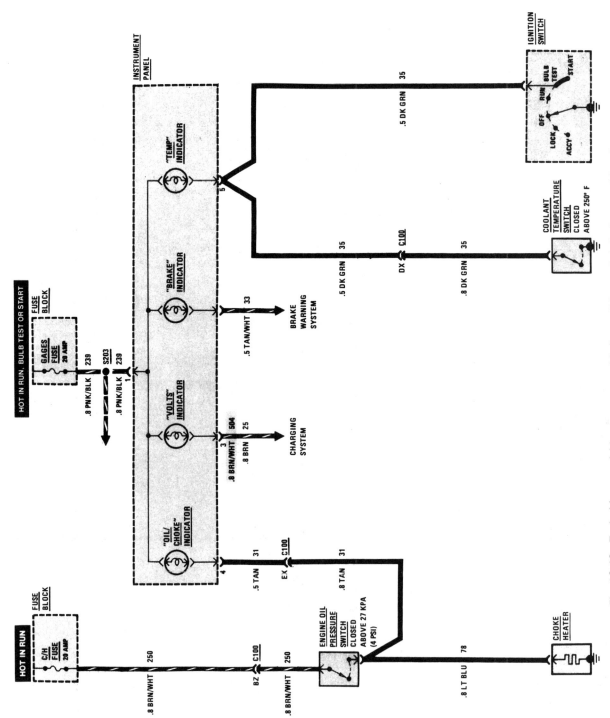

Fig. 13.48 Typical later model instrument panel indicator lights and choke heater wiring diagram

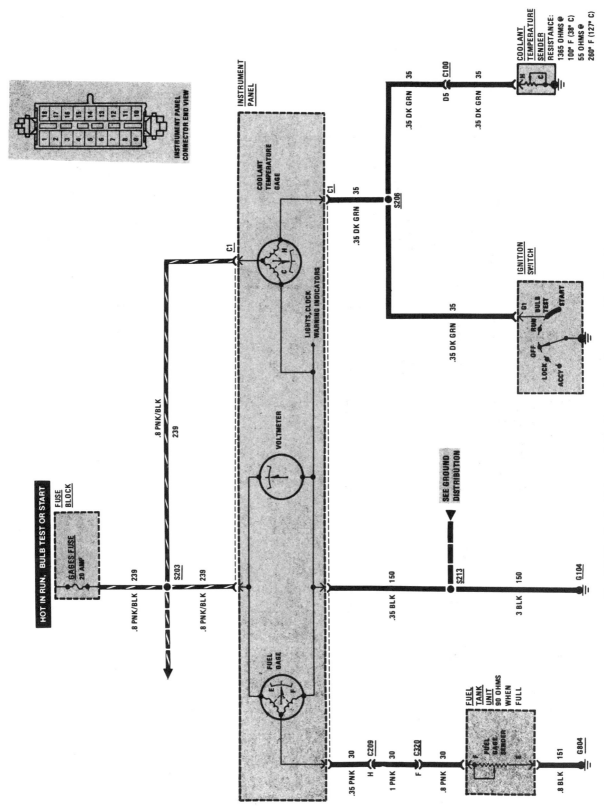

Fig. 13.49 Typical later model instrument panel gauge wiring diagram

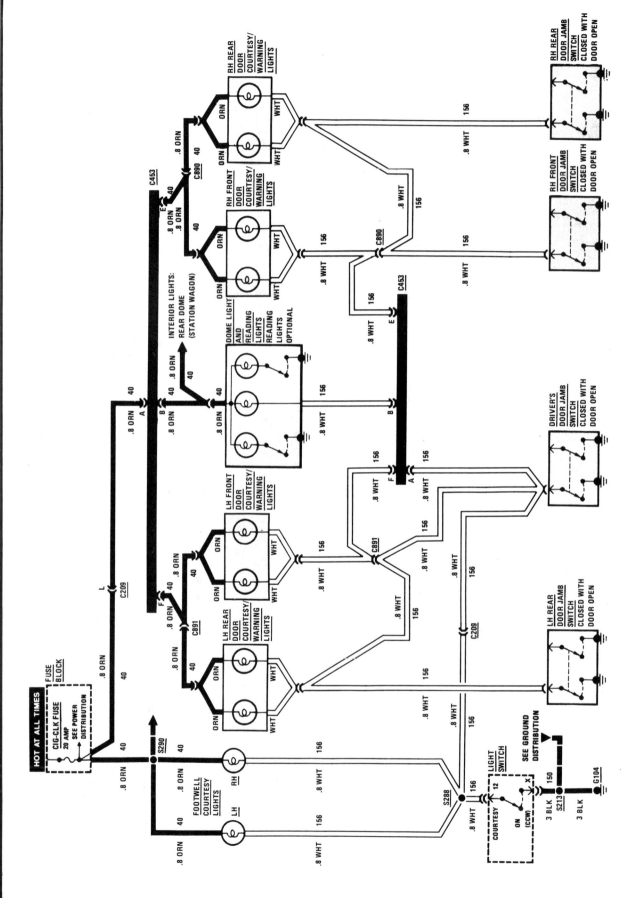

Fig. 13.50 Typical later model interior lighting wiring diagram

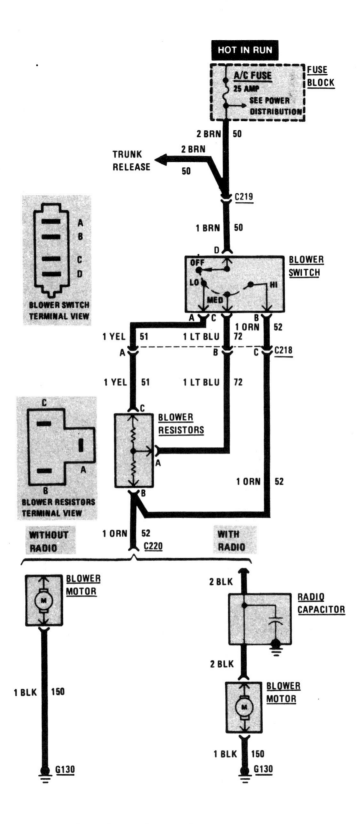

Fig. 13.51   Typical later model heater wiring diagram

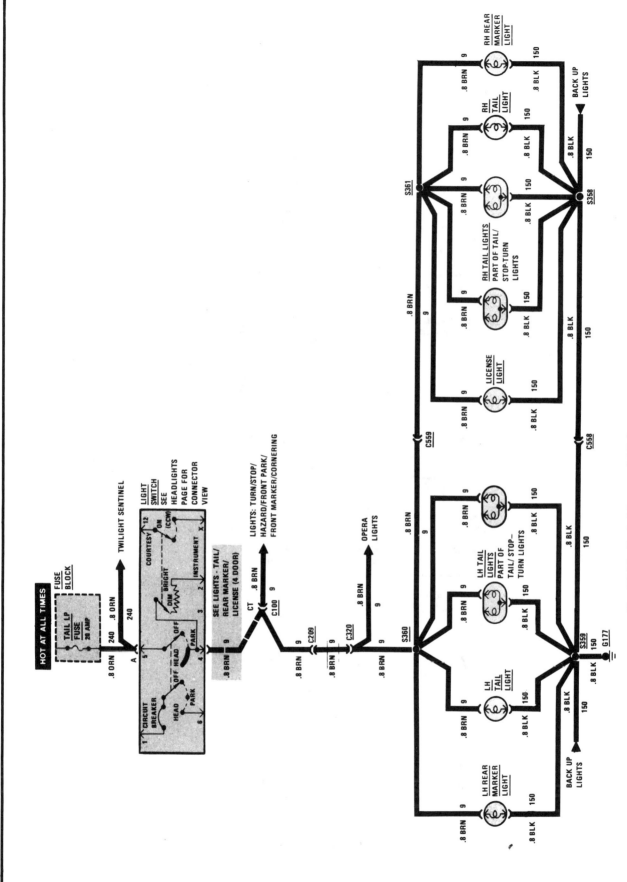

Fig. 13.52 Typical later model 2-door rear lighting wiring diagram

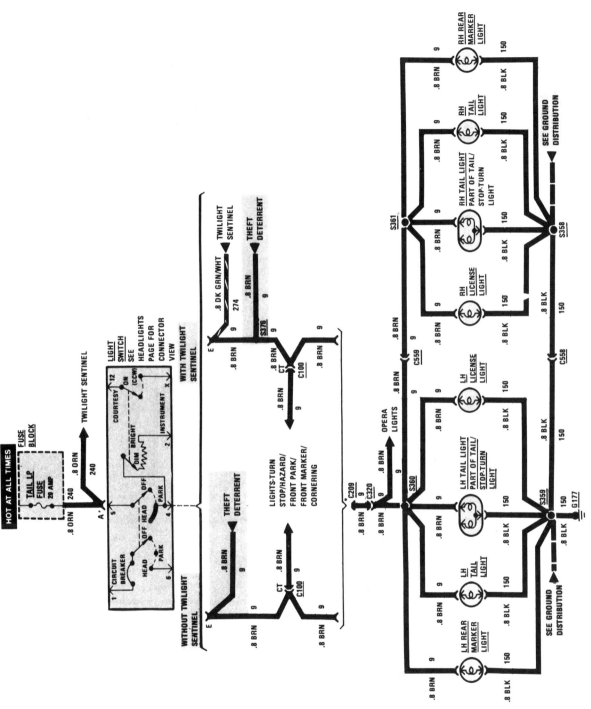

Fig. 13.53   Typical later model 4-door rear lighting wiring diagram

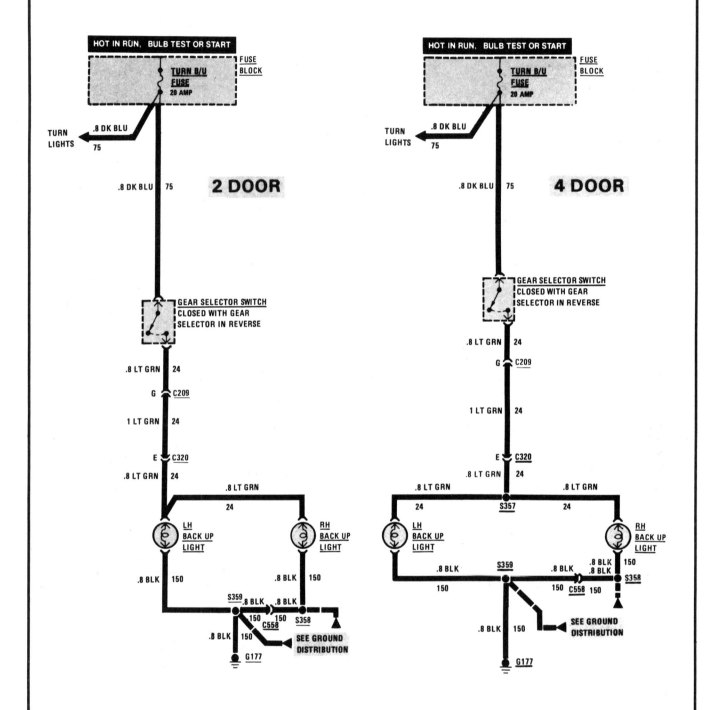

Fig. 13.54   Typical later model back-up light wiring diagram

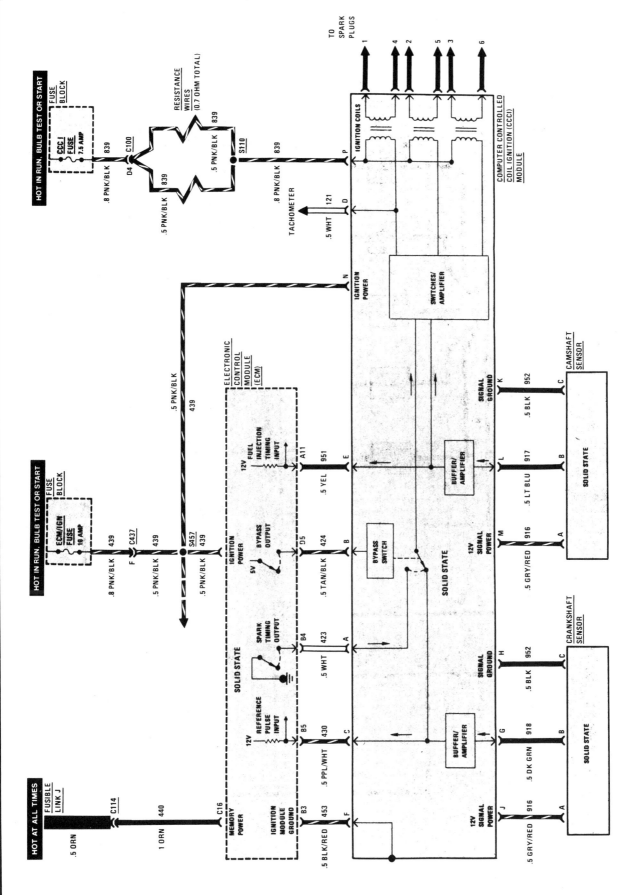

Fig. 13.55   1984 model port fuel injection wiring diagram

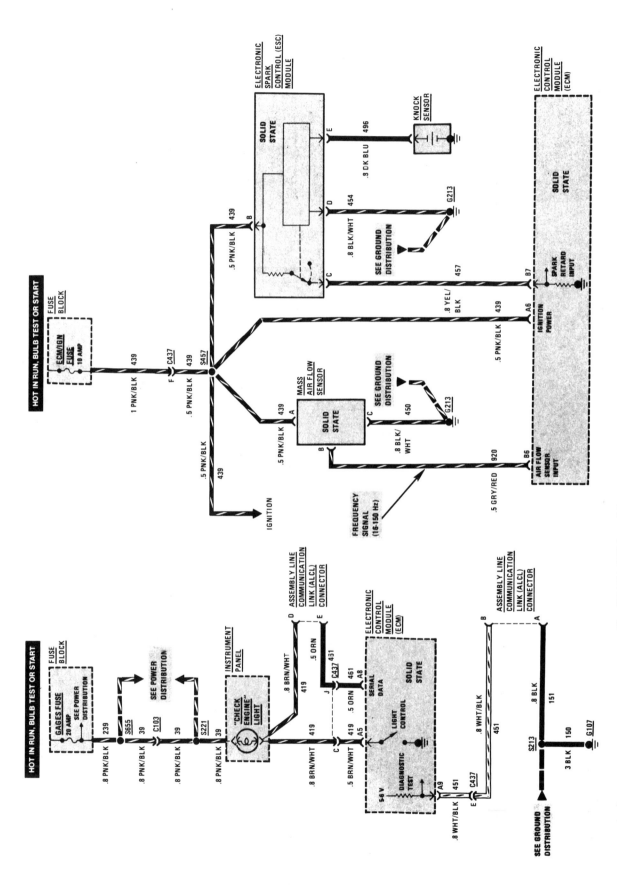

Fig. 13.56   1984 model port fuel injection C4 system wiring diagram

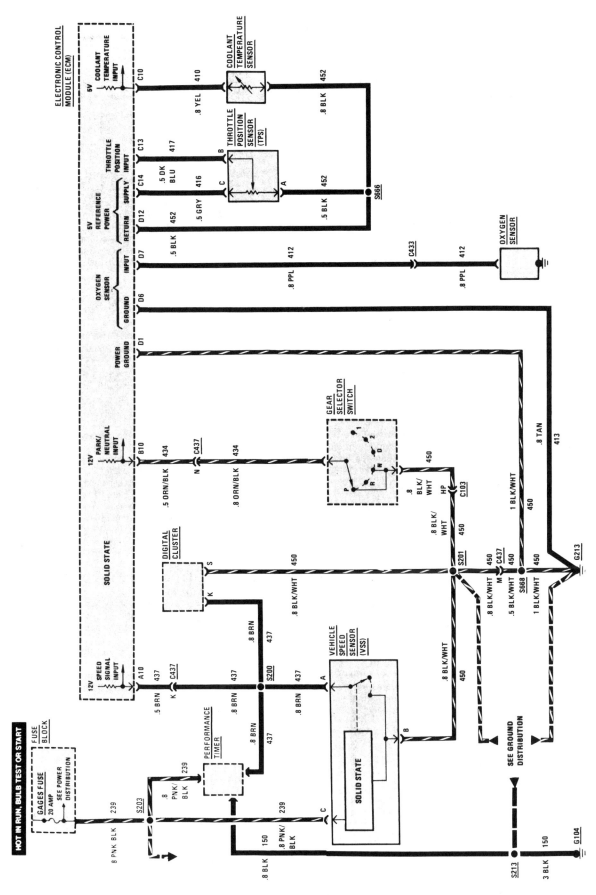

Fig. 13.57   1984 model port fuel injection C4 system sensor wiring diagram

Conversion factors

Length (distance)
Inches (in)	X	25.4	= Millimetres (mm)	X	0.0394	= Inches (in)
Feet (ft)	X	0.305	= Metres (m)	X	3.281	= Feet (ft)
Miles	X	1.609	= Kilometres (km)	X	0.621	= Miles

Inches (in) X 25.4 = Millimetres (mm) X 0.0394 = Inches (in)
Feet (ft) X 0.305 = Metres (m) X 3.281 = Feet (ft)
Miles X 1.609 = Kilometres (km) X 0.621 = Miles

Volume (capacity)
Cubic inches (cu in; in^3) X 16.387 = Cubic centimetres (cc; cm^3) X 0.061 = Cubic inches (cu in; in^3)
Imperial pints (Imp pt) X 0.568 = Litres (l) X 1.76 = Imperial pints (Imp pt)
Imperial quarts (Imp qt) X 1.137 = Litres (l) X 0.88 = Imperial quarts (Imp qt)
Imperial quarts (Imp qt) X 1.201 = US quarts (US qt) X 0.833 = Imperial quarts (Imp qt)
US quarts (US qt) X 0.946 = Litres (l) X 1.057 = US quarts (US qt)
Imperial gallons (Imp gal) X 4.546 = Litres (l) X 0.22 = Imperial gallons (Imp gal)
Imperial gallons (Imp gal) X 1.201 = US gallons (US gal) X 0.833 = Imperial gallons (Imp gal)
US gallons (US gal) X 3.785 = Litres (l) X 0.264 = US gallons (US gal)

Mass (weight)
Ounces (oz) X 28.35 = Grams (g) X 0.035 = Ounces (oz)
Pounds (lb) X 0.454 = Kilograms (kg) X 2.205 = Pounds (lb)

Force
Ounces-force (ozf; oz) X 0.278 = Newtons (N) X 3.6 = Ounces-force (ozf; oz)
Pounds-force (lbf; lb) X 4.448 = Newtons (N) X 0.225 = Pounds-force (lbf; lb)
Newtons (N) X 0.1 = Kilograms-force (kgf; kg) X 9.81 = Newtons (N)

Pressure
Pounds-force per square inch (psi; lbf/in^2; lb/in^2) X 0.070 = Kilograms-force per square centimetre (kgf/cm^2; kg/cm^2) X 14.223 = Pounds-force per square inch (psi; lbf/in^2; lb/in^2)
Pounds-force per square inch (psi; lbf/in^2; lb/in^2) X 0.068 = Atmospheres (atm) X 14.696 = Pounds-force per square inch (psi; lbf/in^2; lb/in^2)
Pounds-force per square inch (psi; lbf/in^2; lb/in^2) X 0.069 = Bars X 14.5 = Pounds-force per square inch (psi; lbf/in^2; lb/in^2)
Pounds-force per square inch (psi; lbf/in^2; lb/in^2) X 6.895 = Kilopascals (kPa) X 0.145 = Pounds-force per square inch (psi; lbf/in^2; lb/in^2)
Kilopascals (kPa) X 0.01 = Kilograms-force per square centimetre (kgf/cm^2; kg/cm^2) X 98.1 = Kilopascals (kPa)

Torque (moment of force)
Pounds-force inches (lbf in; lb in) X 1.152 = Kilograms-force centimetre (kgf cm; kg cm) X 0.868 = Pounds-force inches (lbf in; lb in)
Pounds-force inches (lbf in; lb in) X 0.113 = Newton metres (Nm) X 8.85 = Pounds-force inches (lbf in; lb in)
Pounds-force inches (lbf in; lb in) X 0.083 = Pounds-force feet (lbf ft; lb ft) X 12 = Pounds-force inches (lbf in; lb in)
Pounds-force feet (lbf ft; lb ft) X 0.138 = Kilograms force metres (kgf m; kg m) X 7.233 = Pounds-force feet (lbf ft; lb ft)
Pounds-force feet (lbf ft; lb ft) X 1.356 = Newton metres (Nm) X 0.738 = Pounds-force feet (lbf ft; lb ft)
Newton metres (Nm) X 0.102 = Kilograms-force metres (kgf m; kg m) X 9.804 = Newton metres (Nm)

Power
Horsepower (hp) X 745.7 = Watts (W) X 0.0013 = Horsepower (hp)

Velocity (speed)
Miles per hour (miles/hr; mph) X 1.609 = Kilometres per hour (km/hr; kph) X 0.621 = Miles per hour (miles/hr; mph)

Fuel consumption*
Miles per gallon, Imperial (mpg) X 0.354 = Kilometres per litre (km/l) X 2.825 = Miles per gallon, Imperial (mpg)
Miles per gallon, US (mpg) X 0.425 = Kilometres per litre (km/l) X 2.352 = Miles per gallon, US (mpg)

Temperature
Degrees Fahrenheit = (°C x 1.8) + 32

Degrees Celsius (Degrees Centigrade; °C) = (°F - 32) x 0.56

*It is common practice to convert from miles per gallon (mpg) to litres/100 kilometres (l/100km), where mpg (Imperial) x l/100 km = 282 and mpg (US) x l/100 km = 235

Index

T

U

V

W

HAYNES AUTOMOTIVE MANUALS

NOTE: New manuals are added to this list on a periodic basis. If you do not see a listing for your vehicle, consult your local Haynes dealer for the latest product information.

ALFA ROMEO
531 **Alfa Romeo** Sedan & Coupe '73 thru '80

AMC
Jeep CJ – *see JEEP (412)*
694 **Mid-size models**, Concord, Hornet, Gremlin & Spirit '70 thru '83
*934 **(Renault) Alliance & Encore** all models '83 thru '87

AUDI
162 **100** all models '69 thru '77
615 **4000** all models '80 thru '87
428 **5000** all models '77 thru '83
*1117 **5000** all models '84 thru '88
207 **Fox** all models '73 thru '79

AUSTIN
049 **Healey 100/6 & 3000** Roadster '56 thru '68
Healey Sprite – *see MG Midget Roadster (265)*

BLMC
260 **1100, 1300 & Austin America** '62 thru '74
527 **Mini** all models '59 thru '69
*646 **Mini** all models '69 thru '88

BMW
276 **320i** all 4 cyl models '75 thru '83
*632 **528i & 530i** all models '75 thru '80
240 **1500 thru 2002** all models except Turbo '59 thru '77
348 **2500, 2800, 3.0 & Bavaria** all models '69 thru '76

BUICK
Century front-wheel drive – *see GENERAL MOTORS A-Cars (829)*
*1651 **Buick, Oldsmobile & Pontiac Full-size** all rear wheel drive models '70 thru '88
*627 **Mid-size** all rear-drive **Regal & Century** models with V6, V8 and Turbo '74 thru '87
Skyhawk – *see GENERAL MOTORS J-Cars (766)*
552 **Skylark** all X-car models '80 thru '85

CADILLAC
Cimarron – *see GENERAL MOTORS J-Cars (766)*

CAPRI
296 **2000 MK I** Coupe all models '71 thru '75
283 **2300 MK II** Coupe all models '74 thru '78
205 **2600 & 2800** V6 Coupe all models '71 thru '75
375 **2800 Mk II** V6 Coupe all models '75 thru '78
Mercury in-line engines – *see FORD Mustang (654)*
Mercury V6 and V8 engines – *see FORD Mustang (558)*

CHEVROLET
*1477 **Astro & GMC Safari Mini-vans** all models '85 thru '88
554 **Camaro** V8 all models '70 thru '81
*866 **Camaro** all models '82 thru '89
Cavalier – *see GENERAL MOTORS J-Cars (766)*
Celebrity – *see GENERAL MOTORS A-Cars (829)*
*625 **Chevelle, Malibu & El Camino** all V6 & V8 models '69 thru '87
449 **Chevette & Pontiac T1000** all models '76 thru '87
550 **Citation** all models '80 thru '85
274 **Corvette** all V8 models '68 thru '82
*1336 **Corvette** all models '84 thru '87
*704 **Full-size Sedans** Caprice, Impala, Biscayne, Bel Air & Wagons, all V6 & V8 models '69 thru '88
319 **Luv Pick-up** all 2WD & 4WD models '72 thru '82
*626 **Monte Carlo** all V6, V8 & Turbo models '70 thru '88
241 **Nova** all V8 models '69 thru '79
420 **Pick-ups – Chevrolet & GMC,** all V8 & in-line 6 cyl 2WD & 4WD models '67 thru '87
*831 **S-10 & GMC S-15 Pick-ups** all models '82 thru '87
*345 **Vans – Chevrolet & GMC,** V8 & in-line 6 cyl models '68 thru '87
208 **Vega** all models except Cosworth '70 thru '77

CHRYSLER
*1337 **Chrysler & Plymouth Mid-size** front wheel drive '82 thru '88
K-Cars – *see DODGE Aries/Plymouth Reliant (723)*
Laser – *see DODGE Daytona & Chrysler Laser (1140)*

DATSUN
402 **200SX** all models '77 thru '79
*647 **200SX** all models '80 thru '83
228 **B-210** all models '73 thru '78
525 **210** all models '79 thru '82
206 **240Z, 260Z & 280Z** Coupe & 2+2 '70 thru '78
563 **280ZX** Coupe & 2+2 '79 thru '83
300ZX – *see NISSAN (1137)*
679 **310** all models '78 thru '82
123 **510 & PL521 Pick-up** '68 thru '73
430 **510** all models '78 thru '81
372 **610** all models '72 thru '76
277 **620 Series Pick-up** all models '73 thru '79
235 **710** all models '73 thru '77
720 Series Pick-up – *see NISSAN (771)*
*376 **810/Maxima** all gasoline models '77 thru '84
124 **1200** all models '70 thru '73
368 **F10** all models '76 thru '79
Pulsar – *see NISSAN (876)*
Sentra – *see NISSAN (982)*
Stanza – *see NISSAN (981)*

DODGE
*723 **Aries & Plymouth Reliant** all models '81 thru '88
*1231 **Caravan & Plymouth Voyager Mini-Vans** all models '84 thru '88
699 **Challenger & Plymouth Sapporo** all models '78 thru '83
236 **Colt** all models '71 thru '77
419 **Colt (rear-wheel drive)** all models '77 thru '80
610 **Colt & Plymouth Champ (front-wheel drive)** all models '78 thru '87
*556 **D50 & Plymouth Arrow Pick-ups** '79 thru '88
234 **Dart & Plymouth Valiant** all 6 cyl models '67 thru '76
*1140 **Daytona & Chrysler Laser** all models '84 thru '88
*545 **Omni & Plymouth Horizon** all models '78 thru '84
*912 **Pick-ups** all full-size models '74 thru '88
*349 **Vans – Dodge & Plymouth** V8 & 6 cyl models '71 thru '86

FIAT
080 **124 Sedan & Wagon** all ohv & dohc models '66 thru '75
094 **124 Sport Coupe & Spider** '68 thru '78
087 **128** all models '72 thru '79
310 **131 & Brava** all models '75 thru '81
038 **850 Sedan, Coupe & Spider** '64 thru '74
479 **Strada** all models '79 thru '82
*273 **X1/9** all models '74 thru '80

FORD
*1476 **Aerostar & GMC Safari Mini-vans** all models '86 thru '88
788 **Bronco and Pick-ups** '73 thru '79
*880 **Bronco and Pick-ups** '80 thru '88
014 **Cortina MK II** '66 thru '70
295 **Cortina MK III** 1600 & 2000 ohc '70 thru '76
268 **Courier Pick-up** all models '72 thru '82
*789 **Escort & Mercury Lynx** all models '81 thru '88
560 **Fairmont & Mercury Zephyr** all in-line & V8 models '78 thru '83
334 **Fiesta** all models '77 thru '80
359 **Granada & Mercury Monarch** all in-line, 6 cyl & V8 models '75 thru '80
*754 **Ford & Mercury Full-size,** FORD: LTD ('75 thru '82); Custom 500; Country Squire; Crown Victoria MERCURY: Marquis ('75 thru '82); Gran Marquis; Colony Park, all V8 models '75 thru '87
773 **Ford & Mercury Mid-size,** FORD: Torino; Gran Torino; Elite; Ranchero; LTD II; LTD ('83 thru '84); Thunderbird ('75 thru '82), MERCURY: Montego; Comet; Marquis ('83 thru '86); Cougar ('75 thru '82); LINCOLN: Versailles, all 4 cyl, in-line 6 cyl, V6 & V8 models '75 thru '80
*654 **Mustang & Mercury Capri** all in-line models & Turbo '79 thru '88
*558 **Mustang & Mercury Capri** all V6 & V8 models '79 thru '87
357 **Mustang V8** all models '64½ thru '73
231 **Mustang II** all 4 cyl, V6 & V8 models '74 thru '78
204 **Pinto** all models '70 thru '74
649 **Pinto & Mercury Bobcat** all models '75 thru '80
*1026 **Ranger & Bronco II** all gasoline models '83 thru '89
*1421 **Taurus & Mercury Sable** all models '86 thru '88
*1418 **Tempo & Mercury Topaz** all models '84 thru '87
*1338 **Thunderbird & Mercury Cougar** all models '83 thru '88
*344 **Vans** all V8 Econoline models '69 thru '88

GENERAL MOTORS
*829 **A-Cars** – Chevrolet Celebrity, Buick Century, Pontiac 6000 & Oldsmobile Cutlass Ciera all models '82 thru '87
*766 **J-Cars** – Chevrolet Cavalier, Pontiac J-2000, Oldsmobile Firenza, Buick Skyhawk & Cadillac Cimarron all models '82 thru '87
*1420 **N-Cars** Pontiac Grand Am, Buick Somerset & Oldsmobile Calais '85 thru '87; Buick Skylark '86 thru '87

GMC
Safari – *see CHEVROLET (1476)*
Vans & Pick-ups – *see CHEVROLET (420, 831, 345)*

HONDA
138 **360, 600 & Z Coupe** all models '67 thru '75
351 **Accord CVCC** all models '76 thru '83
*1221 **Accord** all models '84 thru '85
160 **Civic 1200** all models '73 thru '79
633 **Civic 1300 & 1500 CVCC** all models '80 thru '83
297 **Civic 1500 CVCC** all models '75 thru '79
*1227 **Civic** all models except 16-valve CRX & 4 WD Wagon '84 thru '86
*601 **Prelude CVCC** all models '79 thru '82

HYUNDAI
*1552 **Excel** all models '86 thru '89

JAGUAR
098 **MK I & II,** 240 & 340 Sedans '55 thru '69
*242 **XJ6** all 6 cyl models '68 thru '86
*478 **XJ12 & XJS** all 12 cyl models '72 thru '85
140 **XK-E** 3.8 & 4.2 all 6 cyl models '61 thru '72

JEEP
*1553 **Cherokee, Comanche & Wagoneer Limited** all models '84 thru '89
412 **CJ** all models '49 thru '86

LADA
*413 **1200, 1300, 1500 & 1600** all models including Riva '74 thru '86

LANCIA
533 **Lancia Beta** Sedan, Coupe & HPE all models '76 thru '80

LAND ROVER
314 **Series II, IIA, & III** all 4 cyl gasoline models '58 thru '86
529 **Diesel** all models '58 thru '80

MAZDA
648 **626** Sedan & Coupe (rear-wheel drive) all models '79 thru '82
*1082 **626 (front-wheel drive)** all gas models '83 thru '87
*267 **B1600, B1800, B2000, B2200 & B2600 Pick-ups** '72 thru '88
370 **GLC Hatchback (rear-wheel drive)** all models '77 thru '83
757 **GLC (front-wheel drive)** all models '81 thru '85
109 **RX2** all models '71 thru '75
096 **RX3** all models '72 thru '76
460 **RX-7** all models '79 thru '85

MERCEDES-BENZ
346 **230, 250 & 280** Sedan, Coupe & Roadster all 6 cyl sohc models '68 thru '72
983 **280 123 Series** all gasoline models '77 thru '81
698 **350 & 450** Sedan, Coupe & Roadster all models '71 thru '80
697 **Diesel 123 Series** 200D, 220D, 240D, 240TD, 300D, 300CD, 300TD, 4- & 5-cyl incl. Turbo '76 thru '85

MERCURY
See *FORD* listing

MG
475 **MGA** all models '56 thru '62
111 **MGB** Roadster & GT Coupe all models '62 thru '80
265 **MG Midget & Austin Healey Sprite** Roadster '58 thru '80

MITSUBISHI
Pick-up – *see Dodge D-50 (556)*

MORRIS
074 **(Austin) Marina 1.8** all models '71 thru '75
024 **Minor 1000** sedan & wagon '56 thru '71

NISSAN
*1137 **300ZX** all models '84 thru '86
*771 **Pick-ups & Pathfinder** all gasoline models '80 thru '88
*876 **Pulsar** all models '83 thru '86
*982 **Sentra** all models '82 thru '86
*981 **Stanza** all models '82 thru '89

OLDSMOBILE
Custom Cruiser – *see BUICK (1551)*
*658 **Cutlass** all standard gasoline V6 & V8 models '74 thru '87
Cutlass Ciera – *see GENERAL MOTORS A-Cars (829)*
Delta 88, Delta 88 Brougham & Delta 88 Royale – *see BUICK (1551)*
Firenza – *see GENERAL MOTORS J-Cars (766)*
98 Luxury, 98 Regency & 98 Regency Brougham – *see BUICK (1551)*
Omega – *see PONTIAC Phoenix & Omega (551)*

OPEL
157 **(Buick) Manta Coupe 1900** all models '70 thru '74

PEUGEOT
161 **504** all gasoline models '68 thru '79
663 **504** all diesel models '74 thru '83

PLYMOUTH
425 **Arrow** all models '76 thru '80
For other Plymouth models see *DODGE* listing

PONTIAC
T1000 – *see CHEVROLET Chevette (449)*
J-2000 – *see GENERAL MOTORS J-Cars (766)*
6000 – *see GENERAL MOTORS A-Cars (829)*
Bonneville, Bonneville Brougham & Catalina – *see BUICK (1551)*
*1232 **Fiero** all models '84 thru '87
555 **Firebird** all V8 models except Turbo '70 thru '81
*867 **Firebird** all models '82 thru '89
Grandville, Parisienne – *see BUICK (1551)*
551 **Phoenix & Oldsmobile Omega** all X-car models '80 thru '84

PORSCHE
*264 **911** all Coupe & Targa models except Turbo '65 thru '87
239 **914** all 4 cyl models '69 thru '76
397 **924** all models including Turbo '76 thru '82
*1027 **944** all models including Turbo '83 thru '86

RENAULT
141 **5 Le Car** all models '76 thru '83
079 **8 & 10** all models with 58.4 cu in engines '62 thru '72
097 **12 Saloon & Estate** all models 1289 cc engines '70 thru '80
768 **15 & 17** all models '73 thru '79
081 **16** all models 89.7 cu in & 95.5 cu in engines '65 thru '72
598 **18i & Sportwagon** all models '81 thru '86
Alliance & Encore – *see AMC (934)*
984 **Fuego** all models '82 thru '85

ROVER
085 **3500 & 3500S Sedan** 215 cu in engines '68 thru '76
*365 **3500 SDI** V8 all models '76 thru '85

SAAB
198 **95 & 96** V4 all models '66 thru '75
247 **99** all models including Turbo '69 thru '80
*980 **900** all models including Turbo '79 thru '88

SUBARU
237 **1100, 1300, 1400 & 1600** all models '71 thru '79
*681 **1600 & 1800** 2WD & 4WD all models '80 thru '88

TOYOTA
*1023 **Camry** all models '83 thru '88
150 **Carina** Sedan all models '71 thru '74
229 **Celica** ST, GT & liftback all models '71 thru '77
437 **Celica** all models '78 thru '81
*935 **Celica** all models except front-wheel drive and Supra '82 thru '85
680 **Celica Supra** all models '79 thru '81
1139 **Celica Supra** all models '82 thru '86
201 **Corolla 1100, 1200 & 1600** all models '67 thru '74
361 **Corolla** all models '75 thru '79
*961 **Corolla** all models (rear wheel drive) '80 thru '82
*1025 **Corolla** all models (front wheel drive) '84 thru '88
*636 **Corolla Tercel** all models '80 thru '82
230 **Corona & MK II** all 4 cyl sohc models '69 thru '74
360 **Corona** all models '74 thru '82
*532 **Cressida** all models '78 thru '82
313 **Land Cruiser** all models '68 thru '82
200 **MK II** all 6 cyl models '72 thru '76
*1339 **MR2** all models '85 thru '87
304 **Pick-up** all models '69 thru '78
*656 **Pick-up** all models '79 thru '88
787 **Starlet** all models '81 thru '84

TRIUMPH
112 **GT6 & Vitesse** all models '62 thru '74
113 **Spitfire** all models '62 thru '81
028 **TR2, 3, 3A, 4 & 4A** Roadsters '52 thru '67
031 **TR250 & TR6** Roadsters '67 thru '76
322 **TR7** all models '75 thru '81

VW
091 **411 & 412** all 103 cu in models '68 thru '74
036 **Bug 1200** all models '54 thru '66
039 **Bug 1300 & 1500** '65 thru '70
159 **Bug 1600** all basic, sport & super (curved windshield) models '70 thru '74
110 **Bug 1600 Super** all models (flat windshield) '70 thru '72
238 **Dasher** all gasoline models '74 thru '81
*884 **Rabbit, Jetta, Scirocco, & Pick-up** all gasoline models '74 thru '84 **& Convertible** '80 thru '85
451 **Rabbit, Jetta & Pick-up** all diesel models '77 thru '84
082 **Transporter 1600** all models '68 thru '79
226 **Transporter 1700, 1800 & 2000** all models '72 thru '79
084 **Type 3 1500 & 1600** all models '63 thru '73
*1029 **Vanagon** all air-cooled models '80 thru '83

VOLVO
203 **120, 130 Series & 1800 Sports** '61 thru '73
129 **140 Series** all models '66 thru '74
244 **164** all models '68 thru '75
*270 **240 Series** all models '74 thru '86
400 **260 Series** all models '75 thru '82
*1550 **740 & 760 Series** all models '82 thru '88

SPECIALTY MANUALS
1479 **Automotive Body Repair & Painting Manual**
1480 **Automotive Heating & Air Conditioning Manual**
482 **Fuel Injection Manual** Covers Bosch, Chrysler, Ford and General Motors

See your dealer for other available titles

** Listings shown with an asterisk (*) indicate model coverage as of this printing. These titles will be periodically updated to include later model years — consult your Haynes dealer for more information.*

Over 100 Haynes motorcycle manuals also available

9/89

Haynes Publications Inc., P.O. Box 978, Newbury Park, CA 91320 • (818) 889-5400 • (805) 498-6703

Printed by
J H Haynes & Co Ltd
Sparkford Nr Yeovil
Somerset BA22 7JJ England